ABRAHAM AND HIS SON

ALSO BY JAMES GOODMAN

Stories of Scottsboro

Blackout

ABRAHAM AND HIS SON

The story of a story

JAMES GOODMAN

SANDSTONEPRESS
HIGHLAND | SCOTLAND

First published in Great Britain by
Sandstone Press Ltd
Dochcarty Road
Dingwall
Ross-shire
IV15 9UG
Scotland.

www.sandstonepress.com

First published in the United States by Schocken Books,
a division of Random House, Inc., New York,
and in Canada by Random House of Canada, Limited, Toronto.

Commissioning Editor: Robert Davidson

The publisher acknowledges support from Creative Scotland
towards publication of this volume.

ISBN: 978-1-910124-15-4
ISBNe: 978-1-910124-16-1

Jacket design by Mark Ecob, London
Typeset by Iolaire Typesetting, Newtonmore.
Printed and bound by Totem, Poland

TO MY FATHER AND TO MY MOTHER,

WHOM I LOVE

PUBLISHER'S NOTE

The roads a book might take from author to reader are many and various. James Goodman's account of how a story has travelled through time, continuously active and continuously relevant, was already published in America when I visited the desk of his agent in the crowded International Rights Hall at Frankfurt Book Fair.

Its subject matter, the story of Abraham and Isaac (Ishmael to Muslims), meaning not so much the father and son as the history of the story *itself*, was esoteric to say the least. The problems for us were how to identify something so *sui generis*, whether as myth or history, apologia or page-turning narrative, and how to find its likely readership.

The culture I spring from is rather sceptical of authority, almost by definition, with a ready willingness to lampoon that we, generally, get away with in our robust democracy. At least, people do not usually lose their lives over such matters. Here are the four words that spring into my mind: trust, fear, authority, obedience. Trust and authority are inextricable since trust *is* authority. Otherwise obedience is based on fear. When Authority gets its capital 'A' and becomes a person, or an institution, or a committee, hierarchy is introduced and resistance and scepticism are likely to follow.

To modern Western minds, that mistrust of Authority is healthy, but the story of Abraham and his son assumes an unquestioning and complete faith in the authority of God. In this light the story takes on mythic qualities, describing the many ramifications of an essential part of human nature. Ramifications that include the son's unquestioning trust of his earthly father and, by extension, of a given order.

James Goodman digs considerably deeper. As a secular Jew, he writes from a particular mindset with a view to reaching across certain hard, religious boundaries. To widen the spectrum of questioning and invite further comment I asked four individuals, all committed to their faiths, who also write and publish widely, to read the book and give a short response. They are:

Finlay Macdonald, minister and former Moderator of the Church of Scotland, Chair of the Iona Cathedral Trust, who has written questioningly of the Church's attitude to gay clergy and of the modern, Scottish, meeting with Islam in his books *Luke Paul* and *Luke Paul and the Mosque*.

Rabbi Julia Neuberger, who as Baroness Neuberger is a member of the British House of Lords and author of many books including *Is That All There Is: thoughts on the meaning of life and leaving a legacy*.

Qaisra Shahraz, a Muslim who is an educationalist, consultant, teacher trainer and inspector, trustee of Manchester Multi-faith Centre, as well as the author of three novels and a collection of short stories, the most recent being *Revolt*.

Ian Wilson is a Roman Catholic convert now living in Australia. Recognised as an expert on the Turin Shroud he is the author of many books including *Murder at Golgotha, Jesus: the evidence*, and *The Shroud of Turin*.

I am very grateful to all four for their participation and happy to record my thanks here.

After all this, the scene is set for the reader to enter history with James Goodman. To enter also: mythology, tradition, violence and belief. To trace the effect of only a few lines in an old book on generations of humanity whether for good or ill. To peer into the common heart of Judaism, Christianity and Islam. It is an extraordinary tale, and *Abraham and his Son* is an extraordinary achievement. To understand this story is to understand a difficult part of what we are. Whether that part is the best of us or the worst is for the reader to determine.

Robert Davidson
Sandstone Press
Highland Scotland
9th September 2014

This is an absorbing book. It explores the ancient story of Abraham's readiness to sacrifice his son in apparent obedience to God's command, and shows how it has been interpreted, re-interpreted, argued about, understood, misunderstood, applied and misapplied over the last three millennia. We are directed to a rich seam of Jewish, Christian and Islamic commentary and the thinking of philosophers such as Spinoza, Kierkegaard, Kant and Buber; we are guided through the paintings of Caravaggio, Rembrandt, Domenichino and examine Donatello's early fifteenth century marble statue; in further rich seams we explore the part played by the story in literature, music and drama from the English Mystery Plays to contemporary Israeli literature.

Some of the book's most moving sections consider the role of the story in the Crusades and the Holocaust, and the concluding chapters come right up to date with references to the post 9/11 'war on terror'. Particularly chilling is an account of a young Iraqi man found to have been co-operating with the US led invasion. The tribal elders gave his father a choice. Kill your son or we will kill your entire family. Paralleling this we hear of an American anti-war protester challenging pro-war congressmen, asking if they would sacrifice a child for Falujah, a place they had not heard of before 2004.

In eighteenth century Scotland it was frowned upon if preachers changed their text too often. The suspicion was that they weren't squeezing every ounce of Gospel truth out of it, so one Bible verse could keep a minister going for up to year, and these were not short sermons.

I thought of this as I read James Goodman's book. I also thought that it will undoubtedly make a better read than those sermons.

Finlay A J Macdonald

James Goodman makes the reader realise that the story of Abraham's binding of Isaac has been interpreted and reinterpreted throughout the centuries, and used to justify a whole variety of theological positions in at least three faiths. He tells the story of its interpretation most engagingly, and we learn a lot about the story and the editing of the Torah in the process - and also a good deal about James Goodman himself, who has done this as a labour of love, and has allowed others into the world of commentary who would never have got there otherwise.

Rabbi Julia Neuberger

This is not a novel or a piece of fiction; but an academic debate. James Goodman in his book, *Abraham and his Son*, highlights how the question of Abraham and the story of his son Isaac's sacrifice is a difficult one and continues to intrigue people like him. On the one hand, he shows how prophet Abraham is an important religious figure that helps Muslims, Christians, and Jews to recognize certain commonalities among them and also, certain shared heritage. On the other hand, and this is the crux of Goodman's entertaining debate, he highlights that there are real differences in the view about Abraham and the stories surrounding the sacrifice episode in the three religions.

The writing is both erudite and highly entertaining as Goodman presents intriguing perspectives that we find in the three traditions on Abraham. His bantering and semi-sardonic style as he questions, answers and ponders gets us thinking about what actually happened with the story of the sacrifice; and to wonder as to which version is the correct one.

As a historian he treats us to a feast of historical anecdotes crossing centuries and civilizations, as exemplars to illustrate his points relating to the story of Abraham and his family. As a fellow writer, I admired his assured mastery of his writing craftsmanship. In particular, in how Goodman excels at using language as a bantering tool, to speculate, tease, question and entertain the reader. I enjoyed his use of analogies relating to writers and editors. I have both learnt, and been entertained.

Qaisra Sharaz

James Goodman describes himself as 'a reader, a son, a Jew, a father, a sceptic, a historian, a lover of stories and a writer'. Well, with the single exception of 'Jew' (thirty years ago I converted from agnostic to Roman Catholic), I can lay claim to all the same labels. And 'reader', the first on the list, is the most pertinent to Goodman's subject matter.

This is because every regular Catholic Sunday Mass requires lay readers to read passages from the scriptures pre-chosen in a three year cycle. The role that I have generally volunteered for throughout my years of living both in England and Australia. Except that the one reading I have always dreaded being rostered for is that for the 17th Sunday of the Catholic year: Genesis 18: 20-32 - the dialogue between Abraham and God concerning just how few 'just men'* needed to be living in Sodom for the whole town to be spared a fiery fate.

To explain: Abraham's opening gambit is to ask whether fifty just men might be a sufficient number to save the town? God confirms yes. So with every profession of self-abasement, Abraham asks what about forty-five? God reassures him 'I will not destroy it if I find forty-five just men there.' 'Perhaps there will only be forty there?' ventures Abraham? 'I will not do it for the sake of the forty' responds God. Yet even now Abraham is not satisfied. His relentless questioning ratchets the number ever downwards 'Perhaps there will only be thirty?' 'Perhaps only twenty?' then finally 'I trust my Lord will not be angry if I speak once more: perhaps there will only be ten?'

Time and again when I have listened to others delivering this reading I have ached for them to give it some more expression, for them to raise even the merest chuckle from the congregation by injecting a nervous higher pitch to Abraham's final question, and some testiness or weariness to God's final answer. But of course inviting a laugh from your scripture reading is a definite 'no, no' for any reader at a Catholic Mass. Which makes it just as well that I have never been rostered to perform Genesis 18: 20-32.

Nevertheless the relentlessness of Abraham's questions in this particular episode only underscores the oddity of just how *un*questioning will be Abraham's response only four chapters later when God asks him to sacrifice his so long-awaited only son Isaac. And that's the very oddity to which James Goodman addresses himself so exhaustively yet so entertainingly in the pages that follow.

Ian Wilson

---

* This is the Jerusalem Bible translation. Other translations differ.

And it happened after these things that God tested Abraham. And He said to him, "Abraham!" and he said, "Here I am." And He said, "Take, pray, your son, your only one, whom you love, Isaac, and go forth to the land of Moriah and offer him up as a burnt offering on one of the mountains which I shall say to you." And Abraham rose early in the morning and saddled his donkey and took his two lads with him, and Isaac his son, and he split wood for the offering, and rose and went to the place that God had said to him. On the third day Abraham raised his eyes and saw the place from afar. And Abraham said to his lads, "Sit you here with the donkey and let me and the lad walk ahead and let us worship and return to you." And Abraham took the wood for the offering and put it on Isaac his son and he took in his hand the fire and the cleaver, and the two of them went together. And Isaac said to Abraham his father, "Father!" and he said, "Here I am, my son." And he said, "Here is the fire and the wood but where is the sheep for the offering?" And Abraham said, "God will see to the sheep for the offering, my son." And the two of them went together. And they came to the place that God had said to him, and Abraham built there an altar and laid out the wood and bound Isaac his son and placed him on the altar on top of the wood. And Abraham reached out his hand and took the cleaver to slaughter his son. And the LORD's messenger called out to him from the heavens and said, "Abraham, Abraham!" and he said, "Here I am." And he said, "Do not reach out your hand against the lad, and do nothing to him, for now I know that you fear God and you have not held back your son, your only one, from Me." And Abraham raised his eyes and saw and, look, a ram was caught in the thicket by its horns, and Abraham went and took the ram and offered him up as a burnt offering instead of his son. And Abraham called the name of that

place YHWH-Yireh, as is said to this day, "On the mount of the
15 LORD there is sight." And the LORD's messenger called out to Abra-
16 ham once again from the heavens, and He said, "By My own Self
I swear, declares the LORD, that because you have done this thing
17 and have not held back your son, your only one, I will greatly bless
you and will greatly multiply your seed, as the stars in the heavens
and as the sand on the shore of the sea, and your seed shall take
18 hold of its enemies' gate. And all the nations of the earth will be
blessed through your seed because you have listened to my voice."
19 And Abraham returned to his lads, and they rose and went together
to Beersheba, and Abraham dwelled in Beersheba.

—Genesis 22:1–19

I didn't think he'd do it.

I really didn't think he would.

I thought he'd say, whoa, hold on, wait a minute. We made a deal, remember, the land, the blessing, the nation, the descendants as numerous as the sands on the shore and the stars in the sky. You said: through Isaac you'd make my name great. I have kept my word. Don't you go back on yours.

He might not have put it precisely that way. He tended to say what he had to say more succinctly. But you know what I mean.

I didn't think he'd do it, certainly not without asking when, where, how, or why. Why should I sacrifice my son? I readily concede that he answered God's initial call without a moment's hesitation. That was undoubtedly among the reasons that he was so special to him. But I can't help thinking that he came to regret that he hadn't taken some time to consider what he was getting himself into. From then on, almost everything he said to God took the form of a question: a question about God's promise of greatness, a question about offspring and inheritance, a question about land, a question about the likelihood that a child could be born to a hundred-year-old man and his ninety-year-old wife, a question (in the form of a wish) about Ishmael, and most memorable of all a barrage of questions, pointed questions, no matter how humbly couched, about the innocent and the guilty of Sodom and Gomorrah.

So you can imagine my surprise when God asked Abraham to take Isaac to the land of Moriah and offer him up as a burnt offering, and Abraham didn't say a word. Not one word. One question after twenty-five years of questions is all it would have taken. He and God could have talked, and God could have explained what he was up to.

And remember: This is the guy God chose to show the world his way. To do what was just and right. Was Abraham always sure what God's way was? Of course not. Was he always sure that God's way was the right way? Not likely. Did he make mistakes? He did. For instance: he never should have given his wife, Sarah, to another man. Did he always learn from them? Who does? Several years later, he did it again. Did he have days he wished he could do over? Sure. That's literature. That's life. Who doesn't, including God? Remember when he promised not to destroy the innocent along with the guilty of Sodom, to forgive the city of sin for the sake of the good? Not long after, God's angels visited Abraham's nephew, Lot, and the citizenry of Sodom went after them, to a *man*. God reduced the place to cinder and ash, somehow neglecting to include the city's women and children in his calculation.

Still, on his worst day, I didn't think Abraham would do it, not without saying a word. At the very least I thought he'd stall for time, say, hey, wait, wait, give me a few minutes, and I'll get back to you, I simply need to talk it over with the boy's mother. Or, I thought, that in the hours between God's command and bedtime, or bedtime and morning, Sarah would have read God's command on her husband's face. Anyone who has followed the travail of the two of them since they left Ur for Canaan would know that that would have been the end of the matter right then and there.

But he didn't say a word. Not to God. Not to Sarah. Not to anyone. Instead, he rose up early the next morning, saddled his donkey, called for two servants and Isaac, his son. He split the wood and headed out. God led him on and on, made the journey three days, giving him plenty of time to think about it, to change his mind, to figure a way out. I thought one of his servants might catch on, and perhaps he did too. Abraham stopped—when he saw the place from afar—and said, you two stay here, with the donkeys. We'll be back after we go up and pray.

That left Isaac. Whether or not he knew it, he asked exactly the right question in exactly the right way. But Abraham reached deep, and somehow found a way to answer. And for all the awe that readers have expressed at his composure, the simple truth is that all Abraham had to do was not fall apart. Isaac was just a boy, thrilled to be on a special errand all alone with his father. He was not about to parse his father's words for hidden meanings.

Right up to the last moment, I thought, I hoped, I may even have prayed, that Abraham would protest: I can't do it, I can't. I obey you as I obeyed my own father, Terah, but Isaac: he is my son.

But he didn't.

And so God, through a messenger, had to stop him himself: "Do not reach out your hand against the lad, and do nothing to him, for now I know that you fear God and you have not held back your son, your only one, from me."

I was stunned. It was not at all what I had anticipated. I had no illusions about God, not after Adam and Eve, Cain and Abel, the Great Flood, and the Tower of Babel. (I have never been persuaded that the citizens of that apparently peaceful place, working together and getting along, had done anything wrong.) Nor confidence that I could predict his behavior or fathom what he was thinking. Still, I harbored a sneaking suspicion that it was not what God had antici-pated either. But what could he do? He tried to make the best of a difficult situation, adjust on the fly, cut his losses and Abraham's too. Look forward. Move on. Try not to let one bad day spoil the rewards of a good long life. Sometimes events take unexpected turns, even when you are thought to have everything under control.

And what could I do? I was just a reader who thought the story had come out wrong. And a son, like Isaac, who had to try to make sense of and peace with a difficult father. And a Jew, like any Jew who gives any thought to Jewish experience, past or present, who had to decide what to make of, and do with, an enormous inheritance, an inheritance that includes nearly three thousand of years of history, literature, ritual, and law. And a father, another difficult father, who had to figure out what part or parts of that inheritance I wanted to try to pass on to my sons. And a skeptic, by nature and nurture resistant to things we believe simply because (it is said) they have always been believed, things we do simply because they've always been done. And a historian, uncomfortable with the idea that the way things are is the only way they could possibly be. And, as if that weren't enough, a lover of stories, driven to show and share the power and beauty of stories, sometimes even terrible stories. And to do that showing and sharing at a most inopportune time, a time (like so many times) when not a day goes by when someone somewhere doesn't commit some horrible atrocity in the name of the God of Abraham and Isaac, in the name of their scripture or revelation, making it all the more challenging to convey my appreciation for those stories and their history, or even to answer those who see nothing but the dark side, the undeniable dark side, of their long lives.

Happily, I was also a writer, and every writer knows that sometimes a character gets away from you, surprises you, takes on a life of his or her own, even when you think you have a handle on him, even when you appear to be pulling all the strings. Sometimes an entire story gets away from you. It is an occupational hazard, all the more (if you'll pardon a mixed metaphor and then bear with me for a few pages of speculation) when you are called in, as I imagine the author of the story of the near sacrifice was called in, like a relief pitcher, late in the game, without an outline, or even clear signals from the catcher, to finish someone else's story.

So you see, I was a reader, a son, a Jew, a father, a skeptic, a historian, a lover of stories, and a writer. I had no choice, or little choice. Tradition virtually compelled me to write the story of Abraham and Isaac.

2

He was a writer. Of that I am sure.

The rest I am left to imagine. Everyone is.

Here goes:

He was a writer. Some readers have called him a "dictator," by which they (at least the sympathetic ones) mean "one who dictates." Remember, his was still largely an oral culture. The point is that he did what writers do: he made things out of words: put them down, moved them around, added some, took others away, decided which ones had to go and which should stay.

He was, however, no ordinary writer.

To begin with, he was not driven to publish. Precious little of his work has seen the light of day. For every word he published, there were thousands, perhaps tens of thousands, he just discarded, or filed away. Believe me when I tell you that most of what has been attributed to him was the work of others.

What he did publish he published under other people's names, or no one's name at all. Today he would be called a ghostwriter, though he did it for love, not money. He worked behind the scenes—I picture him at a small table in a small room, a bare bright room with big windows looking out on the universe—helping writers who, for one reason or another, were unable to help themselves. In the spirit of the biblical scholars, I will call him G.

Now, obviously G couldn't help every writer in need. For one thing, he wasn't interested in every writer's project. What writer would be? I know historians who don't read fiction, let alone write it. They can't understand why anyone would waste their time reading stories that aren't true. I know poets who read only poetry. I know fiction writers who think "nonfiction" is the Latin word for "memoir." No other form of experience-based prose ever penetrates their literary airspace. G was partial to short stories, family history, and brief lives. When he was young, he dabbled in poetry. He steered clear, despite ample opportunity and plenty of evidence he'd be good at it, of the law.

Even if he had been interested, he would not have had the time. The portrait of an artist in Exodus, dictating from the mountaintop, is magnificently drawn. And it makes me, for one, green with envy, for I know that there are writers out there who, despite every kind of distraction (on Sinai there were pillars of fire and clouds of smoke and enough thunder to make the earth tremble, and between thunder cracks the deafening blast of trumpets), work in white heat, without sleep, at breakneck speed, and (with apparent ease) somehow manage to get it right the first time.

But G was not one of them. Words did not come easy to him. Not the kinds of words that ended up on stone, clay tablets, animal hides, and papyrus. Or even the words read on special occasions in the public square. He could talk up a storm. But there is a big difference between speaking words and writing them. Spoken sentences don't have to be grammatical. They don't even have to be sentences, and they don't have to come in any particular order or lead neatly and logically from one place to another. The truth is that he could, and often did, go around in circles for long periods of time before the people he was speaking to even noticed. And even when they did notice, most didn't mind, because they were busy and his rambling on and on freed them to do other things with their time.

And if, as he talked, he saw them stiffen, frown, wince, shake, groan, glare, or just stare at him without the slightest glimmer of interest, sympathy, or comprehension, he could revise on the fly.

And if he got a word, phrase, sentence, or even an entire passage that was not quite right, or even completely wrong, he hadn't scratched his sentiments or self into stone or a copper scroll that was going to outlive him by thousands of years. They were gone, like the breath that delivered them. And all he had to do was take another breath and try again, with different words or a different tone, or from a different point of view.

Written words are another matter. You know what I am talking about if you have ever tried to spend a day, let alone one day after another, trying to make sentences meant to be read, trying to find just the right word, out of all the words out there, and put them in just the right order. To say enough without saying too much, to leave room for readers to breathe and wander without leaving them lost or bewildered, wondering what's happening and what it means. Everywhere but his writing table everything was so clear. Words came to him in well-turned phrases, which attached themselves to others to make paragraphs with winning beginnings, middles, and ends. But the moment he tried to put them down, they scattered, or came at him so fast he could not possibly keep pace. In the end, they rarely looked as nice, or sounded as sweet, on the page as they first sounded in his head. Hours passed, and every good line seemed like a miracle.

Oh, you write beautifully, he'd hear people say. As if writing beautifully were like being beautiful, or tall, something you are by birth, not something you have to work at. And he'd think: You have never seen a line I've written before I've revised it fifty times. You don't see a page or even a paragraph that hasn't taken dozens of different forms. And those are just the words you see. You can't imagine and don't want to know how many complete sentences, pages, chapters, you will never see, earlier versions in which the voice was wrong or the perspective was wrong or the language or imagery or sound of the words was wrong—or, and this may be the most painful of all, something was wrong he could hear or feel but not name.

It was hard work, and there was no shortage of writers in need. He had to be choosy. But there were some projects that had his name written all over them, and the story of Abraham was one of them.

I don't have a clue who asked him for help, just a hunch what they asked for. A writer or several writers, perhaps a whole team of writers, had written a history, or saga, about a man, his family, and a God. The God approached the man, born Abram, out of the blue, and offered him a deal. Follow me, walk in my way, do what I say, and I'll take care of you. Good care. Really good care. Not just you, but your children, and your children's children, my blessing, a great nation.

Think of it as an insurance policy, full life, plus annuity, fully transferable not just to a few designated beneficiaries but to all of his descendants, through the ages. The first premium was migration. Abram paid it, no questions asked, and almost immediately he discovered that, as always, there was fine print, and in the fine print, gaps in the coverage. The first was famine. Abram left Canaan for Egypt, where, worried about his well-being despite all those promises, he told his wife, Sarah, to say she was his sister, in the hope that Pharaoh would take her and spare his life. Pharaoh did, and God had to bail them out, but that wasn't the last of Abram's troubles. He had to deal with quarrelsome shepherds, warring kings, and his well-meaning but ne'er-do-well nephew, Lot. He had to deal with his and Sarah's difficulty getting pregnant, with the conflict between Sarah and Sarah's maidservant Hagar after he (at Sarah's suggestion) conceived a child with Hagar, with sin in Sodom, with several harrowing misunderstandings with Abimelech, king of Gerar, and with more trouble between Sarah and Hagar after his and Sarah's son Isaac was born. Along the way there were additional premiums, or demands, most notably a name change, from Abram to Abraham, and circumcision at ninety-nine.

Don't let me give you the wrong impression. There were good days, many good days, glorious days. Imagine how Abraham must have felt on his way out of Egypt, escaping from his first close encounter with the Egyptians, not just with his life and his wife, but with a generous portion of Pharaoh's livestock, silver, and gold. Or on his way back to Hebron after rescuing Lot from the alliance of kings who had overrun the cities of the plain. Or as he quizzed God about his plans to destroy those same cities and God seemed to understand what he was saying about justice.

But those bright moments could be short-lived. I think often of the morning, just a few days after that conversation with God, when Abraham stood on the very same spot, a hillside above Sodom, and got a good look at the fate of those who crossed him. Smoke rose from the ashes as if from a kiln.

Inevitably he had questions: When God promises greatness, Abraham asks how. When God promises land, he asks how he would know it was his. When God promises Isaac, Abraham laughs (though it is Sarah's laugh, a little later, that most people remember) and then asks about Ishmael. Inevitably there were misunderstandings. One does not get to know and understand a brand-new God in a day. There were days of doubt and perhaps even regret. Covenant regret. All the more when that God, at once demanding and mercurial, assumes he is completely in charge.

And though we don't know what God was thinking, it would not be wholly unnatural if over time Abraham's doubts became self-fulfilling, generating doubts in God. What was I thinking? Is this guy the real thing? I've got a lot riding on this. Is this another dead end? He is generous. He is magnanimous. He is a magnificent host and a skilled diplomat. When conflict or even the possibility of it arises with his nephew, with neighboring landowners, with powerful political figures, he shrewdly trades land and wealth and even water wells for good feeling and peace. Most important, he does everything that I ask. On the other hand, there is no end to his questions.

This goes on for many years, but it can't go on forever. The man and his wife are getting old and it doesn't take a prophet to figure out that there is a lot of history to come between the end of their lives and the realization of God's promises. One descendant might have been delivered quickly, though he wasn't. But nation building takes generations, and it was time to move on. And the author did move on. After Sarah and Abraham expelled Hagar and Ishmael, Sarah died, and Abraham arranged for her burial, secured a wife for Isaac, remarried, had additional children, and died peacefully and happily of old age.

But either that writer, or group of writers, or more likely his or their editors, or maybe even editors working later (the distinction between writer and editor was much fuzzier in those days than it is today), were not satisfied. There was one action-packed scene after another, and plenty of worry and wonder about whether and when and how God's promises would be realized. But there was nothing to tie it all together. The editors wanted something, somewhere, a scene or series of scenes, a story within a story, to connect the story's past and the story's future. Without that scene, without some sort of climax, they feared that readers might feel as if the story didn't end, but just faded away.

They knew where they wanted to go. but not how to get there, and that's when they came to G. He jumped at the opportunity. What writer wouldn't have? It's a great story, a gripping family saga that took on, in the most unabashed way, some of the great issues of its day, of any day—migration and dislocation; family, sex, and marriage; sibling rivalry and inheritance; might, inequality, and right; crime and punishment; war and diplomacy; honesty and duplicity; jealousy, love, fear, death, doubt, and belief—all complicated by the comings and goings, the commands and the promises, the blessings and curses of an unfamiliar and mysterious God.

G liked what he read but agreed with them that something was missing. After several readings, he even had a hunch about where it should go. You can see it for yourself simply by plotting the events in Abraham's life on a time line. He was seventy-five, Sarah sixty-five, when God called them out of Haran. They traveled to Canaan, then Egypt, then back. A decade passed. Twice God emphatically renewed his promise, yet Abraham remained childless. That's when Sarah suggested he sleep with her maidservant. A year later, Ishmael was born. Another decade passed, thirteen years to be precise. Abraham was ninety-nine when God promised him Isaac, commanded circumcision, and destroyed Sodom and Gomorrah. About a year later, Isaac was born and Ishmael and Hagar were cast out.

Next thing we know, Sarah dies—at the age of 127. And we are led to believe, or expected to believe, that after all those things nothing worthy of note happened between the expulsion of Hagar and the death of Sarah except an easily managed conflict with Abimelech over a few wells. A gap of thirty-seven years. I suppose from a purely practical point of view the structure is just fine. Isaac, the child of God's promise, is alive and well. Ishmael is out of the way (though not so far out, in body or mind, that he does not later join his brother at their father's funeral). Abraham is getting along with his Canaanite neighbors The author could move on to Rebekah, Esau, and Jacob. But if the stories of Abraham and all the stories after them were all work and no play, all function and no form, they would not have taken as many pages to tell or turned out as magnificently as they did.

That is not to suggest G had an easy time of it. At first, he too was unsure how to proceed. He knew it had to be short. The story was already long and in places repetitious, with some of the repetition essential and some not. It had to be dramatic, but not so dramatic that it changed the course of the entire saga, parts of which had (apparently) already been written. It had to reveal something essential about Abraham and his relationship to God, and he had some ideas about that, good ideas he thought, but all the good ideas in the world do not necessarily make one good story, and anyone who has been through it will know what it was like, and probably prefer not to think about it: how many false starts he had, how many times, after getting a second and third line down, he thought, Yes, that's it, I've got it, only to look back later and realize that *it* wasn't it at all.

Even after he decided to make it a test and got the form of the first line right, he couldn't get Abraham's response right. He was certain that he would say something, but he could not figure out what or how, and until he could figure that out, he couldn't move on. It was only after God called and Abraham said simply, "Here I am," and God commanded and Abraham said absolutely nothing, and then rose early the next morning and still said nothing, that the words started to flow, and not as they usually did, in fits and starts, but smoothly, as if some much more fluid writer than he was moving his hand.

And they flowed in a wholly unexpected direction.

And yet he liked the way it came out. He liked the way the opening—your son, your only one, whom you love, Isaac—echoed in language and theme so much of what had come before, starting with God's call—Go forth from your land, from your birthplace, your father's house. He liked the way the plot—the sudden threat and ultimate resolution—at once paralleled and recast and advanced so much of what had come before. He liked God's utter (and very human) capriciousness and Abraham's inhuman intensity (and guile). He liked the pace, the economy, the suspense, the combination of crystal-clear surface and unfathomable depth. He liked (and you tell me what writer wouldn't give something precious in exchange for?) the perfect pathos of Isaac's question about the lamb. He liked the sound of the words and, even more, the space between them, the gaps, the silences. He had imagined the story would be short, but he never imagined that it would be *so* short, or that so much of its impact would come from what wasn't there. He read the lines over and over, aloud, and he would not have been too embarrassed to admit that he was hypnotized by the sound of his own voice.

He made one copy and passed it on to his editors, telling them, "Here's my latest draft. I am still working on it." Then he took a break. He wanted to come at it a few days hence, with a fresh set of eyes. He did, and as so often happens, the spell had worn off. Here I have to be honest, or at least careful. I don't want to let all that has gone down since distort my report. He still liked it, as a story, as words on the page, elegantly arranged. It was a good start, but he wasn't finished. There were things, big things, wrong with it. In the context of the life of Abraham alone, it was deeply flawed. He couldn't leave him or it as they were. He went back to work and came up with a new version, a version he was much happier with.

But it was too late.

The writers he was working for, to a man, liked the draft he shared as much as he had liked it, at first maybe more, but without any of his subsequent reservations.

"Look," G said, "I like it too. But it's no good. Abraham's silence is all wrong."

"Wrong?" they said.

"Wrong that he just set out," he said.

"Wrong that he obeyed God?"

"Not that kind of wrong," G said. "Or not just that kind." He knew that people could disagree about that. They did then. They still do today.

"What other kind is there?"

"I mean I got Abraham wrong. I got Abraham wrong as a character, inside the story. Even if God had wanted him to saddle his donkey, and call for his servants and Isaac, and split the wood, all without saying a word, it was not like Abraham not to say a word. Even if you have no other qualms about his silence, you must admit that it was not consistent with his character."

"Character?" they said. "You are saying that it was out of character for Abraham to do what God commanded?"

"Yes," he said. "His first words to God were a question. His last were a question. And God's last words to him before he asked him to offer Isaac were in answer to his question about Ishmael, meant to reassure him that he would take good care of his firstborn too. It's just not right. Leave it like it is and it will be obvious to everyone that this story doesn't belong."

"He left home without saying a word," they said.

"Yes. He did. I admit it. But think about it: he was a semi-nomad already on his way to Canaan. The command to keep moving was not of the same magnitude or significance as the command to sacrifice his son."

"You are overanalyzing," they said.

They would not think of revising it in any significant way.

3

He protested. He implored. He pleaded. "The story could be, would be, terribly misunderstood," he said. His pleas—we can deduce—fell on deaf ears. There was nothing he could do. But he was not good at doing nothing, so he tried to go back to work. But he couldn't. Every time he sat down to write, he thought of the story and he couldn't think of the story without thinking about the other ways it might have come out. He tried reading, to take his mind off it, but no matter whom he read, no matter what he read about, the sound of the words, the look of the words, the order of the words, made him think of writing, and writing made him think of his writing, and his writing made him think of Abraham and Isaac. And he couldn't think about Abraham and Isaac without a huge wave of restlessness and regret.

Days passed, months, then years. His wife encouraged him to move on, to look forward, not back. It seemed to her that he was letting one disappointment, however large it loomed, spoil the many satisfactions of a pretty good literary life. But he was distraught and didn't even want to talk about it.

The men he had written for, on the other hand, talked about nothing else. They were jubilant, so proud of the final product. They sent him a copy and urged him to read it. They urged everyone to read it.

He couldn't even look at it.

His friends did too.

"Have you read it?"

"I can't," he said.

"Oh, you should. You won't be able to put it down."

"I can't bear to," he said.

"Why not?"

"My story."

"Your story?"

"The story of Abraham and Isaac."

"Which one?"

"The sacrifice story. It came out all wrong."

G's friend shrugged. "It is a great big book," he said, "a huge anthology of the literature of Israel." And it was: not all of it by any means, but the work the editors considered the best of it. There was—in addition to legend—genealogy, biography, and history. There were legal codes, cultic rituals and regulations, poetry, even the lyrics to some songs.

"You should read it," G's friend said. "There is some remarkable writing in there."

He couldn't and didn't.

He ate. He slept. He went to his table but never stayed for long. He walked more. He talked less. His wife was worried. Nothing she could say or do was the right thing to say or do, until what she did, whether out of frustration, or exasperation, or simple curiosity, was to start reading the book herself. She was a fast reader, and in no time she had read it from beginning to end. At which time she joined his friends and editors in urging him to read it himself.

"I can't," he said.

"Why not?" she asked.

"My story."

"Your story?"

"Abraham and Isaac. It will be terribly misunderstood. I can't even think about it."

"It's not two dozen lines," she said. A small part of Abraham's story, which is itself just a small part of whole. It is completely overshadowed by Creation and the Great Flood that comes before it, and after by the saga of Esau and Jacob and Laban and Jacob's wives and his sons, Joseph and all his brothers. Then the drama of slavery and liberation and revelation and forty years of wandering in the wilderness.

"Yes," he said, "but it's the climax, the pivotal moment of Abraham's life."

"Maybe so," she said, "but if it makes you feel any better, you should know that it doesn't seem to have left a lasting impression." In all the history that follows, despite more references than anyone could count to the God of Abraham and Isaac and Jacob and God's covenant with Abraham, Isaac, and Jacob and the land God promised to Abraham, Isaac, and Jacob, there is not one explicit reference to—she paused for emphasis—"your story."

"No mention?" he asked.

"No."

"Not one?"

"Not that I noticed."

That surprised him, and it was only then that he took a look for himself. At first he just scrolled through the book, a passage here, a passage there. Skimming or scanning the way, today, you might see a scholar searching to see if he'd been cited in another book's footnotes or bibliography or thanked in the acknowledgments. Then he scrolled some more. He was a slow reader, but very thorough, and in a few days of searching he found a handful of passages that might conceivably be interpreted as allusions to Abraham's story. One of the authors of the chapters on Isaac's son Jacob refers, cryptically, to the "terror of Isaac." And though he could imagine someone arguing that the phrase was nothing more than a synonym for the "God of Isaac," he had a hard time believing that it was just a coincidence that, with hundreds of references to the God of this and the God of that, it was only when referring to Isaac that the words "God of Isaac" became "terror of Isaac." Elsewhere, God tells Isaac that he would bless him because his father had listened to his voice and obeyed his commandments. And much later Moses reminds God of his promises to Abraham, Isaac, and Jacob, going so far as to mention multiplying Abraham's "seed like the stars of the heavens" and giving his seed all the land forever. He even notes that God himself swore those promises—"You swore by Yourself"—as God had sworn atop Moriah. But Abraham had done many things God asked, and God had made many promises. However clear those allusions seemed to G, or seem to me, in neither instance is there an explicit reference to Abraham's seeming willingness to sacrifice his son. Even in the books that recount the history after Moses and the crossing of the Jordan—the annals of the judges and the kings, the chronicles of the fall of Israel and later Judah, exile and return, then chapter after chapter of prophetic literature, wisdom literature, lots more poetry and song—there is still only fleeting mentions of Abraham and only oblique references to the story of Abraham and Isaac.

She was right. He had to admit it. He also had to make sure she understood that when it came time to decide what to include and where it should go, the anthology's editors had obviously been more concerned with portraying Israel's history as a nation, and ultimately a nation under one God, than with its literary history. Unlike the editors of most modern anthologies of literature, they did not necessarily organize the contributions chronologically. We don't know for certain which parts of the anthology, or even which parts of which parts of the anthology, were written when. G suspected that at least some of what came after his story had been written before it. If large parts of it had been written before, it might mean nothing that it wasn't referred to again.

"It may be that it was not referred to," G said, "because it was not there to refer to. I hadn't written it yet."

"Now you sound sorry," she said. "One minute you moan about how the story came out, about being read and misunderstood. The next you regret not being noticed."

And she was right again. The truth is that he was not wholly without an ego. For all his reservations, when push came to shove, he didn't want to be completely ignored. "What writer wouldn't be a little sorry?" he said.

"Maybe a writer who wrote a story about a father who nearly sacrificed his son—when it is entirely possible that God expected him to object, or at least stop the sacrifice himself," she said.

"Thanks," he said. "I got it wrong. I wanted to revise it. You know I did."

"Relax," she said. "If and when readers do notice, they will do it themselves."

"Do what?"

"They'll revise it."

"Revise it?"

"Yes. They'll revise it. They seem unable not to. Read it. The whole thing, and you will see for yourself."

So he did. He read, several hours a day for several weeks, and he saw. He saw exactly what she meant. With all due respect, it took careful reading, but no prophetic powers. If all you had in your hands was the anthology—no later translations into Aramaic, Greek, Latin, Syriac, Coptic, Arabic, or Persian—no commentary, no theories about how the book was put together, or when or by whom, no inside knowledge of the degree to which editors revised as they combined, juxtaposed, and synthesized writings produced by different schools or different traditions in different places at different times—nothing but the writings themselves, you would know it. You would know that this was one revisionary people.

They revised to elaborate, revised to elucidate, revised to answer questions, revised to interpret, revised to criticize, to accentuate, to update, to differentiate, and to explain. They revised myth, legend, and history. They revised rituals and regulations. They revised legal codes and even commandments (there are two versions of the Ten Commandments). They revised critical elements of their theology. They revised the names of people and places, including the name of the mountain where God gave Moses the Ten Commandments.

They revised the physical relationship between God and the people at Sinai (or Horeb). They revised the name of God.

Now, one might suspect that a people so bent on revising had no reverence for tradition. But just the opposite is true. These people revered tradition so deeply that they did whatever they had to do to keep it alive. So when times and ideas and circumstances and sensibilities changed, they revised it. But even when they revised it dramatically, hoping to substitute one tradition for another, even one image of God for another, the writers and editors—whether priestly editors or scribal editors or prophets or judges or kings or maybe even queens—did not believe that they had the right, or the authority, or the power, to excise that which they were revising or presenting an alternative to.

We don't know, especially for the early years, what got left on the cutting-room floor, or exactly which writers and editors did what to which texts. But one thing is clear: if the editors had been intent on imposing their view, a single view, a party line, intent upon covering up conflicting perspectives, we would not have had the book—then in many scrolls—that G had in front of him. Nor would I have the book I have in front of me today, in anything remotely resembling its current form.

We would not have both Chronicles and the parts of Samuel and Kings it revises. We would not have Deuteronomy and the parts of Exodus (and Numbers and perhaps even Leviticus) it revises. Or all of Deuteronomy, for in several significant ways that book revises, or records multiple traditions, itself. We would not have two versions of Creation, two versions of the Flood, two versions of the rebellion in the wilderness, two versions of Jacob obtaining Shechem, or, closer to home, two versions of God's covenant with Abraham, two versions of the expulsion of Hagar and Ishmael, three versions of Abraham or Isaac giving their wives to a pharaoh or king. In sum, we would not have multiple versions of more stories, and pieces of stories, and laws, and rituals, and reasons for laws and rituals, than anyone could possibly keep track of. Nor would we have so much evidence of the different perspectives, in time and over time, that marked the development of theology and law: Was Israel holy or did it simply aspire to holiness? Was the god of Abraham, Isaac, and Jacob one god of many or the one and only? Was God merciful or just or both? Did God hear Israel's prayers, accept their sacrifices, wherever they were offered, or only in one sacred place? Did we observe the Sabbath to mark Creation or the liberation from Egypt?

If revisionists had been nonchalant about tradition, let alone hostile to it, we would know only the end of the story, not how the nation got there, and the book would have been a small fraction of the length that it is.

What did all that mean for G? These people, his people, revised, but they didn't erase. "Face to face the Lord spoke to you on the mountain out of the fire," Moses says in one famous line of Deuteronomy. "I stood between the Lord and you at that time to convey the Lord's words to you, for you were afraid of the fire and did not go up the mountain," he says in the next. G liked the story but deeply regretted its meaning. He regretted its meaning but didn't want to discourage people from reading it. It was in the anthology—a great book if there ever was one—to stay, but if at any time people took note of it and were bothered by it, they would revise it. Maybe his children, maybe his children's children, maybe their children after them. Sooner or later, someone would revise it.

4

And G's wife was right.

Someone did revise it.

Just not as G had hoped, for it soon became clear that his editors were not the only readers or writers at peace with Abraham's response to God's call.

Consider one of the first surviving revisions of the story, the one that came in the book of Jubilees, a revision of the entire early history, from Creation to Moses. It appeared in the second century BCE and took its name from the calendar reform the author advocated. He wanted to date all of Jewish history (every momentous event, every festival, every birth, and every death) precisely, dividing all time into Jubilees, periods of forty-nine years made up of seven segments of seven solar years.

It may be somewhat misleading to call Jubilees a revision. Every indication is that its author (whom I am going to call Jubilees for the sake of simplicity) or his editor or publisher thought of it as the original. I don't know who believed that. But those who did, however devout, were not seasoned readers. Except in the places, and there are many of them, where the author borrowed verbatim, his voice was different, his style was different, his point of view was different (the biblical narrator is omniscient; Jubilees's is Gabriel, God's angel of presence, channeling God and dictating to Moses on Sinai), his obsessions (among them the calendar and the end of time) were different. Most pertinent, his Abraham was different, different from the Abraham in the pages of the book we call Genesis.

If I have persuaded you of anything—just one thing—I hope I have persuaded you that Abraham was one complicated character. Seventy-five years old and he hitched his wagon to a God who appeared out of nowhere and said next to nothing about who he was, where he'd come from, or how he expected Abraham to behave. It was a bumpy ride and three decades later Abraham was still trying to figure out what he had gotten himself into.

G's hope and expectation was that readers coming along later would see that Abraham's response to God's command was out of character. That they'd ask, "Would he have set out without saying a word?" But what Jubilees saw as out of character were large chunks of the chapters that came before. His Abraham was born halfway between Ur and heaven, with an instinctive sense of how to get the rest of the way. Even as a small boy, he understood (in addition to advanced astronomy and agronomy) the errors of the earth, especially idol worship and uncleanliness. He urged his father to embrace the one true God, and when all else failed, he set fire to the house where Terah's man-made gods were stored. Most strikingly, in Jubilees's telling, Abraham approached God to talk about a covenant—not the other way around. Like the biblical Abraham, Jubilees's Abraham occasionally had doubts, but he never gave his wife to a pharaoh or king (she was taken from him), laughed at anything God said, or questioned God's judgment, not even about the sinners in Sodom.

Some will say the makeover was predictable. Abraham was a founder, and though writers occasionally gain a few minutes of fame and a small fortune by debunking founders, the surer path, at least over time, is to turn them into saints. Jubilees was hardly the first or only writer of his age to apply posthumous polish to a portrait, not even the first to apply it to Abraham. The author of Nehemiah, a fourth-century BCE text and one of last books to be added to the anthology, jumped right from Creation to Abraham, and what he found worthy of note was that Abraham had done exactly what God had asked him to do. Ben Sira, whose extremely influential book of wisdom, composed early in the second century BCE, was ultimately not included in the Jewish canon, gave Abraham pride of place in his passages praising famous men. Sira called him "the great father of a multitude of nations," who, when tested, was found faithful, by which Sira meant obedient and devoted, inclined to walk in God's way.

Then there was the book of Judith, another second-century composition, a gripping work of historical fiction about a beautiful and devout widow—she feared God with great devotion—who used her good looks and charm to single-handedly turn back a brutal siege by Holofernes, a commander in the army of the neo-Babylonian king Nebuchadnezzar. Holofernes's troops had surrounded the Israelites and seized their springs and wells. The streets were littered with the bodies of the dead and dying. The people urged their leaders to surrender, and some of them promised to do so if God didn't show his mercy in five days. Judith would have none of it. She exhorted her fellow citizens not to give God a deadline, not to put him to the test, not to bind his purposes, not to think they could know him or move him as they might an ordinary man. Instead, they should simply be strong to the bitter end: "In spite of everything let us give thanks to the Lord our God, who is putting us to the test as he did our forefathers. Remember what he did with Abraham, and how he tested Isaac . . . For he has not tried us with fire, as he did them, to search their hearts."

Jubilees worked in an adoring tradition. (One poet, a contemporary, boasted that he had heard the story of the "far-famed Abraham" "a thousand times.") Still, Jubilees did as much to elaborate upon and advance that tradition as anyone in his day whose work has survived. His Abraham simply could not have looked better in what Jubilees imagined were God's eyes. Yet his purity and goodness were problematic when it came to the biblical version of the story. If Abraham recognized the one true God from infancy and never wavered, if absolute obedience was his defining trait, the story's first line makes no sense. Why would God need to test him? And, by Jubilees's time, that question rubbed up against another: Even if Abraham wasn't such an angel, why would God need to test him or anyone else? What about Abraham wouldn't Jubilees's all-knowing God know?

Well, Jubilees was nothing if not inventive, and daring, an exegetical escape artist, able to wiggle out of every imaginable jam. He answered those questions by employing a character he'd introduced much earlier in his story, Prince Mastema, a dark fallen angel, a character he may have first encountered in Job. Mastema was jealous of all the swooning over Abraham in heaven, all the talk about his faithfulness despite affliction. So he taunted God, suggesting that Abraham loved Isaac above all else. He told God to test him, to see just how devoted to God he really was.

Now, Jubilees's God was no fool. He knew that Abraham had proved himself through many trials and tribulations: he had left his home, suffered famine, nearly lost his wife to a pharaoh and his nephew to cantankerous kings. He had submitted to circumcision and sacrificed his older son, Ishmael, and Ishmael's mother to the strong will of his wife. "And," Jubilees wrote, "in everything through which he tested him he was found faithful. He himself did not grow impatient, nor was he slow to act; for he was faithful and one who loved the Lord." (Note that the Abraham of old loved Isaac and obeyed God. Love of God, Abraham's and everyone else's, comes a little later in the story.)

So why did God ask him to sacrifice Isaac? Jubilees shows us, but not until after his Abraham rose early, saddled his ass, split the wood, called for Isaac and his lads, and set out on his three-day journey. With Gabriel and Mastema at his side, God watched as Abraham built the altar, placed the wood on it, bound Isaac, placed him on the wood, and stretched forth his hand to take the knife to slay his son. Only then did God tell Gabriel to tell Abraham to stop.

Why?

In Genesis, God's messenger says: "Now I know that you fear me." But in Jubilees's revision we hear God's instructions, and in those instructions God deleted the "now": "Tell him not to let his hand go down on the child and not to do anything to him, because I know that he is one who fears the Lord."

So Gabriel called from heaven and said, "Abraham! Abraham!"

Abraham was startled and said, "Yes?"

Gabriel said: "Do not lay your hands on the child and do not do anything to him, because now I know that you are one who fears the Lord. You have not refused me your first-born son."

Note the return of the "now": coming out of Gabriel's mouth it causes no trouble. If someone now knows something about Abraham that he didn't know before, it is Gabriel and Mastema and the other angels. And sure enough, "the prince of the Mastema was put to shame." And Abraham lifted up his eyes and looked and, behold, he saw a single ram caught by his horns, and Abraham went and took the ram and offered it as a burnt offering instead of his son.

Then, just to make sure that there was no misunderstanding about what God knew and when he knew it, Jubilees altered God's blessing: "All the nations of the earth will be blessed through your descendants because of the fact that you have obeyed my command. I have made known to everyone that you are faithful to me in everything that I have told you. Go in peace." Here Jubilees's trick is the "to everyone," which ensured that the verb "YDTY" would be read as *yidda'tî* ("I have made known") and not *yāda'tî* ("I know"). Biblical Hebrew has no vowels. Without them, Jubilees's "YDTY" could have been pronounced and understood either way. But not when it was followed by "to everyone." We don't "know something" to everyone. We make something known to everyone. We show them.

Jubilees's God knew everything. He was not testing Abraham. He was demonstrating his devotion.

Now let me make it clear just in case it is not. Jubilees was not some woolly-headed religious reformer, softening up God, looking for an end run around religious observance. Or an irreverent writer having fun with sacred characters. Just the opposite: he was a serious fellow, a revivalist at a time when the attitudes, values, ideas, language, even customs and manners that Philip of Macedon and his son Alexander had brought from the West were taking root in Near Eastern sand and soil. I imagine Jubilees speaking to Jews so smitten by Greek ways that they had begun to wonder if they really had to observe all those tiresome commandments in order to be good Jews. Trying to bring the wayward back into the fold, Jubilees stressed the primacy of law and ritual observance. He wrote and revised to show that the law, particularly the calendar, the schedule of festivals, was manifest in the early chapters of biblical narrative as well as in the later chapters that are explicitly concerned with cultic rules and regulations.

Jubilees's Abraham offered Isaac on the fifteenth day of the first month, the same day of the year that Jews in Egypt would later sacrifice a lamb to keep the Destroyer away from their firstborn. He thereby located the origins of the paschal offering in the religious life of the first Jew. His Abraham marked the near sacrifice with a seven-day festival (three days from Beersheba to Moriah, three days back, one day for Sabbath), a festival that just happened to coincide with the seven-day festival Jubilees knew (and we know) as Passover. In his telling, the connection between the events and their commemorations was not the least bit forced: Sarah's firstborn son, and with him Israel's future, was delivered from the machinations of Mastema and redeemed with a lamb. Later, the Jewish people, God's firstborn, were delivered from the Destroyer by the blood of the lamb. The lesson was clear: Obey his laws, do what he tells you to do, and God will take care of you. Abraham observed Passover. You should too.

Jubilees took Abraham's obedience for granted. What needed to be explained was God's command. For Philo, a stoic Jewish philosopher living in Alexandria two centuries later (in the first half of the first century of the Common Era), it was the other way around. If Philo wondered why God asked, or was troubled that he did, he never let on. His attention, like mine, was focused on Abraham's response.

But there we part ways. He was as comfortable as Jubilees was with Abraham's obedience. His project was to explain it, show what it was made of, part of his larger project of demonstrating, in one fell swoop, the greatness of the Jewish tradition and its universal relevance, the harmony between the written law of Moses and the philosopher's unwritten natural law. You see, Philo shared Jubilees's devotion to Judaism but not his aversion to Hellenism. What he did was take Abraham's obedience and translate it into Greek.

God commanded, and Abraham obeyed.

No whining, as Abraham had whined when God said he was going to make his name great and he asked how: How will I be great when I am going to die childless?

No anxious questions, like those Abraham had asked when God promised land and he asked how he was going to know that it was really his.

No qualms, like those Abraham had expressed when God

announced his intention to destroy Sodom, or divided devotion: remember when God promised a son through Sarah and Abraham responded by saying that he hoped that Ishmael would live in God's favor.

No hesitation: I am thinking of the moment Sarah told him to send Ishmael away.

God commanded and Abraham obeyed. Abraham's fondness for the boy—his only legitimate son, the child of his old age, a wonderful boy—was indescribable. Yet Abraham "showed no change of color nor weakening of soul, but remained steadfast as ever with a judgment that neither bent nor wavered." He simply set out to do what God had asked him to do. Isaac's question about the lamb would have reduced most men to tears, or struck them dumb. Either way, Isaac would have known where the lamb was. Not Abraham. He didn't alter his voice, his countenance, or his intention. He looked at his son with a steady eye, assured him that God would provide, and went about his business.

Philo loved the story. He considered it the greatest moment in a long life of great moments. He couldn't imagine a nobler example of the wise man suppressing emotion for the sake of reason, the reason that the stoic philosopher considered the unwritten law of nature and essence of God and the human soul.

Just one thing bothered him: not what Abraham did, but why God says he did it: "Now I know that you fear me." The word "fear" provided the opening for cynics and skeptics whom Philo criticized but didn't name, lowlifes who loved nothing more than dragging everyone down to their level. They either misunderstood the story or intentionally twisted its meaning. "So what?" they said. Many a man had sacrificed a child. Some had sacrificed several. What's so special about Abraham almost sacrificing one?

And Philo, as well versed in Greek history, poetry, and drama as he was in the books he attributed to Moses, would have known the stories.

Leos, one of the founders of Athens, son of Orpheus, sacrificed three daughters in a successful effort to end a famine. By one account, the daughters volunteered and went exuberantly to the altar.

Aristodemus of Messenia sacrificed one daughter when his city was struck by a plague. He didn't have to. The lot had fallen to another man's child. But when the father of that young woman whisked her off to Sparta, Aristodemus (ignoring the protests and pleas of the girl's fiancé) rushed his daughter to the top of the city gates.

Then there was Iphigenia, about whom accounts vary widely. Her father, Agamemnon, had learned from an oracle that Artemis was angry, and in her anger she was holding back the wind that the Greeks needed to get their ships to Troy. Nothing short of sacrifice would appease her. After much back-and-forth between Agamemnon and his brother (Menelaus), then Agamemnon and his wife (Clytemnestra), then Agamemnon, Clytemnestra, and Iphigenia herself, Iphigenia insisted against all argument upon giving her life for her country. Some versions of the story end with her on her way to the altar: "With my own blood in sacrifice I will wash out the fated curse of God." In others, the ax actually falls and blood flows, but it is the blood of a deer, a deer Artemis left behind when she whisked Iphigenia away.

King Athamas of Orchomenus had two wives and four children. His second wife wanted the children from his first marriage, Phrixus and Helle, out of her way. So she ruined (by roasting) the seed for the season's crop, causing a famine, and then, when she learned that her husband had sent a messenger to the oracle to determine what the gods wanted, she bribed the oracle to say that the gods wanted Phrixus and Helle. The children were saved at the last moment by a flying golden ram. Helle fell off en route to safety, giving the Hellespont its name. Phrixus made it safely to the city Aia, where he sacrificed the ram to Zeus in gratitude, was warmly received by the king, and was given the king's daughter in marriage. The fleece of that very ram was later the object of Jason's quest, but that's another story.

Closer to home, in the book we call Judges, there was Jephthah, who in battle with the Ammonites made what most commentators since have characterized as a reckless vow. If God delivered his enemies into his hands and saw to his safe return home from battle, he'd make a burnt offering of whatever or whomever came out to greet him. Much to his dismay, his daughter was the first one out the door. He was bereft, but he kept his vow. Further along in Israel's history, the king of Moab, under siege by Israel, sacrificed a son atop the city gates.

Philo knew men had sometimes sacrificed children. But, he insisted, Abraham's sacrifice was different, not just one more sacrifice but a novel form of conduct. Abraham didn't do it mindlessly, out of tradition. It was not tradition where he came from. Or out of a desire to impress fellow citizens or subjects. He did it without fanfare or witnesses, without telling a soul. Or—as the vast majority of men did it—in a moment of crisis and fear, in the hope of getting something from God.

Abraham did it simply because God asked him to do it. (That God asked may have been the biggest difference, but not one that Philo noted.) Abraham did it solely to demonstrate his perfect piety, his devotion, and his love.

Well, to get from fear to love, Philo had to put aside the book of Genesis the minute Abraham raised the knife, before God stopped him and explained why it wasn't necessary for him to go through with it. And that's precisely what Philo did. He then moved, as he believed any true philosopher ultimately would, beyond or beneath the story's literal meanings, its local meanings, to its allegorical meanings, its universal meanings, the meanings only wise men can see.

Isaac's name, Philo wrote, means "laughter"—not the carnal laughter of the body but the ethereal laughter of the mind. All laughter and joy ultimately belong to God. Only he is completely happy, free of the sorrow that humans so often live with, or the fear of sorrow to come. When God asks for Isaac, Abraham doesn't hesitate. He understands that Isaac, like laughter and joy, belong to God. But for that understanding, for his piety and his love, God rewards him. He stops the sacrifice, thereby sharing some of his laughter and sparing Abraham some fear and grief.

That's ingenious, and lovely in its way, but it is not the story I know or the larger cycle of stories of which it was, and remains, a part. Abraham certainly knew his share of fear and grief. But a purely happy God, without frustration, sadness, or regret? That's not the God of Genesis. Between sunset on the sixth day and Moses's farewell address, you'll have as hard a time finding a happy God as you will have finding a man, woman, or child who loves him.

Don't get me wrong. I have grown fond of Philo. I admire his learning, and though some say his knowledge of Hebrew was minimal or nonexistent, thereby rendering meaningless all his allegory based on the deep meaning of particular words, I, knowing so few languages myself, would be a horrible hypocrite to hold his ignorance of Hebrew against him. Long after his death, many now-famous men adopted his distinction between literal meanings and allegorical meanings, the carnal and the spiritual, to say some really nasty things about the Jews. But I'd be the last writer on earth to argue that a writer is responsible for every last thing posterity does with his or her words. Writer to writer, I regret that he didn't pay more attention to his prose. The language is stuffy and there is a tedious sameness to the structure of his sentences. It can be a small act of stoicism to read him. Still, I can't help but admire the precision, rigor, and dogged persistence of his analysis. He was a reader, a real reader, for whom every writer has a special place in his or her heart.

I only wish he didn't like G's story quite so much. For all his interpreting and allegorizing, for all his effort, perfectly understandable, to turn a story of fear and obedience into a story of reason and love, he actually left it pretty much as he found it on the page. That's partly because he too fell for the story's silences. And even more because he, like Jubilees, took Abraham's response for granted. Philo himself was a brave man. At the age of sixty, in the fortieth year of the Common Era, the final year of the reign of Caligula, he risked his life to protest vicious violence against Alexandria's Jews. Yet it never seems to have occurred to him that Abraham's standing up to God, asking him what he was thinking, might also, in the face of his fear, have been a stirring example of stoicism, reason, piety, and love.

6

~~~

To get a sense of Philo's comfort with the story, all you need to do is turn to Flavius Josephus, the Jewish priest (born Yosef ben Matityahu), general, rebel leader (for a while), later advocate of accommodation with the Romans, and self-proclaimed prophet, who, late in the first century of the Common Era, toward the end of a long and eventful life, settled down in Rome under the patronage of the emperor Vespasian, then Titus, and finally Domitian, to write history: first a history of (and our primary source for) the war with Rome; then a general history of the Jews, starting with Creation; and finally a short memoir—three works to which anyone interested in late Second Temple Judaism or Jewish history will at one time or another turn.

Philo took aim at writers who insisted that there was nothing extraordinary about Abraham. He left the story as he found it but put the great man's deeds in context, revealing what he took to be the story's hidden meanings, showing skeptical or cynical readers what they couldn't see. Josephus, though no less admiring, worried that his readers might conclude that Abraham (and his God) were extraordinary, but in a horrible way, the former bloodthirsty and the latter murderous. To lessen the likelihood, he added scores of lines to the story, many of them lines of dialogue, saying what G had left unsaid.

God appears, enumerates the many good things he has done for

Abraham, and asks for Isaac back in sacrifice, at which point Josephus jumps in to make God's motives clear. " 'He' simply wanted to 'make trial of' and 'manifest his piety'—to show that Abraham had his priorities straight. What better way to do that than to show that he 'put the doing of God's good pleasure even above the life of his child.' " Later in the story, right after God "forbade" Abraham to slay his son, Josephus allows God to explain his motives himself: He didn't ask out of some "craving for human blood." He didn't make him "a father only to rob him in such impious fashion of his offspring; no, He simply wished but to test his soul and see whether even such orders would find him obedient."

As for Abraham, Josephus didn't deny, couldn't deny, wouldn't want to deny, that when God asked for Isaac, Abraham set out without protest or pause, making all the preparations without saying a word to anyone about God's commandment or his own resolve to obey it (thereby demonstrating a readiness that, according to one standard translation, even God found "surprising"). But Abraham's ardor had nothing to do with eagerness. It was simply a sign that he understood that everything he had, he had thanks to God, and as a result "in everything we must submit to his will." And that's why, after he built the altar, Abraham turned to Isaac and launched into a long address, emphasizing that none of this was his plan. He had prayed for Isaac for years and rejoiced when he arrived. He had hoped Isaac would live a long life, take care of him in his old age, be his heir. Unfortunately, God had plans of his own. He, who had given him Isaac, now wanted him back. The silver lining was that now Isaac would not die in an ordinary way, whether in war, from disease, or by accident. Instead, he would be "sped" by his own father to God, the Father of all, through the rites of sacrifice.

Spelling all that out, including some things that seem obvious, Josephus provided an early demonstration that when it comes to storytelling, more is not always better. But he was a historian, with the historian's desire to tell the whole story and the historian's reluctance to let good research, or any research, go to waste. If he had evidence, whether from the teachings of Moses or the traditions that had grown up around them, he would be inclined to use it. If that evidence allowed him to interpret or explain something, he would be inclined to interpret and explain. It is partly a matter of pride. What is the good of knowing something if no one knows you know it? And partly, control. Why take the chance that readers will explain it for themselves—and get it wrong. That's why so many history books are so long.

But there was more to Josephus's verbosity than a professional preference for sound over silence. He wrote a mere half century after Philo. He read him, learned and borrowed from him, admired him, and in writing his history of the Jews he thought of himself as contributing to Philo's project, explaining and extolling the Jewish tradition. But he was writing in a different, and much more dangerous, world. The Romans had laid siege to Jerusalem, destroyed the Second Temple, suppressed the revolt, and set out to extinguish every last bit of Jewish resistance, if not every last Jew. Palestine · was awash with Jewish blood.

Josephus was a survivor. He had survived a shipwreck that took the lives of hundreds of fellow passengers. He had survived the siege of Jotapata, a small hilltop town north of Nazareth, on the Roman general Vespasian's route to Jerusalem. After the breach of the walls, Josephus and four dozen Jotapatans took refuge in a cave. His compatriots concluded that if death and surrender were their only choices, they'd prefer to die. Yet Josephus had mixed feelings about that kind of martyrdom (his elaborate arguments against it anticipate almost every Jewish objection to it in the centuries ahead), and after a suicide pact that involved the drawing of straws and the death of all but the man Josephus was supposed to kill before he killed himself, he and that other man came out of the cave alive. He was captured, imprisoned, and sentenced to death, but Vespasian spared his life when Josephus persuaded him that he, Josephus, would have been dead already, in mass suicide, if God hadn't wanted him alive to deliver an important message: that he,

Vespasian, would ultimately ascend to the throne. Vespasian took Josephus on as his hostage and interpreter, freeing him when his prophecy came to pass. By the time Josephus started writing history, he was a Roman citizen, living on a pension and in luxury at the emperor's expense. But his people were still in trouble. The task of demonstrating, to his Roman audience, the antiquity, the preciousness, and the relevance of Jewish history was more pressing than ever. It might be a matter of life or death. Josephus had every reason to try to explain exactly what Abraham and his God were thinking.

And what Isaac was thinking. In Josephus's hands, even Isaac (whom I have always imagined as a small boy, just old enough to carry the wood and ask, as a small boy might, about the lamb) is loquacious, a young man, fully aware of his duty. Writers before Josephus had implied that sometime before Abraham bound him Isaac had realized that he himself was the lamb. The author of Judith had his (or her) hero urge his or her fellow citizens, suffering miserably and on the verge of surrender, to "remember what God did with Abraham, and how he tested Isaac." A tested Isaac had to have had some time to think about his future, or lack thereof. And Philo interpreted the story's haunting refrain, "And the two of them went together," to mean that they had walked together at the same pace, in the same place, in mind as well as body.

Josephus's Isaac left less to the imagination. He responded to Abraham's address with an address of his own, assuring his father that he understood, and then some. The way he saw it, if he wasn't willing to go along with God and his father—if he "should not resign himself up readily to both their pleasures"—he wouldn't be "worthy" of having been "born" in the first place. The fact is that he would have been willing "even if" the idea to offer him up had been his father's alone. And what father, not wanting to sacrifice his son but concluding that he had no choice in the matter, would not take some solace in the thought that his son understood? With those words, Isaac immediately made his way to the altar.

Just to be sure that readers understood that Isaac was speaking of his own free will and accord (which was also to understand that the middle patriarch, the son of Abraham, the father of Israel, was not simply a prop in this momentous play, a lamb being led to slaughter), Josephus gave us his exact age. Isaac was twenty-five, old enough to argue, fight back, or simply run away if he had had any objections to his aged father's plans.

Josephus's Isaac was a knowing and willing victim, but his knowledge was narrow. He knew one ancient virtue, obedience: son to father; father and son to God. What God commands, you do, even if he commands you to do something that he himself will characterize as "impious" shortly after he stops you from doing it. Other first- and second-century Isaacs knew more, perhaps none as much as the Isaac of the writer we know only as Pseudo-Philo, a Jewish writer whose one extant work, in a Latin translation, was shelved and passed along with Latin translations of Philo of Alexandria and for many years attributed to him, though I don't know how. Their approaches to scripture are nearly as distinct as their styles.

Pseudo-Philo was as drunk on words and scripture as Philo was stone sober. He was an ecstatic rewriter of the Bible, whose retelling of the big story, from Creation to Saul, often reads as if he had found fragments of several sacred scrolls and then, without a copy of the original to guide him, or any interest whatsoever in restoring it to its original form, set out to produce an updated edition. His treatment of the near sacrifice falls into three different chapters. Today a generous reviewer might say that he chose to organize his book thematically, as opposed to chronologically, and there would be much truth to that. From Pseudo-Philo's point of view, there was meaning to the madness.

Pseudo-Philo's God, like the God of Jubilees's, was prodded by

jealous angels to ask for Isaac, and his Abraham set out immediately. When, along the way, Abraham told Isaac the plan, the
boy was momentarily confused, even dismayed. He reminded his
father that it was the sweet smell of burning lamb that God seemed
to love. And the best of the flock was set aside for slaughter in
order to atone for wicked deeds of men. Man, on the contrary, was
supposed to inherit this world. "Why then," he asked his father,
"should you be saying to me now, 'Come and inherit eternal life
and time without measure?'"

We will never know how Abraham would have explained it,
for Isaac answered his own question before his father had a chance
to say a word: "Why if not that I was indeed born in this world
in order to be offered as a sacrifice to him who made me? Indeed,
this will be my blessedness over other men—and in me the generations will be proclaimed and through me nations will understand
how God made a human soul worthy for sacrifice."

Just in case anyone misunderstood what Isaac was saying (and
at least in the English translation of the awkward Latin translation of a text that scholars assume was first composed in Hebrew,
it would be easy to misunderstand or not understand at all), eight
chapters later Pseudo-Philo retells the story of Jephthah, the mighty
warrior of Gilead, who, desperate for an edge in a difficult battle,
vowed to sacrifice to God "whomever comes forth from the doors
of my house to meet me." Alas, it was his daughter, his only child,
and he rent his clothes and moaned and groaned about his fate.

His daughter (who here, unlike in Judges, has a name, Seila)
urged him to get hold of himself. "Who is there who would be sad
in death," she asked, "seeing the people freed?" Remember, she
said, the days of the fathers, "when the father placed the son as a
holocaust"—a whole burnt sacrifice—"and he did not refuse him
but gladly gave consent to him, and the one being offered was ready
and the one who was offering was rejoicing."

Here Isaac is not merely appended to a story about Abraham's
obedience. Or to Jubilees's story of a demonstration of the same, or

to Philo's story of God's sharing his happiness and joy with those who display perfect piety, devotion, and love. Rather, he himself stands at the center of a story about the dignity of human sacrifice, of an innocent boy dying, as a sin offering, for God. And though Pseudo-Philo gave Isaac a voice and theological imagination that would have been impressive even at twenty-five, he was not alone in imagining Isaac that way. If you find that hard to believe and you have a strong stomach, grab a Bible that includes the Apocrypha and take a look at the second and fourth books of Maccabees. The former is an abridgment of a long-lost Jewish history. The latter is an essay in stoic philosophy—a celebration, not unlike Philo's, of the elevation of reason above passion—grounded in a portion of that same history, a graphic account of the earliest Jewish resistance to Antiochus IV, who ruled the Seleucid Empire for ten years, starting in 175 BCE, and whose persecution of the Jews contributed to the Maccabean revolt.

Antiochus defiled the Temple, forbade circumcision and the observance of the Sabbath, and made it a capital crime just to say "I am a Jew." It isn't clear what he was thinking. Some say he stumbled into a Jewish civil war, mistaking the revolt of exurban traditionalists against Hellenized Jerusalem Jews for a revolt against his rule. Some say that after Rome curtailed his invasion of Egypt, he coveted the Temple's gold. Some, including one historian who knew him, say he was not thinking at all. He was insane. Whatever his motivation, his decrees and his deeds made a bad situation in and around Jerusalem worse, and in histories of the revolt against him, and against Greek culture and Greek rule, Jewish writers celebrated the Jewish martyrs who suffered publicly and, when called upon, died for their God.

The second book of Maccabees recounts the murder of two women who ignored the prohibition of circumcision. They were paraded around the city with their newborns at their breasts and then hurled from the walls. Another group of Jews sneaked off to a cave to observe the Sabbath. They were burned alive. Both 2 Maccabees and 4 Maccabees tell the tale of Eleazar, an aged scribe, respected in Jerusalem by pagans and Jews alike. Antiochus's goons force-fed him a piece of pork. He spat it out and led his captors to the rack. Still eager to spare his life, they urged him to substitute kosher meat for the king's. He refused and urged other children of Abraham to die, like Isaac, nobly for their religion. Beaten, scourged, cut, stabbed, burned to the bone, and about to expire, he lifted his eyes to God and said, "You know, O God, that though I could have saved myself, I am dying in these fiery torments for the sake of the Law. Be merciful to your people and let our punishment be a satisfaction on their behalf. Make my blood their purification, and take my life as a ransom for theirs."

Seven other victims of Antiochus were brothers, sadistically and grotesquely tortured—with wheels, joint dislocaters, rack and hooks, catapults and cauldrons, braziers, wedges and bellows, thumbscrews and iron claws—one after another in front of their mother, who was proud to her own dying breath of her sons' piety and resolve. She took strength from the example of Abraham, the first Jewish parent to sacrifice a son to God. Like him, she put religious reason—her love and fear of God—above her sympathy for her sons. Her "sympathy for her children" was great, the chronicler wrote, but it did not sway her, "for she was of the same mind as Abraham." "For God's sake also," she said, "our father Abraham was zealous to sacrifice his son Isaac, the ancestor of our nation; and when Isaac saw his father's hand wielding a knife and descending upon him, he did not cower." Meanwhile, one of that woman's sons implored his brothers: "Remember whence you came and at the hand of what father Isaac gave himself to be sacrificed for piety's sake."

Clearly, we are not in Genesis anymore. Not that all the stories there are suitable for children. Horrible things happened and worse were threatened. But the details were generally left to the imagination. Two writers, at the very least, had a hand in recounting the Flood. Neither thought it necessary to describe a single person drowning. As for blood, there's not much of it. Cain killed Abel. His blood cried out, but just metaphorically. Jacob's sons slew the citizens of Shechem (as they were recuperating from circumcision) in revenge for the rape of Dinah. Without a drop of blood. In Exodus, the blood certainly starts flowing (water turned to blood, the blood of the lambs smeared on the doorposts, the blood of the firstborn), and in Leviticus there is so much animal blood splashed around altars that today the squeamish tend to pass right over those pages. In Deuteronomy, the specter of spilled blood and a whole lot of other really nasty stuff hovers above the would-be disobedient. Nevertheless: nowhere in the first five books is there precedent for the virtually pornographic depiction of that poor mother cheering as the king's henchmen gouge, scalp, skin, fry, boil, and dismember her seven sons.

But here's the essential point: Even if the contributors to those books had been into that kind of thing, it never would have occurred to them to portray suffering or dying young as something that happens to good people who live their lives by God's laws. The chapters of scripture on Abraham, Isaac, and Jacob, like the chapters and books that follow them, are full of mixed signals and outright contradictions. Different writers took different positions on some pretty weighty questions of history, theology, and law. I could show you passages that suggest that God wants false prophets put to death immediately and others that suggest he wants those accused of false prophecy to have fair trials. I could show you passages where God says that the sins of the fathers will be visited upon the children and others where he says they absolutely will not. I could show you passages where it is clear that the author thought that the god of Abraham was one of many and others where it is just as clear that the author thought he was the one and only God. But if there was widespread agreement about anything, it was that God takes care of those who obey him and at the very least abandons those who do not. The blessings in Deuteronomy are reserved for those who walk in God's way. The curses are the punishment for those who go astray. The godly prosper on earth. The ungodly fail. To be sure, those self-effacing children of God in Maccabees, and their mother, insist that they are suffering for their sins. But there is not a hint that they have done anything wrong. If they suffer for sins, they are the sins of others.

Times change. Persecution changes too, and the authors of Maccabees may have been trying to make sense of and give theological meaning to a form of persecution that the Hebrew scriptures didn't fully explain: the persecution of Jews not as Israelites or Judeans, people who occupied a coveted city or plain, or controlled a coveted well, but as Jews, people who worshipped a particular god in a particular way. Antiochus's victims believed in God and observed all his laws. Yet they suffered, suffered for doing exactly what God told them to do. And yet despite their suffering, and perhaps earthly failure, they wanted to believe that God still loved them, that their suffering, individual and communal, was a clear sign that he loved them: He punished them immediately instead of waiting until their crimes reached great heights. He tested them, disciplined them, but did not forsake them. And he would reward them for their suffering with eternal life.

I can see where they were coming from, but as a reader and writer trying to understand Abraham and Isaac, I can't hide my discomfort with the development. I expected Abraham to protest or at least ask God why he had made such an inexplicable demand, a demand that seemed to contradict his promise and confound his own grand plan. I am sorry he didn't. You might think I am dreaming, that in the context of his place and time my expectation of a questioning Abraham is an impossible stretch. But is it any less of a stretch to say, as some writers had begun to say, that Abraham was zealous to kill Isaac and that Isaac was the first Jewish martyr, not just ready but glad to die to sanctify God's name?

Even some writers who celebrated martyrdom understood the point I am trying to make. After the emperor Hadrian suppressed the Bar Kokhba revolt in 135 CE and renewed the Roman crusade against the Jews (those not sold into slavery were prohibited from entering Jerusalem, circumcising their sons, observing the Sabbath, even studying Torah), several writers recast the story of that Maccabean mother and her sons. They gave her a name, Miriam, and portrayed her as resisting not Greek but Roman persecution. But like the unnamed mother, Miriam was perfectly devout, her sons brave and true to God. When the time came for her youngest to die, she urged the emperor to kill her too, right then and there, but he (contemptuously citing Leviticus) refused. Miriam squeezed the baby to her breast and gave him a message for his greatest grandfather: "Do not preen yourself [on your righteousness], saying 'I built an altar and offered up my son, Isaac.' Behold, our mother built seven altars and offered up seven sons in one day. Yours was only a test, but mine was in earnest."

8

Now, someone looking back at all this revising at the turn of the millennium might be struck by an apparent paradox. Writers took every imaginable liberty with the story of the near sacrifice. Some took unimaginable liberties. Yet as they did, they went out of their way to say that the entire anthology, the literature that they revised, was not just complete but perfect—every letter, every number, every word, every phrase, every juxtaposition, every omission, every repetition, every flight of fancy, every seeming contradiction, every error of transmission or translation, every slip of the pen, every compromise with an editor, every surrender to exhaustion or frustration or a deadline or darkness at the end of the day—intentional, purposeful, and meaningful, the completely conscious and perfectly realized design of its author.

And get this: some of them suggested or said (or simply assumed that everyone knew) that the entire thing, not just the cycle of stories about Abraham, not just the stories before and after that cycle, not just the laws, rituals, and regulations, all those building plans and codes, but all the myth, history, poetry, philosophy, and even prophecy—they said all that had been dictated (the first five books to Moses), revealed (to the prophets), inspired, and (according to some) actually written by a single writer, black fire on white fire, a ghostwriter; not my ghostwriter, however, but rather another, in many people's minds the first, last, and greatest of all ghostwriters. God. Not everyone said all that, by any means. But most everyone did.

Wouldn't you know it? Nineteen lines that the author struggled with, then lost control of and wanted to change but was not able to, nineteen lines that he regretted like he had never regretted anything he had written before, in time came to be considered not just perfect, to the letter, but divine.

I take the compliment on his behalf, and appreciate the irony. The history of literature is full of it. But I am less interested in the irony than the paradox—the paradox of divinely inspired writings that (centuries after the Scriptures were redacted and the canon closed) every Tom, Dick, and Harry (or Jubilees, Philo, and Josephus) felt free to revise. Or, to be more precise, the reason why, in the minds of generation after generation of writers, copyists, editors, and translators at the turn of the Common Era, there was no paradox at all: they did not think of themselves as revising a thing. The glory of Jewish literature, Josephus explained, the history no less than the law, was not simply that it comprised exactly twenty-two books "containing the record of all time," each of them written by a prophet who had obtained his knowledge from God. It was also that throughout "long ages" no one had "ventured either to add, or to remove, or to alter a syllable." (The Greeks, by contrast, possessed "myriads of inconsistent books," "mere stories, improvised according to the fancy of their authors.") What we might see as adding (say, in the scores of words of direct speech that Josephus added to his rendition of Genesis 22), Josephus and other writers saw as explicating, interpreting, illuminating, finding the real and true meaning of a text that was difficult, deeply mysterious, even intentionally cryptic, its true significance often shrouded, whether in indirection, hidden meanings, or even baffling contradictions. It was a text that they believed often said something different from what it appeared to say, meant something different from what it appeared to mean, taught something different from what it appeared to teach. Without judges, sages, wise men, priests, and eventually rabbis to interpret, decipher, and explain it, we would be lost.

Ancient interpreters assumed the text was perfect and they assumed it was mysterious, but I don't think there was anything inevitable about the marriage of those two assumptions producing dramatic revision or transformative interpretation. Would it be a crime to leave a perfect story mysterious? I don't think so. In literature, as in painting or music, even history, not every mystery has to be solved, not every enigma has to be interpreted, explained once and for all. There are many stories, to say nothing of poems and even more paintings, that I don't fully understand, or understand at all. It wouldn't occur to me to change a word or a brushstroke. In fact, I would be no more likely to insist on knowing what they mean than I would be to ask or insist upon knowing the cause or meaning of the layers of light—orange, purple, pink, red, azure, and gray—that form in and around the clouds over the river out my window at sunset so many nights. I am not saying no one should ever inquire, nor even that I myself never do, but simply that it isn't a crime just to look and lose yourself in the view, letting go of the need to know, as I often do standing in front of a work of abstract art, or reading some of my favorite poetry—

The palm stands on the edge of space.
The wind moves slowly in the branches.
The bird's fire-fangled feathers dangle down.

—or listening to certain classical music. I enjoy the sound and sense and allow the rest to remain mysterious.

But here's what I have to remind myself. Back then, readers of the Bible were not reading for pleasure, or first for pleasure, or just for pleasure. G did not intend to write an instruction manual—*What to Expect When You Are Expected to Sacrifice Your Son*—but those who translated, interpreted, and rewrote his story assumed not just that it and all the other old stories were perfect and mysterious but also that they were relevant and instructive, their lessons and morals as timely and applicable on the day they were being read as they had been on the day they were written. G didn't write a how-to guide, but they were reading or listening to figure out how to live their lives.

Here one might fairly ask (as friends of mine often do) if I understand that ancient interpreters assumed that their sacred texts were perfect, mysterious, significant in every detail, endlessly instructive, and in one way or another divine. And I understand that those assumptions not only provided an opening for improvisation but actually made it likely, perhaps even necessary, as writers sought to straighten time's crooked lines, bring theological unity and moral clarity to messy biblical characters, plots, and meanings, and tweak texts they took to be perfect until they were perfect for their purposes, in their minds. And I understand that all the straightening and tweaking was not a by-product but often the very purpose of biblical interpretation. If I understand all that, why go on and on about it?

My answer is this: I am still thinking about Genesis 22 from the perspective of poor G, centuries earlier, imagining and eagerly anticipating the day when his story would be revised. That day had come. But put yourselves in my shoes, as I put myself in his: When, at the turn of the millennium, all those Jewish writers decided that suffering like that mother's seven sons suffered could be a sign of God's grace, that sacrificing one's son could be a way of showing one's love, that dying for God could be a way of glorifying him, that the suffering and dying of people in one generation could serve as expiation for people in another, that God's chosen people, however defeated in this world, would all be together in the next, I can't help wishing that instead of revising or reinterpreting the story of the near sacrifice, instead of making Abraham zealous and Isaac willing, they had left the story of Abraham and Isaac alone and come up with one of their own.

"Be careful what you wish for," some sage said. In this instance they did.

Now, there are people, really smart people, who in our day have spent a significant amount of time arguing, in a scholarly sort of way, about whose atoning sacrifice came first: Did the Jews borrow the idea from the early Christians or did the early Christians borrow it from the Jews? All agree that by the time of Jesus, Isaac's role in the story had grown enormously. But had it developed to the point where some readers and writers imagined Isaac not just as a willing victim but a willing victim whose messianic suffering and death would result in forbearance and remission of sins for time immemorial? And, if so, was that Isaac on the minds of the earliest Christians when they tried to make sense of the death of Jesus? Or did that Isaac emerge only after the followers of Jesus imagined that their beloved rabbi was God's beloved son, the messiah who had died for mankind's sins and was raised up again so that through him we could all be saved and reborn?

Believe me when I say that I don't have a stake in the outcome of that debate. I think of it as I might think of some intricate evolutionary puzzle, complicated not just by the absence of key pieces of evidence but also by tremendous uncertainty about the dates of the pieces that we have. Several Aramaic translations of the Bible (called Targums) portray a willing Isaac. They go so far as to explain, perhaps for the first time, why, if Isaac was so willing, Abraham needed to bind him. The reason is that he had asked

Abraham to bind him—so that he would not tremble or flinch, confusing Abraham or causing the knife to slip, or accidentally kick Abraham, or (unintentionally) spoil the sacrifice (which had to be perfect, unblemished) in some other way. What's more, at least one Targum suggests that as a reward for his obedience, Abraham had asked for, and God had agreed to provide, not just deliverance but redemption, a remission of the sins of future generations. But there is no agreement on the dates of those translations, and even if there were agreement—agreement, say, that came after Jesus—scholars would still argue about whether or not translations drew on older sources that didn't survive or older understandings of the story that were never recorded.

Meanwhile, among the Dead Sea Scrolls, the trove of sacred literature discovered in the Qumran caves, there is a brief retelling of Genesis 22. Its technical name is 4Q225–227, but because of several critical correspondences, including a character named Mastema accusing Abraham before God, some scholars call it Pseudo-Jubilees. Pseudo-Jubilees is dated to the turn of the era, and one of its many intriguing aspects is an extra line of speech by Isaac. After he asks about the lamb and Abraham answers, Isaac has more to say. But what? Some scholars believe he says, "Tie me up" or "Bind me well," which would indicate that at least one early Isaac was aware of Abraham's mission and at peace with it. Unfortunately, certainty is hard to come by. It seems clear that after Abraham answered his question, Isaac said something. But we don't know how Abraham answered. The line is missing. (He might have said, "God will provide the lamb." Or he might have said, as he says in some of the Targums, "God will provide the lamb, but if he doesn't, you, Isaac, will be the lamb.") And the supposition that in Pseudo-Jubilees Isaac asked to be bound is based entirely on one Hebrew letter, a letter that might have been the first letter of quite a few words other than "tie" or "bind," words that might well have been followed by words other than "me up" or "me well." What's more, as James Kugel, an extraordinarily wise and trenchant biblical scholar, has recently observed, that one letter, and thus Isaac's imagined request, doesn't come precisely where literary analysis and logic would lead us to expect it to come in the story.

Those are just a few questions about a few pieces of the puzzle. There are scores of them. Even when the words are all decipherable and the dates widely agreed upon, scholars debate the relative influence of what is known: not just ideas about Abraham and Isaac but the whole complex of turn-of-the-millennium Jewish ideas (and contemporaneous pagan, especially mystery cult, ideas) about the son of man, the end of days, the suffering servant, the coming of the messiah; about martyrdom, death, atonement, salvation, and resurrection.

It is a complicated debate and, once you delve into it, fascinating, but my attention is fixed on the rewriting and revision of one short story, and all I really need to say, at least for now, is that in light of the rewriting and revision between Jubilees and the advent of Christianity, you don't need to be a biblical scholar to understand what the first Christian Jews did with it.

The earliest Jewish interpreters, whatever their other differences, all stressed Abraham's piety, his devotion, his love, and especially his obedience, not just to specific commands but to all of God's laws. He was repeatedly tested and he repeatedly passed. At least in hindsight, it should not be surprising that the first Christians, while hardly gainsaying obedience to God, let alone devotion, sacrifice, and love, folded all that into faith. Abraham's greatness lay not so much in what he did—his obedience to God's commandment—but in the faith that made it possible for him to do it, that made the unbearable bearable: the faith that one way or another God would keep his promise.

Not that the very earliest Christian writers made much of the story. As far as I know, no one wrote a treatise on Abraham and Isaac or devoted a chapter to it in a treatise on some larger incident or theme. No one even bothered to retell the story from beginning to end. Abraham appears in crucial places in the Gospel of John

and the Epistles to the Romans, Hebrews, and Galatians, most
notably in arguments about the supremacy of faith and in confident early Christian claims to be the true heirs of Abraham, the
beneficiaries of God's blessing. But the near sacrifice is mentioned
explicitly only in the very Jewish-leaning Epistle of James and the
very Christian-leaning Epistle to the Hebrews, where the author,
whose name we don't know, appears to address a group or community of fellow Jewish Christians, whom he feared, or whom he had
been told, were backsliding, rethinking the meaning of Jesus's life
and death and (more crucially) their commitment to the new community in the face of the demands and dangers of Jewish-Christian
life and faith. At the heart of his Epistle was a carefully constructed
and perfectly polished, if not especially balanced, comparison of the
old Temple sacrifices to the sacrifice of Jesus, the eternal priesthood
of the church to the Levitical priesthood, the new covenant to the
old, of faith to law.

To make the case for faith, "the assurance of things hoped for,
the conviction of things not seen," the author turned to history, the
faith with which men (and women) of old won God's favor. Abel
by faith offered a more acceptable sacrifice. He died, but because he
had that faith he still speaks. Noah, warned by God about events he
could not possibly have foreseen, built an ark and became heir to
the world to come. Abraham left his home for a place unknown, for
a land of pure promise. By faith, Sarah received the power to con-
ceive Isaac, despite her age. And then, "by faith Abraham, when he
was tested, offered up Isaac, and he who had received the promise
was ready to offer up his only son of whom it was said, 'Through
Isaac shall your descendants be named.' He considered that God
was able to raise men even from the dead; hence, figuratively speaking, he did receive him back."

Thanks to Abraham, the story continued: By faith Moses cast
his lot not with Pharaoh but with the people of Israel. By faith the
people of Israel crossed the Red Sea as if on dry land. After them,
men and women of faith "conquered kingdoms, enforced justice,

received promises, stopped the mouths of lions, quenched raging fire, escaped the edge of the sword, won strength out of weakness, became mighty in war, put foreign armies to flight. Women received their dead by resurrection. Some were tortured, refusing to accept release that they might rise again to a better life. Others suffered mocking and scourging, and even chains and imprisonment. They were stoned, they were sawed in two, they were killed with the sword; they went about in skins of sheep and goats, destitute, afflicted, ill-treated—of whom the world was not worthy— wandering over deserts and mountains, and in dens and caves of the earth." They did not receive what God had promised, but they retained their faith in things unseen.

The author of the Epistle to the Hebrews introduced no new characters. Imagined no new scenes. Put no new words in the mouths of Isaac, Abraham, or God. He neither added nor took away. He contributed just two lines to a growing body of exegesis. But to change the meaning of words is to change the words, and two lines of New Testament Epistle, long attributed to Paul, were not just any two lines of exegesis. By the time Augustine got to them in *City of God,* most of the church fathers had had their say, and many people read the story in a whole new way.

~~~

My feelings about all of the early Christian talk of faith are mixed.

Naturally, I understand that many readers had a difficult time with the story.

I have had a difficult time with it myself.

And though my particular reservations may not have been widely shared, I can't help thinking that many people, including some of those who loved to crow about Abraham's greatness, actually had a hard time imagining, from the inside out, how he could have done what he did. Think about it: A sick child is enough to cause, in parents, intense anxiety if not the deepest despair. But we don't always get to choose our trials, and in his shoes (asked to do the last thing on earth I wanted to do, yet afraid not to) I'd consider the kind of faith imputed to Abraham to be the greatest of blessings. I can't help thinking that the idea that Abraham's response to God was rooted in faith (faith that God would keep his promise, faith that he'd ultimately get Isaac back) made it more comprehensible, a difficult story easier to bear.

And it wasn't as if those who talked and wrote about Abraham's faith didn't have evidence. Commentators had long noted that Abraham was faithful, by which I think they meant devoted and obedient. It was, for many, his defining trait, and though being completely obedient to God is one thing and having complete faith in God is quite another, the distance between them was not great, especially to people writing and reading Greek, where the same word—*pistos*—could easily convey either of those two different ideas about Abraham. What's more, earlier in Abraham's life, some time after the battle with the kings, in a passage the early Christians frequently cited, Abraham appears to have had faith and been rewarded for it. The word of God had come to him in a vision: " 'Fear not, Abram, I am your shield. Your reward shall be very great.' And Abram said, 'O my Master, LORD, what can You give me when I am going to my end childless.' " God told him to look toward the heavens, and then promised him descendants as numerous as the stars. "And he trusted in the LORD, and He reckoned it to his merit."

I could argue until I was red in the face, reminding people that chapter 15 is one thing and chapter 22 another. The former mentions trust explicitly. The latter mentions fear. If trust were the key, God would have said so when he stopped him—would have said, "Now I know that you have faith in me." And he would have rewarded him for keeping that faith, rather than for obeying his command.

I would argue in vain. Abraham's faith lay at the root of everything else, the early Christians would say. On the way to Moriah, it was simply assumed. And if you can't grasp that, recall the words with which Abraham took leave of his servants: "You stay here with the ass. The boy and I will go up there; we will worship and we will return to you." Not "I" but "we."

I might point out that there are other ways to interpret those words, obvious ways, as even some Christian commentators acknowledged. But it would be more than a little presumptuous of me to insist that one couldn't legitimately read them as trust or faith. In the third century, Origen, the Alexandrian scholar and theologian, imagined a perplexed observer asking Abraham what he was actually saying to his servants: "Are you saying to the servants in truth that you will worship and return with the child, or are you deceiving them? If you are telling the truth, then you will not make him a holocaust. If you are deceiving, it is not fitting for so great a patriarch to deceive."

"I am speaking the truth," Origen's Abraham replied, "and I offer the child as a holocaust. For this reason I both carry wood with me, and I return to you with him. For I believe, and this is my faith, that 'God is able to raise up even from the dead.'" In fact, Christian interpreters said, it was Abraham's faith that allowed him to see ahead: "His character was considering the slaughter," Bishop Succensus wrote, two centuries later, "but his faith declared and spoke the truth about the outcome." When Isaac, observing that his father had the fire and he had the wood, asked about the lamb, Abraham's faith spoke the truth again: "God will see to the sheep for the burnt offering, my son." If that was not an expression of faith, Christian commentators asked, or prophecy grounded in faith, what would be?

I could say, again, that faith is not the only way to read Abraham's response. That I don't think that was the author's intent as he was writing, nor his or his editors' or first readers' impression as they read. But it should be pretty clear by now that neither the author nor his editors nor his first readers got to say what the words meant once and for all. And that's a good thing. Among the wonderful things about the story is the work it leaves for readers to do.

Faith that God would not make Abraham sacrifice Isaac is one thing, faith in resurrection another, and there's no evidence that Abraham knew anything about it. In his world, as I understand it, individuals died. Families, communities, and nations lived on. His hope for posterity was grounded in God's promise of descendants as numerous as the grains of sand on the shore. That's why he was so upset when it seemed as if he wasn't going to have any. But if Jubilees's Abraham could know some of God's laws even before God approached him (and all the rest of them five hundred years before Sinai), I suppose there is no reason why the Christian Abraham couldn't understand God's power to raise the dead.

I can see where they were coming from and where they ended up. I can understand how they got there. Yet I still read the story, above all else, as a story, and I can't help thinking that when the author of Hebrews recast it as a story about faith, he robbed it of its drama, or what was left of it after Jubilees decided that God, knowing everything, knew that Abraham would do exactly what he had asked him to do.

Now Abraham knows the outcome too.

Sure, it was difficult for him to go through the motions, to rise early, saddle the donkey, gather and split the wood, hike for the three days with the boy bounding, obliviously, at his side, ditch the servants, answer Isaac's question, and finally build the altar and bind him. But if the outcome was not actually in doubt, if Abraham believed that in the end God would keep his promise, what distinguishes the story from a dog-eared children's story where the harrowing beginning and middle are made palatable by the knowledge, foreknowledge after the first read, that everything works out in the inevitable end?

And then, along the same lines, there is the problem of God's blessing. If God knows that Abraham is perfectly faithful and Abraham has unshakable faith, what is God testing or demonstrating? However arbitrary or unknowable the grounds for Abraham's initial election (and Noah's before him), God made these people work for their blessings. Jubilees's God might have been able to read Abraham's mind, but there is no evidence that Abraham could read God's. And even if he could, why would God reward him so richly for doing something that Abraham knew he was not going to have to do? Years later a wise man would speculate that God doesn't throw dice. The jury is still out on that one, but I think it even less likely that he plays charades.

To Christians in the first few centuries of Christianity, it wasn't a game. It was history, sacred history, and if you knew how to read it, there was no mystery about its meaning. The Hebrew past was a shadow, a prefiguration of things to come: In Sarah's miraculous pregnancy, they saw Mary. In her beloved son, Jesus. In Abraham's willingness, God's own. In the three-day journey, the three days between crucifixion and resurrection. In the wood that Isaac carried, the cross. In Abraham's promise that God would provide a lamb, the lamb of God. In the ram, Jesus again. In the thicket the ram was caught in, his crown of thorns. In Moriah, Golgotha. In the sacrifice, the Eucharist. In Isaac's offspring—singular, Jesus. In the descendants of Isaac, the child of promise, Christ's church.

That's a dicey way to do history. When we look to the past, our expectations and desires shape when they don't determine what we see. If I go looking for evidence that Abraham had questions and doubts about God, I'll find it. But if I am not careful, I'll miss or minimize the importance of the moments he appears to have had none, all those times he did just what God asked when God asked it. If I go looking for evidence that the present was prefigured by the past, I'll find it. But if I am not careful, I'll miss or minimize the importance of all the floats that don't seem to have a place in history's inevitable parade. If I reduce people and events to their conscious contribution to a future that they themselves didn't nec-essarily anticipate, plan for, or even dream of, odds are that I will not understand them. Christians, elevating the ideal of faith in their own time, looked back and found it everywhere, including in Abra-ham's words to his servants ("We will return to you") and to Isaac ("God will see to the sheep"). But isn't it possible that the poor man was simply dissembling, with every good reason not to say "You stay here, I'll be back after I sacrifice Isaac" or "Actually you are the sacrifice, my son"—so that the former didn't stop him and the latter didn't flee.

That said, historians make that kind of mistake all the time. The early Christians may have taken a tendency or temptation and transformed it into a theory and method, but they were hardly the first or only or last people to read the present back into the past, to look back and see nothing but earlier versions of themselves. (Many Jewish interpreters would also come to see the Jewish present pre-figured in the Jewish past, types in the patriarchs and anti-types in their descendants.) If I seem cranky, or crankier, about the Christian interpretation of the near sacrifice, I am. But it is not because of their presentism, or my sense of what makes for a good story, or their idea of faith. I can live with all three. What I can't live with, or what I would prefer not to live with, what bugs me and often infuriates me, is not the idea of prefiguration but rather supersessionism. The idea that the present superseded the past, the Christians the Jews. The idea that with the sacrificial death and resurrection of Jesus, God's blessing had passed from the descendants of the flesh to the descendants of the spirit, from people of the law to the people of faith, from the people enslaved in the earthly Jerusalem to the people living free in the Jerusalem above, from the people of God's promise to the people of God's curse, from the physical offspring of Isaac to the spiritual offspring, Jesus, and through him the church.

Recall that in Genesis all the nations of the earth were to be blessed through Abraham and his descendants. But the authors of several of the texts we know of as the Gospels insisted that not all of Israel was of Israel—or as Paul, author of the Epistle to the Romans, put it, not all the descendants of Abraham and Isaac were the children of Abraham. The Jews made the mistake of pursuing righteousness through the law rather than through faith. They stumbled over the law and never made it to faith. As centuries passed and the church fathers studied ancient history, they found that that stumbling, the Jewish spiritual blindness no less than the Christian scrambling toward Christ, had been foretold. And they found that stumbling even on the way to Mount Moriah. The Jews, wrote Cyril, the powerful patriarch of Alexandria from 412 until his death in 444, followed God by law but were unwilling by faith to follow Christ, who went to his death for all. "For 'from part of Israel there was rigidness,' which is signified by means of the ass present with the servants. For the ass is the representation of their final unreasonableness. And their rigidness is the child of unreasonableness." The Jews were the ass: the earthly, the dumb, the blind, the servants Abraham left behind.

Yikes. Philo, whose ideas had an enormous influence on early Christianity, had written doggedly of the distinction between the physical and the ethereal, the carnal and the spiritual, the body and the soul, the literal and the allegorical, the earthly and the heavenly, and there's no doubt what the philosopher took to be the higher realm. But there is also no doubt that Philo, a devout and fully observant Jew, believed that the body, the letter, the literal, was here to stay. To say that you prefer your church and its stories to another church and its stories is one thing. But to say that your church annuls another church (completes it, voids it, supersedes it) is quite another. And when that other church and its people are still with you—in other words, when the superseded past is still with you—well, that reading of history is a recipe for disaster.

Now, remember that when I speak of the early Christians, I am speaking not of men and women on the street but their chief spokes-men, the men we call the church fathers, several dozen different writers living over several centuries in dozens of places all over the Mediterranean world. Gather together even a small sample of their writings about Abraham and Isaac and you will find a magnificent variety. Some were interested in God's command. Some, Abraham's response. Some, the journey. Some, the servants. Some, Isaac. Some, the near sacrifice itself. Some, the ram, and some, God's blessing. Some imagined what an ordinary man might have felt, or even said to God. Some imagined what Abraham might have said to Sarah to comfort her or calm her down. Some explained why Abraham hadn't said anything to Sarah. Some imagined how his spirit would have warred with his flesh on the three-day journey, which, like the teasing form of God's command, was intended to make the test harder to bear. Some imagined that Isaac had known everything. Others, that he had known nothing at all. Some dug deep into the details of story. Others scoured the old for clues to the new.

When I step back from the story, I am reminded that the early Christians argued about everything: They argued about the divinity of Jesus. They argued about the relationship between Father, Son, and Holy Ghost. They argued about Jesus's incarnation and his body (was it earthly flesh or some more heavenly substance?). They argued about whether flesh and the Jewish deity who created it was good or bad. They argued about whether the God of the Israelites and the father of Jesus were one and the same. They argued about where the spirit and light and word of God resided and how, if they didn't reside in each of us, one gained access to them. They argued about the relative importance of faith and works in the attainment of God's grace. They argued about whom God spoke to and who could speak for God. They argued about the status and role of bishops. They argued about whether Christians should share a specific set of beliefs and, if so, what those beliefs should be. They argued about which books should be included in the canon, and they argued about how those books should be interpreted, according to the plain sense or by means of symbol, type, figure, or allegory. They argued about who gets to say.

They argued a lot about the Jews. In the second century, Marcion was among those who considered the story of the near sacrifice and every other story in the Old Testament vile, the god of the Jews a lower god, perhaps a false one. Huge portions of the New Testament also drew Marcion's scorn. He liked Luke and ten letters, all of which he attributed to Paul.

How often Marcion and other early Christians actually argued *with* the Jews is not entirely clear. Some scholars say that Christians and Jews had nothing to do with one another after the first century, not even disputation. They say that the Christian polemic that looks the most like argument—explicitly anti-Jewish polemic—was actually aimed at other Christians, those who clung to Jewish practices, or at pagan converts who adopted Jewish practices, or at pagans who used Jewish history or theology to refute Christian claims. Others say that on the ground, even in churches and synagogues, there was every kind of encounter, argument, rivalry, coexistence, identity, and exchange. The latter believe that the Gospels were not just originally Jewish but fundamentally Jewish, grounded in Jewish tradition and teaching and belief. The very distinction between Christian and Jew, some say, remained blurred for centuries.

Marcion was excommunicated, but over the next two centuries

other forms of heresy and every sort of schism convinced many clergymen that the church needed canon, law, and binding creed. Yet in the fifth century, the bishop of Hippo, Augustine, was still doing battle with dualism, and in his arguments against Manichaeism, a heresy he himself had flirted with before his conversion to Christianity, he defended the literal truth of the Old Testament and insisted that the God of ancient Israel and the God of the new Israel were one and the same. He also argued against the likes of John Chrysostom of Constantinople and Severus of Minorca, who insisted that Christ's teachings led inexorably to the elimination of the Jews. "Slay them not," Augustine famously said. Jews should be allowed to live and practice Judaism, but his reasons are telling: The Jews were living, physical evidence of the truth of the teachings of Moses, the authenticity of antiquity. They actually existed. At the same time, their subsequent exile, dispersion, misery, and degradation were daily living proof of the fate awaiting those who rejected Christ and remained slaves to the law.

The sacrifice of Isaac, as the church fathers were inclined to call it, did not figure in that or any other major debate among Christians. Notwithstanding many differences in emphasis and some differences in interpretation, they all agreed that the story was about a father, Father Abraham, a lover of God and a man of perfect faith, who set out, at God's command, to sacrifice his beloved son. Whether his and his son's willingness merely prefigured God's sacrifice or actually precipitated it, the outcome was the same: God stopped him, but for his faith God rewarded him and his offspring. The Father of all fathers so loved the world that he gave his only Son, his own beloved son, so that whoever believes in him should not perish but have eternal life.

I I

~~~~

I understand why, looking back over the four centuries between the death of Jesus and the appearance of Augustine's *City of God,* centuries in which the church won converts, worked out creed and canon, and became the religion of the Roman Empire, so many people have been inclined to see Christianity exactly as the Christian faithful themselves saw it, as the latest and the greatest. Israel's covenant of Moses's law was the past; the Christian covenant of faith, the present and future. Jews were the aging parents, Christians the vigorous child. There was an obvious chronological logic to that view of the relationship—the Jews had been around longer—and, to Christians, an equally obvious appeal.

What that view missed was that the religion of Israel was not in decline or frozen in time. With the destruction of the Temple in 70 CE, the suspension of daily ritual sacrifice, and the dispersion of the priesthood, Jews certainly did hold on to one part of their past—the revelation at Sinai—as if it were their last remaining connection to God. But it was less a desperate clinging than a passionate embrace, and like so many of those it was fruitful. By the time Augustine characterized the Jews as artifacts, flesh-and-blood fossils, irrefutable evidence of biblical truth, Jewish interpreters were deep into a long and remarkable renaissance, a renaissance in which they paid homage to the past, to revelation and to tradition, by using it to create something new. So much so that instead of thinking of Judaism and Christianity as parent and child, it might be more useful to imagine siblings, siblings in a large, fractious family, struggling for the attention and affection of their parents—or Parent—and their share of the inheritance, which included not just a priceless set of sacred texts but the power and authority to say what they meant.

Now, a person living today or much closer to our time than to late antiquity should be excused for thinking that those Jewish interpreters, however often at odds with Christian interpreters, all thought about Abraham and Isaac (and every other Bible story) the same way. That's because when people speak of the Jewish interpreters of late antiquity today, they often refer to them not by their names but simply as "The Rabbis." When people speak of the fruits of their labor, they often refer to "Rabbinic Tradition" or "Jewish Tradition" or just "Tradition."

Sometimes that is nothing but an innocent form of shorthand. It is easier, especially when referring to the rabbis of the first millennium, to say "the rabbis" ("according to the rabbis," "in the words of the rabbis," as "the rabbis liked to say," or simply, "the rabbis said") than to drop a name (Gamaliel "the Elder," Yishma'el b. Elisha, Meir, Judah ha-Nasi, Haninah bar Hama, Shmuel bar Nachman, Mar Shemuel, or scores of others) in the instances when we have a name, a name few laypeople are likely to recognize. Other times it is a rhetorical sleight of hand, an attempt to end a debate, clinch an argument, settle a dispute, link one's position on a matter of ethics or ritual or law to an unassailable authority. In either case, the phrase suggests that Tradition is singular, monolithic, and perfectly clear; that the rabbis (one generation after another, one century after another, producing more than a thousand years of interpretation, not just in Palestine and Babylonia but in Syria, Greece, Italy, Spain, France, Germany, Macedonia, Asia Minor, Byzantium, Persia, Alexandria, and everywhere else on earth there were Jews) thought or spoke as one, walked in lockstep.

Yet as anyone who has taken even a cursory look at the lit-

erature the rabbis produced knows, nothing could be further from
the truth. What we call rabbinical or Jewish tradition was, from the
first, just like biblical tradition: multiple, dialogical, polysemous,
sometimes even riotous. The Mishnah and Tosefta are voluminous compilations of (and ongoing debates about) the oral law,
the law God spoke at Sinai but Moses didn't record, transmitted
from generation to generation and ultimately organized into six
orders (seeds, festivals, women, damages, sacrifices, and purity)
and sixty-three tractates (topics like blessings, Sabbath, marriage,
divorce, torts, oaths, courts, offerings, and ritual slaughter). The
Gemara is the commentary on the Mishnah and Tosefta, and the
two Talmuds, one redacted in Palestine and one in Babylonia, com-
bine the Mishnah and the Gemara. The *midrashim* are the body of
literature that has recorded or re-created century after century of
commentary (midrash) on the written Torah itself, whether the narrative portions of the written Torah (*midrash aggadah*) or the law
(*midrash halakhah*).

Because the Talmud is the commentary on the Mishnah and the
Mishnah is often the commentary or elaboration upon the written
Torah, the Talmud inevitably contains commentary on the written Torah. In other words, it contains midrash, and in the Talmud's
midrash, Abraham and Isaac come up from time to time. In one
instance, a question about the appropriate penalty for a person who
ignores the words of a prophet sparked (or was later linked to)
a discussion of the surest ways to distinguish true prophecy from
false, which sparked (or was later linked to) a discussion about the
attentiveness with which Isaac listened to Abraham, which sparked
a discussion about the possible reasons for God's test. But from
the middle of the first millennium, most of the Jewish commentary
on Abraham and Isaac came in midrash proper, interpretation of
the written scriptures themselves, interpretation drawn from lessons and homilies delivered and discussions that took place in the

schools and Torah academies and synagogues that were fast becoming the center of Jewish life.

First-millennium midrash has come down to us in many different forms. Some of it reads like raw transcripts of conversations, some like collections of sermons, some like loosely connected collections of short stories, some like pumped-up parallel narratives of entire books of the Torah. But invariably it, just like the commentary on the oral law, was a literature of dialogue and debate launched by questions: questions about word choices, questions about juxtapositions, questions about repetition, questions about inconsistencies, questions about contradictions (including contradictions between different versions of the same biblical story and contradictions between how biblical characters behaved in the past and how readers were supposed to behave in the present), questions about the meaning of obscure, archaic, confusing, puzzling, or just plain troubling passages, questions about gaps, questions about practical ramifications of passages in ethics or ritual or law, questions about the tension between oral and written Torah, questions about exactly what happened in a story and why.

One of the first questions rabbis asked was an old one: Why did God test Abraham? He already knew he was righteous. When rabbis wanted to, they answered it without adding or taking away a word.

Some answered, as Jubilees had answered, that God had simply wanted to demonstrate Abraham's obedience, to elevate him, like a banner, for all the world to see. Perhaps God also wanted to justify, a hundred years after the fact (one form of biblical backdating), his initial call and blessing. Abraham's performance made it more difficult for readers (turning from the end of Genesis 11 to the opening of Genesis 12) to conclude that God's choice had been arbitrary.

Others said that God always tests the righteous, the way a potter tests the strong vessels (the weak would shatter) and a farmer yokes the strong cow (the weak would let him down). When it comes to people, the philosophically minded added, such tests allow the righteous to transform potential into actual, good hearts into good deeds. God was pretty sure and maybe even certain that Abraham was good. But Abraham was not without a will of his own. He didn't have to be good. God gave him the opportunity to see what he was made of.

Others said it was simpler than that: God tested Abraham to increase his fear of him.

Why did Abraham, who had plenty of servants, saddle his own ass?

Because love upsets the natural order of things, just as hate does. One rabbi hoped that one would counteract the other: "Let the sword taken in the hand of our father Abraham" when he stretched forth his hand to slay his son "come and counteract the sword grasped by Pharaoh" when he threatened to destroy the Jews.

Why did Abraham take two servants with him?

Several reasons, two of which were quite practical. If he had taken only one and that servant became ill, Abraham, in caring for him, would have become the servant of his own servant.

Another reason: If he had taken only one and that servant needed to leave his side to relieve himself, Abraham would have been left on his own.

Why did God lead him on for three days?

So no one could diminish Abraham's deed by saying that he had obeyed in shock or confusion at God's command, rather than carefully considered obedience.

Another reason: Because God always comes through on the third day. See Jacob in Genesis. The three spies in Joshua. The books of Jonah and Esther. Or the prophecy of Hosea: "After two days he will revive us, after three days he will raise us up, so we can live in his presence."

. . .

Other questions, or variations on those very same questions, prompted rabbis to modify or elaborate on the words on the page, starting with questions about the meaning of the story's very first words: "After these things." Most early Christian commentators encouraged readers to skip right over that phrase. They said it was merely a way of moving the narrative forward, a little like "Next thing you know." If those words referred to anything, it was all the things that had happened since God first called. Most rabbis, by contrast, believed that only momentous "things" could have triggered so momentous a test.

"What things?" they asked, which was another way of asking "Why? Why did God ask?"

The first move many rabbis made was to employ a second meaning of *ha-devarim* ("these things"), which, from the Hebrew root *d-b-r* ("speak"), also means utterances or words. "After these words," God tested Abraham. God's command came in response to something someone said and, at least since Jubilees, Satan was a prime suspect. Some imagined him accusing Abraham of taking God for granted, throwing a great feast to celebrate Isaac's weaning but neglecting to set aside even a single bullock or ram for God.

God scoffed. Come on, Satan, if I were to tell him to sacrifice his son, he would not refuse.

Others said it was the "words" of Abraham himself, full of remorse for celebrating without making an offering to God. God told him to relax. I know that you are worthy. Watch, I'll show you and everyone else, once and for all.

Others imagined Isaac and Ishmael arguing about who was the more beloved son.

"I am more beloved than thou, because I was circumcised at the age of thirteen," Ishmael said.

Isaac said no, it was he, circumcised at eight days.

"I could have protested, yet did not," Ishmael said. "You had no choice."

"All you did was lend God three drops of blood," Isaac said.

"Were the Holy One, blessed be He, to say unto me, 'Sacrifice thyself before Me,' I would obey."

God said, "This is the moment!"

And Abraham rose early in the morning.

Why early?

Some said: Because he delighted in God's commandment and was eager to do what God had asked. Others: Because all God's chosen rise early. Jacob rose early in the morning. Moses rose early in the morning. Samuel rose early in the morning.

Others still: Because Abraham wanted to leave before anyone tried to stop him.

What prompted Isaac to ask about the lamb?

Satan. The last thing he wanted to see was a demonstration of Abraham's greatness. He approached them along the way. Abraham first. "Are you crazy?" Satan asked. "God gives you a son at one hundred, and you are going to sacrifice him?"

Abraham ignored him.

"And what if he asks you something harder?" Satan asked.

"I'll do what he asks," Abraham said.

"And tomorrow he is going to say, Ha, you are a murderer."

"I will live with it."

Getting nowhere, Satan turned to Isaac.

"I doubt that's where we are going," Isaac said, "but if so, so be it."

"You mean you don't care if all that was due you will go to Ishmael?" Satan asked.

Isaac did a double take, and it was only then that he asked about the lamb.

In some versions, Abraham tells him that God would provide the lamb. In others, that he himself would be the lamb. After which, in every version, both of them walk on together.

The moral of that story in the minds of many rabbis: Evil doesn't have to do all that it is intended to do to cause trouble.

Once atop Moriah, "Abraham built an altar," suggesting to the rabbis that he built it alone, without any help from his vigorous and ever-obedient son. Many wondered why. Some said it was because Satan had not surrendered after appealing to the two of them directly. Rather, he turned himself into a river, blocking their path. When they tried to ford it, the water rose, which tipped off Abraham. He chased the angel away, but he was still wary, and that's why, when they arrived at the site, Abraham told Isaac to hide, fearing that Satan would try to maim him in some way, perhaps by pelting him with stones, leaving him unfit for sacrifice.

It was one question after another, and some of the answers to the simplest questions surprised me.

At long last, some rabbis had come to see the unlikelihood—what I took to be the unlikelihood—that, in response to God's command, Abraham would have said nothing more than "Here I am." Many imagined a dialogue to explain why God had taken so many words ("Pray, take your son, your only one, the one you love, Isaac") to introduce his command when just two—"Take Isaac"— would have done the trick.

"Take your son," God said.

"Which son?" Abraham asked. "I have two sons."

"Your only son," God answered.

"Isaac is the only son of his mother and Ishmael is the only son of his mother."

"The one you love."

"Is there a limit to the affections? I love them both."

"Isaac!" God said.

There were (always) other explanations. Some said, as some church fathers said, that God was simply trying to increase the suspense, make the test harder, bring Isaac ever closer to Abraham's heart. Many noted that God had employed the same tactic in his very first words to Abraham: "Go forth from your land, your birthplace, and your father's house." He could simply have said, "Go. I'll show you where."

Others said just the opposite: that he had used the extra words to soften the blow.

How those lines of imagined dialogue were first delivered or received, I can't say. It is not impossible—in fact it seems likely—that at least some rabbis were going for a laugh, gently mocking Abraham (who had somehow divined God's will) for stalling. No matter. We mock people for their human foibles. If it was mockery, I'd be happy to think that in every generation there have been some who have acknowledged the mystery, strangeness, even inhumanness, of Abraham's silence.

Other rabbis imagined Abraham's attempt to buy some time coming after God told him what he wanted him to do.

"Sacrifice Isaac?" he asked. "I can't. I am not a priest."

Get on with it, God said, citing one of David's psalms: "You are a priest forever."

At last someone besides Satan was giving voice to what some, yesterday no less than today, might consider reason, trying to slow the mad march to Moriah. Abraham ultimately departed, but God's good angels picked up where he left off. They protested the unfairness of it all. They wept. It was unnatural for a man to kill his son, they cried. Especially a man like Abraham, who showed hospitality to strangers, observed the Sabbath, remained true to Jerusalem. If he was not a man of merit, no man ever was, or would be. In some versions, Abraham wept too and his tears fell into Isaac's eyes, blinding him momentarily and thereby saving his life. The heavens had opened up above him. Had he gotten a good look at the Shekhinah—the divine presence—that look would have been his last.

Several rabbis, whose words have been preserved in the one of the oldest tractates of the Mishnah, suggested that on the way to Moriah, Abraham had prayed for Isaac's life. Atop the mountain, God answered his prayers. Nonetheless, subsequent generations of rabbis imagined that after God stopped him, Abraham called him out on his prevarication: "Yesterday you said that through Isaac my seed would be acclaimed. Then you retracted and said, 'Take now thy son.' Now you say, 'Do not raise your hand against the boy.'"

And God (anticipating Psalm 89) said: "Oh Abraham, I will not violate My covenant, or change what I have uttered. I said, 'Take now thy son, etc.' But did I tell you to slaughter him? No, I said to 'take him up.'" (The literal meaning of the word for sacrifice, *olah*, is "what is brought or taken up.")

"You have taken him up," God said. "Now take him down."

Other rabbis found other ways to demonstrate that Abraham had completely misunderstood God's command. Rabbi Samuel ben Nahmani, in the name of Rabbi Jonathan, did so by unpacking a powerful passage in Jeremiah, in which God chastises the people of Judah for sacrificing children to Baal. Those were sacrifices, God insists, that "I never commanded, never decreed, and which never came to My mind." The word "commanded," the rabbi said, referred to the king of Moab (who had sacrificed a son in the heat of battle). The word "decreed" referred to Jephthah (who had sacrificed his only daughter after returning home safely from battle). "Never came to My mind" referred to Abraham. The idea that God had commanded Abraham to sacrifice Isaac was preposterous. The thought had never even entered God's mind.

Abraham, however, was not mollified. When God's angel stopped him, he asked, "Who are you?"

"I am an angel."

"God told me to do this," Abraham said. "God Himself will tell me to stop."

Which is why God said and the Bible reads, "By My own Self
I swear."

Another interpretation for the word "swear": After Abraham
stopped and sacrificed the ram, he insisted that God himself swear
that he would never test him like that again.

God swore, repeating his promises, at which time Abraham said
to him: You've had your say. Now I would like to have mine. You
told me to sacrifice Isaac. I could have protested. I didn't. When
you said take your son, I might have said: Yesterday you promised
to make my children as ubiquitous as dust. Through Isaac. Yet now
you say sacrifice him. Yet "I did not do this, but suppressed my
feelings of compassion to do your will." I bound him and laid him
on the altar, and I hope that when Isaac's people are in trouble, you
will "remember that binding in their favor and be filled with compassion for them."

God promised to remember—or to respond to a reminder. He
knew, he said, that in the future, Isaac's descendants would fall into
the clutches of sin and, as a result of their sins, become the victims
of persecution. He would judge them on Rosh Hashanah. If they
wanted him to remember the binding of Isaac, they should blow
upon the shofar: "On the New Year they take the shofar and blow
on it, and eventually they will be redeemed by the ram's horn."

Abraham and Isaac's descendants have paid heed, and then
some. They sound the shofar not only on Rosh Hashanah but
also every day (but the Sabbaths and the last day) of the entire
month of Ellul, which leads up to it. They have incorporated Abraham's plea—"Remember"—not only into the penitential prayers
and liturgical poems they recite from the first day of that month
through the last moments of Yom Kippur, but also into their daily
and weekly prayers throughout the year, including the prayers that
immediately precede and follow the reading of Genesis 22 in week-
day morning services: "Just as Abraham our forefather suppressed

his mercy for his only son and was willing to slaughter him in order to do Your will, so may Your mercy suppress Your anger from upon us. . . . May You overstep with us the line of Your law and deal with us with the attribute of kindness and the attribute of mercy. In Your great goodness may You turn aside Your burning wrath from Your people, Your city, Your land, Your heritage."

All that cheers me. Even the demand for redemption in the future based on Abraham and Isaac's merit cheers me. It isn't so much the idea of it. I came of age, perhaps naively, thinking that we all earn our own blessings and curses. I understand now that way back when, the issue was hotly contested. Read the book of Exodus, where God, in blazing anger over the Golden Calf, threatens to destroy the Israelites and Moses implores him not to: "Remember Your servants, Abraham, Isaac, and Israel, how You swore them by Your Self and said to them: I will make your offspring as numerous as the stars of heaven, and I will give to your offspring this whole land of which I spoke, to possess forever." For a different view, turn to the book of Ezekiel. The prophet argues that "the righteousness of the righteous shall be accounted to him alone, and the wickedness of the wicked shall be accounted to him alone."

What I welcome in Abraham's insistence that God remember is not so much the idea of the merit of the fathers—how could I be happy that we all benefit from Abraham's willingness to do something I wish he hadn't done?—but rather the unmistakable implication in Abraham's words that God had made an excessive and mind-boggling demand. After all, God had already reaffirmed his promise—his blessing and the descendants—even sweetening the deal with the reassurance that Israel would seize its "enemies' gates." But here and elsewhere Abraham, and the rabbis through him, suggest that as payback for the test that Abraham has just endured, all God's previous promises weren't enough. Abraham wants pardon for future crimes, absolution for the ages, a guarantee that the covenant and the promise at the heart of it would be irrevocable.

There is more, and I could go on, along similar lines, for pages. But if I did, I might mislead you, contributing to just the kind of distortion I have warned you against. For every late-antique take on the story that suggests that (as far back as the first centuries of the first millennium) there were rabbis who believed that God should not have asked and Abraham should not have obeyed, there are several other takes that remind me that theirs was a minority view. In fact, some of the very riffs I find reassuring resist glib readings. Recall that some rabbis imagined Abraham weeping, his tears flooding Isaac's eyes. But just to make sure that no one mistook his compassion for reluctance, those same rabbis or their editors quickly added: "Yet even so, his heart rejoiced to obey the will of his creator."

So much so that sometimes God had a hard time getting him to switch gears. That's why, in the minds of many rabbis, God said, "Do not raise your hand against the boy" when the mortal danger to Isaac came not from Abraham's hand but from the cleaver he held in it. It turns out that the tears of God's angels had ruined the knife.

"Then I will strangle him," Abraham said.

"Lay not a hand upon the lad."

"Let us bring forth a drop of blood from him," Abraham pleaded.

"Don't do anything to him," God said. "Nothing. Not a blemish"—punning on the words *me'ummah* ("anything") and *mum* ("blemish").

Abraham stopped. But he was disappointed, and in his disappointment he prayed:

As he sacrificed the ram, he said: "Do Thou regard the blood of the ram as if the blood of my son were being poured before Thee."

As he skinned the ram, he said: "Do Thou regard this as though it were the skin of my son Isaac, which is being flayed before Thee."

As he coated the ram with salt, he said: "Do Thou regard this as though the salt were being poured on my son Isaac."

As he offered the limbs of the ram, he said: "Do Thou regard this as though these were the limbs of my son Isaac being offered to Thee."

As he burned the ram, he said: "Do Thou regard this as though the ashes of my son Isaac were heaped up on top of the altar before Thee."

In those prayers and others like it, the rabbis, through Abraham, wanted God to see the ram not in place of Isaac, not instead of Isaac, not as a substitute for Isaac—a valid exchange, a ram instead of a boy—but the ram as if he were Isaac. To help God see it that way, some rabbis imagined that the ram's name was Isaac. Others imagined that Abraham had asked God to pretend that he had sacrificed Isaac first and then, after Isaac, the ram, the ram in addition to, not instead of, Isaac.

And that's not all. In addition to rabbinical riffs in which Abraham asks God to let him take some blood, and riffs in which Isaac expresses his hope that a portion of his blood would suffice for the atonement of Israel, there are riffs in which Abraham actually takes Isaac's blood: "And Abraham bound him on the altar and then took the knife in order to slaughter him, until a quarter of his blood left him."

And another: "And there were Abraham's eyes on Isaac's eyes, and Isaac's eyes on the very heavens, and tears falling, pouring, from Abraham's eyes until he stood virtually to his height in a pool of tears. He said to Isaac: My son, since you have already begun to give up a quarter of your blood, may your Creator appoint some other victim in your place."

Exegesis of crucial passages of Scripture moved in the same

direction, including the interpretation of Exodus 12:13 ("When I see the blood I will pass over you, so that no plague will destroy you when I strike") and Exodus 23 ("For when the Lord goes through to smite the Egyptians, He will see the blood . . . and the Lord will pass over the door and not let the Destroyer enter and smite your home"). What blood? Anyone who knows the story of the exodus from Egypt would swear it was the blood of all those lambs smeared on the lintel and doorposts of Jewish homes. But it was not only that blood: it was also, according to many rabbis, "the blood of Isaac's binding (*akedah*)." "That is the blood meant, for it says, 'Abraham called the name of that place, the Lord will see.'" What did he see? "He saw the blood of Isaac's sacrifice."

Then there's the line in Chronicles that explains another crucial moment of deliverance, when God was about to destroy Jerusalem on account of the census that David had ordered. He "sent a pestilence upon Israel, and 70,000 men fell." Then he sent "an angel to Jerusalem to destroy it, but as he was about to wreak destruction, the LORD *saw* and renounced further punishment and said to the destroying angel, 'Enough! Stay your hand!'"

"What did he see? The blood of Isaac's sacrifice."

Other writers, including those who translated the book of Chronicles into Aramaic, had a slightly different view: What did the Lord behold? "He beheld the ashes of the Akedah of Isaac."

And where, rabbis asked, did God see Isaac's blood and ashes? On Ornan the Jebusite's threshing-room floor, some answered, where, after God's angel retreated, David built an altar and offered a sacrifice and vowed to build the Temple: "Here will be the house of the Lord and here the altar of burnt offerings for Israel." And that's where his son, Solomon, built the Temple, on the threshing-room floor. And where was the threshing-room floor? Where else? On Mount Moriah.

And centuries later, after the return from exile in Babylonia, when the Israelites rebuilt the Temple, how did they know where to put the altar and what to do with it? "Said R. Eleazar: They beheld the altar all built and Michael, the Great Prince, stood by it sacrificing on it." But R. Isaac Napaha disagreed: They rebuilt it themselves, and they knew they had found the right spot when "they beheld Isaac's ashes, that these lay on that spot. Isaac's ashes were the foundation of that altar."

And why were ashes placed on the head of each and every one of the participants in a public fast? There was "a difference of opinion" between "Rabbi Levi bar Hama and Rabbi Hanina," two authorities cited in the Babylonian Talmud. One said it was to show God that we know that before him, "we are all like dust and ashes." The other, to call to mind "for our sake Isaac's ashes."

If only I were not so squeamish about sacrifice, especially human sacrifice, I could just relax and take quiet satisfaction in the thought of all that those nineteen lines had wrought, the legacy of one very short story in history and literature, from Exodus to the establishment of Solomon's Temple to the establishment of Temple service to the rebuilding of the Temple and beyond. Who, now, would have the audacity to say that the story—which many rabbis now referred to as the "Binding of Isaac" (*Akedat Yitzhak*) or just the *Akedah*—had been neglected or ignored?

But I am who I am. I am appalled by many of those takes on the story, and I can't help wondering how many first-millennium rabbis felt the same way. Unfortunately, I have no way of knowing. I am not, in most instances, reading transcripts of conversations, or complete sermons, or even narratives written by a single author. Far from it. I am reading edited compilations of conversations and passages from sermons and scenes from stories, perhaps edited compilations of compilations, exegesis passed from rabbi to rabbi, rabbi to students, rabbi to congregations, for generations and sometimes centuries before it was collected by editors who cut and pasted and added and updated with abandon and only occasionally cited their sources and only inadvertently dated them. One interpreta-

tion follows another with the simplest transition ("another interpretation"; "Rabbi So-and-so said") or no transition at all, and
it is the same whether the latter interpretation supplemented the
former or complemented it, implicitly dissented from it or flatly
contradicted it.

Every once in a while I get a hint (in a word—"No!"—or
phrase—"Enough of that!") of one rabbi's view of the interpretation of another. But most of the time I come away only with each
rabbi's own view, set before or after the view of another (and that
other might well have lived long before or long after). I know (any
reader would know) that the rabbis loved language, loved puns
and other fun with words and numbers, loved multiple meanings,
loved associations and interpretations based on the juxtaposition
of words, and on the sound of words, and on the repetition of letters and roots and words and phrases in passages near and far. But
whether particular rabbis loved or were at peace with explanations
and associations and revisions that were mutually exclusive, or simply different from their own, I can't say.

I have no idea what the rabbis who imagined Abraham stalling thought of the stories in which he rose early and rushed to do
the deed. What those who imagined him weeping as he took leave
of Sarah thought of the stories in which he was giddy with excitement, eager to obey God's command. What those who imagined
him praying to God to spare Isaac (let alone taking God to task for
asking) thought of the stories in which he pleaded with God to let
him go through with it. What the rabbis who imagined God with
a good reason to ask and a determination to see Abraham obey
thought of the stories in which God contended he hadn't asked and
never would.

I don't know. I don't even know what the rabbis who associated Isaac's deliverance with the sacrifice of the paschal lamb and
redemption of the Jewish firstborn in Egypt thought of the rabbis who associated it with the shofar and atonement of Rosh
Hashanah. Or what any of those rabbis thought of the rabbis who

believed that the twice-daily lamb sacrifice in the Temple, built on
Mount Moriah, was a reenactment of Abraham's substitution of a
lamb for Isaac.

What I do know is that the rabbis who compiled and edited the
collections of rabbinical commentary we call *midrashim* brought
the widest range of interpretations and narrative together on the
page, offering us many different, often contradictory ways of thinking about the story without trying to resolve the contradictions or
get us to think about it one way or another. It bears repeating that
neither they nor the rabbis whose words they purported to preserve
thought of themselves as revising Scripture. But in their endless asking and answering, they created a vast archive of anecdote, of lexi-
cography, of scene, of dialogue, of cognates and analogy, countless
precious nuggets of narrative, commentary, and exegesis. Or, more
accurately, they contributed volume upon volume to the existing
archive, an archive that in one form or another (the histories of
Josephus and 2 Maccabees; the rewritten Bibles of Pseudo-Philo
and Jubilees; the philosophical essays of Philo and 4 Maccabees;
the historical fiction of Judith; the interpretative translations beginning with the Aramaic Targums; the self-conscious revision of early
parts of the Bible by later biblical writers, copyists, translators, and
editors; and the explanations of the text offered by teachers at public readings of the Torah going back a thousand years) was nearly
as old as the texts themselves. Recall the scene, the gathering before
the water gate after the return from exile in Babylonia, recorded in
the book of Nehemiah. Ezra was asked to read from the teaching of
Moses, and while he did, the Levites explained the teaching to the
people: "They read from the scroll of the teaching of God, translat-
ing it and giving the sense; so they understood the reading."

That archive was a great repository of tradition. It was tradition. And yet, as each succeeding generation of exegetes drew,
commented, and elaborated upon the material in it, consciously
or unconsciously transformed minor keys into major, selected elements of interpretation and narrative that made the most sense to
them and combined those elements into single-author commentar-

ies or wove them in creation-to-nation narratives, elevated some
motifs, neglected others, brought new ways of thinking and new
tools to bear on old problems, or simply saw old stories and old
problems in a fresh light, that repository of tradition was also the
raw material out of which new tradition was made.

Consider the small and simple contribution of Johanan ha-
Kohen, a liturgical poet who lived in the land of Israel in the seventh
century. Drawing on both Bible stories and midrash, he imagined a
dialogue between God and his daughter, the Torah, about possible
suitors. She surveyed the field and found a lot to love, but she also
found reasons (Noah drank too much and cursed his grandson,
Canaan; blind old Isaac was like a judge who took bribes; Jacob
deceived his father) to reject one after the other. In the end she
chose Moses, but I can't resist noting her reason for passing over
Abraham, for whom her father had made a strong case. She, too,
thought the world of him, and she, too, knew that he was "good
and perfect in his ways":

> But he did not beg for mercy for his only son.
> He wished to spill his blood like a cruel man
> In order to fulfill your will wholeheartedly
> As he was certain that God is good and merciful.
> He should have, however, begged to spare his only son
> And save him from the burning coals.
> No mercy would have been shown his son if the Lord of
>   mercy had not taken pity.

In just a few lines of verse (*piyyut*), Johanan transformed a story
about Abraham's responsibility to God into a story about his irre-
sponsibility to his son.

That was not a common way of looking at the story or Abraham
in the middle of the first millennium. Yet the poem was out there.
Later it was incorporated into Shavuot services in Ashkenazic syna-

gogues, where it remained for centuries. It was out there, along with the rest, and I love that it was there, and I love the reason it was there, which I have to admit is the very same reason that the commentary that disturbs me was there. I love that the rabbis had so much to say and weren't afraid to say it. I love that they weren't cowed by the age or authority of the story or any other ancient story, by its status or stature in anyone else's eyes, or by their own tremendous reverence for it or by their reverence for their teachers and for the teachers who had come before them. I love the attitude even when I don't love the expression; love the form—the way they talked about the story and the way they did things with it—even when I don't love the content.

Scripture was Scripture, holy, sacred, divine. But teachers and students, preachers and congregations, writers and readers, shaped the way people understood it, sometimes altering the meaning by altering the plot (a story in which God says he never intended for Abraham to sacrifice Isaac means something different from a story in which God explicitly rewards Abraham for his willingness to do so), sometimes altering the plot by altering the meaning (a three-day journey in which Abraham is silently scheming to come up with a way out means something different from three days in which he is eager to obey God's command, and both are different from days in which he is certain—"We will worship and come back to you"— that God was not actually going to make him sacrifice his son).

Scripture was Scripture. The law revealed in it, oral and written, though also subject to seemingly endless debate and (over time) subject to all sorts of revision, was, at least by the Middle Ages, thought in each moment of time to be fixed and binding.

But the stories in Scripture were neither fixed nor binding. Their meaning was plainly not (and has never been) the meaning for all.

The archive I am imagining was not exclusive to Jews. Christian interpreters made contributions to it throughout late antiquity, and every indication is that as they prepared sermons and lectures and wrote pastoral letters and apologies—arguing among themselves and explaining to others who they were and what they believed— they drew on it too. Their first contribution was the late first-century idea that the story was all about Abraham's faith. Several centuries later, some turned their attention to Sarah.

They didn't have much to work with. G had left her out of the story, and the earliest Jewish interpreters, from Jubilees to Josephus, had followed his lead. And by their lights who can blame them? The story wouldn't have been much of a story if the sacrifice had been aborted in the first few lines. How do you say "Over my dead body" in classical biblical Hebrew? And though Abraham might have been torn, God would have understood. He might well have said exactly what he had said a chapter earlier, when Sarah ordered Abraham to cast out Hagar and Ishmael, and Abraham was distressed: "Whatever Sarah tells you, do as she says, for it is through Isaac that offspring shall be continued for you."

The first rabbis were no more inclined than Second Temple sages to tangle with her. But questions remained. How, for one, did Abraham get away from a mother so protective of Isaac and his prerogatives that she banished his older brother for misbehaving at the boy's weaning? They imagined Abraham scheming. He thought: She never allows the boy out of her sight. "After all, she was a woman, with a woman's mind, and she flew off the handle at every little thing; imagine if she got wind of this." But if he was just to leave with Isaac, without saying a word, she'd kill herself. So late in the afternoon on the day Abraham received God's command, he asked her if it would be okay for him to take Isaac for religious instruction. There was a school a few days away. He himself had known God since the age of three. The boy was ready. Sarah was pious, and she agreed. "Go in peace," she said. But he didn't want to take any chances that she'd change her mind. So "Abraham rose early the next morning."

The more pressing question was how Sarah died. Her death is reported in the very first lines of the very next chapter of Genesis, and the proximity of two such momentous events simply could not have been a coincidence. To explain it, many rabbis turned, once again, to Satan, who, having failed to persuade either Abraham or Isaac that what they were doing was crazy, figured Sarah was his last hope. Some said he had approached her disguised as an old family friend and told her where her husband and son had gone. She cried out, the same cry that she imagined would soon come from her son—three short sobs (explaining one way of sounding the shofar, the three short blasts called *shevarim*). Her heart stopped on the spot, and her soul flew out of her. Others said Sarah had taken off after them, making it only as far as Hebron, where she learned that Isaac had been spared, and she died, on the spot, of joy. Others still said she had awaited their return at the door of her tent. But Isaac lagged well behind Abraham, and when Sarah saw Abraham approaching without him, she assumed her son was dead. She fainted, and never came to. In a fourth version, she lived long enough to hear Isaac tell the tale:

"You mean if it were not for the angel you'd already be dead?" she asked.

"Yes," Isaac said, and she shrieked six times (explaining the six additional blasts of the shofar required as a minimum in addition to the three mentioned in the Torah). Then she died.

Thus Genesis 23:1: "And Sarah's life was a hundred and twenty-seven years, the years of Sarah's life. And Sarah died in Kiriath-Arba, which is Hebron, in the land of Canaan, and Abraham came to mourn Sarah and to keen for her."

"And where did Abraham come from?" many rabbis asked. "Why wasn't he with her?"

"He came from Mount Moriah."

And how old was Isaac at the time of the binding? Each of the versions linking God's test and Sarah's death had the additional virtue of allowing rabbis to answer that question definitively, and with a mature Isaac. Born when his mother was ninety, he would have been thirty-seven.

(And, for curious close readers wondering what Sarah was doing in Hebron when she died, when Abraham left for Moriah from Beersheba and returned there: see the second Satan version above.)

If there was a first-millennium rabbi who considered the possibility that Abraham might have taken Sarah into his confidence, his words have not been preserved. A few bishops, by contrast, did consider it, only to conclude that Abraham had had no choice but to keep her in the dark. Writing in the fifth century, Basil of Seleucia detailed Abraham's deliberation: " 'She is pious,' he thought, 'but I fear her nature. Although seeing the piety, I fear the love. The woman is pious, but she is a mother. It is a terrible thing when mothers are overpowered by the weakness of nature. I fear lest she defile the sacrifice through weeping. . . . Lest beating her face, she ruins the sacrifice and does violence to God.' "

The church fathers could be nasty about Sarah's nature. Gregory, bishop of Nyssa in the last quarter of the fourth century, believed that Abraham had considered her "entirely untrustworthy," a judgment in which he concurred, noting that Adam had not been "aided in the least by accepting Eve's advice." But for many commentators, especially in the Christian East, nastiness about Sarah's nature was tempered by typology. If Abraham was a type of God and Isaac a type of humanity saved by the lamb of God (or linked with the lamb as a type of Christ), there had to be a role for Sarah, and there was: she prefigured Mary, and however faint the shadow in the eyes of those with the dimmest vision, she was worthy of representation if not always respect. Even Gregory paid her the respect of imagining what she would have said to Abraham had he confided in her: "Do not become a wicked story for the world. This is my only born son . . . my first and last child. Whom will we see after this one at our table? Who will call his sweet voice to me? Who will call for mother? Who will attend my old age? Who will wrap up my body after my death? Who will heap up a mound over the body?" He's the "bloom of youth," fruit of great prayer, branch of our succession, remnant of our people, staff of our old age. She asks Abraham to kill her first: "Let the eyes of Sarah see neither Abraham as a child killer nor Isaac killed by his father's hands."

I like Sarah's warning about the wicked story, and her last line too. (And I am struck by the echoes of Homer and Sophocles in the writing of a bishop who suggested that his education was unadulterated, all Christian.) Still, I can't help thinking that the main reason Gregory gave Sarah a voice was to use what he took to be her weakness as a foil, magnifying Abraham's strength.

I much prefer the Sarah of the fifth- and sixth-century verse homilists and hymnists, Christians whose literary and liturgical language was Syriac, a dialect of Aramaic. These writers, perhaps inspired by the great Syriac theologian and hymnist Ephrem (who maintained that the only reason Abraham hadn't told Sarah about the sacrifice was that God hadn't commanded him to), not only imagined what Sarah might have said to Abraham but also let her say it for herself. And say it she did, in verse homilies so dramatic and so full of direct address, dialogue, and physical movement that some scholars believe they might have been acted out on a stage. It seems certain that they were sung in church, and on feast days in Syriac churches they may well have been sung by women.

In one homily, Sarah, seeing Abraham and Isaac packing up, asks where he is taking her only son. She reminds him that she has never discouraged him from doing what is good. You brought in the poor, she says, and I looked after them. Some of the poor "turned out to be angels." You fetched a calf; I kneaded the unleavened bread. "We were as one person, with a single love." But now, "when you have in mind a journey, why is the child going with you, and why are you not revealing your secret to Sarah your faithful wife who in all the hardships of exile has borne trials along with you?"

"I wish to slaughter a lamb and offer a sacrifice to God," Abraham replies.

Sarah asks him to leave Isaac behind. If anything is to happen to him, she says, I'd be "unjustly deprived of the single son to whom I have given birth. . . . You are drunk with the love of God—who is your God and my God—and if He so bids you concerning the child, you would kill him without hesitation."

Don't worry, Abraham says. Like me, you are "pure and full of faith." God is in charge. He does what he wants, on earth as well as in heaven. If he wants Isaac back, he'll take him. I have vowed to do what God asks. And I will. But it is a lamb I plan to sacrifice. Don't delay us any further with all your talking. "I shall take with me two young men so that you will not worry over Isaac, (thinking) that I am handing him over to slaughter."

They set out, but Isaac has overheard all that, and after Abraham orders the servants to remain at the foot of the mountain, he begins to pepper his father with questions. Where are we going? Why are we going alone? What are you going to do to me? You said we were going to slaughter a lamb, but where on this mountain are we going to find one?

The Lord will provide the lamb, Abraham says. So Isaac begins to gather wood and Abraham begins to build the altar and tend to the fire. They work together, rejoicing in their respective tasks, but in the hymnist's telling, they are emphatically not of one mind. They have entirely different ideas about the work they are doing and entirely different expectations, and when Abraham grabs Isaac, binds him, and raises the knife, Isaac cries out, first to his father— "Instead of the lamb you have made me the lamb"—and then to God.

Another hymnist, the Syrian-born Romanos, who is believed to have lived in the sixth century, wrote in Greek and began his hymn in the traditional Greek fashion, with hypothetical speech. His narrator asks Abraham, "How did you not say?" and then goes on to suggest what Abraham might have said to God. Then Abraham introduces Sarah, warning God to be careful, lest Sarah overhear them. Abraham tells God that she wouldn't believe that he had understood him correctly.

"If he who gave were to take away," she would ask, "what has he given? Old man, just leave to my care what belongs to me; when he who called you wants him, he will let me know." She would remind her husband that God had sent an angel to inform her that she would soon bear a child. He would send another to inform her that her son would soon die. "I will not trust the child to you; I will not give him to you." If God wants a sacrifice, let him take a sheep. She would promise Isaac that it would not happen: Abraham would have to kill her first. Then he could murder his son. But he won't, she would say. Your father won't.

Among the remarkable things about Romanos's hymn, and among the things that has led scholars to suspect that his influences included the Syriac hymnists or a common source, was that from that point on in the hymn, the apparatus of hypothetical speech falls away and Abraham and Sarah talk directly to each other. Abraham warns her not to anger God by speaking that way. "He asks of us what belongs to him already." Don't blemish the sacrifice with tears. "God wants him, and who can keep him from God?" He is strong enough to slay him while he's locked in your embrace. Show him your good will by giving him up. I could cry too, he says, "wet all earth with my tears. . . . Or does it seem to you that it is only your offspring that is doomed? Isn't he my son as well to whom I gave life?"

"You have been his begetter and you will be his slayer also?" she asks.

God rules over all, Abraham replies. "He has demanded of me a gift of that which was given to us only for a short time."

Like the Syriac hymnists, Romanos gives Sarah her say, but neither he nor they were done with her. In Romanos, she turns to Isaac and tells him to go. If God wants you alive, she says, he will not kill you. "Now I will be glorified: I will be called blessed for offering a gift of my womb to him who gave you to me." Go, she tells Isaac, "and become the victim of God, together with your begetter—or rather, your murderer." She has faith that as he left her, he'd find his true father. And she had faith that he'd be back, one way or another. If not in this world, then in the world to come.

One Syriac homilist imagined that Sarah had begged Abraham to allow her to go along with them: to carry stones for the altar, to bind Isaac with locks of her white hair, to dig the hole for his grave. If he would not permit her to go all the way, she would "remain at the foot of the mountain until" he had "sacrificed him and come back." She grabs Isaac and tells him to listen to his father, to do what he says. "If he should actually bind you, stretch out your hands to the bonds, and if he should actually sacrifice you, stretch out your neck before his knife, stretch out your neck like a lamb, like a kid before the shearer. See my son that you do not put your father under oath when he draws out his knife against you, lest his mind be upset and there be a blemish in his offering. And listen my son to the words of your mother, and let your reputation go forth unto generations to come." In tears, she embraces him and kisses him and says, "Go in peace."

Part of me wishes that Romanos and that Syriac writer had stopped with lines like "I will not give him to you" or "You are drunk with God." But if they had, their innovation would actually have been less notable than it was, limited to the way they gave Sarah a say, in direct speech, and the words they gave her to say. That's because what I welcome today, what looks to me like Sarah's good sense, was actually firmly established tradition, deeply devout writers diminishing her by giving voice to her motherly instincts and womanly nature, her lesser understanding and love of God. In the middle of the first millennium, at least a few writers moved beyond that tradition, making Sarah Abraham's equal in faith— and, no less remarkably, making Abraham her equal in doubt.

In Romanos, Abraham is at first as reluctant as Sarah to obey God's command. He worries that anyone who were to see him slaughtering his child would think him mad. He wonders how he could possibly bind and murder the boy whose "swaddling clothes" he had "untied," the boy he had nurtured and hoped would be his heir. He goes so far as to say that he will not do it, leaving it ambiguous whether he intended to refuse or he knew that he ultimately wouldn't have to.

Sarah's argument with Abraham is the extension of his argument with himself, and Romanos devotes the same amount of space to the two of them, and the same amount of space to her change of heart as to his insistence that she should have that change of heart. Then he does something equally striking: he gives Sarah the last word. She had predicted that Isaac would return safely, and when he does, she dances "with joy" and says: "May he who made you appear before me, my child, receive my spirit."

Here, again, Romanos may have taken his cue from the Syriac homilists, who also end with Sarah. One Syriac writer imagined that, upon his return, Isaac had reported right to his mother, telling her what had happened, and insisting, rather unconvincingly, that she need not have been worried. God sent the lamb, Isaac says, and Abraham offered it in my place. "He stretched out his hand to the knife, and it reached the very neck of your darling, and had there not been the voice, I would yesterday have been killed, and they would have been looking for my bones in the fire."

Sarah faints, and when she comes to she is sobbing, speaking to Isaac as if he had died. "Welcome in peace slain one come alive, upon whom the Lord's right hand had compassion. The fingers which fashioned you in my womb have now delivered you from the knife." You were slain by Abraham, but "God in His mercy gave you back."

A second Syriac homilist imagined an even more dramatic ending. Early on, when Sarah had asked where he and Isaac were going, Abraham told her not to mind: "This secret to-day women cannot be aware of." Sarah groaned. She not only wanted to know, but to go, to participate. Abraham ignored her, but on his way home, he decides to call her bluff. He tells Isaac to stay behind, so he can "spy out her mind and her thoughts."

Sarah receives him ("Welcome, O happy one, who has sacrificed my only child on the pyre"), fetches water to wash his feet, and asks him to tell her what happened. "Did he weep when he was bound, or groan as he died?" She imagines that he was looking for her, his eyes wandering over the mountains, expecting her to save him. Now she wants to know everything.

Isaac did not cry or groan, Abraham reports, but he did ask for you.

"I was wishing I was an eagle or had the speed of a turtle-dove," she says, "so that I might go and behold that place." She would have liked to see the fire and to "bring back a little of his blood to be comforted by its smell," and a lock of his hair and an article of his clothing and some of his ashes. As she speaks those words, Isaac appears. She embraces him and welcomes him back to life. Isaac explains what has happened and she thanks God for giving him to her "a second time."

Once again, Sarah had the last word, and that is not the only sign of her elevation. Abraham has been tested once, but she has been tested twice, once by God and then again by her husband. She passes with an unimaginably high score: "I do obeisance to that voice which delivered you, my son, from the knife," she says in the hymn's final lines. "I praise Him who saved you from burning on the pyre. Henceforth, my son, it will not be Sarah's son that people will call you, but child of the pyre and offering who died and was resurrected."

. . .

I marvel at those strange hymns, and sometimes I ask myself why. After all, their authors took the Sarah of the Hebrew Bible, a woman who, though hardly without faults, would at least have had the good (and to me wholly imaginable) sense to say no to God, and transformed her into a woman of almost unimaginable Christian faith. One minute she calls Abraham drunk with God. The next she is at least as drunk as he is, "burning," as one Syriac writer put it, with a desire to sacrifice her son.

But history moves in unpredictable and often surprising ways. I am grateful for Sarah's voice and the depth and complexity of her feelings, and the complexity of the feelings she brought out in Abraham, and I am grateful for the esteem in which these writers, whether women or men, held her. All the more in light of the condescension of so many of their Jewish and Christian contemporaries. I myself am not moved by the hymnists' and homilists' ideas or feelings of faith, let alone by their burning desire, but if their ideas and desire were to be held up as the highest virtue—heralded and rewarded—I think that it is a virtue that Sarah should have the right to choose. Above all, I take solace in the thought that once her angry and incredulous words were out there, added to the archive, and once Abraham's doubts were out there with them, and even Isaac's anxiety and sense of betrayal, there was no telling what others might do with them.

14

~~~

That Sarah was new to me. So was that one hymnist's anxious Isaac. But so much else was familiar that as I read, I felt as if I had been transported to a great reunion, held in the middle of the first millennium, to mark five hundred years or more of biblical exegesis. Syriac Christians hosted, but they invited Greek-speaking Christians from near and far (including Ephrem Graecus and Gregory of Nyssa and John Chrysostom of Constantinople and Basil of Seleucia and Amphilochius of Iconium and Irenaeus of Lyon and Clement and Origen of Alexandria). And, hard as it may be for some to believe, they invited a host of Jews.

Looking around the room, I recognize men who told the story as a test of obedience and men who told it as a test of faith. Men who imagined that Isaac was a wise and willing victim and men who imagined him wondering, anxiously, what in the world his father was up to. Men who understood why Abraham didn't say a word to Sarah and men who didn't—believing that she too would have proven to be a model of Christian faith. At one table Jews who translated Hebrew scripture into Greek and Aramaic shared trade secrets with Christians who translated it into Greek, Latin, and Syriac and, after that, Greek to Coptic. At another, bishops who (perhaps influenced by Melito, bishop of Sardis) devoted their days to identifying typology, all the bits of history that pointed to and culminated in Christ, mingled with bishops (including Irenaeus) who borrowed the Jewish concept of *zekhut avot*—the merit of the fathers—to make sense of the sweep of sacred history: Abraham's sacrifice didn't merely prefigure God's, it brought it about. Because Abraham was willing to sacrifice his son, God actually sacrificed his.

In the ballroom's low light, a pair of priests, who (like many rabbis) imagined Isaac asking to be bound and angels crying out to God as Abraham reached for the cleaver, might have been mistaken for rabbis, who (like many priests) saw, in the wood that Isaac carried, the cross that condemned men carried to their own executions. And if that wasn't surprising or confusing enough, after a few drinks, Greek and Syriac Christian commentators, who could be vicious about Jews in their writings and sermons (as Romanos himself, probably Jewish-born and later baptized, was in his homilies about the Passion), took to the stage and sang songs of Abraham and Isaac with lyrics that might have been written by a rabbi.

Swept up in the revelry and feeling a little bit giddy, I was tempted to offer a toast. Here's to the very height of biblical hybridity and interdenominational exchange. How could anyone read those hymns and still say that the early Christians weren't paying close attention to the Jews?

Afterward I would have felt silly—not on account of what I'd said about the priests and rabbis but for imagining I could know the height of anything like that. Only when we are hiking or mountain climbing, and even then only on clear days far above the tree line, do we know the summit the moment we are there. Those Syriac hymnists (and probably Romanos too) had sung their last song before Muhammad was born. At most the future prophet was a little boy, and no one could have seen the man and Islam coming.

And even if I had received a hot tip, had known that he was on his way and about to take the Arabian Peninsula by storm, had somehow got my hands on an advance reading copy of the Qur'an, the bounty of Islamic exegesis would still have taken me by surprise. Unlike the priests and bishops, who claimed that their new covenant and testament had fulfilled the old, Muhammad insisted his revelation was nothing but a midcourse correction, a reminder of a kind of submission to God that had preceded slavery and Sinai and the whole history of ancient Israel. He expressed great respect for the Hebrew prophets, right through Jesus, and the great books. His simply thought that the revelation those books recorded had been distorted and corrupted, by word and by deed, and that as a result the People of the Book, all the people of all the books, had lost their way. "There are illiterates among them who do not know the book," he said, "but only fancies, and they do nothing but conjecture. Woe to them who write the book with their own hands and then say: This is from God."

When I first read those words, in the opening pages of the Qur'an, I assumed the people Muhammad called illiterates were the very same ones I call exegetes: the ancient interpreters, the rabbis, the priests, all the people I've been telling you about, from Jubilees to the Syriac hymnists and Romanos. Muhammad's project was to set the record straight, return to revelation uncorrupted by interpretation and revision, to get back to basics, fundamentals, original intentions. That isn't my project, but that is what I assumed he was up to.

What I discovered, as I kept reading in the Qur'an, and then volume after volume of Islamic exegesis, especially the Hadith, the authoritative record of the words and deeds of the Prophet, is that neither Muhammad, who died in 632, nor the Muslim exegetes (scholars, jurists, theologians, and historians, one generation after another) who came after him were opposed to all interpretation and revision and elaboration and embellishment. They were opposed only to the interpretation and revision they were opposed to, elaboration and embellishment they didn't like. Muslims produced every manner of interpretation, every manner of revision, every manner of story about Abraham. They told about his emigration (from Babylonia to Syria), about his close encounter with a tyrant (who tried to steal his wife), about his relationship with Hagar and their son Ishmael; about Hagar and Ishmael's relocation to Mecca; about Abraham's visits to Ishmael and Hagar; about Abraham and Ishmael's building of the Kaaba, Islam's holiest shrine; about Abraham's calling on Muslims to make the pilgrimage to Mecca; and about Abraham's own first pilgrimage. And they told scores of stories about the near sacrifice of his son.

They told and recorded stories. If you were to read them, you would find not just liberal revision of ancient stories but familiar revision, starting with an Abraham who never had a question or doubt, never made a mistake, never wavered; an Abraham about whom Jubilees himself would have found an enormous amount to admire. You'll find an articulate, talkative, willing Isaac, and an Ishmael who (as in many rabbinic sources) maintained a close relationship with his father long after he left home, married, and began to father a great nation of his own. You'll find a crafty Satan, who tried to stop Abraham but was thwarted at every turn, often by Sarah, a woman of few words but almost all of them right there with her man. You'll find a "noble substitute" for Isaac. And for Abraham and Isaac's steadfastness in the face of a terrible trial, you will read about a reward that will make you think, at once, of Christian notions of vicarious atonement and Jewish notions of the saving merit of the fathers.

I don't mean to suggest in some sort of chauvinistic way that Islamic stories were completely derivative, cut and pasted from Jewish and Christian sources. They weren't. Like so many of the stories of the rabbis and priests, like so many of the biblical stories themselves, they were composites, made of prebiblical traditions, pre-Islamic Arabian oral traditions (including pre-Islamic monotheistic traditions), Jewish and Christian biblical traditions, and emerging and evolving Islamic traditions. There were many parallels, many borrowings, many adaptations, and in no time there were notable new directions.

For example: Several influential Islamic authorities cut through the confusion of countless rabbinic explanations of what prompted

God to ask. Turns out, he got the idea from Abraham, who had been so moved by the news of the imminent arrival of a pious son, and so grateful, that he immediately made an oath to God: When the boy came of age, he would sacrifice him. Several years later, Abraham dreamed that the time had come. He asked his son what he should do, and his son said: If that's what God wants, let's do it.

Islamic writers also contributed the fullest and most graphic descriptions of the story's climatic moment. Jewish exegetes didn't shy away from it—recall Isaac asking to be bound, angels weeping, Abraham expressing his frustration when God said stop. But the form of the early midrash, the painstaking examination of the meaning of single words, phrases, and discrete verses (and the movement from those words and verses to distant words and verses in Scripture and distant places and times in history in order to explain them) tended to provide a merciful distraction. The emphasis on typology or allegory in Christian interpretation had precisely the same effect.

In dozens of different Islamic versions, we do not stray.

Isaac asks Abraham to tighten his bonds so that he cannot squirm, to pull his shirt out of the way so it won't get soaked with blood and later cause his mother grief, to sharpen the knife and be quick so his death will be less painful, to return his shirt to his mother to provide her with comfort, and to give her his best wishes. Only then does Abraham draw his knife across Isaac's neck. But unbeknownst to Abraham, God has slipped a sheet of copper between knife and neck. The knife doesn't break the skin. Frustrated, Abraham flips Isaac onto his forehead (thereby helping readers understand why the description of the near sacrifice in many sources, including the Qur'an, deviates from the standard Islamic sacrifice ritual, where the victim is always placed on its side).

God commands Abraham to stop. He does, and he and Isaac sacrifice a ram instead. Not long after, father and son return to Sarah, who greets them and asks about their day. Abraham tells her where they have been, and her response, in one paradigmatic version, sounds like an Arabic version of the punch line of a Jewish comedian's joke: "You would sacrifice my son and not inform me?"

In other versions Isaac asks Abraham to lay him on his forehead (providing a second explanation for the deviation). Abraham heaps praise on his son for his obedience and grabs the knife, but God (or sometimes Gabriel) turns it to its dull side and then informs Abraham that he has already fulfilled his vision. In unison, Gabriel, Abraham, and Isaac shout, "God is most great."

To say that Isaac is a willing victim in these accounts does not say enough about his role. He seems to be calling the shots from the moment Abraham wakes from his dream.

"Are you obedient?" Abraham asks, vaguely.

"Yes," Isaac says. "Even if you wanted to sacrifice me, I would not try to prevent it."

Abraham retrieves rope and knife and off they go. Satan, taking the form of an old man Abraham recognizes, tells Abraham that he is doing the devil's work. Abraham tells him to get lost, so Satan tells Isaac that his father is about to sacrifice him. "If that's what God wants, so be it," the boy says. Satan leaves, thinking his last best chance is to find Sarah, and Abraham and Isaac go on their way. When they arrive, Isaac delivers a complete set of instructions:

Take my shirt off so it will not be bloodied, causing my mother to cry over me. Tie me up so I don't squirm in your arms, causing you pain (note that the Islamic Isaac's concern is for his father's comfort, not the Levitical requirement that a sacrifice be completely unblemished). When you place the knife at my throat, don't look, or you might be overcome by compassion. Give Mother my greetings, but spare her the details of the sacrifice so that she will not be sorrowful over me. "And when you see a young boy like me, do not look at him, so that your heart will not grieve on my account."

Hearing all that, a voice from heaven calls out, "O friend of God, how can you not be compassionate for this small child who speaks to you with such words."

"Don't distract me," Abraham says, thinking it is Satan speaking. He gets back to work, removing Isaac's shirt and binding him. As he puts the knife to Isaac's throat, he prays, "In the name of God the powerful and excellent."

God flips it.

Abraham turns to sharpen it.

God flips it again, and says, "O Abraham, take this ram and redeem your son with it. Sacrifice it as an offering. God has made this day a holy festival for you and your children."

The ram joins in: "O Friend of God, sacrifice me instead of your son, for I am a more appropriate sacrifice than he. I am the ram of Abel, son of Adam, who gave me as an offering to his Lord and whose offering was accepted. I have grazed in the meadows of the Gardens for forty autumns."

All that was left was God's blessing, and many Islamic interpreters, like many rabbis, implied, without coming right out and saying it, that in the biblical version of the story God is a little stingy. Abraham has nearly sacrificed his son, and God rewards him simply by reiterating promises he has made several times before. But the Islamic Abraham doesn't demand more. God, unprompted, offers it, and not to Abraham but to his son. In some versions he offers him a wish, any wish. In other versions, he offers him a choice, one of two: Either I'll forgive half the Muslim people, or I'll respond to your petition on anyone's behalf. Isaac chooses the latter: "Whenever a sinner who believes in you appears at the gates of heaven," he says, "pardon him on my behalf, and let him into paradise."

Who could resist the charm of Isaac's generous calculation? Or not appreciate the echo of a passage in the Talmud in which a rabbi imagined a future day when God, unhappy with his chosen people, would appeal to the patriarchs, starting with Abraham, to see if any of them were willing to take upon themselves responsibility for the sins of the current generation?

"Your children have sinned," God says.

Wipe them out, to sanctify the name of God, Abraham advises.

God turns to Jacob, thinking that a man with so many difficult children of his own might be more compassionate.

Wipe them out, Jacob advises.

Frustrated with both grandfather and grandson, God turns to the man in the middle and Isaac doesn't let him down. On behalf of the sinners, Isaac takes several different tacks: First, he chides God for saying "Your children have sinned." Plainly, Isaac reminds him, the sinners are your children too. Then he uses some fancy math to point out that they really hadn't sinned for very long. Finally he plays his trump card: He tells God that if he, God, himself would "bear all" the sin, it would be great. If he won't, Isaac says he would be happy to split the burden with him, half and half. But if God should say that he, Isaac, must bear it all, he would say: "I offered myself up before Thee as a sacrifice!"

Before I am accused, by a reader familiar with Islamic interpretation, of missing the forest for the trees, let me make one thing perfectly clear. I understand that most readers, settling into an easy chair with a representative sample of Hadith, would find all these small details, and even all the remarkable echoes and correspondences, less significant than one huge innovation, or correction: in many Islamic versions, Ishmael is the son whom Abraham promises to sacrifice. Ishmael is the son Abraham dreams God wants him to sacrifice. Ishmael is the son he nearly does sacrifice. And Ishmael is the son who asks God's pardon for his descendants through the ages.

How could that be?

Easy, as anyone who has stuck with me for this long should see. Even if an Islamic exegete's only source was the Hebrew Bible, he could have substituted Ishmael for Isaac with less effort than it had taken earlier commentators to imagine Abraham (to say nothing of Sarah) eager to see the sacrifice through or Sarah welcoming Isaac back from the dead. The word "Isaac" appears five times in Genesis 22. All it would take is a quick search-and-replace.

In fact, it was even simpler than that, for Islamic exegetes weren't working from the Bible. Their starting point was the Qur'an, God's words to Muhammad by way of Gabriel, and Muhammad recounted the story in his own inimitable way, at once more concrete and cryptic, a jazzy mix of figurative and literal, poetry and prose (that many Muslims insist is neither). In it, Abraham asks the Lord for a righteous son and his wish is granted. When the boy comes of age, Abraham dreams that he is supposed to sacrifice him. He asks his son for his view:

> He said, "My father, do as thou art bidden; thou shalt find me, God willing, one of the steadfast." When they had surrendered, and he flung him upon his brow, We called unto him, "Abraham, thou hast confirmed the vision; even so We recompense the good-doers. This is indeed the manifest trial." And We ransomed him with a mighty sacrifice, and left for him among the later folk "Peace be upon Abraham!"
>
> Even so We recompense the good-doers; he was among Our believing servants. Then We gave him the good tidings of Isaac, a Prophet, one of the righteous. And We blessed him, and Isaac; and of their seed some are good-doers, and some manifest self-wrongers.

You see: The trial had taken place even before the good news of Isaac arrived. The nearly sacrificed son would have to have been Ishmael, the older son, Abraham's only son at that time.

Of course not everyone read it way. For starters, whether within chapters or among them, the Qur'an only occasionally proceeds chronologically. What comes first is not necessarily what happened first. The narrator circles around and jumps around, usually putting stripped-down versions of biblical stories or brief references to biblical characters and stories in the service of the pedagogy, the point, the lesson, the argument, thereby leaving ample room for creative reading and interpretation. Generation after generation of

Muslim scholars and sages rushed in to fill that space, and they created myriad versions and variants of versions, including versions of what happened (in some Abraham does exactly what Isaac asks and in others he refuses to, insisting that he'll do only what God commands) and where it happened (Mecca, where Ishmael and Hagar lived, or Syria, where Isaac and Sarah lived) and exactly when it happened in relation to the building of the Kaaba and the call to pilgrimage (Shiite scholars have tended to set the sacrifice in the context of the very first pilgrimage to Mecca, and both sacrifice and pilgrimage in the context of Arabian pilgrimages and sacrifices that preceded Islam) and even what animal Abraham sacrificed in Isaac or Ishmael's place.

The earliest exegetes considered Isaac the victim, and they weren't embarrassed, as some later exegetes may have been, to cite Israelite tales (Torah) and the Gospels as authorities. Yet the appeal of the Ishmael in Mecca versions of the story is not mysterious. In the Bible, God made his covenant with Abraham and confirmed it (because you have done this) at Moriah. Ishmael, though banished, would be taken care of. He would be the father of many great nations, but the covenant was with Isaac and his children through the ages.

The early Christians started there, but they altered the definition of Abraham and Isaac's descendants, casting the Jews off as Abraham and Sarah had earlier cast off Hagar. One of the ways that Paul did that was by allegory: Abraham, he wrote in Galatians, had two sons, one by a slave woman and one by a free woman. Hagar represented the covenant enacted at Sinai, in Arabia. The Jews were her children, and she and her children, children of the flesh, all those who rejected Christ, were slaves in the earthly Jerusalem. Sarah represented the new covenant. Her children, children of the spirit, were free in the Jerusalem above. "Cast out the bondwoman and her son: for the son of the bondwoman shall not be heir with the son of the freewoman. So then, brethren, we are not children of the bondwoman, but of the free."

Ishmael was the genealogical link between Abraham and the Prophet, the progenitor of the Arab people. Is it any wonder that as Islam took root in the Arabian Peninsula and spread from there, many Muslims, scholars and lay, preferred the version of the near sacrifice that made Abraham's older son the son whose submission to God defined their faith and secured God's blessing? In favoring Ishmael, Muslims simply did what, for so many, comes naturally. They redirected the course of sacred history so that God's blessing ran their way.

Many, but hardly all. The debate between those who favored Ishmael and those who favored Isaac continued for centuries, with exegetes on both sides citing respected authorities (sometimes the very same authorities), ideally a chain of authorities with links extending all the way back to the Prophet. Some arguments were polemical and pointed:

"The Jews claim that it was Isaac, but the Jews lie."

"The proof for those who say that it was Isaac is that the Christians and Jews agree about it. The answer to that is that their agreement is no proof and their view is not acceptable."

The Jews "forced this understanding because Isaac is their father while Ishmael is the father of the Arabs."

But late in the first millennium and early in the second when Islamic scholars began compiling collections of oral traditions, many of them were as comfortable as the rabbis who edited compilations of midrash with disparate and contradictory accounts and explanations, laid out one after the other. It was not uncommon for Islamic scholars to report the arguments for opposing views accurately and at length before making the case for their own. And they appear to be have been at peace with multiplicity, or at least a certain kind of uncertainty: "Some people say that it was Ishmael," wrote al-Ya'qūbī (a Shiite historian and geographer in the third century of Islam), "because he was the one who settled in Mecca, while Isaac remained in Syria. Other people say that it was Isaac because Abraham sent him (Ishmael) and his mother out when Isaac was a young boy, and Ishmael was a grown man with children. There are many traditions about each view and people disagree about them."

By that time the literature of Islam was as vast as the empire, and Muslims had a body of sacred exegesis they thought of as all their own, exegesis that, notwithstanding all the Qur'anic criticism of the fancies, lies, and conjectures of the Jews and Christians, was full of innovation and of invention, full of insight borrowed from the archive of oral and written exegesis, full of creative reading and writing—said to be, by way of the Prophet, the word of God.

One man's revelation was another's impossible fancy. One man's fancy, another man's revelation. It is a truth that's been churned into a truism, yet not a trite one when it comes to sacred stories and religious differences more generally. No one could be more attuned to it than I. Yet when I step back from all the narrative twists and interpretive turns I so enjoy tracking, from all the versions and variations and authorities and traditions, from the arguments about whether it was Isaac or Ishmael whom Abraham nearly sacrificed, or a ram, goat, or lamb that he ultimately did, it seems to me that there is at least one way in which most Islamic versions of the story really did deliver what Muhammad had promised: a return to fundamentals, foundations, a simple story of command, response, and reward.

No questions. No hesitation. No doubt. No gut-wrenching appeals from Sarah. When Satan told her where Abraham had taken their son, she was skeptical. She said that the boy's father was even more compassionate to him than she was. But if God had truly commanded Isaac's sacrifice, Abraham would go through with it. In one version she blames herself—for mistreating Hagar. But she does not try to stop it. Nor, after God stops it, does the Islamic Abraham ever take God to task for asking.

What is the Islamic version of the story about? It is not so much about faith. Nor the ideal of human sacrifice. Nor a prefiguration of a great sacrifice to come. Nor martyrdom. Nor even the saving merit of our forefathers. Rather, most Islamic versions of the story are, at root, about listening to God's voice. What God asks, his chosen people do. It was a trial, a test, and Abraham passed it, and in passing it, he became first and forever after the paradigmatic Muslim, the very definition of a Muslim, one who submits to God.

~~~

You don't have to look hard to find them: the Jewish riffs in early Christian commentary and the Christian riffs in the rabbinical commentary of late antiquity and the Jewish and Christian riffs in the Islamic commentary. They are hard to miss, and they would not be so striking to me if, over the centuries, Jews, Christians, and Muslims had always spoken the same languages, shared the same libraries, read the same books, and then gathered for ecumenical Bible study, tolerated difference in theory and practice, treated one another as equals, at least under the law, or lived together in peace.

But notwithstanding periods of calm and even tolerance (some say early Muslim Spain was as good as it got), they did not. Even when there was not punishing proscription or gross inequality, there was tension and periodic violence at the core of even the most tolerant communities. It is the history of conflict among Muslims, Christians, and Jews, and the widespread perception of difference, of separation, of sharp distinctions, of high walls and fences topped with wire, that makes instances of convergence and exchange worthy of note. If all were sweetness and light, we'd expect it and take it for granted. But we don't, because there were so many ways of seeing and thinking about sacred history each group wouldn't acknowledge, so many lines each group wouldn't cross (or imagine itself crossing), so many places each group insisted it would never go.

The rabbis responded to all the talk of Abraham's faith by making explicit what they hadn't thought needed to be said: the story of the Binding of Isaac was about listening to God's voice. They believed, just as the priests did, that God tested Abraham to search his heart. But what God was searching for was not some abstract sense that he himself would keep his promises but active obedience. In the words of the author (or editor) of the *Pirke de Rabbi Eliezer*, a rich rewriting of and commentary on Genesis and Exodus put together in the late eighth or early ninth century (though attributed to the late-first-century Eliezer, teacher of the great Akiva), God said he wanted to know if Abraham would be able "to keep all the commandments of the Torah."

Christian commentators insisted the sacrifice of Isaac had nothing to do with Moses's law, that shadow of better things to come. Someday, perhaps, the Jews would outgrow it, accept Christ, and leave the old Israel for the new.

Islamic scholars, meanwhile, shrugged off all Christian talk of shadows, of prefiguration, of types. What use could a Muslim possibly have for the idea that prophecy and sacred history culminated in Christ—five hundred years before Muhammad arrived on the scene? Unlike the Jews, they considered Jesus an important prophet, a messenger of God. But like the Jews, they believed that he had been a man. God was One. That may be why, when God granted the Islamic Isaac (or Ishmael) a wish as a reward for his and his father's submission, the boy wished that everyone who believed in God would be welcomed in heaven—except those who believed God had a son or some other partner.

Neither rabbis nor priests took the idea that Ishmael was the nearly sacrificed son seriously. To them, it was one more sign that when it came to history and sacred literature, the Muslims had a few screws loose. Whether they showed respect for Ishmael or mocked him, they all elevated Isaac. But not the same Isaac. Jews and Christians each had their own, and considering that by the end of the first millennium Jesus had come to be the biggest sticking point between them, what is remarkable about the Jewish Isaac is how much like Jesus he had become.

The rabbis had abandoned (if they had ever entertained) the Isaac I imagine, the small boy with no real role or obvious understanding. Their Isaac was a young man, thirty-seven years old, sharing the stage with his father, a knowing victim and a willing victim and sometimes not a victim at all, but rather an agent in the drama that nearly took his life. Sometimes he asked to be bound. Sometimes he stretched his neck toward the knife. Sometimes he bound (and thus nearly sacrificed) himself. Perhaps nowhere is his privileged place in the story clearer than in the version in which he, lying on his back on the altar, obtained a view of the divine presence that his father, standing above him with the knife, did not.

Christian exegetes were no less in awe. Isaac's miraculous birth was annunciated by angels. He bore his own cross. He was bound like a lamb. He was returned to his father (and mother) unscathed. He was the beneficiary of God's blessing, and in all those ways and more he was a type of Christ, of the church, of the body of Christ's faithful. In all those ways he remained dear.

But the story was about his father, who was tested through him. Not every exegete went as far as Melito, the bishop of Sardis, who in the second century insisted that Isaac had been completely "silent, bound like a ram, not opening his mouth nor uttering a sound." You may recall that a few hundred years later several Syriac hymnists imagined him asking a slew of anxious questions on the way up the mountain and then, upon his return, nearly killing his mother with a blow-by-blow account of his ordeal. But even at his most articulate, he remained a young boy who never usurped his father's role. "Abraham was fervent for the killing of Isaac," one hymnist wrote, while Isaac was "looking out for the lamb . . . both readily became workers for God . . . though their labors were not equal."

And no matter how much Isaac said or didn't say, knew or didn't know, he absolutely did not suffer. "Christ suffered," Melito wrote, "whereas Isaac did not suffer; for he was the model of the Christ who was going to suffer." Christ suffered, Cyril of Alexandria wrote two and a half centuries later, but Isaac, "having been placed on the wood," was "stolen away from death and suffering."

To understand the Christian insistence that Isaac did not suffer is in part to understand the power of typology, which limited the range of things commentators could say about him just as surely as it enlarged the range for Sarah. For Christ's death and resurrection, unharmed and unblemished, to be fulfilled, there had to be something unfulfilled; for his sacrifice to end all sacrifice and atone for the sins of humankind, there had to be a near sacrifice, a dress rehearsal, a ritual sacrifice that didn't quite do the trick. Isaac is "a type of the Lord," wrote Clement of Alexandria, "a child as a son; for he was the son of Abraham, as Christ the Son of God, and a sacrifice as the Lord, but he was not immolated as the Lord. Isaac only bore the wood of the sacrifice, as the Lord the wood of the cross." Isaac did "everything but suffer, as was right, yielding the precedence in the suffering to the Word."

But the more time I spend with the priests and bishops of late antiquity, the more I suspect that there was more at work than typology. After all, the Christian Isaac could have been stolen away from death without being spared pain and suffering. He could have suffered some without suffering as much as Christ. My hunch is that the Christian Isaac didn't suffer partly because of typology and partly because of exegetical competition between Christians and Jews. The Christian Isaac never suffered because the Jewish Isaac often did.

The rabbis said he had wondered, worried, and trembled. Sometimes he trembled exceedingly. They said he had asked to be tied so that his involuntary movements would not spoil the sacrifice. In at least one version he protested: "So this is the Torah you talked about to my mother Sarah when you said, 'I am going to take him to the schoolmasters!' In more than one he cried. He sustained knife wounds, and he bled. Eventually, in some exegesis, he died.

Sometimes he died of fright.

Sometimes the moment the blade touched his throat his soul took flight.

Sometimes the sight of the heavens killed him.

Sometimes it was a loss of blood.

Sometimes he succumbed to the flames.

Sometimes it was, matter-of-factly and without elaboration, simple sacrifice: he was "slaughtered according to the rite."

In every instance God revived him, and when he came to, he realized that he had just been given a preview of the manner in which the dead would live again. He opened his mouth and recited the second benediction: "Blessed art thou, O Lord, who quickeneth the dead."

Today, friends and family and colleagues and neighbors and sometimes total strangers look at me in disbelief when I tell them that some rabbis imagined that Abraham had killed Isaac.

"No he didn't," they say.

"They imagined that he did," I say.

"What do you mean, they imagined that he did? The story is clear about that. God said stop."

"It's not what I mean," I say. "It is certainly not what I expected, or wanted; not how I hoped the story would be revised."

"It is not what happened," they say. "Everyone knows that Isaac didn't die. It is Jesus who dies, the Christians who celebrate a father actually sacrificing his son."

I understand their surprise and incredulity. The stories of death and resurrection are not the ones people are likely to learn in Hebrew school, or even in seminary. They realize that I am in a better position to know than they are, but they still insist I must be mistaken. How, they ask, could the rabbis or anyone else have come to that conclusion from the story as they remember it?

I send them back to the Bible, urging them to keep a few of the questions that some rabbis asked in mind:

Why the second angelic address? Why couldn't God have said everything he had to say the first time?

And why, in that second address, did God say, "Because you have done this and have not withheld your son, your only one"?

And most of all: How are we to understand the story's last line: "Abraham then returned to his servants, and they departed together for Beersheba." Where was Isaac?

The story left readers with questions. Some answered them with stories in which Isaac died:

God called again because Abraham didn't stop the first time.

Or Abraham did stop—he didn't lay a hand on him—and it was his literal obedience that sealed Isaac's fate. Remember that Abraham knew the rules the Torah prescribed for sacrifice as well as any Levitical priest. (Never mind that those rules would not be revealed, the priesthood established, for four hundred years.) He knew that the fire went first and the wood went on top of it. In Genesis 22, Abraham built an altar. He laid out the wood. He bound Isaac and placed him on the altar on top of the wood. If that's how it happened, if Abraham put the wood on the fire and Isaac on the wood, and then, as God commanded, he stopped and did not lay a hand on him or do anything to him, the incident would have ended with Isaac's ashes.

And that explains why God said, "Because you have done this thing and not withheld your son, your only one." Because one way or another, Abraham did do it, had done it. He had sacrificed his son.

And that explains why Isaac was not with Abraham when he returned to his lads and they rose and went together to Beersheba.

Some rabbis imagined that Isaac had been washed into heaven by the angels' tears, staying there until God brought him back to life and earth. Others imagined that God had lifted him into the Garden of Eden, where he remained—for three days, for three years (just in time to hook up with Rebekah), for however long it took him to recover from fear, from shock, from knife wounds, from the flames.

All reasonable people will acknowledge that there were, and are, other explanations, simple, straightforward answers to those questions. And they'll be relieved to know that one rabbi or another employed them all. Two examples should suffice. When God said, "Because you have done this thing and have not withheld your son," he meant only that Abraham had demonstrated his willingness—not that he had actually offered him. He had sacrificed the ram instead. As for Isaac at the end: Some said he had lagged behind. Some, conversely, that he had taken a shortcut home, eager to assure his mother that he was safe. Some said that Abraham had sent him to study Torah at the academy, the very academy he had told Sarah he was taking him to in the first place. And some (thank heavens, including no less an authority than Abraham Ibn Ezra) said what I would say if someone asked me: Isaac was right there, together with Abraham, in his charge. The author was simply thinking about Abraham and God.

The rabbis' questions provided a convenient opening for those who wanted to kill Isaac, but they did not make his death and resurrection inevitable. His death had to solve a larger problem than the problem posed by those lines, and I think it did. At least since 2 Maccabees, Abraham and Isaac had been associated with Jewish martyrdom, being prepared to die for God. They'd also been associated with the merit of the fathers, a merit that resulted not only in deliverance in times of trouble—from Pharaoh in Egypt, from the angel of death, from the Red Sea, from the destroying angel in Jerusalem after David's census—but also in the pardoning of sin, starting with the sin of the Golden Calf.

According to the author of Chronicles, Solomon built the First Temple atop Mount Moriah. According to many rabbis, the Jews returning from exile in Babylonia built the altar for the second atop Isaac's ashes. The Passover sacrifice, the two daily *tamid* sacrifices, perhaps all Temple sacrifices, were thought to be reenactments of Abraham's sacrifice, and after the Second Temple was destroyed, the daily and festival sacrifices were often evoked in and replaced by ritual and prayer: "Let our lips compensate for the bulls." The memory of Abraham's sacrifice was everywhere. Isaac, more than any other Jewish figure, was associated with the resurrection of the dead.

And yet, in Scripture and most early revisions and interpretations of Scripture, Isaac didn't die. Or didn't seem to die, and that left a gap, a growing gap, and perhaps a nagging gap between the meaning and significance in people's minds and the story as it appeared on the page. It was a gap that exegetes as early as Philo seemed to acknowledge (when he said that even though God had stopped the sacrifice, he accepted it as a complete sacrifice) and a gap that the creators of a significant body of midrash (when they imagined Abraham begging God to let him do it, or to let him extract a bit of blood, or at the very least to imagine that he had killed his son and then the ram) seemed intent to bridge.

And even if I am wrong in imagining intramural fretting, even if the gap were a gap that the rabbis could have lived with if they were living all by themselves (there were, after all, an infinite number of gaps between Scripture and interpretation), it was also a gap between a near sacrifice and the sacrifice to end all sacrifices that century after century of Christian commentators, in the pulpit, on the pages of their commentary, and in anti-Jewish polemic, would never let them forget: The Jewish Isaac didn't suffer. Without blood there is no atonement. Your sacrifice was just a shadow of the real thing, your merit not saving.

In a letter to his churches written a few weeks before Easter in 334, Bishop Athanasius of Alexandria went out of his way to warn Egyptian Christians not to observe Passover with Egyptian Jews. The bishop wanted to be sure they realized that the Jewish Passover (a Passover not of the Lord but of the Jews) was a ritual that God no longer approved of. Jews continued to celebrate the paschal offering only because they failed to understand that when Abraham offered his son, he was worshipping the Son of God, and that the ram he ultimately sacrificed represented Christ, and that while Abraham was tested through Isaac, it was not Isaac who was ultimately sacrificed but Christ: "For the sacrifice was not properly the setting to rights of Isaac but of Abraham who also offered, and by that was tried. Thus, God accepted the will of the offerer but prevented that which was offered from being sacrificed. For the death of Isaac did not procure the freedom of the world but that of our Savior alone."

So some rabbis imagined that Isaac, too, had died, had died on Mount Moriah.

I can't tell you who first imagined that, or even when. The blood and ashes go way back ("on account of his blood I chose them," God said of Isaac in Pseudo-Philo, probably in the first century). But the precise dating of particular motifs in first-millennium midrash is difficult when not impossible.

Nor can I tell you how many rabbis and laypeople imagined that he had died.

And notwithstanding my suspicion about competition between rabbis and priests, I can't access the relative importance of that competition compared to, say, developments within each tradition (rabbis and priests arguing among themselves) in particular places at particular times. To do that, I would need a proximity to writers and readers, teachers and students, preachers and congregations, theological debates and their specific settings, that I, leaping from one place and time to another, rarely have.

What I can tell you is that at the end of the eleventh century, the church's war of words against Jews and Judaism turned into the real thing. The pope, responding to a plea from the emperor of Byzantium, called for a Crusade, and an army of Christian soldiers, mustered throughout western Europe, set out to repel Muslim advances in Anatolia and then liberate Jerusalem. Jews were not the crusaders' initial targets, but it was not long into their journey that it occurred to them that while they traveled thousands of difficult miles to fight infidels, the greatest enemies of Christ were closer to home. They assaulted one Rhineland Jewish community after another.

Vastly outnumbered and virtually unarmed, the Jews had a limited number of choices. Some appealed to local clergy to protect them. Some tried to buy off the crusaders. Some fought. Some hid. Some fled. Some converted. And some, seeing no hope for survival as Jews, simply chose death. Of those, some killed family members and then themselves before the crusaders had a chance to. In the decades afterward, writers returned to those dark days in chronicles, memorials, penitential prayers, poems, and hymns, and when they did, they paid an extraordinary amount of attention and great homage to the men and women who took their own lives. They invariably likened them to Abraham and Isaac. And they sure seemed to be attempting to contest Christian calumnies against the Jews.

Several writers recount the killing in Mainz, where the Jews were set upon by a huge and (compared to some) highly organized band. The first martyrs "stretched their necks" to their tormentors, or simply let the crusaders kill them. Witnesses, seeing the first to die, concluded that because there was "none like" their "God," they would be better off taking their own lives. "The women girded their loins with strength and slew their own sons and daughters, and then themselves. Many men also mustered their strength and slaughtered their wives and children and infants. The most gentle and tender of women slaughtered the child of her delight. They all arose, man and woman alike, and slew one another. The young maidens, the brides, and the bridegrooms looked out through the windows and cried out in a great voice: 'Look and behold, O Lord, what we are doing to sanctify Thy Great Name, in order not to exchange You for a crucified scion who was despised, abominated, and held in contempt in his own generation, a bastard son conceived by a menstruating and wanton mother." Thus "the precious children of Zion, the people of Mainz, were tested with ten trials as was our Father Abraham. . . . They bound their children in sacrifice, as Abraham did his son Isaac, and willingly accepted upon them-selves the yoke of fear of Heaven, the King of Kings, the Blessed Holy One. . . . Let the ears hearing this and its like be seared, for who has heard or seen the likes of it? Inquire and seek: was there ever such a mass sacrificial offering since the time of Adam? Did it ever occur that there were a thousand and one hundred offer-ings on one single day—all of them comparable to the sacrifice of Isaac, the son of Abraham."

In the ponds around the village of Wevelinghofen, "men, women, and children, grooms and brides, old men and women, slaughtered themselves and exposed their throats for their heads to be severed in sanctification of the One Name." One man, a saintly man well on in years, together with his son, "fled together into the water, and the youth stretched out his neck to his father for slaugh-ter as they stood in the waters." The father recited the benediction for ritual slaughter, and the son answered, "Amen." And all those around them cried out, "Hear, O Israel, the Lord is our God, the Lord is One." "Behold, all ye mortals, the great valor of the son who, though not bound, submitted himself to slaughter, and how great was the fortitude of the father who was not softened by pity for so pleasant and handsome a youth," an only son. "Who will hear and not weep? The offering and he who offered him up were unanimous in their desire that their life-breath be stilled."

Writers not only likened the martyrs to Abraham and Isaac, they also went to great lengths to show that the martyrs had done so themselves. One chronicle describes a rabbi in Worms, where eight hundred lost their lives in two days, who cast his sacrifice of righteousness, his killing for the unification of God's name, not in the vernacular of his time and place but in the very language of the Bible. The man called out to his wife and all those nearby: "God gave me this son; my wife Zipporah bore him in her advanced age.

His name is Isaac. I shall now offer him up as a sacrifice as our father Abraham did his son Isaac." Zipporah asked him not to lay a hand on the lad—not yet. "Slaughter me first and let me not see the death of the child." The rabbi didn't want to delay. "He bound his Isaac, his son, and took the knife in his hand to slaughter him," reciting the appropriate blessing. The lad responded, "Amen." "And he slaughtered the boy. He took his shrieking wife and together they left the room. The errant ones slew them."

These were smart, learned, seasoned writers, and their analogies to Abraham and Isaac and other biblical heroes are not lacking in nuance. They call attention, in the most heartrending way, to differences between past and present, between Speyer, Worms, and Cologne, on the one hand, and Moriah on the other. They ask why the skies did not darken, as so many midrashists insisted they had darkened over Moriah. They ask why no angels cried: "Once over one Akedah, Ariels cried out before thee. But now how many are butchered and burned! Why over the blood of children did they not raise a cry?" They observe that, unlike Isaac, the victims of the Rhineland slaughter did not ask or need to be bound.

Over and over they note the difference in numbers:

> On the merit of the Akedah at Moriah once we could lean,
> Safeguarded for the salvation of age after age—
> Now one Akedah follows another, they cannot be
>   counted.

Repeatedly they suggest that while Abraham's sacrifice was great, theirs was even greater: "When were there ever a thousand and a hundred in one day, each and every one of them like the Akedah of Isaac son of Abraham?"

Considering how inclined chroniclers were to note differences, it could not have been an accident that none of them pointed out the biggest difference of all. No chronicler contests or qualifies or laments the analogy, argues that it is misleading, that Abraham didn't actually kill Isaac, that Isaac did not die. No one says what Miriam, the mother of seven sons in Hadrian's Rome, reenacting the martyrdom of the Maccabean mother, said to the last of her sons to die: "Go and tell father Abraham not to let it go to his head: 'Yours was a trial, mine was an accomplished fact.'"

We can't know, from the Crusade Chronicles or any other surviving source, precisely what the victims said in their final moments, let alone what they were thinking. Historians have been of many minds about the relationship between the experience and the stories told about that experience afterward. Nor can we know how many people took their own lives and the lives of loved ones, how many others were murdered, and how many converted to avoid certain death. And even if we knew the numbers, it is possible that our ability to comprehend their meaning has been impaired by the forced conversions, mass expulsions, blood libels, pogroms, inquisitions, mass murders, and attempted genocides in the centuries since. Even the highest estimates, in the low five figures, might seem small. Nonetheless several vital Jewish communities—Rashi had studied in both Worms and Mainz—were wiped out, and several others were devastated. It was a catastrophe, and whether chroniclers wrote in its immediate aftermath or decades later, they lived in its shadow. They couldn't see the future, but they feared that there was trouble ahead.

The crusaders had an explanation for Jewish degradation and defeat, and it was akin to their justification for their attacks on the Jews in the first place. Jews were being punished for their sins, especially the rejection and murder of Christ. Their suffering was a sign not of God's redemptive love but of his abandonment. The crusaders were simply the agents of God's wrath on earth, holy warriors, on their way to repel infidels and avenge crucifixion. All they had to lose was their lives, a victory in defeat that would earn them a remission of sins and eternal life.

Jewish survivors had a choice. They could concede their enemies' argument or use all the tools at their disposal to turn it on its head.

The story of Abraham and Isaac was one of their tools. The Jews had not been abandoned. They had been singled out, like Abraham, to do God's work. They were not being punished but rather tested, ten trials exactly like Abraham's. They had not sinned. They were the righteous, suffering for the sins of others. They were not defeated. Rather, they had sacrificed themselves exactly as Abraham had sacrificed Isaac. It was Abraham's sacrifice, not Jesus's, that was the greatest in the past, and theirs, not the crusaders', that was the greatest in the present. And theirs would be the greatest reward: "Happy is he who is slain or slaughtered and who dies attesting the Oneness of His Name," one chronicler wrote. "Such a one is destined for the World-to-Come, where he will sit in the realm of the saints." The martyrs had exchanged "a world of darkness" for "a world of light," a "world of sorrow for one of joy, a transitory world for an eternal world." Their chroniclers wondered how God could possibly restrain himself: "It was for You that innumerable souls were killed! May You avenge the spilt blood of your servants, in our days and before our very eyes—Amen—and speedily."

It was a multipurpose tool, a shield, a spear, a spur, and a standard against which they could measure their own achievement. Chroniclers used the story to contest Christian chauvinism. They used it to establish sacred precedent for the words and deeds of the Rhineland dead, for the line between acceptable and unacceptable forms of Jewish martyrdom remained contested, and not everyone believed that taking one's own life—as opposed to having one's life taken—fell on the acceptable side. They used it to glorify the Jewish tradition, and thereby persuade fellow Jews, including friends and neighbors who had converted, that their faith, its great past and its even greater present, was worth suffering and even dying for, a task that might have been complicated by their very own existence. After all, some of the early chroniclers were almost certainly among those who had decided not to sacrifice their lives. They used it to steel themselves for sacrifices to come. They used it to prod God into battle on their side ("May You avenge the spilt blood of your servants in our days and before our very eyes").

I deeply regret the stories in which Abraham killed Isaac. I regret the stories in which orgies of human sacrifice were staged to resemble Temple services, or baptisms in water and blood. I regret that in the wake of the First Crusade the weapon of choice was often a Jewish version of the passion, of righteous suffering and bloody atonement. Or a Jewish channeling of the spirit of the crusaders themselves, who were on their way to Jerusalem in the service and imitation of Christ, to take back the Holy Land or die the most glorious death trying.

It should go without saying that there is no moral equivalence between suicide and murder, the deeds of those who killed themselves and loved ones rather than convert and the deeds of those who murdered strangers because they refused to convert. Still, I regret the celebration of any kind of violence in God's name, and I despise the idea that the willingness to kill and die for God is the greatest form of devotion. There are places in the Hebrew chronicles and memorials where writers display understanding and sympathy for those who made other choices, including conversion, and places where they reveal, in the way they tell their stories, perfectly understandable mixed feelings about both martyrdom and survival. I wish that it had been possible for someone to figure out a way to use the story to celebrate or elevate the rabbinical imperative to live, which came, among other places, in the Talmudic interpretation of Leviticus 18:5 ("You shall keep My laws and My rules, by the pursuit of which man shall live: I am the Lord"). God doesn't want people to die by his rules and laws, many rabbis insisted. By his laws, he wants them to live.

But what writer, what chronicler, what memorialist, what poet, what composer of prayers, ever bore such a burden? What words had to do so much work in rallying a wounded and dispirited community in the wake of tragedy and in the face of ongoing threats from an unpredictable and merciless foe? How could I, with centuries of hindsight and so much safe distance, simply condemn them for borrowing some ideas about suffering and salvation, about water and blood, about punishments and rewards, from those among whom they lived and with whom they struggled, especially when some of those ideas or earlier versions of those ideas might well have belonged to them in the first place? Above all else, how could I blame them for wanting to believe that they, not those who persecuted them, were the agents of God in history, doing his work on earth? Who could blame them for wanting to demonstrate, in the complete absence of concrete evidence (the skies didn't darken, God's messenger didn't say stop, his angels did not weep), that their God was on the scene and on their side. I could regret the story but still try to understand it, and I did. I could hate the story but still feel for, even love, the storyteller, and I do.

Don't let the way I tell my story fool you. History does not unfold neatly, a chapter at a time. It is a great big carnival, a circus, a mall, a multiplex, a market, a bazaar. At the very same moment that some commentators said or suggested that Abraham had killed Isaac, others practiced and promoted ways of reading Scripture that made his death much less likely.

One was Egyptian-born Saadia Gaon, the first rabbi born outside of the land of Israel to head the great Hebrew academy in Sura. In tenth-century Iraq, he translated the Bible into Arabic and wrote commentaries in which he championed the plain sense (*peshat*) of Scripture. The Bible, he insisted, means what it says, and we should leave it as it was written—except in those instances when our senses, observation, experience, or intellect tell us that the plain sense can't be so. Or when the plain sense, "the popular explanation," of one passage contradicts the plain sense of another, the meaning of which is perfectly clear. Or when the plain sense contradicts Jewish tradition.

Here is one of his examples: A child could tell you that Eve was not the mother of all living things. Not the mother of the lion or the tiger or the bear. So Saadia maintained that it was fine to amend Genesis 3 to read: Eve was the mother of all living "and speaking." Similarly, anyone with an iota of intelligence could tell you why God couldn't, literally, be a "consuming fire." Fire is often man-made. It is sometimes feeble. It comes and goes. The author of Deuteronomy was using a metaphor, and therefore it was acceptable for interpreters to turn from the literal (*peshat*) to the figurative (*derash*) to understand and explain it.

And when, in the story of the near sacrifice of Isaac, God says, "Now I know that you fear me," every imaginable alarm goes off. Common sense, reason, our understanding of other biblical passages, and tradition all tell us that there is nothing that God doesn't know. The common emendation, "Now I have made known to the people that you are faithful to God," makes the story clearer, the Bible more internally consistent.

Coming after a millennium of every kind of interpretation and alteration, the liberties Saadia proposed might strike you, as they strike me, as tame. But he had to defend them, for in his day there were exegetes who insisted that even he strayed too far from the plain, literal, original sense of Scripture in which they thought all interpretation and Judaism itself should be grounded. Critics contended that the rabbis of the great academies and their oral Torah were merely handmaidens, valuable when they illuminated written Torah, superfluous when they did not.

The insurgents were called Karaites, and their movement, born in Iraq in the ninth century and later based in Jerusalem, had many adherents. But the rabbis, whose interpretations they often ridiculed and whose authority over the meaning of the words they rejected, didn't go away. They insisted that there was no reason to choose between interpretive freedom and tradition, oral and written. The challenge was to strike the proper balance between them.

In many minds, then and ever since, no one struck that balance better, or more gracefully, than Rabbi Shlomo Yitzchaki, or Rashi, the dean of the northern French school in the second half of the eleventh century. Rashi had a powerful yet playful intelligence, a command of classical midrash, and an ear for several languages and the meanings that emanate from the sound of words, all of which he conveyed in the loveliest prose. Today, rabbis often credit him for insight that he himself gleaned from the rabbis of late antiquity, from learned conversations that had taken place centuries before he was born. But his genius, when it came to Abraham and Isaac, was not revisionist daring or even interpretive originality, but rather the brilliant selecting, editing, and employment of earlier material, the winnowing of a universe of possibilities down to a beautifully arranged, interpretively sharp, and always morally instructive few.

Every Talmud features Rashi's commentary, and for centuries so did many Bibles. He was, and he remains, one very popular rabbi. But in his day his blending of figurative, homiletical, and literal— his use of figurative and homiletical to get to the literal—earned him many critics. One contemporary critic was Joseph Kara. "One should know," Kara wrote, "that when the prophecies were written they were written complete, with nothing missing and with adequate interpretation, so that subsequent generations would not be led astray by them. It is not necessary to bring a proof from anywhere else, including the midrash, because the Torah was given and recorded in perfect form, lacking nothing." Rashi's most famous critic was probably his own grandson, Samuel ben Meir (Rashbam), who lived in France in the first half of the twelfth century and insisted that readers could understand both the plain sense and the context without the sages.

Why is Abraham's knife called *ma'akhelet*? Rashi had given three reasons. First, because the root of the word (*akhal*) is the verb "to eat," and the knife eats the flesh it cuts. Second, because (as Rabbi Hanina had put it in the first century) the knife, through ritual slaughter, makes food (*okhlin*) fit for eating. Third, as many rabbis before him had noted, because Israel "eats" from the knife's reward. All the benefits that Israel enjoys it "enjoys only in the merit of that knife."

Rashbam insisted that Rashi's first explanation was sufficient in and of itself: "A knife is called a *ma'akhelet* based on the idea expressed in the phrase," in Deuteronomy, "My sword shall eat (*to'khal*) flesh." He didn't deny the legitimacy or occasional value of the figurative, but he believed that the figurative and literal should be kept separate. Rashi's mistake was mixing them on the page.

Abraham Ibn Ezra, the twelfth-century Spanish poet, astrologer, philosopher, grammarian, and philologist, pictured the plain sense of Scripture as a point at the center of a circle. That point was the meaning, in many cases a single meaning, consistent with reason, logic, and context (by which Ibn Ezra meant the meaning of surrounding passages). To get at that point, you had to start with a deep knowledge of Hebrew grammar and the precise meaning, in time, of particular Hebrew words. Unhinged from Hebrew, interpretation took flight, as it did when the rabbis of the great academies, sometimes with great philosophical insight, wandered round and round the circle but never zeroed in on it. Or when the Karaites ignored it, interpreting passages as they saw fit, according to their own needs. Or when the Catholic priests and not a few Jewish sages imagined that the point at the center of the circle was a riddle or a mystery, anything but what it appeared to be, at which time they invariably lost sight of it or buried it in a fog of explanation. Or when homilists, troubled by a difficult passage or a straightforward passage that was troubling, changed one word into another, one meaning into another, one story into another, a story simpler for them to explain and simpler for their students and congregants to understand.

Consider, as Ibn Ezra did, three words in the story's first line, "God tested Abraham." So simple, yet, he thought, so often misunderstood. Many rabbis said that what God had done was to elevate Abraham, raise him up, like a banner or a flag, for all to see. Some, from antiquity right through Saadia, said that God had demonstrated Abraham's obedience (even though the dimmest reader would realize that no one, not even Abraham's own servants, was there to see it). Others said that Abraham had misunderstood: God simply meant for Abraham to bring Isaac up to Moriah. As soon as he realized that Abraham had misunderstood him, he said, "Put him down." Those misreadings followed not only from an inattention to language and context, but also from an inability or unwillingness to admit that God would deliver and then rescind a command. But God did and God does. *Nissah* means "test." God tested Abraham, in order to reward him. Live with it, Ibn Ezra said.

Equally illustrative are Ibn Ezra's comments on Isaac's age. He acknowledged the tradition that Isaac was thirty-seven, and as tradition, he accepted it. But from a logical point of view he found it "unacceptable." If Isaac had been an adult, "his piety should have been revealed in Scripture and his reward should have been double that of his father for willingly having submitted himself to be sacrificed. Yet Scripture says nothing concerning Isaac's great self-sacrifice." Others put his age at five. That, too, Ibn Ezra found unacceptable. A five-year-old couldn't have carried the wood for the sacrificial pyre. Logic led to an approximation, something "close to thirteen," and to the conclusion that Abraham had "overpowered him and bound him against his will." The proof, Ibn Ezra wrote, lies in what Abraham said and didn't say: He "hid his intention from Isaac and told him, 'God will provide the lamb for a burnt-offering, my son.' Abraham knew that if he said, 'You are the burnt-offering,' Isaac would quite possibly have fled."

David Kimhi (Radak) was a distinguished rabbi and scholar from a distinguished family of rabbis and scholars, a family that, in response to the invasion of Spain by Moroccan Muslims (Almohads) in the middle of the twelfth century, and the subsequent persecution of Jews, literally carried the Spanish tradition to Provence. In Radak's view, there were times when Ibn Ezra went a little too far, reading more literally than Moses wrote. Radak was a rationalist who perceived multiple levels of meaning, and he believed that Moses fully intended to convey them all, a surface meaning for the masses and for the learned all kinds of depth. Radak brought history as well as philosophy, philology, and linguistics to his influential exegesis, and his sense of the place of Scripture over time provided him with a context for his understanding of the plain sense. In response to Ibn Ezra, he conceded the obvious: there were no witnesses on Mount Moriah. But to move from that observation to the conclusion that God had not intended to demonstrate Abraham's obedience was to miss one of the story's purposes for all those who heard or read it after it was recorded. It was a demonstration for the ages.

I could go on. I haven't mentioned Ramban (Nachmanides), back in Spain in the thirteenth century, who tried to tie it all together, South and North, Spanish, French, and German, classical and modern, philology, linguistics, theology, psychology, history, typology, and even what he took to be human nature. Or Rambam (Maimonides) in twelfth-century Spain, Morocco, and finally Egypt. In his *Guide of the Perplexed,* Maimonides used the story to correct what he took to be a widespread misunderstanding of the purpose of biblical tests. God tested not to learn something himself or to afflict in order to reward but rather to show men what they ought to believe and how they ought to behave. He tested Abraham and Isaac to show how far we must be prepared to go in the love and fear of God. Nor have I mentioned any of the other philosophically minded exegetes who followed in Maimonides's footsteps. One was grammarian and logician Joseph Ibn Kaspi, who was born in Argentière in 1280 but—driven by a unquenchable thirst for knowledge, an unhappy marriage, and children in far-off places—spent much of his life elsewhere in France as well as in Spain, Majorca, and (in search of instruction from Maimonides's family) even Egypt. Or the Kabbalists, who, beginning in the twelfth and thirteenth centuries, dug so deep into classical midrash in search of metaphysical meanings and especially the emendations of God that they sometimes left the rabbis of late antiquity looking literal. And even if I paused to identify and characterize each of them, my survey would still be superficial and skewed. There was also a vast body of Islamic exegesis in the first centuries of the new millennium and Christian exegesis in four modes (literal, allegorical, tropological, and anagogical) even before Martin Luther and all the other reformers entered the fray.

I fear trying your patience. What's more, for all the variety—the various approaches of the academies in Iraq, Palestine, North Africa, Spain, France, and Germany, the competing ideas about the value and authority of the oral law and rabbinical interpretation, the different approaches to the plain sense of the text (from the narrowly grammatical to the boundlessly mystical), the contentious debate among exegetes (including Saadia's criticism of the Karaites, Ibn Ezra's criticism of Saadia, Rashbam's criticism of Rashi, and Ramban's criticism of just about everyone)—I want to highlight something a great many of the medieval exegetes had in common, or a direction in which many of them seemed to be moving.

Where earlier generations of rabbis had reveled in multiple meanings, many medieval exegetes engaged in a more sober search for the one meaning. While earlier generations had focused on the relevance of Scripture, its value as instruction the day it was being read, many now focused on what they took to be its original meanings and contexts, its meaning to Moses and God. Where earlier generations had been comfortable with the boundless association of passages written at different times and describing different times (where something that happened in Moses's Egypt or Josiah's Jerusalem could be used to explain something that happened a thousand years before), now many were engaged in a disciplined and often quite literal analysis of vocabulary, grammar, and syntax in time. Where earlier generations of editors had produced compilations of fly-on-the-wall rabbinical conversations and collections of sermons, some now began to produce carefully edited commentary of individual interpreters.

That shift in orientation neither began nor ended with medieval Jewish interpreters. The rabbis were heavily influenced and encouraged by innovations in the study of science, medicine, philosophy, and especially language, innovations that had their roots in the Islamic world and spread (sometimes when Jews chose to leave or were expelled) north and west from there. Then, too, if you will allow me a rabbinical leap in space and time, what was Martin

Luther if not a Christian Karaite, calling for a return to the text and the spirit guiding each person's interpretation of it? Out with allegory, out with the hierarchy of priestly interpreters dictating meanings, and of course out with indulgences. Back to Scripture, Scripture alone.

I don't want to push the contrast between old and new, classical or medieval, too far. Rashi's commentary is rich with rabbinical riffs, direct quotations, or close paraphrases, which he often let stand without elaboration or comment of any kind. And for all their criticism of Rashi's use of classical midrash, neither Rashbam nor Ramban eschewed it entirely.

And, as always, literal and figurative were often only so in the eyes of each exegete. Writing in the early twelfth century, Rashbam criticized commentators who spun elaborate yarns to explain what had prompted God's test in the first place, including stories about Satan's goading and Isaac's bragging. They had all failed to recognize that the word *ahar* ("after," as in "after these things" in the story's first line) always referred to events immediately preceding the event at hand. Then he used that understanding of the word to spin an elaborate yarn of his own. God, he wrote, was punishing Abraham for swearing an oath of peaceful coexistence with King Abimelech, as Abraham had done in the scene immediately preceding God's test. That oath was a clear violation of the command (which God delivered some four hundred years later as Abraham's descendants wandered in the wilderness) *not* to make peace with any of the previous inhabitants of the Promised Land.

Three hundred years after Rashbam, Martin Luther insisted that the truth of the Bible and Christianity resided in the text alone. But if you open Luther's lectures to the chapter on Genesis 22, you will see that he didn't return to the text alone so much as the reinterpretation of it that came in the Epistle to the Hebrews, forever after the foundation of Christian talk of Abraham's faith. When the exegesis of the "saints" or even the Jews (whose writings came to him by way of the Frenchman Nicholas of Lyra) made good sense, he borrowed. When it didn't, he took off on his own. Often way off, as when he put himself in the story, telling us what he could or could not have done in Abraham's place, or when he imagined scenes that he was sure Moses must have left out of the historical record.

And what choice did he and all the other rebels have? As they elevated text above tradition, they created an interpretive vacuum, which they themselves then stepped in to fill. The Karaites' contribution to the archive of biblical exegesis was enormous, including some of the earliest line-by-line commentaries produced by individual authors. Luther's contribution to the archive was also enormous. His lectures on Genesis alone run to eight volumes, ninety-five pages of which are devoted to my nineteen lines.

Finally, and perhaps needless to say, the turn to individual commentary aimed at the plain sense of Scripture did not mean that every exegete arrived at the same plain sense, in matters large or small. When the angel of God called out ("Abraham, Abraham"), Rashi imagined that the repetition was a sign of love. Ibn Ezra and Radak imagined that it was a sign of urgency. And Ibn Kaspi imagined that it was a sign of relative significance: God and Moses signaling that the command to desist was more insistent than the command to sacrifice, that it was the command that really mattered. Nor did it mean that the rabbis who were in the business of editing collections of midrash believed that it was their job to separate the wheat from the chaff. The compilations of midrash published in the Middle Ages, including the *Midrash Ha-Gadol,* were as inclusive as ever, and when printing presses started churning out Bibles, each publisher tried to include more individual commentaries—alongside, above, and below the biblical text—than the next.

Nevertheless, exegetes who emphasized the literal and the contextual were here to stay, and they added immeasurably to the archive of biblical interpretation. They also contributed to a shift in the assumptions about the proper relationship between reader and Scripture. For the longest time, interpreters had tried to get close to the text by bringing it, quite consciously, to them, wherever they were. Now some of them were trying to move toward it. That didn't mean that they always succeeded. Nor did it mean that in moving toward it they were no longer interpreting it, remaking it in their own image, seeing things that weren't originally there. But it did mean that they had come to believe that it was their responsibility to move toward it and they imagined themselves doing just that.

What was in all that for me? Why would I, so long a champion of biblical revision, make so much of, let alone welcome, the arrival of exegetes so partial to what they took to be Scripture's plain sense? Those are fair questions, and my answer has several parts.

For starters, not even the most dyed-in-the-wool homilist is likely to resist the gift of a plain-sense interpretation when that interpretation corresponds to his or her own plain sense, or even more to his or her fancy. I love it when rabbis, reading literally, suggest that the meaning of the phrase "the two walked on together" is not that father and son walked as one, in mind as well as in body, but rather that Abraham kept Isaac close to ensure that he didn't try to run away. And I love it when Ibn Ezra tersely dismisses "those who say that Abraham slaughtered Isaac and left him on the altar and following this Isaac came to life": they are, he writes, "contradicting Scripture." And when the thirteenth-century Spanish mystic Ibn al-'Arabi argues that Abraham misinterpreted his dream, that God wouldn't and didn't command him to kill his son. And when Ibn Kaspi argues not just that the story's purpose was to uproot, undermine, and weaken the heathen practice of child sacrifice, but also that Abraham himself (even before he looked up and saw the ram in the thicket and decided, on his own, to offer it) understood that child sacrifice was an abomination to YHWH. I even applaud when Martin Luther, whose writings often make me want to scream, imagines that there had to have been a conversation between Abraham and Isaac at the altar, a difficult conversation, in which Isaac, "struck with amazement," reminded his father of God's promise. In any context I can imagine, Luther's scenario (like Ibn Ezra's before him) seems more likely—and more likely literal—than Isaac egging his father on.

But there's more. Attention to a story's plain sense can serve as a useful check on reckless revision, and a check also on destructive forms of typology, the explicit or implicit argument that the past is merely a shadow of things to come, always about something other than what it seems to be about, something in its future, something better. In the right hands it can encourage a proper respect for the past as the past, for distant and different ways of thinking and behaving (however much that thought and behavior contains the seeds of what's to come, however often even the simplest words and deeds have ethical, philosophical, theological, metaphysical, and mystical implications and dimensions).

Finally, remember where I started: remember that I was thinking about context before I was thinking about revision. It was my reading of Genesis 22 in the context of the ten chapters that came before it, in the context of that tumultuous quarter century of Abraham's life, all the questions he had asked God, all the worries and doubts that he had expressed, that made me think that Abraham wouldn't have done what he did in the way that he did it in the first place. That Abraham wouldn't have set out for Moriah without saying a word was the plain sense of the life and character of Abraham to me.

That is not to say that I have switched teams, gone over to the other side for good. I believe there are many different paths to interpretive enlightenment. I can bear long and learned explications of the origin and significance of single words with the best of them. Say, Ramban on the word "Moriah," which the author of Chronicles identified as the Temple Mount.

Why Moriah? Where did that place-name come from? Was it, as some Talmudic sages had said, that the word is a compound of the word for "instruction" and the divine name—and Jerusalem is the place from which instruction in the ways of the Torah spread around the world? Or that Moriah comes from *mora*, fear, and it was on Moriah that the ancients feared God and worshipped before him. Or, as Onkelos (the name associated with one of the most influential Aramaic translations of the Torah) and Rashi after him had said, that the incense offered in the Temple contains myrrh (*mor*) and other spices. Or, putting all the ancient *midrashim* aside, was it that the word "Moriah" meant "mountain of Myrrh," as in Song of Songs, "I will go to the mountain of myrrh and the hill of frankincense." That was probably the plain-sense explanation, Ramban concluded, for one simple reason: in Abraham's time there was myrrh on the mountain, but there was no Temple.

What I wouldn't give for that kind of command of the language and literature. But I would not be completely honest if I didn't confess that sometimes while reading passage after passage of that kind of analysis, my eyes glaze over and my attention strays. I might even daydream, almost irreverently, and imagine another commentator less concerned about where the word came from than how Abraham responded to the command to go there. "Excuse me, sir," he might have said. "I am but dust and ashes, a man of few words, and as such often misunderstood. Do you happen to remember, back before Isaac was born, when we stood on that hillside overlooking Sodom and I asked, 'Will not the Judge of all the earth do justice?'

"What part of my question didn't you understand?"

I have yet to find that Abraham in the literature of the late Middle Ages. But one of the remarkable things about the life of the story is that even though you can't always get the Abraham and Isaac you want when you want it, or even the Abraham and Isaac you need, you can always get something different from what you have. All the more if you are willing to turn to people working in different fields and forms. One obvious place to turn is the walls.

Visual artists were drawn to the story early on. The wall painting in the synagogue at Dura-Europos and the frescoes in the catacombs of Callisto and Priscilla go back to the third century. By the end of the fourth, bishops Gregory of Nyssa (in modern Turkey) and Augustine of Hippo (in modern Algeria, fifteen hundred miles to the west) had each noted that likenesses of the story—on wall paintings, mosaics, sarcophagi, and frescoes—were everywhere. Abraham's deed, Augustine wrote, was "so famous that it recurs to the mind of itself without any study or reflection, and is in fact repeated by so many tongues, and portrayed in so many places, that no-one can pretend to shut his eyes or his ears from it." Several hundred images from late antiquity survive.

Gregory believed that the artists of his day were out ahead of the exegetes who worked with words. Whether or not that was the case, the early artists frequently went their own way. They invariably pictured Isaac as a small boy. Either they had not heard, from the rabbis, that he was a young man, or they didn't believe it. And though it is hard to read the expression on the face of the small, simple figure of Isaac on the mosaic floor of the sixth-century synagogue at Beit Alfa, if pressed, I'd have to say he looks at least a little alarmed. The ram, by contrast, is relaxed and ready, and the early artists gave him a place, front and center, as a symbol of God's providence and deliverance, that he rarely attained in the stories or commentary of the rabbis or priests or (before too long) Islamic exegetes.

At least a few early artists gave Sarah a prominent place too, right up there with Abraham and Isaac atop Moriah. She is definitely in two of the late fourth- or early fifth-century images of the sacrifice on the walls of the chapel of the necropolis at El Bagawat (Egypt), standing right next to or just above Isaac, with a hand or hands raised in prayer. And she may well be on the scene in the sixth-century sarcophagus in a church in Lucq-de-Béarn. If so, she has her hand over her mouth, as if looking on, aghast. But the figures in that sarcophagus are indistinct, lacking essential detail, and is it hard to know for sure—hard to know if it is actually Sarah, hard to know if she is actually looking aghast. Someone wanting a close look at Sarah in the fifth or sixth century would do better with Romanos or the Syriac homilists.

What a difference a millennium could make. By the middle of the second, a veritable who's who of Byzantine, medieval, Gothic, Romanesque, Renaissance, baroque, and Dutch Golden Age artists had drawn or painted or etched or carved or shaped what they or their Christian patrons almost always called *The Sacrifice of Isaac*. They rarely added characters (in fact, most dropped Sarah from the scene) or dramatically altered the story's plot. They nonetheless managed to use ink, marble, wood, bronze, ceramic tile, stained glass, and oil to plumb the story's depths, its interiors, in distinctive ways.

Consider Abraham's demeanor. Many interpreters took great pride, in fact delight, in describing Abraham as unflappable, completely at ease. Neither his face nor his words gave any hint of reluctance, uneasiness, or dread, something that might have tipped Sarah off, made the servants suspicious, or alarmed Isaac. Painting that composure was no problem so long as artists imagined that he had been as calm and cool on the inside as he was on the outside, and some painters did. Expressionless, or nearly so. Moved only by the voice of God's angel. You can see that in the late oil paintings of the Florentine Andrea del Sarto, fascinating paintings in which there is certainly surprise in Abraham's face the moment the angel arrives, but a surprise that is as carefully controlled as the movement of the muscles in his big hands and arms and shoulders and neck and head. You can see the same self-control in the work of another Florentine, Alessandro Allori, a different and somewhat unusual take in that Allori painted a parade of scenes in one large canvas. In the penultimate scene, Abraham points up and ahead to the site of the sacrifice as if he were proposing a suitable spot for a picnic. Or Domenichino's *Sacrifice,* which looks like a still from a graceful dance. Even—or especially—in Caravaggio's rendering of what would have been Isaac's last moment of life, where Abraham's knife, shimmering with light coming straight from the heavens, is a blade's length from Isaac's neck and Abraham's hands are as steady as his gaze. Abraham looks at the angel intently, without revealing a bit of emotion, as if to say: If you've got something to say, say it, and quickly. I've got work to do.

But if you thought, as many writers did, that Abraham's composure, however impressive, simply had to be a cover, concealing inner turmoil or just plain fright, you had a problem. Or a choice, between inner turmoil and outer calm. Many artists sacrificed the latter for the former, painting an anguished Abraham, the inside on the outside, sad, sorry, frightened, torn, in despair, if not half mad. I am thinking of the sadness and perhaps resignation in the eyes and mouth of Donatello's marble Abraham, an early fifteenth-century sculpture all the more haunting for the subtlety of Abraham's expression. Or, less subtly, but not without great power of its own, the polychrome wood sculpture carved a century later by the Spaniard Alonso Berruguete, where a Christ-like Abraham holds the bound and kneeling Isaac, as he so often held him, by the hair, his own head thrown back, his eyes looking up toward the heavens. Or Rembrandt's famous oil, of 1635, in which Abraham looks puzzled, confused, maybe even a little dazed, his huge hand covering Isaac's face, whether to blindfold him or to smother him we don't know. The angel, who has grabbed Abraham's right hand with his own, looks as if he were about to smack him with his left, though it is more likely that he is simply pointing to the heavenly source of his words. Abraham has dropped his knife, but Rembrandt leaves it suspended in mid-flight, painted, like Abraham's face and every bit of Isaac, in light, its tip still pointed where it was pointed when it was in Abraham's hand, toward Isaac's naked neck.

Twenty years later, in an etching, Rembrandt imagined a much quieter scene, a psychological foil to the oil's high drama. He gathered the movement of muscles, arms, angel, and knife and turned them into feeling. Abraham looks utterly defeated, torn and grieving inside and out, but he is calm, his hand gently wrapped around Isaac's head, his fingers again covering Isaac's eyes but now barely making contact. Here the angel seems to be comforting Abraham as much as restraining him, comforting him just as Abraham tries to comfort Isaac, who is on his knees, bent over one of Abraham's, his hands at his sides. Abraham has the knife in his hand, but he holds it, firmly and deliberately, at a distance, its tip turned safely away from Isaac, on its way out of the painting's frame. Still, Abraham looks ancient—shrunken and ghostlike—as if he were ill or about to be, and it is hard to imagine him providing Isaac with much comfort. This is not the Abraham of the church fathers, or of Luther, let alone the Abraham of John Calvin, who repeatedly calls God's test torture and goes to great lengths to describe Abraham's anguish and grief, yet who nonetheless insists that he remained completely composed and tranquil. Nor is it the Abraham of the rabbis who imagined a dry-eyed Abraham looking forward to the sacrifice or, after God stopped him, praying for permission to go through with it.

Then there was Isaac. Most Christian exegetes working with words imagined him as knowing and willing, quiet if not completely silent, and above all else not suffering. There are so many examples of visual art in which he is portrayed that way that I hardly know where to start. How about the Isaac in the twelfth-century mosaic on the north wall of the cathedral in Monreale, Italy. Granted, he does not look comfortable. Well clad, just like his dad, in Roman garb, he is perched on his back on the edge of a high altar, his hands bound behind him. Only Abraham's firm grip on his hair keeps him from tumbling to the ground. But the awkwardness of the pose only makes the look of calm on Isaac's face all the more striking. Or the Isaac in the thirteenth-century Gothic picture Bible known as the Crusader Bible, where the boy crouches with his bound hands clasped in front of him in prayer, as nonchalant about the surprising turn of events as is his father.

In the lavishly illustrated fourteenth-century edition of Guyart des Moulins's Bible Historiale, Isaac is on his knees, head bowed slightly, hands again clasped in prayer. Abraham appears somewhat taken aback by the arrival of the angel, who has a stern look on his face and a firm grip on the tip of Abraham's knife, but Isaac's face reveals little or no emotion. His poise is all the more remarkable in Donatello's sculpture, for Abraham's knife has already met Isaac's flesh and there is no angel on the scene. Abraham is distressed, his features somehow both marble and in motion, yet Isaac's face is perfectly still. If he is anything but fully accepting of his fate, we can't see it in his astonishingly lifelike face. In Simon Bening's sixteenth-century book border, painted bright in tempera and gold on parchment, Isaac's head is bowed and he looks lost in his prayers, while Abraham, standing behind him, prepares, like a logger, to swing a long sword down on his neck. In Cigoli's oil, Isaac is back up on the altar, nude now except for a shroud across his waist, his left leg extended to the ground, his right leg crossed under it. His head is cocked, his arm pinned behind his back, and his whole body again held in balance by Abraham's grip. The knife is on its way, yet he is at peace. In Jacopo da Empoli's oil, by contrast, there is tension in his cheeks and eyes, and his eyes roll heavenward in uneasy supplication. But his body still speaks of acceptance, with a knee resting on the altar, his head cocked upward, his arms bound loosely where, in a crucifixion, nails might be. A few years later, one of Empoli's students, Felice Ficherelli, painted Isaac nearly flat on his back, his wrists bound, his hands crossed. Yet his raised arms look to me like the arms of a young man stretching as he wakes from an afternoon nap. And then, in Rembrandt's late etching, Isaac is back on his knees, his arms at his side, muscles tense but not straining.

In all those images, and hundreds of others (in Christian art alone), you can find those Isaacs. But despite so many models to learn from and imitate, and endless talk about Isaac's quiet acceptance of his fate, not every artist imagined him that way. The wide-eyed Isaac in the York Psalter (a twelfth-century illuminated edition of Jerome's revision of his own Latin translation of the book of Psalms) looks more than a little alarmed, especially when you compare the expression on his face to the expression in the story's first scene. His hands, uncharacteristically, are unbound, and it seems no more likely that he was praying than trying to push his father away. In Berruguete's sculpture, Isaac's hands are bound high and tight behind his back; his arm and chest muscles strain against his bonds; his mouth is open as if he were crying out in pain or calling for help. In Del Sarto's oils, his mouth is still. It is his eyes that express his alarm, all the more because he is looking not up to the heavens but out of the frame at us, as if we might be able to help him, or at least explain what in the world his father is doing.

In Titian's action-packed and colorful oil, which if you were not familiar with you might assume was the creation of Disney, we look up, from below, at a small boy, already kneeling atop the altar, lorded over by a Hercules-like Abraham, whose huge biceps, forearms, and wrists push down on his head, as if he were trying to hold him underwater. In Caravaggio, the ram looks willing, but Isaac is in obvious distress, held down by the force of Abraham's arm, by the grip of Abraham's hand on his face and around his neck, and by the thumb pressed into his jaw. Isaac's open mouth looks like that of a dying or dead fish, and his eyes are dark and dull. In Pedro Orrente's *Sacrifice,* another baroque oil, the muscles in Isaac's arms, chest, even abdomen, are all bulging. The veins in his neck alone belie acceptance. Looking away (Abraham is always looking away), Abraham pins his head to a slab of stone with the tail of a red blindfold. In Rembrandt's oil, Isaac looks only slightly less miserable, the muscles in his upper body taut, his neck bent back, his face smothered, and the back of his head pressed into the wood of the altar by Abraham's huge hand.

I don't know what those painters intended to show or say about Abraham's state of mind or Isaac's emotions, let alone what viewers saw. I don't know how much or in exactly what ways those images were shaped by their moment in art history, the conventions, the expectations, the cost or status of colors, the works artists imitated or reacted against, the creative avenues opened up or closed off by new materials and techniques, the internal logic of forms. I don't know how much my vision has been shaped by my sensibilities, my ideas, my desires, my place, and my time. Today there are art historians who look at Lorenzo Ghiberti's magnificent bronze relief, designed for a competition in Florence in the very first years of the fifteenth century, and see mixed feelings in Abraham's pose: his torso backing away from Isaac as his arm thrusts at him with the knife. And yet I, who would like nothing more than to see mixed feelings, see nothing but resolve: the contrast between the flex of Abraham's body and the movement of arm and knife a somewhat awkward attempt to represent the body's natural movement, Abraham putting his weight behind the knife blow.

The winner's panel was to adorn the east door of the Baptistery. The competition came down to Ghiberti and Filippo Brunelleschi. Ghiberti won, and afterward he boasted that even the men he had defeated ("without any exception") conceded that his work was the finest. Many scholars believe he made better use of the quatrefoil frame, and the materially minded note that he shrewdly reduced the weight of his relief (it was seven kilos lighter than Brunelleschi's), increasing its appeal to judges calculating the cost of each in bronze, which was then ten times more expensive than marble. Still, I can't help think that the classical order and Gothic elegance of Ghiberti's relief—Abraham's fierce determination, Isaac's hard-bodied, stoic acceptance—also contributed to his victory. Brunelleschi's panel was messier, less harmonious, more natural. Notwithstanding the orderly horizontal and vertical lines, the scene fills the frame only haphazardly, and there is no mistaking Abraham's confusion and the fear, if not agony, in Isaac's face.

It is possible that Brunelleschi, like Caravaggio two centuries later and many others in the years in between, could not imagine the scene without imagining that Isaac had suffered. It is possible that some artists and sculptors realized that Isaac could have suffered some without overshadowing the sacrifice to come. It is possible that his suffering, or at least his struggling, solved a formal problem that arose when a painter or sculptor set out to portray a narrative that takes place over three days. How do you generate drama or add to the suspense? In words, the suspense builds in the movement from command, to response, to preparation, to journey, to the ditching of the servants, to Isaac's question about the lamb. Ghiberti shows us the last moment of that movement. The angel is on his way, but not yet there. He is racing to beat the knife. But in many of the images the angel arrives ahead of us, with a hand (a hand that is not mentioned in the Bible) locked on Abraham's arm or knife. We know that Isaac is safe the moment we set eyes on him (though I must admit that in Brunelleschi it is a really close call). But Isaac can't see the angel—he never can. He doesn't know he is safe, and the tension in many of the images resides in his not knowing.

What I can say is that when I look at those paintings and sculptures, I see familiar scenes in fresh ways. Christian commentators said that Isaac hadn't suffered, and so it is not surprising that in their writings they did not show him suffering. Many rabbis suggested that he had. Yet they rarely showed him in any real pain or distress. Crusade chroniclers told stories of martyrs who considered themselves Isaac's heirs, but it was the martyrs, not Abraham and Isaac, whose gruesome deaths they described. Even in the stories in which it was said or implied that Isaac had died, it might be more accurate to say he fainted or, like a cartoon character, had the wind knocked out of him. One minute he's down and out cold; the next he springs back to life, recites the benediction for the dead, and races off to the Garden of Eden or the academy of Shem. Compare the Isaac of Caravaggio, Donatello, Berruguete, or Brunelleschi to the Isaac in the fifteenth-century Second Nuremberg Haggadah, where he is falling headfirst, his arms outstretched in front of him, "from the Garden God planted for our protection." Drawn or etched simply, he looks like a yeshiva student playing Superman at recess.

It is not that rabbis consciously downplayed suffering. Their commentary, like the story itself, left readers free to imagine it. And there are places—whether in Abraham's or Isaac's words or simply in their tears—where they evoke it. But the rabbis didn't force you to dwell on it. For most of them, Isaac's suffering, like his blood and ashes, was an abstraction. They pondered its meaning and significance, not the experience itself. Some of those oil paintings and sculptures forced me back to the experience. There isn't blood in any of them, nor even a hint that the sacrifice was carried out. All are highly stylized. Most are utterly unreal. Nonetheless, the best of them break the spell cast by dreamy discussions of theology and philosophy and grammar and theories of interpretation and the derivation and meaning of words. Whatever the intent or outlook of the artist, I look at some of those paintings and say to myself: My heavens. This is a story about a father who is about to sacrifice his son.

I guess with so many people celebrating from such a comfortable distance, without seeming to reckon, really reckon, the cost, I simply wanted someone to acknowledge that it hurt. I wanted someone to say or show that a father could not set out to sacrifice a son, could not nearly sacrifice a son, without causing real pain and suffering, leaving wounds. In a few of the English mystery plays, popular dramas drawn from Bible stories, Abraham and Isaac say as much themselves.

The mysteries grew out of the liturgical drama of the medieval church, which itself had roots in dramatic hymns. Like liturgical plays, the earliest versions of each of the mysteries were written by clerics. Unlike them, they were written in the vernacular and performed out of doors, on major feast days (including Corpus Christi and Whitsunday) and at festivals and fairs. Some performances were overseen by local officials and performed by play masters, one at a time, on stationary stages. Others were overseen by craft guilds and performed by craftsmen, either singularly or in cycles that ran from Creation to the Last Judgment and lasted all day or even several days. A different guild—the barbers did Abraham and Isaac in Chester, the papermakers and bookbinders did it in York—would be responsible for each Bible story, or "pageant." Players would perform on a "pageant wagon," which could be rolled around town for multiple performances in a single day.

Whether stationary or processional, amateur or semiprofessional, the sets, staging, props, and costumes were all elaborate and inventive. The wagons often had two or three tiers. The ground might serve as a fourth. The lowest level might represent hell, but sometimes hell was up on the stage, a huge dragon's mouth. Many angels managed to fly. Public records point to performances in the late fourteenth century, though it is unlikely that those were the first. The earliest extant manuscripts are dated closer to the end of the fifteenth, by which time they were a popular form of theater all over Europe. In England they remained popular through the middle of the sixteenth century, when Queen Elizabeth banned them and every other form of religious drama.

There are six surviving Abraham-and-Isaac scripts, more of them than of any other single Bible story. Yet anyone taking a cursory look might well wonder what the plays add to the archive of interpretation and revision, to the things people have said about and done with the story. On the surface there isn't a more predictable representation of traditional Christian themes: of God's testing and the trials that mark earthly life; of obedience and the often painful demands of faith; of the drama of God's promise to Abraham and the threat to that promise posed by Abraham's sword; and running through all that, the prefiguration of the birth, life, death, and resurrection of Christ. Even someone who reads only the opening and closing pages will get it, for the last words in each play go to a learned man, who takes the stage to sum up the play's meaning and significance. In the Brome play it is a "Doctor," who prescribes keeping, as best we can, God's commandments. He advises women, especially, not to make the mistake, when their children are taken away, "to grouch against God." Whatever God sends, the doctor says, whether wealth or woe, remains true, for as the story of Abraham and Isaac shows, if you keep a good heart and serve him faithfully, he'll take care of you: "Now Jesus that weareth the crown of thorn" brings "us all to heaven-bliss!"

The learned man in the Chester play picks up where the Brome doctor left off, reminding us that the drama we just witnessed signified "Jesus, sacrificed to win mankind's grace." "By Abraham," he understood "the father of heaven," who undid the devil's work with his son's blood. By Isaac, "Jesus," who was obedient, always, to his father, and on account of that obedience managed "death to confound."

The point of the plays could not be clearer, but reading them, what I have to remember is that these plays weren't read quickly or skimmed. Once they were written or revised (and they were revised with abandon), they weren't read at all. They were seen and heard, which made them, like frescoes, tile floors, manuscript illustrations, stained glass windows, sculptures, and decorative lamps—and also like sermons and dramatic hymns—books for those who could not read. And while a play's typological truths and moral lessons could and often were revealed by a learned man in a few lines at the end (just as they had been revealed in a few lines of the Epistle to the Hebrews or a long paragraph in *City of God*), the plays themselves were "books" of hundreds of lines of carefully composed dramatic verse, in which an old man and a young boy (except in the York play, where Isaac is the young man of so much Jewish exegesis) say (and do) things to each other, to themselves, to their audience, and to God.

The Brome play opens with Abraham out in his field, singing Isaac's praise. The boy is not only his beloved son but also his sweetest, and Abraham prays for his good health and long life. God, looking down, decides to test him. An angel conveys his command. Abraham says that he "never loved anything so much" on earth. But God he loves much more. He's sorry, but he'll do it. The angel assures him: So long as you do God's work, you will have no reason to worry.

Abraham calls for Isaac, who is busy praying. Whatever you ask, Isaac says, I'll do with "glad cheer." But it is not long (the stage is small) before they arrive and Isaac notices that his father looks dreadful. Abraham tells him not to worry. But Isaac worries. He wants to know why his father's sword is drawn. He wants to know where the beast is. Abraham asks him to stop talking. Your words, he says, are breaking my heart. Isaac wants to know if he is to be harmed. Abraham says he can't tell him. Not yet. But Isaac wants to know.

"I must kill thee," Abraham says at last.

"Kill me, father?" Why? If I've done something wrong a rod should do. But "with your sharp sword kill me not," for "I am but a child."

Abraham says he's sorry, but it is not up to him.

Isaac wishes his mother were there. "She would kneel for me on both her knees," he says. But she isn't, so Isaac prays that his father will change his mind.

Abraham tells him he must do it. Otherwise, he'll offend God. He's afraid to do that.

"And is it God's will that I should be slain?" Isaac asks.

"Yes," Abraham says. That's what makes it so hard.

Isaac gets it and says he will never complain about God's will. Sure, God might have sent him a better ending. But what will be will be. He tells his father not to grieve. That he has other children. That he will soon forget him. He insists that they should do the Lord's bidding and asks only that Abraham pray for him after he's gone and tell his mother he has left for another country.

Reading those lines and all the others, I see what so many readers before me have seen. I see the role of typology, which is everywhere, not just in the spoken words but also the stage directions, costumes, makeup, and props. A bearded and ancient Abraham looks like God the Father. A nearly nude Isaac sometimes rides the donkey and always carries a bundle of wood tied into a cross. I see the tension between the story's allegorical meanings and its literal meanings. I see why some critics believe the former limits the latter, inhibiting the development of sophisticated dramatic structures, characters, plots, and themes. I see the clash of ideals (such as obedience, acceptance of earthly suffering, and faith) and day-to-day niceties and desires (such as a reluctance to sacrifice one's child), a clash medieval writers could not get enough of. I see the sentimentality. But what holds my attention is something else: the way the story changes when playwrights, without ever drawing our attention away from Abraham and Isaac, slow it down, set the plot in time, the time it takes to recite all those lines.

The Brome Isaac is willing, but he throws his father off with his questions and unwittingly torments him with his good nature. He asks to be forgiven for his sins. He asks to be blessed. He asks Abraham to cover his eyes and give his best wishes to his mother. And he repeatedly asks Abraham to do it and get it over with. The delay, he says, is killing him.

Yet when Abraham asks him, a second time, to stop talking— just to stand for one last kiss—Isaac doesn't understand the request. We have only a little time left, he says.

Your meek words scare me, Abraham says. He asks Isaac to kiss him once more, but Isaac tells him to go ahead.

Not yet, Abraham says. I must bind you.

Just go ahead and do it, Isaac says. I won't hinder you. He is sorry to die but can't bear the waiting. He reminds Abraham not to tell his mother, and then he himself bids her farewell.

Abraham is in tears.

Isaac apologizes for upsetting him and asks for mercy.

Enough, Abraham says. He assures Isaac that he has done nothing wrong. He'd rather die himself, if only God wanted him for an offering.

Stop, Isaac says. Mourn no more. Your weeping hurts as much as the thought of my own death. Afraid of the sword, he asks Abraham to cover his eyes and lay him facedown. He cries out to God, asking him to receive him.

The time has come, and Abraham wants to do God's will. But he can't. "Oh! Father of heaven, what shall I do?"

What are you waiting for? Isaac asks again.

"Now, heart," Abraham cries, "why wouldest thou not break in three?" He raises his sword. The angel snatches it away and thanks Abraham on God's behalf. Abraham tells Isaac to get up, shares the good news, and kisses him. But Isaac, assuming Abraham is still stalling, begs him to kill him. Abraham explains that he doesn't have to. Isaac doesn't believe him, but he comes to and explains his salvation to the ram: "Thou shall this day die for me, in the worship of the Holy Trinity."

God still commands and controls, but Abraham has been transformed by Isaac's distress. In the play's opening scene, he is merely a symbol of obedience, coldly weighing his love for his son against his fear and love of God. By the story's climax, he is a character, a man whose heart is broken, a father who thinks he has no choice but to sacrifice his son.

The author of a third play, the Northampton play, added Sarah to the script, and it is Abraham's exchanges with her, actual and imagined, that give his character its depth. No sooner does Abraham respond to God's angel—"Here I am" and "His will be done"—than his thoughts turn to his wife. He knows she is not going to like the idea of his leaving with Isaac, and she doesn't, relenting only when he argues, as so many of the Abrahams of first-millennium *midrashim* had argued, that it was time for Isaac to learn how to worship God.

Off they go, but Abraham isn't free of her. As soon as he tells Isaac of God's plan, Isaac asks him what his mother will think of it. There is no need to tell her, Abraham says, but Isaac is not so sure. He wishes she were with them, as she had wanted to be. Abraham reminds him that she can't always have her way. He loves him as much as she does. But every time the boy speaks, he evokes her, reminding his father how much she loves to hold him close and kiss him, how much she will miss him, how much he hopes he will bid her farewell for him, and how important it is that he discard his clothes in a way that ensures that she will never see them.

The angel stops him. Abraham thanks God. The test caused him great distress, he says, but he is grateful nonetheless. Then without pause he tells Isaac to dress, quickly, and to say nothing to his mother. Please. Not a word.

The moment they arrive home, Abraham invites Sarah out for a walk, and once alone he fills her in. Where was your mind? she asks. On God, he says, and he tries to explain, but his explanation doesn't square with what we have just seen. We saw his mind on her, and she represented not simply woman's nature but also the part of himself that doubted that he should go through with it. In the end, she concedes that he had no choice—what God wants, God will get—but as a depiction of a type of Mary, her performance is not persuasive. And though Abraham spins his own experience as faith, his words come off as little more than retrospective gloss. In the scenes we've just observed, obedience is what moved him up that mountain.

By the end of a fourth play, the Towneley, even that obedience, bare-bones but still dependable, is strained. Audiences would not have guessed it would be. When God first called, Abraham was almost murderously enthusiastic: "Both wife and child," he had said, "if he bid kill." But for reasons that aren't clear, he never tells Isaac that the sacrifice was God's idea, and so Isaac, though obedient, asks all the questions I imagine that Abraham would have asked of God. He is ready to go where Abraham goes, to do what he wants done, but he wants to know why. He begs for mercy. He wonders, if he has trespassed, whether a good beating might not suffice. The increasing urgency of his questions and the brutal economy of Abraham's answers wreak artful havoc on the play's poetry, especially its carefully metered and measured eight-syllable English lines.

Isaac!
  What, sir?
    Good son, be still!
Father!
  What, son?
      Think on thy get [offspring]!

What have I done?
        Truly, no ill.
And shall be slain?
        So have I het [promised].
Sir! What may help?
        Certes, no skill [For sure, there's nothing].
I ask mercy.
              That may not let.
        When I am dead, and closed in clay.
Who shall then be your son?

Abraham can't stand it. Who could? But he doesn't let on to Isaac. He turns away from him and up to the heavens and says, "Ah! Lord, that I should abide this day!"

"Who shall do what I used to do?" Isaac asks.

Abraham asks him to be quiet. But he can't.

What have I done, father, what have I said?
Truly, no kind of ill to me.
And thus, guiltless, shall be arrayed?
Now, good son, let such words be!"
I love you.
        So do I thee.
Father!
        What, son?

Isaac cries out for his mother. Abraham tells him to stop. It won't help in the way you imagine it would, he says. Then he turns away again, this time to the audience, his eyes filled with tears, which he doesn't want Isaac to see. He wishes more than anything the boy were unkind. But he's not. He's perfect. He'd die for him if he could. "To slay him, thus, I think great sin." He'll never be out of my mind. What shall I say to his mother? he asks. He fears her reaction.

All the while Isaac lies, still as can be, on the altar.

Only after God tells the angel to stop him and the angel is on his way does Abraham try to pull himself together. The crying only makes it worse, he says. The angel rushes in, wrestles him to the ground, and tells him to stop. Who says? Abraham asks. But once persuaded that the angel speaks for God, Abraham thanks him, in a few words, and excuses himself: "To speak with thee have I no space." He needs to talk to his son.

He tells Isaac that he's been saved.

"Sir! Shall I live?" Isaac asks.

Yes, Abraham says. You've escaped "a full hard, grace—thou should have been both burnt and broken."

"But, father, shall I not be slain?" Isaac asks.

"No," Abraham says.

"Then am I glad! Good sir, put up your sword again."

Abraham tells him not to be afraid.

"Is all forgiven?" Isaac asks.

Yes, Abraham says, for certain.

"For feard, sir, was I nearhand mad."

The Towneley play ends there. The manuscript's final pages are missing. We don't know if a learned man took the stage to help clear up the confusion, answer some of Isaac's questions, help dry Abraham's tears. He might have noted that in keeping God's command to himself, Abraham bore the full burden of his faith. Or that typology works by contrast as well as identity: the bewildered Isaac, lying still on the altar, reminds us of Jesus, not knowing why his father has forsaken him. But if Abraham, about to break under the pressure, seems somewhat less than God, it is because he still needed to be completed, perfected by him. The learned man might then have pointed out that God's testing had increased Abraham's love for Isaac. Or that God's ways are not always comprehensible. There is often no explanation for suffering. Or that grace often moves in tandem with obedience, but not always in ways that we can see. He may, finally, have brought the play back to its beginning, the very beginning, noting how Abraham's obedience and stoic faith were just the kind of obedience and faith that it would take to repair the rift created by Adam.

No way to know. Nor, as the play ends with Isaac reporting that he had been nearly mad with fear, do we know whether or not, before the doctor arrived, there would have been a short scene like the scene in the Brome play that comes right after the angel stays Abraham's hand. There, Isaac grabs the ram and is about to blow on the fire to raise the flames when he hesitates and asks:

But, father, while I stoop down low,
Ye will not kill me with your sword, I trust?

Abraham tells him not to worry.

Isaac says he won't, but he still wishes that Abraham would put the sword in its sheath. It frightens him terribly.

Abraham offers the ram. God rewards them, and Abraham is overjoyed, proud that they have obeyed God without complaint. Isaac, however, refuses to join in the celebration.

I was never so afraid before
As I have been at yon hill.
But, by my faith, father, I swear
I will nevermore come there,
But it be against my will!

He never wanted to do anything as much as he now wanted to go home to his mother.

The rabbis were not unaware of the toll the near sacrifice might have taken. They invariably referred to Isaac's fear, and they often traced his blindness in old age back to that fateful day. Some attributed it to the tears (of angels, of Abraham) that had fallen into his eyes. Others, to the blinding light of the heavens. But nowhere in

first-millennium Jewish, Christian, or Islamic literature is there so
subtle or sensitive an attempt to imagine Isaac moments after the
sacrifice, a boy who is afraid to bend down in front of his father
and swears never to leave home alone with him again. Abraham's
obedience, we are reminded in several plays, helped to repair the
rift between God and man caused by Adam's sin. But it also caused
a new rift between father and son.

At the risk of repeating myself, I must say that I do not know
why some of these plays open up the story in the ways that they
do. The form, the time that a playwright took to develop character
and plot, certainly contributed, but the form alone, the movement
from traditional exegesis to play, from page to stage, can't explain
it. Despite hundreds of lines of dialogue and a leisurely pace, some
of the mystery plays are mechanical, static, and wholly unbeliev-
able. Neither typology nor the moral lessons of history required so
much art.

Nor can I hear the actors' voices, read their body language, or
see the expressions on their faces, the light and look in their eyes,
infer meaning from the pace and timing with which they delivered
their lines. There is subtle humor and even farce, or at least ample
opportunity for farce, in many of the mystery plays, and I would
not be surprised to learn that some of the scenes or exchanges that
I find most poignant on the page were sometimes played for laughs
on the stage. One is the moment I just mentioned in the Brome
play, after the danger seems to have passed. My sense is that the
playwright found a simple way to demonstrate Isaac's complete loss
of trust. But I can picture two actors hamming it up, making light
of the boy's reluctance to bend down (to feed the fire's flames) so
long as his father stood above him with his sword drawn. Like-
wise, in the Northampton play, there is an exchange I feel sure was
intended to bring down the house: Abraham tells Isaac he's to be
sacrificed. Isaac asks him if his mother knows of his plans. Abraham blurts out, "She? Mary! Son, Christ forbid?" And that's just
one of many lines in the Northampton play that makes me suspect

that audiences walked away thinking less about obedience or faith than about women, how they were always getting in (or threatening to get in) men's way.

What's more, and this I feel sure of: Just because a playwright (or painter or sculptor) imagined Abraham's anguish or Isaac's invisible wounds or strains between the two of them doesn't mean they disliked the story, thought the test was regrettable, shared my discomfort with Abraham's response, wished Abraham had protested or that the story had unfolded in some other way. Quite the contrary: they may have concluded that pain and suffering, isolation and anguish, are the price that people pay for their faith. What distinguished the authors of a few of the mystery plays was the sensitivity with which they entered the scene and then found the dialogue to dramatize, to give life to, any number of vast abstractions.

Their art was enhanced by a sort of double vision, or comfort with two contradictory ideas: the near sacrifice was horrible, the sacrifice was sublime. That comfort will not strike those familiar with images of the crucifixion (or with passion plays, stories, and songs) as exceptional. Artists did not shy away from explicit substantiation of Jesus's suffering. "With what rapture," Methodist hymnist Charles Wesley wrote in the middle of the eighteenth century, "with what rapture / Gaze we on those glorious scars!" But befitting the shadow of things to come, the warm-up, most Christian representations of Abraham and Isaac were tamer, and I can't help thinking that one reason for one of the big differences between stories and images of the near sacrifice of Isaac and stories and images of the crucifixion of Christ is as simple as this: Jesus's father allowed it to happen; some say he even willed it. Yet however painful it was for him to watch, God himself didn't actually do the deed. He didn't lead his son to Golgotha. He didn't nail him to the cross. Abraham, by contrast, was commanded to do it, set out to do it, and was about to it. He was about to do it himself.

No one struggled harder to understand how horrible madness, a father setting out to kill his son, could be holy than Søren Kierkegaard, the early nineteenth-century Danish philosopher, whose now-canonical essay, *Fear and Trembling,* part fictional reenactment, part philosophical meditation, part cultural criticism, and part cri de coeur, at once celebrates Abraham and explicitly asks—actually, it insists—that those who would celebrate also acknowledge the "monstrous paradoxes" that follow from his faith:

Abraham had to give up Isaac to have him, to get him back.

Abraham had to believe that he could both give him up (sacrifice him) and get him back (resurrection), a belief that was "absurd," beyond reason, beyond even thought: "Faith begins," Kierkegaard wrote, "precisely where thought leaves off."

Abraham had to place himself, one man, above the community (the universal with which Hegel and others believed that all individuals ought to strive to be in harmony), above the norms, duties, and laws (that we should love our children more than ourselves, that we should not kill) that ought to shape our lives. Faith—the sacrifice of Isaac—required the suspension of the ethical in the name of something higher, Abraham's singular relationship to God.

Crow about Abraham's faith all you want, Kierkegaard said. But recognize that it transformed murder into a holy act, infanticide into sacrifice, well pleasing to God. "So let us either forget all about

Abraham or learn how to be horrified at the monstrous paradox which is the significance of his life."

It was difficult and it was dazzling, right from the start, when Kierkegaard's pseudonym, Johannes de Silentio, wishing he had been there with Abraham in order to better understand him, imagined four different scenarios. In the first, Abraham tries to explain it all to Isaac, but Isaac doesn't understand. He protests and then begs for his life. In frustration, Abraham throws him down, grabs him by the throat, and says: " 'Foolish boy. Do you believe I am your father? I am an idolater. Do you believe this is God's command? No, it is my own desire.' Isaac trembled, and cried out to God. 'If I have no father on earth, then be Thou my father.' But below his breath Abraham said to himself: 'Lord in heaven, I thank Thee; it is after all better that he believe I am a monster than that he lose faith in Thee.' "

In the second, Abraham travels with his head down, goes through all the motions, raises the knife, sees the ram, and sacrifices it instead. He returns home and grows old. Isaac thrives, but Abraham's "eye was darkened, he saw joy no more."

In the third, Abraham thinks of Hagar and Ishmael along the way, and afterward returns again and again to the mountain, alone, asking God's forgiveness for forgetting his duty to his son. He can't understand why it was a sin to offer God the best he had, but if it was a sin, he could not understand why he would ever be forgiven.

In the fourth, Abraham appears calm on the outside, but the muscles in his hand, clenched in anguish, give him away. Isaac loses his faith. They return home and say nothing to anyone about what transpired, ever.

Again and again, de Silentio returns to the scene, but he can't get inside it. Only when he starts to unpack Abraham's faith, distinguishing it from mere obedience, and especially resignation (the Abraham of the mystery plays, who does what he thinks he has no choice but to do, all the while assuming that all is lost, at least in this life and world), does de Silentio make any progress at all. What moved Abraham, what made him the "knight of faith," was the movement beyond resignation, the combination of obedience and hope:

> All along he had faith, he believed that God would not demand Isaac of him, while still he was willing to offer him if that was indeed what was demanded. He believed on the strength of the absurd, for there could be no question of human calculation, and it was indeed absurd that God who demanded this of him should in the next instant withdraw the demand. He climbed the mountain, even in that moment when the knife gleamed he believed—that God would not demand Isaac. Certainly he was surprised by the outcome, but by means of a double movement he had come back to his original position and therefore received Isaac more joyfully than the first time. Let us go further. We let Isaac actually be sacrificed. Abraham had faith. His faith was not that he should be happy sometime in the hereafter, but that he should find blessed happiness here in this world. God could give him a new Isaac, bring the sacrificial offer back to life.

I marvel at the precision and the passion with which Kierkegaard explores the movement of Abraham's faith. So many before him just threw the word out there and assumed that their audience knew what it meant. His distinction between faith and resignation, and later between a tragic hero's sacrifice in the public interest (Agamemnon) and Abraham's purely private undertaking, makes sense to me. Yet for all of Kierkegaard's philosophical fireworks, and the equally explosive power of his prose, the rhythm and repetition, the marvelous range of literary, historical, and theological reference, the grounding of every abstraction in some vivid example, Kierkegaard's interpretation of the story, his idea of what moved Abraham, was less a dramatic departure than an elaboration of a line of thought at least as old as the Gospels. His narrator's speech in praise of Abraham echoes—literally—the Epistle to the Hebrews, and his subsequent analysis of obedience, resignation, and hope owes every kind of debt to Luther, right down to his astonishment and awe, his repeated confession that he not only couldn't have done what Abraham did. He couldn't even understand him.

"I have said however that we cannot comprehend this trial," Luther wrote, "but we can observe and imagine it from afar."

"Abraham I cannot understand," Kierkegaard wrote; "in a way all I can learn from him is to be amazed."

Kierkegaard's idea that faith justifies the suspension of the ethical was also an idea with a long history. Augustine, writing in defense of Hebrew Scripture and Jewish history in the face of Faustus the Manichean's slanders, noted that Faustus didn't bother to try to use the sacrifice to smear Abraham. Everyone knew that Abraham's deed, which would have been considered unnatural and even mad if it had been his own idea, became, by God's command, a model of submissiveness and faith. But Augustine was writing around 400 CE, defending biblical characters who he imagined had lived in an age when what was right was largely defined by God's commands and revealed law. He was not defining the relationship between faith and ethics in his own time, let alone Kierkegaard's nineteenth century.

I can see (the text makes it plain) that Kierkegaard was sticking it to Hegel and perhaps the Danish clergymen whose theology and Sunday sermons were influenced by Hegel. One and all, he thought, they failed to see the contradiction between their identification of the ethical as the highest stage of individual development and their talk of faith. If there was nothing higher than the ethical, and if the individual, acting as an individual against the ethical, was always (as Hegel suggests) in a state of sin or temptation to sin, Abraham shouldn't be celebrated: "He should really be remitted to some lower court for trial and be exposed as a murderer."

Kierkegaard was also sticking it to Kant, who saw the essential harmony of reason and religion, our ethical and spiritual lives. Kant had used God's command to Abraham to argue that even if God were to speak to a man, that man could never be sure that the voice was God's. The infinite is simply beyond our apprehension. But in some instances, Kant says, we can know when a voice we hear is not God's. And one of those instances is when that voice commands us to do something that reason tells us is wrong.

That logic made no sense to Kierkegaard. Or it made sense only if it was true that each man was supposed to determine his relationship to God by way of his relationship to other human beings. If that was the case, God would be nothing but an empty vessel, which men fill with categorical imperatives, moral obligations, and duties. God's role or function would be purely symbolic, even decorative. To have faith in him would mean nothing.

Kierkegaard thought it was the other way around. A man's relation to other men ought to be determined by his relationship to God, a God for whom all things are possible, including making himself known and heard. "God is God for me because he speaks to me," Luther had said. Part of Abraham's terrible trial was, and part of the terrible loneliness of faith is, the knowing and not knowing, the certainty that lies so close to doubt, the proximity of the sacrifice that would be holy to the temptation to sacrifice that would be sin.

I can see that Kierkegaard was arguing with Hegel and Kant, and (reading his essay alongside his journals) I can also see that he was arguing with himself, trying to make sense of, justify, and explain his own choices, his own faith, his own duty, his own sacrifices, especially his decision not to marry Regine Olsen, a woman he seems to have truly loved. Sometimes he wondered if, in breaking off the engagement, he had demonstrated his own lack of faith, the faith that it would have taken to leap into marriage, fatherhood, and family. Other times, he wondered if he had sacrificed Regine, or himself, or both, sacrificed worldly pleasure and reward to something higher, whether philosophy, theology, writing, or God. Or conversely, if in breaking off the engagement, he, like Abraham, had leapt into the absurd. He broke off the engagement and yet he continued to imagine, absurdly, that somehow, later in life, he would end up with her.

I can see where he is going, but I can't go there with him. Marriage is sacrifice, often compounded by children. Not marrying is sacrifice too. Most commitments involve both embracing and letting go. But to the degree that Kierkegaard turned to philosophy to help make sense of his own life, he failed to see that to acknowledge that every choice calls for sacrifice, and every long-term commitment is a leap of faith, is decidedly not to say that all sacrifices are equal. To obey God when he tells you to sacrifice worldly pleasure for philosophy or religion is not the same as obeying when he tells you to sacrifice your child, however similar the chemistry and mechanics of the faith that feeds each instance of obedience.

As for Kant, it is complicated. He wanted ethics and law grounded in reason, always coming from within. Judaism, he thought, was little more than the sum of its cold, spiritless, externally imposed rituals and laws, a mindless form of heteronomy perfectly exemplified by Abraham's mute acquiescence to God's command. The man knew nothing about the richness of the legal tradition or the philosophical tradition or the variety and fluidity, the heart and soul, of the interpretive tradition I've been tracking here. Nevertheless, Kant's conviction that religion and reason, divine commandments and ethics, were in harmony had resonance in age-old Jewish thought and practice, and in the centuries since his death, his influence on Jews and Judaism has been considerable. There was no place for Judaism, as he understood it, in the universe of human reason he imagined. Yet when he proposes what Abraham should have said to God—"That I ought not to kill my good son is quite certain. But that you, this apparition, are God—of that I am not certain, and never can be, not even if this voice rings down to me from (visible) heaven"—Kant sounds more than a little like a rabbi, including at least a few rabbis long before his enlightened time.

Kierkegaard's understanding of Abraham's faith is wholly familiar to me. It is as old as the Gospels. It is electric Luther. His ideas about the suspension of the ethical alarm me. His effort to understand the story from Isaac's point of view is attenuated. Yet I keep going back to his essay, and not simply because I can't resist mind-bending philosophy when it comes in lyrical prose.

No one goes—or seems to go—to greater lengths to celebrate Abraham's faith. Yet no one before him went to greater lengths, with such empathy or imagination, to resist the lazy understanding and idealization and celebration of that faith, the bombastic but ever-so-easy evocation of testing, of obedience, of a father's willingness to give up a child he cherished and could not replace. No one was as dismissive of commentators who cheapened the story, who drained it of all its drama and significance, by saying that God didn't mean it, that it was just a test, the outcome of which was never in doubt. Or as dismissive of the storytellers who rushed Abraham from command to deliverance and reward as if he were traveling on a winged horse as opposed to an ass. No one looked down with such scorn on those who shirked the hard work of recalling that the journey was three days, of trying to imagine Abraham's thoughts and feelings along the way, his anguish, his desperation, his loneliness, his fear and trembling, the temptation to stall on the one hand and to hurry and get it over with on the other, to turn back, to scream, to run away, to cry, to curse one's bad luck, and most of all to give up, to give up.

Abraham arouses Kierkegaard's admiration, and at the same time he appalls him. ("He who has explained this riddle," he wrote in a notebook, "has explained my life.") I don't share his particular admiration of Abraham, or what sometimes seems to be his longing for the kind of faith he ascribes to him, or any other faith that trumps the ethical, any more than I am moved by the moral lessons of the mystery plays, or the theology of so many of the great drawings and sculptures and paintings. I have my own ideas about Abraham and my own ideas about the story. But if it is to be a story of that kind of faith (the faith of the author of Hebrews, of Augustine, of Luther, and of so many others whose ideas of faith they shaped), I prefer Kierkegaard's adult version to all those that read like lazy children's stories. I prefer, and even take some solace in, the versions that deliberately and painstakingly show the beginning and middle of the story before they show the end, and even at the end, those that account for the cost as well as the reward.

I can spend a lot of time with Kierkegaard, and for that matter Kant, without thinking much about where the story came from and what it meant at the time. Kant plucked it out of Scripture to make a point about the proper relationship, in theory, between divine revelation and human reason. The relationship between the two in ancient Near Eastern history was beyond his purview. Kierkegaard argued that faith like Abraham's trumped reason, transforming murder into a holy act. If it ever occurred to him that in Abraham's time—or the time the story was written—child sacrifice might not have needed to be transformed, might have been perceived as a holy act in the first place, he didn't let on.

Kierkegaard thought as hard as anyone about Abraham's experience. But in his mind, that experience existed outside of history. He brought it into his own time. Abraham might well have returned from Moriah just a few days before he put pen to paper. There is nothing wrong with reading a sacred story that way, and anyone who thinks there is is bound to be frustrated. That is how ancient interpreters read Scripture. In fact, that's how ancient interpreters transformed an anthology of ancient literature into Scripture, and that's also how many church fathers and rabbis of late antiquity read it, and that's how generation after generation of Islamic interpreters read the sacred books of the Christians and Jews as well as their own. That's how many if not most people read sacred history and, to be honest, secular history too. We remake it, shape it to our needs, our interests, and our desires. I call attention to it here simply to draw a contrast between all of them—between most of us—and the readers and writers who in the seventeenth and eighteenth and nineteenth centuries believed there was another way, a better way, to read. Their first questions weren't theological (Why does God test the righteous?), philosophical (Does reason create God or God create reason?), ethical (Should Abraham have protested? Did he have a responsibility to tell Sarah and Isaac what he was up to?), typological (What does the story tell us about the life, death, and resurrection of Christ?), or even practical (If God pulls the strings, why not rail against him when misfortune strikes?) so much as historical: Who wrote the Bible? When? What did it mean to the authors and their earliest readers? What does it tell us about the world in which they lived?

"What took them so long?" people ask me. "Nothing, really," I reply. Those questions didn't arrive, full-blown, in the eighteenth century, with the rise of rationalism and empiricism and the great leaps forward in the sciences that we call the Enlightenment. Or even a century earlier with the Dutch philosopher Baruch Spinoza, whose work contributed so much to both the Enlightenment and modern biblical scholarship. For centuries some readers—Muslim, Jewish, and Christian—had been asking questions about the plain sense of the text, and some of those questions led them to questions about the author's meaning and intent. But what readers did when they got there, whether they pursued those questions or ducked them, depended on what they wanted to know.

Think about it: No one was closer to the origins of the words than the writers who first composed or recorded them. However inspired they felt, wherever they thought their inspiration had come from, they knew something that people coming after them didn't necessarily know about how and why particular parts of the anthology had come to be. Some of the early editors and redactors must have known too. Time passed and Second Temple sages began to attribute the anthology, in whole or part, to Moses. The moment they did, questions arose. It was some of those questions (about repetition, about seeming contradictions, about strange word choices, about anachronism, about seemingly ungodly behavior, about the things God didn't seem to know, even about the name of God) that had moved the rabbis of late antiquity to midrash in the first place. They asked difficult questions and they came up with elaborate answers. Some of those answers took the form of explanations: God tested Abraham to demonstrate his fear of God, not to gauge it; Moses used "Elohim" to signify God's justice and "YHWH" to signify his "mercy," or Elohim to signify any one of his several attributes and YHWH to signify his essence. Some took the form of stories. We may see some of those explanations and stories as far-fetched, but if a person's primary concern was what the text, literally or figuratively, meant to them, how they might explain it to their students and congregation, how it might help them get close to God, questions about authorship were largely beside the point. They still are. Those who wanted to believe, believed. Martin Luther frequently paused to speculate about the relationship between the author's intent and the text's meaning, about what the author was thinking and feeling when he wrote a particular passage, why he included this insight or detail or excluded that. Luther simply assumed that Moses was the author. Those who didn't want to believe, didn't. And those who wanted to believe but had doubts ended up somewhere in between.

Back in the twelfth century, Abraham Ibn Ezra had called Isaac Ibn Yashush, a fellow Jew in Muslim Spain, "Isaac the blunderer" for asking how Moses could have known anything about the kings of Israel and Judah. Yet Ibn Ezra's own reading, his close attention to the meaning of words, Hebrew words, in the context of the words around them, surely anticipated the critical study of the Bible. It also left him with questions of his own. Why, he wondered, did the author, writing about the patriarchal age, write a line like "at that time the Canaanites were in the land" when the Canaanites were still in the land when Moses died on the east side of the Jordan. Similarly, why did Moses begin his valedictory address, "These are the words that Moses addressed to all Israel on the other (east) side of the Jordan," as if the writer were on the west side when he was writing? Moses never made it to the west side, the Promised Land. Why, for that matter, did Moses refer to himself in the third person and to people and places and things that didn't exist in his day, including, in Genesis 22, a mountain Jews referred to as Zion? Moses wrote: "as is said to this day, 'on the mount of the Lord there is sight' "—clearly evoking (in Ibn Ezra's mind) the mountain on which Jerusalem and its Temple were built, the place where God sees or is seen. But Moses couldn't have known about Zion. Ibn Ezra suspected that those who read carefully would "recognize the truth." But he didn't advocate broadcasting it far and wide: "He who understands," he wrote, "will keep silent."

That was wishful thinking. Those who study, and from their study think they know things others do not, are often inclined to speak. As the centuries passed, more and more readers were swept up in the enthusiasm for the plain sense and original meaning of Scripture. And in the heightened interest in the history of the early church (and religion more generally) that the enthusiasm for the plain sense of Scripture sparked. And in the thirst for knowledge of ancient languages, including Hebrew, that the study of both the plain sense and its context in church history contributed to. And in great leaps forward in astronomy, physics, and biology, and in the rise of rationalism and empiricism in philosophy. In the midst of all that ferment, what some people wanted to study and speak about, in the same way that they studied and spoke about other works of ancient literature, was the origins of the Bible.

Theories multiplied like Israelites in biblical genealogies. Some readers tried to square new findings with old traditions. One fourteenth-century interpreter, identifying what he considered unmistakable similarities between the prose style of Moses and later biblical writers, concluded that the prophets had completed a project that Moses had begun. Several sixteenth-century scholars, by contrast, credited Moses with all five of the books attributed to him. Scribes coming along after him, they believed, had simply edited them, updating here and there. Other readers were prepared to jettison tradition. Thomas Hobbes was among those who, in the seventeenth century, argued that the evidence pointed to an author, an original author, some time after Moses, though Hobbes himself couldn't say with any certainly how long after.

In the middle of the seventeenth century, Spinoza gathered the evidence of previous commentators and added evidence of his own—all the anachronisms (including references to the future that had to have come from the pen of a writer working later), the repeated use of the phrase "to this day," and the sentences that simple common sense suggests Moses didn't write: Would Moses have told the story of his own death? Would the humblest man who ever lived have described himself as the humblest man who ever lived? It is clear "as the sun at noon," Spinoza concluded, that the Torah of Moses was written by someone "who lived long after Moses."

Questions about authorship invariably irritated those who believed that every word came directly from the mouth of God. They still do. But that wasn't their only purpose, and in many ways they were the least potent part of the challenge Spinoza posed to traditional ways of reading the Bible. He and those who shared his assumptions believed that the text, which the ancients and so many after them had assumed was intentionally cryptic, was simply distant, the product of a different place and time. Its relevance lay not in eternal and universal meanings and truths but rather in the meanings it authors originally meant to impart. The interpreter's job was not to iron out or explain away wrinkles, contradictions, duplications, obvious errors of fact, difficult passages or dubious characters, but rather to try to understand them all as objects of history. To do that, interpreters needed to cast aside the distracting, often mystifying, commentary of the rabbis and priests and turn their attention to the words on the page, learn all they could about who wrote them, compiled them, and arranged them, and how they went about doing all that. Knowing something about the authors and their editors, or at least the world in which they worked, was essential to knowing what Spinoza most wanted to know: what the words actually meant.

Those assumptions turned traditional assumptions—especially of scriptural inscrutability, perfection, and timelessness, assumptions about the reading of sacred texts that many Jews, Christians, and Muslims shared—on their heads. The Jews of Amsterdam censured him, and after the fact Protestants and Catholics condemned him too. Others were ostracized for lesser critical crimes. Richard Simon, a French priest and Hebraist whose aim, in the late seventeenth century, was to rebut Spinoza, tried to persuade his readers that Moses had indeed written the laws. Later, the prophets, guided by the spirit of God, had merely organized and polished them. Simon was expelled from the church and most copies of his book were burned.

But neither the questions nor the intellectual ferment behind them could be contained, and in eighteenth- and nineteenth-century Germany, a small but determined group of scholars, some amateurs, some academic, even a clergyman here and here, turned their attention to Hebrew Bible stories (starting with the story of Creation itself, and then the Flood) that seemed to be told two or more times (doublets and triplets). They moved from an analysis of the differences between the two versions—one that was hard to miss was the name of God—to an analysis of other passages and parts that seemed to be written in different styles or voices or from dramatically different points of view. Then they used those differences to develop theories, some competing, some complementary, about the "documents" they believed the Bible was made of, when those documents were written, and what they revealed about the history of ancient Israel.

If you know the name of just one of those scholars, it is probably Julius Wellhausen, a professor of Old Testament history, Oriental languages, and theology at Greifswald until 1882, when he dropped theology from his teaching portfolio, having concluded that his scientific approach to Scripture, "despite all caution" on his part, rendered his students unfit for the Protestant clergy. Four years earlier he had published his *History of Israel,* in which he synthesized several centuries of "higher criticism."

Wellhausen imagined that the Five Books of Moses actually comprised four different documents, written over the course of several centuries, beginning a few hundred years after Moses. J was the writer whose God was called YHWH, and YHWH looks and often acts a lot like the gods of old: he walks around in the Garden of Eden; after he curses Adam and Eve, he clothes them. Religion in J's time was a cult of nature and fertility, its festivals predominantly agricultural. E's God was Elohim, and he wrote just after J. His faith was also primitive, but in his pages, where God often appears in dreams and visions, there are hints of elevation, of the spirit to come. D wrote in the age of the prophets, the height of Israelite spirituality and ethics. Festivals marking firstfruits, the barley harvest, the wheat harvest, and the ingathering, were now and forever after linked to the history of Israel and its God. P came last, and everywhere his pen touched papyrus or parchment, he revealed a priestly concern with temple cult and ritual, sin and guilt, sacrifice and law. The divorce of the religion of Israel from nature, the common man, and perhaps reality itself, was complete. Judaism, a mature but dry, legalist, spiritless faith, came not in the beginning, with Abraham, Isaac, and Jacob, or later with the revelation at Sinai, the conquest of Canaan, the establishment of the monarchy, or even the building of Solomon's Temple, but with the priestly redaction of the Torah and the rise of the rabbis at the end.

Like the documents it analyzed, like every work of history and literature, Wellhausen's work was replete with traces of the world in which it was made, nineteenth-century Europe. Its evolutionary framework was of its age, as was its denigration of Judaism. In the years since, some scholars have challenged specific conclusions and others have challenged his whole approach. There has been debate about the number of sources (soon there were several Js and Es and Ds and also a K and L and S and either several Ps or a P and an H, the latter contributing what many considered a distinct Holiness Code in Leviticus). There have been debates about the dating of sources: an Abraham cycle that was written in Israel in the time of David or Solomon bears a very different relationship to the underlying history than an Abraham cycle written during the Babylonian exile or after it in an archaic form and style. A theory that D preceded H who preceded P provides one picture of the history. A theory that the three writers, who expressed dramatically different views on fundamental questions of theology and law, were contemporaries, quite another. There have been debates about the very nature of the sources, with some insisting that Wellhausen's documents are themselves collages of smaller documents, perhaps even fragments. The key to understanding the Bible's relation to history, they say, or if not history then at least oral tradition, is the study of the smallest units of composition within it. "Form" critics focus on the genre of each unit of composition, whether genealogy, law, prophecy, etiology, saga, legend, or song. "Tradition" critics focus on the shared understandings of the past that linked one portion of the text (one or more story, or entire story cycles, or legal codes, or collections of rituals, or chapters of history) to a particular community, whether a family, a tribe, a priestly circle, a king and his court, a political or religious reform movement, a cult, a city or city-state, or an entire nation.

The debates continue to this day. For many biblical scholars the documentary hypothesis, modified here, supplemented there, remains the point of departure. And even those who consider the idea of a handful of documents written by a handful of writers to be as quaint as the idea of Moses taking dictation in the desert would acknowledge the many lasting contributions of the documentary school and all the other early biblical scholarship—including one of the ideas at the heart of the whole enterprise: the idea that the

Bible is a book that was written and revised by men over the course of several centuries, men with particular passions and interests in particular places at particular times, a book with a past, a past that is worth trying to imagine even if it is a past that we may not (as history) ever know.

To put it another way: In the beginning, all Scripture was local. To some that idea is obvious, unremarkable, even trite. To others it is utterly appalling. It sullies the sacred by dragging it down from the heavens and into the muck. Yet from where I stand, it looks to me as if the rise of biblical scholarship simply and rather dramatically enlarged the sacred and the heavens, creating a whole new galaxy in the universe of narrative, interpretation, and analysis, with practitioners, approaches, perspectives, and methods as numerous as a galaxy's stars. The fear was that scholarship would break Scripture's spell. But scholars cast spells of their own, and for every connection between the word of God and the words on the pages that scholars severed, there were countless other connections between the words and the world that they established or repaired.

~~~

Naturally, I was curious to see what scholars had to say about the story of Abraham and Isaac, starting with what they had to say about who wrote it.

For a long time the critical consensus was that it was E, the Elohist, a writer who left his signature first and foremost in the divine name: there's the Elohim (God) who puts Abraham to the test; the Elohim who tells Abraham where to go and whose chosen place Abraham goes to; the Elohim who (Abraham assures Isaac) will see to the sheep; and Abraham's fear of Elohim, which God comes to know. Supporting evidence includes the messenger of God, a figure scholars associated with E. Beersheba, a place scholars associated with E. And all the parallels in setting, plot, character, and theme that link the story of the near sacrifice to the story of the expulsion of Hagar and near death of Ishmael, which immediately precedes it and which scholars were sure was an E story.

Was there any doubt? By the source critics' own criteria, there was room for it. After all, the messenger who saves Isaac—unlike the messenger who saves Ishmael—is an angel of YHWH (the Lord), and after Abraham sacrifices the ram Abraham calls the place "YHWH-Yireh—as is said to this day, 'On the mount of YHWH there is sight.'" And that same messenger of YHWH delivers the second address, and YHWH himself swears Abraham's reward. That makes five YHWHs in all, one for every Elohim.

And yet so sure were the early source critics that the story of Abraham and Isaac was an E story, the debate among them was not about who wrote it but how all those Yahwehs got into an E story.

The fourth and fifth YHWHs were easily dispatched. Just about everyone assumed that the second angelic address was "secondary," meaning that it was tacked on later. The first three were more troublesome, but one way or another they were explained away too: Some imagined an older layer of tradition appropriated by E. Some imagined an E story revised by a post-Elohist editor. Some imagined two parallel (perhaps regional) traditions, a northern E tradition and a southern J tradition, combined after the fall of the northern kingdom, Israel, by the author who combined J and E or later by R, the redactor. Some imagined two sharply divergent traditions, a sacrifice and a near sacrifice, combined in a similar way.

When, in the second half of the twentieth century, a few scholars had the temerity to challenge the attribution of the core of the story to E, they made note of the debate about the divine name but quickly moved beyond it. However and whenever the Elohims and the Yahwehs got there, the final version is a J story in its vocabulary and its phrasing, J in its particular sense of God's testing and Abraham's fear of God, J in its concern for God's promise and provenance, and J in its inimitable style.

Some of the champions of J are among the revisionists who doubt that there was an independent E source, as opposed to, say, an E editor of various earlier sources. Be that as it may, they insist that J was the author of the story of the near sacrifice. They don't deny the echoes in form and content of the story of Hagar and Ishmael. But they argue that there are many plausible explanations for those echoes, the most obvious of which is this: J wrote that story too.

I took all this in from a considerable distance, and with a certain mischievous pleasure. That pleasure increased as time passed and I realized that even the boldest scholars of the documentary school—the ones who are sure that J was from Judah and E from

Israel and P (coming before, not after, D) was an Aaroneid priest
in the court of King Hezekiah (appalled by JE's elevation of Moses
and his lack of respect for their ancestor Aaron in the story of the
Golden Calf) and D (the author of the entire history from Moses
to the fall of Judah) a priest (like E) of Shiloh (probably Jeremiah,
contemptuous of the northern kingdom and kind to Josiah) and R
another Aaroneid priest, probably Ezra—even they are circumspect
when it comes to the story of the near sacrifice.

Still, I couldn't help wondering if, after more than a century of
scholarship, there were anything (just one thing, about authorship,
composition, and dating) upon which everyone who gave or gives
any thought to such matters agrees.

Early on there was widespread agreement that the story was
among the earliest Hebrew Bible stories, perhaps written or
recorded as early as the tenth century BCE. But before long, some
scholars, including some of the same people who challenged the
attribution to E, turned the chronology upside down, arguing that
it, along with many of the other J stories in Genesis, was a late one,
masquerading as an ancient story, late in style, late in reference to
places, people, things, late (a lot like Deuteronomy) in outlook, perhaps as late as the Persian period, which began in 539 BCE when
Cyrus defeated the neo-Babylonians and Israelite and Judean exiles
began to return to Zion and rebuild the Temple.

Similarly, there was once agreement that God's second address,
through his angel, was written long after the rest. Some considered
it an awkward addition, clumsily appending God's earlier and oft-
repeated promises to a story that stood perfectly well on its own.
Others thought it a profound and subtle commentary on the story
of the near sacrifice, the very earliest commentary, which not only
knit God's test into the complete cycle of stories about God's promise and God's providence, but also raised it to a higher theological
plane: If God's initial call, his choice of Abraham, could fairly be
called arbitrary (What, one might ask, did he do to deserve God's
blessing?), after Moriah it could be called arbitrary no more. From

then on, God's promise, Israel's chosenness, was firmly grounded in Abraham's deeds, and those deeds and human agency itself had an obvious place in God's plan.

Eventually that consensus also broke down. Prominent scholars, while in complete agreement with the "earliest commentary" arguments about purpose and profundity of the second angelic address, have come to see it as essential to the rest of the story as God's command, Abraham's response, the angel's retraction, and the ram.

That leaves just one small but not insignificant area of agreement.

There are, as I have said, scholars who think that J wrote the story. And, though I have not had reason to mention them, there are scholars who think it possible that J was a woman, a writer in the court of Solomon's son, Rehoboam.

But I've yet to find a scholar who believes both that J was a woman and that J wrote the version we know. Which means that everyone who has weighed in believes that the story was written by a man.

But what was he trying to say?

Something about child sacrifice, it has long been assumed.

Evidence of the practice comes not just from the myriad reports and references in the Hebrew Bible but also from Canaanite literature (much of which was uncovered in the early twentieth century in the ancient port city of Ugarit), from Greek and Roman history and literature, from archaeology (especially studies of Carthaginian burial grounds, cremation urns, and bones of infants that seem to have been burned white), from suggestive ancient Near Eastern inscriptions and even a few suggestive works of art.

None of that evidence is conclusive. The vast majority of the literary evidence is polemical, people accusing other people of sacrificing children, and the physical evidence, including the most damning of it, the human remains in Carthage and other neo-Phoenician cities and colonies in North Africa, has been the subject of ongoing debate. Some anthropologists are certain that the bones are the remains of sacrificed children. Others suspect that they are third-trimester fetuses and perinates. Still, many scholars believe that the weight of the evidence suggests that the practice was not entirely a figment of the polemical imagination. A king, in a moment of public crisis, might sacrifice a child in the hope of appeasing an angry God and thereby saving a city. A warrior with his back to the wall might sacrifice in the hope of drawing God into battle on his side. And just about anyone, grateful for a bountiful harvest or healthy herd or brood, might have been moved to give back some of what God had bestowed.

But what was the story trying to say about the practice?

The spectrum of respectable opinion has been wide.

At one end are those who, yesterday and today, believe that the story was a polemic against it—its critical moment not when God asked or when Abraham set out but when God said stop and Abraham obeyed. In the telling, the author put God and the very first Hebrews on the side of the angels (and later the prophets) in the effort to eradicate the scourge of human sacrifice from the ancient Near East. At the other end are those who believe something approaching the opposite: that the story is a narrative expression of an old and essential element of Israelite theology, God's claim to every firstborn son. "You shall give Me the first-born among your sons," God says in Exodus 22. It was a matter of consecration and donation. Like the firstfruits of the field and the firstborn of the flock, the firstborn son belonged to him. He didn't always take what was his. (In all but that one of the several instances in the Torah where God lays claim, he quickly and neatly adds unmistakable instructions for redemption.) But he could and there were times when he did.

In between the extremes are the historical and tradition-minded critics who imagine that the story signaled the transition from one moment or ideal to the other, preserving the memory of a change in cult practice, perhaps even an actual event that prompted the change, early in the second millennium BCE, the age of Abraham, Isaac, and Jacob. And the form critics who, while agreeing that the story preserved a memory, believe it preserved the memory not of an event but of a story—perhaps pre-Israelite or non-Israelite oral tradition—a story (etiological) that explains the origins of something. It is possible that it originally explained the origins of a cult site or place-name, but more likely the combination of place and practice, perhaps answering the question "Why was it that at this particular place it became permissible, or even desirable, to substitute an animal for the firstborn son?"

But what place? As far as anyone knows, neither Moriah nor YHWH-Yireh was the name of an actual place. Those inclined to see layers of older tradition behind the story imagined a Canaanite cult site and story. Others imagine Judean or Israelite sites (some propose Jeruel, some El-Roi). In either case, the original name of the place was lost when a later writer or editor came up with the story's final place-names. Others still, digging deep into the roots of words, exploring associations based in meaning and associations based in sound, mapping Abraham's movement around Canaan, calculating distances, conclude, as many rabbis concluded centuries before, that the site of the near sacrifice, the place where the Lord saw, was always understood to be Jerusalem. Which is why when the author of Chronicles got around to the building of the Temple, he wrote: "Then Solomon began to build the House of the Lord in Jerusalem on Mount Moriah."

The scholars who have assumed that the story was originally about sacrifice, one way or another, have dominated the debate, but there are others who believe that they may well be mistaking the story's plot for its meaning. By the time the story was redacted, and perhaps even by the time the version we know was written, prophecy and law had eliminated child sacrifice. Readers understood it was detestable to God and his people. The practice was no longer at issue.

What was at issue, they say—after the Assyrians overran Israel in late eighth century BCE, or while the Babylonians threatened Judah in the early sixth, or after the Babylonians captured Jerusalem in 586, razing the Temple and carrying many Judeans off into exile, or even after the first exiles began to return from captivity a half century later, when the population was sparse, the boundaries uncertain, the Temple rebuilding project faltering, the great nation seemingly small and weak and forever at the mercy of great empires—was God's promise.

Wherever it came from, these scholars insist, whatever it once looked like, the story we know can only be understood in the context of that promise and the threats to it, which means in the context of the entire Abraham cycle. It begins with God's first call and command (give up your past) and God's promise (I will bless you) and proceeds from there, ever so slowly, characterized by confusion about both the promise and the plan, by questions about who was going to get what and when, by uncertainty and doubt, by snares and detours, by heartaches, grave threats, and near death. Nothing is for certain. Nothing comes easy—without testing, without trial, without degradation.

Imagined from the perspective of Abraham and Isaac over the course of three days, the story might be said to distill to its essence and recapitulate all the Abraham stories that come before it. The God who calls and promises is also the God who seems capable of going back on his promises, the God who gives life is also the God who can withhold life and even take it away. It is harrowing, but in the end that God, the one and only, shows mercy to and rewards those who fear him. God returns Isaac to Abraham and then reaffirms his promise: because you had done this, Israel would be delivered. Israel would be redeemed.

And what about the "this," the thing that Abraham has done,

the command he has obeyed, the aborted sacrifice at the heart of
the plot? The scholars who read the story that way would say that
if, somehow, we could ask the author what he was thinking, he'd
likely take the question in stride, maybe even shrug. He wouldn't
deny the monumental place of sacrifice in the imagination of many
ancient Israelites, or the possibility that tradition and form critics
were right when they say there were older versions of the story
and older layers of meanings that the author may not have been
conscious of. But, hard as it might be to believe, he would say: I
was not thinking about child sacrifice one way or another. I was
thinking about Abraham's future and looking for something hard,
really hard, for him to do.

Among the scholars inclined to see the story deeply embedded in
the entire Abraham cycle are those who considered themselves critics of the Bible as literature. The literary critics acknowledge and
make use of the findings of the source critics, the tradition critics,
the form critics, and all the others critics who identify and study the
sources and documents from which they think the Bible was made.

And they make use of the findings of the redaction critics, who
study the art of the editors who cut and spliced and wove and joined
and sometimes wrote the parts together.

And the textual critics, who study the differences—variants—
among all the extant versions of the redacted text, variations across
languages and time, variants in different languages at the same time,
and variants in the same language at the same time. Sometimes
those differences are huge, including entire sections of Jeremiah,
Job, and Daniel. And sometimes they are small. The late-antique
and medieval rabbis went to great lengths to explain the significance of the word "behind" (*ahar*) in the line "Abraham looked
up and saw a ram behind." Today scholars believe that *ahar* was a
transcription error: in the ancient text the word was *ehad,* meaning
"a" or "one" ram: Abraham looked up and saw "a" ram.

And they make use of the findings of linguists and philologists and anthropologists and archaeologists and historians of the ancient Near East, who identify all the parallels between the stories, covenants, vassal treaties, languages, laws, rituals, social practices, and even the gods of ancient Israel and all the peoples (the Canaanites, Egyptians, Hittites, Phoenicians, Assyrians, Mesopotamians, and Persians) among whom so many ancient Israelites were born, lived, and died.

The literary critics of the Bible learn from and acknowledge the work of all those scholars. But their own work is grounded in their conviction that no matter how many people had a hand in it, how long it was in the making, how many earlier forms it took, how much of it was borrowed from neighbors, how many different kinds of imperatives shaped it, how often and how dramatically transcription, translation, and exegesis transformed words and meaning, the final product (which happens to be the only version of most of it that for many years now anyone has actually set eyes on) is, in addition to everything else, and perhaps above all else, a work of literature.

The literary critics are too tactful to point out that much of the evidence offered in the brief against divine or Mosaic authorship displays a dismaying innocence of the history of literature, from the ancient Greeks to the whole gamut of modern and postmodern writers. What if Moses were a precursor of Dickinson or Joyce or Beckett or Faulkner or Woolf? What if God were a writer who couldn't stop revising?

There is no point. Few of the literary critics attribute the books to God or Moses.

But where other scholars see doublets and triplets, they see the clever development of plot, character, and theme.

Where others see inconsistency and contradiction (and in that contradiction evidence of competing traditions and schools and circles and courts), the literary critics see multiple points of view, artful appropriation and juxtaposition, and every kind of ambiguity.

Where others look behind the text in the hope of finding oral tradition, political and theological orientation, and historical facts, the literary critics look right at it and find carefully composed poetry and lyrical prose.

Where others see fractures and fragments, pieces and parts, smudges and crooked seams, J and E and D and H and P and G, literary critics see the Teaching of Moses and the Holy Scriptures—remarkably coherent works of ancient literature, literature without which it is simply impossible to imagine or understand the literature, to say nothing of the graphic art, music, religion, and politics, of the past two thousand years.

All that and, what's more, they have great taste. To a man, they have had nothing but the highest praise for my story:

"The most perfectly formed and polished of all the patriarchal stories"—Gerhard von Rad

"The profoundest recorded experience in all the history of the patriarchs and the telling of it soars to comparable literary heights."—E. A. Speiser

"One of the peaks of ancient narrative."—Everett Fox

"A masterpiece of biblical literature."—Robert Alter

"A masterpiece of economy, psychology, and artistic subtlety."—Jack Miles (not only a former Jesuit seminarian but also a biographer of God)

One of the pioneers of the literary approach, a German philologist and critic named Erich Auerbach, set the tone. Living in exile in Istanbul in the early 1940s (after the Nazis forced him out of his post at Marburg), Auerbach went to work on a sweeping study of (nothing less than) the representation of reality in Western literature. In his opening chapter, he uses the story to demonstrate how ancient Hebrew writers harnessed the awesome literary power of the unseen and the unsaid.

Think about it: we don't know where God was when he called

out to Abraham or where Abraham was when he answered, "Here I am." That one Hebrew word (*hi-ne-ni*) at once reveals, with characteristic concision, Abraham's attention and readiness, while it completely conceals his physical location, where he actually was. We don't know when they spoke. Was it the afternoon or the evening before the morning Abraham rose early, or in the middle of the night? We don't know Isaac's age, or the ages of the two servants or even their names. We don't know anything about the lay of the land they all passed through on the first two days. In fact, we know nothing at all about those days, not even the weather. Did a bright sun and clear sky mock Abraham's distress, or did dark clouds and sand-whipping winds make for a perfect harmony between what he saw and what he felt? We don't know. We don't even know if Abraham was distressed. We don't know anything about what he was feeling or thinking, and we know next to nothing about what Isaac was feeling or thinking. We don't know what Sarah knew or even where she was. Only through the eyes of artists, working later, can most of us begin to picture the scene of the sacrifice, the altar, or the knife.

In short, we are told or shown only what we absolutely need to know to follow the action. Everything else, Auerbach writes, is "left in obscurity; the decisive points of the narrative alone are emphasized, what lies between is nonexistent; time and place are undefined . . . thoughts and feelings remain unexpressed, are only suggested by the silence and the fragmentary speech; the whole, permeated with the most unrelieved suspense . . . and directed toward a single goal, remains mysterious and 'fraught with background.' "

Auerbach's analysis of Genesis 22 comes in a close comparison of the biblical style to "the genius of the Homeric style" as it is displayed in chapter 19 of the *Odyssey,* a chapter in which every element of plot, character, and theme is set in the foreground, every scene is fully illuminated, every connection made explicit, every thought is expressed, and every act takes place in the story's present, right in front of our eyes, and is fully explained. And while I can imagine some less-enamored critic spinning all of Auerbach's talk of background as a backhanded compliment ("what is memorable about your writing is what you didn't write"), he doesn't mean it that way. He warns us not to mistake the skeletal structure—the withholding of detail, description, and dialogue, especially detail and dialogue that reveals interiors—for evidence of a primitive stage in the evolution of storytelling. Rather, he sees it as evidence of a sophisticated sense of memory, thought, emotion, and action, all set squarely in the flow of time—so sophisticated that unlike Homer, whose stories can be analyzed but resist interpretation and allegory, biblical literature cries out for interpretation. In fact, Auerbach argues, it must be interpreted or transformed by allegory to be fully understood and explained.

Not every critic accepts all of Auerbach's premises. Or considers Hebrew Scripture so singular. Or shares his estimate and appreciation of its literary value. But many do, and the point is that before Auerbach, most critics would have found the idea that the literature of the ancient Israelites could be spoken of in the same breath as the *Iliad* and the *Odyssey* laughable.

How could I not appreciate Auerbach and all those who have followed in his footsteps? But the truth is that I was smitten by scores
of biblical scholars, and I (just like the literary critics themselves)
have learned from loads of them. I have learned from those who
study the parts, the fragments and supplements, as well as those
who, studying the final product, never give the parts a thought.
From those who study law, ritual, and theology as well as those
who study narrative, poetry, and song. From those who study huge
themes as they developed over centuries and those who study parts
of speech, tenses, prefixes, suffixes, word roots, letters, and vowels
in a particular text or at a particular moment in time. From those
who believe that the interpretive tradition—the vast body of literature that Scripture gave rise to—is one thing, and modern biblical
scholarship quite another. (The story that Abraham smashed his
father's idols, narrowly escaped death by fire at the hands of an idol-
worshipping tyrant, and left home to separate himself from those
who refused to heed the word of the one true God is tradition. The
idea that the historical Abraham was part of a great migration early
in the second millennium and that the stories about him were written early in the first millennium BCE to help legitimize monarchy,
empire, and the centrality of Jerusalem to both is scholarship.) And
I have learned from the scholars who believe that when it comes
to the Hebrew Bible, a book that took shape over centuries and

contains within its pages most of what we know about its context, there is (more than) a little rabbi in every biblical scholar.

In time, scholars began to study the interpretive tradition with the same energy, intensity, and rigor they studied Scripture. Needless to say, I have learned from them too, and it has been my good fortune that one of the first to turn his attention to Abraham and Isaac, Shalom Spiegel, a professor of Bible, medieval Hebrew poetry, and midrash at the Jewish Theological Seminary, was blessed by a slew of muses. Born in Romania and educated in Vienna, Spiegel came to New York by way of Haifa in 1929. Two decades later (at about the same time, coincidentally, that Erich Auerbach published *Mimesis*), he was asked to contribute an essay to a volume that was to be published in honor of a fellow seminarian, the librarian and historian Alexander Marx. Spiegel contributed a critical edition of a previously unpublished twelfth-century poem, Rabbi Ephraim's *Akedah,* and an introduction to the same, *Me-aggadot ha-akedah,* the legends of the *Akedah,* which in Judah Goldin's inspired translation is called *The Last Trial: On the Legends and Lore of the Command to Abraham to Offer Isaac as a Sacrifice: The Akedah.*

Spiegel's original Hebrew subtitle, "A Liturgy by Rabbi Ephraim of Bonn about the Slaughter of Isaac and His Resurrection," revealed exactly which "legends" Spiegel was most interested in. Drawing upon a stunning range of sources (from Scripture and other ancient literature to the earliest understandings of it in law, ritual, and liturgy to the latest biblical scholarship), he examines a series of moments and interlocking themes, starting with the rabbis' questions about Isaac's whereabouts at the end of the story and concluding with questions about God's second call from heaven. In between, he looks closely at all the *midrashim* that leave the impression that Abraham actually sacrificed Isaac—or that makes it clear that many ancient and medieval rabbis imagined that he had.

The pleasure Spiegel took in the excavation of versions and variants is palpable. To tag after him as he chases an explanation (for Isaac's absence), or a motif (Abraham begging God to let him do

it), or a recurring image (Isaac's blood or ashes), or an association (Temple sacrifice, synagogue prayer), or an obscure, fleeting,
forgotten, and perhaps (Spiegel suggests) sometimes even suppressed reference, hint, or slip back toward its first trace, seeming to exhaust every possibility before darting off in an entirely
different direction with the same or some intimately related end
in sight, is literally thrilling. Unlike the rabbis (who rarely even
tried), Spiegel somehow manages to make the most abrupt and
artificial transitions in his narrative and analysis seem smooth
and natural. Just like them (or their editors), he was never satisfied
with a single way of seeing, saying, understanding, or explaining, when two or more were at hand. When we are through, we
grasp not only the early association of the binding of Isaac and the
deliverance of Passover but the likelihood of an even earlier connection between the rituals of Passover and the rituals intended to
provide people with protection and deliverance from the demons
and destroyers who wreaked havoc after dark in the first full moon
of spring. We grasp not only the later association of the binding
and Rosh Hashanah (atonement for all owing to the merit of the
fathers, the Akedah Merit) but the reason why, in the nineteenth
century, in the midst of the Jewish enlightenment, some scholars
insisted that the whole of idea of the Akedah Merit was a corrup-
tion by way of Christianity.

When Spiegel is through, what began as an introduction to a
poem is at once an imaginatively organized and richly annotated
history of midrash, a penetrating midrash on midrash, and an
unforgettable work of art, at once solemn and playful, passionate
and wise, dripping with lament and yet maybe not entirely despair-
ing, chock-full of learning yet unfailingly lyrical, a prose poem that
pays homage, in its word choices, its sentence structure, and its irre-
pressible inquisitiveness, not just about the substance of his sources
but also about their sound.

Spiegel devotes his longest chapter to the relationship between
the story of Abraham and Isaac and the story of God and Jesus.

He touches upon but he doesn't dwell on the question of which came first. That is partly because he is confident that key pieces of the Christian story predated Christianity. It is also because he is confident that the lines of influence ran more than one way: "Is this to say that the Christians learned their lessons from Judaism and the Jews picked up nothing from their Christian surroundings? Not at all! Beliefs and opinions float from place to place and pass over from one religion to another wittingly and unwittingly. There are conceptions like the Akedah Merit that start out at first to act as influence and end up being influenced themselves." But it is mostly because he believes that the roots of both Jewish and Christian stories lay deep in the pagan world. The Canaanites, for example, also appear to have had stories about the death and rebirth of gods and the sons of gods.

Common origins didn't necessarily mean common destiny, and Spiegel identifies crucial differences between the two sets of stories: the Satan who tried to stop Abraham, unlike the devil, had no autonomy; he was always under the control of God. The merit of the binding of Isaac, unlike salvation through Christ, was not literally derived from the deeds of one man, or even two. It was the merit of all the fathers and sons that encouraged God to show mercy to their descendants. What's more, Jewish atonement was not permanently fixed. God always wanted more. Good deeds had to keep coming. The biggest difference of all, in Spiegel's telling, was that the remnants of paganism, the heritage of idolatry, "which in Judaism remained peripheral," grew to become dominant in Christianity. The ancient Israelites worked slowly and hesitantly and often with mixed feelings to suppress or sublimate or transform the ideal of human sacrifice. Then Christian Jews came along and put a bloody human sacrifice at the center of their faith.

But, Spiegel insists, for Jews no less than for Christians, the weight of the past, all that blood and all those ashes, all the deaths and resurrections, were not easily thrown off. The pull of habit, of tradition, was strong. "The ancient pagan demand for the actual sacrifice of children was not uprooted from the world, nor perhaps from the heart either." Persecution alone kept the ideal alive, the fire burning, the sacrificial knife honed.

It is not until several pages before the end of his essay (67 pages in Hebrew; 135 in English) that Spiegel first mentions Rabbi Ephraim of Bonn's *Akedah,* the 105-line poem all those pages were intended to introduce. Ephraim, writing several decades after the Second Crusade, drew on a thousand years of midrash and may also have made an original contribution to it when he provided what appears to be a new answer to an old question, "Why the second address from heaven?"

Some said that Abraham had interrupted God's first address (when he looked up, spotted, and sacrificed the ram). Others said that Abraham had demanded to hear from God himself, not one of his angels. Others said, more simply, that God had had more to say.

Rabbi Ephraim imagined an entirely different scenario:

He made haste, he pinned him down with his knees,
He made his two arms strong.
With steady hands he slaughtered him according to the
   rite,
Full rite was the slaughter.

Down upon him fell the resurrecting dew, and he revived.
The father seized him then to slaughter him once more.
Scripture, bear witness! Well-grounded is the fact:

And the Lord called Abraham, even a second time from heaven.

The ministering angels cried out, terrified:
Even animal victims, were they ever slaughtered twice?

Where, Spiegel wondered, did Ephraim get the idea that Abraham had nearly slaughtered Isaac twice? He had just shown that ancient midrash was full of evidence that Abraham had been eager to do it, and full of hints that he had done it—once. But Spiegel suspected that the idea that Abraham had tried again was born closer to home. Scattered among the chronicles of the Rhineland martyrs, he found accounts of men and women who had evoked Abraham as they slaughtered their children. And he found accounts of men and women who had sung the *Alenu* as fires burned around them, just as Isaac, in some midrash, sang amid his flames. And he found accounts of brides and bridegrooms who had gone to their deaths "together," as Abraham and Isaac had walked together and in some commentary even built the altar together, like a Jewish father building a wedding canopy for his son. And he found accounts of children who, like Isaac, had lost blood from wounds. But it was another motif altogether that helped him make sense of Ephraim's poem: accounts of men and women who, figuratively speaking, had twice sacrificed their lives to God.

One chronicle of the massacre at Mainz records an incident in which crusaders discovered, among piles of corpses, Jews who had somehow survived their wounds. Renounce your faith, they said to them, and you'll be saved. The wounded hadn't the strength to speak. Instead, they raised a finger toward the heavens. The crusaders finished them off. There were similar stories in the chronicles of the massacres at Mehr and Elnere, instances where attackers had left people for dead, returned to find them alive, and then killed them again. In one, a man who had killed his wife and three sons before stabbing himself survived his wounds. Crusaders converged upon him and asked if, now, he would convert. When he said no, they dug a grave. He buried his wife and sons and then lay down himself. They buried him alive, but still he didn't die. They dug him up and asked again. Again he refused. So they put him in the grave a second time.

"The boundaries between midrash and reality get blurred," Spiegel observes. The idea that Abraham had tried twice may have had its origins in those accounts. But it also may have had its origins in Rabbi Ephraim's own personal experience. He was born in 1133, thirty-seven years after the First Crusade. In the early days of the Second Crusade, his father sought refuge for his family in Wolkenburg, under the protection of the bishop of Cologne. Spiegel imagines them and their neighbors huddled there, waiting for the "fury of those who had gone wild with destruction of the Jews" to die down. They would have recalled that it had been fifty years since the last great slaughter, and they might have told stories of all those who had "sprayed their own blood and the blood of their dear children, and underwent many an Akedah, and built altars, and prepared sacrifices." Ephraim was thirteen at the time. Later he wrote poems about the martyrs, and a memoir, full of facts he had gathered about the decrees and persecutions of his own time. "Perhaps," Spiegel wrote, "from what his ears had picked up while he was still of a tender age, fear-ridden and impressionable, years later when the commentator and poet tried to resolve the difficulties in the biblical Akedah narrative, there rose to the surface, from the hidden recesses of his soul: 'The father seized him then to slaughter him once more. Scripture bear witness! Well grounded is the fact': if not in Scripture, then in the experience of the Jews in the Middle Ages."

And then again in the experience of the Jews in the middle of the twentieth century.

Spiegel never mentions it, never even hints at it, not even in

those final pages, pages filled with pained Jewish responses to persecution and gruesome death in the Rhineland, but he wrote in the
immediate aftermath of persecution and death in Germany, Poland,
Belarus, Lithuania, Latvia, and Estonia the likes of which not even
the Jews had ever known. Which is to say he wrote a history of
the stories of Isaac's death and resurrection just as evidence for the
latest chapter of that history began to accumulate. Even before the
outcome of the war was clear, before the camps were liberated,
before the last ghetto was razed, before the death marches and mass
executions were halted, victims and witnesses had begun to make
the connection between the Shoah, the catastrophe in Europe, and
the Olah, the holocaust demanded of the very first Jews.

Among them was a prisoner in Auschwitz, a father there with
his son. It was the eve of Rosh Hashanah, 1944, and the Nazi commander had ordered a selection. The teenagers above a certain
height, large enough and strong enough to work, would live. The
rest of the group, of sixteen hundred, would go to the gas. Under
such circumstances, the father of a younger or shorter boy had just
one hope. He could try to bribe a *kapo* to pull a boy from the group
condemned to die. Since that *kapo* himself would be held account-
able if the numbers didn't add up, for every boy he pulled he would
have to find a substitute from among the boys who, for the time
being, had been spared.

The father approached a rabbi, a distinguished Hungarian
scholar of Jewish law. The father had some money stashed away,
and he wanted to know if, under the circumstances, it would be
permissible for him to offer that kind of bribe: "May I save his life
at the expense of another?" The rabbi wouldn't answer him. He
said he couldn't. To do so would require consultation with other
rabbis and perhaps an appeal to a higher authority. It was complicated. He didn't even have his books. He urged the man not to ask
again. The father persisted. The rabbi remained mum. The father
concluded that he had done all that was required of him. He had
asked a rabbi, and the rabbi's refusal to answer was his answer:

it could not possibly be lawful for him to offer the bribe. If it were, the rabbi surely would have told him so, allowing him to redeem his son, his only one. So the father did nothing, and he passed the next day, the rabbi remembered, in a kind of euphoria, joyful that he had had the privilege of "giving his only son's life in obedience" to God. "He prayed that his act might be as acceptable in the sight of the Almighty as Abraham's binding of Isaac," which also happened on Rosh Hashanah and which we are reminded of in our "Torah reading and prayers."

That story would be too good for a sermon to be true—if there weren't so much evidence that others saw it the same way. Here's Rabbi Simhah Elberg: "I think that Isaac, the eternal Jew, was never taken down from the Akedah. Mount Moriah has always been transferred from one land to the other," from Spain to France, from France to Germany, from Germany to Poland. Elberg had studied in Warsaw and was back there, from Paris, for his sister's wedding when the Nazis invaded. He managed to flee. The rest of his family died in the camps. "The Akedah of Treblinka was to the people what the Akedah of Isaac was to a single individual. Both sanctified our history, our existence. Treblinka is the culmination of Mount Moriah. The Akedah-of-Isaac nation has survived the test. The wretched voices of millions have been ripped forth from the flaming red fires." Elberg looked ahead to redemption, but he warned that it had yet to come, not even with the exodus of hundreds of thousands to the land of Israel. The nation remained in limbo, somewhere between exile and redemption.

"The Akedah of Isaac, of multitudes upon multitudes of the children of Israel, was created in our generation before our very eyes," wrote Reuven Katz, a rabbi who had studied in Belarus, Lithuania, and Vilna and led congregations elsewhere in Eastern Europe before he emigrated to Petah Tikvah in the early 1930s. "It has killed six million brothers and sisters without any pity for the beauty of Jacob. More than a million children and babies among them. Since the destruction of the Temple, Israel has had no Olah (burnt) offering of so many Akedahs, dying in the purity of sanc-tification of God and land." Yet Katz believed the community had stayed true to God and, like Isaac, would be reborn: "The people of Israel have earned a country and a life of sovereignty and free-dom, with the promise of 'Unto thy seed will I give this land.' " Just as the ashes and blood had once led to freedom from bondage, so the latest sacrifice would lead to the Promised Land. "The blood itself is absolution of Israel. The blood of the holy ones and heroes who brought Israel freedom and the country itself. The blood of the righteous functions as the desired conciliation for the sin of the generation."

But what was the sin? There was no agreement. Some said assimilation. Some said neglect of Torah. Some said it was one or more of the age's "isms": secularism, socialism, humanism, nation-alism, scientific Judaism, and other forms of Reform. Some said it was Zionism. Some said it was opposition to Zionism, or simply finding peace in exile. Some said, as the authors of the Crusade chronicles had said, that it was the sins of generations past. What made the present so much more frightening was not just the mag-nitude but the agent. In antiquity, Abraham, Moses, and Jeremiah had led the way, even to the altar. "Today," Rabbi Elberg wrote, "Hitler has spoken in the name of God. For us, that is the bitterest punishment of all."

Others accepted the analogy but rejected the idea that the Jews had done anything wrong. History, they said, showed that the Jews did not need to sin to suffer and die for their God. It started with Abraham and Isaac, said Kalonymus Kalman Shapira, the Hasidic rabbi of Piaseczno, Poland, in a lesson he taught in a secret syna-gogue in the Warsaw Ghetto. When Abraham demonstrated his desire to bind, and Isaac his desire to be bound, they inaugurated "a form of worship that requires total self-sacrifice for God and the Jewish people." Shapira spoke those words in early October 1940, one year to the day after his only son succumbed to injuries he had sustained in the German bombing of the city, which also took the lives of Shapira's daughter-in-law and sister-in-law. His own wife had died shortly before the war. His mother died soon after his son, of grief. Shapira's only daughter would be sent from Warsaw to Treblinka in 1942. The rabbi himself was the last to go, deported to a work camp at the time of the ghetto uprising, and then shot to death in late 1943. He left three years of Torah commentaries back in Warsaw, buried in a milk carton. A construction worker found them after the war.

God's angel stopped Abraham's sacrifice, Shapira said, and for that reason every murder of an innocent Jew by a gentile is "in absolute antithesis to the *Akedah*." Yet it is an antithesis that "actually consummates" it. The *Akedah*s of Warsaw, Treblinka, Auschwitz, Bergen-Belsen, Dachau, Babi Yar—of all the blood-soaked lands of Eastern Europe—were simply the latest and by far the greatest instances of consummation, of Jewish self-sacrifice, of suffering and dying to sanctify God's name. The Torah does not say "God tested Abraham." It says "After these events, God tested Abraham." Why? "Because," Shapira said, all these events, "all murdered Jews, comprise the final act of the *Akedah*. Their martyrdom turns God's wrath away from the Jewish people, and so the murdered ones die for all the Jewish people, in an act that rises to the level of the *chesed* (loving-kindness) of Abraham."

The predictability of that response did nothing to lessen its sting. It was a way of thinking that was at least a thousand years old at the time of the Crusades, and it was fed by ideas about the relationship between sin and suffering, blood and absolution, that were much older than that. What's more, old as it was, it was not static, some rusty relic dragged out of storage in the aftermath of disaster and then again on days of remembrance. It was still vital and in flux in the early decades of the twentieth century, employed by a variety of people in a variety of ways, the secular no less than the religious, nowhere more than in Palestine, where Jewish pioneers and subsequent waves of Jewish settlers, many of them chased out of their homes and homelands by pogroms and other forms of persecution in Europe, faced hostility from their new neighbors.

"We are all bound here," Yitzhak Lamdan wrote, in a poem he called "Upon the Altar." Lamdan had come from the Ukraine in 1920, part of Zionism's third wave. Six years later he published "Masada," the poem for which he is best known, an epic that takes its title from the name of the hilltop desert fortress where, according to Josephus, a thousand Jewish rebels under siege committed mass suicide rather than surrender. Masada fell to the Romans in 73 CE, three years after the fall of Jerusalem. Now, after nearly nineteen hundred years in exile, Jews were returning, and Lamdan was prepared for more of the same: "We are all bound here, and with our own hands we brought wood here." This time there was no question about where the lamb was or whether the sacrifice would be accepted. "Therefore let us silently stretch out our necks over the altar."

"Hah, it's not me," Lamdan wrote, in another poem, playing on the coincidence of his name and that of his subject:

another Isaac was there.
The fire was different, and different was the binding.

I knew where I was being led from the start,
Not for testing's sake did God command the one who
*   led me.*
I loved to walk and walk, and I didn't ask for a ram.

Many writers of Lamdan's generation imagined themselves as the sacrificed sons or (as they grew older and had children of their own) the fathers of sacrificed sons or even the sons of sacrificed mothers and fathers in a life-and-death struggle for a national homeland and a future for the Jewish people. Some celebrated the sacrifice, or at least saw it as necessary, as Natan Alterman did in a poem in which Abraham is a little Polish boy sleeping, upright, on his stone front steps. The boy's murdered parents and younger sister urge him to "come home," but he is afraid to move. Enemies still threaten. The night is full of daggers and blood. He cries out. His mother cries back: "I am glad! Were it not for the knife in my breast / My heart would break in two." Here the sacrifice comes first, and it is only when God calls—when the ancient thunder comes from on high—and says, "Do not fear," and then promises to make the boy mighty and "bless those who bless you" and "curse those who curse you"—that the boy is willing to go forth to the new nation: "For the command that thundered to Avram the father / Still thunders to Avram the lad."

Others resigned themselves to what they took to be the inevitability of sacrifice, a resignation famously dramatized in the diatribe of Amichai, one of the characters in *Days of Ziklag,* S. Yizhar's thousand-page novel of Israel's war for independence. Amichai is a soldier, part of a small squad struggling to hold a remote desert outpost under enemy siege. At one point he says he hates "our father Abraham for going to bind Isaac." He wants to know "what right" he has "over Isaac." If Abraham wants to offer a sacrifice, "let him bind himself." He hates "the God who sent him." He hates that Isaac is "nothing" but the "object of a test" between "Abraham and his God." He hates the "sanctification of God in the *Aqedah.*" He hates the killing of the sons as "a test of love!" He hates the world that stands still and does not cry out: "Villains, why must the sons die?" He hates all that, and yet in the end Amichai concedes that there is "no evading the *Aqedah.*" It "only seems you could leave everything and run." But you cannot: "This is what life is like. . . . If you're not ready to be killed and kill—there'll be no good in the world. No justice, no love, no beauty."

Some distinguished between passive and active martyrdom, elevating the latter, the militant martyr. Others denied the value of the distinction: "The Aqedah too," Zalman Shazar, a poet, journalist, Labor Zionist, and later the third president of Israel, wrote in the early 1940s, "when it occurs out of free choice, is an expression of supreme heroism, and it is no less active than standing at the gate with a gun in one's hand." But either way, Abraham and Isaac were alive and on the scene—even before the arrival of news and refugees from Hitler's Europe or, just a few years later, the invasion of Arab armies that began hours after the new state of Israel declared its independence.

Yet if the turn to the story of the near sacrifice and the history of martyrdom to explain the Holocaust was wholly predictable, the vehemence with which that reading of the story and that explanation of Jewish catastrophe were contested was not. Today, many people are likely to find the dissenting views commonplace. That's because after more than half a century of relentless reconsideration, reinterpretation, and recasting—reinterpretation and recasting that has come in waves, taken every imaginable shape and form, and shows no sign of abating—for many people it has become commonplace. Views that for ages were unorthodox have become part of the mainstream. But it is useful to remember that in the context of the life of the story, they have not been mainstream or commonplace for long.

Some argued that the analogy between the binding and the Holocaust failed, on the simplest level, as analogy.

For starters, God commanded Abraham to sacrifice Isaac. He didn't command the murder of Jews. The idea that he did, that Hitler and his soldiers were doing God's work, was abhorrent, contemptible, not the least of which because it echoed the apologetics of all those who, whether they welcomed the final solution or regretted it, said that genocide was punishment for deicide and the continuing rejection of Christ. Or those who put it more subtly but no less repulsively: a divine reminder of Christ's sufferings. The whereabouts of God, the God of history—whether he stood by and watched the whole thing unfold, or he went into hiding, or (as some writers said) he was dead—were irrelevant. The murder of six million Jews and millions of others was wholly the work of men.

Second, Abraham set out, in response to a divine command, to sacrifice a son he loved. The Jews of Europe didn't set out to sacrifice their children or themselves. They were murdered. By people who hated them.

Third, the angel of God said stop, and Abraham stopped. He didn't sacrifice Isaac. Neither God nor anyone else stopped the Nazis. They killed for years.

Most of the writers who rejected the analogy entertained the details only long enough to sweep them aside. That's because they rejected the very idea of it. There was, they said, no useful analogy. The attempt to exterminate the Jews of Europe, all the Jews of Europe, simply because they were Jews, stood alone as a catastrophe in kind and degree. Pinchas Peli, a scholar of Hebrew literature and Jewish studies and a widely read essayist, worked his way through one possible biblical precedent after another—from Cain and Abel to Job—before concluding that none would suffice. "The Shoah stands out in its uniqueness in Jewish history and the history of Jewish martyrdom," he wrote. "The sacrifice of Isaac, with all its mystery and all the variety of interpretations given it, will always remain a world apart from the Shoah." The philosopher Emil Fackenheim reminded his audience in a series of lectures, later published as *God's Presence in History,* that the Rhineland martyrs, like most Jewish martyrs in history, had chosen to die rather than to convert. The crusaders had killed them because of their faith. The victims of the Holocaust weren't given a choice. Hitler killed them in an attempt to exterminate "a race."

Fackenheim believed that those who likened the binding and the Holocaust misunderstood both—and Jewish theology to boot. Jews don't die for God or to glorify God. They live for God. In fact, Fackenheim argues, the imperative to live is among the most important lessons of the Shoah, an imperative he imagines in the form of a 614th commandment: Thou shall survive as Jews, thou shall not contribute to Hitler's project by dying, by giving up, by cursing God (however much we have to wrestle with his angels), let alone by abandoning him. What Fackenheim calls the "commanding voice of Auschwitz" demands the end of the exaltation of martyrdom. Jews are "forbidden to hand Hitler yet another, posthumous victory," he writes. "They are commanded to survive as Jews, lest the Jewish people perish." They are commanded to remember the victims, "lest their memory perish. They are forbidden to despair of man and his world, and to escape into either cynicism or otherworldliness." And finally they are "forbidden to despair of the God of Israel, lest Judaism perish." Fackenheim concedes that a secularist can't make himself believe or be commanded to believe. And that the Holocaust might well force believers into an entirely new relationship with God. But "one possibility," he insists, is "wholly unthinkable: A Jew may not respond to Hitler's attempt to destroy Judaism by himself cooperating in its destruction."

Elie Wiesel, who survived slave labor, a death march that took the lives of thousands, the loss of his mother and one of his sisters to the gas chambers of Auschwitz, and of his father (who was with him almost all the way to the end) to dysentery, starvation, exhaustion, and several brutal beatings in Buchenwald, insists that the notion that Jews died to sanctify God, just like the idea that Isaac died on Mount Moriah, is contrary to both the spirit and the letter of Scripture, a confusion of Christian and Jewish stories. "In Jewish tradition man cannot use death as a means of glorifying God," he writes. "Had he killed his son, Abraham would have become the forefather of a people—but not the Jewish people." Fackenheim advocated the end of martyrdom. Reading Wiesel alone, you might think that it never existed: "For the Jew, all truth must spring from life, never from death. To us, crucifixion represents not a step forward but a step backward: at the top of Moriah, the living remains alive, thus marking the end of an era of ritual murder. To invoke the Akedah is tantamount to calling for mercy—whereas from the beginning Golgotha has served as pretext for countless massacres of sons and fathers cut down together by sword and fire in the name of a word that considered itself synonymous with love."

Wiesel, like many writing before him and many writing after, prefers to ponder Abraham's small victories: his argument on behalf of the innocent of Sodom, his insistence (in midrash) that God himself rescind the command, his refusal (in midrash) to leave the altar before he had given God a piece of his mind. Nor is he alone in noting that Jews are more inclined to commemorate good days, days of liberation, exodus, revelation, deliverance—Passover, Shavuot, Purim, Hanukkah—than the many disasters. The commemoration of the latter are bunched into one, Tishah b'Av. Wiesel doesn't deny, he would be last to deny, that the story of Abraham and Isaac seems to contain in its small frame so much Jewish destiny. Or that it has repeatedly been employed to describe and explain one catastrophe after another. But, he insists, the story doesn't end with catastrophe. It ends with Isaac, still alive. Isaac is a hero not for suffering, not for almost dying, but for surviving. "Suffering, in Jewish tradition, confers no privileges. It all depends on what one makes of that suffering. Isaac knew how to transform it into prayer and love rather than into rancor and malediction." His reward, in Wiesel's mind: "The Temple was built on Moriah. Not on Sinai."

2 5

Once again, change came with catastrophe. It came in waves.

Sometimes it came quietly and unobtrusively, as it did when commentators carried bits of biblical scholarship out into the wider world. Back in the 1860s, Abraham Geiger, a German rabbi, a scholar, and a founder of Reform Judaism, was among those who had argued that the story's meaning was simple and clear: "Lay not thy hand upon the lad." That was the "true worship" of God. Geiger's interpretation infuriated his former Bonn University classmate and friend Sampson Raphael Hirsch, a founder of Modern Orthodox Judaism. Hirsch charged that Geiger, "in his raving madness," had turned the moment on Moriah—Abraham and Isaac's "free will surrender of their own beings," the very height of Jewish spirituality—into its opposite, a trite epiphany. A century later, Geiger's interpretation was everywhere: in Bible commentaries, catechisms, sermons, popular histories and encyclopedias of religion, guides to religious literacy, and Bible stories for children. In *The Story of the Jew,* one of my Hebrew school textbooks, published in 1964, the story is characterized as a "bitter cry" against the pagan practice of child sacrifice. Abraham demonstrated his ("and the Jews' ") heroic willingness to accept God and his law, and God made known that "He could not accept human blood." Nearly fifty years later, in his book on the city of Jerusalem, James Carroll, a former priest and prolific writer, put it precisely the same way: "The point of the story is that on the holy mountain God intervened to end human sacrifice."

Sometimes it came in riotous song, including a burst of up-tempo sixteen-bar electric blues, with Robert (ben Abraham) Zimmerman, a.k.a. Bob Dylan, belting out the lyrics above Mike Bloomfield's slide guitar, Al Kooper's piano, and Sam Lay's drums. Between verses, Dylan blew on a whistle that mimicked a siren, and the cacophony of sounds expressed Dylan's so-it-goes cynicism at least as much as the street slang and sarcasm of his words:

> Oh God said to Abraham, "Kill me a son"
> Abe says, "Man, you must be puttin' me on"
> God say, "No." Abe say, "What?"
> God say, "You can do what you want Abe, but
> The next time you see me comin' you better run"
> Well Abe says, "Where do you want this killin' done?"
> God says, "Out on Highway 61"

Dylan's Abraham is, briefly, a sixties rebel, but note that neither the angel of God nor any other form of deliverance is on its way. Sacrifice becomes killing in a setting that is less Genesis than the end of days.

Sometimes it came when commentators concluded that God would not have tested Abraham in that way, not even to teach him that he abhorred child sacrifice. One was G. Henton Davies, a distinguished Baptist minister and Oxford Old Testament scholar. In a commentary on Genesis commissioned in the late 1960s by the educational arm of the Southern Baptist Convention, Davies surveyed a wide range of traditional interpretation and modern scholarship before concluding that God would not have asked so cruel a sacrifice of anyone but himself. What happened was that Abraham, afraid that his love for Isaac, his inability to imagine his life without him, had compromised his connection to God, decided to give him back. The ram was the savior, but God did not stop a sacrifice he had set in motion. Rather, he saved Abraham from his own obsession and his own misunderstanding of God.

Not everyone could or would so cavalierly discard the story's first line. And surely, others said, God tests us. The question is how he wanted Abraham to respond. Change came when commentators began to answer that question by arguing that Abraham (and Dylan) got him wrong. God had actually wanted Abraham to argue, protest, even resist. He had *expected* Abraham to say, "You must be putting me on." And while any number of comedians played the gap between expectation and response for a laugh—Woody Allen's God asks Abraham how he could do such a thing and then interrupts his answer. "Never mind what I said," the Lord spake. "Doth thou listen to every crazy idea that comes thy way?"—most commentators portrayed it as tragedy. It was a test, and Abraham failed. The proof: he lived for another seventy-five years and prospered, but God never spoke to him again.

Change came when exegetes explicitly took on earlier exegetes, none more than Kierkegaard, as if that tortured soul had not suffered enough. Jean-Paul Sartre and Martin Buber, following Kant, parted ways with him at Abraham's first "Here I am." "If I hear voices," Sartre asked in 1945, "what proof is there that they come from heaven and not from hell, or from my own subconsciousness, or some pathological condition? What proof is there that they are intended for me?" When we prepare to suspend the ethical, Buber warned in the early 1950s, we had better be sure we have been "addressed by the Absolute" and not "one of his apes." "Ever and ever again, men are commanded from out of the darkness to sacrifice their Isaac."

The French philosopher Emmanuel Lévinas was more patient, sticking with Abraham for the entire length of the three-day journey. He imagines the determination it must have taken to get from tent to mountaintop. But in light of that determination, the gathering momentum, the fear and the trembling, the sheer force of Abraham's faith, Lévinas is certain that the critical moment in the story is not God's initial command, or Abraham's response, or even the angel's retraction. It is when Abraham puts down the knife.

Unlike the painters, who to a man picture Abraham's head turned away from his son, his gaze fixed on God's angel or the heavens, Lévinas imagines Abraham looking right at Isaac, face-to-face, and what he sees shows him that he should not kill him. Where Kierkegaard went wrong was in thinking that our singular relationship with God somehow exists independently of (and above) our singular relationship with others, our responsibilities to others, when in fact our relationship with others (in this case, Isaac lying on that altar) ought to mediate our relationship with God.

The story, Lévinas argues, is not about the suspension of the ethical, but rather its birth: "That Abraham obeyed the first voice is astonishing: that he had sufficient distance with respect to that obedience to hear the second voice—that is essential."

Others gave Abraham even more credit than that. Some saw in his painstaking preparations and roundabout route (why else would the journey have taken him three days?) a subtle form of resistance. He was stalling, a tried-and-true "weapon of the weak." But all along he was confident that if he gave God enough time, he would come to his senses. All along he had faith that God would not stand idly by while he violated his law. Claire Elise Katz, an American philosopher as wily as any late-antique rabbi, does not go quite that far, but her Abraham still discovers the ethical before God's angel says a word: he looks at Isaac's face, sees the difference between right and wrong in his eyes, and drops the knife. That (not Abraham's desire to strangle Isaac!) was why the angel said, "Don't lay a hand on him." The knife posed no danger. His hands were all he had left. Neither God nor his angel needed to stop the sacrifice. Abraham had stopped it himself.

Omri Boehm, another extraordinarily resourceful young philosopher, whose analysis of Genesis 22 is grounded in his reading of Maimonides and Ibn Kaspi as well as Kant, employs source criticism (who wrote what, when, and why) to argue that the idea of an ethical Abraham was not simply a figment of the late twentieth-century imagination. Rather, it had ancient roots. The original story, Boehm believes, comprised verses 1 through 10, followed immediately by verses 13 and 14. Verses 11 and 12 were added later, probably by the same writer who added verses 15–19, the angel's second address. If you skip from the end of verse 10 to the beginning of verse 13, you will see what Boehm means: just as Abraham is about to sacrifice Isaac, he looks up, sees the ram in the thicket, and decides to sacrifice it instead of Isaac. All his own doing. God doesn't say anything. He does not have to.

Jack Miles contributed a forward to Boehm's book, and he appreciates it for the same reasons I do: Boehm's fearless elevation, perhaps even excavation, of a religious model of disobedience to an "unlawful command." But Miles's own retelling of the story, in *God: A Biography,* is somewhat more open-ended.

Miles sees the binding as the climax of a protracted power strug-

gle, a struggle with many dimensions but control of human reproduction at its heart. Who was calling the shots? God, the creator
and destroyer who repeatedly promised Abraham offspring but
took forever to deliver? Or Abraham, the man who (while waiting)
handed his wife over to a pharaoh; fathered a child with Hagar;
laughed when God said that he would soon father a second child
with his ninety-year-old wife; spoke up for Ishmael even after God
had informed him that Isaac was on his way; gave Sarah to a second
man, this one a king; and made the case for sparing the sinning cities of the plain? No accident, Miles believes, that the thunderclap
of a command to sacrifice came so soon after Abraham's brief on
behalf of the Sodomites. God demanded deference. Evidently, the
sacrifice of his foreskin was not enough.

Abraham calls his bluff. He sets out but never says he will do it.
He tells his servants that he and Isaac will be back. He tells Isaac
that God will provide the lamb. As we read, we have no way of
knowing whether he is on his way to sacrifice his son or just playing
a high-stakes game of chicken, instructing God, pleading with him,
cajoling. Abraham goes through all the murderous motions before
God stops him and declares victory—"Now I know that you fear
God, for you have not withheld your son"—and "for the seventh
and final time, promises Abraham abundant offspring." But, Miles
writes, "it is as much God who concedes defeat as Abraham," for
Abraham's obedience has "actually been far more ambiguous than
God chooses to believe. He has not, after all, slain his son, and perhaps he would never have done so."

All that, and yet in it—and in untold variations—there was very little aid or comfort for Isaac. No matter why God asked, or how he hoped Abraham would respond, or what Abraham was thinking, or who ultimately stayed Abraham's hand, the boy remains in the shadows, an afterthought, wounded even when Abraham doesn't touch him, left only with scars and the memory of one immortal line.

Change came when commentators, many of them in Israel in the 1960s, began to identify with Isaac's experience as a victim and to launch their critique of the story from his point of view. Theirs were not the dorky, willing Isaacs of ancient and late-antique commentary and narrative. Nor were they the militant and heroic Isaacs of the pioneers and second and third waves of Jewish settlers in Palestine. Nor the often weary but stoic Isaacs of the War for Independence— all of whom had only yesterday (and sometimes still) revered their fathers (at least on paper) and accepted the role even when they did not celebrate it. No, these were unwilling Isaacs, furious at their fathers, at all the fathers, who in the name of God or land or state could not stop sacrificing their sons.

The sacrificing father in "The Way of the Wind," a stark and chilling short story Amos Oz published in 1965, is Shimshon Sheinbaum.

Sheinbaum is an intense, driven, and ruthlessly self-disciplined Labor Zionist, utterly sure of himself and his every belief, conviction, even instinct. He walks up to an open window and knows instantly where the wind is coming from, and when and how it will arrive. Although he is a patriarch of the labor movement, a movement intent on making not only a new nation but also new kind of Jewish man, late in life he himself has no heir. So he "conquers" Raya Greenspan, a woman thirty-three years his junior, and three months after their wedding, a son, Gideon, is born. But Gideon, however beloved, turns out to be "something of a disappointment." He is, in his father's eyes, weak, bewildered, vacillating, sniveling, lovesick, slow, the author of sentimental poems and cruel parodies, "not the stuff on which dynasties are founded" but rather a perfect representative of a whole generation, exuding "an air of shallow despair, of nihilism, of cynical mockery. They can't love wholeheartedly and they can't hate wholeheartedly, either. No enthusiasm, and no loathing."

When Gideon announces his intention to join the paratroopers, his father assumes it is one more of the boy's bad jokes. But he is serious, and though his mother refuses to give her permission (an only child seeking assignment to a combat unit needed both parents' consent), Sheinbaum goes over her head and gets an exception to the rule. Redemption would come on Independence Day, when Gideon's unit was scheduled to perform in an air show, jumping in front of family, friends, and neighbors and landing on the soil of his very own kibbutz. His father can't wait.

The day comes. Gideon jumps. But the wind takes an unexpected turn and blows him off course. His chute gets caught in power lines, and though spectators believe he will survive the fall, he is afraid to let go. He dies hanging on those lines, electrocuted, crucified upside down on the cross of his father's ideology, obsessions, virility, dreams, and desires.

. . .

It is not supposed to be that way. Sons are supposed to bury fathers, not fathers sons. Moshe Berfel, the protagonist of Yariv Ben-Aharon's 1966 novel *The Battle,* worries that the burying fathers, endlessly sacrificing sons "on the altar of war," were engaged in a futile effort to evade their own death sentences. "Should not a father die for his ideals?" Berfel asks. "Is it not my duty to bury him before he buries me? I mean, before his ideals are realized?" Two years later, in a symposium that took place on Kibbutz Givat Haviva, the poet and essayist Eli Alon argued that honesty requires that we, all of us, evaluate our ideals and our very lives not just from the point of view of Isaac, but "from the point of view of the dead Isaac, from the point of view of the dead." If we do, he said, "we'll be surprised to discover that many of the slogans and values that seem necessary to us, in order 'to give meaning to our lives,' and for which we were ready to die, will suddenly seem to us vanity and folly."

The poet and playwright Hanoch Levin took Alon's call literally, or felt the same impulse at the same time. The perspective of the dead Isaac is exactly what a few audiences got in his wickedly satirical cabaret piece *The Queen of the Bath*. (Golda Meir is the queen.) In one scene, Levin's Abraham is frail and deeply apologetic: God wants it, he tells Isaac. What can I do? Levin's Isaac, edgy and articulate, tries to reassure him, and urges him to go ahead and do it, if that's what God wants. It is not a big deal, he says, the slaughter of one kid, just a kid. They go back and forth in that way, until, finally, the angel calls out. Unfortunately, Abraham is hard-of-hearing. It is Isaac who hears God's voice, and now, with their roles reversed, he must persuade his father not to kill him. The scene ends with Isaac wondering what will happen if God calls out to other fathers, commanding them not to sacrifice their sons, but none of them can hear.

The next thing we know, Isaac is in his grave, singing a song as

Abraham buries him. The dead Isaac rejects the idea that there was
anything honorable about his father's obedience to God's whim:

Father dear, when you stand over my grave,
Old and tired and forlorn here,
And you see how they bury my body in the earth
And you stand over me, father dear,

Don't stand then so proud,
  . . .

And don't say you've made a sacrifice,
For the one who sacrificed was me here,
And don't say other high-flown words
For I am very low now, father dear.

Father dear, when you stand over my grave
Old and tired and forlorn here,
And you see how they bury my body in the earth—
Then you beg my pardon, father dear.

In 1970, Levin's play was stillborn. Shortly before opening
night, the censorship board demanded the removal of two scenes,
including the exchange between Abraham and Isaac, which it considered offensive to the fathers of soldiers. The theater appealed
and won, but many of those in the audience for the initial performances were indeed offended, and religious members of the Tel
Aviv city council put pressure on the theater to shut down the show.
Actors began to fear for their safety, and the show closed after nineteen nights. But Isaac continued to speak, and over the next two
decades, a period marked by a surprise Arab attack and traumatic
war in 1973, the continued occupation of East Jerusalem, the West
Bank, the Gaza Strip, the Golan Heights, and (until 1979) Sinai, the
invasion of Lebanon in 1982, the Sabra and Shatila massacres, the

rise of the antiwar movement and the First Intifada, Isaac's point of
view informed almost every discussion and debate. So strong and
so widespread was the identification with him that a whole generation of writers and artists became known as "the generation of
Isaac."

Not that there haven't been times when patience with him has worn
thin. How, writers wondered, after all these years, could he be so
naive? How could he go marching off to Mount Moriah, fooled
again? How, with only rare exceptions (Leonard Cohen's Isaac,
who threatens to kill to stop senseless sacrifice, was one) could he
not protest? How could he forget that he and his Arab brother
faced the exact same threat?

In a poem first published in 1982, Yitzhak Laor calls his name-
sake an idiot—"This Idiot, Isaac." Yet Laor saves his bitterest words
for Abraham, whom he likens to Amalek, Israel's ancient arch-
enemy. Recall Moses's warning, in his farewell address: "Remember
what Amalek did to you on your journey, after you left Egypt—
how, undeterred by fear of God, he surprised you on the march,
when you were famished and weary, and cut down all the stragglers
in your rear. Therefore, when the Lord your God grants you safety
from all your enemies around you, in the land that the Lord your
God is giving you as a hereditary portion, you shall blot out the
memory of Amalek from under heaven. Do not forget!"

Now the poet warns the patriarch:

To pity the offering? . . . The ass?
Thus to surrender? From the Negev to Mount Moriah to
    be sacrificed?
To trust a father like that? Let him kill him first. Let him
    slam his father
his only father Abraham
in jail in the poorhouse in the cellar of the house just so

he will not slay.
Remember what your father did to your brother Ishmael.

At least one poet, the magnificent Yehuda Amichai, did pity the offering, the actual offering, in a poem he published the following year. Amichai's protest is less explosive than Laor's, more sardonic than furious. But it is every bit as subversive of the story's traditional meanings. In Amichai's hands, the binding becomes a simple stunt or photo op. The shofar, blown for thousands of Rosh Hashanahs to remind God to remember Abraham and (in remembering) to contain his wrath, becomes a bugle or party horn. And the substitution of the ram for Isaac, for so long and to this day widely understood as a giant step toward civilization, a reason for religious pride, becomes just another form of barbarism. While all around him rabbis, priests, clerics, and laypeople continued to ask, and argue about, whose sacrifice was the greatest and why, Amichai concludes that

> *The real hero of the sacrifice was the ram*
> *Who had no idea about the conspiracy of the others.*
> *He apparently volunteered to die in place of Isaac.*
> *I want to sing a memorial song about the ram,*
> *His curly wool and human eyes,*
> *The horns, so calm in his living head.*
> *When he was slaughtered they made* shofars *of them,*
> *To sound the blast of their war*
> *Or the blast of their coarse joy. . . .*

Fifteen years later, Amichai imagined that Abraham had "had three sons" and he riffed on the root meaning of each boy's name. Ishmael was saved by his mother, Hagar. Isaac was saved by God's angel. But Yivkeh, a third son, we've never heard of "because he was the youngest" and, "much-loved," "wasn't saved by anyone." When he was small

his father called him affectionately Yivkeh will cry
my little cutie-pie. But he sacrificed him on an altar.
And in the Bible it is written, "the ram," but it was
    Yivkeh.
Yishmael never heard again of God his entire life.
Yitzhak never laughed again his entire life.
And Sarah laughed only once and never again.
Abraham had three sons.
He will listen, he will laugh, he will cry.
Yishmael (Let God listen), Yitzhakel (Let God laugh),
    Yivkehel (Let God Cry).

Here the ram survives, and there is no hero of the *Akedah*.

I am not sure any writer has returned to Mount Moriah as often as A. B. Yehoshua. He seems as unable as Kierkegaard's de Silentio to stay away. Yet unlike Silentio, who as a child found the story beautiful and grew to admire it more and more, Yehoshua found it intolerable from the first. He thought God's command was an outrage. No God worthy of worshipping would make such a demand. He thought Abraham's willingness was an outrage. It made no moral sense whatsoever. Yet Yehoshua understood that the story was the bedrock of God's blessing, the linchpin of the covenant, the reason, on the Day of Judgment and every other day that justice and mercy hangs in the balance, that God suppresses his wrath.

Secular himself, it naturally occurred to Yehoshua to see what would happen if he took God out of it—as the instigator of the sacrifice, the first cause. He imagines Abraham as an old man, with Isaac coming of age, remembering how, when he was Isaac's age, he had mocked his father's gods and ultimately left his father's house. What if Isaac came to mock his God, the God to whom he had devoted his life, and sacrificed so much? It was through Isaac that the covenant would be passed. What if he rebelled, continuing the line but not the covenant?

So Abraham took Isaac up. Bound him. Raised the knife, and then dropped it. He told Isaac: "God stopped me, and saved your life." From that moment on, whatever else he thought of Him, Isaac would believe that he owed his life to God.

Yehoshua took God out. He calls what remained the "knife game," a game in which fathers bound their sons, their futures, the future of their nation, to their ideals and their faith by submitting them to life-threatening dangers and then saving them at the last moment. But, Yehoshua quickly concluded, that was not enough. The game was too dangerous. Who knew where the knife would ultimately fall? And what kind of damage would be done, so long as the game—ending in Isaac's deliverance—could be idealized, held up as the metaphor for all of Israel's experience, for all of Jewish experience, used as evidence that no matter how bad things got, how many lives were lost, how much suffering there was, God would ultimately come through.

Yehoshua had conveyed that danger and damage, the near-death happening over and over, in *Early in the Summer of 1970,* a nightmarish early novella. It is the story of a Bible teacher, several years past retirement age and under pressure to retire, but unwilling to, because of the war. He insists that he can't leave the school and students now that they—all the teachers, all the fathers—are sending them to their deaths. The head of the school doesn't see the connection. But the old man just keeps showing up for class, until the day the head pulls him out to inform him that his son, the old man's only son, has been killed in action in the Jordan Valley. In a daze, the father travels to Jerusalem to recover his son's body, but there's been some mistake. The body in Jerusalem is not that of his son, and when he travels east into the valley, toward the river, it is not his son again and again. Along the way, he prepares the speech he'll deliver at graduation to students about to leave school for the army: "On the face of it, your disappearance is nothing, is meaningless, futile. Because historically speaking, however stubborn you are, your death will again be but a weary repetition in a slightly different setting. Another tinge of hills, new contours of desert, a new species of shrub, astounding types of weapons. But the blood is the same, and the pain so familiar"

Two decades later, Yehoshua published *Mr. Mani*, the story of one family over several generations, from the middle of the nineteenth century to the end of the twentieth. Yehoshua tells the story backward, which means that the novel begins at the end and ends at the beginning, begins with a mysterious suicide and ends with a mysterious sacrifice, or more precisely a father confessing— to a rabbi—to the sacrifice (on the steps of the Dome of the Rock, the Temple Mount, Mount Moriah) of a wayward son, a son with a dangerous (in the father's mind) obsession: reuniting the sons of Ishmael and Isaac. The danger is not simply that the boy has elevated the value of peace among different people in a particular place, Palestine, above the value of his distinct religious tradition, but also that as he struggles to remind the Ishmaelites of what they have forgotten (that they are actually Jews, or were once Jews), the young man has himself forgotten that he is a Jew.

It is a disorienting novel, a distressing novel, a difficult novel (the story is told in five conversations we hear only one side of), and often an enigmatic novel, an epic large parts of which we are left to imagine for ourselves. Critics and other readers do not even agree who ultimately wields the sacrificial knife, the Jewish father in hot pursuit of his son or the Muslims guarding the shrine. Yet from beginning to end it is an extraordinary evocation, at once utterly fantastic and utterly realistic, of the powerful sway that our ancestors hold over us, whether or not we know who they were or what on earth they have to do with who we are. Yehoshua traces the Manis all the way back to Moriah not to celebrate ritual or obedience or faith or sacrifice to (or for) God or country (in war after war "of no choice"), but to try to break its spell or at least loosen its grip, to undo the costly inheritance once and for all. But I can't imagine who would know better than he—a novelist who has enacted the binding in the hope of eradicating it, killed Isaac in the hope of saving his children—just how difficult a task that is going to be.

27

~

And then there is Sarah. I left her for last simply to try to convey a sense of the way the waves of commentary came. If one of the first was generated by revulsion (revulsion against genocide and the blind obedience to authority that was widely believed to have contributed to it, revulsion against the interpretation of that genocide as martyrdom), that wave broke among many others, as one postwar social movement after another generated challenges to one form of authority after another and each new challenge gave rise to new questions, or new answers to old ones. Yet it was only with the feminist movement, when the authority of men—divine and human—over women was added to the list, and when women began to enter the rabbinate and ministry and the academy in ever-increasing numbers and increasing numbers of women poets and fiction writers began to make their voices heard, that the ancient question—Where was Sarah?—was raised anew. In the late second millennium, as in the early first, Sarah came last.

Writers turning to her have had a lot to work with. She is as clearly defined a biblical character as Isaac is indistinct, as active in defense of her interests as he is passive, as strong as he is weak. So strong and so decisive that though the poet Eleanor Wilner's Sarah (a late second-wave feminist, right down to her perfectly correct consciousness of caste and class) may be a bit of a stretch, the gist of her initial response to God would not have surprised third- and fourth-century rabbis and priests. God said, "Go," and she said, "No." Abraham was asleep in his tent. She stepped out of hers and stood between "the desert and the distant sky." Then, speaking in a soft voice, words "the canon does not record," she told God she wouldn't be chosen, and if she could help it, neither would her son. In light of God's promise, the sacrifice was a sham or a sin. "Shame," she said to him, who must have known she would choose Isaac: "What use have I for History—an arrow already bent when it is fired from the bow?"

She wakes Isaac and tells him what she knows. She plans to leave, before Abraham wakes, to track down Hagar, whom she ("drunk with pride") cast out. She gives Isaac a choice: to come with her or go with Abraham, to choose or be chosen. He's confused, uncertain how he'll greet Ishmael, wondering what, if he's not chosen, he will be. She tells him he must choose. He wants to know what will happen if they go. "I don't know," she says. "But it is written what will happen if you stay."

We don't find out what Isaac decided. Or maybe we do, if Scripture accurately records it. But in other poems, and sermons, and songs, and commentary, Sarah doesn't leave the choice to Isaac. Sometimes, she and Isaac flee. Sometimes, she prevents Abraham from leaving, as the rabbis worried (and Satan hoped) she would. Sometimes she goes after them and stops them before they reach Moriah. In one novel, she follows them all the way to the mountaintop, where she finds Isaac piling wood on the altar and Abraham "standing to one side, an absent look in his eyes." Sarah urges Isaac to run, but before he can, Abraham scoops him up into his arms. She appeals to God, making her case as a party to the covenant, as a convert to his idea of justice, and most of all as a mother. Then she spots the ram and cries out, "Abraham, Abraham, look at the ram behind you." Afterward Abraham claims he did not hear her. What he heard, he says, was the voice of God. Sarah tactfully concludes that she and God must have cried out together.

Sarah has been written into the story in every which way. In one recently discovered midrash, a midrash attributed, with fitting license, to Rashi's sister, it is all a bad dream of Sarah's, a working out of the trauma of leaving her home and her father's house, of wandering endlessly, of being handed over to lecherous men in Egypt and Gerar, of having Isaac taken out of her arms for circumcision. In another, more recent take, a Colorado rabbi audaciously explains the old mystery of Sarah's absence, or whereabouts, not just in chapter 22, but for all the years between the weaning of Isaac, in Beersheba, and her death, in Hebron (when Abraham still resided in Beersheba and clearly was not with her when she died). It turns out that she, alarmed by Abraham's increasingly bizarre behavior, had decided to leave him shortly after Isaac was born. Hagar's banishment was nothing but a ruse, the first step in a scheme that ultimately allowed the two of them to get away with their sons. Afterward they arranged an early form of joint custody with the boys' father.

Other readers, writers, critics, and scholars, while generally sympathetic to the spirit and intent of those who wrote Sarah into the story, have devoted their own efforts not to adding Sarah to the biblical story but rather to exploring what her exclusion from it tells us about ideas about men and women in the world that made the Bible and the world the Bible made. Among the first was the philosopher Carol Ochs who, in a brief essay written in the late 1970s, touches upon a wide range of responses (rabbinical, historical, psychoanalytical, and philosophical) before concluding that at the heart of the story and the entire cycle of Abraham stories was the conflict between matriarchy and patriarchy. In the former, a man's primary allegiance was to offspring and blood relatives. In the latter, to an abstraction, the voice of God. Abraham has to prove himself, especially after he had argued with God about Sodom, prove that he has left the old tradition behind. "God demands that he denounce the most fundamental tenet of the matriarchal religion and kill his own child," Ochs wrote. "Abraham passes the test and is pronounced fit to be the father of a new, patriarchal religion."

Two decades later, the anthropologist Carol Delaney surveyed an even wider range of readings, Jewish, Christian, and Muslim, en route to her own. She agrees with Ochs (and the scholars who had weighed in after her, most notably Nancy Jay) that the struggle for power at the heart of the story was not between Abraham and God but between Abraham and God on one side and Sarah on the other. Delaney agrees that the story conveyed a powerful message about the outcome of that struggle, about who was in charge. But in her mind its essence was what it said about why Abraham was in charge, what it said about the intellectual underpinning, in particular ideas about reproduction, of male power. Patriarchy, she argues, was built upon the idea that men are the Gods on earth, creating human life when they plant the seed. Women merely provide the womb, the soil in which the seed grows. Delaney is dubious about much of the evidence used to support the idea that child sacrifice was widespread in the ancient Near East. But whether it was or wasn't, she believes that the story had less to do with idealizing or prohibiting it than with answering another set of questions entirely, then and long afterward: Whom does Isaac belong to? Whose seed is he? Who gets to decide whether he lives or dies? The legacy of the earliest answers to those questions of power and authority, Delaney argues, has been century after century of child sacrifice through child abuse, poverty, inequality, and war.

I don't think that Sarah would have agreed that Isaac belonged to Abraham. That is why she had to be left out of the story. There would have been a wicked fight. Abraham himself suggests as much in Alicia Ostriker's poem "The Story of Abraham," a parody in which the covenant takes the form of an eye chart, with the command to sacrifice coming (right after the command to circumcise—"a mark of absolute / Distinction, it would only hurt for a minute") in the fine and blurry print at the bottom. When Abraham hesitates, saying he needs to talk "some of this out" with his wife, the print suddenly turns bold:

> NO WAY. THIS IS BETWEEN US MEN.
> AND IF YOU HAPPEN TO BE THINKING
> ABOUT LOOPHOLES
> FORGET IT, MAN. It said they preferred
> Not to use strong arm techniques. It said
> I'd already signed on.

Right up to that moment, Ostriker reminds us, in an essay titled "Out of My Sight," Sarah has played a pivotal role in the story cycle. It is she who twice saves Abraham's life by pretending to be his sister. It is she who comes up with the idea of the coupling that produces Ishmael. It is she who gives birth to Isaac, and after Isaac was born, it is she who insists upon the banishment of Hagar and Ishmael. But with Ishmael out of Isaac's way, Sarah is no longer essential to the story, and with God's big test ahead, she may well have been an impediment to the fulfillment of God's grand plan. Neither Sarah's absence from Genesis 22 nor her death in the first line of Genesis 23 was an accident. Like Rebekah and Miriam and any number of other strong biblical women who follow, she has to be silenced and removed from the scene. And in Ostriker's analysis, nothing could be more telling or sobering than the words (in the traditional Hebrew version of the text, and maintained in the Septuagint, the King James Bible, and the Jewish Publication Society translation until its most recent, 1985, revision) with which Abraham twice asks the Hittites for land to bury his wife: "I am a stranger and a sojourner with you: give me a posses-sion of a burying-place with you, that I may bury my dead out of my sight."

The biblical scholar Phyllis Trible is no less frustrated by Sarah's absence. But she is less impressed than Ostriker and other feminist critics by Sarah's role in the previous chapters. Trible wants her in the story of the near sacrifice, but for a different reason. God tested Abraham, she argues, to see if he could let go of Isaac, let go of the human attachment most precious to him, let go of every-thing but God. But Abraham had already left his native land, his father's house, and his father. He had twice handed Sarah over to other men. He had risen early to see Hagar and Ishmael off. He has nothing to prove. It is Sarah who has repeatedly failed God's tests. It is she who needs to be encouraged to detach, to disavow her idolatrous worship of Isaac, and in doing so to find God. "The dynamic of the entire saga," Trible writes, "from its genealogical preface on, requires that Sarah be featured in the climactic scene, that she learn the meaning of obedience to God, that she find libera-tion from possessiveness, that she free Isaac from maternal ties, and that she emerge a solitary individual, non-attached, the model of faithfulness." In the spirit of the Syriac songwriters fifteen hundred years before her, Trible wants Sarah in the story not as a mother desperately clinging to her only son but as a woman fully prepared for God's test—Here I am—and thus completely worthy of God's blessing.

Others don't want Sarah in the story on those terms, and some don't want her in it at all. Among the latter is Wendy Zierler, a profes-sor of modern Hebrew literature, who recently went searching for a feminist reading of the *Akedah* and found it in the juxtaposition of Genesis 22 and Deuteronomy 6: "And you shall love the Lord your God with all your heart and all your being and with all your might." What Trible sees as Abraham's "liberation from possessiveness" en route to proximity to God and some great future, Zierler sees as costly detachment from and even the sacrifice of the people closest to him, the living sands and stars. Abraham passes God's test but ends up all alone. Zierler wants Sarah to remain outside the story as an alternative to Abraham's attachment to God by fear and awe. She wants Sarah as a "model of love," love of family and neighbors as well as (and as a form of) love of God. Zierler notes that the very next time the word "love" appears in the Bible, at the very end of Genesis 24, when Abraham's servant brings Rebekah to Isaac, Sarah is there: "And Isaac brought her into the tent of his mother Sarah and took Rebekah as his wife. And he loved her, and Isaac was consoled after his mother's death." "Even after her death," Zierler writes, "Sarah is the one who keeps the notion of love alive in the text."

All that was left was the funeral, which the Israeli poet Benjamin Galai, early among those to write from Sarah's point of view, evokes in his rewriting of the opening of Genesis 23, *Hayei Sarah*:

> *And the life of Sarah*
> *was*
> *a hundred years, twenty years, seven years.*
> *. . .*
> *The years of Sarah's life.*
>
> *And she died—*
> *But really,*
> *Her candle had gone out many days, many before*
> *Her last resting place was dust.*
> *And the coffin she lay in was made of all the years,*
> *The memory of wood cleft on another mount,*
> *On another mount, in the Land of Moriah.*

Sarah rested, but not always, even today, in peace. In the sea of sympathy, there has also been criticism, including criticism for her treatment of Hagar, which has occasionally been laced with the old but still chilling thought that the near sacrifice was punishment or payback, an instance of Sarah reaping what she sowed. In Shin Shifrah's "Hagar," an Israeli mother tries to allay her daughter's fear of the Arab other:

> *Do not fear, my daughter,*
> *Hagar,*
> *Only the name is strange,*
> *A storm in the desert*
> *A dry throat,*
> *Do not fear*
> *Hagar*
> *Because the destiny of Hagar*
> *Is waiting in ambush at the entrance*
> *To Sarai's*
> *Tent.*

Criticism has also come from Isaac, whose complaint is sometimes that his mother cooperated with his father ("Butcher me and bring my flesh back to my mother," one of Hanoch Levin's angry Isaacs commands Abraham) and sometimes simply that she failed to protest. In Israel, even the question "Where was Sarah?," which since the 1970s has so often been the starting point for sympathetic storytelling and analysis, has occasionally been turned against her, against all the mothers, as it is in a poem Yehudit Kafri published in 1988. Kafri's narrator wonders why Sarah depended on a God so tyrannical to protect Isaac, and why (as Abraham saddled the donkey) she herself did not say, "Do not raise your hand against the boy," and finally (if Abraham had ignored her):

> *Why did she not stand*
> *In the middle of the road*

And whisper through pursed lips:
You will not pass through this way
As long as I live!

I understand where Kafri and the others are coming from, but I
am old-fashioned enough to believe in authors and to hold them
responsible for who is and who is not in their stories. It was not
Sarah's fault she wasn't there. I am more inclined to put her in
and give her the chance to deliver those very lines or, as so many
have tried to do, to explore the meaning of her absence. Or the
cause of her death. You may recall that some rabbis imagined
her dying of shock when she learned where Abraham and Isaac
had gone. Others, her dying of joy when she learned that Isaac
had been spared. My favorite interpretation suggests a third
possibility. It comes from Rabbi Kalonymus Shapira, who found
himself having to explain Sarah's death to fellow worshippers and
students in the Warsaw Ghetto in early November 1939, one month
after a German bomb took the life of his son. "The Torah," he
said, "may also be telling us" that Sarah "died in order to show
God that a Jew should not be expected to suffer unlimited levels
of anguish. Even though a person, with the mercy of God, survives
and escapes death, nevertheless elements of his capability, his mind,
and his spirit are forever broken, and as a result of his ordeal, lost
to him. In the final analysis, what difference does it make, whether
all of me or part of me is killed?"

   If all else fails, as it so often does, I would try to find one more
way to express sadness and regret, as Eli Alon does in a poem he
published in 1989:

   In the beginning there was this story:
   a father
   his son
   the God
   and the sacrificial knife.

Sarai? Where is Sarai?
A small footnote
in an dreamed-up land
nothing but a springboard to
the Father
the God
taking over the stage.

What Sarai? Where is Sarai?
Have we ever had a mother
to protect us
to have mercy?
. . .
And when a son is born to us
What we will give him? What is there in our hearts
Besides that knife?

Alon's final question begins with an echo of Isaiah and ends with a shout-out (part tribute, and perhaps also part rebuke) to Haim Gouri, whose poem "Heritage" is a quietly devastating expression of resignation and fate, first published in 1960. Gouri was a young man, but his Abraham is old and the day is late. The ram arrives last, to answer the boy's question. Abraham sees the angel. The knife slips from his hand, and he turns to go. Isaac sees only his father's back. But the story doesn't end there. Recall Yehoshua's worry about the knife game. Look again at Rembrandt's oil.

Isaac, as the story goes, was not sacrificed.
He lived for many years,
Saw what pleasure had to offer, until his eyesight dimmed.

But he bequeathed that hour to his offspring.
They are born
With a knife in their hearts.

   Sarah was not there, in that poem, but half a century later,
toward the end of his ninth decade, Gouri closed a cycle of new
poems with the haunting cry "if only," if only she had been, the
nagging thought that perhaps "everything could have been different
on that Mountain, / if we had only listened to her voice."

28

~~~

The author of Ecclesiastes was exaggerating when he said there is nothing new under the sun. Either that, or he was a writer who prized sound more than precision, and he realized that it was more elegant to say that there is nothing new than to say that there is nothing new that doesn't have some old in it. For all the innovation, the careful analysis and the wild and crazy speculation, the clever application of critical theory and biblical criticism, the subtle and not-so-subtle subversion in poems and stories and songs, the measured criticism and boundless fury, the recasting of collective religious experience as secular national experience, family drama, even individual trauma and angst—for all that, the "new" more often than not had "occurred long before." Changes in context could be enormous. Changes in the meaning of words in the minds of writers and readers could be enormous. Changes in the uses to which words were put could be enormous. Changes in a particular commentary's currency could be enormous. Antecedents might be near. Or far. Or both, a chain extending back to antiquity. The new may be fully cognizant of the old. Or completely oblivious. All that I know for sure is that the day it is written or spoken, all commentary is modern commentary. And all commentary is rooted in the past, in tradition, often more than one.

. . .

The new didn't come out of nowhere, or all at once, or once and for all. It didn't extinguish or (always or everywhere) even displace the old, for history is not half a superhighway with all the cars and trucks traveling in the same direction at roughly the same speed. Nor is it a raging river or swollen stream, nor an arrow or straight line of any kind, nor even a stampede. At every moment, there were people on the shoulder, along the bank, above or below or to one side of the line, outside the fray; at every moment there were people who went about their religious lives in blissful innocence or studied ignorance of the ferment going on all around them. And at every moment there were people who paid close attention and in one way or another pushed back, or even stepped back, making history—like tradition—much more of a conversation, a conversation in time and across time, a dialogue, a dialectic, a debate, an argument, sometimes even a bit of a brawl.

What that means is that there have been, and there still are, commentators, Muslim, Christian, and Jewish, who insist that God didn't ask, wouldn't ask, and there have been, and still are, commentators who insist that he most certainly did. Among the latter were dozens of Southern Baptist ministers and church newspaper editors who, in 1969, were outraged by G. H. Davies's commentary on Genesis, commissioned for them by the Baptist Convention's educational board. They had many objections, but they were particularly incensed by Davies's interpretation of Genesis 22 (he had said that the sacrifice was Abraham's idea, not God's), which they believed "clouded a clear divine directive," and, like the historical scholarship that infected the whole volume, would only undermine Baptist belief in the literal truth and infallibility of the Bible. Davies was not without his defenders. Nonetheless, at the national convention the following year, messengers voted overwhelmingly to withdraw the volume, destroy all unsold copies, and find another writer to revise it. Two years later the revision appeared. Its author assured readers that today God certainly would not ask a man to sacrifice a son. In fact, from Abraham's day on, God's people could point to Mount Moriah as evidence that he didn't want human sacrifice. But Scripture got history right: the command had come from God.

What that means is that there are some who say that God should not have asked and there are others who reply that there is no "should" independent of God. Who could blame the latter for quoting the remarkable Kalonymus Shapira, who, in one more of his Warsaw sermons, had expressed that reply so trenchantly: The nations of the world, he said, even the best of them, believe that "truth exists in and of itself, and that God commanded the truth because the truth can be nothing but true." The Jewish people, on the other hand, believe that all the "truth that exists in the world" is true only "because God commanded it so, and wanted it so." When God commanded Abraham to sacrifice his son, "the binding of Isaac became the truth, and if He had not later commanded Abraham not to harm him, then the truth would have been to slaughter him."

More than half a century later, Seyyed Hossein Nasr, a distinguished scholar of Islam, in conversation about the story with a handful of Jews and Christians, seemed puzzled by all the hand-wringing, the fretting about God asking and Abraham obeying. Some clergymen and women even wondered how they could believe in such a God and celebrate such a man. Abraham, Nasr countered, was a friend of God, imbued with his spirit and presence, as close to God as a human could be. Isaac—or Ishmael—was a prophet who willingly chose to participate. We can't ask how we can believe in a God who asked for such a thing without asking "Where do we get our ethical norms? If we have a source of ethical knowledge that is independent of God, then we are not living in the biblical or Qur'anic world."

That means there are some who, teaching the Old Testament to Christian children, omit the near sacrifice altogether, skipping from

Isaac's birth to his marriage, or who tell the story quickly and talk a lot about Abraham's love of God. And there are others who explain it bluntly, asking kids to "try to imagine going out and killing" a beloved pet dog or cat "with a knife because some voice" in their head told them to. It would be very scary and might even seem impossible, but "God wants to see that we trust Him all the way," the way "Abraham trusted God enough to kill his only son." Another writer explains that because of Abraham's trust and his willingness, God was willing to sacrifice his son on that same hill and to let his son's blood wash away the sins of ordinary women and men. But only the sins of those who reached out to him, who let Jesus into their hearts: "This morning," he told them, "you are on the top of the hill. The lamb is there waiting to take your place. God is waiting to save you. The Holy Spirit is whispering into your ear to get saved. Will you this morning? Or will you burn in the fire of hell someday because you said no to God?"

There are some readers who diagnose Abraham as depressed or accuse him of abuse (a reenactor of his own childhood trauma) and there are others who insist that those who do say less about Abraham than their own lack of historical and religious imagination. Among the latter is Jon Levenson, a prolific scholar of Jewish studies and ancient Hebrew literature, with a deep and abiding passion for the theology of the Hebrew Bible. Levenson is a mild-mannered professor and public lecturer, fond of puns ("there was lots of sects in Ancient Israel") and wisecracks with a critical edge ("Some say that after returning from Moriah, Abraham and Isaac never spoke again. Show me where they spoke before.") But in response to commentators whom he believes have abused Abraham, he can wield a fearsome pen. The mistake Abraham's critics make, he argues, is to think of the patriarch as they would think of a father today who sets out to sacrifice a child. That father would be acting in flagrant disregard—in Jewish tradition alone—for the provisions for substitution in Exodus; the prohibition of child sacrifice in Leviticus and Deuteronomy; and the Talmud's elevation of law over oracle and prophecy. To diagnosis that father as deranged or abusive, Levenson acknowledges, would be fair, "but it is a symptom of acute myopia and mind-numbing parochialism to think that this must also have been the case in a society that practiced sacrifice (even, on occasion and for a while, child-sacrifice) and did not confuse it with murder."

That means that there are writers who are furious at their fathers, at all the fathers. Remember Yitzhak Laor, who in the aftermath of Israel's first war in Lebanon had likened Abraham to the Amalekites and warned all the Isaacs to watch out for him. And there are others, including Laor a decade later, who remember their fathers as hardworking and comforting to them when they were sick and when, with military service looming, they were afraid to die. If there is a crime now, it is not against a people. Nor is it the attempted sacrifice of a son. It is much more mundane, but painful all the same: a father's inability to understand his son's experience, especially in war, and his inability to see that however much he would like to protect him—

> *I won't let them take you, my son*
> *I am the ram*
> *I am the angel*
> *I am your father*

—he can't.

That means that there are still some who imagine that Abraham killed Isaac, including the biblical scholars who believe or suspect that the story was an E sacrifice story (verses 1–10 and 15–

19) transformed into an aborted sacrifice story by a later editor or redactor, perhaps with the simple addition of verses 11–14 and the phrase "a second time" in verse 15. Take those lines out and you will read a sacrifice story too. Like so many readers before them, the scholars who hold this view note Isaac's absence at the end of the story. Source criticism provides them with another intriguing clue. As Richard Elliott Friedman puts it, "Isaac never again appears as a character in E."

And there are others—many others—who are as sure as they are sure of anything that Abraham stopped and sacrificed a ram instead. One is the father of a twenty-eight-year-old Iraqi who in the early years of the second Iraq war was accused of collaborating with U.S. forces. The young man was said to have provided the information, tragically inaccurate, that resulted in a botched raid. Civilians were killed. The young man's tribe was humiliated. Villagers, fearing insult and retribution from the tribe of the victims, gave the father an ultimatum: "Close the door" on the matter, they said, or we'll kill your entire family. Otherwise an outsider would close it for them, sparking a long and bloody cycle of violence. The father and another son did the deed. Not long afterward, Anthony Shadid, the indefatigable Lebanese-born American journalist, sat with the father. He spoke quietly, with tears in his eyes. "I have the heart of a father and he's my son," he said. "Even the prophet Abraham didn't have to kill his son."

That means that there are some who struggle to make sense of what they take to be the baffling contradiction between Abraham's eloquent questions after God revealed his plan to destroy Sodom (first he asks if he'll punish the innocent along with the guilty, then he asks if he won't spare the guilty on account of the innocent) and his abject silence after God commanded him to sacrifice his son. And there are those who insist there is no contradiction at all. In the first instance, God confided in Abraham and perhaps sought his counsel. In the second, God commanded him to do something. In the first, Abraham raised questions of justice in the context of sin. In the second, he understood that Isaac's innocence was imperative: the victim was supposed to be without blemish. In the first instance, Abraham argued and God listened. In the second, Abraham did exactly what God had asked him to do—he served God—even when doing so meant, in the words of the Israeli scientist and philosopher Yeshayahu Leibowitz, separating that service from "all human needs, feelings, and values, even from the great historical ends," the nation God had promised him. As Leibowitz sees it, the sequence of events made perfect sense, for it is the service to God, not the ethical argument, on which Judaism stands: "The highest symbol of Jewish faith is the stance of Abraham on Mount Moriah, where all human values were annulled and overridden by fear and love of God."

There are Catholic and Protestant clergy, theologians, and scholars who speak and write against the idealization of senseless sacrifice, the fixation on pain and suffering, the reveling in violence and bloodshed. And there are ministers and priests who deliver sermons (depending on the denomination, on Holy Thursday, Good Friday, Easter Vigil, or the third Sunday of Pentecost in the first year of the lectionary cycle or the second Sunday of Lent in the second year) about the purity of Abraham's heart, the primacy of his faith, and the magnificence of the sacrifice that his sacrifice led to: "The image of Isaac carrying the wood of the sacrifice tips us off that this story points beyond itself to a future sacrifice beyond all comprehension. The ram caught in the thicket is not the true substitute, and the true sacrifice does not take place upon Moriah. It is the Lamb, not the ram, God's Son, not Abraham's, that is offered. Like Isaac, he carried the wood of the sacrifice up the slope of Mt. Calvary. But unlike Isaac, he did so freely, knowing what that sacrifice would cost him. And his sacrifice accomplishes what no animal sacrifice could possibly accomplish—the eternal salvation of all willing to accept this free gift of love."

What that means is that there are Muslim parents who when asked by their children to explain the Festival of the Sacrifice (which comes on the tenth day of the last month of the Islamic calendar, at the height of the Haj, and during which, to this day, millions of Muslims sacrifice a goat, a cow, or a lamb, or arrange for someone to sacrifice one for them—one-third they eat, one-third they share with friends, one-third they give to the poor) quickly change the subject. Or explain that the lamb they have just sacrificed is the same one that will someday lead them to paradise over the knife-blade-narrow al-Sirat Bridge. Or tell them that Abraham knew that God wouldn't make him go through with it—no one he loved so much would hurt him or his son. And there are those who explain that they are commemorating Abraham's willingness to sacrifice what he loved most in the world without any expectation of reward, his demonstration that there was nothing he would not do for Allah.

That means that there are Jewish commentators who argue that Jews don't suffer or die for God, that Jews live for God, that the God of pain and suffering is a false god. And there are Jewish commentators who argue that they most certainly do. For the latter, Rabbi Joseph B. Soloveitchik, one of the twentieth century's seminal Jewish philosophers, Talmud scholars, and teachers of Modern Orthodoxy, is an irresistible authority. Soloveitchik once said that he "recoiled" from all the talk of how "the observance of *mitzvot* is beneficial for digestion, for sound sleep, for family harmony, and for social position." The religious act may end in joy, but it "is fundamentally an experience of suffering." God says: "Offer your sacrifice!" It started with Abraham: "He was not to fool himself in thinking that he'd get another son." Or that he would ever forget Isaac: "Out of your sleep you will call for Yitzchak, and when you wake up you will find your tent desolate and forsaken." Nevertheless, God demanded that sacrifice, and what began on that mountain continued in the great Temples built upon it and then in the synagogue and throughout our religious lives today: "Build an altar, arrange the pieces of wood. Kindle the fire. Take the knife to slaughter your existence for My sake. Thus commands the awesome God. This approach is the basis of prayer. Man surrenders himself to God. He approaches the awesome God and the approach expresses itself in the sacrifice and *Akedah* of oneself."

What that means is that there are mothers who blame God, as a mother does in Chava Cohen-Pinchas's poem "A Request." She's a nursing mother, baby in hand, her arms stretched out like the ram's horn in the bush. She asks God to listen, to make his "Sukkah of mercy / Like the shade of the vine and the fig." She asks him not to test her, not now of all times, not to play hide-and-seek. She calls out to him, as God called to Adam and Eve in the Garden, "*Ayekah?*" But he's not around:

> *With my short hand I cover my eyes*
> *My voice is lost in a scream*
> *With no Sound*
>
> *Where are you (Ayekah).*

And there are mothers, like the mother in Shin Shifrah's "Isaac," who blame themselves:

> *For me no ram was held in the thicket.*
> *I bound*
> *And I slaughtered.*

God did not pay attention.
He laughed.

Not even the notion (seemingly as benign as it has been ubiquitous) that the story was originally a polemic against child sacrifice has gone uncontested. In recent years, Jon Levenson has made the most wide-ranging case against it, arguing that it is a kind of wishful thinking or apology that can't survive a close, critical, and clear-eyed reading of the text in the context of the Hebrew Bible and numerous other ancient Near Eastern sources. God says in Exodus: "You shall give Me the first-born among your sons." "Most fathers," Levenson writes, "did not have to carry out this hideous demand. But some did. Abraham knew it was his turn when he heard God in his own voice, ordering the immolation of Isaac."

At some point in time it became permissible, perhaps even preferable, to substitute an animal for a child. At some point, revealed law proscribed the sacrifice of children. In the seventh and sixth centuries BCE, prophets, usually attributing the practice to the influence of neighbors and their gods but in at least one instance (Ezekiel) attributing it to bad laws given as punishment by God, vehemently condemned it. But the very terms and the vehemence with which Ezekiel and Jeremiah waged war against child sacrifice suggest that the proscription did not take hold overnight.

Even as practice yielded to law and polemic, the religious idea behind it remained strong. So strong that Levenson considers it more precise to say that child sacrifice was not eradicated so much as it was transformed, transformed into rituals of donation (paschal offerings, consecration to the priesthood, circumcision, and prayer) and into narratives: Stories that express the idea that the beloved son belongs to God. Stories that express the idea that God's promise to Israel was grounded in a father's willingness to sacrifice his son. Stories that express the idea that the dire threat to Isaac, and Israel, was inseparable from the blessing, that God's chosen always suffer humiliation before they exult in redemption. And in Levenson's telling, that humiliation and redemption (death and resurrection) of latter-born but beloved sons in conflict with their older brothers did not end with Ishmael and Isaac and Esau and Jacob and Joseph and all his brothers. Rather, it ended up animating the great and long-lasting conflict between at least two more siblings: Judaism ("Tell Pharaoh that Israel is my firstborn son") and Christianity ("This is my beloved son, with whom I am well pleased").

Like just about everyone who has written about Genesis 22 since the publication of *The Last Trial,* Levenson is indebted to Shalom Spiegel. Spiegel, too, had seen child sacrifice behind the story and ancient understandings of it. He, too, had seen the celebration of an eager Abraham and a willing Isaac, of blood and ashes, of death and resurrection, rooted in the transformation or sublimation of practice into ritual and narrative. But whereas Spiegel identifies the practice as pagan and the idealization of it as an atavism that Jews sought to suppress, Levenson sees both practice and idealization as essential to Israelite and rabbinic theology. Whereas Spiegel is among those who imagine that the primary purpose of the story was to attach a great name to a new norm ("abolish human sacrifice, substitute animals instead"), Levenson demurs. God does not command the substitution. The story lacks the kind of phrase that often signals a biblical explanation ("and Abraham offered up the ram as a burnt offering instead of his son, as is done to this day"). And later tradition does not refer back to the incident as the reason for the redemption of the firstborn. Might the story have signaled the *permissibility* of substitution? Perhaps, Levenson says. But only modern distance from and enlightened distaste for the ideal of sacrifice could make it possible for readers to imagine that a story in which God commands Abraham to sacrifice Isaac and then rewards him for his willingness to do so was intended to reveal God's unequivocal opposition to human sacrifice.

· · ·

It is a challenging and utterly absorbing interpretation. In some places it is simply dazzling. In others, merely profound. But it is not the last word. Heavens willing, that won't come until the end of time. There are others who believe that just because the story wasn't a polemic against or even a straightforward etiology of substitution doesn't mean it was, in the beginning, an explicit idealization of child sacrifice. Stories, they say (and Levenson himself repeatedly shows), work in such complicated ways. It is possible that it was neither a polemic nor celebration, but rather a story about God's care for all those who obey him, penned in a moment of deep despair about Israel's fate. It is also possible that, written or redacted long after the arguments about child sacrifice were settled, it was both a celebration of *and* a polemic against the practice. Israel gets to demonstrate that its God doesn't want it, and Israel also gets to celebrate the idea of it. Remember: there was a lot of talk: endless accounts of this king or that group of wayward people passing children through the fire; passages in Exodus in which God seems to ask for the firstborn; and one instance—the king of Moab, fighting against Israel—in which the sacrifice of a son appears to have been effective. Yet there is not a single instance in the entire Hebrew Bible in which an actual human sacrifice is celebrated.

Idealization is one way of reading the story, but it is just one of many possible ways of reading it, and even in Levenson's own account it is a reading that gets stronger as time goes on. Late Second Temple interpreters and then late-antique rabbis were more enthusiastic than anyone before them—or anyone whose sentiments we are aware of. Their enthusiasm reveals a lot about the theology of rabbinic Judaism, and perhaps, also, the relationship between it and early Christianity, but the later that enthusiasm comes, the less it tells us about earlier readings and meanings and contexts. When evidence comes from a dizzying number of times and places—and when so much of that evidence is difficult to interpret and some of it is difficult to date—it is almost inevitable that even the most critically and historically informed Bible scholars will be reading some of it backward, or at least in several different directions at once. I'd be the very last—the thought would never come to my mind—to fault Levenson for using rabbinic enthusiasm to suggest things about the story's ancient meanings and context. Nor for occasionally getting carried away and interpreting like a great medieval or late-antique rabbi himself, as he does when he says that when God called, "Abraham knew it was his turn."

We don't know that and can't know that from the story or its context. There is no other hint of child sacrifice in Abraham's day or anywhere else in Genesis. That Abraham knew exactly what to do when God called tells us no more than that he knew exactly where to go. God could have shown him one as easily as he showed him the other. Whenever it was written or redacted, whether we read it as actual history, an ancient folktale, or a sacred story, it is set in the imagined age of the Patriarchs, centuries before the appearance of the ritual, literature, archaeology, mythology, and law on which every possible historical argument for the practice or transformation of child sacrifice is based. We'll never know what Abraham was thinking. All we know for sure is what, in a story, he says and does. His silence is one that we, as historians, can't fill.

That means that there are some who can imagine themselves responding to God's call just as Abraham did, just as the poet Uri Zvi Greenberg imagines himself responding, in his impassioned tribute to Jerusalem, "city of the Father's glorious trial," where even on a rainy night, "that fire, kindled at dawn, still burns on the hill":

"If God were to command me now, as once He did
My ancient Father—I would surely obey,"
Sing my heart and my flesh on this night of rain,
As the Angels of Peace stand at the head of my sleeping
   children!

What can equal this glory, this wondrous zeal—
Alive since that ancient dawn to this very moment—for
the Mount of Moriah?
The blood of the covenant sings on in the father's fervent
body.
He is prepared to offer his sacrifice on the Temple Mount
at dawn.

And there are others, like Ra'yah Harnik, a poet and (after the first Lebanon war) a grieving mother who, writing just three decades later, in the early 1980s, turns Greenberg's and Abraham's "Here I am" into an equally emphatic "Here I am not":

I will not offer
My first born for sacrifice
Not I

At night God and I
Make reckonings
Who can claim what

I know and am
Grateful
But not my son
And not
for sacrifice

29

There is no end to it. Not a day goes by when someone, somewhere, doesn't add to it. Not a day. And even now, after all these years, I still haven't had my fill. But it wasn't all the biblical commentary or scholarship or even the ever-widening circle of conversation that initially drew me to the story or prompted me to write about it.

Awkward as it is to admit, I knew next to nothing about any of that when I began.

I came to it from an entirely different direction.

It was early in the third millennium. Dark days. Terror attacks had sparked a global war on terror and there was no end to either war or terror in sight. Wherever I turned, I heard the word "sacrifice." Eulogists praised soldiers for making the ultimate sacrifice. Proponents of staying the course in Iraq in the face of a fierce insurgency and the threat of civil war argued that if we withdrew, our dead would have sacrificed their lives in vain. Opponents called for the repeal of recently enacted tax cuts, and perhaps even a reinstatement of the military draft, to ensure that the sacrifice exacted in two surreally distant conflicts was not borne entirely by a few. Americans accused the parents of Afghani, Pakistani, and Iraqi suicide bombers of sacrificing their children. Afghanis, Pakistanis, and Iraqis accused coalition commanders of doing the same. One American antiwar activist, video camera in hand, stalked pro-war congressmen and prominent political commentators, asking them if they would sacrifice one of their children to retake Falujah, a city they had not heard of before 2004.

I started reading about sacrifice, and then child sacrifice, in history and literature, sacred and profane. I wanted to know who had sacrificed children and when and why. I found a slew of accusations (one group of people accusing another of sacrificing children) and a lively scholarly debate (truly heroic efforts to tease experience out of scant evidence) about which of those accusations were true. I also found the story of Abraham and Isaac, the ground zero of Western child sacrifice stories. Before long I had turned from books and essays *about* the story to the story itself, and then to all the Abraham stories in Genesis, and then to commentary on those stories, starting in antiquity.

It was an unexpected turn, but I was hardly the only one who had taken it. A lot of people were reading, talking, and writing about religion, especially religious extremism. And though the conversation was dominated by talk of Islamic extremism, fair-minded observers couldn't help but notice that here at home it was not only militant Muslims who posed a threat to pluralism, equality, freedom, and secular democracy. Right-wing Christians campaigned against gay rights, women's reproductive rights, sex education, contraception (even when it meant AIDS prevention), stem cell research, climate science, the teaching of evolution, and any number of other ungodly manifestions of the separation of the Christian church and the state. And when they turned their attention from social issues to mosques, madrassas, Qu'ran-carrying magistrates, and sharia law, they confirmed the fears of many, not all of them Muslim, that our wars near and far were at least part crusade. Jews had their extremists too, if just a few, a small minority of a small minority, but some of them—like the religious nationalists in the occupied territories and their allies in Israel proper—were worrisome way out of proportion to their numbers because, I'd like to think, of the tinderbox in which they lived and the roadblock they seemed to pose to Mideast peace. I couldn't help notice that many settlers based their claim to the West Bank on God's covenant with Abraham. Some threatened to die as martyrs before they gave up their land, no matter who, Arab or Jew, tried to take it away.

In the midst of all that, one small but exceedingly loud group of writers insisted that religion itself, not just resurgent fundamentalism, was at the root of all the trouble. Moderate and even liberal religion simply provide cover for the crazies, masking the unreason and the truly deleterious influence of the ideas and beliefs at religion's core. As they do, they end up legitimating and reinforcing reactionary religious authority. Once you grant texts (or gods) authority, they said, you can't complain when people do things with them that you don't like.

In every indictment, Abraham was named. The charges extended well beyond his mistreatment of Isaac, a few bad days in a distant land a long time ago. Critics considered him culpable for what they took to be the long half-life of his perfect performance on God's gratuitous test: centuries of patriarchy, persecution, and abuse; crusading, jihad, and holy war; blind, deaf, and dumb obedience and faith. Who, they asked, could calculate the damage done by the idea (that we must be prepared to sacrifice what we hold most dear) at the heart of Abraham's devotion? When more sanguine observers objected to all that and maintained that he, the common father of Muslims, Christians, and Jews, was actually the last best hope for interfaith dialogue, reconciliation, and comity, his critics scoffed, pointing out that Abraham's descendants have fought over his inheritance, God's blessing for the ages, much more than they have gathered in peace around his table. What he really was was the father of killing in God's name. (And his apologists: they were the first to invoke the Nuremberg defense.) In every argument, the near sacrifice was introduced as evidence that God is a monster, or a delusion, or at best not so great. That people should give up their faith.

I had nothing in common with and little sympathy for fundamentalists or fanatics of any denomination, least of all for those whose absolute certainty contributed to their turn to violence. I had a host of things in common with even their harshest critics. Some of them were family and close friends. On many days I myself wondered what kind of God would, for no good reason, command a man to sacrifice his son, and why so many people would celebrate, as the patriarch of patriarchs, a man so prepared to obey. There were all sorts of things about Islam, Christianity, and Judaism, past and present, that rubbed me the wrong way, though I would be quick to add that I didn't and don't know remotely enough about any one of them to render a good or fair judgment. The idea of my judging religion, en bloc, was out of the question.

But by that time I did know something about Abraham and the story and, much to my surprise, I found myself inclined to stick up for him and it. I did not expect to persuade everyone to read the story as I read it. I do not now. But I did expect that at least a few would find, as I have found, more than a little consolation, perhaps even reason for hope, in the life of the story. I feel sure that even those who despise the story and dismiss as beside the point all my talk of Abraham as a character, the story as a story, and (most ludicrous of all) the author as an author (let alone an author who got the story wrong), will acknowledge that what people have made of Abraham and the story is much more complicated than the harshest criticism allows.

For one thing, readers have had misgivings from the beginning. If there was ever a time when people paid close attention to the story and were completely comfortable with it, as it was, on the page, a time readers didn't think it in need of repair, there is no record of it. But the devout didn't think they could get rid of it. Or take some wide detour around it. It stood between creation and nation, or salvation. So they asked questions, and answered them with commentary, interpretation, and stories, which in turn generated more questions, and more interpretation, and more stories.

Out of all that, dissenting traditions were born. In the second half of the eighth century BCE, the prophet Micah laid out a long list of things that God might want from him (calves a year old, thousands of rams, myriad streams of oil, his firstborn) before concluding that all he really wanted was for him to "do justice, and to love goodness, and to walk modestly" with his God. A century later Jeremiah went even further, saying that the idea of human sacrifice had never even entered God's mind. Some scholars say Micah paid homage to the ideal of child sacrifice in the very way that he argued that it wasn't what God wanted, and that Jeremiah protested way too much. Both, they say, were rewriting history, God's and Israel's early years. But even if they were, it is telling that they wanted people to believe their revisionist history and theology, and it is also telling that the rabbis who called attention to their words in the Mishnah and Talmud wanted people to believe it too. Just as it is telling that there were rabbis in late antiquity who imagined Abraham stalling, and rabbis who imagined him praying along the way that he wouldn't have to perform the sacrifice, and rabbis who imagined God's angels weeping at the injustice of it all, and rabbis who imagined God's daughter, the Torah, rejecting Abraham as a suitor because he didn't plead with God on behalf of his son.

Abraham has had critics forever. The story has been used as evidence that God abhors human sacrifice for nearly as long. And if martyrdom had not been hotly contested, apologists probably would not have gone to such great lengths to turn it into sacred historical precedent. Any honest appraisal of the merits and demerits of our religious traditions would have to take our interpretative traditions, all those questions and answers, all the things that people have done with what they have inherited, into account.

In fact, I couldn't imagine a better foil for the fiction at the heart of fundamentalism, in all its varieties, than the fluidity, multiplicity, and variety of revelation over time, the thinking and rethinking, the talk and the argument, the writing and rewriting, the vast array and mélange of meanings, the engagement with troubling texts, and the marriage (at times happy, at times troubled, at times both) of tradition and innovation. Nor could I imagine a better way to display that variety and fluidity than to shine some light on the long and protean life of nineteen lines of ancient literature, a story that many (including the vast majority of the people who have taken it into their own hands as if it were a clump of soft clay) believe to be the work of God.

It was then that it first occurred to me to write a brief history of the story, a book about some of the things that people have done with it, Muslims, Christians, and especially Jews, who have returned to it more often and have revised it in more different ways.

30

No sooner did that thought occur to me than I began to have doubts.

Where would I start? How would I ever get a handle on two thousand years of commentary and two hundred years of scholarship, to say nothing of all the ritual and liturgy and literature and drama and music and art? How would I figure out where to survey and where to take soundings, how to strike a balance between depth and breadth, when I would need to know more than I knew about a commentator's life and times to understand a particular commentary, when I would need to show or tell more to explain? Who would stick with me? How many at this late date would care? I felt a little like Kafka's Abraham: He has faith. He wants to do what he has been called to do, in the right spirit, in the right way, but he simply can't believe that it is he who has been called to do it.

It didn't help—though of course it did—that every single time I mentioned the project to anyone—every time, to anyone—he or she recommended a take on the story I just had to see, watch, listen to, read:

- An illustrated catechism one of my students had saved from Sunday school.
- An essay on the interpretation of dreams in medieval Islamic exegesis.
- A play written by the Calvinist theologian Theodore Beza, who put the devil in the costume of a monk.

· A public radio program on young people who are "losing" their religion. One thirty-three-year-old, who was raised a Muslim but is now an atheist, recalls hearing the story of Abraham when he was in the fifth or sixth grade: "His God tells him to sacrifice his son. Then he takes his son to sacrifice him, and he turns into a goat." And even back then he thought: "That's crazy! Why would this guy do this? Just because he heard a voice in his head, he went to sacrifice his son and it turned into a goat? There's no way that this happened. I wasn't buying it."

· Oratorios of Carissimi and Charpentier.

· A poem of Emily Dickinson.

· The commentary of the Lubavitcher Rebbe, recommended to me by a young Lubavitcher in Bryant Park. He had asked if I wanted to wrap tefillin. I said, "No, thank you," and then asked him if he wanted to talk about the *Akedah*. He lit up and asked: "Do you know why Abraham's sacrifice was the greatest of all sacrifices, greater even than all the martyrdom that came after?"

"Why?" I asked.

Because, he explained at great length, the martyr sacrifices his life in order to preserve his self: his beliefs, his ideals, his understanding of God, all the things he is and lives for. Abraham sacrificed his very self, thereby demonstrating that at the core of one's being lies not that self but the connection to the creator, the spark of divinity within. "Check out *Vayera*," he said, "at chabad.org." Later, I did. The entry is several thousand words, most of which he had recited by heart.

· Goldfaden's opera. Britten's canticle. Stravinsky's sacred ballad.

· The commentary of one imam, also posted on the Web, delivered in a Friday sermon during the Festival of the Sacrifice, recommended to me by another young man as I stood outside a midtown Manhattan mosque. The prophet's greatness, the young man explained, was his willingness to sacrifice not just his life but his entire self to Allah.

· Agnon's *Only Yesterday*. Mossinsohn's *In the Negev Plains*. Makiya's *The Rock*. Saramago's *Cain*.

· Several recent Rosh Hashanah sermons in which rabbis have hypothesized that Isaac was living with Down syndrome or some other form of developmental disability.

· The drawings, paintings, sculptures, and photographs of Shoshana Heimann, Avraham Ofek, Menashe Kadishman, Natan Nuchi, and Adi Nes.

· "The Parable of the Old Man and the Young," penned by Wilfred Owen, an English poet and, in 1918, a soldier on the western front. Decades before his theme became a regular trope of antiwar protest ("It's always the old to lead us to the war, it's always the young to fall"), Owen's Isaac is a young soldier in the trenches, "bound" by his father "with belts and straps." Abraham stretches forth his knife. The angel says stop, points to the thicket, and commands him to offer the Ram of Pride instead:

> *But the old man would not do so, but slew his son,*
> *And half the seed of Europe, one by one.*

Owen's turn came as his unit crossed the Sambre-Oise Canal, at Ors, one week before the armistice ending the war was signed.

· The sculpture of George Segal, commissioned to commemorate the killings at Kent State, which sits in the shadow of the apse wall of the Princeton University Chapel. Sometime before I last visited, a vandal or prankster or found-art exegete placed a condom on Abraham's thigh-high knife.

· Any number of psychoanalytical interpretations, starting with that of Erich Wellisch, who sees in the near sacrifice

Abraham's effort to resolve the Oedipus conflict and overcome the death instinct with love.

· A rap song, a rock band, a clever British sketch comedy skit, countless comic strips (including *Peanuts*), a memoir (*The Last Testament*) attributed to God, and now (I kid you not) a video game called *The Binding of Isaac*. The object of the game is to keep Isaac away from his mentally ill mother, who believes God wants him as a sacrifice.

· The *Encyclopedia of the Bible and Its Reception,* in which the entry on the *Aqedah* is forty columns of fine print.

· A sixteenth- or seventeenth-century Cretan play, in verse.

· Sari Nusseibeh's *What Is a Palestinian State Worth?*

· A pivotal scene in Fatih Akin's *The Edge of Heaven,* in which a Muslim man, long estranged from his father, explains the Festival of the Sacrifice to a Christian friend.

   "We have the same story," she says.

   He recalls that as a child he was frightened by it. His mother had died young. He asked his father if he would sacrifice him if God asked.

   "What did your father answer?" his friend asks.

   "He said he would even make God his enemy in order to protect me."

· Avivah Zornberg's *Genesis: The Beginning of Desire.*

· Daniel Mendelsohn's *The Lost.*

· Orhan Pamuk's *The Museum of Innocence.*

· David Grossman's *To the End of the Land.*

· Yael Feldman's *Glory and Agony.*

· Chinua Achebe's *Things Fall Apart.*

I started writing. My doubts lingered. I wasn't the only one who had them.

My mother, heretofore the most loyal and indulgent fan of my work, repeatedly asked my wife and siblings why I was writing about "that" story, and she made no effort to hide her distress from me. Isaac's line alone ("the saddest line in all literature," she once said) was more than her heart could bear. It was visceral. Every time she overheard me talking about it, she would grab her head by the hair, as if she were trying to pull it out, and say, "Stop, stop. I hate that story. I can't listen to another word."

A trade book editor, another fan, said he was fascinated by the subject and intrigued by my take on it, but he wondered if I was qualified to write the book. "You have no training or special expertise in any relevant area," he said. "You don't even have the languages you would need."

"It is worse than that," I said to him (and forever afterward to anyone who would listen). "The real problem is not that I am not qualified. It is that I know how much I do not know."

A neighbor of mine, whose observance of Judaism includes the study of a page of Talmud a day, was even more skeptical. "There are limits to interpretation," he said, "boundaries you can't cross." He calls my approach "everyone gets a say" and "anything goes" and he thinks it makes the past a simple projection of the present. What I am doing, he believes, is substituting individual preference ("my story") for received tradition, the authority and collective wisdom of the men who have transmitted Scripture and revelation from generation to generation and together, as a religious community, continue that work today. "Don't surrender to the zeitgeist," he says. "Don't succumb to the rot that all truths are relative, interpretations equally valid, authorial intentions meaningless. Before you know it you'll be saying that the words belong to readers, that writers are merely the first of them, that the author is dead."

I assure him that reports of the death of the author are greatly exaggerated. Not even the rage for sampling, pastiche, homage, collage, impersonation, copying, pasting, mash-up, and flat-out plagiarism that has characterized the early digital age has killed him—or her. He's as alive as he has ever been, maybe more so.

Another neighbor, equally observant, objects (with a wry smile) every time I refer to the story as a story. "It is not a story," he says.

But I was determined or stubborn or foolhardy or simply in thrall with the material. And I thought the time was right. So I plowed ahead, reading and writing and talking (or so it seemed) about nothing else. Still, it did not come easily. Pages accumulated. If I told you how many it took to produce each one of these, you wouldn't believe me. If I showed you, you would worry. By the time I had a rough draft of the whole thing, years had passed and I could not call my history brief.

"How will you know when you're finished?" one friend asks me, about once a week. "When you have read enough?"

"It's hard to know," I say. "There is no end to it."

"Maybe not," he says, "but more does not equal better."

"Time's up," another says. "Put down your pen. Let go of it."

Those two could not be more enthusiastic about the project. Others are less so.

"You really want to celebrate this story?" one friend asks. We talk a lot. Sometimes we argue.

"I am not celebrating," I say. "I am showing what people have done with it."

"What they've done with it? You want to celebrate? You need to get out a little."

"Not everything," I say.

"What then? When?" another friend asks. "Not a day goes by that I don't see a photograph of the gruesome aftermath of a suicide bombing or some other form of religious violence. Haven't we had enough sacrifice? Enough doing in the name of God?"

"You are cherry-picking a meaning," I say.

"It's not as if it is an obscure meaning," he says.

"But it's just one," I say.

"Yes, one. What God asks, you do. What you think God wants, you do. Even kill."

"But we are not stuck with any one meaning," I say. "Not the original meaning, not the literal meaning, not the latest meaning, not the dominant meaning, not the meaning to a historian, not the meaning to a theologian, not the meaning to the most orthodox or the most reformed."

"I think a lot of people have been stuck with one meaning," he says. "Or struck. It is time to move on."

"Would that we could," I say.

"We can," he says. "But even if we couldn't, you are not just acknowledging lineage, deviant genes in our cultural pool. You are full of pride. You're trying to rehabilitate a terrible tradition by excavating and restoring a few rare artifacts."

"Some of those artifacts have become common currency," I say. "Others remain promising possibilities."

"You have drunk the Kool-Aid. Or turned Talmudic. You are so caught up in the minutiae, in the esoteric, in the tiniest twists and turns of text and interpretation, that you've completely lost sight of the big picture."

"Big pictures have their place," I say. "But so do the minutiae. The twists and turns. The give-and-take."

"One doesn't have to be an in-your-face atheist to dislike this story, you know. Or to be alarmed by your fondness for it."

"I want to keep the conversation going. It still—"

"Occasionally it inoculates someone against religion," he says. "That's the only good it does today."

"It still turns readers into writers," I say. "It forces us to think through and beyond what is written, and given. It makes us add and take away."

"Listen to you. Soon you'll be reciting Micah and Jeremiah. You love the story. You defend it as if you wrote it yourself."

And what could I say? I wanted to revise it and have it too.

I did, and I do.

Acknowledgments

My greatest debt is to the scribes, translators, commentators, scholars, writers, and artists, only a small fraction of whom I have managed to mention in all these pages, who have wrestled with this story before me. Three scholars I must mention here are David Nirenberg, Barry Walfish, and Steve Whitfield. At the eleventh hour, each of them took the time to read the manuscript and provide essential encouragement, criticism, and suggestions for revision. No one, mentioned or unmentioned, bears any responsibility for my errors and missteps.

Two terrific institutions, one small (Paragraph, the writer's workspace on Fourteenth Street) and one large (the New York Public Library on Fifth Avenue and Forty-Second Street), provided me with a place to work at two critical moments toward the end. Thanks to Lila Cecil, Ally Collier, and Joy Parisi at Paragraph, and Jay Barksdale, Allen Room liaison at the library, for facilitating my residencies, and to so many fellow writers and scholars for fine and fun company during breaks.

My agent, Anne Edelstein, and my editor, Dan Frank, have once again been great readers, critics, and friends. Their support and their patience illuminate the limits of our understanding of both reason and faith. At Schocken Books, I am also grateful to Jillian Verrillo, Lindsey Ross, Muriel Jorgensen, Nicole Pedersen, and so many others whose names I do not know.

Ongoing support from chancellors, provosts, deans, department chairs, and department administrators at Rutgers University, Newark, where I teach history and creative writing, has made my writing life possible. These colleagues have not only tolerated my waywardness but actually cheered me on. Special thanks to David Hosford, Steve Diner, Phil Yeagle, Sallie Kasper, John Gunkel, Jack Lynch, Deborah Williams, Fran Bartkowski, Gary Farney, Clement Price, Christina Strasburger, and fi nally two dear friends as well as inspired leaders, Jan Lewis and Beryl Satter.

Writing books is hard. Getting them to readers is harder. Robert Davidson has had some inspired ideas about how to go about the latter, starting with the symposium with which the book now begins. I could not be more grateful to him for those ideas, but also for thinking the book worth his efforts in the first place. I hope this is just the first of the books I work on with him and his terrific colleagues at Sandstone Press.

I have been working on this book for a long time, and there are so many others to thank, for so many different kinds of things: Noah Bickart, Barry Bienstock, Omri Boehm, Deb Bohr, Alice Dark, Naomi Danis, Vivian Dietz, Bruce Dorsey, Greg Downs, Dan Ernst, Joy Ernst, Jody Falco, Ruth Feldstein, Richard Gaskins, Rigoberto Gonzales, Rachel Hadas, Ellen Herman, Martha Hodes, Tayari Jones, John Keene, Diane Klein, David Lelyveld, John McGreevy, Jani Masur, Lou Masur, Matthew Moore, Jim Oakes, Jayne Anne Phillips, Aaron Sachs, Bob Sadowsky, Akhil Sharma, Brenda Shaughnessy, Jeffrey Steinman, Ezer Vierba, Sean Wilentz, Jeff Fischer, Eliza McFeely, Karen McFeely, Drake McFeely, Mary McFeely, Bill McFeely, Len Tesler, Wendy Goodman, Sue Weil, Sandy Goodman, Deb Bernstein, Bob Goodman, Jon Mohrer, Jill Mohrer, Jackson Goodman, Samuel Goodman, Jennifer McFeely, Burton Goodman, and most of all my mother, Rachel Lehr. She really did hate the story, but she still would have loved this book.

Notes

~~~~~~~~

CHAPTER 2

14 the way the opening: Genesis 12:1 and 22:1.

CHAPTER 3

23 "Face to face the Lord": Deuteronomy 5:4–6.

23 someone would revise it: For a lively and concise introduction to the voluminous literature on biblical origins and authorship, see Richard Elliott Friedman, *Who Wrote the Bible?* (San Francisco, 1997), and Friedman, *The Bible with Sources Revealed: A New View into the Five Books of Moses* (San Francisco, 2003). For a sense of how fluid our understanding of the sources remains, even in the work of individual scholars committed to one approach or another, compare both books to the first edition of Friedman, *Who Wrote the Bible?* (New York, 1987). For a guide to reading the Bible that also provides an engaging introduction to the documentary hypothesis and source criticism and teems with useful insight and references to recent scholarship, see James L. Kugel, *How to Read the Bible: A Guide to Scripture, Then and Now* (New York, 2007). My ideas about inner-biblical exegesis and revision have been shaped by Kugel, as well as by Michael Fishbane, *Biblical Interpretation in Ancient Israel* (New York, 1985), and numerous contributions to the *Jewish Study Bible,* especially Benjamin D. Sommer, "Inner-Biblical Interpretation," and the introductions and annotations to Genesis, Exodus, and Deuteronomy, written by Jon D. Levenson, Jeffrey H. Tigay, and Bernard M. Levinson, respectively, all in Adele Berlin and Marc Zvi Brettler, eds., *The Jewish Study Bible* (New York, 2004). Two other translations and commentaries are also ragged from daily use: Robert Alter, *The Five Books of Moses: A Translation with Commentary* (New York,

2004), and Everett Fox, *The Five Books of Moses: A New Translation with Introductions, Commentary, and Notes* (New York, 1995). I have taken my epigraph from Alter.

CHAPTER 4

24 Jubilees: R. H. Charles's translation (1917) is readily available online at http://www.sacred-texts.com/bib/jub/. But see also the translation of O. S. Wintermute, in James H. Charlesworth, ed., *The Old Testament Pseudepigrapha,* 2 vols. (New York, 1983), 2:35–142. My translations come, as noted, from Wintermute; from James C. VanderKam, ed. and trans., *The Book of Jubilees,* 2 vols. (Lovain, Belgium, 1989); and from the more readily available excerpts in James L. Kugel, *Traditions of the Bible: A Guide to the Bible as It Was at the Start of the Common Era* (Cambridge, 1998); Kugel, *How to Read the Bible: A Guide to Scripture, Then and Now* (New York, 2007); and also Kugel, "Exegetical Notes on 4Q225 'Pseudo-Jubilees,'" *Dead Sea Discoveries* 13 (2006): 73–98.

25 she was taken from him: Jubilees 13:10–15.

25 the author of Nehemiah: Nehemiah 9:7–8.

26 Ben Sira: Sirach (Ecclesiasticus) 44:20.

26 book of Judith: Judith 8:26–27.

26 One poet, a contemporary, boasted: Philo the Epic Poet, fragments 1–2, in Eusebius, "Preparation for the Gospel" 9.20.1, reprinted in H. Attridge, "Philo the Epic Poet: A New Translation and Introduction," in Charlesworth, *The Old Testament Pseudepigrapha,* 2:783.

27 "one who loved the Lord": Jubilees 17:17–18, in VanderKam, *The Book of Jubilees,* 2:105.

28 "one who fears the Lord": Jubilees 18:9, in Kugel, "Exegetical Notes."

28 "your first-born son": Jubilees 18:10–11, in Kugel, "Exegetical Notes."

28 instead of his son: See Jubilees 18:12. See also Wintermute, in Charlesworth: "And Prince Mastema was shamed. And Abraham lifted up his eyes and saw a ram was caught in the thicket by his horns. And Abraham went and took the ram and placed it up for a burnt offering instead of his son. . . . It is Mount Zion."

28 "Go in peace": Jubilees 18:16, in Kugel, "Exegetical Notes." See also Wintermute, in Charlesworth: "And all the nations of the earth will bless themselves by your seed because you obeyed my word. And I have made known to all that you are faithful to me in everything that I say to you."

28 We show them: Kugel, "Exegetical Notes."

29 Abraham observed Passover: James C. VanderKam, *The Book of Jubilees*, a volume in the series Guides to Apocrypha and Pseudepigrapha (Sheffield, 2001), 52–53; Shalom Spiegel, *The Last Trial: On the Legends and Lore of the Command to Abraham to Offer Isaac as a Sacrifice: The Akedah* (New York 1967), 51–59 and passim; Jon D. Levenson, *The Death and Resurrection of the Beloved Son: The Transformation of Child Sacrifice in Judaism and Christianity* (New Haven, Conn., 1993), 176–199.

CHAPTER 5

30 Philo: Philo, *On Abraham* 32–37 (Colson, Loeb Classical Library, 289). See *Philo*, 12 vols. (Cambridge, 1929–62). *On Abraham* is in volume 6.

31 "neither bent nor wavered": Philo, *On Abraham* 32.170.

31 would have known the stories: For Leos and Aristodemus, see Pausanius, *Description of Greece*, 1.5.2; Jerome, *Against Jovinianus*, 1.41; and Diodorus Siculus, *Library of History* 17.15, all cited in Shalom Spiegel, *The Last Trial: On the Legends and Lore of the Command to Abraham to Offer Isaac as a Sacrifice: The Akedah* (New York, 1967), 9–12. For Athamas, Phrixus, Helle, and Jason, see Apollonius of Rhodes, *Jason and the Golden Fleece*, trans. Richard Hunter (New York, 1993).

33 Jephthah: Judges 11.

33 king of Moab: Kings 3:27.

35 he risked his life: Josephus, *Jewish Antiquities* 18.8 (Thackeray, LCL, 242); Philo, *On the Embassy to Gaius* (Colson, LCL, 379).

CHAPTER 6

36 Flavius Josephus: Flavius Josephus, *Jewish War, Jewish Antiquities*, and *The Life*. See *Josephus*, 13 vols. (Cambridge, Loeb Classical Library, 1926–65). The story of the near sacrifice is told in *Jewish Antiquities* 1.222–236 (Thackeray, LCL, 242).

37 "find him obedient": Josephus, *Jewish Antiquities* 1.233–234 (Thackeray, LCL, 242).

37 God found "surprising": See Josephus, *Jewish Antiquities* 1.234, in William Whiston's translation, in *The New Complete Works of Josephus*, revised and expanded, translated by William Whiston and commentary by Paul L. Maier (Grand Rapids, Mich., 1999), 68.

37 the rites of sacrifice: Josephus, *Jewish Antiquities* 1.228–231.

38   awash with Jewish blood: See, in addition to Josephus himself, Martin
     Goodman, *Rome and Jerusalem: The Clash of Ancient Civilizations*
     (New York, 2007).

39   "how he tested Isaac": Judith 8:26.

39   in mind as well as body: Philo, *On Abraham* 32.172 (Colson, LCL,
     289).

39   made his way to the altar: Josephus, *Jewish Antiquities* 1.232.

40   his exact age: Josephus, *Jewish Antiquities* 1.227. Scholars using
     Jubilees's calendar and chronology to calculate Isaac's age have come
     up with both fifteen and sixteen. Rabbis would later estimate both
     twenty-six and what would become the most common rabbinical esti-
     mate, thirty-seven. See *Genesis Rabbah* 54:6 and 56:8, in H. Freed-
     man and Maurice Simon, eds. and trans., *Midrash Rabbah,* 10 vols.
     (New York, 1939, 1983). See also Ibn Ezra on Genesis 22:4 in Abra-
     ham Ibn Ezra, *Ibn Ezra's Commentary on the Pentateuch* (New York,
     1988), 224–225.

CHAPTER 7

41   Pseudo-Philo: *Liber Antiquitatum Biblicarum (L.A.B.)* 18:5, 32:1–4,
     and 40:2. See D. J. Harrington, "Pseudo-Philo: A New Translation
     and Introduction," in James H. Charlesworth, *The Old Testament
     Pseudepigrapha,* 2 vols. (New York, 1983), 2:297–377, and How-
     ard Jacobson, *A Commentary on Pseudo-Philo's Liber Antiquitatum
     Biblicarum with Latin Text and English Translation,* 2 vols. (Leiden,
     1996).

42   "eternal life and time without measure": Pseudo-Philo, *L.A.B.* 32.3,
     as quoted in James L. Kugel, *How to Read the Bible: A Guide to Scrip-
     ture, Then and Now* (New York, 2007), 26, and Kugel, *Traditions of
     the Bible: A Guide to the Bible as It Was at the Start of the Common
     Era* (Cambridge, 1998), 175. See also Harrington, "Pseudo-Philo"
     ("Come and inherit life without limit and time without measure")
     and Jacobson, *A Commentary on Pseudo-Philo's Liber Antiquita-
     tum Biblicarum* ("Come and inherit a secure life and time without
     measure").

42   "a human soul worthy for sacrifice": Pseudo-Philo, *L.A.B.* 32.3,
     as quoted in James L. Kugel, *How to Read the Bible,* 126, and
     Kugel, *Traditions of the Bible,* 175. See also Jacobson ("The
     Lord has deemed the soul of a man worthy to be a sacrifice") and
     Harrington ("The Lord has made the soul of a man worthy to be a
     sacrifice").

42   Jephthah: Judges 11.

42   "seeing the people freed?": Pseudo-Philo, *L.A.B.* 40:2 (Harrington).

See also Jacobson ("Who is there who would be sad to die, seeing the people freed?").

42 "the one who was offering was rejoicing": Pseudo-Philo, *L.A.B.* 40.2 (Harrington). See also Jacobson: "Or have you forgotten what happened in the days of our fathers when the father placed the son as a burnt offering, and he did not dispute him but gladly gave consent to him, and the one being offered was ready and the one who was offering was rejoicing."

43 Antiochus IV: Martin Goodman, *Rome and Jerusalem: The Clash of Ancient Civilizations* (New York, 2007), 49.

43 hurled from the walls: 2 Maccabees 6:10–18 and 4 Maccabees 4:23–26.

43 burned alive: 2 Maccabees 6:11.

44 Eleazar: See 4 Maccabees 8:1–18:24 and 2 Maccabees 7:1–42.

44 "take my life as a ransom for theirs": 4 Maccabees 6:1–31, in H. Anderson, "4 Maccabees: A New Translation and Introduction," in Charlesworth, *The Old Testament Pseudepigrapha*, 2: 531–564. See also 2 Maccabees 6:18-31.

44 "the same mind as Abraham": 4 Maccabees 14:20 (NRSV).

44 "did not cower": 4 Maccabees 16:20 (NRSV).

44 "sacrificed for piety's sake": 4 Maccabees 13:12 (H. Anderson).

47 They gave her a name, Miriam: *Lamentations Rabbah* 1.16.50, in H. Freedman and Maurice Simon, trans. *Midrash Rabbah,* 10 vols. (New York, 1939, 1983), 7:133.

CHAPTER 8

49 The glory of Jewish literature: Josephus, *Against Apion* 1.37–47 (Thackeray, Loeb Classical Library, 186). Josephus added that every Jew not only abides by those books, but if need be would cheerfully die for them. But the Greek: "Even to save the entire collection of his nation's writings from destruction, he would not face the smallest personal injury."

50 we would be lost: Those who have read anything by James Kugel, or heard one of his engrossing public lectures, will know that I have borrowed and I am employing his "four assumptions," the assumptions about the biblical literature that so many ancient interpreters shared, assumptions with which ancient interpreters not only read sacred texts but, in Kugel's telling, actually created one, by which he means took an anthology of ancient literature and made it, interpreted it, into the Bible. See Kugel, *Traditions of the Bible: A Guide to the Bible as It Was at the Start of the Common Era* (Cambridge, 1998) and

How to Read the Bible: A Guide to Scripture, Then and Now (New York, 2007).

CHAPTER 9

52 whose atoning sacrifice came first: For a relatively recent and relatively concise (considering the extent and complexity of the debate), overview, see Edward Kessler, *Bound by the Bible: Jews, Christians and the Sacrifice of Isaac* (Cambridge, 2004), 8–36. For a deeper immersion I have learned from Geza Vermes, "Redemption and Genesis XXII" in *Scripture and Tradition in Judaism* (Leiden, 1961), 193–227; Philip R. Davies and Bruce D. Chilton, "The Aqedah: A Revised Tradition History," *Catholic Biblical Quarterly* 40 (October 1978): 514–546; Hans Joachim Schoeps, "The Sacrifice of Isaac in Paul's Theology," *Journal of Biblical Literature* 65 (December 1946): 385–392; Robert J. Daly, "Soteriological Significance of the Sacrifice of Isaac," *Catholic Biblical Quarterly* 39 (January 1977): 45–75; Alan F. Segal, " 'He Who Did Not Spare His Own Son': Jesus, Paul, and the Akedah," in *From Jesus to Paul* (Waterloo, Ont., 1984), 169–184; and Segal, "The Akedah: Some Reconsiderations," in *Geschichte—Tradition—Reflexion* (Tubingen, 1996), 99–116. Absolutely essential for understanding the relationship between Jewish and Christian stories and scripture more broadly is Jon D. Levenson, *The Death and Resurrection of the Beloved Son: The Transformation of Child Sacrifice in Judaism and Christianity* (New Haven, Conn., 1993). Levenson's latest book, *Inheriting Abraham: The Legacy of the Patriarch in Judaism, Christianity, and Islam* (Princeton, N.J., 2012), was published just as I was putting this book to bed, but I am certain it will also be essential to our understanding of the similarities and differences between the Abrahams and the "sacrifices" of Judaism, Christianity, and Islam.

52 Targums: See, for example, "Vayera," in J. W. Etheridge, *The Targums of Onkelos and Jonathan Ben Uzziel on the Pentateuch, with the Fragments of the Jerusalem Targum from the Chaldee* (New York, 1968), and Michael L. Klein, *The Fragment-Targums of the Pentateuch: According to Their Extant Sources,* 2 vols. (Rome, 1980), 2: 16–17, 103–104.

53 James Kugel: James L. Kugel, "Exegetical Notes on 4Q225 'Pseudo-Jubilees,' " *Dead Sea Discoveries* 13 (2006): 73–98, and Geza Vermes, "New Light on the Sacrifice of Isaac from 4Q225," *Journal of Jewish Studies* 47 (Spring 1996): 140–146.

55 Epistle to the Hebrews: Hebrews 11:1–39.

CHAPTER 10

58 *pistos:* James L. Kugel, *How to Read the Bible: A Guide to Scripture, Then and Now* (New York, 2007), 122–123, and, in even more depth, Kugel, *Traditions of the Bible: A Guide to the Bible as It Was at the Start of the Common Era* (Cambridge, 1998), 308–311.

58 "Fear not, Abram": Genesis 15:1–6 (Alter).

58 Origen: Origen, *Homily on Genesis* 8.5, in *Homilies on Genesis and Exodus,* vol. 71 in the series The Fathers of the Church (Washington, D.C., 1982), 140.

59 Bishop Succensus: Succensus, *Catena* 1250, quoted in Edward Kessler, *Bound by the Bible: Jews, Christians and the Sacrifice of Isaac* (Cambridge, 2004), 94.

60 no mystery about its meaning: For the typological understanding of the story, the best place to start is with Melito of Sardis. I arrived by way of Kessler, *Bound by the Bible,* and then moved on to Robert L. Wilken, "Melito, the Jewish Community at Sardis, and the Sacrifice of Isaac," *Theological Studies* 37 (1976): 53–69. But cf. Paul R. Trebilco, *Jewish Communities in Asia Minor* (Cambridge, 1991).

62 The Jews were the ass: Cyril of Alexandria, *Glaph. in Genesis,* PG 69 141B-C, quoted in Kessler, *Bound by the Bible,* 93. See also B. Lee Blackburn Jr., "The Mystery of the Synagogue: Cyril of Alexandria on the Law of Moses" (Ph.D. diss., Notre Dame, 2009).

63 the early Christians: Kessler, *Bound by the Bible,* looks at the responses of the church fathers to Genesis 22:1–14, line by line.

63 argued about everything: For a lively and accessible introduction to many of these arguments, see virtually any of Elaine H. Pagels's books, but especially *The Gnostic Gospels* (New York, 1979); *The Origin of Satan* (New York, 1995); and *Beyond Belief: The Secret Gospel of Thomas* (New York, 2003).

65 Augustine: I started with Peter Brown, *Augustine of Hippo* (Berkeley, 1967, 2000) and more recently I have benefited from Paula Fredriksen, *Augustine and the Jews: A Christian Defense of Jews and Judaism* (New York, 2008). Two review essays helped me put Fredriksen's interpretation in the context of the existing literature and history: Jeremy Cohen, "Revisiting Augustine's Doctrine of Jewish Witness," *Journal of Religion* 89 (2009): 564–578, and David Nirenberg, "Slay Them Not," *New Republic* 240 (March 18, 2009): 42–47.

CHAPTER 11

68 midrash: I started with several terrific introductions, most of them written by scholars for general readers, and went from there to trans-

lations of the primary sources, especially H. Freedman and Maurice Simon, eds. and trans. *Midrash Rabbah,* 10 vols. (New York, 1939, 1983) and Menahem Kasher, *Encyclopedia of Biblical Interpretation: A Millennial Anthology (EBI)* (New York, 1953). See Yaakov Elman, "Classical Rabbinic Interpretation" and David Stern, "Midrash and Jewish Interpretation," both in Adele Berlin and Marc Zvi Brettler, eds., *The Jewish Study Bible* (New York, 2007); Lawrence H. Schiffman, *From Text to Tradition: A History of Second Temple and Rabbinic Judaism* (Hoboken, N.J., 1991); Shaye J. D. Cohen, *From the Maccabees to the Mishnah* (Philadelphia, 1987); and Adin Steinsaltz, *The Essential Talmud* (New York, 1976). Also useful, each in its own way, are George Robinson, *Essential Torah: A Complete Guide to the Five Books of Moses* (New York, 2006), and Jacob Neusner and Alan J. Avery-Peck, *Encyclopedia of Midrash: Biblical Interpretation in Formative Judaism,* 2 vols. (Leiden, 2005).

68   the Talmud's midrash: See, for example, b. Sanhedrin 89b.

69   to elevate him, like a banner: *Genesis Rabbah* 55:1,6.

69   tests the righteous: *Genesis Rabbah* 55:2. See also Ramban on Genesis 22:1, in Ramban (Nachmanides), *The Torah with Ramban's Commentary,* translated, annotated, and elucidated by Yaakov Blinder et al. (Brooklyn, 2004).

70   "counteract the sword grasped by Pharaoh": *Genesis Rabbah* 55:8.

70   leave his side to relieve himself: *Leviticus Rabbah* 26:7; *Genesis Rabbah* 55:8; *EBI,* 3:137.

70   "live in his presence": *Genesis Rabbah* 55:6, 56:1.

71   Isaac and Ishmael arguing: For three older versions of this oft-repeated-and-revised midrash, see b. Sanhedrin 89b; *Genesis Rabbah* 55:4; and *Tanhuma, Wayyera,* 4.42, in John T. Townsend, ed. and trans., *Midrash Tanhuma* (Hoboken, N.J., 1989). See also *EBI,* 3:128–129.

72   before anyone tried to stop him: *EBI,* 3:135–137.

72   "Are you crazy?": My paraphrase of *Genesis Rabbah* 56:4.

73   leaving him unfit for sacrifice: *Genesis Rabbah* 56:5; *EBI,* 3:139.

73   "Take your son": b. Sanhedrin 89b; *Genesis Rabbah* 55:7; *EBI,* 3:12–17 and 132–133.

74   "I am not a priest": *Genesis Rabbah* 55:7.

74   that look would have been his last: *Genesis Rabbah* 56:8; *EBI,* 3:143 and 145.

75   God answered his prayers: b. Ta'anit 2. What follows "prevarication" is my paraphrase of Abraham's complaint in *Genesis Rabbah* 56:8.

75 "Now take him down": *Genesis Rabbah* 56:8; *EBI*, 3:132. See also *Tanhuma, Wayyera*, 4.40, in Townsend, ed., *Midrash Tanhuma*.

75 never even entered God's mind: b. Ta'anit 4a; Jeremiah 19:5.

76 "By My own Self I swear": *Tanhuma*, cited in Jacob Culi, *The Torah Anthology*, Me'Am Lo'ez (New York, 1977), 2:336, and Louis Ginzberg, *The Legends of the Jews* (Philadelphia, 1909–1938), 1:282.

76 never test him like that again: *Genesis Rabbah* 56:11.

76 "filled with compassion for them": *Genesis Rabbah* 56:10.

76 "redeemed by the ram's horn": *Genesis Rabbah* 56:9.

77 "Your city, Your land, Your heritage": *ArtScroll Transliterated Linear Siddur* (New York, 1998), 81–87.

CHAPTER 12

78 Exodus: Exodus 32:11–14.

78 Ezekiel: Ezekiel 14 and 18.

79 the promise at the heart of it would be irrevocable: See the notes to Exodus 11–14 in Adele Berlin and Marc Zvi Brettler, eds., *The Jewish Study Bible* (New York, 2004), 184–185.

79 "the will of his creator": *Genesis Rabbah* 56:8.

79 "Nothing. Not a blemish": *Genesis Rabbah* 56:7.

80 "on top of the altar before Thee": See the text and notes in Shalom Spiegel, *The Last Trial: On the Legends and Lore of the Command to Abraham to Offer Isaac as a Sacrifice: The Akedah* (New York, 1967), 60–62 and passim, and *Genesis Rabbah* 56:9.

80 not instead of Isaac: *Genesis Rabbah* 56:9 in H. Freedman and Maurice Simon, eds. and trans. *Midrash Rabbah*, 10 vols. (New York, 1939, 1983).

80 "until a quarter of his blood left him": *Tanhuma, Wa-Yera* 23, quoted in Spiegel, *The Last Trial*, 48.

80 "some other victim in your place": *Yalkut* 101, quoted in Spiegel, *The Last Trial*, 48.

81 "the blood of Isaac's sacrifice": Menahem Kasher, *Encyclopedia of Biblical Interpretation: A Millennial Anthology (EBI)* (New York, 1953) 3:156, and Spiegel, *The Last Trial*, 51–59.

81 "'Enough! Stay your hand!'": 1 Chronicles 21:14–15; Spiegel, *The Last Trial*, 51–59; and *EBI*, 3:156.

81 "the ashes of the Akedah of Isaac": Spiegel, *The Last Trial*, 38–44.

81 On Mount Moriah: Ibid.

82 "the foundation of that altar": Ibid., 43–44.

82 "for our sake Isaac's ashes": b. Ta'anit 16a, cited in Spiegel, *The Last Trial*, 42–43.

84 the gathering before the water gate: Nehemiah 8:1–9.

85 Johanan ha-Kohen: Abraham I. Shafir, "'Az Terem'—A Piyyut by Yochanan Hacohen." *Hebrew Studies* 45 (2004): 232–252. See also Abraham Shafir, "Akedat Yitzhak—New Perspectives," Bar-Ilan University's Parashat Hashavua Study Center, Parashat Va-Yera 5767 (November 11, 2006), online at http://www.biu.ac.il/JH/Parasha/eng /vayera/sha.html.

CHAPTER 13

88 "Abraham rose early the next morning": See, for example, Samuel A. Berman, *Midrash Tanhuma-Yelammedenu: An English Translation of Genesis and Exodus from the Printed Version of Tanhuma-Yelammedenu with an Introduction, Notes, and Indexes* (Hoboken, N.J., 1996), 143.

89 Then she died: See, for example, Avivah Gottlieb Zornberg, "Cries and Whispers: The Death of Sarah," in Gail Twersky Reimer and Judith A. Kates, *Beginning Anew: A Woman's Companion to the High Holy Days* (New York, 1997), 174–200; David Goldstein, *Jewish Legends,* rev. ed. (New York, 1987). See and compare to Louis Ginzberg, *The Legends of the Jews* (Philadelphia, 1909–1938).

89 "And Sarah's life": Genesis 23 (Alter).

89 "He came from Mount Moriah": *Genesis Rabbah* 58:5.

89 Basil of Seleucia: *Orat.* 7, quoted in Edward Kessler, *Bound by the Bible: Jews, Christians and the Sacrifice of Isaac* (Cambridge, 2004), 75.

89 Gregory, bishop of Nyssa: Gregory of Nyssa, *De Deitate* PG 46 569A, quoted in Kessler, *Bound by the Bible,* 75–76.

90 fifth- and sixth-century verse homilists: I first encountered references to Romanos and the Syriac homilies in three books, Louis A. Berman, *The Akedah: The Binding of Isaac* (Northvale, N.J., 1997); Burton L. Visotzky, *Reading the Book: Making the Bible a Timeless Text* (New York, 1996); and Kessler, *Bound by the Bible.* From there I found my way to Mikhalis Moshkos, "Romanos' Hymn on the Sacrifice of Abraham: A Discussion of the Sources and a Translation," *Byzantion* 44 (1974): 311–328; R. J. Schork, *Sacred Song from the Byzantine Pulpit: Romanus the Melodist* (Gainesville, Fla., 1995); Sebastian P. Brock, "Genesis 22 in Syriac Tradition," in *Mélanges*

Dominique Barthélemy (Fribourg, 1981), 1–30; Brock, "Genesis 22: Where Was Sarah?," *Expository Times* 96 (October 1984): 14–17; Brock, "Reading Between the Lines: Sarah and the Sacrifice of Isaac (Genesis, Chapter 22)," in *Women in Ancient Societies* (New York, 1994), 169–180; and especially Brock, *From Ephrem to Romanos: Interactions Between Syriac and Greek in Late Antiquity* (Brookfield, Vt., 1999). Also essential is Susan Ashbrook Harvey, "Spoken Words, Voiced Silence: Biblical Women in Syriac Tradition," *Journal of Early Christian Studies* 9 (2001): 105–131.

91 "borne trials along with you?": All my paraphrases and quotations from this homily, which Sebastian Brock refers to as "Memra I," are based on or taken from Brock's translation from the Syriac, in Brock, "Two Syriac Verse Homilies on the Binding of Isaac," in Brock, *From Ephrem to Romanos,* 108–112.

92 and then to God: Memra I, in Brock, "Two Syriac Verse Homilies," 110.

92 Your father won't: All my paraphrases of and quotations from Romanos are based on or taken directly from Moshkos, "Romanos' Hymn on the Sacrifice of Abraham." Cf. R. J. Schork's engaging and enlightening translation and commentary, Schork, *Sacred Song from the Byzantine Pulpit.*

93 "a short time": Romanos, in Moshkos, "Romanos' Hymn," 322–323. Cf. Romanos, in Schork, *Sacred Song from the Byzantine Pulpit,* 153.

93 the world to come: Romanos, in Moshkos, "Romanos' Hymn," 23–24.

93 "Go in peace": Memra II, in Brock, "Two Syriac Verse Homilies," 123.

94 ultimately wouldn't have to: Romanos, in Moshkos, "Romanos' Hymn," 320.

94 "receive my spirit": Ibid., 326–327.

94 "bones in the fire": Memra I, in Brock, "Two Syriac Verse Homilies," 111.

94 "gave you back": Ibid.

95 "her mind and her thoughts": Ibid., 124.

95 "I was wishing I was an eagle": Ibid., 125.

95 "who died and was resurrected": Ibid.

96 no telling what others might do with them: Those interested in Sarah in mid-first-millennium exegesis should also look at the Bodmer Poem. For a recent reading, see Ton Hilhorst, "The Bodmer Poem on

the Sacrifice of Abraham," in Edward Noort and Eibert Tigchelaar, eds., *The Sacrifice of Isaac: The Aqedah (Genesis 22) and Its Interpretations* (Leiden, 2002), 96–108.

CHAPTER 14

98 Islam: This entire chapter takes off from and owes an enormous debt to the scholarship, prodigious as it has been pathbreaking, of Reuven Firestone. See Firestone, *Journeys in Holy Lands: The Evolution of the Abraham-Ishmael Legends in Islamic Exegesis* (Albany, N.Y., 1990); Firestone, "Merit, Mimesis, and Martyrdom: Aspects of Shiʿite Meta-historical Exegesis on Abraham's Sacrifice in Light of Jewish, Christian, and Sunni Muslim Tradition," *Journal of the American Academy of Religion* 66 (Spring 1998): 93–116; Firestone, "Comparative Studies in Bible and Qur'an: A Fresh Look at Genesis 22 in the Light of Sura 37," in *Judaism and Islam: Boundaries, Communications, and Interaction: Essays in Honor of William M. Brinner* (Leiden, Boston, 2000); and Firestone, "The Qūr'ān and the Bible: Some Modern Studies of Their Relationship," in *Bible and Qūr'ān* (Atlanta, 2003), 1–22. Also useful and enlightening are F. Leemhuis, "Ibrahim's Sacrifice of His Son in the Early Post-Koranic Tradition," in Edward Noort and Eibert Tigchelaar, eds., *The Sacrifice of Isaac: The Aqedah (Genesis 22) and Its Interpretations* (Leiden, 2002); F. V. Greifenhagen, "Cooperating Revelations? Qur'an, Bible, and Intertextuality," *ARC* 33 (2005): 302–317; Ayaz Afsar, "A Comparative Study of the Intended Sacrifice of Isaac/Ishmael in the Bible and the Qūr'ān," *Islamic Studies* 46 (2007): 483–498; and Mishael Caspi, *The Binding (Aqedah) and Its Transformations in Judaism and Islam: The Lambs of God* (Lewiston, N.Y., 1995).

99 "This is from God": Qur'an 2:78–79, cited in Firestone, *Journeys in Holy Lands,* 15. See also Arberry, 2:72: "And some there are of them that are common folk not knowing the Book, but only fancies and mere conjectures. So woe to those who write the Book with their hands, then say, 'This is from God.'" A. J. Arberry, *The Koran Interpreted* (New York, 1955).

101 If that's what God wants, let's do it: Firestone, *Journeys in Holy Lands,* 107–115.

101 we do not stray: Ibid., 116–128.

103 "let him into paradise": Ibid., 129–134.

104 "I offered myself up before Thee as a sacrifice!": b. Shabbat 89b. See also Firestone, *Journeys in Holy Lands,* 133.

104 pardon for his descendants through the ages: Firestone, *Journeys in Holy Lands,* 135–151.

105 Their starting point was the Qur'an: Qur'an 37:99–115 (Arberry).

106 Galatians: 4:21–31.

107 polemical and pointed: All three of the quotes that follow come from Firestone, "Merit, Mimesis, and Martyrdom," 99–100.

108 "people disagree about them": Firestone, *Journeys in Holy Lands,* 135. For another view of the debate, especially the chronology, see Leemhuis, "Ibrahim's Sacrifice of His Son in the Early Post-Koranic Tradition." For the place of the conflict between Shiites and Sunnis in the debate about the identity of the nearly sacrificed son, see Firestone, "Merit, Mimesis, and Martyrdom."

CHAPTER 15

110 as good as it got: For the best of times, see Maria Rosa Menocal, *The Ornament of the World: How Muslims, Jews, and Christians Created a Culture of Tolerance in Medieval Spain* (Boston, 2002). For an extraordinarily sophisticated and nuanced view of the complicated relationship between anti-Jewish violence and community, see David Nirenberg, *Communities of Violence: Persecution of Minorities in the Middle Ages* (Princeton, N.J., 1996).

111 *Pirke de Rabbi Eliezer: Pirke de Rabbi Eliezer (The Chapters of Rabbi Eliezer the Great) According to the Text of the Manuscript Belonging to Abraham Epstein of Vienna,* translated and annotated with introduction and indexes by Gerald Friedlander (New York, 1965), 223.

112 nearly sacrificed himself: See *Sifre Deuteronomy* 32.

112 view of the divine presence: See *Fragmentary Targum,* quoted in Geza Vermes, "Redemption and Genesis XXII" in *Scripture and Tradition in Judaism* (Leiden, 1961), 194–195.

112 "nor uttering a sound": Melito, fragment 9, in Melito, *On Pascha and Fragments,* trans. Stuart George Hall (Oxford, 1979).

112 "labors were not equal": Memra I, in Sebastian P. Brock, "Two Syriac Verse Homilies on the Binding of Isaac," in *From Ephrem to Romanos: Interactions Between Syriac and Greek in Late Antiquity* (Brookfield, Vt., 1999), 109.

113 "the Christ who was going to suffer": Melito, fragment 9, in Melito, *On Pascha and Fragments.*

113 "stolen away from death and suffering": Cyril of Alexandria, *Glaphyra in Genesis,* PG 69 144A, quoted in Edward Kessler, *Bound by the Bible: Jews, Christians and the Sacrifice of Isaac* (Cambridge, 2004), 132.

113 Isaac is "a type of the Lord": Clement of Alexandria, *The Paedagogus*

(Christ the Instructor) 1.5, quoted in Kessler, *Bound by the Bible*, 131.

113 "So this is the Torah you talked about": quoted in Shalom Spiegel, *The Last Trial: On the Legends and Lore of the Command to Abraham to Offer Isaac as a Sacrifice: The Akedah* (New York, 1967), 49. Spiegel discusses all of these versions and many more. His essay remains, more than half a century after it was published, the standard work on the *midrashim* in which Isaac dies.

114 "slaughtered according to the rite": Ephraim (of Bonn), "Adekah," in Spiegel, *The Last Trial*, 148.

114 "quickeneth the dead": *Pirke de Rabbi Eliezer* 31, p. 228.

115 would have ended with Isaac's ashes: Spiegel, *The Last Trial*, 36–37.

115 from knife wounds, from the flames: Ibid., 3–8.

116 simply thinking about Abraham and God: *Genesis Rabbah* 56:11; Ibn Ezra to Genesis 22:19, in Abraham Ibn Ezra, *Ibn Ezra's Commentary on the Pentateuch* (New York, 1988), 226–227.

116 "Let our lips compensate for the bulls": See Hosea 14:3: "Instead of bulls we pay [the offering of] our lips."

118 "our Savior alone": Athanasius, *Epistle 6,* in *The Festal Epistles of S. Athanasius, Bishop of Alexandria,* vol. 38 in the series A Library of Fathers of the Holy Catholic Church Anterior to the Division of the East and West (Oxford, 1854). See also Kessler, *Bound by the Bible*, 133.

CHAPTER 16

119 "on account of his blood I chose them": Pseudo-Philo, *L.A.B.* 18:5.

119 difficult when not impossible: The first complete account of Isaac's death and resurrection that can be dated with any precision (though hardly definitively: there is ongoing debate) appears in the *Pirke de-Rabbi Eliezer,* which scholars believe, based on internal evidence (references to contemporary events), to be a late eighth- or early ninth-century text, but it clearly contains material much older than that. See, most recently, Steven Daniel Sacks, *Midrash and Multiplicity: Pirke de-Rabbi Eliezer and the Reinvention of Rabbinic Interpretive Culture* (New York, 2009). See also Edward Kessler, *Bound by the Bible: Jews, Christians and the Sacrifice of Isaac* (Cambridge, 2004), 127–130. I myself, following Shalom Spiegel, *The Last Trial: On the Legends and Lore of the Command to Abraham to Offer Isaac as a Sacrifice: The Akedah* (New York, 1967) and Jon D. Levenson, *The Death and Resurrection of the Beloved Son: The Transformation of Child Sacrifice in Judaism and Christianity* (New Haven, Conn.,

1993), assume that the death-and-resurrection motif was much older than the end of the first millennium.

120 one Rhineland Jewish community after another: For my understanding of the Crusade chronicles and Jewish responses to the First Crusade more generally, I am deeply indebted, in addition to Spiegel, *The Last Trial,* to Robert Chazan, *God, Humanity, and History: The Hebrew First Crusade Narratives* (Berkeley, 2000), and to Jeremy Cohen, *Sanctifying the Name of God: Jewish Martyrs and Jewish Memories of the First Crusade* (Philadelphia, 2004). I would also recommend Alan L. Mintz, *Ḥurban: Responses to Catastrophe in Hebrew Literature* (New York, 1984), and Susan L. Einbinder, *Beautiful Death: Jewish Poetry and Martyrdom in Medieval France* (Princeton, N.J., 2002). On Jewish martyrdom more generally, see Shira Lander, "Martyrdom in Jewish Traditions," *Catholic-Jewish Consultation Committee Meeting* (St. Mary's Seminary, Baltimore, Md., Bishops Committee on Ecumenical and Inter-religious Affairs and the National Council of Synagogues, December 11, 2003), online at http://www.bc.edu/dam/files/research_sites/cjl/texts/cjrelations/resources/articles/Lander_martyrdom/index.html. On Jewish memory and history making more generally, absolutely and always essential is Yosef Hayim Yerushalmi, Zakhor: *Jewish History and Jewish Memory* (Seattle, 1982). For a more deeply contextualized look at memory in general, and memories of the First Crusade in particular, see David Nirenberg, "The Rhineland Massacres of Jews in the First Crusade: Memories Medieval and Modern," in *Imagination, Ritual, Memory, Historiography: Concepts of the Past,* ed. G. Althoff et al. (Cambridge, 2001), 279–310. For consistency, unless otherwise indicated, my quotations from the chronicles come from Shlomo Eidelberg, trans. and ed., *The Jews and the Crusaders: The Hebrew Chronicles of the First and Second Crusades* (Madison, Wis., 1977). You can find nearly identical versions of the same quotations in Spiegel, *The Last Trial.*

120 the killing in Mainz: "Solomon bar Simson Chronicle," in Eidelberg, *The Jews and the Crusaders,* 32–33. See also Spiegel, *The Last Trial,* 18–20.

121 the village of Wevelinghofen: "Chronicle of Eliezer bar Nathan," in Eidelberg, *The Jews and the Crusaders,* 86–87. See also Spiegel, *The Last Trial,* 22–24.

121 a rabbi in Worms: "Narrative of the Old Persecutions (Mainz Anonymous)," in Eidelberg, *The Jews and the Crusaders,* 103–104. See also, Spiegel, *The Last Trial,* 24–25.

122 "Why over the blood of children": Spiegel, *The Last Trial,* 20.

122 "they cannot be counted": Ibid., 20–21.

122 "the Akedah of Isaac son of Abraham?": Ibid., 19–20.

124 "May You avenge the spilt blood": "Chronicle of Solomon bar Simson," in Eidelberg, *The Jews and the Crusaders,* 31, 33, and then also 49: "May the blood of His devoted ones stand us in good stead and be an atonement for us and for our posterity after us, and our children's children eternally, like the Akedah of our Father Isaac when our Father Abraham bound him upon the altar."

125 By his laws, he wants them to live: b. Sanhedrin 74a.

CHAPTER 17

127 others practiced and promoted ways of reading Scripture: My understanding of medieval Jewish interpretation began with and depends throughout on Barry Dov Walfish, "Medieval Jewish Interpretation," in Adele Berlin and Marc Zvi Brettler, eds., *The Jewish Study Bible* (New York, 2004), 1876–1900. From Walfish's terrific essay I went to the available English translations of individual commentators, cited in the notes below.

127 Saadia Gaon: Sa'adia ben Joseph, *Rabbi Saadiah Gaon's Commentary on the Book of Creation* (Northvale, N.J., 2002), 29–34.

127 a "consuming fire": Ibid.

128 more internally consistent: Abraham Ibn Ezra discusses Saadia on Genesis 22:12, in Abraham Ibn Ezra, *Ibn Ezra's Commentary on the Pentateuch* (New York, 1988), 222.

129 Joseph Kara: quoted in Walfish, "Medieval Biblical Interpretation," 1888.

129 Abraham's knife called: Rashi to Genesis 22:6, in *The Torah with Rashi's Commentary,* translated, annotated, and elucidated by Yisrael Isser Zvi Herczeg et al. (Brooklyn, 1994), 234; *Genesis Rabbah* 56:3, in H. Freedman and Maurice Simon, eds. and trans. *Midrash Rabbah,* 10 vols. (New York, 1939, 1983).

129 Rashbam insisted: Rashbam to Deuteronomy 32:42; Rashbam to Genesis 22:6, in *Rabbi Samuel Ben Meir's Commentary on Genesis,* translated and annotated by Martin I. Lockshin (Lewiston, N.Y., 1989), 98.

130 Abraham Ibn Ezra: Ibn Ezra, *Ibn Ezra's Commentary on the Pentateuch,* 1–19.

130 "God tested Abraham": Ibn Ezra to Genesis 22:1, 222–224.

131 "Isaac would quite possibly have fled": Ibn Ezra to Genesis 22:4, 224–225.

131 David Kimhi (Radak): Eliyahu Munk, ed., *Hachut Hameshulash: Commentaries on the Torah by Rabbeinu Chananel, Rabbi Sh'muel Ben Meir (Rash'bam), Rabbi David Kimchi (R'dak), Rabbi Ovadiah Seforno*, 2 vols. (New York, 2003), 2:434–438.

132 Maimonides: Moses Maimonides, *Guide of the Perplexed*, 3:24.

134 Rashbam criticized commentators who spun elaborate yarns: Rashbam to Genesis 22:1, in *Rabbi Samuel Ben Meir's Commentary on Genesis*, 94–96. See also Munk, *Hachut Hameshulash*, 432–434.

134 Martin Luther insisted: Luther to Genesis 22:9, in "Lectures on Genesis, Chapters 21–25" in *Luther's Works*, ed. Jaroslav Pelikan et al., 69 vols. (St. Louis, 1955-), 4:112–113.

135 "Abraham, Abraham": Rashi to Genesis 22:11; Ibn Ezra to Genesis 22:11 (225); Radak to Genesis 22:11 (441); Joseph Ibn Kaspi, *Gevia' Kesef*, chapter 14, in Joseph Kaspi and Basil Herring, *Joseph Ibn Kaspi's Gevia? Kesef: A Study in Medieval Jewish Philosophic Bible Commentary* (New York, 1982), 230.

136 to ensure that he didn't try to run away: Menahem Kasher, *Encyclopedia of Biblical Interpretation: A Millennial Anthology (EBI)* (New York, 1953), 3:145–46.

136 "contradicting Scripture": Ibn Ezra to Genesis 22:19, 226–227.

136 Ibn al-'Arabi: See Sara Sviri, "Dreaming Analyzed and Recorded: Dream in the World of Medieval Islam," in Guy G. Stroumsa and David Dean Shulman, eds., *Dream Cultures: Explorations in the Comparative History of Dreaming* (New York, 1999).

136 an abomination to YHWH: Ibn Kaspi, *Gevia' Kesef*, chapter 14:219. Kaspi also believed that the learned also understood that God didn't ultimately desire animal sacrifice either, but that's another dimension of his interpretation and my story. See Kaspi, *Gevia' Kesef*, chapter 14:225.

136 Isaac, "struck with amazement": Luther to Genesis 22:9, in Luther, "Lectures on Genesis," 4:112–113.

137 Ramban on the word "Moriah": Ramban (Nachmanides) to Genesis 22:2, in *The Torah with Ramban's Commentary*, translated, annotated, and elucidated by Yaakov Blinder et al. (Brooklyn, 2004), 497–501.

CHAPTER 18

139 One obvious place to turn is the walls: The literature on the visual representations of the story is large and growing, but for this chapter, I have looked much more than I have read. For invaluable inventories, see Isabel Speyart van Woerden, "Iconography of the Sacrifice

of Abraham," *Vigiliae Christianae* 15 (December 1961): 214–255, and Princeton University's *Index of Christian Art*. For Augustine, see *Against Faustus* 22.73, quoted in Edward Kessler, *Bound by the Bible: Jews, Christians and the Sacrifice of Isaac* (Cambridge, 2004), 155. For Gregory of Nyssa, see *De deitate,* quoted in Kessler, *Bound by the Bible,* 155. Kessler provides a useful introduction to the early years in *Bound by the Bible,* 153–174. But see also Joseph Gutmann, "The Dura Europos Synagogue Paintings and Their Influence on Later Christian and Jewish Art," *Artibus et historiae* 9 (January 1, 1988): 25–29; Gutmann, "The Sacrifice of Isaac in Medieval Jewish Art," *Artibus et historiae* 8 (January 1, 1987): 67–89; and Gutmann, "The Sacrifice of Isaac: Variations on a Theme in Early Jewish and Christian Art," in *Sacred Images: Studies in Jewish Art from Antiquity to the Middle Ages: Collected Studies* (Northampton, 1989). See also the symposium that begins with Marc Bregman, "Aqedah: Midrash as Visualization," in *The Journal of Textual Reasoning* 2 (June 2003), online at http://etext.lib.virginia.edu/journals/tr/volume2/index.html. Also useful is Jo Milgrom, *The Binding of Isaac: The Akedah, a Primary Symbol in Jewish Thought and Art* (North Richland Hills, Tex., 1988).

140 El Bagawat: Matthew Martin, "Observations on the Paintings of the Exodus Chapel, Bagawat Necropolis, Kharga Oasis, Egypt," in John Burke et al., eds., *Byzantine Narrative: Essays in Honour of Roger Scott,* Australian Byzantine Studies Conference 2004, University of Melbourne (Melbourne, 2006).

140 Consider Abraham's demeanor: Andrea del Sarto: *The Sacrifice of Isaac* (c. 1527–1529); see also del Sarto's *The Sacrifice of Isaac* (1506); Alessandro Allori: *The Sacrifice of Isaac* (1601); for a similar pastoral view, see Domenichino's *Abraham Leading Isaac to Sacrifice* (1602); Domenichino: *The Sacrifice of Isaac* (1627–28); Caravaggio, *The Sacrifice of Isaac* (1603).

141 an anguished Abraham: Donatello, *The Sacrifice of Isaac* (1418); Alonso Berruguete, *The Sacrifice of Isaac* (c.1526–32); Rembrandt, *The Sacrifice of Abraham* (1635) and *The Sacrifice of Abraham* (1655).

143 Then there was Isaac: Cigoli, *The Sacrifice of Isaac* (1605–07); Jacopo da Empoli, *The Sacrifice of Isaac;* Empoli lived from 1554 to 1640, and while some date the painting to the 1590s, others date it to the 1620s; Felice Ficherelli, *The Sacrifice of Isaac*, dated to the early-to-mid-seventeenth century.

144 not every artist imagined him that way: Berruguete, *The Sacrifice of Isaac* (1526–32); del Sarto: *The Sacrifice of Isaac* (c. 1527–1529);

Titian, *The Sacrifice of Isaac* (1542-44); Caravaggio, *The Sacrifice of Isaac* (1603); Pedro Orrente, *The Sacrifice of Isaac* (1616); Rembrandt, *The Sacrifice of Abraham* (1635).

145 mixed feelings in Abraham's pose: See, for example, Jules Lubbock, *Storytelling in Christian Art from Giotto to Donatello* (New Haven, Conn., 2006).

145 the east door of the Baptistery: See Rona Goffen, *Renaissance Rivals: Michelangelo, Leonardo, Raphael, Titian* (New Haven, Conn., 2002), 6-7: "The committee's decision was surely influenced by the fact that Ghiberti's panel weighed 7 kilos [approx. 15½ lbs] less than Brunelleschi's, savings in bronze that signified considerable savings of money." Also engaging and informative is David Drogin and Beth Harris, "Brunelleschi & Ghiberti: The Sacrifice," video, *Smart History* (Khan Academy), online at http://smarthistory.khanacademy.org /brunelleschi-ghiberti-isaac.html. See also "A Peek behind Ghiberti's Florentine Baptistery Doors," *ARTstor Blog*, n.d., online at http:// artstor.wordpress.com/2012/05/29/a-peek-behind-florences-gates-of -paradise/: "The photographs of the backs of the panels clearly show how Ghiberti saved those 7 kilos."

147 Second Nuremberg Haggadah: See Louis A. Berman, *The Akedah: The Binding of Isaac* (Northvale, N.J., 1997), 140. See also the "Nuremberg Haggada II," National Library of Israel, online at http://web.nli.org.il/sites/NLI/English/gallery/jewish/Pages/nuremberg -hagada.aspx.

CHAPTER 19

148 English mystery plays: There are six: Brome, Chester, Coventry (also known as N-Town), Towneley (also known as Wakefield), Dublin (also known as Northampton), and York. See Rosemary Woolf, *The English Mystery Plays* (Berkeley, 1972), and Jerome Taylor, *Medieval English Drama; Essays Critical and Contextual, Patterns of Literary Criticism* (Chicago, 1972). In sorting all this out, I benefited from the brief notes of Gloria J. Betcher, "See How Much Our Understanding of the Middle English Biblical Plays Has Changed Since 1956," in Class Notes on Early Drama in Britain, online at http://www.public.iastate.edu/~gbetcher/373/MEDrama.htm. For consistency, my quotes come from R. T. Davies, ed., *The Corpus Christi Play of the English Middle Ages* (Totowa, N.J., 1972), but I have cross-checked the text of the Dublin play with Osborn Waterhouse and Norman Davis, eds., *Non-cycle Plays and Fragments* (New York, 1970), the text of the Towneley (Wakefield) with Martial Rose, *The Wakefield Mystery Plays* (New York, 1969), and the text of the

Brome play with the version in Waterhouse and Davis as well as with
a third version, based on the Beinecke Library manuscript, with help
from Waterhouse and Davis, which appears in M. H. Abrams, ed.,
The Norton Anthology of English Literature, 3d ed. (New York,
1974), 395–406.

151 typology: Rosemary Woolf, "The Effect of Typology on the English
Mediaeval Plays of Abraham and Isaac," *Speculum* 32 (October
1957): 805–825. Peter Braeger, "Typology as Contrast in the Middle English *Abraham and Isaac* Plays," *Essays in Medieval Studies* 2
(1985): 131–153; Clifford Davidson, "The Sacrifice of Isaac in Medieval English Drama," *Papers on Language & Literature* 35 (Winter
1999): 28–55; Thomas Rendall, "Visual Typology in the Abraham
and Isaac Plays," *Modern Philology* 81 (February 1984): 221–232.
Also useful, in the context of the broader themes of this book, is Allen
J. Frantzen, "Tears for Abraham: The Chester Play of Abraham and
Isaac and Antisacrifice in Works by Wilfred Owen, Benjamin Britten,
and Derek Jarman," *Journal of Medieval & Early Modern Studies* 31
(Fall 2001): 445–476.

153 added Sarah to the script: The Northampton Abraham and Isaac is
the only English mystery in which Sarah has a part.

156 typology works by contrast as well as identity: Braeger, "Typology as Contrast in the Middle English *Abraham and Isaac* Plays,"
131–153.

159 "those glorious scars": Charles Wesley, "Lo, He Comes with Clouds
Descending."

CHAPTER 20

160 Kierkegaard: My quotes come from Søren Kierkegaard, *Fear and
Trembling: Dialectical Lyric by Johannes de Silentio,* trans. Alastair
Hannay (London, 2003). But I cross-checked them against and also
made much use of Howard V. Hong and Edna H. Hong et al., eds.
and trans., *Fear and Trembling; Repetition* (Princeton, N.J., 1983).

163 Augustine: *Against Faustus* 22.73.

163 Kant: Immanuel Kant, *The Conflict of the Faculties,* trans. Mary J.
Gregor (New York, 1979), 115.

166 just a test: For a Christian theologian's reading of the word "test"
as "just a test," something God never intended to see through, see
Gerhard von Rad, *Genesis: A Commentary* (Philadelphia, 1961), 234;
for a nearly identical Jewish version, see Nahum M. Sarna, *Understanding Genesis* (New York, 1966), 161–162, or Sarna on Genesis
22, in Sarna, *Genesis: The Traditional Hebrew Text with the New
JPS Translation* (Philadelphia, 1989).

166 Abraham arouses Kierkegaard's admiration: Kierkegaard, *Fear and Trembling*, 89–90.

166 "has explained my life": See "Selected Entries from Kierkegaard's Journals and Papers Pertaining to Fear and Trembling," in Hong and Hong, *Fear and Trembling*, 242.

CHAPTER 21

169 the world in which they lived: James L. Kugel, *How to Read the Bible: A Guide to Scripture, Then and Now* (New York, 2007); Richard Elliott Friedman, *Who Wrote the Bible?* (San Francisco, 1997); and Kevin Madigan, "Catholic Interpretation of the Bible," in Donald Senior and John J. Collins, *The Catholic Study Bible* (New York, 2006), 54–67.

171 "on the mount of the Lord there is sight": Genesis 22:14 (Alter).

171 Ibn Ezra suspected that those who read carefully: Friedman, *Who Wrote the Bible?*, 19.

171 origins of the Bible: Kugel, *How to Read the Bible*, 2–46, and from Kugel to his very useful source notes. See also, and most recently, Joanna Weinberg and Anthony Grafton, *"I Have Always Loved the Holy Tongue": Isaac Casaubon, the Jews, and a Forgotten Chapter in Renaissance Scholarship* (Cambridge, 2011).

171 Theories multiplied like Israelites: Friedman, *Who Wrote the Bible?*, 18–21; Kugel, *How to Read the Bible*, 2–46.

172 Spinoza concluded, that the Torah of Moses: Friedman, *Who Wrote the Bible?*, 21.

173 Richard Simon: Ibid., 20–21. See also Kugel, *How to Read the Bible*, 30–33.

173 Wellhausen: Julius Wellhausen, quoted in Kugel, *How to Read the Bible*; Wellhausen, *Prolegomena to the History of Israel*, trans. J. Sutherland Black and Alan Menzies (Edinburgh, 1885).

CHAPTER 22

177 who wrote it: There are good summaries, introductions to arguments, and references to a gigantic literature in Shalom Spiegel, *The Last Trial: On the Legends and Lore of the Command to Abraham to Offer Isaac as a Sacrifice: The Akedah* (New York, 1967), 122–126; John Van Seters, *Abraham in History and Tradition* (New Haven, Conn., 1975), 227-240; E. A. Speiser, *Genesis* (New York, 1964), 166; and in G. W. Coats, "Abraham's Sacrifice of Faith: A Form-Critical Analysis of Genesis 22," *Interpretation* 27 (1973): 395–396. See also Richard Elliott Friedman, *Who Wrote the Bible?* (San

Francisco, 1997), 247, 256–257, and Friedman, *The Bible with the Sources Revealed: A New View into the Five Books of Moses* (San Francisco, 2003), 165, 160. For biblical scholarship on Genesis 22 more generally, there is an invaluable summary and bibliography of the scholarship up to 1980 in Claus Westermann, *Genesis 12–36: A Commentary* (Minneapolis, 1985), 351–365; and a bibliography of work published between 1980 and 2003 in the categories of "human sacrifice, exegesis, and reception history" in Edward Noort and Eibert Tigchelaar, eds., *The Sacrifice of Isaac: The Aqedah (Genesis 22) and Its Interpretations* (Leiden, 2002), 211–223. Also essential are Hermann Gunkel, *Genesis* (Göttingen, 1910, 1977), and Gerhard von Rad, *Genesis: A Commentary* (Philadelphia, 1961).

178   J wrote that story too: See, for example, Van Seters, *Abraham in History and Tradition,* 227–240.

179   turned the chronology upside down: See, for example, ibid. But cf. Ronald S. Hendel, *Remembering Abraham: Culture, Memory, and History in the Hebrew Bible* (Oxford, 2005). See also Noort, "Genesis 22: Human Sacrifice and Theology in the Hebrew Bible," in Noort and Tigchelaar, *The Sacrifice of Isaac,* 14–20.

180   an obvious place in God's plan: R. W. L. Moberly, "The Earliest Commentary on the Akedah," *Vetus Testamentum* 38 (July 1988): 302–323.

180   essential to the rest of the story: See Van Seters, *Abraham in History and Tradition,* 237–240, and Jon D. Levenson, *The Death and Resurrection of the Beloved Son: The Transformation of Child Sacrifices in Judaism and Christianity* (New Haven, Conn., 1993), chapters 11, 12, and 14, especially 138–142 and 173–174.

180   J was a woman: Friedman, *Who Wrote the Bible?,* 85–86, and *The Book of J,* translated by David Rosenberg and interpreted by Harold Bloom (New York, 1990).

180   Something about child sacrifice: For a brief introduction to the literature, I would start with Levenson, *Death and Resurrection,* especially but not only 3–52 and 111–124. Then I would move by way of Levenson's notes to some of the dissertations, books, and essays he cites and wrestles with, including Roland de Vaux, *Studies in Old Testament Sacrifice* (Cardiff, 1964); Paul G. Mosca, "Child Sacrifice in Canaanite and Israelite Religion: A Study in Mulk and [Molech]" (Ph.D. diss., Harvard, 1975); George C. Heider, *The Cult of Molek: A Reassessment* (Sheffield, 1985); and John Day, *Molech: A God of Human Sacrifice in the Old Testament* (Cambridge, 1989). From the monographic literature I moved on to two recent anthologies, Noort and Tigchelaar, *The Sacrifice of Isaac,* and Karin Finsterbusch,

Armin Lange, and Diethard Romheld, eds., *Human Sacrifice in Jewish and Christian Tradition* (Leiden, 2007). Also extremely interesting and useful is John S. Rundin, "Pozo Moro, Child Sacrifice, and the Greek Legendary Tradition," *Journal of Biblical Literature* 123 (Fall 2004): 425–447. For the scholarship that puts ideas of gender and relations among women and men at the center of sacrifice, child sacrifice, and Genesis 22, start with two essential books: Nancy B. Jay, *Throughout Your Generations Forever: Sacrifice, Religion, and Paternity* (Chicago 1992), and Carol L. Delaney, *Abraham on Trial: The Social Legacy of Biblical Myth* (Princeton, N.J., 1998). For two (of a number) of the post-9/11 takes of the legacy of the story and sacrifice in Judaism, Christianity, and Islam, see Yvonne Sherwood, "Binding-Unbinding: Divided Responses of Judaism, Christianity, and Islam to the 'Sacrifice' of Abraham's Beloved Son," *Journal of the American Academy of Religion* 72 (December 2004): 821–861, and Bruce Chilton, *Abraham's Curse: Child Sacrifice in the Legacies of the West* (New York, 2008). For stories of child sacrifice in a Hindu context, see David Dean Shulman, *The Hungry God: Hindu Tales of Filicide and Devotion* (Chicago, 1993). For a very recent, and also very lucid and persuasive, essay on sacrifice, focusing on the differences between sacrifice *to* and sacrifice *for*, see Moshe Halbertal, *On Sacrifice* (Princeton, N.J., 2012).

181 old and essential element of Israelite theology: Jon Levenson has a clear and concise overview of the existing scholarship alongside his own views in *Death and Resurrection*, especially but not only 3–17 and 111–124.

182 "to substitute an animal for the firstborn son": See, for example, Van Seters, *Abraham in History and Tradition*, 227–240, and also Westermann, *Genesis*, 351–365.

182 But what place?: Levenson, *Death and Resurrection*, 114–124. See also Gunkel, *Genesis*.

183 Israel would be redeemed: Among the scholars who see the story as about something or some things in addition to or other than child sacrifice, see von Rad, *Genesis: A Commentary*; Noort, "Genesis 22: Human Sacrifice and Theology in the Hebrew Bible," 1–20; Moberly, "The Earliest Commentary on the Akedah"; and Delaney, *Abraham on Trial*.

185 literary critics of the Bible: I started with Robert Alter and Frank Kermode, *The Literary Guide to the Bible* (Cambridge, 1987); Alter, *The Art of Biblical Narrative* (New York, 1981); and Alter's introductions and commentary in Alter, *The Five Books of Moses: A Translation with Commentary* (New York, 2004).

186 Auerbach: Erich Auerbach, *Mimesis: The Representation of Reality in Western Literature* (Princeton, N.J., 1953).

CHAPTER 23

190 *The Last Trial:* In addition to Goldin's introduction, I have learned from Arnold J. Band, "Scholarship as Lamentation: Shalom Spiegel on 'The Binding of Isaac,' " in Band, *Studies in Modern Jewish Literature* (Philadelphia, 2003); Yael Feldman, " 'The Most Exalted Symbol for Our Time'?: Rewriting 'Isaac' in Tel Aviv," *Hebrew Studies Journal* 47 (2006): 253–273; and Feldman, *Glory and Agony: Isaac's Sacrifice and National Narrative* (Stanford, 2010).

192 "which in Judaism remained peripheral": Shalom Spiegel, *The Last Trial: On the Legends and Lore of the Command to Abraham to Offer Isaac as a Sacrifice: The Akedah* (New York, 1967), 116–117.

193 "The ancient pagan demand": Ibid., 129.

CHAPTER 24

197 Auschwitz, a father there with his son: Irving J. Rosenbaum, *The Holocaust and Halakhah* (New York, 1976), 3–5.

198 Simhah Elberg: "The *Akedah* of Treblinka," in Steven T. Katz, Shlomo Biderman, and Gershon Greenberg, eds., *Wrestling with God: Jewish Theological Responses during and after the Holocaust* (New York, 2007), 192–197. This useful volume includes biographical sketches of each author, illuminating introductions, and a bibliography.

198 Reuven Katz: "Torah Portion *Behukotai*: Israel's Misery and Israel's Redemption," in Katz et al., *Wrestling with God,* 107.

199 "the bitterest punishment of all": Elberg, "The *Akedah* of Treblinka," 192.

199 Kalonymus Kalman Shapira: See Nehemia Polen, *The Holy Fire: The Teachings of Rabbi Kalonymus Kalman Shapira, the Rebbe of the Warsaw Ghetto* (Northvale, N.J., 1994), and Kalonimus Kalmish ben Elimelekh (Kalonymus Kalman Shapira), *Sacred Fire: Torah from the Years of Fury, 1939–1942,* trans. J. Hershy Worch, ed. Deborah Miller (Northvale, N.J., 2000). My quotes here come from Shapira, *Sacred Fire,* 140.

200 nowhere more than in Palestine: Yael Feldman's *Glory and Agony: Isaac's Sacrifice and National Narrative* (Stanford, 2010) is absolutely essential for anyone interested in the complicated place, uses, and power (especially the psychological and psychoanalytical place and power) of Genesis 22 (and ideas of sacrifice more generally) among Jews in Palestine and the state of Israel in the twenti-

eth century. I have also benefited enormously from Mishael Caspi, *Take Now Thy Son: The Motif of the Aqedah (Binding) in Literature* (North Richland Hills, Tex., 2001); Yoseph Milman, "The Sacrifice of Isaac and Its Subversive Variations in Contemporary Hebrew Protest Poetry," *Religion & Literature* 23 (Summer 1991): 61–83; Stanley Nash, "Israeli Fathers and Sons Revisited," *Conservative Judaism* 38 (Summer 1986): 28–37; and Abraham (Avi) Sagi, "The Meaning of the *Akedah* in Israeli Culture and Jewish Tradition," *Israel Studies* 3 (1998): 45–60.

201 "silently stretch out our necks over the altar": Isaac Lamdan, "Upon the Altar." I have used the translation of Ruth Kartun-Blum, in Kartun-Blum, "'Where Does This Wood in My Hand Come From?': The Binding of Isaac in Modern Hebrew Poetry," *Prooftexts* 8 (1988): 296. Compare to Mishael Caspi's translation, reprinted in Caspi and John T. Greene, eds., *Unbinding the Binding of Isaac* (Lanham, Md., 2007), 137. For the Hebrew original, see Isaac Lamdan, *Kol Shire Yitshak Lamdan* (Jerusalem, 1973).

201 "I didn't ask for a ram": Isaac Lamdan, trans. and quoted in Kartun-Blum, "'Where Does This Wood in My Hand Come From?,'" 296. For the Hebrew, see Lamdan, *Kol Shire Yitshak Lamdan*.

201 Natan Alterman: This is the translation of Vivian London, which appears along with the Hebrew in Ruth Kartun-Blum, *Profane Scriptures: Reflections on the Dialogue with the Bible in Modern Hebrew Poetry* (Cincinnati, 1999), 28–29.

202 *Days of Ziklag*, S. Yizhar: I've relied on two translations (and fascinating discussions): Yael Feldman's, in *Glory and Agony*, 171–176, and Avi Sagi's, in "The Meaning of the Akedah in Israeli Culture and Jewish Tradition," 46–47. For the Hebrew, see S. Yizhar, *Yeme Tsiklag* (Tel Aviv, 1958). For another example of the same take, see the Polish-born American poet Jacob Glatstein's "Isaac," in David Curzon, *Modern Poems on the Bible: An Anthology* (Philadelphia, 1994).

202 Zalman Shazar: quoted and discussed in Feldman, *Glory and Agony*, 100–104.

203 wholly the work of men: There are endless examples. For one, see Emil L. Fackenheim, *God's Presence in History: Jewish Affirmations and Philosophical Reflections* (New York, 1970).

204 Pinchas Peli: "Borderline: Searching for a Religious Language of the *Shoah*," in Katz et al., *Wrestling with God*, 244–262, quote on 258.

204 in an attempt to exterminate "a race": Fackenheim, *God's Presence in History*, 69–79.

205 Elie Wiesel: *Messengers of God: Biblical Portraits and Legends* (New York, 1976), 76. For one more example, of countless possible examples, of Jewish writers drawing the sharpest possible distinction between Jewish and Christian foundation stories, see Ignaz May-baum, "The Face of God after Auschwitz," in Katz et al., *Wrestling with God,* 402–408.

206 "built on Moriah, not Sinai": Wiesel, *Messengers of God,* 97.

                              CHAPTER 25

207 biblical scholarship out into the wider world: Abraham Geiger, *Juda-ism and Its History* (New York, 1865, 1911), 64; Hirsch to Genesis 22, in *Hirsch Commentary on the Torah,* 2nd ed., revised and corrected (Gateshead, 1966), and *The Hirsch Chumash: The Five Books of Torah* (New York, 2000); and Harry Gersh, *The Story of the Jew* (New York, 1964), 16. Gersh's book is a rewriting of Lee J. and Elma Ehrlich Levinger's 1928 volume, which has next to nothing to say about the patriarchal age. James Carroll, unlike Gersh and Geiger, understands that some ancient Israelites, like some "pagans," probably practiced child sacrifice. Otherwise Carroll's understanding of the story (Abra-ham's willingness to sacrifice and God's merciful rejection of the prac-tice) is identical. See James Carroll, *Jerusalem, Jerusalem: How the Ancient City Ignited Our Modern World* (Boston, 2011), 15, 69–72.

208 Bob Dylan: *Highway 61 Revisited,* 1965.

208 G. Henton Davies: Gwynne Henton Davies, "Genesis, Introduction and Commentary on the Text," in *The Broadman Bible Commentary* (Nashville, 1969), 196–199. For an Islamic version of the idea that God would never ask such a thing, would neither command a Mus-lim to sin nor test a Muslim by commanding him to break one of his laws), see "Abraham and the Sacrifice: God Never Ordered Abraham to Sacrifice His Son," *Submitters Perspective* 15 (April 1999), online at http://www.masjidtucson.org/publications/books/SP/index.html.

209 Woody Allen's God: Allen, *Without Feathers* (New York, 1975), 26–27. Allen's God, by contrast, tells Abraham to get some rest and check back in the morning. For one of myriad recent midrash in which Abraham fails God's test, see Avraham Burg, *Very Near to You* (Jeru-salem; New Jersey, 2012), 30–32.

209 Jean-Paul Sartre and Martin Buber: Sartre, "Existentialism Is a Humanism" (1945–46), in John Kulka et al., *Existentialism Is a Humanism* (New Haven, Conn., 2007), 26, and Buber, "On the Suspension of the Ethical," in Buber, *Eclipse of God: Studies in the Relation Between Religion and Philosophy* (New York, 1952, 1999).

210 Lévinas: Emmanuel Lévinas, *Proper Names* (Stanford, 1996), 77, quoted and discussed in Claire Elise Katz, "The Voice of God and the Face of the Other," *The Journal of Textual Reasoning* 2 (June 2003), online at http://etext.lib.virginia.edu/journals/tr/volume2/index .html.

210 a tried-and-true "weapon of the weak": a concept many commentators borrowed from the political scientist James Scott, or imagined in one form or another for themselves. For the former, see Ron Krebs, "Rosh Hashana 5768," *Divrei Torah*, Congregation Darchei Noam, online at http://darcheinoammn.org/Learning/Learning.htm. For the latter, see all five essays in the first part of Lippman Bodoff, *The Binding of Isaac, Religious Murders, & Kabbalah: Seeds of Jewish Extremism and Alienation?* (Jerusalem, 2005), 27–92.

211 Claire Elise Katz: "The Voice of God and the Face of the Other." See also Joan Baez, "Isaac and Abraham" (1992). Baez's Abraham doesn't stop the sacrifice himself but wishes he had: "Said 'My darlin' son, I wish I was the one / Who spared you, spared your precious life.' "

211 Omri Boehm: Boehm, *The Binding of Isaac: A Religious Model of Disobedience* (New York, 2007). See also Boehm, "The Binding of Isaac: An Inner-Biblical Polemic on the Question of 'Disobeying' a Manifestly Illegal Order," *Vetus Testamentum* 52 (January 2002): 1–12; and Boehm, "Child Sacrifice, Ethical Responsibility and the Existence of the People of Israel," *Vetus Testamentum* 54 (April 2004): 145–156. For a complementary interpretation, forcefully argued, though lacking most of Boehm's evidence, see Harold Bloom's commentary in *The Book of J*, translated by David Rosenberg and interpreted by Harold Bloom (New York, 1990).

211 Jack Miles: Miles, *God: A Biography* (New York, 1995), 47–66.

CHAPTER 26

213 "The Way of the Wind": in Amos Oz, *Where the Jackals Howl, and Other Stories* (London, 1981). The story is reprinted in Nitza Ben-Dov, ed., *The Amos Oz Reader* (Boston, 2009).

215 "before his ideals are realized": Aharon, *The Battle*, quoted in Avi Sagi, "The Meaning of the Akedah in Israeli Culture and Jewish Tradition," *Israeli Studies* 3 (1998): 47. For the Hebrew, see Yariv Ben-Aharon, *ha-Kerav, Sifriyah La-'am*, 102 (Tel Aviv, 1966).

215 Eli Alon: quoted in Ruth Kartun-Blum, *Profane Scriptures: Reflections on the Dialogue with the Bible in Modern Hebrew Poetry* (Cincinnati, 1999), 58, and quoted and discussed at length in Yael Feldman, *Glory*

and Agony: Isaac's Sacrifice and National Narrative (Stanford, 2010), 229–31: "I would not want Abraham to be the father of my nation and such a God to be my God. God in this story is a Moloch and Abraham is simply an idol-worshipper."

215 *The Queen of the Bath*: On Levin and the play, see Hanoch Levin, *The Labor of Life: Selected Plays,* trans. and ed. Barbara Harshav (Stanford, 2003), xiii–xx; Feldman, *Glory and Agony,* 235–240; Kartun-Blum, *Profane Scriptures,* 55–58; and Sagi, "The Meaning of the Akedah in Israeli Culture and Jewish Tradition," 49–50.

216 "Father dear": Levin, *The Labor of Life,* xix–xx.

217 Yitzhak Laor: "This Idiot, Isaac." I've used the translation of Avi Sagi, in Sagi, "The Meaning of the Akedah in Israeli Culture and Jewish Tradition," 50. For a second English translation and discussion, see Feldman, *Glory and Agony,* 278–281. For the Hebrew, see Yitzhak Laor, *Rak ha-guf zokher* (Tel Aviv, 1985).

218 "the real hero of the sacrifice was the ram": Yehuda Amichai, *A Life of Poetry, 1948–1994,* trans. Benjamin Harshav and Barbara Harshav (New York, 1994), 345. See also Yehuda Amichai, *The Selected Poetry of Yehuda Amichai,* ed. and trans. Stephen Mitchell and Chana Bloch (New York, 1986), 151.

219 "Let God Cry": Amichai, "Abraham Had Three Sons." This is the "free translation" of Tova Forti, in Forti, "The Topos of the Binding of Isaac in Modern Hebrew Poetry," in Mishael Caspi and John T. Greene, eds., *Unbinding the Binding of Isaac* (Lanham, Md., 2007), 144. For the Hebrew, see Yehuda Amichai, *Patuah Sagur Patuah* (Jerusalem, 1998).

220 he owed his life to God: Abraham B. Yehoshua, "Mr. Mani and the Akedah," *Judaism* 50 (2001): 61–65.

220 *Early in the Summer of 1970*: Abraham B. Yehoshua, *Early in the Summer of 1970* (Garden City, N.Y., 1977).

221 *Mr. Mani*: Abraham B. Yehoshua, *Mr. Mani* (New York, 1992). In addition to Yehoshua's own commentary on his writing, I have found invaluable Yael Feldman's writing on *Mr. Mani* and many other twentieth-century Israeli novels. See Feldman, *Glory and Agony.*

CHAPTER 27

222 Eleanor Wilner's Sarah: "Sarah's Choice," in *Sarah's Choice* (Chicago, 1989).

224 she and God must have cried out together: Marek Halter, *Sarah: A Heroine of the Old Testament* (London, 2004), 290–293.

224 Rashi's sister: Dvora Yanow, "Sarah's Silence: A Newly Discovered

Commentary on Genesis 22 by Rashi's Sister," *Judaism* 43 (Fall 1994): 398–408.

224 a Colorado rabbi: David J. Zucker, "The Mysterious Disappearance of Sarah," *Judaism* 55 (Fall–Winter 2006): 30–39.

224 Carol Ochs: *Behind the Sex of God* (Boston, 1977), 45–46.

225 Carol Delaney: *Abraham on Trial: The Social Legacy of Biblical Myth* (Princeton, N.J., 1998). For an earlier, and overlapping, interpretation of the relationship between gender and sacrifice, see Nancy B. Jay, *Throughout Your Generations Forever: Sacrifice, Religion, and Paternity* (Chicago, 1992).

226 Alicia Ostriker's poem: "The Story of Abraham," reprinted in *Invisible Light: Poems about God* (New York, 2000), 23–24, and also in Delaney, *Abraham on Trial,* 132–133.

227 "bury my dead out of my sight": Alicia Ostriker, *Feminist Revision and the Bible* (Oxford, 1993), 38–50.

227 Phyllis Trible: Trible, "Genesis 22: The Sacrifice of Sarah," in Alice Bach, ed., *Women in the Hebrew Bible: A Reader* (New York, 1999), 285.

227 Wendy Zierler: Deuteronomy 6:5 (Alter); Zierler, "In Search of a Feminist Reading of the Akedah," *Nashim* (June 2005): 10–26. This translation of Genesis 24:67 is Robert Alter's.

228 Benjamin Galai: "The Life of Sarah," translated by Ruth Kartun-Blum and reprinted along with the Hebrew in *Profane Scriptures,* 44–45. For a second translation, see Bernhard Frank, ed. and trans., *Modern Hebrew Poetry* (Iowa City, 1980), 71. For the original collection, see Benjamin Galai, *Mas'a Tsafonah: Shirim* (Tel Aviv, 1968).

229 Shin Shifrah's "Hagar": translated by Irit Aharony, in "The Outcry, Question, and the Silence—Sarah and the Akedah in the Midrash and in Contemporary Israeli Literature," in Mishael Caspi and John T. Greene, eds., *Unbinding the Binding of Isaac* (Lanham, Md., 2007), 174. For the Hebrew, see Shin Shifrah, "Hagar," *Sipurei Bereshit* (Stories of Our Beginnings), ed. Zion Tanyah (Tel Aviv, 2003).

229 Yehudit Kafri: "In the Beginnings," translated by Irit Aharony, in "The Outcry, Question, and the Silence," in Caspi and Greene, *Unbinding the Binding of Isaac,* 177. For a second translation, and the Hebrew, see David C. Jacobson, *Does David Still Play Before You?: Israeli Poetry and the Bible* (Detroit, 1997), 216–217. For the volume in which the poem originally appeared, see Yehudit Kafri, *Mal'an shel layits: shirim* (Tel Aviv, 1988).

230 "whether all of me or part of me is killed?": Kalonimus Kalmish ben Elimelekh (Kalonymus Kalmish Shapira), *Sacred Fire: Torah from the*

Years of Fury, 1939–1942, trans. J. Hershy Worch and ed. Deborah Miller (Northvale, N.J., 2000), 14.

230 Eli Alon: "*Beresheit,*" translated by Jonathan Mohrer, with the generous assistance of Naomi Danis. For another English translation and discussion, see Yael Feldman, *Glory and Agony: Isaac's Sacrifice and National Narrative* (Stanford, 2010), 277–278. For the Hebrew, see A. Eli, *Ba-derekh la-arets ha-muvtahat* (Tel Aviv, 1989).

231 Haim Gouri, whose poem, "Heritage": in T. Carmi, trans. and ed., *The Penguin Book of Hebrew Verse* (New York, 1981), 565. For a second translation, see Haim Gouri, *Words in My Lovesick Blood: Poems,* trans. and ed. Stanley F. Chyet (Detroit, 1996), 27.

232 "if we had only listened to her voice": the final lines of Gouri's "Eyval," translated by Jonathan Mohrer, with the generous assistance of Naomi Danis and Noah Horowitz. For another English translation, see Feldman, *Glory and Agony,* 318. For the Hebrew, see Haim Gouri, *Eyval: shirim* (Tel Aviv, 2009), 52.

CHAPTER 28

235 the command had come from God: Clyde T. Francisco, "Genesis, Introduction and Commentary on the Text," in *The Broadman Bible Commentary,* vol. 1 rev. (Nashville, 1973), 187–189. For the controversy, see Jerry Faught, "Round Two, Volume One: The Broadman Commentary Controversy," *Baptist History and Heritage* 38 (Winter 2003): 94–114; Carl L. Kell, *Against the Wind: The Moderate Voice in Baptist Life* (Knoxville, 2009), 27–45; and Jeff Rogers, "Genesis 22—'The Sacrifice of Isaac' or 'Finding the Way Out,'" *PulpitBytes,* online at http://pulpitbytes.blogspot.com/2006/09/genesis-22-sacrific -of-isaac-or.html.

235 Kalonymus Shapira: Kalonimus Kalmish ben Elimelekh (Kalonymus Kalmish Shapira), *Sacred Fire: Torah from the Years of Fury, 1939–1942,* trans. J. Hershy Worch and ed. Deborah Miller (Northvale, N.J., 2000), 131–132.

235 Seyyed Hossein Nasr: in Bill D. Moyers, *Genesis: A Living Conversation* (New York, 1996), 233.

236 a beloved pet dog or cat: Dr. Gene Scott, "Heroes of Faithing: Abraham," n.d., online at http://asis.com/users/stag/heroes/abraham.html.

236 "because you said no to God": "Abraham and Isaac," *Mr. Kent's Devotional and Sunday School Lessons,* n.d., online at http://www .mrkent.com/devotionals/sschool/abe_isaac.htm.

236 diagnose Abraham as depressed or accuse him of abuse: See, for example, Joanne Carlson Brown and Rebecca Parker, "For God So

Loved the World?" in Joanne Carlson Brown and Carole R. Bohn, *Christianity, Patriarchy, and Abuse: A Feminist Critique* (New York, 1989), 26; Michael Lerner, *Jewish Renewal: Path to Healing and Transformation* (New York, 1994), 39–46; and Burton L. Visotzky, *The Genesis of Ethics* (New York, 1996), 104. See also Alice Miller, *The Untouched Key: Tracing Childhood Trauma in Creativity and Destructiveness* (New York, 1990).

236 Levenson: Jon D. Levenson, "Abusing Abraham: Traditions, Religious Histories, and Modern Misinterpretations," *Judaism* 47 (Summer 1998): 259–277. See also Terence E. Fretheim, "God, Abraham, and the Abuse of Isaac," *Word and World* 15 (1995), 49–57, and Andrew S. Yang, "Abraham and Isaac, Child Abuse and Martin Luther," *Lutheran Quarterly* 19 (Summer 2005): 153–166.

237 Yitzhak Laor: "This Idiot, Isaac (Late Version)." This translation is my own. For Gabriel Levin's, together with the Hebrew, see David C. Jacobson, *Does David Still Play Before You?: Israeli Poetry and the Bible* (Detroit, 1997),129–130. Levin's translation originally appeared in *Modern Hebrew Literature* 11 (Autumn–Winter 1993): 32.

237 Abraham killed Isaac: Shalom Spiegel, *The Last Trial: On the Legends and Lore of the Command to Abraham to Offer Isaac as a Sacrifice: The Akedah* (New York, 1967), 122–126, and Richard Elliott Friedman, *Who Wrote the Bible?* (San Francisco, 1997), 247, 256–257. See also Richard Elliott Friedman, *The Bible with Sources Revealed: A New View into the Five Books of Moses* (San Francisco, 2003), 65.

238 Anthony Shadid: *Night Draws Near* (New York, 2005), 260–291.

239 Yeshayahu Leibowitz: *Judaism, Human Values, and the Jewish State,* ed. and trans. Eliezer Goldman et al. (Cambridge, 1992), 14 and passim. On Sodom and Gomorrah, see also Levenson, "Abusing Abraham," 272 and 277n53. Also provocative in pondering Leibowitz's way of thinking about the story is Richard S. Ellis, "Human Logic, God's Logic, and the Akedah," *Conservative Judaism* 52 (Fall 1999): 28–32. In sermons, essays, and Bible commentary on the World Wide Web, there are countless other examples of this perspective (and every other). One that echoes Leibowitz and Ellis that has stuck with me over the years is Hillel Goldberg, "What Did Abraham Hear?," *Genesis Project,* 1999, online at http://www.torah.org/features/genesis/topic7.html.

240 "this free gift of love": Marcellino D'Ambrosio, "The Sacrifice of Isaac," The Crossroads Initiative, online at http://www.crossroadsinitiative.com/library_article/907/sacrifice_of_isaac.html.

240 Muslim parents: Orhan Pamuk dramatizes each of these responses

and explanations and several more in a just few pages of *The Museum of Innocence* (New York, 2009), 34–42.

240 Joseph B. Soloveitchik: The Rav (or Rov), quoted in Harold Schulweis, "The Sculpture of George Segal: Skirball Museum Lecture—May, 1997," online at http://www.vbs.org/page.cfm?p=870&newsid=187, posted January 28, 2011; in Schulweis, "Obedience and Conscience, Rosh Hashanah 1999," online at http://www.vbs.org/page.cfm?p =870&newsid=233, posted February 11, 2011; and in Chaim Navon, Lecture #24: The *Akeida, Theological Issues in Sefer Bereishit,* The Israel Koschitzky Virtual Beit Midrash, Yeshivat Har Etzion, online at http://vbm-torah.org/archive/bereishit/24bereishit.htm.

241 Chava Cohen-Pinchas's poem: "A Request," translated by Irit Aharony and reprinted in Aharony, "The Outcry, Question, and the Silence," in Mishael Caspi and John T. Greene, eds., *Unbinding the Binding of Isaac* (Lanham, Md., 2007), 178. For the Hebrew, see Chava Cohen-Pinchas, *Masa' Ayalah* (Tel Aviv, 1994).

241 Shin Shifrah's "Isaac": "Isaac," translated by Irit Aharony and reprinted in Aharony, "The Outcry, Question, and the Silence," in Caspi and Greene, *Unbinding the Binding of Isaac,* 178–179. For the Hebrew, see Shin Shifrah, *Shir Ishah: Shirim* (Tel Aviv, 1962).

242 "Abraham knew it was his turn": Jon D. Levenson, *The Death and Resurrection of the Beloved Son: The Transformation of Child Sacrifice in Judaism and Christianity* (New Haven, Conn., 1993), 17.

243 Levenson demurs: See Spiegel, *The Last Trial,* especially 63–64, and Jon D. Levenson, *The Death and Resurrection of the Beloved Son: The Transformation of Child Sacrifice in Judaism and Christianity* (New Haven, Conn., 1993), 3–17 and 111–142.

245 Uri Zvi Greenberg: "On a Night of Rain in Jerusalem," in T. Carmi, ed., *The Penguin Book of Hebrew Verse* (New York, 1981), 530–531.

246 Ra'yah Harnik: translated by Ruth Kartun-Blum and reprinted along with the Hebrew in Ruth Kartun-Blum, *Profane Scriptures: Reflections on the Dialogue with the Bible in Modern Hebrew Poetry* (Cincinnati, 1999), 5. For the original Hebrew collection, see Ra'yah Harnik *Shirim le-Guni* (Tel Aviv, 1983).

CHAPTER 29

251 Micah paid homage: Jon D. Levenson, *The Death and Resurrection of the Beloved Son: The Transformation of Child Sacrifice in Judaism and Christianity* (New Haven, Conn., 1993), 10–11.

Index

in *Prooftexts* Vol. 8, No. 3. Excerpt from the poem "This Idiot, Issac" by Yitzhak Laor, translated by Sagi, from the essay "The Meaning of the Akedah in Israeli Culture and Jewish Tradition" in *Israel Studies* Vol. 3, No. 1. Reprinted by permission of Indiana University Press as administered by Copyright Clearance Center.

National Association of Professors of Hebrew: Excerpt from "'Az Terem'— A Piyyut" by Yohanan ha-Cohen, translated by Abraham I. Shafir. This translation originally published in *Hebrew Studies* 45 (2004). Reprinted by permission of the National Association of Professors of Hebrew.

Stanford University Press: Excerpt from *The Labor of Life: Selected Plays* by Hanoch Levin, translated and edited by Barbara Harshav. Copyright © 2003 by the Board of Trustees of the Leland Stanford Jr. University. All rights reserved. Reprinted by permission of Stanford University Press, www.sup.org.

University Press of America: Excerpt from the poem "Abraham Had Three Sons" by Yehuda Amichai, translated by Tova Forti, from the essay "The Topos of the Binding of Isaac in Modern Hebrew Poetry" by Tova Forti. Excerpt from the poem "A Request" by Chava Cohen-Pinchas; excerpt from the poem "In the Beginnings" by Yehudit Kafri; and excerpts from the poems "Hagar" and "Isaac" by Shin Shifrah, all translated by Irit Aharony and from the essay "The Outcry, Question, and the Silence" by Irit Aharony. These two essays published in *Unbinding the Binding of Isaac*, edited by Mishael M. Caspi and John T. Greene. Reprinted by permission of the University Press of America.

W. W. Norton & Company, Inc.: Excerpt from *The Five Books of Moses: A Translation with Commentary,* translated by Robert Alter. Copyright © 2004 by Robert Alter. Reprinted by permission of W. W. Norton & Company, Inc.

Yitzhak Laor: Excerpt from "This Idiot, Isaac" (Late Version) by Yitzhak Laor, translated from the Hebrew by James E. Goodman. Reprinted by permission of the author.

THE BLUE BOOK

THE BLUE BOOK

A.L. Kennedy

WINDSOR
PARAGON

First published 2011
by
Jonathan Cape
This Large Print edition published 2012
by AudioGO Ltd
by arrangement with
The Random House Group Ltd

Hardcover   ISBN: 978 1 445 85998 9
Softcover   ISBN: 978 1 445 85999 6

British Library Cataloguing in Publication Data available

11785525

Printed and bound in Great Britain by
MPG Books Group Limited

For

W. F. N.

But here this is, the book you're reading.

Obviously.

Your book—it's started now, it's touched and opened, held. You could, if you wanted, heft it, wonder if it weighs more than a pigeon, or a plimsoll, or quite probably rather less than a wholemeal loaf. It offers you these possibilities.

And, quite naturally, you face it. Your eyes, your lips are turned towards it—all that paleness, all those marks—and you are so close here that if it were a person you might kiss. That might be unavoidable.

You can remember times when kissing has been unavoidable. You are not, after all, unattractive: not when people understand you and who you can be.

And you're a reader—clearly—here you are reading your book, which is what it was made for. It loves when you look, wakes when you look, and then it listens and it speaks. It was built to welcome your attention and reciprocate with this: the sound it lifts inside you. It gives you the signs for the shapes of the names of the thoughts in your mouth and in your mind and this is where they sing, here at the point where you both meet.

Which is where you might imagine, might even elicit, the tremble of paper, that unmistakable flinch. It moves for you, your book, and it will always show you all it can.

And this is when it needs to introduce you to the boy.

This boy.

This boy, he is deep in the summer of 1974 and

1

by himself and cutting up sharp from a curve in the road and climbing a haphazard, wriggling style and next he is over and on to the meadow, his purpose already set.

No, not a *meadow*: only scrub grass and some nettles, their greens faded by a long, demanding summer and pale dust.

So it's simply a field, then—not quite who it was in its spring.

A field with an almost teenager live inside it.

He is, taken altogether, a taut thing and a sprung thing, free and also rattled with being free, and there is no particular path across this field, but the boy knows his way and heads for its most distant border. Hands quick, feet quicker, plimsolls and a washed-out yellow shirt, shorts that are greyish and fawnish, that have a torn pocket at the back. His clothes are too small and yet also slack in a way that suggests he is both longer and leaner than when they were bought. He is running as if pursued.

Ahead of him, the air shrugs with afternoon heat, distorts—he likes this. He mainly likes uncertain and changeable things—they seem to offer more chances for comfort, success. And sometimes they're all that he gets so he has to make the best of them.

His footfalls jar, drum, as he drives into a harder and harder pace, fists lifting as high as his throat, head back. He is as brown as all the island's children, dark from months of swimming, running, rowing, scrambling, months of bicycles and horses, little boats, months of hoarding stones and noting birds and of the pleasures in simple exhaustion. The boy's expression is currently thin and fierce. At a distance, it isn't easy to judge if this comes from effort, or emotion.

He reaches the opposite fence, swings himself over easily, fluidly, fast. His body is made of long, hard balances and strengths which take constant practice: there are days when he stumbles, breaks things, fails. Today, though, he is neck and neck with his own growth. Tomorrow, it will probably beat him again, muffle him up in clumsiness. In the end, he will be the bobbing head-and-shoulders-above in almost any group, will feel his height as a responsibility, a potential trap. He is already beginning to know this, but the knowledge is still light and he has taken to the pleasures of being visible, selected, dominant. His hair also draws the eye—fair, currently close to white at its tips, a salt white that deepens into honey against his scalp, his skin. He is not unattractive, but will always assume he is simply passable, scraping by. This will often seem charming.

He takes the only possible track onwards—a snug route between high blackthorn hedges, like the start of a maze. He enjoys being hidden in the din of bees, the scuffles of dunnocks and wrens, of fugitive lives. His feet run in the centre of the path where the cropped turf dips as if it were being bowed, stretched down beneath his special weight. Trees reach across and shadow him. With the green below and the green above, he could be in a tunnel, could be bulleting into the secret of something, unlocking it. And the tunnel leads down, tilts headlong down, until it balks at the cliff's edge and flexes into a sudden turn, then tacks back and forth across the face of a sharp descent, plunging on in a kind of crouch, huddling as far as it can from the threat of winds and the bright sea's watching.

The tunnel is no longer constant from here on: the boy sometimes breaks out across tawny exposures

3

of stone, lopes beside tumbled drops and distances and the wide blare of sealight. Sometimes the branches clasp in over him again with a thick press of humid air, cobwebs, bramble tears—they touch him like music, stroke and cling and prick. Inside he is mostly filled with music, seems to himself that he shudders and glows with it, with so many beautiful details: names and lyrics, sleeve notes, playlists, artwork, mystically important anecdotes. On his best days, he is racked with music to the point of helpless smiling.

Only once, the boy pauses in the crook of a naked turn, is shaken by his own breath, folds over to touch his knees and stares at the howling, unsteadying blue of water. He feels its breath rise and brush him, sees the white gnaw and fumble of it against rocks and the seam where it fits under the sky. The blue stares back, bullets clear through him and out the other side. The boy feels it does not care about him, is only a terrible, hungry dazzle.

And then his intentions take him again, harry and press, and the grass underfoot steepens, sheers away deep into a final slither, an excuse to be out of control before he reaches the brink: the metal post, the first of the fixed ropes. He almost grins.

Descending is difficult—he has learned it is much easier to climb. Here, he can't see where his toes kick in and bounce, has to control his body as it swings, one line dropping to another, from post to post, threading the twists of the route and winding him lower. He bears his own weight safe, hands clever round the fat, stiff strands. He likes the effort, sweat, wishes it were more, for torn hands and bleeding, for the test of a fall.

Below him is the Pot: a tiny cove pocketed in

4

behind a high, containing wall and floored with a fawny-grey chaos of rocks. The boy makes his last spring, looses the rope and lets his feet land with a grinding clack amongst the wreckage and cold echoes. There is a sense here of something temporarily absent, a power that will return and overwhelm. The boy feels his shins tickle with its thrill and wishes he could properly savour the fear, believe it and be transported by its possibilities. He stepping-stones across the foreheads of the flatter boulders, aiming for an archway to his left.

At one time, he supposes, the Pot must have been really like a pot, a round little space sealed up from the tide, but the fabric of the island is never reliable. The whole place has worried itself into passages, landslips, caves, stacks. And long ago the miners worked at it: he imagines them, imported strangers with candlelit talents, grimly burrowing down between *magnetite*, *haematite*, *sphalerite*, *bornite*— the boy keeps the rhymes hot under his tongue like a spell. He likes to whisper the musical complications of *argentiferous pyrite* and *hornblende gneiss*. He belongs to the island, because he can name its bones. But it is unforgivably delicate: even the granite headlands seem shattered by some terrible, ancient impact. They are more shocked heaps of weight than permanent features.

And the Pot's feet-thick defences have been breached: a dark, lithe passageway leads along a fault line and will let in the high water. It lets the boy go out. He scrambles to one side of a huge, dropped boulder, fits between stones smoothed into contours that might be the flanks of some strange living thing. Above him is the nice threat of other faulting, sudden falls—ahead is sunwarmth on

5

surfaces, the rasp of limpets and a small shore which is his: in its heart, it is his and should be his and was meant to be forever his. This was the only certainty he wanted. There will only be one other he ever will.

Back in the cottage his mother will still be packing. Although she is very familiar with moving, she will take hours to fill and then unfill her bags, to rearrange and start again. The boy has told her he will deal with his own things. He always does.

This afternoon, he lies down on his back amongst the lowest rocks, settles and shifts until they can properly dig in and bite him. There are buttresses and thrones here ready for him, granite platforms that lift him so he can observe, but today he won't use them. He shuts his eyes and lets the roar of daylight bleed through and the reek of the sea is already tight around him, nearly wicked—it has the hotmetal, weird, stark taste of himself doing bad, himself at the start of sex, of his whole, red lifetime's allowance of sex. It's the scent, to be truthful, of being beyond the start and lost in a newness of want, of blurred demands and lapping, tidal fears.

But today is about something else—not being scared, not being a body, not about coping with any of that.

The boy swallows and he pauses and he parts his lips and then he is angry. He is furious.

At last.

At last, he is beside himself. He is raging.

And he's also determined that he won't be sad, or cut, or split, or harmed in some way that is bewildering and lodged in his stomach and his lungs and in his face—but mainly in his stomach, in this emptied place where he had a stomach. Those feelings would

6

be bad, so instead he is fully and hopelessly raging. He claws his fingers into the pebbles and gritty damp and he is never going to cry, never going to be the boy who has to leave here and not come back, lose this and then have to remember it, never going to be the boy who was stupid and let this in and loved it, who made plans.

Instead, he will be the boy who climbs down the ropes into his secret, into his perfect place and makes sure, before everything changes, that he is changed first. He has decided that he will be somebody else. He is going to lie here until he gets faster than death, until he is nothing but velocity. He is going to summon his future so powerfully that it will weather the cliffs in moments, boil their crystals, shock their strata until they break. The day when he steps from the harbour to the boat, the day when he walks to another new school, the day when he gathers his mother's clothes and folds them, tidies her away and finds he is only thinking of whether he'll make a sandwich when he's done—those times will have passed him, hardly touched him, and he will be grown smoothly older, will be fine. Before he stands up again, brushes off the sand from his adult self, he will have gathered powers, dignities and skills— he will be a man and complete.

This is his wish. He believes it so hard that his arms shake and he feels sick and, if the world were fair, his efforts ought to be rewarded.

The boy's breath speeds, is shallow, injured and animal. He frowns. Sandflies bounce and cloud, closed anemones shine like blood clots in shadowed fissures, the whole shoreline seethes mildly with thoughtless life. He puzzles on, leans against nature, needs it to give.

7

An hour passes, more.

The boy keeps on. He is a determined person.

But in the end he is tired and thirsty and not altered and the evening is coming and with it the tide and, because he does not want to drown, the boy eases himself back through to the Pot and stands for a while where the late sun is prying amongst the rubble and he braces his feet and then yells his name. He screams it. He intends the word to catch and stain somewhere, to hide itself away for later, like a spell. Then he grabs hold of the rope and begins to pull his body up.

He knew his intentions would fail him, but they were all he had.

He was right about this, though—it is much easier to climb.

Later, more than thirty years later, a man and a woman wait to board a boat—a liner, to be more accurate. They stand in a nicely murmuring and generally well-dressed queue while suffering a sense of gentle disappointment. They had expected and, only half jokingly, discussed the quayside bustle in which they would want to be immersed before embarkation: stevedores hefting cabin trunks through the clean tang of seaside air, other couples walking up brisk wooden gangplanks in handmade shoes and waving.

The woman has hair like her father's: a thick black with illogical spasms of curl. She would rather this were not the case. She has also inherited what is pretty much her mother's figure, so at school she was mildly dumpy and, having spent her twenties and thirties getting away with being more curved than actually fat, she imagines that her forties and a slowing metabolism will force her into increasingly vague knitwear and mail order slacks with elasticated waistbands. She does not anticipate that she'll enjoy this, although in some ways she'd have to admit that she's had a good run. Her full name is Elizabeth Caroline Barber and she is thinking—*I could just fancy a bit of waving. I have no idea who we'd be waving to, though. Or to whom we would be waving. There's something about queuing for a liner that makes you want to get your grammar right . . . No one ashore we **could** wave to. Except the stevedores—and I wouldn't be sure about waving to them—all greasy caps and Mickey-Finned drinks with Humphrey Bogart, your stevedores.*

I think.

But not really a job that exists any more, is it? Or it does exist, but not in Britain, because we don't have docks, not really. Shore porters—do we still have them? Do we still have real jobs here at all? Ones you need to train for, that have titles, special hats? Jesus, the postman had a uniform when I was a kid—now he looks like the man who mugged the man in the uniform and stole his sack. Not that he has a sack any more either.

The jolly postmen's Christmas race with loaded sacks—they used to show a bit of that on telly every year—the light-hearted end to the news. Or did I make that up? I'm fairly sure it used to happen. A manifestation of postal pride—vaguely servile and sweaty, but pride, nonetheless . . .

Is this the way I'll be now? I'll climb aboard, get more and more nostalgic, then judgemental, then

9

terrified of change and eventually I'm going to be right wing? Just happily fixated on the noose and the birch, detention centres for foreign miscreants, sterilisations for the poor and/or thick?

It's because I'm annoyed.

Being annoyed is almost indistinguishable from being right wing.

Correction: being annoyed **in a queue** is almost indistinguishable from being right wing. That kind of unpleasantly bottled fury and tedium isn't going to break out in celebrations of your brotherhood with one and all and the commonality of human experience— not when one and all are in your way and your own experience is uniquely pissed off with every other human on earth.

If State Socialism had been more sensible, it wouldn't have generated all those queues—that's what cut its throat in the long run—everyone a bloody fascist before they got their four-ounce loaf of bread. I would imagine.

Naturally, I'm thinking of State Socialism because that will make me even less comfortable when I'm already, as I might say, exquisitely aware that only contemplating—from a distance—the outside of this luxury bloody liner has made me feel slightly filthy, a bit **wrong**.

Behind us, the country is being cut up and auctioned off for meat and we couldn't care, apparently—we're just sailing away.

Guilty, that's what this makes me. I'm starting to feel sticky with it.

Probably not starting—could have been building for a while.

Has been building.

I want to wash. Lie down and wash and then lie

10

down again. And then wash.

And, of course, I am undemocratically irritated by the utter lack of luxury at this stage in the proceedings— cheap carpet, prefab walls, grey-sounding announcements relating to technical/nautical difficulties and delays—which may or may not be alarming: I understand none of them—and a rank of vaguely shoddy check-in desks, behind which women in uniforms do almost nothing very slowly.

*Why are we **here**? We're not **cruise people**. We're **not quoits and gin slings and rubbers of bridge people**. Or **being driven past monuments at speed with optional commentary people**, we are not **tonight will be the 1974 theme disco in the Galaxy Room people**. We will not be getting tattoos while in altered states, or buying Moroccan boys, or toppling wealthy aunts over the side, and we will not be—hopefully—dying in an unfortunate but historic mid-Atlantic calamity.*

Why are we here?

Why am I here?

Why am I here with Derek?

Why is Derek here with me?

Why are we standing in a non-moving queue which, at best, threatens to funnel us into a holding area equipped with unadventurous vending machines and a lady who seems to be selling tea and shockingly rudimentary sandwiches. She may also have biscuits, I can't tell from here.

At least there are toilets.

Currently out of reach, but it's good to know they've been provided.

Over there.

Where we can't use them.

Not that I couldn't nip away and ease discomfort should I need to, although Derek might not like that—

11

my leaving him.

He's in a mood.

Hasn't said so, doesn't need to, doesn't speak during moods. Self-explanatory, his bad temper, by dint of its heaving great silence.

Nevertheless, without using the medium of language he is still making it plain that he doesn't want to be surrounded by the staggeringly ancient as they whine about their pills and their luggage and their feet, or— should they, by some miracle, have actually been processed—as they shuffle between the tea lady and the toilets while mouthing sandwiches and apparently coming close to coughing their last.

We are, by miles, the youngest couple here. We are also the tallest. Well, Derek is the tallest. Just about. No doubt, should he—like our queue-dwelling neighbours—live to be 180, his own vertebrae will have collapsed into powder and aches and he will be smaller, or else hooped over like that guy there who is practically, for goodness' sake, peering back at life through his own knees. Which must be novel. Then again, at his age, would he want to keep on having to look ahead?

In front of Elizabeth, Derek hunches and shrugs his shoulders inside his jacket, then rubs one hand into and through his hair.

Dirty blond.

And she remembers this morning and lying on her side, newly awake, still softly fitting back into herself and being bewildered by a thought, by the idea of holding—she had this perfectly clear sensation of holding her arms around warm, breathing ribs, a lean chest—her hands meeting over his breathing—a dream of her resting in tight to the curve of his spine. But she wasn't holding anyone.

Hypnopompic hallucination. It's not uncommon.

12

Might be linked to stress.

I have stress.

My stresses are considerable.

A long spine, clearly enunciated, and then the dream had closed and made her miss him.

Silly.

More than silly—quite a lot more than that.

More than silly being currently the absolute best I can muster.

Derek had been out of bed and clattering about in the hotel shower, trotting to the sink, tooth brushing, spitting, throat-clearing, shaving, forgetting and then not forgetting to comb his hair. He had been readying himself while Beth was quietly left with a hot illusion, finding it deep, convincing.

Later, she'd held his hand in the taxi as they headed for the docks. She'd felt his knuckles, she'd suffered that tiny bump of nervousness as the pale side of the ship approached them, a higher and higher slab—like a building, like something too large to float.

Although it will. I have every confidence that it will. Massive boat for a massive ocean, that's not a problem.

And it's not as if we've had to pay for this—not exactly. This is a—what would you call it?—windfall. A possibly fortunate happenstance.

Then again—no such thing as a free cruise. Which isn't a popular saying, but could be—it might be appropriate . . .

Not that we're on a cruise, not honestly what we could say is a cruise. This will be **transport**—*Southampton to New York—like catching a bus.*

Well, not so much like a bus.

More like being taught to appreciate the romance of taking tea at four and cabin stewards and sunsets off

13

the stern before an early night.

Sunsets off the bow. Heading west—it would be the bow. Where you'd be exposed, wind-lashed, freezing. Not romantic.

Just the early night then.

Like willingly falling unconscious in a vast disaster movie with a cast of the virtually dead.

Christ, I don't know why I'm doing this.

I just do not.

'Boring, isn't it? Or else, perhaps not so much boring as *unsettling*. I mean, *I'm* unsettled . . . Can't speak for anyone else. Sorry . . .' This is the man who has ended up standing behind her in the line.

Behind him is the brittle lady with aggressive jewellery—the one Elizabeth has decided to think of as a quietly alcoholic widow, the one who genuinely does seem to be accompanied by what might once have been called A Companion.

Bet she'll turn out to be less quietly alcoholic.

Elizabeth is starting to gather hypotheses about many of her relatively-soon-to-be fellow passengers.

She has no theories about the man. He does not seem to be anything in particular. He has one hand in his trouser pocket and whatever bags he is travelling with must have been handed over for loading, because he is carrying nothing beyond a dark brown overcoat. It is a noticeably good coat, although he does not seem to care about it, keeps it haphazardly folded across one arm.

It'll crease.

And he'll be sorry if they lose his luggage.

No. No, he won't.

His suit, although vaguely ill-kempt, fits him suspiciously well.

Made for him.

14

He would buy other luggage, if they lost his. There's nothing he couldn't replace.

That's what I'd guess.

Even though she knows this is unfair, she believes there is something despicable about a person who can't appreciate his own belongings, who doesn't need his clothes.

Should this happen to be the case. Judging the book by its cover—which one never should.

'I do apologise. Perhaps you didn't want to talk.'

'What?' She doesn't want to seem rude. Saying *what* to a stranger would be rude, in almost anyone's opinion. Ignoring someone when they speak to you and thinking about them instead is rude, too. 'Um . . .' Doing it again would be ruder. 'I'm sorry.' Whether you know them or not.

'Ah. So we're both sorry.' He rummages violently in the pockets of his coat and then stops. He inclines his head and apparently gives his entire attention to the notch in her collarbone. He addresses it earnestly. 'I . . . by myself, you see. Long voyage ahead . . . not incredibly long and there's the cinema, shows, entertainers . . . probably far too much going on to deal with, in actuality, *uncomfortable numbers* of possibilities—but familiar faces . . .' He breaks off to gaze beyond her, as if he is searching for something troublesome and fast moving. He is pale in a way that suggests fragility, illness. He sighs, 'There are occasionally times—*will be*, I beg your pardon, occasionally times when one would like to chat—when *I* would. Apart from *this* time, of course, which is *excruciating*—but hardly a time at all, more a type of solid, liquid maybe, that *has to be got through*. Probably, though, you don't *want* to chat and so everything I've said is . . . *irrelevant*.' The

15

man blinks, considers. 'Or else . . . chatting might not be involving, *distracting* enough.' He shakes his head briefly and steps towards her, his left foot splaying very gently, not inelegant, but outwith his control. He walks as if his shoes are too stiff, or too heavy, or not his.

Or as if he's afraid. I would say he's afraid. He walks like a man on glass, on ice.

He falters to a halt. 'Are you good at maths?'

'I beg your pardon?'

'Maths.' He smiles past her, aims the expression quite carefully at her partner's doggedly mute back. 'Arithmetic? Numbers? One and one equalling two. As an alternative to eleven. Or three. In the binary system, three—but not in the decimal, not in the one we'd be used to using. So many ways of saying so many things. Two would be what we were dealing with here and now.'

'I know one and one is two, yes.' She tries to smile calmly, because this might be the correct response.

When he looks at her directly there is something about the deep of the man's eyes which makes her reach and find Derek's hand, tug him round by it to stand beside her. Elizabeth is not absolutely surprised when this doesn't make her feel more at ease. She seems only to be demonstrating a public weakness, a lapse in taste.

The stranger continues, apparently concentrating on forcing himself inside his words, increasing their density, and yet staying as motionless as he can be while still managing to speak, 'Then what would be the number you would pick—just a game—can we play a game?—one number between one and ten— what would you pick?—you might want to think for your number carefully, search, maybe discount

16

inappropriate options—or else you could choose the first one, your very first choice, the one that seemed right, that immediate choice. Or you could change your mind. Because everyone's free to do that. Of course.'

He could be an entertainer.

Either very successful, or very not.

'No. Really. Indulge me. Genuinely think of a number between one and ten. You can't be wrong. Just give me a number.'

He waits politely.

A paid entertainer.

He continues to wait, but with no suggestion that he doubts she will eventually oblige him.

'Seven.'

'Really? Seven. You're sure?'

Stage clothes and pretending. An act.

When she says it again, 'Seven,' she sounds sharp and has the sense that she has become a small focus for others' interest. She wishes the man would go away.

Instead, he very carefully smiles at her. 'And another? He shows her exactly the face of an understanding friend, a man to whom she could say anything in any way and be entirely understood, a gentle man and a gentleman, a rare thing. He shows her precisely and tenderly calibrated fellow feeling. For the space of two words it roars and flares and is unpreventable. It comforts. It is built to do nothing but. Then he puts it away. 'Another? If you wouldn't mind.'

'Two.'

'And another?'

She can feel Derek's arm leaning against hers, but he says nothing to help her. She is the one that

17

speaks. 'Five. No, eight. Eight.'

'You're good at this. Now reverse them—those numbers. Do you need a piece of paper to work this out? I think I have a piece of paper . . .' He contemplates his coat and its pockets again severely.

'Seven five eight in reverse is eight five seven. I can remember that much.' Which didn't seem petulant and ungrateful before she'd said it, heard it, but it clearly was—undoubtedly she is being a bad sport. No, she is being put in the wrong—when none of this is anything she asked for.

The man blinks, takes himself close to the edge of a grin, conspiratorial, charming. 'But you chose seven *two* eight . . .' He pauses to clear his throat. 'If seven *five* eight would be better . . .' The amusement flickers in again.

'It would.'

'Beautiful.' Although for an instant he frowns, considers, then, 'So now you can subtract them from each other—seven five eight from eight five seven. What would that make ?'

'That would be . . . Nine . . . That would be ninety-nine.'

'As opposed to sixty-six, if we picked another point of view . . . And if you add those numbers together— nine and another nine—that would be . . .'

'Eighteen.'

'And then subtract the one from the eight. Because we can't leave it be. Poor eighteen.'

'Seven.'

'Seven. Which is the number you first thought of, isn't it . . . ? Oddly. Seven. And I'll show . . . I'll show you seven. In a manner of speaking. I have it here.' This time he is more assured as he manhandles his coat and fetches out a thumbed book from one of its pockets—she can't see the cover. 'Would you say you were determined, a determined person? If you don't mind my asking . . .' The man angles his head towards Derek and grins, rapidly boyish and then smoothed again. 'Is the lady determined? I have no idea, but she does seem that way—admirable, if I can say so—which is why I asked—I wouldn't ask if I thought it wasn't probable—determination, that shows in the face—like . . . *mercy*, for example—*kindness*—betrayal, grief . . .'

He can't shut up. He's stuck in this, talking it through to the end. Patter. Spitting out the patter, no matter what. A man who memorises nonsense and then inflicts it.

'You're her husband? Boyfriend? None of my business—but *lovely* idea, to go on a cruise together. Nothing better, I would say.'

And the stranger nods back at Elizabeth, refocuses, winks, while he speaks and speaks, voice quiet but unavoidable. He hands her the book and tells her, 'Determination can change who you are. Changing who you are can alter almost anything. Do you believe that?' And no space for her to answer, because rattling, bolting in after it comes, 'I can prove it. In a way. In a trivial, though perhaps diverting, way. If you take the book and you think of your number, you think of *seven*, strongly enough— if you feel *seven* in your chest, in your pulse, if inside your head you scream it—if you internally *yell*—and that seven becomes so *true* that its *essence*, its *strength*, is irresistible—and when you do that and keep doing that, then you can open up the book and turn it to page seven and you will see . . .'

Obedient, she opens the book where she's told to and sees nothing unusual.

'And you keep on screaming and you turn over that page . . .'

Which she does and finds that neatly, predictably, there is no page eight. There are only two pages, one after the other, both numbered seven—as if seven were somehow contagious, had soaked through the paper.

'And page eighteen, as we might imagine . . .'

Delivers itself as another page seven.

'The numbers.' She passes him back his trick. 'Clever. Thank you.'

'Don't mention it.' And he puts on his coat, which seems unnecessary—the waiting area is bleak, but not cold.

'It must be odd to read—a book like that.'

'Maybe.' He repockets the book which is maybe odd to read, shakes his sleeves, his lapels, until whatever order he sought to impose has been established. 'Books aren't about numbers, though, are they? They're stories—words. They're people's stories. The numbers wouldn't be the part you'd notice, I'd have said. Even if you ought to . . .'

The man forces out his hand abruptly and surprises Derek into shaking it.

And, perfectly normally, Elizabeth is next for the chill, smooth pressure of his grip, the tamp of his thumb in the heart of her palm. There is something overly naked about the man's skin, as if it is a terrible, white secret. She tries to disengage a moment before he allows her to which makes her feel rude again, intolerant. She tells him, 'Some people would notice.' Which is intended to sound placatory, but is mainly patronising and also mumbled.

'Many wouldn't. Many, in fact, *would not*.' This as he turns from her, as he is leaving with that faintly

20

dragged and staggered walk, that atmosphere of discomfort, the uneasy head.

All at sea.

Elizabeth intends to keep an eye on him, watch where he goes, but then the queue fusses around her in a kind of irritated ripple and manages to propel itself forward by at least a yard. The excitement of this means she loses the man completely.

'God save me from amateur magicians.' At least the incident has broken Derek's sulk. 'I think we're getting somewhere finally, though . . .'

And he's right. As mysteriously as they were trapped by inaction, they are now bustled through and can fully partake in the joys of flip-up plastic seating and sturdy tea, no biscuits. Elisabeth feels she might want to buy a bag of chocolate nuts from the machine, but then reconsiders her intention, does nothing.

Docile blocks of humanity are summoned from their benevolent detention and disappear through doorways which smell of oily mechanisms, fuel and—unmistakably—salt water.

Almost on our way.

And this thought squeezes her with panic, raises a true, sick welt of fear that means, when the appropriate passenger grouping is called, Elizabeth almost stumbles from her seat. She has small difficulties with her hands as she picks up her bag. Over to her left she can hear voices.

'And if we subtract two hundred and thirty six from six hundred and thirty two . . . ? We get?

'Um . . . three hundred and ninety-six . . . ?'

'And three plus nine plus six?'

'That's . . . seventeen.'

'That's . . . ?'

21

'Oh, eighteen. Yes. Eighteen.'

'And we can't leave poor eighteen alone, though, can we? Poor eighteen. One from eight?'

'Is seven.'

The second time around it's less impressive: the working starts to show and maybe she's sorry for the man and his puzzle which no longer does.

*   *   *

And maybe you're sorry for him also, have compassion for his inadvertent and public failing. Perhaps you would find it uncomfortable if your book mentioned the way Beth continues to watch the man until he shakes his head, glances away from his work and—before Beth can stop this—meets her eyes again. He tries to construct a type of smile, but his face is soft suddenly, perhaps ashamed, and he turns away and seems to sink slightly. He drops his book, has to stoop and fumble for it—nervous fingers.

This is unfortunate for him and you can imagine how he feels.

You're aware of how easy it is to make these minor errors.

There are times when you've personally known things to misfire—the sentence that fell badly, the dull gift, slapdash comment, hobbled punchline, tight-fisted tip—trying to be too stupid, trying to be too clever, too silly, too carefree, too caring, too free. You can think back to those long and hollow pauses when you realised that you'd misjudged a mood, weren't paying attention, had taken the wrong risk.

You don't worry about these occasions, or not that much. There are a few past humiliations which,

22

yes—if you ponder them, truly enter in—can still raise a significant sting and that queasy and sticky ridiculousness of you being inappropriately yourself. But there's nothing destructive about your reflections and you can laugh at them with ease. You can enjoy allowing others to laugh, too. You don't stand on your dignity, you aren't stuffy or prickly unless you've been given good cause and this means you can be relaxing company. Those who know you would say this, if they were asked.

And those you know, the people you care about—mistakes with them can be more serious. Going wrong can hurt so much when you're only beginning to care, when you're delicate and don't know your situation and something extraordinary could be ruined before you reach it. But it's probably worse when you love, fully love, what you've got and yet could still crash in and spoil it. You want to avoid that—anyone would.

You cope, though. In some areas, you excel. For this and many other reasons there's a good deal about you that others could admire. You're a survivor, although people might not notice this and you don't make a fuss.

You're a good person at heart.

You're sure of this and your book's sure of it, too.

There are things good people shouldn't do. Most of these are well established, codified as precepts, but you can be certain that—with laws or without them, overseen or unobserved—your own nature would prevent you from straying too far into harm.

You wouldn't consciously injure, wouldn't murder, wouldn't steal.

Although stealing can sometimes be difficult to define: more than your fair share of mints in a restaurant, hotel soaps, ashtrays in bars—some objects can seem ownerless, lost, attractive. This doesn't mean that you would take crockery from the restaurant, or light fittings from the hotel, or fire extinguishers from the bar—any more than you would walk out with the mirror from a changing room, or a coat set down for an unguarded moment on a chair, or drive away with someone else's car.

You wouldn't study a person who, in a strict and pedantic sense, belonged to someone not yourself— you wouldn't slip into wanting them, imagining, overtures. Just as you wouldn't defraud an insurance company, or falsely claim a benefit, or avoid paying any portion of your taxes.

Not to an unacceptable degree.

You only have these ideas, just very occasionally these quite natural ideas. When, for instance, the person ahead of you in the bank queue is carrying bags of money, just obviously a great weight of unmarked cash, or when security guards stroll past you with simple, tidy boxes of who can say how much—you do very slightly have this impulse to find out how heavy solid wealth could be, to make yourself better informed on that small point—

to grab, to snatch and run.

This doesn't imply that your integrity is tarnished. You have thought a thought, no more than that.

And maybe you have picked up coins, banknotes in the street, or from the floor of a shop, a cab, a bus, in the car park at the back of a rowdy pub—so many people have paused there—rendered careless, eccentric, helpless by their pleasures—and have burrowed into pockets and bags for their keys, have ended by dropping, losing everything as they search. This wasn't money which was yours and yet you kept it. Like a stranger's little gift.

But there was no fault involved, not on your part.

And you would never damage an animal or a child. Unless, of course, it was to spare them greater hurts. And perhaps animals are frightened, sacrificed in the production of your food, even though you do everything reasonable to avoid this. You assuredly have good will, but also distractions—it is sometimes hard to apply yourself for others' sakes and to stay comprehensively informed. Child labour, for instance, can ooze into places you might not suspect and undoubtedly ruins lives, but you may unknowingly support it, buy its fruits. Nevertheless, if you heard of a young individual who was growing without the benefit of an adequate education, who was forced to work, who lost a finger in machinery, or an eye perhaps, then you would act. You would make complaints.

You have defended those weaker than yourself. You were pleased to discover you couldn't do otherwise.

You have a great capacity for kindness.

That's why you give to charities—you can't donate to everyone, wouldn't be foolish about it, but you still try your best. And there have been times when you have enjoyed doing something for nothing and payment would have been unwelcome, if not insulting.

You like the way it feels when you can help.

It's clean.

It makes you feel useful and clean.

And you can rest assured that you're more honest than most people.

Which means you'd prefer to be careful about your employment and it could only seem strange to you, quite terrible, if you slipped into earning your living by doing wrong.

You wouldn't choose to be associated with an unethical company, or criminal behaviour, deception.

So you wouldn't do this.

You wouldn't stand in a moderately spacious civic theatre (with poor acoustics) and address 750 people (the place is full to capacity this evening) having assured them that you have knowledge of their dead. You wouldn't present yourself as being controllably possessed, rattled by the voices from buried throats, gone flesh. You wouldn't peer off beyond yourself into what observers might believe to be a stirring but vaguely melancholy space in which you'll seek out messages of love.

You wouldn't do this.

But your book has to show you the man who would.

This man: tall, pale, golden-headed, and an ache in him that's plain when he raises his hands—long fingers, delicate, uneasy—and when he paces, rocks. He offers his audience—mainly female—a pain that's as bright as his hair, as his skin under the lights. He is alone for them and burning in the bleak space of the stage and any reasonable spectator

26

might want to help him, to touch him, to believe.

And none of this happens by accident. He is not an accidental man. He is prepared. He is never, if he can avoid it, outside in the day—night walks at home and sunscreen with the homburg when he's on the road. No red meat, not ever—rarely meat in any form—a diet he constrains to thin essentials, minimums, as poor in iron as can be survivable. The anaemia refines him, tunes him, lets him flare.

Because appearances matter. Everyone judges the cover before the book.

The man wears a good suit, elegant, his tastes beginning to turn more and more expensive. A quiet tie which he may loosen but not remove. And the jacket stays on, no matter what. Dark, hard leather shoes with a good shine, an uncompromising impact at each step. Dark socks. Plain cufflinks. Shirts of a definite colour, not distracting, not flamboyant and not white—he needs a firm contrast to his skin, a way of quietly showing he's almost translucent, all fragile veins and watered milk. A sense of austerity in his haircut and a hint of service, also the suggestion of precious thinking, perhaps, of heat in the stubble gleaming at his neck.

And his thinking, if not precious, is certainly precise.

Deception is only unforgivable if it is incomplete. Leave any access for doubt, for exposure, bad revelations, and then you're much more than failing— you're committing a type of delayed assault. Be utter and undetected and then no forgiveness will ever be required.

The man's job is to be the perfect liar, because that's what his audience needs. Blood, words, skin, face, eyes, breath, bone—he must lie in his entirety.

The enquirers deserve nothing less. So that when he names out relatives and pets, describes familiar jewellery and clothes, episodes of romance, pleasant outings, birthday parties, misfortunes, habits, griefs, coincidences, arguments, birth signs, jokes, uncommon journeys, illnesses, cars and motorbikes, hospitals, buses, armed intrusions, injuries, scrambled efforts at evasion, running and narrow paths, terminal bewilderments—most particularly when he speaks of the terminal things, of deaths—they will be true. He will give them, most particularly, true deaths.

His job to be the window that lets them see through, the door that will open so they can walk back to the times and the places he'll resurrect. And when he tells his enquirers worlds, they will seem true worlds. They will be truer and better than the world they have.

Tonight 750 strangers have watched him convincingly let other souls slip into his blue-white self and then speak through him. Over and over, he's brought loves closer, invited them, called them in. This has been his little gift to everyone.

And he's the best. No one is like him.

Not sure that anyone would want to be.

And almost done and tired and tired and tired, he's shaken his head as if freeing himself and let his shoulders drop, he's sighed and rubbed his cheeks and felt his audience lean their will against him, the broad, warm press of how they still want more, could easily stay here—row on row—and drink him all away. But this is it, show's over: a nod and a handful of sentences, an appropriately small and quiet bow and he'll walk to the bland little dressing room and wash his face and sit, lean back and sit.

'You didn't let me speak to Billy. When you were

here before you let me speak to him.'

Woman right at the front—quite naturally right at the front and in the centre—directly at his feet, in fact, only the height of the stage between them. 'Why didn't he want to speak to me?' She has left her seat, is tensed almost on tiptoe.

Pink sweater—polo neck to deal with slightly ageing skin, overly glamorous jewellery, trying too hard—and she is yelling. The man assumes that she is mentally unable not to yell. The man has met this kind of thing before.

'Didn't he want to?'

The theatre stiffening, clinging round him while he remembers his previous visit—it was in the spring—and having made this woman happy about her dead son. This time, for three hours—plus interval—she has been carefully avoided. Too anxious, too bereft.

Female, 35–45, single and childless: difficult, they lack the usual entry points, are all needs and lacks and fretting and last-minute hopes, they suffer cruel and salty lunges of impossibility. So you offer them dreams.

Female, 35–45, divorced after her child was taken: easy. Give her back the boy.

But just because it's easy that doesn't mean I should.

The room waiting for a proper remedy, the man's authoritative resolution.

If I help her now she'll come to every session when I'm in town, she'll start to follow me about.

The man can taste her: something sour from her like illness and panicky—the flavour of instability there and obsession. He always understands things partly with his mouth, is currently swallowing bitter metal and earth, something moist and stagnant

29

mixed up with dark earth. Having paid attention, he would know her in great detail if they were ever to meet again.

'No.' And a beat while the rest of the audience almost relaxes, prepares for more trust. He pulls in a breath and lets his hand twitch. 'Last time I was here Billy said his goodbye. He said he loved you.'

She cries at this—happygreedy tears—hands curled and lifting near her lips.

'He told you what he couldn't, what he didn't have the chance to say. That satisfied him and put him at rest.'

Nobody is with her, she came by herself, is pursuing this by herself—arms falling to flutter at her sides: if someone was here for her to hold, they would catch the signal and step in, she would be embracing and embraced. Grief seeping around her, rises in clouds, travelling.

'He told you.'

She nods, little girl nod, all compliance and listening.

The man straightens his spine, widens his attention to take in the room. 'We do have to finish.' He watches this make her tremble. Of course, it would. 'But if he gives me more for you I will tell you afterwards.' He's firm when he looks at her, pauses until her eyes lift, and is firmer still until she sits and the man can roll on into the final phrases, can coil up his performance and tidy it away.

He's slightly too fast as he walks for the wings.

And he won't tell her anything afterwards.

He won't see her.

He'll use the office exit and be in his car and gone before she gets outside. No stage door rendezvous in the rain.

30

The man feels this is for the best.

He wants to be a good person. He wants to find the right ways to do wrong.

There are fireworks.

Naturally.

There would have to be fireworks.

Elizabeth stands on her cabin's balcony.

She has a *balcony*.

For that matter, she's *in a cabin*—and she watches mildly impressive fizzes of rising colour, detonations, splayed fire. Without a crowd to appreciate it, the effort seems slightly peculiar, if not sad. Derek is paying no attention—he's inside unpacking, *stowing* their belongings—or actually, now that she looks, he's sitting on the end of their bed and holding a life jacket, peering at it, as if it is failing to reassure.

Elizabeth knows how he feels.

Passenger Emergency Drill—scare the bloody life out of you, that would. Maundering herds of visibly breakable pensioners and couples with ideological reasons for never consenting to walk—being self-propelled letting their side down in some way—and yet they're out and tottering about in what amounts to a communal suicide pact—every stairwell just an accident in progress, just a slow-motion invitation to crushing injuries and fractured hips—and nobody getting anywhere, it's simply this huge release of the bewildered.

And myself amongst them—no use pretending—myself more than confused and liking it that my head's run to a blur, because then I don't have to deal with

31

it, don't have to cope with any part of my fucking brain. I need only be trapped and watch strangers coagulate while the words plunge by.

Distracted.

Exactly what I'm after.

Exactly what I am. Pretty much.

Except for this bit—which is too close to being aware and will need to be stopped.

So.

There I was with Derek and there Derek was with me and both of us having mistaken the unspoken rules of the occasion and not dressed up for a cocktail party with optional death later. Derek, in fact, might have ambled in from weeding, or light DIY, perhaps something electrical and I'm there in my current moderately smart slacks but slovenly jumper, weak blouse peering apologetically out at the collar and garish shoes—plus, the sea air had made my hair frizz. Red shoes and amateur clown hair, accompanied by a passing handyman—we were getting looks—cornered in this area of wall-to-wall piss-elegance and tweed while no doubt other scruffy souls were easing along unremarked.

*And these guys in their Elegant Casual Dress Code get-ups, they wanted to barge—clearly they wanted to ram their wives softly ahead of them like delightfully scented and tolerant little snowploughs, but they couldn't—or rather they weren't sure if they should— they were genuinely conflicted about shoving a way through, because they're the type who are meant to win at everything and be survivors, but the ship **wasn't** actually going down—was still at anchor, in fact—and nothing was at stake and everyone's status was as yet ill-defined and there was always the risk of causing significant—and later disastrous—offence and*

32

meanwhile they'd hoped to appear as sporting, likeable, gallant, which tends to preclude punching out old ladies—life's so difficult . . .

And all of us, bumbling along together and hugging our orange buoyancy aids as if they were wallets, or kittens, or children and locked in this big, thick, dreamy inability to save ourselves.

Even when we finally dribbled into our Assembly Station—the stylishly appointed theatre: wartime good cheer from the stage and advice from ex-Navy passengers about donning jerseys before immersion and two pairs of socks: you would want to drown comfortably, not be cold—even then, it took half an hour for everyone involved to actually place their life jackets over their heads.

We would die.

We would horribly die and be lost because of our sheer inadequacy.

We would deserve it and good riddance to us. We are clearly of no use.

And there was me trying to remember if it was the forearms or the buttocks of fellow unfortunates that open-boat-drifting and starving mariners are meant to eat.

Although we'd never get as far as that; bobbing and bloating, we'd be, and no one left to fish us out and snack.

Oh, Christ.

It doesn't bear thinking about.

So I won't.

Would rather not.

Forearms and buttocks of women—I think that's what's recommended.

And sadly I have both—all four.

Imagine.

No idea what I'd do to live, to be alive and stay that way.

Below her, over the handrail, are the layered edges of other balconies and fat rows of plastic pods which she supposes would expand in some startling way and turn into what would be, given the passengers' manifold incapacities, relatively pointless lifeboats, should the need arise. Here and there she can also see the calm metal side of the ship. Out of her sight it must drop into the water, clean down and vanish, angle in through the cold and the dark until it meets the rest of itself, folds and seals monumentally into the hard depth of a keel. Around them the yellowish spill of their lights spreads across gently progressing water: a careless halo pouring out into the night, showing the white gleam where they cut the water's skin.

For a while, she'd had the wavering impression that somewhere a band was playing brass instruments with a degree of vehemence—this was when the quayside was still safely tied beside them and a stirring march and uniforms could have been thought an appropriate farewell gesture. She couldn't be that sure of what she'd heard, because of the explosions ongoing overheard. And there was a breeze rising— enough to tousle sounds and make them unreliable. The music's stopped now, anyway—they've left it behind. Although she supposes that the pianist who played as they strolled aboard may be playing still, or could perhaps have been replaced by some combination of other musicians and instruments, maybe a harp. She feels sure that a harp will appear at some point. And on broad, soft-carpeted decks fruit machines are winking beside the type of green baize tables that promise exciting loss and there are bars and lounges, the theatre, the programme of stimulating lectures and lessons and entertainments and then there are the restaurants and the tiny, pricey shops and the spa and there is, of course, the library—currently closed, but on two storeys with a communicating spiral staircase, which must count for something—and, in short, there is an overwhelming sense that she has entered an environment prepared for people who are quite terribly afraid of being left to their own devices.

But Elizabeth likes her own devices.

Sometimes.

'She's got money then, Margery.' Derek emerges and leans beside her at the rail, slips his arm around her waist and nestles—she can feel the hard shape of his hip. Probably because she is slightly chilled— she's not wearing her coat—his temperature is surprising, warmth caught in his pullover. He kisses the top of her head and it makes her shiver. 'Hello.'

'Margery? No . . . Not particularly . . .'

'She pays for a pair of these . . . That's a four-figure cabin in there. That's two grand. Twice two grand.' Derek likes to say that kind of thing—to mention money obliquely, disrespectfully, as if he understands it and can't be impressed.

Not that he doesn't have money himself. A man of substance, Derek. And all his own work, doesn't take it for granted.

'It wasn't a special effort, was it? She hasn't got cancer or something—wants to leave everything to you.'

'She's my friend, Derek. I was worried enough about her when she had to cancel. I don't need you . . . adding that jolly idea.'

'Sorry. Only kidding. Sorry. Really.' He peers at

35

her until she can let him see he is forgiven. 'I am.'

'Her husband—second husband—he had money. And then he died. He was older . . . And . . . she doesn't have that many friends. And she, ah . . . likes me.'

'Oh, I see . . . Me, too.' Derek squeezes her waist in a way that suggests they'll have sex later under their mustard coverlet, in their fawn with additional mustard and really quite—it has to be said—1970s accommodation which is not moving, not absolutely—not pitching or rolling, they're still only creeping along the Solent, after all—but, nevertheless, the walls, the floor, their surroundings, are unashamedly *lively* with engine throb, and beyond that is the faintest, faintest give, a sway, like an anxiety—or rather, a tease, a promise to be surprising in days to come.

January in the Atlantic—we have to be out of our minds.

Derek kisses her again, moist heat against her neck. 'Bet I like you more than she does . . .'

She wonders how cold she feels to him, how strange. 'You both like me in different ways . . .' Her hair flutters, unhappily disturbed—it stings slightly when it hits her cheek. 'Since the husband, she does have money, I suppose. Not *her* money, though. Well, it is hers, since he . . . So . . . yes. She's well-off.'

'Shame she couldn't come in the end—I'd like to have met her. Someone you went to school with—bet she's got stories . . .'

'Not that kind of stories, no.'

'Stories about lovers . . .' He puts the words in close to her ear and they flicker, nudge.

'I didn't have a lover at school. I didn't even have

36

boyfriends.'

'Yeah, I've never believed that *late starter* stuff. I think you're just being modest.'

'I have lots to be modest about.' This odd desire he has occasionally to rework her as a sexually rapacious teenager—all pouting and gymslips. Sometimes it's sweet and sometimes it's just annoying and borderline weird. 'My dad wanted me to be academic. So I was.'

'Always did what your dad said . . .'

'Always.'

Not absolutely always, but that's nothing to discuss at this juncture.

Derek begins to steer her indoors and she allows it to be comforting that she gives him control, steps inside and is waylaid by the awful decor, the seafaring neatness, smallness, the practical lack of clutter to pre-empt rough seas and breakages. The effect is claustrophobic, but also endearing.

Derek sits on the tiny sofa, his legs aimed mostly at the bed and thus avoiding the minute table, his whole frame slightly compressed, designed according to a different scale. 'Not fair, though . . .'

'What isn't?'

'That she pays for you to come along—for us both—and then she ends up being stuck at home herself. Do you think she got a refund?'

'I didn't ask . . . Couldn't be helped, though—when it's your heart, you have to . . . well—take it to heart. Sorry.'

Hate doubled meanings—once you start them, they don't bloody stop—inferences, references, cross-references—then everyone turns into the sad bloke at the party who thinks it's his job to chuck in puns, focus the room's loathing.

'And is she OK now, Beth?'

And, right enough, a punster does draw out the hate. Eventually even the nicest people would succumb to their darker longings and just fillet him, cut him up— still punning—and throw him into the tajine, on to the barbecue, into freezer bags for later—depending on the brand of party.

I don't hate them because they're not funny, I hate them because they mean nothing you say can stay innocent.

'Beth?'

'Yes. Yes, she called and said the tests were, you know . . . reassuring. It's just the long sea voyage thing and the insurance thing—in case they have to winch you off by helicopter, improvise on you with jump leads, that kind of stuff. They like you to be healthy.'

Elizabeth removes her shoes, lies on the bed. She looks over at Derek as he reaches for the paper and starts to read. He is folded neatly in the available space—the limbs and joints and angles of a long and wiry man, that particular shape. And in her mind she lets herself think

Love.

Such a terrible word—always demands you should be its accomplice, should comply—can't even say it without that sense of licking, tasting, parting your lips to be open, to welcome whatever it is that slips in beneath your breath, and then you find yourself closing to keep it, mouth it, learn its needs—this invisible medicine, this invisible disease.

It takes a hold.

Not like sex. Sex is a slip of a word, a slither—and it can be so simple, uncomplicated as it sounds.

Not that it wasn't a cause for concern at the

*start—because I **did** reach it later, I **was** a slow learner and usually, initially unsure—but then hasn't everyone been unsure? I don't think it's remotely unique to suffer those young, young endless doubts—If he's kissing me, actually kissing me—which is nice—absolutely nice—even so, am I quite sure of why?*

Does he like me? Find me attractive? Because I'd be hoping that both of those things is what we'll be about.

Or is he kissing me the way he kisses everyone, is he just the friendly type? Or curious? Or bored? Or has he stumbled and coincidentally fallen against my mouth?

Which is preposterous, naturally, but need not be mistaken. My insecurity may only signal that I am both ugly and right.

Right about being wrong—romantically mistaken.

Am I, for example, being kissed because there is something delicious on my face—my lips—possibly gravy, perhaps jam—it could be jam . . . Is he just hungry? Is this just to do with jam? I want to believe this is mainly about me, but I could be deluded.

I can't feel my irresistibility is likely.

Then again, what I can feel is blinding, incandescent, and offers no names for itself and is eating, is swallowing, all of my names for me—and the more I keep doing what we're doing—because he's still doing it, too: we're doing it together, in fact—except he's doing it in the opposite direction—and this works, really works—and I wouldn't have thought that a body, anybody's body, could be that, well, entertaining—the more we do this, whatever it is, the less I know about it, the less I know about everything, and the less I am able to care about not knowing.

I am perfectly happy and also evaporating.

Who'd have thought?

But eventually you're wholly free of thinking and can begin to uncover who you are with him, touch against touch.

And you make beauties together.

You and whoever he happens to be.

It does seem wrong to say so, but who he is can seem slightly irrelevant.

Not in a bad way—although it does sound bad—the specific identity of the gentleman does not, to be honest, matter that much.

*This isn't your fault. It's nearly **their** fault: the number of—eventually a not excessive but still significant number of—gentlemen's fault, because they have been, as it were, not that outstanding or differentiated and, therefore, in order to have any fun, any modest pleasure, you have become **very** differentiated. Your heart, your mind, your body, they have become discrete. You have separated into fragments that no longer communicate and which get curious and bored and stumble, and your condition is patently not ideal, but equally you're never disappointed.*

You do sometimes have a sense of waiting by which you are almost overwhelmed, but this shows you are not pathological or numb. And you bear none of the gentlemen ill will. You would smile at them in the street, be quietly fond: you would commiserate should they receive unpleasant news. This isn't love, though— this is not love, this is not in any way that word.

This is safe.

You are safe.

You are lucky and not confined—not really—it's rather that you enjoy prudent limitations, almost always have.

You are not unaware of love's damages, that chaos,

and realise you have been spared, are sparing yourself. You get to pursue what are not relationships, more a series of hobbies, indoor games for rainy evenings and afternoons.

So, on several legitimate levels, you are content.

Only then, for instance—just for instance—you may stand beside a man, a not unfamiliar man, and—sharp and hard and for no reason—every shade of him will strike in through you: his angles and his musics and the subtleties of his scents: and you cannot touch him, but want to—cannot respond, but want to—cannot move, but want to. He has, in the course of doing nothing, suspended you in want and want and want. And through you come reeling these dreadful truths: that you respect him and fully intend to be proud of him hereafter and to see him both happy and well— and you'll need him kept warm in the winter and cool when it's hot and will let no ugly breeze come near him and no wanker be permitted to annoy him and you wish for him to be comfortable, at the very least comfortable, for ever. And these are desires that ache in you deeper than sweating, or bending, or sucking, or any of the thin and predictable memories or the fantasies that might defend you from the present, too present, reality of him.

*The tiny idea of naming him **darling** is almost unsurvivably arousing.*

Which is beyond preposterous.

You are turning innocent and selfless to such a degree that if your absence would please him, you'd disappear.

You would have to go.

But you can't go.

You couldn't go.

You couldn't leave while his voice is purring in your skull, purring and curling and thinking your thoughts

41

and you look at your hands and feel his fingers, as if you have become each other's gloves—and the sound of his breath and when he swallows could set you falling, could take you to a place where you might weep, where you are far out of your mind, but still at home in it, at liberty inside yourself as you have never been.

Many people take to this, are delighted to be found and lost, possessing and possessed.

You are not one of those people.

*You **were** not one of those people.*

But your selves have bled together now, blurred and joined. He has made of you a unified need, a piece of desperation, by being here and existing—effortless.

And his manner of existing means you will not be having sex with him.

*Which is to say, you **will** have sex with him, but you also will not.*

You will be complicated.

You will touch—will begin with touch—will slip and slither and hold and rock and cling. You will fuck—but you wouldn't, you truly wouldn't, if it wasn't entirely impossible to say what you need to in any other way.

*It won't be **sex**, it will be **speaking**.*

*And—God help you—it will also be admiration, tenderness, concern—this excruciating list of necessities which are all chained to **making love**.*

*You will **make love**.*

*You are **in love**.*

You weren't when he was leaning in the doorway.

Then he stepped over here and you were.

You are.

It isn't fair.

It isn't fucking fair.

Because you know what it will mean.

42

*You will lie down with him and be naked—not en route to the usual somethings and, for the sake of practicality, undressed—no, you will be irrevocably naked, stripped—you will be all skin and jolts and talking and—for fucksake—**honesty** will break out and that's when you will come unhinged, because you aren't going to leave him while he sleeps, sneak off and never come back, and you won't act as if you expect him to smother you in the night, or that you'll wake up in a quarry later with a head injury and no shoes. And you're not going to keep it brutal and light in the morning, say **you'll call**. You're going to rest unconscious in the almost unbearable mercy of his arms and want the trust of that and like it—you're going to stretch and turn into the day for more of the same and for enquiries and delicate smiles and whispers in case he's not awake, except he **is** awake—why else would you be talking to him?—he's awake and listening and whispering as well and you both keep on whispering so you can still dream each other and be not yet in the world.*

And then you'll have breakfast when it's time for lunch.

*And suddenly, unforeseeably, how much you will have to do: memorising mutual preferences, habits, frustrations, ticks—and you'll discuss—you will **have** to discuss—God knows—futures and kittens, or dogs, or stealing a baby from outside a shop—you probably won't have the time to make one of your own—and, if not that, then certainly there will be carpets and curtains to consider and accommodation, gardens, flats, renting, mortgages, life insurance, drawing up your wills—and what if he dies before you?—then you'll be upset—and planning how many you'll have at the wedding breakfast—although you might want*

43

*something quick, a quiet affair with the cabby who drove you in as a handy witness—I mean, why not?—it could happen—it genuinely, horrifyingly might—when, Jesus Christ, you don't want to get married, not **you—marriage**, that's an institution—since when did you want to spend life in an institution?—this whole thing is unpicking you, reworking you into someone else—which means he will, in actuality, be marrying someone else and how could you possibly cope with that?—the jealousy alone would kill you—and the invading burdens, responsibilities, the claustrophobia, the shock, they are in the room with you like sump oil, they are rising to your chest—and this isn't how it should be, how you should be, because you love him, he is the closest you will get, the dearest, and surely this should not have to guarantee that being with him terrifies you more than dying—more than if you might die before him and end up making him upset.*

He mustn't be the man you'll never have, purely because he seems to be so meant, has perfections, ends your waiting, because he opens you up to your spine and doesn't hurt.

So, although you might beg to, you don't run.

You stay and can stand with the back of your hand near enough to the back of his for you to feel him, read him, the magnificent argument of his blood, and you tremble and do nothing and this is fine.

Except.

Then your lungs fill with having to dress so you'll please someone else and vice versa—and this doesn't choke you, but is unfamiliar, is odd—and then there's going to the pictures together, which you're bound to try eventually, it is something you see all the time and completely normal, yet somehow a threat—and there's wanting to buy a sofa, because that's what lovers *do—and you are lovers—you **do**, there is no saving you from it, **love**—and undoubtedly you'll end up going with him to buy the sofa and looking in lots of places and not being able to see the perfect one—when only perfection can represent your love—or, indeed, be the decor and furnishings of your love—and eventually it's not improbable that you'll get tired—you don't want to imagine this, wouldn't wish it to be the case—but if you are both exhausted and perhaps your blood sugar is low then it's almost inevitable that you'll fight— perhaps not badly but then maybe worse, and this free-floating resentment and discontent will follow after—and maybe in the final furniture shop there's also a table lamp that you don't like—you despise it and you can't help your opinions, they are yours and your personal expression is protected under international law—but your lover **does** like the lamp, that is **his** opinion of it—he adores it, insists that it's superb, and this reignites your disagreement, kicks it into bitterness and rage and additionally looses the welling of commitment and undertakings and regulations and sameness and exposure, hideous risk, and the awful heap of this is insurmountable and sweeps hard down at you and before you can scream or prevent this, you've picked up the lamp—the tragic, frustrating, adorable, loathsome lamp—and you've hit him, you've knocked him right on his wonderful head and he's bleeding—he's crying and you're hitting him again— you're causing him pain and making him afraid and it's a nightmare, you would rather shoot yourself— although, of course, you don't have a gun, you're dangerous enough without one—and, Christ knows, you haven't a clue how this came about, but you are still hitting him, your darling, because this way you won't have the new wait for the failure of everything* *sweet in your life, its most beautiful thing, you have instead brought it neatly to a close.*

You have killed him.

Because he was far too extraordinary.

You have murdered the one man you've ever tried to love.

And it takes a long breath to picture this, to see it, mourn it, understand.

And for this and many other reasons, you should save him from yourself.

You shouldn't take his hand and shouldn't kiss him. Your mouths shouldn't make and echo and make the shape of **love**.

But you do take his hand and you do kiss him.

Of course.

'Oh, you can't do that, though . . .'

Elizabeth opens her eyes and discovers that she is lying on her back.

All nonsense.

I'm full of nonsense.

The ceiling is neatly above her, inoffensive cream and calm.

And where would I be without nonsense.

Here.

She is frowning, puzzled by this feeling of having run in from somewhere without warning, of losing her breath. 'I can't . . . ?'

'You can't go to sleep. Not yet.' Derek sits on the bed beside her. The mattress only dips a little—it is made of stern and seafaring stuff. 'We have to stroll about and see the premises. Then we should have dinner. If you want.' He lifts her hand, kisses her knuckles. This is nice, but also gives her the slow and far impression of punching him in the mouth. 'I'm quite hungry. You hungry? We've missed our sitting for the wassername—for the captain's table dining palaver—but there's a buffet somewhere. I'd prefer the buffet . . .'

'Ahm . . . I'll be hungry once we've strolled.' She looks at her watch. 'Christ, it's half past nine. Did I sleep? I didn't think I'd slept, but I must have. Anyway . . . Yes. Let me have a shower and then we'll go and check what's what.'

Before she can sit up, he nuzzles his face to her neck. 'This'll be good, won't it?'

He's a lovely man, can be very sweet-natured and he wants to enjoy an enjoyable thing, a watery jaunt in good company. That's not unreasonable of him.

'Yes. It'll be good.'

On what Beth thinks of as the Mingling Level she finds herself walking through trails of aftershaves and perfumes she hasn't encountered in years.

And why not? Choose one you like and stick with it. Eau Sauvage. My dad wore that. I'll bet you someone's wearing Hai Karate, too. And there'll be Old Spice and Brut and 4711 and Charlie and Aqua Manda and Tramp and straight Lavender and Lily of the Valley, because you know exactly where you are with them. Yes, you do.

I do not know exactly where I am.

Perhaps I should start wearing lavender.

No, where I am is on a boat.

That's exact.

In an ocean, a wilderness, a chaos—but I am also undoubtedly here and on this boat.

Somebody who, for want of a better term, may be

47

called The Ship's Photographer—not a position Beth would have considered essential—has commandeered a less-frequented corner near the lifts and has unfurled a quite extensive backdrop, reproducing the setting sun at sea. Couples are having their photographs taken in front of it—the actual setting sun having disappeared much earlier in more al fresco and unpredictable surroundings.

The photographer gently poses his subjects in a small range of sentimental configurations: the gentleman rests his arm round the lady's shoulders, the lady leans in and lays her hand on the gentleman's chest, the gentleman enfolds the lady from behind, while both peer off beyond themselves into what observers might believe to be a stirring but vaguely melancholy space.

Derek doesn't understand her interest in the proceedings. 'We shouldn't stay.' He's getting bored. Loathes hanging about, our Derek.

'They don't mind. They want to be looked at, in fact.'

'But not by us—by their relatives, or whoever—later.'

'Why don't you nip off, get hold of a list for what's on in the cinema. I'll stand here and stare at them till you come back and then we'll eat.'

He shakes his head and she can tell that he is wondering briefly if their journey will be marred by her strange preoccupations. For a moment he hovers, as if his disapproval, correctly applied, will be able to change her mind. She rubs his arm and gives him a smile until he returns it.

'I just . . . they're endearing, you know? It's endearing.'

'You don't want *us* to do that?'

'*Christ* no. Are you insane?' She rubs his arm again. 'Go and check out the films. I'll be here.'

It isn't true—she doesn't believe the photography's endearing—so many couples unable to touch without also apparently clinging in desperation, the hands slipped over husbands' hearts as if to make sure they're still beating, the oddly unconfident flaunting of savagely younger wives. The singles—grimacing, over-brave, over-dressed. It seems possible to hear them inwardly reciting—*This could be me on the night when I meet my husband / an incredible girl / an utterly boring bastard who renovates properties in Kent . . .*

There's only one pair among them who don't depress Elizabeth, to whom she has warmed: older guy, mildly elegant, and a wife who matches and he stands half in his partner's shadow, presents her, because she's still lovely and ought to be first, and he holds her, light as light, to show admiration while letting her be—her being, plainly, very much what he likes—and she rests easy against him and is happy and her face full of the sense that in a moment she will turn and look at him and they'll grin, share the secret of who they are, one with the other.

'So how are you this evening?'

Fuck.

It's the man from the queue—stepping in from her left and halting as sharply as if a wall had sprung up to fox him.

No wall, though—nothing in his way.

Elizabeth knew she would see him again.

He's the sort to be unshakeable.

She wonders how he managed to approach without her noticing.

Although his feet are apparently fixed, he twitches,

shifts, inclines his body, positions himself to obscure the photographer, the backdrop and the subjects: their nervousness, their excuses, their attempts to dilute reality's disappointments.

So he'd rather I looked at him, then—is posing himself instead. As what? Lonely and stealthy. Not a combination I'd recommend.

And we're on this fucking boat for seven days . . .

'Are you well?' He's changed into jeans and a shirt, but his shoes are still formal—shiny black oxfords—and he seems, if anything, less relaxed—there are flickers and starts of tension in his arms and the rise of his chest.

Looks like an off-duty policeman. Or a soldier—an officer trying to be in mufti—the scruffy isn't scruffy, it's still a discipline, a plan.

He glances at his feet, his shins, then shakes his head. 'I'm Arthur Lockwood, call me Arthur, and *yes*, I don't dress down well—I'm much better with up, but *still*, at least I don't have . . .' He slows his sentence to the pause where she might help him finish . . .

And Elizabeth would rather *not* help, but it turns out that she does in any case: . . . 'creases ironed into your jeans.' Her intentions were too fixed on not cooperating.

Thinking summons doing, brings it on—you know that—and what you most forbid yourself is bound to linger, is bound tight. It'll hang about like a bleak and uncomfortable man.

'Yes, I'd be the type, wouldn't I? The way your husband would be the type to wriggle and pull himself into his jerseys as if he's five and needs his mum to get him through it. *Endearing*, one would imagine.' Arthur Lockwood, call him Arthur, smiles

50

at her with unalloyed sincerity and it is difficult to feel insulted or disturbed by someone who does this effectively and warmly and with care.

'He's not my husband.'

'Really? I'd have thought he was. Did you personally know, by the way, that three hundred and sixty-one people have been photographed so far. Not your husband?'

'No. Three hundred and sixty-one. I'd have thought that was too much, too many. He's not.'

'I could be wrong. Often am. Well, not often.' He shrugs, shivers like a man with a pain in his neck and flutters his attention beyond her, possibly into a stirring and melancholy space. 'But when I *am* wrong . . . I do then go *fantastically astray*. If he's not currently your husband then he has, *of course*, lured you off to sea and into all of *this* with the intention of proposing. What I would do. If I were him. Which I am not.'

Elizabeth knew this, knows this:—that Lockwood is not Derek and that Derek has been building towards something—tetchier than usual, more needy and delicate—she hadn't wanted to notice it, name it—*marriage*—but that is almost certainly the destination her partner has hauled on board with them. There is going to be a time when he will ask and she will have to answer. No doubt champagne is stored somewhere for just such occasions. 'I don't think that's true.'

'He didn't lure you?' Lockwood snaps a wide, clear glance right in at her. He winks. 'Ah well then . . . *you* lured *him*.' And he bowls his interest away against the wall over her shoulder. 'How extremely—I'm not quite sure of the word . . . *informative*. Oh, and yes . . .' Lockwood swivels on

51

his heel and Elizabeth follows him round until she catches sight of Derek, who's approaching with a slip of paper in his hand. He holds it aloft—this causing Lockwood to dip forward and near and murmur to her, 'Like Chamberlain after Berlin . . .' before he strides a pace away and hard into a handshake with Derek which slightly crushes—although it does not render useless—what turns out to be a handwritten list of tonight's film screenings.

'Hello. Arthur Lockwood, call me Arthur—were you going up to the buffet, because I don't mean this to sound in any way uncomplimentary, but you do both seem to be avoiding the evening's dress code for dining and me, too, of course, to the best of my ability, and so we might go along together, if you didn't *mind*.' He contemplates both of them and Elizabeth briefly believes that if she interrupts him, if she can shut him up, then her fists will unclench and whatever wrong thing is on the way will turn aside and seek out other people, but she hasn't any sense left in her mouth, nothing to tell him, to bundle up against him, and so he digs out at her again, at Derek—these small, harsh movements of his skull, his forearms, each keeping time with the drive of his words, 'I travel a great deal by boat—freighters, liners—hate to fly—late-onset phobia—very common in middle life—and I can recommend the buffet *experience*—it's *the one consistent, one reliable element*—they're good with *meat*—have a lot of *meat*-eaters on board and they cater for them—excellent *meat*—do you like *meat*? Profess vegetarianism and you'll be the lowest of the low, they will be *stern* and brusque and give you boiled potatoes only and a talking-to . . .'

Elizabeth hears Derek admit that, yes, he isn't

averse to meat, and this establishes enough of a connection to mean it's too late for them now.

Far too late.

Beyond saving.

We'll have to go with him.

And they proceed, the three of them together, as if they are friends. They work their way over the softly untrustworthy floor and then up the softly untrustworthy stairs, while Elizabeth tells herself—*far too, far too, far too late and we should do anything but this*—and notices she pats at Lockwood's elbow, perhaps because she hopes to make him safer.

Mild shirt and beneath the cloth is bone—the unprotected hardness of bone—he is down to his bone—little bone, big bone, little—bared and taut and listening—there it is, listening—requiring.

And a jolt in the muscle.

Another.

It's waking up.

She raises her hand from him. Folds her arms across her waist as they continue to climb.

It's waking up—it said so.

I noticed it and it knows.

*   *   *

'The one thing I do love—meat.' Lockwood unloads his tray on to their table and has, indeed, collected a disturbing weight of meat—correctly pink and tender beef—which obscures a more restrained selection of vegetables.

Outside the restaurant's windows are blank water and blank air, this vast cave of night determined to confront them with their own reflections. Elizabeth watches a yellowed version of her body trying to eat lasagne, faltering cutlery, childish mouthfuls. The yellowed Lockwood shovels beef into himself intently, nods and encourages Derek into elaborate descriptions of his business, of how he first met Elizabeth, of other journeys they have undertaken, of his parents and schooling, hobbies. Derek nudges at his food, but barely alarms it. Lockwood consumes. Lockwood swallows in a way that seems near to pain, to choking.

In the end, Derek stops talking, exhausted. He blinks. He is pale, quickly paler than when he sat down, than the minute before this one. 'Excuse me.' He runs his fingers along the back of Elizabeth's wrist, gets up and walks away—tight steps, the ship adding a minor stagger on uneven beats. The sea is making itself felt.

Lockwood watches Derek go, then lowers his knife and fork, crosses them on his plate.

Elizabeth angles herself to face the window—she can feel him, though—Lockwood—his living and sitting and watching and thinking all prickle on her skin.

There are small rattles of crockery that nag. The ship is beginning to flex, play.

Oh, God.

Whatever that means.

Whatever does God mean?

Elizabeth is dropping fast into a headache and also tired, tired, tired and so hollowed, so indefensible, undefended, when she needs to be something else. When she needs to be she isn't sure of what.

'*Merciless.*' Lockwood waits until she turns to him and then repeats, '*Merciless.*' He is studying the window and may be commenting on the ocean, which is certainly swelling visibly, tangibly.

54

'I'm sorry?'

'No. No, you're not.' He pushes away his plate and takes a sip from his water glass, rubs his face with his free hand, 'Will you, Elizabeth . . . Elizabeth, will you fuck him tonight. Will you fuck him and will you say *yes*—will he hear your voice saying *yes*—and will he be inside you, hearing your voice—*yes*—and imagining—*yes*—that perhaps, that perhaps you'll agree to be his wife—*yes*—and his prick in you, moving in you—*yes*—when you tell him will that make him come . . .' He turns his palms down and then up and then down and studies them and seems bemused by his extremely clean, well-tended fingers, his buffed nails.

Elizabeth half stands to get away, but he simply wags his head—quietly, deeply furious—a rage so confined and so injured that it scares her: these quick shadows and signs that it makes in his eyes, the tensions in his face—and she cannot help but sit again. It is clear that even he doesn't quite know what he'll do—that the further she goes from him, the louder he's likely to ask, 'Do you use protection, or does he come right into you, can you feel it push and run uninterrupted—his semen, seminal fluid, cum, spunk—and his little—what would they be: grunts, pants, hisses? Damp words? Is that how it is with him? Pushing and damp?' As it is, with Elizabeth so near him, he grinds out his sentences, flat and soft, to somewhere beside her, some shape in the air that he can bear to look at, fix. He's unable to bear her.

Unable, perhaps, to bear anything.

He coughs, clears his throat, coughs again. And this time it's Elizabeth who wags her head and she isn't sure of why.

Wrong move—like trying to make fun of him—trying to mirror him.

Mirror and you show him you'll follow his lead, give him sympathy and dominance, you prove you're alike. People like people they're like. People remember their fathers, mothers, the peering down of family faces, smile answering smile, leading smile—seeing their own muscles apparently move someone else, a proof of mind-in-mind, of love.

Which is completely fucking obvious and he's not stupid.

Fit his shape and you might understand him, though . . .

Lockwood notices her efforts and only smiles—this young, gentle look which meets her and isn't answered, which pierces and leaves. After this he seems to relent, there's a sort of sinking in his spine, a withdrawal of engagement. His head falls and he murmurs to the tabletop, 'No, don't answer. Don't. Personal question. All personal questions and inappropriate from a stranger. My comments have been an unsuitable intrusion and I should apologise but will, of course, not.'

He pauses and the floor bucks, shivers, rests.

Then Lockwood fades himself close to whispering, each word sounding on the same low note before breaking into breath, raw breath. 'You touched my arm.'

Elizabeth can't swallow. Inside she is filling with silence. It tastes like milk—yes, it's milky and thick in her mouth.

So concentrate on that.

'You touched my arm.'

Milk and stillness.

Not that it isn't hard to hold.

Stillness.

It's the worst thing to keep, but I do want it—a rest from the gabbling, the nonsense, keeping up the pace and always being tired from not sleeping because of the noise—my noise—because of the rubbish just spooling away in here beneath the hair, the skin, the bones, just mazing around and around in the brain.

Distraction.

A distraction that doesn't distract me enough—an inadequate misdirection from the forthcoming panic, which might as well panic me now because I know it's on the way.

Then again, I no longer need the gabble. No more diversions required, because right here is the perfect fear for me and I can step out of hiding.

Should be a relief.

'You touched my arm.'

No more guesses, worries: the real thing.

And at that same moment, both of them—Elizabeth and Lockwood—become aware of Derek. He's weaving back from the toilets, greyish and heavy-limbed, skin shining with water or sweat. He is obviously ill. Both of them—Elizabeth and Lockwood—follow his progress and, if he were inclined to give them his attention, he might perhaps be puzzled by their very similar expressions of true concern.

Another and a better worry: altruistic, practical. He's poorly, seasick. He's plainly a priority.

And a reason to leave.

Thank fuck.

Elizabeth gets up from the table, 'I'll have to . . . He needs . . .' and she motions to Derek that they will go—head for the cabin and peace, take care of his ills.

Give him the tablets to settle him—he should have taken them before—and then he can lie down.

See how things are in the morning.

Not a fucking clue about the morning.

Lockwood snaps into the actions and the tones of a man who is saying goodbye to an acquaintance. He meets her eye and then quickly states, 'You touched my arm.' Before Derek is near enough to hear. Then Lockwood shakes her hand, releases, nods to Derek, nods to her.

As she goes, Elizabeth does not nod and does not tell anyone—*Yes. Yes, I did touch your arm. For 361 reasons, I touched you.*

Derek wants to lie. Nothing but that. He says so.

Like a kid.

He is curled in their bed, arms folded around his own shoulders although—if he wanted—Elizabeth would hold him. Derek doesn't want. He is miserable. They didn't make it to the cabin without him throwing up again. And he has thrown up since. Horizontal, he isn't sick, but says that he feels as if someone is squeezing his skull. Because he can't tolerate seeing, she has darkened the room and so she sits in a generalised gloom on the miniature sofa beside their broadish and expensive window, through which is clearly visible a pattern of stars and cloud, rain spatters, the idea of a moon, hints of its greater light. And the shipglow—there's always that—if she went outside she could see how they burn as they go. But she has to stay in with Derek. She draws the curtains.

Derek breathes as if doing so annoys him.

The room is too hot, smells sweaty and sour—oddly like the back of a late-night taxi—and the floor is pressing up beneath them and then flinching away. They have entered a storm, or perhaps simply the ocean's accustomed state: no more pretending, a week of this.

Derek is a dim curve, there's a deeper shade of shadow where he is slanted across the bed—on his side, knees tucked—the shape is vague, more a suggestion, but he's familiar all the same.

I should think so, by now—we've been together for nearly a year.

More like thirteen months. And they didn't move in with each other until quite late. She went to him.

Slightly surprising.

His place was nicer than mine—bigger.

Surprising nonetheless.

Beth still has some furniture in storage, odds and ends—that's mostly to do with lack of space, not to provide her with resources should she ever wish to bolt. Derek lives in a thirties bungalow with strangely extensive gardens, even a stream transecting it and adorned with a Japanese-flavoured bridge. The interior is markedly less generous, because of the clutter. Derek inherited a plethora of ugly pieces from his mum and dad—vast sideboards, grandfather clock like a coffin—and he hasn't been able to throw them away so far—sentimental.

Sentimental man. Soft areas. He's still cautious in case I damage one.

And I'm not absolutely unguarded myself.

And this is not a disadvantage—it means I can be clear-headed and take care of everyone. It means that I know Derek shouldn't see Lockwood again—we'll dodge him. He's the sneaking type, but we'll manage so there'll be no more enquiries—nothing about what Derek and I may or may not do, or how.

It's nobody's business who I fuck.

Or that I do fuck.

And I do fuck—we do—we do fuck.

Lockwood's voice still there in the verb, his taste— so she uses it to spite him, tries to.

Derek's like a kid when we fuck—when we do fuck— and once he's over, once we're there, he's all pleased, like a boy—happy the way he would be if he'd learned a trick and showed it and you'd been honestly amazed.

Cute.

Not that he knows any tricks.

But still cute.

Sort of.

Cute could describe it.

In the distances of the ship, components she cannot name are chafing and whining. There is, intermittently, the reverberating slam of big water against the bows and—although she can't currently say so—this sense of struggle is enjoyable and what she'd hoped for. She wanted the din and fight of a genuine journey, of something large being achieved.

Derek, in contrast, is much quieter than he has been and she guesses he's fallen asleep.

Good. So I can stop failing to comfort him.

Her efforts have been mainly useless and uninspired. She has cleaned up the bathroom, set a cool cloth on his forehead—which he liked—refilled his water glass.

Which he did not like—the water bounced back up and out of him as soon as he drank it.

Horrible how sad he's got about this—a bit of his holiday spoiled by a misfortune and him not feeling the way that he'd want. He's disappointed—as if he's five and needs his mum to get him through it.

Horrible and—again—cute.

So he's abject and I find it appealing. Does that mean I'm peculiar?

I don't think so. We tend to those we love and more so when they're troubled.

Not that I'm being his mother. Not that.

Too many wardrobes and antimacassars and ottomans involved with that.

Ottomans or ottomen?

Undoubtedly there are stewards and sundry other members of staff who are practised in the ways of *mal de mer* and its relief and she should probably call them—but Derek really wouldn't want strangers pestering in at him.

Tomorrow morning—we'll check on his progress then and decide the best course.

And meanwhile—because he's well out of it—she won't have to keep on throwing him perky sentences of invalid-encouraging stuff.

It doesn't matter.

It's all right.

There's no need to worry.

You'll be fine. It'll all be fine. You'll be all right.

She didn't necessarily believe these things were true, but they seemed constructive, padded out uneasy pauses and have been—naturally—a distraction.

Can't beat me for that. Past master. Past mistress, I suppose, except that sounds louche.

And distracting Derek has prevented her from being forced to hear what she's saying and saying inside—the slither and pelt of that.

Noise is all I'm full of and no one should have to

tolerate noise. It's harmful to health and safety.

She folds her arms, adjusts, clutches her shoulders. There's a shiver in her breath and she can't stop it, has no way to halt the fretting as her time sheers by.

Let me yammer away for long enough and I'll maybe just drown myself out.

Which doesn't make any kind of sense—my only emergency plan and it makes no sense.

She's been talking crap again, inside and out—but it doesn't matter. It's all right. There's no need to worry. She'll be fine. It'll all be fine. She'll be all right.

Some people whistle, or doodle—Beth chatters. It doesn't mean that she's silly, or callous, or weak.

You understand about this. You're an understanding person.

And, like Elizabeth, you've attempted to lighten a mood when no positive information was to hand— so you've made something up, built it out of optimism and eagerness to please and if you thought of it as mainly music rather than meaning, you've been able to absolve yourself for passing on information that's actually false. And if the information is good—has good intentions—then it might even end up making itself true. Any word can work a spell if you know how to use it.

Plus, honesty does have its savage side—you're well aware, quite frankly, that it wouldn't always be your first or even last option. The fabrications of kindness, of courtesy, of optimism: they're very necessary—and, by accident, or in a pressured circumstance, there may have been occasions when you haven't been utterly accurate in what you've said.

This can feel ugly and uncomfortable to you, alien—because you have integrity, and dishonesty doesn't suit you, how could it? But nobody is fastidious all the time, unremittingly brave: you can be scared off to this or that edge of the truth—like anyone. And if, for example, you did in actuality do some unfortunate thing and it was completely unlike you—the word, the thought, the act, the total mistake—if it was so far from who you are that describing it, admitting it, would be misleading— then a deception might be called for, a silence might be justified.

And what if you're simply finding a way of practising your dreams, letting them play, sharing? What if you're pronouncing incantations, inventing happy prophecies? That surely must be pure and harmless. The friends, the relatives, the loves, the ones who know you: they can see through to your heart no matter what you tell them, so your fantasies can be something they'll enjoy—secrets that join you closer to them, enlarge their definitions of who you are—a person's choice of lies being dependably diagnostic.

Not lies, though—that's too harsh a term. When you thoroughly study yourself, you know that you're better than that, than a liar. You've only avoided being truthful, pedantic, when it would hurt somebody—somebody including yourself—and self-defence is nothing shaming.

It's an indication of your moral sensitivity that you do sometimes feel ashamed.

You have in the course of your entire life occasionally erred, drifted, been too instinctive. You admit that.

And not everyone would admit that.

Also, there were days when you said the true thing even though it would hurt. You withstood the injury. You could make yourself admired for that, but instead you don't talk about it. There are several things—when you reflect—that you don't talk about and it's significant that the very good aren't mentioned any more than the very bad. They can both unnerve you.

You tend to give others your middle ground. Which is prudent. Human beings are not intended to be comprehensive in their expression of themselves. If they were, they would be terrifying. They would always mean too much.

There would be layers revealing layers and meanings that double and on and on and where would it end?

It would end in a room.

It would end with a man standing in a doorway and walking back into a room.

It would end with this room.

He's in this room.

The man is in this room.

In another hired-for-the-evening stuffy little room—stage at the far wall, away from the door, and the rows of stackable seating set out neatly with an aisle—a shuttered hatch to one side that will roll up and open through to the tiny kitchen where someone will make the tea and coffee, serve up biscuits in the interval.

And every room will never be anything but stuffy—what the man does perhaps affecting the atmosphere's density, he can't be sure—and the biscuits will never be anything but stale—snack density *not* down to him: it's because they buy cheap biscuits—no matter who or where they are, they go in for own-brand, nasty biscuits and ignore the sell-by dates, don't bother to store them in a tin, which shows a breathtaking lack of foresight. Tight-fisted town after town and in every venue the fund-raising raffle to open the evening and the prizes of unconvincing electrical goods, or personal readings at later dates, free healings, the sending of amplified prayers on the winner's behalf.

And the man is there with her—with the woman, with his love—and they are there together and smiling where no one can see it, giggling just beneath the skin. They are being the secret of who they are, one with the other, and everything of them that's important is tucked out of sight. The man and the woman are hidden in amongst these strangers and having their fun, a tight fit so that they're cosy, no matter what. They could do this forever, the pair of them—if forever could be reached—swapping and making the codes: the counting, the signals and counter-signals—like kiss against kiss.

They'll give the full show tonight, a good one—no one will ever understand how good. A night to remember all ready and dancing in them, wanting to start now, to play: they can feel it like breath on their necks.

A night made of what they have on file from last time and what the man's found out since he arrived—this in the days before Facebook, Twitter, before lives were bent over for better inspection everyfuckingwhere. The man has to work for what he knows, gather overhearings and gossip and newspaper cuttings and In Memoriams and graveyard tours and averages, statistics and guesses that are always educated—unless he and his love just busk it, improvise—unless they're riding

65

the room and it's racing them somewhere and they let it. And they like the riding and racing—it's what they perfectly do and—for this evening—they'll be doing it in the Church of Eternal Love, Light and Hope.

Says so on the posters and the song sheets— Eternal Love, Light and Hope upstairs and to your left, second floor of the Municipal Hall.

Have to be upstairs if you're after Eternal Love, Light and Hope, stands to reason.

He takes it they didn't go for the Hope, Eternal Light and Love option—H.E.L.L. not being quite the initials they'd prefer.

Shouldn't knock it, though—either you tour the churches or else it's the pub function suites—clattery stage and a star cloth background if you're lucky— might as well be a stripper, ventriloquist, some shaky-handed magic boy wadding silks into his thumb tip, clanging a dove pan—no dignity there.

Not much here, unless you bring it—which we do.

His crowd's in and he's had a look round—it's the usual selection of regulars, virgins, occasionals, desperates: big women in sparkly tops, short sleeves on hefty arms, purple spangles and silvers and pinks, butterflies, starbursts, little girl images of fun.

No black, you won't see black unless it's on a sceptic: the way they insist on mourning for everyone else: all pain, no consolation and fucking smug.

But no sceptics tonight—tonight is leather jackets, smokers' coughs—lockets and bracelets and necklaces with names on and even more so for the men—they get the heavy gold, thick links, substantial watches, the sovereign rings and Mason's symbols, Pioneer symbols, Union symbols, AA symbols, lettered fingers and swallows inked on the webs of

66

thumbs and solo earrings—whole libraries of themselves set out on offer—and the loud shirts and fastidiously well brushed hair. Mainly women here, though—this a matter for women, a women's mystery—chatting women, raucous women, thoughtful women—little love heart tattoos, or coloured stars—in couples and groups and outings: family resemblances, office parties—borrowed clothes, shared clothes, pinched clothes, eBay clothes—styles of make-up—special friends—and they're giddy, nervy, anticipating—good night out— they'd like to be entertained and have no commitment, not noticeably: they're keeping it light-hearted, they imagine—but odd silences, nevertheless—curiosity, mild interest is what they'd admit to—they'd explain how they're nobody's fools, would love it to happen, a contact, they'd be overjoyed, they'd be put at rest, but nobody's bought and sold them—even the man hasn't bought and sold them—they're going to keep an open mind—this being, although they don't know it, the Great Requirement—just open the mind.

Then we'll open it wider still, until it trembles, until you couldn't stop us if you tried.

And you won't try.

And then we come in.

And we'll work in you until we've split you, fathomed who you are, until your everything is different, absolutely—which is what you want, what everyone always wants—to be naked and opened and seen and touched, but still loved—to be absolutely known and proved absolutely lovable.

Not in spite of ourselves, but because of ourselves, our whole terrible selves—that's how we all want to be loved.

We know it would change us, make us complete.

And in underneath the smiling and excitement, the man is already harmonised with his audience, the enquirers—he understands them and he does love.

And he's taken the time to examine them, to be comprehensive and find it—their truth. Because it is there: the grey in their faces, the void in every dawn, the scream in the eyes, the howl, the moment, the one and forever moment, the instant when they heard, felt, knew that the world had left them, had fallen away—these intolerable losses they carry with them, unspeakable. Anyone could see what he does, if they tried—it isn't hard to notice the humiliation of too great a pain. There's no hiding the indignity of that.

There's no bearing the indignity of that.

Which is why the man and the woman are so needed.

The man and the woman together.

Double act.

He assumed they'd work better if they masqueraded as brother and sister. A kind of a joke, this—he's not remotely like her. She's rounder—or rather, fuller—has a smaller nose—her body, hands, mouth, they are modest, but suggest capacities for pleasure, sensuality. He tends to be attenuated, has a body that might be brittle, that's near to alarming and alarmed. He has dyed his hair until it's dark as hers—if less enthusiastic—but this has left him startling, bleach-skinned, like some kind of warning—an illustration of symptoms arising from an ill-judged life, bad habits, excess.

As a pair, they don't match. But the ways they move, the ways they *are* with each other—that convinces.

They don't go on stage pretending they're husband and wife, or admitting—truthfully admitting—that they are lovers. They try to be more, to offer themselves as two people born for other worlds. They spread rumours of childhood visions, terrified neighbours, baffled parents, hypnotised cats.

This was the man's decision and he's sticking with it. Ever since they became completely partners in their types of crime, he has insisted they put a pretence around the pretence, around the pretence.

It seems a good idea. Because he's young.

Complications taste sophisticated to him—like salt and protein, acquired preferences, treats—and he thinks they're harmless. And he is packed with ideas of invulnerable success and the illusion that being definite in his planning will somehow aid his progress, impress reality. He imagines a clandestine marriage at some point and then a life of enjoyable narrow escapes, of passions that always stay feverish because they are pressured, denied.

And he's still affecting the long hair and a beard—anxious to seem a Victorian, a wannabe Golden Age psychic in an off-the-peg twentieth-century suit. As a gesture it's faintly pathetic, but he does enjoy acknowledging former practitioners, traditions, the faked niceties and restraints of another time—all frock coats and surnames until the lights go down, then seance rooms that filled with busy fingers, licensed reliefs and sticky little trinkets hauled out from places propriety couldn't mention. He feels he is wearing a private joke—one even she doesn't really get. In fact, almost no one appreciates the reference and meanwhile, it has to be said—has been said—he looks like General Custer. Custer, only not blond—not any more.

So he is, in a way, ridiculous.

And aping a man who is famous for losing.

But he loves his persona, embraces its implied fragility.

Because he's young.

And he's assuming—and the woman is agreeing—that people wouldn't trust a married team, any kind of romantic team. So the man and the woman have created their own niceties and faked restraints. They say they are family and wandering together in a happy no man's land, called to serve, to ferry messages across. And this means they do have to be absolutely sexless—not the vaguest hint of anything untoward can be permitted—the consequences of a lapse apocalyptic—excitingly so—rumours of incest would finish them. Even a brotherly squeeze of her shoulder might leak heat, a hand-clasp could show inappropriate thought—they couldn't come back from that. So discipline has to be total, merciless.

And he loves that, too.

Because he's young.

No options for either of them but to seal what they are and need into the brief conclusions of their nights. The strain of this assists them, he thinks—makes their demonstrations, their readings, thrum with opaque and yet unnerving energies. They both savour them, translate them later, race and ride with them in hotels, in B&Bs, in the flat where he sleeps and stays awake with her, because they are lovers: not related, not married, but lovers—lovers who hide to keep strong, to stay effective.

So very often, as the bedroom door closes, while it's still on the swing, they're already tasting each other, releasing. Prohibition has become a necessity,

70

infallible foreplay, the deepest tease.

Because he's young.

He lets the work stroke him, raise him, keep him raw so he can feel.

And he does feel—everyone and everything—he feels like a flayed man, a burning body, like the end of himself so that he'll be right for her and right for them, the enquirers.

For tonight.

And every night.

Tonight.

This night the man and the woman are side by side, tucked in the kitchen with the polystyrene cups and the twitchy strip lights and the curls and peaks of conversations tumbling in from outside.

And they are telling you, if you will listen—and how many people ever listen—how much pace they need, or laughter, if they can concentrate, if they'll be arsey, boisterous, sad.

You shouldn't ever meet an audience, meet anyone, for the first time—not when the second time's better. Prepare and you can be their friend already, close as blood.

And it's time.

They stride outside and into nowhere, into forever, into every fucking thing that should be and never will.

Easy.

He introduces his sister, establishes a peace, respect, ground rules: the dead will be returning— were never gone—but have no fear, they are more known and knowing, more familiar than they were— also, they are eccentric and they wish for reconciliations, they hide small objects about the house, they spend slightly inexplicable hours

71

overseeing driving tests—that's mainly a little laugh for the family in the corner—daughters, mother, aunt—they'll get advice about something: not paying too often for others' meals and drinks—and what about the drinks?—they do have a few too many, every now and then, well don't they?—and relaxing is one thing, but don't let it slide, be cautious. And don't buy unnecessary shoes. And don't buy uncomfortable shoes. Older relatives speak their minds, they're often feisty once they've passed and forthright and they appreciate practical footwear, traditional undergarments, their grandchildren, unexpected pregnancies, rainbows, penetrating and inexplicable sensations of delight—they are, in perpetuity, holding their new offspring and overwhelmed, promising bonds of affection to conquer time.

This is reliable, expected.

And the man has told his lover what he heard while he strolled about beforehand, had a non-smoker's convenient cigarette. So she's ready.

She does the work, mostly. He does the minding, guarding, watching—mostly—the actual readings tire him, leave him feeling too unusual.

He's already reported that second row, centre, girl in the criminal sweater, she's on-the-nose already asked for her grandmother: unfinished business, sore stuff, guilt, it's running off her—and the dyke couple at the back, there's clearly some unhappy person they want: a young and troubled, druggy thing, smells of suicide, dark contemplations, insecurity—tact required and gentleness.

New procedure this time—he's always tinkering with changes, improvements—now if he pats his hands together, that's when she'll start to count the

72

silence, she'll stop and register the number when he touches his ear—he'll potter up and down the aisle for that, keep an eye out for tensions, focuses, half-motions: the special ring, medallion, the small something that matters, that has a memory. If it's named by miraculous processes then he can take a hold of it, pass it up to his love and she'll tell what it transmits.

They'd both fancied a spot of psychometry—object-bothering, he calls it—and it sits well in the current repertoire. Take the object, reveal its owner, histories, emanations, importances. When he hands it back, it's something to keep the enquirer warm and confident, it's the charm to bring them luck.

Some luck—they're either dead or here.

But they'll go home happy. They'll be absolved, accompanied, and loved. They'll be fucking loved.

We'll see to that.

*   *   *

And it's running well. So far, they've had two grandmothers back from the beyond and an uncle who's like a father and a grandfather who seemed more like a friend—two watches and a bracelet of heated significance.

And then a mother.

And she's a good one and a deep and a genuine hit. The idea of her returning, the possibility of her thinking, being, watching in the room beside her living daughter—this thickens the air around them—and the congregation truly silent, listening into their spines—and this hauls at the daughter where she sits, jerks her.

And then—here it is—it really is—here's the Six

73

Inch Jump—reality springing forward, paying attention differently, more closely, fitting tight at the man's skin.

It's wonderful.

And then the daughter cries. Of course she cries. Everything demands it. There was some terminal misunderstanding, some apparent wrong that's unforgiven and she carries it, has carried it for years. And how easily, beautifully, matters unwind and are how they were meant to be: time and truth annihilated by will, united will—and the daughter is little Irene again—she is little Irene and she has her mum—she is Irene and happy again, because here's her lovely mum: tiny memories in splinters, the photograph that should be framed now, the burned dinner, a fight at Christmas, the incident with the pet—a dog, she was a dog lover—Irene's mum in the kind years, the sweet time—and this is the nonsense and smallness that means the room can understand we will stay human—that both sides of death will be human, the still-dying and the dead, but they declare themselves eternal also. This proves it—this is living beyond doubt.

A miracle; handmade, perfectly fitted. And a Good Mother, which is to say a Bad Mother—and they're the best—something for everyone, for players and spectators.

Very easy to love this—what the man does.

Times like this, he is almost nothing but love.

Because he's young.

And then—last enquirer—five minutes left—and the man is standing in the aisle—tired, tired, tired—and this Vicki woman is up on her feet and talking about a cousin—he's distracted and Vicki's a bit of an anticlimax, she's barely upset—or oddly upset—there's something about her that may be unspoken—and Vicki's leaning infinitesimally forward and to her left and her hand is in her pocket—and her mind is elsewhere, just as the man's mind is slipping away to mouths and breaths and being finally unsecret: not long to go—but then his enquirer is thinking harder, louder, biting in and distracting his distraction—in her head, there's **right hand, right pocket, big shape, heaviness, car keys**—he's close to hearing a tiny noise of metal—the man is being saturated with this **car keys** thing, **car keys** taste, he is at the edge of seeing them they're so sharp and Vicki continues to lean and gives a tiny glance—it's aimed at a guy in front—over there and in front—a guy on his own—unlikely spot for a rendezvous, but that's what it is—undoubtedly—they are waiting for mouths and breaths, too—and Vicki's bloke is listening too much, twitchy, bluffing casual—the pair of them acting solo, but they're lying.

They live where the man lives. They are made out of fucking and hiding and planned surprises.

And the joy of this opens in the man's chest, it sparkles—and the service, the evening's session, is nearly done, Vicki's consultation dribbling to a half-hearted close: it turns out she's called Vicki Konecki, which is just odd enough to be true—and what she actually wants, loves, what shouts in her is **car keys, lying, sex**—and the man needs to touch her, suddenly and urgently needs to confirm how she is, what she's told him without speaking—he wants to know what her kind of interesting feels like—and his palm is held open towards her back—as though he might comfort her if required—and onstage his partner is winding up and Vicki the liar, this conductress of

75

affairs, this tangible excitement, she's starting to sit down, so he chances it—her change of position excuses a small goodbye and he indulges in this little brushing pat and she'll forgive him, does forgive him—she hardly registers him, to be honest and why should she—but the man is roaring with her after one contact—**door, lying, muscle, door**—and like a red thing in his thinking, she's **pushing** and **coiling** to **kick** down the **door** and she is the **door** and **sex** is there, **sex** will be there—**keys**—and she will **follow** and he has her pulse, she has soaked him with her pulse.

Vicki leaves him shaking.

When he remounts the stage, he is still unsteady.

This doesn't prevent him producing the blessings expected and the kind summation.

And after this the sacrament, the demonstration, the evening's entertainment is concluded and he runs.

He makes his apologies—his lover puzzled—hints that he's ill, that he'll head for the guest house and maybe an all-night chemist first and he runs.

He shakes off the stragglers, sleeve tugs, unfulfillable enquiries, scrabbling requests and emerges outside, breathless and **following—car keys, lying, sex**—darkish street, inadequate lamps and there she is—**lying**—there's Vicki—**sex**—the crowds about her dissipating—the audience, the congregation, the gullible going home.

But there's no sign of her bloke.

I could be wrong.

She turns right and right and right again and then a final turn before she's inclining, stalling, last-minute ducking in for the door of a car and unlocking it. She sits inside.

Lying.
But she won't drive off, not yet.
She won't.
I'll bet anything that she won't.
The man has to pass on, walk by her and keep going.

He crosses to the opposite pavement, turns left and left and left and left and there's the car, still parked—no engine, no lights, but Vicki is there in the driver's seat.

She's waiting so hard it distorts the street, makes his palms tingle.

He slows up and studies the window of the solitary available shop—it is, thank God, an estate agent's and invites consideration. He brings out a piece of paper and pretends to take notes with a pen which is still in his pocket, because he's good at pretending.

Lying.
Car keys.
Sex.
There's a sound, an impact, a door snugged shut, maybe, maybe, he can't be sure.
Don't look.
He hears an engine start. But, if it's her car, she can't be driving away—and not alone—she can't be, he won't believe it.
I can't be wrong.
I won't be.
Oh, and there they go, they fucking do and I am not fucking wrong.
Her car pulls tenderly past him and he can peek: two inside—Vicki and her bloke—same bloke—he's beside her.
I was right. Exactly right.
Nailed it.

77

A hit.

The elation—it's on every surface like the shine from a new rain.

I unlocked her—I fucking read her—been pushing towards this so long that it's finally let me, given way and I'm through—I'm free—I'm mid-air and not fucking falling—I am in fucking lovely flight.

The man walks—faster and then faster—hungry for other people and deeply and tenderly struck by every face, each body that moves past him, by the opened catalogues they offer as they pass beneath the street lamps, as they modify and amplify their states, confess their natures: drunk, drunkhorny, oddanddepressedwildpain, absent, drunkscared, recklesshorny.

He understands.

He knows them.

And he knows he's a phenomenon.

Sad to think that he's almost unique, because everyone ought to be willing to let themselves see, find one another.

But everyone can't, won't, can't and I can.

And he adores it.

Jog-trotting across the late pavements: here he is and here is his species anatomised, luminous with information, secrets, wishes, fears—enough to enchant him, turn him giddy.

He can read anyone.

He is a burning man and reads by his own light.

*   *   *

Somehow it's after midnight when the man sneaks up and into his shoddy B&B—optional shower room across the landing, no TV—and wakes his love. If anyone can join him in this—and somebody must, to be alone would rob out his delight—then it will be her.

It will be her.

Shaking her shoulder and gabbling while she doesn't quite listen, is not overjoyed. No codes, no cheats, no significant numbers, just ordinary talk—the straight experience—but she won't have it, is barely interested. His lover doesn't want to hear him, is out of step.

A cool weight settles against his ribs and doesn't shift.

Eventually, they have a fight and no amends after.

Not what he expected.

Can't read everybody, then.

The lack of connection tightens his skin, pains it.

For a moment he's scared she is too far away, irretrievable.

And more scared that he's lost his new talent, that it wasn't permanently his and tonight was simply an accident, or a mirage he'll never regain or even be able to describe.

The man and his lover lie on their backs, separate and unsleeping in narrow twin beds. At last they stumble up into the morning when it arrives—no tolerance for food, no chatting—more silence on a bleak drive to their flat.

But the man believes that his lover continues to have him and hold him, whether or not they seem close—he is bound through and through her and she through him—no undoing that.

He will solve this—their first real difference of opinions—and they'll carry on—the man and the woman together, side by side.

That's what he expects.

Because he's young.

After a while, the cabin is so oppressive—and so tedious, because Derek is so unconscious—not his fault—and Beth is so tired of sitting and staring, or creeping about, or easing out on to the balcony for a dose of salt and oceanic rage—that she decides she has to slip away. Her going won't disturb him and will therefore do no harm.

Elizabeth eases out into the passageway, delicately pulls the door to and lets it lock. She's bundled her coat out with her like a foldable shame and puts it on in the corridor where it won't disturb.

I need a walk. That's a perfectly normal impulse. I've been pent up all day, one way and another—and I have this energy, spare energy, rattling energy and it ought to be burned or it'll turn septic, run to fat, some terrible something will happen.

And air—Christ I could do with some of that.

Elizabeth has the idea that a whole storm of air might do her good. She isn't exactly rushing but—side to side and occasional stammers—she is progressing rapidly. She is moving like a woman with a goal.

Which, fuck it, I am.

Fuck, fuck and fuck it.

Just let's be practical about this and head outside.

Fuck.

Elizabeth is full of shouting, but she ignores it, takes the stairs, moves on.

It isn't so late that the communal areas are deserted, but there is a sense that somewhere a party

80

has finished and the guests are wavering home. Little cliques are ambling and in spite of the rolls and plunges underneath them, they keep hold of loose formations as they chat, conspicuously elated they've already found themselves usable friends for their trip. They can relax, go to bed with tentative schedules for bridge, or poker, the sewing circles, gossip, a stamp collectors' get-together, the before-dinner drinks.

The opportunities for Entertainment and Experience Enrichment are severely curtailed at this hour and the closed bars and emptied seating, while not forbidding, have certainly ceased to invite. Elizabeth is relieved when she reaches an exit that leads to an external door. A warning sign states that she shouldn't be out here, that prevailing conditions may prove unsafe, then she's pushing the door and it's giving, it allows her through and on to the narrow and relatively sheltered path that circumnavigates the ship.

The Promenade Deck—that sounds likely. Maybe.

I should learn nautical terms, preoccupy myself with that.

She battles into the open and is caught by a sidelong blast that stops her and chastises.

Definitely refreshing.

A turn around the deck. That's supposed to be the bracing cure-all, isn't it . . .

Fuck.

So she heads off into the ransacking slam of it, mackintosh clattering round her legs, but no rain— just the taste of wilderness.

Fuck.

Fuck.

I'm here, though.

81

So this must be where I intend I should be.
Fuck.
Unless I'm just some kind of accident. Waiting to happen.

When she reaches the stern, the wind is muffled. And here it's impossible not to feel—only gently, gently—that every option but the last has been exhausted, that she's run out of ship, and meanwhile, the wide, pale tug of their wake both soothes and invites. A little camera has been positioned to observe, in case anybody succumbs to the attraction, plummets in to join the creamy, long perspective.

And here he is.
Waiting to happen.
Fuck.
Last option.
Fuck and fuck you and fuck you very much.
Here's Lockwood.
Call him Arthur.

He's leaning on the rail, arms braced wide and facing out, staring. He gives the impression the weather may be a product of his will.

Of course. That's how he'd want her to find him—looking authoritative.

Fuck.

An additional pitch in her stomach, because whatever does happen will be undiluted, no interruptions, no distractions, they will *meet*.

And how long before he makes a point of giving his authority away . . . ? Smart manoeuvre, that, to snag you in.

'You're late.' He's quiet, intending that she strain slightly to hear him. He shuts his eyes, lets the breeze press at his face, fair hair lifting, hands deep in the pockets of his long, brown overcoat. It flaps

82

expensively. Now that everything else is moving, he can be still.

And Arthur is always beautiful when he stops to let you see.

Which is appalling, so it's important for Elizabeth to be angry. 'I'm not late. You cued me in and then repeated it four times—and this is four hours after I left you.'

He smiles at this—*after I left you*—as if he has more delicate emotions than she does, as if every doubled meaning cuts . . .

'And could you have said the word *meat* any more loudly? I'm neither deaf nor imbecilic. Neither is Derek.' She offers him a pause within which he does nothing to help, so she has to begin again. 'Well, we're *meeting,* aren't we? This is what you asked for.'

He turns and catches her with a hot look. He's good at that kind of thing. 'I'm so sorry. I was thinking four hours after we *met*. And sorry for the dreadfully unsubtle repetition. I'm out of practice.'

So he's going to be the calm, calm gentleman. Which means I have to be the unreasonable bitch.

'You're not out of practice, Art. You're never out of practice.'

'Try not to make that sound quite so accusatory. I'm out of practice with *you.*'

'And could you make *that* sound less accusatory . . . ?'

'No, I don't think I could, actually.' But, somewhere, he *is* calm. Somewhere he is just glad to be looking at her and he's letting it show, leaking signs and tells like an innocent, like a civilian. 'It's not as if I *meet* you often and it's not as if I'm *meeting* anyone else, or have been for a while—ever really do—and it wouldn't be like this if I was, so it wouldn't be practice, Beth . . .' Of course, he isn't an innocent—when he gives out tells, he means to.

'But you can *meet* someone else if you want, Art. We're allowed other people.' Which is not the direction she should take. Their terms and conditions have never been clear-cut and shouldn't be discussed for fear of savagery and damages.

But Arthur doesn't argue, is only firm with a dash of sad. 'Yes, I know that. I can *meet* people and you can do that, too. I know that.' He wants her to face him and sympathise, to let him in, but she angles her head to the side, says nothing and deflects him, so he continues, 'You're *meeting* Derek. I've been watching that all day.'

'Not *all* day.'

'Strangely, it feels like all day.' He winces. 'I do apologise again. I'm not allowed to say that sort of thing. I withdraw it. Consider it unsaid. Blame it on the unaccustomed protein—heavy meal, rush of blood to the head.'

Elizabeth won't feel guilty—has no plans to be anything like guilty. Nothing here is her fault.

It isn't my fault this is insane, that when we meet it's always going to be insane.

And this was his idea.

Therefore insane.

*A weekend, two or three times in a year, forever and ever and ever, irremovable—that's bad enough. To keep on **meeting**, for ever and ever and with no amen, that's fucking futile—corrosive—infuckingsane—but a **cruise**? This long together on a fucking **boat**? I should just have said no. And then Derek—Derek who is normal—he wants to come along. And how to explain why not? I'm heading out with, as far as Derek knows, my school chum Margery—the Margery that I've been* *meeting for years, since long before I met Derek—so why shouldn't he come and join us? Hang the expense, he'll sort out the details—it'll be fun . . .*

Fuck.

And if Art isn't meeting other people, that isn't my fault, either. I've never asked him to be lonely.

The gale is humming and crying through some gap, around some obstacle—it's singing and the sound is almost wonderful and she would like to listen to it and not deal with Arthur, or anything about him.

I did leave it late to tell Art—didn't want to mess him around—I never want to mess him around—but I do and he does me—and then Margery's falling on her sword—this isn't my decision, but she won't attend—Arthur provides her with an illness—dodgy heart—and we'll ignore that double meaning—fuck, is there a meaning he doesn't multiply, is anything ever just itself? And the lie about the heart—the heart lie— that meant we'd solved the problem—or not solved, but altered . . . me stuck on a boat with Derek who wants to propose instead of being otherwise stuck with Art who never will, or who might if I would let him, but I won't. I can't. I couldn't . . . Main point, main fucking point—my fucking question would fucking be . . .

'Why the fuck tell me you weren't going to come on the cruise and then still fucking come?'

'You knew I would.'

'You said you wouldn't.'

'But you know me.' He's smiling again—putting a melancholywounded spin on it.

'Stop it.'

'Stop what? I'm not doing anything. Beyond reminding you we have *met* before. Have been

85

meeting for years. My body has been *meeting* your body for y—'

'Stop it.'

'I'm saying you know me. That's all. And anyone like me in my circumstances would be predictable. I'm not a story that's hard to tell—not for you. No surprises . . .'

He is standing closer to her. They are propping themselves against a white-painted metal wall—*bulkhead*, maybe, she isn't sure of the right word—it keeps them steady. And this desire to be steadied has drifted them in nearer to each other, tighter—that, and the hope to be warm.

And there may be nothing more to this: simple comforts required by them both and allowed to exert their influence without manipulation.

But Elizabeth has begun to feel pressured, as if she can taste him, working in. She isn't easing herself away again, it's true—although she'd partly like to—and she's aware that Arthur chose the boisterous location, the tempestuous cold—he could have predicted their effects. He'll always have her story worked out, too.

This being the kind of behaviour for which there's no excuse—like his rant about fucking—like saying he wouldn't be here and then being here—like being Arthur Lockwood—makes her—she feels, quite reasonably—angry and an angry woman is allowed to say, 'You cunt.'

'That's uncalled for.'

'And your . . . what would you say it was? Your *oration*? Your speech in the restaurant? That was called for? And lying to me?'

'I didn't lie.'

'I wouldn't have come if I'd thought you'd be here.'

86

'If you remember, our original arrangement was that I would be here and that's why you'd come—sorry, for the double meaning, we can act as if it didn't happen. Of course.'

And he is making her be—letting her be—furious, which she doesn't want. Any large emotion would be bad—it would let the others in.

'I wouldn't have dragged Derek along to be—'

'Oh, I think he's been dragged along from the start, hasn't he? Doesn't realise he's being dragged, but that's hardly putting you on the moral high ground . . .'

'Cunt.'

'Sorry, that's not very specific—are you just saying that I'm generally a cunt? I'm not allowed to . . . *intuit* what you mean, so you'll have to explain.' And he gives her that flinching, wearied look—consistently very effective—and he moves to face her, stands between her and the ocean, and he holds her forearms, pulls her forward so they both stand free of the wall, balance and sway with each other in the ocean's great, grey twists of thought. 'I didn't lie, Beth. I don't lie to you.' And he lets her see he's giving up and won't fight her any more—that she can win if she wants. There will be no argument.

He'll be beaten if she wants. 'I said that I wouldn't enjoy the trip without you, Beth. I said that I wouldn't enjoy it if you were with him. Which is true: I am not enjoying it, but why assume that I won't do something because I'll be hurt—why, of all things, assume that?'

And she would like to reach for him but can't because his hands are fastening more intently and, anyway, she shouldn't.

'I didn't absolutely say I wouldn't be aboard, Beth

. . . and *Christ* what do you want me to . . .' And he's blinking and it's hard to be sure, although not hard enough to be sure that he won't start crying.

No. Not crying. He wouldn't allow that, not when I'm with him and have to watch, when it's something too effective to ever be used. We wouldn't stoop to that.

So it would be the worst trick he could pull.

Or not a trick at all.

And perhaps it isn't a trick.

Because he takes care to avoid breaking completely and makes himself unsympathetic, fends her off. 'I can smell him on you. I can smell his pedestrian little cock.' He studies her expression then releases her, appears satisfied, sets the heels of his hands to his eyes and rubs.

She should get away now. She knows he would let her go, but she's already begun, 'Art. I can't deal with this. Derek's a good man. He's a reliable man. He doesn't do appalling things.' Before she can prevent herself or regret it.

Before they can both regret it.

And he tells her, *'Please.'*

He is so particularly eloquent with that word— *please.* No one should be able to ask so well, it lets them grow accustomed to more than they deserve.

'Please.'

She fails to leave and this means he can say, 'Beth, just let me . . . I was rude and I'm sorry and I apologise and I will be perpetually sorry if you want and I will apologise and apologise . . . I was . . . Let me . . .' He reaches out and then she discovers she's holding his hand. Anyone who saw them would think they were lovers—hand in hand in the privacy of night.

But I'm so cold I can't feel him.

And then Arthur frees her, unbuttons his overcoat—this takes a clumsy while, he's clearly also numbed. He turns himself away from the hardest edge of the weather and opens the long, brown cloth of his coat before he folds her in, hugs her in with the sky blue lining which is probably silk and shouldn't be near salt water. He gives her what's left of his heat.

And anything but this and anything but this and anything but this she can deal with.

Anything but him.

Like lovers.

We were lovers.

We are.

We were.

We are.

Cold cheeks, cold lips, like a dead man's, his words fumbling a little for this reason, or for other reasons. 'Beth, I didn't tell you where I live.' But his voice in her hair, quick beside her ear, and it feels like inside, it has the temperature of inside who he is, of who they have been together—it touches her like a long time ago and like their being other people, like her being someone else and with him. 'You don't know where I live, Beth.'

'What?'

'Ssssshhh. Why should you? You didn't want to. You don't want to. Sound decision—you needn't. But . . . I have the flat in London, that you . . . there was that afternoon when you nearly visited and I can see why you wouldn't—that's all right—and I also have regular hotels . . . but that's not where I live, not home, I . . .' He's shivering—a delicate instrument, Arthur, tends to show his shocks, his unfavourable circumstances. He's built to indicate

89

distress. He needs gloves. They both ought to have gloves, and his fists should at least be in his pockets, but Beth feels them knotted close at the small of her back. Her fingers are against his chest, his ribs, his breathing, the way that he's thin, broken back to his final limits, to the fights in his thinking, his intention. 'Listen, Beth. Listen. There are bluebells. In the spring. Campion, sea campion, primroses, thrift, violets, bird's-foot trefoil, wild garlic in white drifts—all kinds of flowers—but I love the bluebells—in the dusk, they glow—they return all the shine of the day and I walk out past the bank around my house—high, high bank—and that's what I see there and I can smell that blue—it has a smell—and the powdery, perfumey, sugary gorse: it's like cheap sweets and face powder and I love it, too—and under that is the scent of the island—like a big dog—a big, warm animal—woody and clever and dusty and living and salt and I love it the most—boots covered in live dust and after the first night I smell of the island, too, and I forget who I am and what I do and I tramp—yes, still avoiding the sun, I am mostly still avoiding the sun—you know I have to, because of . . . and I'd burn—blonds burn and it's forever since I was out in the summer, fully under it—because of the other things, too—but I can stop—I could stop, I . . . and sometimes I sit in the garden under the tree—but mainly I tramp out at night with a torch or by memory—there are no street lights on the island, not anywhere, so we're good at the dark—we all keep our secrets—we all know them, but we keep them, we're polite—and I go along the cliffs, judge where I'll be safe by the ocean's breathing—the same way it's breathing here—a dark that's alive in the dark—not too near the edge and not too far, that's what I aim for, I don't want to fall—same ocean as this—and I'm on paths that are warm still, that are skin heat—and it is dangerous—slightly— occasionally—depends where I go—but not so much so, because I remember, I have learned the shapes of places and how they are and what they want—and then I get home again safe and behind my bank, inside my bank—the place is set back from the deep of a path—it's been worn in, you see, feet and carts, cutting it down for so very long—and the house above—all hidden and hedged—wrens nesting in the hedge—blackthorn and brambles and honeysuckle, the tangle they like . . . Did you ever see a wren in spring? He's so tiny you could lose him in your hand and with the ticked-up tail and he'll sit and pour out music—huge music—flares his wings, bristles with it, all unfolded by the way he is, has to be—he wants to be bigger and he is—I have a wren—a pair—they live in next to me—and I have my house, walls of pink and grey granite made feet thick for the winters and with stones for the witches to sit on built into the chimneys, so you won't have them pestering you in your house—believe that you could have the witches and then you'll believe you need the stones—the fact that you don't see the witches means the stones repel them—that's how it works—matters of faith—I am aware you understand, even if you no longer want to—and I have a porch for boots and with hooks for hanging up—my boots, my coats, my hats—serious fireplace in my living room—the stone is old, is huge—fat mantelpiece, not much on it, I like it as itself—no ornaments on it and no photographs—no photographs—and rugs, two armchairs—mine and a spare, or rather mine and another, but only for balance because I don't

91

have visitors—lots of whitewash—and my desk is in the study with a sensible chair and some cabinets you'd want me to be rid of—you wouldn't like their contents—some books that you wouldn't like either—and a big kitchen you can sit in and eat breakfast on the table—eat whatever you like— which is what I do—and upstairs there's a bathroom which looks out to the ocean and another little room with just ordinary, good books for reading and then my bedroom with wardrobes and a double bed—and I don't need a double bed—and I can lie in it, if I prop myself up, and I can watch the sunset and everything there is perfect—it is fucking perfect— and remember that summer bedroom? Remember the rose scent from the garden at that hotel and the big squares of sun on the carpet and nobody saw us, because we never left the room. Remember? The first time after Beverley, remember? And my house is ready and it's nice and you should just once, just once . . . there are so many stars, thick stars—I can get drunk with staring at them . . . just once . . . You know I wouldn't . . . I don't . . . That's what I wanted to talk about, to tell you in the buffet. Not the other stuff. But I couldn't tell you, so you got the other stuff, because I couldn't, that's why . . . I wanted you to be here on the ship, so that I could tell you about my house. That's what I wanted.'

And what answer could there possibly be to this? It is unforgivable.

'It's . . . Art, please, I—'

'It's a kind place. All prepared and if it's comfortable for me and we're alike—and we *are* alike . . . It's a kind place.'

And Beth can't accept this and she can't refuse, so she tries, 'You really live there?'

92

'Yes!' It hurts her when he yells, seems to hurt him too, and they stand apart again and he refastens his buttons while, 'Jesus, Beth. Yes. I really live there. I don't lie about everything. I hardly lie at all. The bare minimum. And not with you.'

'Because lies don't work.'

'That's *not why*.'

'On your island—do they know who you are?'

'What?' And for a naked second he is baffled, simply a man she ought to help because he is overwrought. 'No. Not really . . .' And then he is Art again, defended, describing a way in which he lies. 'As far as they're concerned I'm some eccentric with money—a lot of that about on the island—and I have vague health trouble, pay a servant who gathers supplies, oversees repairs and gardening, is sworn to secrecy and who therefore lays down inaccurate gossip which is, in turn, not believed. But, no, they don't know who I am.'

'And they don't know what you do.'

'Fuck, Beth—nobody knows that. The only one who might is you.'

'Because when you tell me 361 people have been photographed . . . Look, we have to get out of this cold or we're going to get hypothermic.'

'If we go in then we can be seen, so we can't . . .' He's shuddering, they both are—perishing. 'Yeah, we'll have to go in. Yeah . . .' And he hunches his shoulders and returns very mildly to the halting twitching man he'd decided to be in the queue.

Elizabeth follows him round to the nearest door, shouts into the wind before he opens it, 'Three six one. I remember.'

'On the Right Hand List.'

'three six one.'

And then they are tumbled through to an aching quiet, a preposterous warmth. Ahead of them is the internal door and then the expanses of carpet, the efficient lighting, the possibilities of—although it is late—inquisitive observation. Elizabeth's cheeks and ears are stinging, being hurt with comfort.

Arthur looks raw and diminished. He is frowning down towards her and bending a touch forward, crossing and uncrossing his arms. '361 on the Left Hand List would be—'

'*Loss. Betrayal. Please listen.* But that's not what you meant. On the Right Hand List **three** is *Touch me*. And **six** is . . .' Swallowing and this airless drop that seems to take her as if she's seventeen and nothing has ever happened to her and she has been academic and a late starter. '**Six** is *Fuck me*.' Can't say it without saying it.

They stand between the doors and Beth wishes she could feel like crying, because that would be something to do and not a trick—not meant as a trick—just something for her to be with.

Arthur rubs his hand over his face in a long, anxious swipe. 'And **one** is *Look at me*.' He lowers his eyes and says very softly, 'And you did touch me when I asked, you touched my arm and I have a suite—I have a *Grand Suite*—and it's comfortable and warm and we could be comfortable and warm in it together and we could undress and we could be in my bed and you could fuck me, because I asked and you haven't done that yet and you can't start a number and not finish, you have to do the whole number and you could fuck me and then I would be with you and I would be naked and you could look at me.'

His head swinging away from her while he speaks,

94

as if he expects to be found offensive, and he doesn't
look at her, is only turning for the final door, pushing
it open into the dry, anxious scent of the ship.

Arthur simply walking himself away: 'You could
look at me.'

Which means he isn't being simple.

He isn't being fair.

He shouldn't say things like that.

Any word can work a spell if you know how to
use it.

Prepared.

The man sits in a bland hotel suite, curtains drawn
for the third day running. Resting in the other room
is a woman nobody can mend, but he will try to.

The man is hot with the idea of saving her and
has already entirely committed himself to the first
of his offerings: the undermining of his own fabric,
the imposition of stresses, minor pains. For the
woman—she's called Agathe—he has made himself
unnatural. For Agathe there is nothing natural that's
left.

He offers as much to every one of them, to each
enquirer.

For quite a while now he's only worked with
individual enquirers—the platform gigs didn't feel
right to him, they lacked control. By himself in a
roomful of strangers and their lacks, that never was
what he'd intended.

This is better.

This is the last of three days.

The man gives enquirers three perfected days,

95

tailored to their needs.

Bespoke service.

Three days and then no more for ever, a definitive end.

Three days prepared by a man who is prepared.

Before the start of every session, he's careful to think—*I am a man who is prepared.* Then he fits his hands one into the other and imagines the smell of caramel and sunshine on his face and reflecting on water and the sound of an easy tidal swell—that kind of breathing, the breath of a calm sea. He revisits a number of comforting places and sensations.

Nothing too pleasant, but enough.

Because I need to be defended.

I need to be prepared.

For this morning he has drunk too much coffee and taken one over-the-counter decongestant. This, combined with his anaemia, will re-pace his heart, make it gallop in his chest. And he will shake.

Which is sometimes an unavoidable requirement.

Appearances matter.

He's in an excellent suit. He can afford it.

Bespoke service.

He's been wearing it for two days straight, though, letting it wrinkle—his shirt's fresh, but wrinkled too—because he's working, shut in with Agathe and the hours racking round, accumulating. And he won't be shaving until he stops.

Here am I, gone to pieces, lost and harried in my single-minded care for you.

Symbolic devotion to their cause.

Normally he's immaculate, keeps cleaner than clean. Shaves twice a day. Manicure once a week.

But if he's got a gig then he has to be more subtle— dishevelled but not distasteful—so no iron, and unscented soap, unscented antiperspirant. Unwanted scents can be confusing.

Additional antiperspirant for his hands.

Because he *is* devoted to their cause and his care *is* single-mindedly for each enquirer.

And, most of all, because they'll hold his hands.

They will touch him.

They will become familiar with the small knock of his pulse, its eloquent suggestions. But always formality with them, restraint.

Jacket stays on, no matter what, and have to be careful, maintain the proper distances. Be a gentleman. Be especially a gentleman for the ladies.

The work is easier with women. Their orientation doesn't matter, it's just simpler for him and smoother with the gender he should love, should be allowed to love—all those echoes of experience, the terrible paths of tenderness that still lead into him, he can use them—they insist on his attention, focus him—and they mean he doesn't have to fake affection. It's a pre-existing inclination.

Plus, women live longer, survive—he gets more practice with them.

Ladies' man.

Which would be funny at another time and in another place.

And if I were another man.

But here I am, myself and working.

And here's Agathe.

Her last name is undoubtedly a cautious invention, but Agathe—that's honest. That rings in her when he says it and he can watch her hollow with the wish to hear it as it once was, familiar and spoken by lost mouths. She aches. When he sits beside her the man aches, too.

97

At first she was excessively wary with him, furious with a desire to be gone, numb, other than she is.

The man can understand this.

And safety: Agathe still wants safety beyond speaking.

But she doesn't believe in it, of course. She has no faith in sanctuaries.

She has seen what will happen to people who do.

A challenge then, Agathe.

Not that she was beyond him.

Very few people have managed to stay beyond him.

And, when he came down to it, with Agathe there was only one real barrier to cross. This made his process simple—either break her, which he would not ever do, or find her line and then respect it, spend their first two days showing it humility and restraint: don't cross it, not until invited.

Kindness.

All done with kindness.

We are all of us done with kindness.

Right now, she will be lying on her bed, but not asleep. Agathe rarely sleeps. She will have heard him showering in his bathroom and the mild din of his feet, his ungainly knock—tired—against a chair that sent it over and on to the carpet. Every noise will have meanings for her, sensible explanations, but each will be a horror, too. Each will be the inescapable, finally here to claim her. Even a cough can jolt her, or the clatter of restless pigeons, outside on the window ledges.

He had guessed this before he met her.

No.

He had been certain.

Because he began by letting her story overwhelm

98

him—the outrage of her experience and a sense of being stunned, robbed, splintered, hauled down towards weeping and giddiness: his, hers, his. He saved the flavours of this and its unfathomable size, its slipping into fury and an attentively waiting nothingness. In her absence, the patterns of what happened to her began to coalesce.

This is the least he would expect, because he has learned how to nourish facts, how to feed them and let them grow into usefulness. Threads, suggestions, scraps, they make him ready for First Sight.

Which was watching her walk out of the frost and into the milky fug of a coffee shop on the Rue Saint-Denis.

Always like the Montreal gigs—such a crazy town, so full of damage, anxious for release. And there was Agathe—the whole of her—the buried and unburied.

So there I was to be with her.

She was angular, clean-limbed, and there would have been something fluid and dignified in her walk, but it was stiffened now and locked. The upright head was anxious, throat taut. Cheap skirt to her ankles and comforting, protecting boots for warmth— nothing dainty, nothing female, not any more, just a defence against Quebec, the cold. A type of thin anorak, faded, not originally hers; quite likely that nothing was meaningfully hers except the scarf.

Karkade red, hibiscus red—impractical synthetic chiffon—hand touches it often—threat to the neck—a memory of threat to the neck—a knot, a fear, a choke in the throat made of words, impossible to swallow and impossible to scream.

That's OK, though.

I only deal with the impossible.

It's what I like.

Red bound around and around her neck. But not blood. To her it's not blood—more like giving, sharing, passion recalled, types of heat—it's something gentle near her lips, I can see her almost tasting it, a sort of response—and it isn't heat, it's primarily warmth, there's a difference, a more lasting penetration.

She has clever fingers—we can share that, don't need to translate it—only her touch has lost assurance—it's blinded—so think of gloves, keeping gloves on you, muffling constantly—and she's directionless.

There's no point to touching when what you want to touch is gone.

Hair cropped to a haze, no longer hides the skull— lovely curve there, but it's a mortified beauty. She has an impulse towards simplicity, scouring and punishment—not starting again, but freezing at nothing. No longer hiding because there is nowhere to hide. No hat. It's bitter outside but no hat.

No hiding.

But she did once, didn't she? Agathe tried to hide and it was bad. She was bad. Time enough for that, though . . .

Her mouth was used to smiling: taken altogether, she has a face that would once have been comfortable, opened, ready to show an intelligence and charm.

Charm is rare and shouldn't ever be extinguished.

Intelligence is rarer, but also more difficult to like and she's intelligent—she's bright, bright, bright.

Silly too, she could be silly, she could play—sexual play and just daftness. I would have enjoyed her. We might have flirted, talked.

She would have laughed a good deal and quite probably clapped her hands together softly when she did. She'll have covered her lips, shielded her grin for a moment, enjoyed having overstepped some tiny mark.

She hasn't been able to change her eyes—they have stayed challenging, curious. They look too much—it's almost a form of self-harm. She is learning to curb them, focus on table legs, pavements, floors, to behave like a refugee. But she has brave eyes, that's irreversible.

Brave and tired, tired, tired—she can no longer trust what they'll force her to see. They are beyond her.

But I'm not.

I'm right here—here with the over-priced cookies and the sugar-heavy syrups—symptoms of safe city living, this masochistic urge to spend too much on shit. We have been consistently persuaded to buy what will do us no good.

Agathe bought me.

She asked for me.

So she gets what she asked for, what she wants. People should.

She'd told him on the phone—very quiet but precise—that she wanted to meet him and to try him.

He hadn't sent for her, she'd asked.

And then he'd lifted his head on that initial afternoon, so that she could find him, and he'd sat calmly, fixed his whole strength into restfulness and tender breathing and hampered glances. He'd reached out and matched the beats and pauses of how Agathe is Agathe.

It's an animal thing, a wilderness thing—flesh echoing flesh and leading, a sense of large defence—or the child and the parent and the parent and the child, the home they make between them—and it's a sex thing and a shared will thing and a human thing and a rest thing: it's come unto me and I will give you rest. It's a relief.

This felt, as it always does, like hunger and freedom

and finding and wearing and racing and dancing and burning and having and laughing and fucking and bracing himself in the tide of who she is, the slap of it against his chest.

He began to fix her in his mind as the scent of syruped coffee and also green mornings, the aftertaste of Fanta—popular in Rwanda, Fanta—and the nag of over-happy music and motor taxi exhausts. There was Montreal in her, too—those flattened Québécois vowels and a park bench, sitting, being startled away by clutching mission drunks, being disproportionately frightened, scared of her multiple weaknesses and how they show themselves: that was yesterday. She had that at her surface, but he pressed until she dipped into years ago and Kigali and the sway of rounded hills—no anxiety, no shocks—simply pooled mist and dust that is a pinkish khaki, that washes down on to the pavements and the tarmac when it rains.

He chooses not to admit that Rwandan earth is a colour that makes him think of taint, of spillage, of humped soil that moves, seethes, becomes remarkable with covering too much slaughtered meat. He keeps her from that—seals every thought of her away from the slip of putrefaction, tangled cloth, unbreathable streets. The least he can do.

He's seen other countries, other places that remember selections and thefts, houndings, flights, pits—Guatemala, Poland, Bosnia, Spain—an older and newer and larger list of countries every year. The man is aware that different violated earths have different colours, so he shouldn't let chance mineralogy mislead him, or trouble her.

In his thoughts, she will see no blood, not where he saves her. His mind doggedly takes her to live in

102

a flawless space in a sunlit room in an upper storey in a row of many mansions—he's going to keep her there. Every one of his enquirers is settled safe inside imagined houses, together with the details that made them real. They are stored away with dignity, accurate tenderness.

He doesn't forget them.

They are held under love.

This is important.

As important as the fact that he works for them and then never sees them again.

No exceptions.

His necessary loneliness.

The right way to do wrong.

The man hears Agathe stirring through the wall, a toilet flush, taps running for a bath. The accommodation they share is not luxurious, but it is pleasant, allows for privacy and space. It brought her near to her earlier existence when she saw it. There was the start of tears, an anger, a shame.

He has given her salts and oils for bathing. Neither of them believes they confer any New Age benefits. They're having none of that crap. They do make her feel indulged, though, womanly and pampered and, by now—two days gone—this is something she can tolerate again. Guillaume, her husband would have bought her similar treats at their beginning, on one of his attentive, unbusied days.

Difficult to get the scents just right—musk, Egyptian sandalwood, frankincense, tuberose, Givenchy Pi for Men and Amarige—very 1990s. He gives her ways in which Agathe can recall Agathe, ways in which Agathe can recall Guillaume.

Michel, her son, is more difficult, further away.

It hurts both the man and Agathe that Michel is

staying mainly out of reach.

The cruelty of sons with their mothers never ceases to disgust.

While she bathes, the man waits and leans his elbows on the table, shuts his eyes and shifts his head, nuzzling the conditioned air. Then he swallows and frowns and drops into a sense of her skin—this isn't a sexual process, this is knowing—this is, in a way, being known—this is water over her surface, their shared surface, over the no-longer-needed body, the attempting-to-forget-itself body, over the scar on her collar bone. Cupping liquid warm in her left hand.

Agathe's right hand is gone. So she can't be right-handed.

Shame, because she was.

Could be worse. And it's not as if she's pretending she'd have prospered as a cleaner, a nanny, a waitress, been happy in some abject, practical, double-handed job. Agathe is not practical. Journalism suited her: ideas, concepts, a discipline of the mind, of uncovering and talking, shaping, driving, late-night calls and letting her name be printed—her byline exposed where the radio broadcasts could find it in those poisonous last days. The new kind of journalists started work: the ones who coach murderers then set them loose to play— and they wanted her. They wanted everyone. They were ready at RTLM: nailed her up on air with her husband. She is unable to forget the adolescent, happy music, the fresh voices—Georges Ruggiu, Valerie Bemeriki—all those knowing and persuasive voices, authoritative threats, exhilarating threats, the fucking and fucking and fucking energy of threats— bloodthreats, fuckthreats, young men's threats.

104

Some days, she could see them shading the air above her like greasy smoke.

They only broadcast for a bit more than a year, so their influence was remarkable. What might be called their productivity was highly impressive. Then again, it was a highly productive genocide—efficient beyond imagination.

Kill rates have never been exceeded.

Not yet.

And the Brits did what to intervene? Helped the delays, assisted evasions. Eventually we sent some trucks. Old ones. Fifty trucks. To save a whole country. Every mechanism slowly failing. Doesn't bear thinking about.

But I do think about it. My job to bear.

I bear nothings, ghosts, thoughts.

A British (non-domiciled, non-taxpaying) citizen just doing what he can.

To help.

To help her.

After the killing's stopped.

Sort of stopped.

Agathe, clearly, was not killed. She was mutilated and raped.

Agathe survived, which is an extremely misleading word.

Agathe can type slowly, freelances with some francophone work, some English. She writes whatever she can, agrees to be an expert on the whole of Africa, to pretend that everywhere on the continent must be fundamentally alike. Agathe pretends she is from Burundi, which is almost true. She comments on Rwanda, on President Kagame, on how many potential *genocidaires* you can select and choose to kill before you yourself will become a *genocidaire*—

on how the poison still frets in the earth.

Agathe knows she had a son.

Not now.

Agathe knows she had a husband.

Not now.

Agathe had that one strong border around the privacy of her mourning and the guilt that she'd been slow once, had not understood her situation—she'd been a journalist and clever but she hadn't adequately predicted, hadn't pre-empted a single terror, had not saved anything.

And after that Agathe had decided that nobody else would mislead her, that she would be ready, even though she believed that she shouldn't be living, that every breath was unforgivable. She was walled up alone inside her watchfulness and sin.

So the man simply sang out her pain, made a methodical inventory for her, so that she could grow used to his being correct. He didn't even murmur against her defences—he sat outside them and stretched in the sunlight and searched through his pockets for redemption, held it coddled in his hand and warm and let her see.

If she wanted it, then she would break herself open for him and ask him in.

Eventually, everyone does.

Because we all need mercy, how could we not?

And I have the finest for her, because I make it.

Hand-crafted for one careful owner.

None better.

And he's set her fingers firm on his wrist, made her hold him so she can't help but notice when he's squeezed his pulse slower, flattened it, when he's raced his heart, trembled. Yesterday—his arm all gimmicked, ready—they went a little further. It

106

wasn't a cheap trick necessarily, only a plain thing, an apposite addition which would deepen confidence—it's not like he'd stooped to blood-writing, nothing shabby. Time was, he was going for 10/11 forces with Tarot cards, nonsense like that—deserved a spanking.

Now he stops his heart.

He did that for Agathe: gave her a death reversed. Nothing flash, just a sufficient halt, no showing off. She would have felt him slow, then stop, then start back up. And it wouldn't have seemed unlikely: he generally looks like death, bloody awful.

Fucking headache all the fucking time.

He'd squeezed the gimmick, let his blood apparently falter and stop, and then he let her search his intentions, eye-to-eye. He parted himself for her, let her peep in. And then he released the pressure on his arm, restored his pulse, stuttering, struggling, fighting to be with her. After that, three decongestants and his lack of effective blood had guaranteed him palpitations, something unfakeable—unless you know how to fake it.

And then The Gift.

He'd brought her Guillaume.

He'd summoned her husband, made Guillaume beyond convincing, let him find her smile—that early-love, most beautiful and delicate of her smiles. The man gave Agathe exactly what her husband would have if he still existed and wasn't bullshit and could have returned from the beyond. The man let Guillaume forgive and forgive and forgive.

Agathe had that one strong border.

Not now.

And today Agathe will wear the mishinana the man bought her—*karkade red*—and together they

107

will finish this before tomorrow morning.

Once she's opened her bedroom door she pauses, stands and is lovely and almost knows it. The cloth of the dress drapes conveniently—tradition leaving her perfect side revealed and concealing the damaged shoulder, the shortened limb.

The man seats her at the table, deft and attentive as a maître d', and then he lights the final candle— *hibiscus red*—turns out the lamps and sits down opposite.

He always uses three candles: the black, the white, the red. His enquirers decide on each colour's significance, a logical order. Very few of them choose to end with red.

Brave eyes and brave to the bone.

No food no drink, not for either of us—only this.

He sets both forearms flat on the tabletop, allows her to mirror him, which she does and tells her, 'Mwaramutse.'

Kinyarwanda—I've not had to use that with anyone else. A nice task, picking it up—adds an extra layer, perhaps a resource for the future—Christ knows, they've got enough widows . . . And speaking it has pleased her, really delighted her in some tiny way. I'm slightly proud of that.

'Is it still the morning?' She smells of roses. She settles, meets his gaze. She is asking for everything this time—whatever else he can do.

Which will be The Final Leaving and The Beginning.

Leaving is easy—it's starting again that's intolerable, deciding to walk out into your life, the way it promises and then fumbles.

I used to say I'd give them hope—but no one should have to deal with that.

Even so, he says, 'It's another morning. Last day.

Amakuru?'

'I'm fine, thank you.'

'We got through the night.'

'We got through the night.' Her voice is deeper, her words are slower than when she arrived, they seem younger, nearer, snug and unselfconscious as they touch her lips. 'We got through the night.'

Night is when the young men ran and played with their swooping, exhumed blades, their stockpiled determination to remove the *inyensi*, the *ibyitso*, accomplices of the rebels, the *inkotanyi.* They made roadblocks which could not be passed, constructed gauntlets that clotted with bodies, breathing heaps and parts. They laid waste. They took neighbours and teachers, broadcasters, politicians, shopkeepers, journalists, anyone, anyone, anyone who was marked, who was listed as a collaborator, cockroach, moderate, threat. And the running men, the playing men—they denied the rules of homes and cities and hospitals and churches and villages and farms, the rules of human beings facing other human beings. They raped in the way they might smoke a cigarette, or take a drink. They raped to prove their point—that they were raping nobody, doing nothing—that appetite and liberated thinking are invincible. They were an absolute, carried out their *umuganda* as if it was truly *clearing brush, cutting down the tall trees*— fast as *pulling out the bad weeds*—as if their country ought to be reworked into one vast, manicured landscape—like the grounds of a stately home, or perhaps a golf course. Machetes and bullets and fears so great that everyone must die before the morning.

Each time Agathe has closed her eyes it has been night. Six years of night inside her skull and the noises that people make when they stop being people.

This morning she will watch the man's face and he will talk her back into April and living in Kimihurura—up the hill by the diplomatic compounds, in amongst the curved roads and woodlands—good for parties and gossip, good for sweet air.

But the President's plane has exploded and what couldn't be happening is; beyond any limits, it is. There was a plan. All along, the men with machetes, the broadcasters, the politicians who moved them— they had a plan—there were strategies and contingencies and diplomatic considerations and she never found the red, wet truth of them. So it found her. It found everyone.

And the man and Agathe and Guillaume—they are there together.

And running up the middle of the road is a naked woman and then she falls the way she might if she had tripped. She will have hurt herself, skinned her knees. There's an odd stain on her back, it glistens. A presidential guard ambles towards her, shoots her once more, this time in the head, moves on.

Agathe is three minutes away—a three-minute leisurely walk—caught in her dangerous, pretty house that has simple doors and unarmoured windows, a pleasant garden, decking for the evening sun, an inadequate fence.

None of what she has is any use to her, not now.

Guillaume wants Agathe to hide. He tells her in one hot whisper, 'Genda!' He sounds the way he never has: so small, so scared, tearing with love. And she won't go and he begs and the men are next door—outside and next door—*Abakuzi,*

110

Impuzamugambi, Interahamwe—the names of her coming death.

And when she remembers this, drops into this, Agathe shivers and the man shivers and when she cries—this bereft, immobile weeping—the man weeps, too.

And she's going, she's going there—completely there—and so stay with her and love her and stay with her and here she goes, all of the way.

And the man tells her that Guillaume is in the room with her—imagines a sense of being filled with this breath, with this scent, this years-ago air—and the man takes her husband's words into his own mouth—'Iruka!' The last word—good guess, lovely guess—beautiful job.

So follow up, keep hold.

The husband must have watched while Agathe hid somewhere . . . no thought of being tortured for her whereabouts—he's going to be murdered, not interrogated—and he wants to see the last of his wife, he wants her face there firm in his thinking when he's by himself and the horror comes.

Somewhere—look at her—it was somewhere tiny, hopeless, flimsy . . . she's shrinking into it, thinking of hugging herself like a girl—somewhere low that was like a cupboard—at the level of the soldiers' shins, boots—flinching, flinching, flinching—loud boots once they were indoors and kicking.

Because this is fucking obvious, the man tells her the intruders took money and jewellery and pawed through her clothes.

Mention bedding—I'd rip bedding—if I was a cunt like that.

Confusing, intoxicating—being the violated and the violator—the killer and the killed.

111

I'll sleep well tonight—bloody exhausted.
I'll sleep well or not at all . . .

Agathe frozen somewhere when he mentions the bedding.

Bedding.

The word hits.

Lovely.

So she was in a linen cupboard. Smell of bedding, fresh, intimate, owned—no way to sleep for her, ever after—no way out of dark and wakefulness—or there hasn't been—but I'll make her a way. I will.

Agathe hid in the linen cupboard and listened to the sounds of metal and her husband's bones.

Guillaume didn't shout, didn't want to upset her, stayed unexpressed—comes across as an odd man, very gentle, slightly distant—more suited for academia than journalism.

Either way, they'd have fucking killed him.

Agathe holding her breath in the cupboard—has kept holding her breath ever since—the only sounds letting her understand Guillaume's murder.

She heard the breaking of her husband's body—what she kissed, learned, fucked, loved. They killed Guillaume.

This would be the point where she went very reasonably insane.

And afterwards—*being the perpetrators again*—the man imagines and describes searching, giggling, drunk men, stoned men, breaking things, foulness in Agathe's house.

Naturally, they found her—cruel to dwell on that and it might push her too far, lock her beyond herself again, so be gentle over it—be gentle anyway—*fuck*—of course, be gentle.

Agathe was not Tutsi like her husband and her

112

rapists knew that. Because she was Hutu, they exercised perverse restraint, permitted everything except her murder. Or else it was premeditated torture—this leaving her alive, alone, making her see.

Trying to overwhelm those eyes. Make them shut.

The last thing they did was to cut off her hand.

The man thinks of her hoping she'd bleed to death.

Not allowed—none of those thoughts, not any more—no more dying, no rushing into destruction. Can't let the bastards make her kill herself, reach out and murder her with her own will.

The man makes Guillaume tell her that her self is sacred and mustn't be harmed, has to be held in beauty. The man allows a type of poetry to break out in his narrative because, husband and wife, they were people of words and found them impressive.

And the man talks about the way Agathe was sure Guillaume was with her and still alive when she fainted—that he was there—and then that terrible re-education when she awoke: metally bloodsmell and shit—lying in her own blood, husband's blood—broken glass, boot prints—things she cannot look at but has to, has to remember, has to eat up because they are all she has left. They were her everything.

Details, the probative details, that's what gets them and she is got.

Which is good because the man has to make her believe that she wasn't mistaken: that Guillaume did watch and wait. The man portrays her husband, invents him as being adamant on this point: that he was there beside her, beyond touching but there.

Something else for her to eat: a better everything.

And this is a type of perfection—a tenderness, but she doesn't stay with it, because her chronology is

113

leading to her son. First her husband was murdered and then her son.

Guillaume is lighting in her, he is convincing and she wants him—but she needs her son.

The man can taste her need—he makes it like chocolate in his head—hotsweet—and she never did really know what happened to her son. Michel, her only boy.

Down in Butare it was diggers and soldiers. No more tolerance for students, no more education required. Not much we can stand to see of that.

The man says he can feel Michel, that he is running along a track in open country. He isn't properly dressed, may have lost clothes, or been woken and driven from his bed. Michel is in a crowd. The men behind the crowd are quiet and busy—they have a long day ahead—they either shoot at the crowd or hack individuals down as they wish. Michel doesn't hear what happens to him, barely understands the start of it—out of breath, dust in his throat and then gone.

This feels unconvincing, not comprehensive enough. Agathe wants to understand completely: at least be with Michel, even if she couldn't do as a good mother should and save him.

Motherlove, motherguilt, motherblood—they all fuck you up.

And I'd like to please her—I would, but Michel, he'd be sodding awkward, he'd resist. Can't get a handle on more of his dying and I'm not going to try and that will work better—it really will work better than having him torn apart for her to watch.

Guillaume—he's the best bet—he's her way out of this. He's salvation.

And she should fucking have that, so I will fucking

114

arrange it, so fucking there.

The man lets her know how Guillaume watched her navigating Kigali. Her husband was why she didn't bleed to death and wasn't caught again. He is why the UN jeep paused where it did and she could reach it. He is why the checkpoints showed no interest in her—already dealt with.

Apparently.

Such love from him.

Bundled—always see the love in bundles, soft armfuls of the stuff.

Because I am a sentimental bastard.

But Agathe gets more than bundles.

She gets a real goodbye.

Guillaume needs to kiss her.

Yes, he does, my love, my darling. Come on Agathe, you can do this. We can do this.

The man suggests Agathe close her eyes and that the darkness will be recast, secured from this day forwards, peaceful. And her love so near her that she can smell his skin, his hair, the things of his that are forever now.

The man wants her to purse her lips.

Deep. A deep kiss. Thoughtkiss. Move for it. Please. Come on. For me. For him. Most natural thing in the world.

If she purses her lips for the ghost of a kiss, this will work.

Leastways, it ought to work. I dunno.

Pimping her for a corpse.

Come on, girl. For me. You can kiss him.

Sweet Agathe.

Open all the secrets of your lips.

She does like her poetry—shame I'm not in the mood myself—too excited—never tried this before.

But he does try talking her back to the excellent pain that was wanting and needing, that was love.

Kiss.

Sweet Agathe and a kiss.

The man leans forward and whispers, 'And he takes your hand, Agathe. You kiss him and, as proof, he'll touch your hand.'

The nerves get confused after amputations, they reconfigure, so—this can be possible, should be possible—a movement of her mouth, her cheek, can summon up what's gone: she'll feel her lost husband holding her lost hand.

And how fucking good would that be? That would be fucking good.

Not exact as a procedure.

Never tried it before, in fact.

But I did want to.

But unpredictable.

But fuck it. You can do this, Agathe. I know that you'll feel it, because you should feel it. You should have this.

You can.

And then he sees her, sees her smile and he is sure—he sees who she was and who she will be and that she is more and clean and more and strong and more and is in love.

Ecstasy. For you and me. Endlessly.

Fuck, yes.

She weeps without noticing. It rocks her, harrows her, and she lets it and still smiles. She burns.

Hurts to look.

Anything this wonderful, you shouldn't look.

Have to take care, though, stay alert.

What's left of her forearm rises from the table and her eyes still shut while she concentrates beyond the

116

man—beyond the world—and grips, clings, touches with fingers that do not exist. She is holding her husband's hand, she can feel it, recognise it.

This is true.

Fucking true.

And this gives the man a joy approaching hers.

Fuck, yes.

*   *   *

It wasn't her husband, though.

Good thing the man only steered her, lightly kept her company and didn't crash in with a name.

Getting it wrong at this point would have been inexcusable.

Michel was the one she imagined returning, whose wounds undid themselves and fled, whose hair smelled of paradise when he touched her and of himself, of the total of his first cry, first look, first step, first hurt, first fight, of his known and secret life, of his mother's knowledge of his life.

Between them—she's between them—I can see it in her, in the sway of the head, the urge to lean on air, to rest her head on fantasies and let them love her.

Happy for you, Agathe.

She trusts, utterly trusts, that her man and her boy are to either side of her and she is breathing them in—greedy.

The red candle burning down.

I have explained.

I do make it very clear.

When the last candle gutters and goes out, then this is over. Permanently. The dead won't be home again, not for me, not for anyone else—so none of the other fuckers will take her, charge her, hook her up to the

weekly fixes of counterfeit affection and silly tricks.
She's had me.
Had the best.
And I've given her everything she needed.
Safe hands, me. A pair of safe hands.
*I **gave** her this. No charge—that's **giving**.*
And no one here but us to know. No one but me.
I saved a life today.
Well done, me.
And no one to know.
The man's safe hands shaking so that he has to flatten them against the tabletop.
She can sit for as long as she wants.
We'll let it all consolidate and calm.

*　　　*　　　*

When Agathe finally opens her eyes, she looks at the man as if she has slept and been awoken and he clasps her hand gently between both of his and waits until she recognises him and this time and this place.
Sorry. You have to be here and they have to be gone.
The way things have to be.
And it will rip you in places that I haven't got, but this is the end and unavoidable.
And I won't do any more—I won't make you need me. I won't do that.
Here you are and only you, and I am only me, but together we made what you wanted. Please take the love in that. Be satisfied.
She is flushed, early morning bewildered—for a moment he feels her appetite, that hungry confusion—so he lets her go. He begins to re-establish a useful distance.

Sodding candle's got a way to burn, but we can snuff it out.

Or she can, that might be better. Maybe . . . Not sure . . .

Can't just hang about here getting morbid, that's for sure.

And this is the point where advice is required and suggestions, ways to proceed into a future.

Advice from me on anything . . .

Laughable.

But nobody laughing.

Why would we.

Then off we go to our lonelinesses. No need to mention them, though. Obvious. Each to our own.

But she has her consolation, yes she fucking does.

From me.

What little there could be—from me.

Keep things brisk, definitive. Check she's fine, solid, no vulnerabilities left without at least some kind of covering.

Talking of which—will she want to take the dress off? Keep it?

She'll keep it.

I'm betting she'll want to walk out wearing it.

And undressing at this juncture is to be avoided, I would say.

This game that he's played: she never understood the rules and he could end with anything, could require anything of her and probably get it, steal it, con it out of her.

But I won't. Have to end it well for you, Agathe. Something special for brave Agathe.

So he stares at the wall beyond her and mentions she has the suite for another three days—this isn't true, but can be very easily arranged—and there is

119

no arguing about this, there can't be: his delivery lets her understand that it is necessary, that it preserves her from the rigours of her new world until she is ready for them. The rest of her transition will take place here.

Then he bows his head for a moment and produces an appropriate smile. When he faces her again he makes it more than readable that somehow he has withdrawn from her at depth, that this is painful and troubling, will leave him less and her more, will leave him solitary, folded back into pale isolation.

He lets himself give in to being tired.

Because I fucking am.

He reaches out and levels his right hand above the candle flame—his last gift.

*Fuck the pain—there isn't any pain—I don't need to fake it, I can think it gone—and she'll like this, she'll **get** it, she'll remember.*

Then he crushes out the fire with his burned palm, marks himself with ash and hot wax, and he pushes back his chair, rises, stands. He bows to kiss her cheek, while she attempts to organise her fretting for him, her thanks and rehearsed goodbyes, but he's already up again and walking, leaving, no more to say, no more permitted—one last glance expressing confidence, affection, his gratitude—he makes himself bright as bright—and then he's out, he's over, free.

He'll send someone later to gather his things—meanwhile, she may want to inspect them, or she may leave them be. He'd like to think she might be curious about him, perhaps a touch fond of who it seemed he was. His belongings are all neutral, provide no clues, just a vague sort of intimacy about them: aftershave, laundry, a mildly used bed.

But she isn't like that. She won't check.

On Wednesday morning, he'll be in the foyer, tucked out of sight for when she leaves.

Just observing, making sure of the gig, the finale.

He expects her to be carrying the new holdall he bought her—important to have a fresh bag for fresh journeys, nothing patronising about it, not a present—and she'll still have that dreadful coat, but underneath it and blazing, singing, he'll want to see hibiscus red: a dress from home, a proud and impractical thing.

That would be a result.

Higher than average chance that she'll carry it off.

Make me cry, that would.

Women—they make me cry.

*   *   *

The man will stand and hide himself from the end of his work, another job done, and he will watch another stranger walk away and he will wonder how he came to be here. He will wonder how he came to be so far from love.

It's easily done.

You take your thumb and press it, nestle it, into the heart of your other hand. Where it most naturally rests, that's the sweet spot, the place where any touch will always raise a tenderness.

Consider whoever you love, ponder them, allow yourself to dwell, and a quiet ache will begin there—the longing you hold instead of their skin, that other skin. Clench your fists and it's that space you'll be defending—both hands curled around a lack, a thought, a tiny mind that you are out of and that your love is in.

And it's a light sleeper, your sweet spot, almost impossible not to wake it in spite of yourself—or because of yourself—not to set it off demanding satisfactions, to be touched—the little well that speaks, asks to be filled.

Best to train it if you can, start early and at least placate it, provide alternative interests to entertain. As a child, an oddly sensible child, you might start by setting a coin there, or a pebble, a medal, a talisman, charm, badge, ornament, folded paper, ticket, earring, seashell, marble, ring—pick any one of the small and precious, small and worthless objects that might litter a room, a jacket's pockets, a usual life.

And then you can teach the hollow of your palm to hold them, hide them, make them disappear. So the absence you feel can conjure up another, earn its keep.

If you would like.

Some children like.

Some people like.

And liking leads to doing, leads to practice—and a way of being compulsorily, usefully self-contained. Through evenings and weekends and holiday afternoons and on into the nights, you'll clench and furl and smooth your grips, you'll pace the beats and off-beats of any motion. The back of your hand will grow innocent, completely fair, its sides will be irreproachable, you'll even be able to offer up its soft, clean face while a marvel stays locked behind your knuckles—then you simply shift your treasure to the ledged base of your fingers, or the fold at

122

your thumb's root, to fingertips, or into the snug of your palm, your gentle, educated palm. You'll start to be made up of refuges from every observation, all angles pre-empted, because this is how you will fabricate invisibility. You will study yourself in your mirror as if you're a dangerous stranger until, finally, you'll see you've managed it, you've changed, become completely secret, a deception. Your skin knows without seeming to know, your muscles and tendons work without seeming to work, your fingers flex and drop and catch and place and never show it.

You are magic.

You are definitively sure there's no such thing, but you can be it anyway.

You can believe yourself wonderful and enough and beyond helping.

If you would like.

If you would want that.

And the boy did want that.

The boy.

Our boy.

The boy was an early starter, in several ways precocious, and most of all with his hands, in his hands. When he is older he won't absolutely remember, but he is perhaps seven, nearly eight, when he first attempts their training. His dad can move cards to the top of the pack and can put the Queen of Hearts in any order with two of her cousins, will dance her about as he lays her down on the kitchen tabletop—first, third, first, second, second . . . wherever he wants. His dad explains that when someone else does this, it's a bad thing to do, because people can use it for cheating at bets and taking cash away from idiots. This is cruel because idiots need their cash more than most. And his dad also has a special card with holes in it which can be pulled along its sides—movable holes punched right through it which the boy cannot look at, except from far away, and isn't permitted to touch.

This leads the boy to conclude the holes are a gimmick built into the card and not a special cleverness of his dad's. The boy works this out.

So his dad has three tricks.

And only with cards.

The boy has already decided that people who think they can trust cards, or anything cards do, are idiots and should be left alone with their cash and not interfered with. He is waiting to be a grown-up and fool the other grown-ups who are like him, who can see things and can work them out. Personally, the boy would only be impressed if something amazing happened with his special piece of amber, or one of his model commandos, or his tiny dinosaurs—with reliable, familiar items. And so he intends to surprise the world with strictly proper stuff: the clean and plain and pure.

He has saved up and bought a book from a lovely and crowded, disreputable shop. It's a manual and contains instructions and thick-lined, authoritative drawings of hands and gestures and men with short haircuts and slyly concealing trouser cuffs—very serious, vintage men: ones like the black and white detectives in old films. But they're always ready to astonish with handkerchiefs and tumblers and American coins. They'd be fun to have round in your house. They are, he assumes, American men and not just being awkward on purpose by vanishing and producing inconvenient currency. He guesses about which British coins would be the same as the

124

ones they're using, stares at the diagrams, imagines his fingers into their shapes. He stands and repeats the passes over his bed so that no one will hear when he fumbles, lets something drop. Eventually, he doesn't need the bed.

And the boy saves up again, this time for the mirror which he carries carefully, painfully back from the high street and into his room. It makes his mother laugh and talk about girlfriends while his dad frowns and the boy feels jangled and compressed.

The following Sunday, as they walk to the paper shop, his dad describes girls and girls' habits. The description requires three circuits of the play park with the rusty swings—right to the bottom trees and back, three times—because it is long and detailed. Although the boy has met girls at school and mainly not given them much thought, his father makes of them dangerous strangers and causes for concern. They will not grow into women like Dusty Springfield, someone the boy is very fond of and believes would be nice, even if she does wear spacewoman dresses and have frightening hair. In fact, perhaps *because* of that, he really does quite fancy her a bit. His father says the girls will have nothing in common with Dusty, won't be *gorgeous.* Or, if they are, this *will not be good news.*

Once they have made it to the shop, his dad asks the boy if he would like to spend this week's chocolate and comic money and the boy tells him that it's all right for today and *no* and *thank you*— because he has plans to buy a thumb tip and other indecently, nakedly misleading and deceiving stuff from the wonderful shop that smells of cigarettes and men and badness and which is called *J. Cooper & Son's Magic*, although there is no J.

Cooper and there aren't any sons. His dad gets him a Crunchie anyway, which isn't normal and so the boy eats it too fast on the way back home before anybody can notice and doesn't enjoy it.

When they are just inside the cool of the entrance— looking at where Mrs Barker keeps her flower tubs which the squirrels dig at *because they are bastards*— the boy's father hugs him and closes a hand around one of his ears and rubs it a bit, as if he might make it disappear, and then his dad looks at him and whispers, 'Arthur, always be careful.' And he kisses the top of the boy's head and asks him, almost too quietly to be heard, 'Will you do that?' And Arthur— the boy's name is Arthur, an old-fashioned name, it gets him grief at school—he nods, although he feels that he won't manage. His magic won't be adequate for girls.

Arthur lives in a ground floor flat beside a roundabout which has daffodils on it in spring and once a bloke on it in the summer, pretending to sunbathe for a laugh. The flat is in London—sort of—but not so that Arthur can notice. He is a train and a bus ride or two bus rides and an Underground away from anything notable or on postcards. There is no Big Ben and no ravens and no palace at the end of his street and when he goes to visit these things they do not belong to him any more than to anyone else and this means they make him annoyed, rather than proud or excited. His mother lives with him. She is unhappy. And his dad is there—his tall and blond and wiry father who is striking but will eventually be quite difficult to recall. His father is also unhappy.

But Arthur is happy—he makes sure to be.

And Arthur's hands are both delirious. They are

overjoyed.

And Arthur loves them.

First night aboard and Beth dreams in numbers. She has edged herself into the bed, curls on her side away from contact, takes care that her chill won't wake Derek, her salt chill.

Which it would—I would disturb him.

Because I'm frozen. I haven't a warm place.

Not really.

And he needs to rest.

And he doesn't need to feel there's something wrong with me, all over me, and he won't, because I'm the only one who'll notice that. My secret.

And Arthur's.

No. Just mine. I allow it to happen and it belongs to me.

I used to share it and now I don't.

*I used to be . . . walking in the street and nothing showing, respectable—riot inside, though, mayhem—with any memory of him, every memory of him—I couldn't predict what of Arthur would hit me or when—as if I'd walk straight into him, like rain—his hands on my shoulders and the press of him behind—or the shape of his fingers—confident, talkative fingers: snug. Trying to stroll and worrying I might fall with the sense of him, the knowledge of him. And I'd smile, because no one could tell and I would think—**Here's me and I'm covered in him and nobody knows it.***

He clings and aims to be ingrained.

Like smoke.

Like water.

127

Like the scent of him.

Not that he doesn't take care to be unperfumed, neutral. But he's there all the same, he's there on you when he's left—delicate.

He finds your bones, soaks in.

Bastard.

And she has no hopes of sleep, expects simply to lie and recite and recite: *loving the unlovable is stupid, is self-harm—loving the reasonable is what I need and I can have that. I do have that. I can prefer that because I am not an idiot.*

Which depresses her because she won't believe it.

I am not an idiot.

Except when I am an idiot.

Bastard.

Sleep does arrive, though, unexpected—a strangely rapid kindness she pushes into, under. But then it turns shallow, of course, and relentless. The force of unease turns her on to her back and the bed nags and sickens beneath her and Arthur—

Bastard.

Creeping bastard—always pesters.

Arthur stands there in her mind. He's fidgeting and wears his overcoat and is occasionally crying, which she would rather not see. And with salt fingers, cold and blunt fingers, dead man's fingers, he reaches forward and summons numbers from the air—empty hand passing them deftly to empty hand—and then he puts each figure in her mouth.

She hasn't forgotten—couldn't forget—the lists of meanings, the translations for each one.

One.

Listen, please.

It's useful, one. It can slip into any sentence, any one you choose, and it can ask you.

128

Please listen.

It marks out the start of the story and Arthur's a man who wants all of the story, all of the time. He wouldn't like to miss a word.

And, then again, he's happier yet when it can mean **Look at me**—*when we're working from the second list, the personal list: The Code for Peculiar People in Public Places.*

He loves it if you look—shy and then not, absolutely not, lying out for your attention, blazing with it.

Favours dark sheets: purples, blues—he brings them with him to every hotel, asks the staff to remake the bed with them—give us something other than the standard white. He's the one paying—paying too much—paying for special attentions—so he gets to pick.

And once he brought black: black sheets, black towels, black curtains, black everything.

Like being exiled into night.

And Arthur lying on the night, showing the light of himself, the milk light.

Look at me.

For special occasions.

Buttoned tight, otherwise. Won't even roll up his sleeves. Then it's clever talk and numbers and playing games.

Look at me while I'm hiding, find me, come hunting, and then I'll know you love me, that it's true.

He knows too many games.

And he's too much work.

And he **ought** *to always hide and be ashamed. And why* **should** *I fucking find him? He's nothing to do with me: shouldn't be anything to do with me. He's a Bank Holiday shag, he's play-acting pickups in hotel lobbies, he's a duplex suite with a fruit bowl and two* tellies when all we need is a bed, because we just fuck—no more to us than fucking, not now.

Every night a one-night stand.

Look at me.

But then she swallows **Five** which is peppery and has thin edges and is **Help** which is what she needs, but doesn't get. Or else it's **Come**, which is what she needs, but shouldn't get, because people can use it for cheating and taking things away from idiots.

Time was, they could both be together—Beth and Arthur in company—and they could ask this of themselves and make an answer. **Come.** They could both deliver and request. They could watch for the twitch of a smile, or the colour rising, the approach. They could enjoy understanding and being understood.

Out of my mind, but into yours, very into yours, and your wish is my command and vice versa.

Takes training.

And the insanity to think of training.

And no cheating—because we'll know . . .

Beth and Arthur.

In her dream she wants to see his face, because she believes it might be informative, but all she gets a sight of is his wrist, the flat back of his wrist.

And no more commands and no more wishes—they don't come true.

Arthur never did a true thing in his life.

A man you should not look at, except from far away, should not be permitted to touch.

Man is **Two**.

Tastes sweet—over-sweet—a memory growing, laid on her tongue, and it ought to be salt, it ought to be forgotten.

Man.

Long-shinned, long-footed—soft give of the skin at his throat: feels all alive—and the tuck of the muscle in over his hip: that curve, that line—and he's blond, but then a little darker, coppery too, where the strangers don't see him, what they don't get.

Two.

Clean, clean shaven—or the bristle of him in the dark—early morning—and kissing the insides of his thighs and breathing him in—hot—roaring—the shine of the boy—pale boy—silky boy—like saying silk—to lick.

Two.

And otherwise, and naturally, it's **Smile at me**.

It bloody would be.

And it would be easy to keep herself in this now, concentrate on the pictures of how he can be. This once, she would risk it, indulge it—half awake and with Derek beside her—but the dream of him feeds her **Eight**—pushes it in with his thumb—fat and slippy—**Accident**.

Always needed it for the punters—got to cue each other in so we can tell them how their loved ones left: the car, the motorcycle, ambushing workplace, fate—acknowledge the endlessly amputated plans. Rude of them, the dead—hurtful to rush away without ever saying, ever mentioning, ever finishing what they started. Untidy. We do hate to have it untidy. And we hate to know our dead have torn things that we can't survive without. They have stolen who we are when we are with them—our good selves, our beauty.

*And **Eight** is No.*

No.

*The other **Eight**.*

An almost entirely powerless word in life. You can scream it as long as you want, but matters will still work on as they must, reality will still ignore you. You're flesh in the mechanism, caught in its gears.

No.

But when it meant **Later** and **Persuade me** and **At the moment, I'd like it if I was in charge**, then we loved it—horny word—the **no** in between us—tickling.

Christ.

Christ, we fucked up.

He fucked up.

He is fucked up.

And she dreams herself away from Arthur, tears things about which she does not wish to think and moves away, free. Relatively free.

Bastard.

Awake. I want to be awake.

I'm not, though.

It's that thing—I'm in that thing you get when you can't move and you're not awake, you only think you're awake, but you're wrong. You're dreaming.

I think I'm wrong.

She's in a fluid version of her past. Its edges ripple and dart forward. It makes her tense.

And she's queuing to board the boat again and outraged for some unnamed reason—she's close to retching with disgust—and she picks up a little bag, heavy bag—which isn't hers, or else it is, but she can't recognise it—and then she flings it—intends to make a large and savage gesture but releases too early, her effort swinging wild and to her left and then she spins round after it and sees him—Arthur—again Arthur—and he's sitting—gently sitting—and the bag has hit him, landed in his lap, and he is instantly, immeasurably sad, which is her fault.

Hit him in the balls with my baggage—my baggage which is emotional.

132

Well, whatever could I possibly mean by that?
Fucksake.

And, although she is additionally outraged by her subconscious's lack of finesse, she responds to the scene and tries to make amends for Arthur's hurt—but there's no way through to touch him, only sudden crowds that intervene. She can't offer consolation. There is only this obvious, accusing damage: him sobbing with his arms hugging the bag and rocking, shuddering—and then he's scrabbling in his pockets, he's desperate, he wants to show her something but can't find it.

Seven.
Not my fault.
Seven.
It was an accident.
Eight.
Or else it was his fucking fault for being in the way, for being here in the first place.
*He's looking for **seven.***
I'm not. I don't expect it.
And it's not my fault that he's in the way.
It's not my fault we're in each other's way.

His hands are clearly fighting with pockets that seal and shrink.

That's what you get with tailor-made: bespoke and wilful.

He lifts his head and blinks at her and is panicking and lost. He wakes her with a look.

Love.
Always the same on any list.
Seven.

Forget every other number, you could still manage a sitting, an evening, a seance, with just that.

Not that it needs a number. It's the constant.

133

No matter how well the enquirers lie, you can still see it in them—**seven**'s what they want, their heart's request. Why else would they come? They need you to *tell them the loves they felt were real, that the cruelty was love misunderstood, the absent affection was only hidden, that every love has been continued, will be endless. They want the dead bound hand and foot to them, chained in love.*

Which is expecting a lot of the deceased. One minute they're live human beings: fickle, silly, irritating, gorgeous, flawed—the next they're supposed to be perfect and content to adore us for ever. Nothing better to do with eternity than watch us, see everything we are and worship it.

When nobody ought to see everything we are, because they couldn't stand it.

Seven.

The best of the games and somewhere in every one of the games. Passing it between them like a note. Arthur and Beth. Beth and Arthur.

'Snow White and the Seven Dwarfs—scared me witless when I was a kid—something about the dwarfs' hats—and the pickaxes.'

Civilians not included.

'Canal holiday—boating on the Avon. Or the Severn. No, the Avon. No, the Severn. Perhaps both. It's big, the Severn. Fucking huge.'

Becoming somewhat notorious for babbling and non sequiturs, mispronunciations . . .

'I don't know if that seven is legal.'

Civilians not capable.

'Five Seven Eleven—my gran adored that. Any time of day, you'd go in—the bedroom would be full of it.'

Changing the name of the perfume to fit. Not Four Seven Eleven. That wouldn't suit them. So it's

Five
Seven
Eleven
Come
Love
Be beautiful
But people change.
They can't endlessly be what someone else requires, it wears them out.

So I am tired, tired, tired. I have 888 reasons for being tired, tired, tired.

Beth gets up, showers quietly, goes and sits in her complimentary bathrobe and watches the next day arrive in shades of slate. The irregular shatter of large weather is comforting as it jars the ship's spine and then hers.

She stares and imagines nothing, a beige blank, until she hears Derek stirring. Then she calls up room service for coffee—no breakfast, they'll neither of them want it—and she steps over to start coaxing at her partner—her registered with US Immigration and the shipping line official partner, the man she is supposed to be with, the man that she currently *is* with—starts cajoling her partner into sips of water and another pill.

Outside Beth's cabin, passengers stagger and shoulder walls as the ship bounces, shrugs. There are little impacts and the blurred melodies of hearty chat, or sympathy, or good mornings. And the staff will smile, because this is compulsory and they will polish and dust and varnish and paint unendingly, because this is also required and the seafaring way—otherwise chaos would triumph, water and hard weather would eat the ship.

Inside Beth's cabin, she is trying to be both hearty and sympathetic and has already said good morning. 'You're rallying.' Keeping the chaos at bay.

'I'm fucking not.'

'You don't look as green.'

'I've got a headache like you wouldn't believe.'

'Dehydration. Drink some more.'

'If I drink any more I'll be sick.'

They decide that being dressed might raise their spirits and so Elizabeth helps Derek to abandon his sweated-through pyjamas, encourages him into the shower and nods when he props himself back on the bed in a soft checked shirt and old cords.

He draws up his knees, glares weakly. 'What are you nodding about? Passed inspection, have I? I'm the one who had to do it all. That shower's a fucking joke—like being pissed on by an ugly bird.' He isn't usually coarse in this way—he is trying to annoy her.

And it's good that he has the energy to be annoying—although it is also annoying.

She rubs his arm. 'They say looking at the horizon—'

'Who say?'

'I don't remember. I heard it on the radio, I think.'

'You think . . .'

He is being petulant and insulting, but that's all right; she knows him and is sure he would be noble with a broken leg or a serious infection, something dignified with which he could contend. Seasickness is distasteful and pathetic and yet overwhelming, it has him rattled.

Nevertheless, she permits herself, 'If you're going

136

to be an arse about this, you can fucking well stay as you are. But getting outside and focusing on the horizon is meant to be good and we could have a go, couldn't we? And you could cope with the yard or so from here to the balcony and then we'll see what happens.'

'I'll get pneumonia is what'll happen.' He grins, though—makes a brave little halfway attempt—the good lad doing his best.

He's a fighter, Derek: gets in the ring and keeps swinging, even when there's nothing to hit.

A fighter, not a lover.

And why is it those are the rock and roll choices?

*Why not, **I'm an actuary, not a fighter** . . . ?*

And why don't you fucking focus on the task in hand?

She wavers across the carpet with Derek, arm-in-arming it, the pair of them in no fit state.

Lover: fighter—they picked the maiming occupations. Obvious. There's more drama in the fatal undertakings, the wastes.

And what are we? One of each? Two of both?

She almost falls and, as might have been expected, complicates the possible reasons why.

It's not the ocean. I'd be unsteady in any case.

Bastard.

Recovery time—you shouldn't need it just because you've looked at someone, listened to him, touched his arm.

I used to think I'd end up feeling ruined because of the physical thing, the exertion—nice word for it— because of the two or three days of fucking against his choice of high-class backdrops. I thought that's what it was.

The luxury screwing.

137

And Christ knows where he's staying on board—or what he originally planned. He maybe intended a hideaway here for me, while his suite has the resident unicorn, the lapis lazuli bathroom and Fabergé bed . . . Or maybe he'd have coffined us in together and no pretence: six nights and seven days, same bed.

Did Fabergé ever make beds ?

Oh, fuck this.

Beth cracks her knuckles against the frame of the balcony door, just hard enough to order her thoughts.

'Careful.' Derek produces a grin. 'We don't have to punch our way out.'

'Hm? No, no, of course . . . Silly. And here we go . . .'

Needle rain catches them once they've emerged in the open air. But mostly the air isn't open, or too unruly: they're boxed in by secluding panels to either side and sheltered by the balcony above. They are only mildly buffeted unless they actually crane out over the rail and ask for punishment. Which Elizabeth does.

Like being slapped.

Which I don't.

And I have nothing to be penitent about.

Already been punished. Meeting Arthur is always its own punishment—pleasure and pain and immediate payment for both.

He prefers things to be self-contained—even when they're my things.

I'm self-contained enough to scream—which makes it easier to leave him—and almost impossible. Every time.

***Seven** days and **six** nights.*

That would have been unsurvivable. Don't know what he was thinking—but I can guess. At his bloody

138

games again.

Love days.
And Fuck me nights.
Love days.
And Betrayal nights.
Comes up a good deal with punters—six—betrayal being so commonplace in life. Like fucking. Hand in glove.
And seven and six is too long no matter how you say it.
Seven and six makes thirteen and that's unlucky.
It's all unlucky.
Because it's him that's the problem, not what we do—it's being too close to him—it makes me ill.
Fucking Arthur—he's like catching flu.

Ideally, Beth should sit with Derek on the two metal chairs provided—just right for a couple—with matching metal table—and gaze out in refreshing circumstances. She's even brought a towel with them to wipe everything down, but the rain dodges back to whichever surface she dries off and, after a while, Derek tells her to stop. 'We can lean. It's good, leaning.' And he rests against the closed door, folds his arms, studies the far horizon with what do indeed appear to be beneficial results.

Elizabeth returns to the rail, sees the ocean mounding round them and faulted into ridges, lines of stress, as if the ship is caught and sliding in a bowl of black glass, hammering and hammering against such a depth and height of glass.

And she shouldn't have drunk all the coffee, methodically worked down the pot to busy herself, because the caffeine is scrambling in her now, dialling up intensities she can't afford.

Get yourself over your sleepless night with exactly

what will guarantee your next and also set a panic rubbing underneath your skin. I never learn.

Clearly.

'Do you want to try exploring?' Derek seems pinker and more assured. 'I might be able . . .'

Which is a good idea. Exercise will be calming.

And avoiding the rest of the ship would be eccentric, inexplicable. Why wouldn't it be entertaining to survey the decks? That should prove both informative and bracing. There could even be the risk of lunch. An attempt . . .

'Elizabeth?'

Somehow the day has slipped until it is almost late enough for lunch.

She can hear Derek shifting, pulling open the balcony door. 'I hope we don't see that guy again, though—the meat-eater. I could do without him.' Feral weather leaps in the cabin's curtains, lifts the ship's newspaper, starts up small howls as it fills their room and hunts and searches for ways further into the ship.

Beth nods, still facing the ocean, letting it hurt her.

The liner has kept itself amused without them. They have already missed classes in bridge and computing, several talks on health and beauty (naturally for the ladies) and on maritime history and engineering (even more naturally for the gents) and at least one quiz.

And the bingo.

But nowhere is quite as photogenically busy as it

140

should be. There is about the decks, the areas for leisure opportunities and the shops, an air of relinquished hope. Hunched passengers sit here and there in frozen contemplation of their own unreliable interiors. Healthy wives mouth news of their afflicted husbands over said husbands' mournful heads. Healthy husbands bashfully destroy plates of sandwiches in the lovingly recreated Olde Englishe Pub while their wives stare fixedly out of windows full of grey unwieldy shapes and disturbances. There is little chatter and the good cheer of the untroubled is slightly too strident. Nobody's plans are going to plan.

Elizabeth leads Derek on a mild ascent through the vessel's layers until they emerge in the gentlest location for more coffee: what appears to be a large hothouse for the propagation of geriatrics. Beyond the glass walls there are sturdy funnels, cables, antennae and receivers murmuring or bleating as they part and bewilder the wind. Overhead the sky raccs fiercely and underfoot the floor misbehaves as it seems set to for the duration, and yet here is only moist warmth and generous pot plants, cane chairs with footstools, cane tables, motionless figures under rugs and a bar decorated along tropical lines, forlornly suggesting late nights, cleavages, reckless cocktails and Caribbean flirting. A small man with a moustache lurks behind the bar, resigned to preparing tea, coffee and possibly cocoa, perhaps even Ovaltine. Elizabeth imagines him spending his evenings in a storeroom somewhere, stroking his boxes of novelty plastic straws and coloured paper umbrellas, counting the jars of unused maraschino cherries, wishing himself or his circumstances gone when neither can be altered.

141

'Shall I order you a banana daiquiri, just to cheer him up?'

'What?' Derek hasn't responded well to his journey and has laid himself flat and closed-eyed on a sun lounger.

'To cheer up the barman—a daiquiri . . .'

'Would kill me.'

'Bovril?' Which wasn't funny, so she shouldn't have said it. She shouldn't have said it, even if it was funny. He's upset—like the rest of the passengers: all of them being shaken until they break.

Derek has started taking each jolt personally, grim. 'It's not going to stop, is it?' He is gripping the sides of his seat.

'I don't know. I mean, I can ask. But the last announcement was . . .' The last announcement was uncompromisingly certain that the storm would continue today and then worsen tomorrow and be unabated the day after that. They both heard it—that was the point of the Ship's Announcements— everyone was meant to hear them. Although if you were suffering dry heaves at the time, you might be inattentive.

'I'll get you some warm water.'

And Elizabeth keeps her word—is honest and does just that—brings him back a cautiously half-full mug of something comforting and hydrating and sits beside him and wonders if she should give him another pill, because that might help, but it does say on the 'read before taking' leaflet that they might provoke headaches—headaches and nightmares, in fact, among other things—and the next dose allowed would be three hours from now and an overdose would probably be awful.

An overdose of nightmares.

So she goes and finds the stack of blankets and brings one to unfold across his legs, this joining him to the rest of the room, to the sense that some catastrophe has happened elsewhere, is still occurring, but here are the survivors and a peace to contain them and an idea of waiting.

Unclear if we're waiting for worse things or for better.

She strokes the flat back of Derek's wrist and he smiles, so she continues, takes sips of a coffee the barman made her—the last thing she needs, more coffee, should have had decaf—and an elderly woman with very red lipstick and overly whitened skin reads an Agatha Christie by herself and another, larger lady—nicely dressed, but with swollen ankles and feet: ugly shoes for her misshapen feet: and this means she is probably dying, is being murdered by a failing heart—scribbles at a puzzle book and there are yawns and there is dozing and there is full and deep and unembarrassed sleep—faces turned softer and younger, parted lips, the grace of unselfconsciousness.

And Beth remembers being with her parents at Blackpool, way out at the end of a pier in a glass garden like this—filled with deckchairs and with sleepers and with mediated daylight.

Black tie and ball gowns for the evening, but what is the ship when we come right down to it? Just the end of a pier in motion, cast adrift. Shows with a chorus and pretty bets you shouldn't make, and wear and tear dulling the glamour and souvenirs and someone who'll tell you your fortune, someone who'll pretend that he knows who you are, what you'll do.

Enough of that.

Eventually, she feels Derek's muscles surrender, his forearm drops and he's away with the others—dreaming.

I hope simply dreaming—not anything bad. No nightmares.

This means she is left to be hungry and—why not?—she goes to the buffet—why not?—it's on the same level, not far, and she needs to eat. She has no suspicious motivations.

I can get a roll, or something. Soup. Derek wouldn't want to watch me deal with soup. I'll give him peace.

And she wanders in between the largely deserted counters of vegetables under heat lamps, noodles, rice, meat—no one here she recognises—tiny oblongs of gelatinous desserts, meat, pastas, fruit platters, meat—no one she knows—an obscenely generous selection of untouched foods, fastidiously arranged. Meat.

I suppose in a while they'll take away the stuff no one ate for lunch and replace it all with stuff no one will eat for dinner.

A few souls gaze out at the storm, picking at cakes, sipping unruly liquids. She does not particularly try to find last night's table, but there it is, in any case— empty and apparently no more or less pleasant than its neighbours, no different.

While Elizabeth waits for a sandwich to be constructed from the freshest possible ingredients according to the line's traditions of fine dining, someone pads in to stand beside her.

Not him, though. It's not him.

'Hello.'

This knowledge swooping so hard through her that, for the first time, she does feel herself unsteadied by the ship, assaulted.

By her shoulder is the older gentleman from the photo shoot: this time dressed in a navy jacket and

144

comfortable planters and just faintly amused by how he has come to be in such a costume—blazer and slacks—and of an age when it might be deemed appropriate. He grins. 'I'm Francis.'

The good husband.

'Never Frank. Don't like it.' He is laden with packages of crackers, some of which he now pockets so that he can shake her hand. 'Hello. Yes.' He leans in, comfortable with being conspiratorial. 'It always seems like theft when you put them in your pocket—even though we have already paid . . . Even though we could eat it all and ask for more and they would have to let us . . .' And at this he gives her the full smile of someone who is decent and prefers to be kind and have fun and who can no longer be bothered hiding it. 'You know . . . if you're by yourself, we're just round there—past the very, very empty pizza stall—nobody inclines to pizza in a Force Nine gale, apparently—and my wife is round there and I will be directly—we're having cheese with many more crackers than we need and not quite enough fruit.' He begins to assume the role of dithering old man, enjoying it. 'Do you think if I gave you some grapes to carry . . . ? I really should just find a tray . . . Only if you'd like company. Only if you're alone.'

Elizabeth is alone.

'Bunny and I, we've heard everything that we could possibly say to each other by now. We long for strangers.'

Elizabeth is exhausted and badly wired with caffeine and quickly, sour and quickly, intolerably alone.

He cocks his head, pauses, and Beth knows he is seeing something in her that she would rather he could not. 'We draw the line at kidnapping, of course.'

And he pauses again, blinks, softly cups her elbow with his hand.

So he'll feel the bone—little bone, big bone, little bone . . . But please don't wake me.

'Your sandwich is ready—looks very nice. You should have it with us. Is that decided? I think it should be decided.' Saying this while he looks away and is overly pleased with what should be her lunch. He concentrates on it utterly and so allows her to be unobserved, but strengthens his grip for an instant to show her she's still thought of before he lets go. 'Perhaps if you wanted to fetch the grapes . . . ?' And this allows her to be in motion and only to glimpse enough of his next smile to be sure that it's too intent. If he's actually concerned about her she shouldn't see it. Otherwise she knows she'll have to cry.

Francis gathers a tray and welcomes the grapes, checks Elizabeth's eyes once and sharply and then hands her the finished sandwich and walks her across to share his table, along with a lady who does indeed turn out to be called Bunny.

Classy silver necklace—he bought it for her: she has other things, but this will be her favourite—it is obviously meaningful and sweet—Arthur would classify it as literally sweet, he'd file it away in his mind as candyfloss, toffee, syrup: make it memorable like that—and I bet it has earrings to match it and they'll dress up tonight and she'll wear them. They'll dance. They'll both be movers—there and grown up for the sixties and taking part, so they'll know how. Elegant, though—you don't often see that, not for real. But she shouldn't wear black—it makes her look poorly.

146

Bunny is poorly.

'It's silly, we do realise.' The wife as pleasant as the husband. 'You can laugh if you want. It's all right.' Hair drawn back, but not severely, in a complicated curl.

He'll like when she lets it down. Will always have liked it. **Bunny, let your hair down. That's the way. Thank you.**

The husband as pleasant as the wife, 'Why would she want to laugh? If you were called Ermintrude, she might want to laugh. But Bunny is a perfectly reasonable form of address for a person.' And he fires a lopsided glance at Bunny, hot and fast. 'More suitable than Doreen, which—as you very well know—we never took to.' His voice delicate as the sentence ends. 'There being a number of things to which we don't take.'

'Francis . . .' Bunny scolding without scolding, pursing her lips so she doesn't laugh. 'We mustn't alarm our new friend.'

'No. No, we mustn't. And we won't.'

Neither of them doing it by numbers. They don't need them.

Elizabeth concentrates on biting, chewing, swallowing, biting again on bread and meat and meat—while Bunny and Francis continue to be cleanly and plainly and purely just what they appear to be and also remain determined to accept her as herself.

They are kind to her.

They are honestly and uncomplicatedly kind to her.

Which is why she does, finally, weep.

And then Elizabeth ran away.

Which is a thing she doesn't do.

Not often.

*I didn't scare them—worried them, but didn't scare them—crying too much. Francis, he expected it and that made Bunny expect it, too and **No, no, not all—we quite understand.***

Francis anxious to ease and excuse. 'It's this weather. Quite atrocious, I'll speak to the captain and have it changed.' So that her sobs start to shudder her more effectively than the deck and she has to go, to bolt.

Couldn't make him watch me fragment. Couldn't do that to a decent man, a normal man.

'We've done as much.' He's determined to understand.

Bunny also: 'I've done more.'

'Both of us have gone quite completely to pieces and in front of people we didn't know from Adam. Honestly.'

'So do stay.'

'Yes, please stay. It's all right.'

Not a chance of it, though. Battering out through the tables and down and down and down.

Fuckit.

Still going.

Fuckit.

I am not just getting clear of them and clear of the help they might want to suggest which can't actually be of any help and which I can't stand because I'm beyond helping, but would rather not remember that.

I am not just running, I'm looking.

I'm looking for him.

Idiot.
Idiot.
Idiot.
Always the same.

And every window that she blurs past is monochrome and raging and around her the lights are trying to be golden, but seeming sad and there is music from the floor below—ridiculously pretty music—and Elizabeth is too dishevelled, she is having too large an emotion not to be noticed, remarked upon, but this doesn't matter, because she is searching and not finding—this is her humiliation, that she is clearly scouring, chasing after something she can't get—this is her paying the proper penalty, her shame.

For sin, or for rejecting sin.
For him, or for rejecting him.
And there is no sign of him.
He hasn't left a trace.
Predictable.
He disappears.
Another game.
Or the end of the games.
I didn't go to his room with him and so he's staying there without me.
He is somewhere without me.
Predictable.
And he loves predicting.
*He puts a piece of paper in his pocket every day. He writes the day's date on it and then—**On this date I predict that Arthur P. Lockwood will die. Yours sincerely, Arthur P. Lockwood.***
He'll carry on until he's right.
Has a game for all occasions.
Even the one he'll never see.
He showed me the note once and explained it. But

149

he didn't predict that I'd slap him as soon as I read it.

Only time I ever hit him—terrible to hit him—never should. It was the shock. Arthur there and promising to die.

She jars herself through the drop of another staircase, then paces beside the dance floor—a dozen or so couples are dipping and bending inside piano music, accommodating to the ship as it kicks and slides, gives them new steps, propels them. Their bodies remember the turns and reverses and beats they learned decades ago, they fill the ghosts of how they moved and smiled at weddings, dinner dances, parties, birthdays, anniversaries.

Not at funerals—not the custom.

The women are dignified and competitive, dressed to make the most of what they no longer quite have, and they're tenacious, brisk—echoing who they were with stronger bones and different skins. They largely dance with each other, because there are not enough men.

The men die fast, die soonest, leave us. We are made to be durable and therefore abandoned.

Except Bunny. She'll die before Francis. It wasn't just the black of the pullover, she has something quietly hollowing her out and they are here for the last cruise, the grand gesture—they are making him something to hold, for afterwards.

The feel of her palm wrapped round his finger and tight and the pulse in it and the heat—like fitting himself inside her, but discreet—they'd enjoy that: could promenade anywhere and no one need understand it, or notice it but them.

It would be something to remember.

A thought to burn him later—to hurt in his own

150

palm, crucify him with her being nowhere he can reach.
Poor Francis.
Poor all of them.
However much money, however much they own or want to own, outside the cold is beating a way in, has all of their names.
I really shouldn't hate them as much as I do.
And she fights to slow herself—breathe, walk—until she sees them properly: all the silly, distracted people who are like her: who will die. They will dress up for special occasions and be pompous, or lovely, inadequate, languid, dull and they will make mistakes and be afraid and enjoy jokes and treats and surprises and maybe their children and then they will stop.
Which makes them wonderful.
Think of how rare they are and tender, of how they are extraordinary—no chance of escaping and still they do all this.
Makes you love them.
Makes you unable not to offer them a broad, indiscriminate love.
That's Arthur's trick, though—so he can love his enquirers into openness, trust. When he actively considers their frailty, it becomes irrelevant if he dislikes them, loathes them—because love is his only appropriate response. He loves them and they know it and that means they will let him burrow in.
He'd be ready for Francis. He'd take the good husband's hand and fold his own around it, press his thumb into its heart, touch where it's bleeding.
That's how he'd start.

Some people can sit in a café and drink coffee by themselves, be nakedly alone, eat teacakes, or something quite fiddly like pasta and they'll be fine.

But you might not be—not every day, not no matter what.

Sometimes you'll look at the café people, their bodies assured and all being well with them, as far as you can judge, and you'll think—*Who are you? How do you manage?* Because it appears they do manage very nicely, while it can seem, now and then, that you do not.

Walking across foyers, into unfamiliar rooms, half-empty restaurants, waiting for the first steps of a first date, being in parties with too many faces you don't know—you can find it taxing. But social anxiety is commonplace, a kind of bond, because you've worked out, of course you've worked out, that your discomfort is often caused by the equal, if not more profound, unease of others. And you've wished you could just announce—*we are scared here in this situation—whatever it is—all of us nervy and being tender-skinned precisely when we should not and although we are adults we feel we would like to run now or burst into tears—big children in stupid clothes who ought to be well-presented but aren't and can't think how they could be and this is, quite literally, painful and we should stop*—but you never have mentioned a word of this: you have only talked nonsense while voices pitched oddly and objects were dropped and the room became irritable or desperate for a drink, for several drinks, for anybody it could really talk to.

Because it can be complicated, having fun.

Not that you can't go out alone: to browse in a furniture store, for example, or anywhere else you might wish—take a stroll in the park, or see a movie without the bother of somebody else—it's possible to relish that kind of thing, as a change, as a rest.

The café situation, though—it can niggle. You have, if you're honest, sat there and wondered if maybe your hands weren't properly angled, if you didn't quite fit, if people who glanced at you wouldn't be horrified, wouldn't find you somehow appalling. You have felt that your aloneness might look entirely justified, deserved.

Which is why you need games—Games for Unpeculiar People in Public Places—and your book can provide them here, would like to help.

c) You can sip your coffee, tea, or beverage of choice—perhaps decaffeinated—and believe you are taking a short break from pressing busyness. This will always be, to some degree, the case and not a thoroughgoing lie—and, as your belief convinces you and others, check your watch with an air of gentle irritation, indulgence: you wish your life weren't so demanding, but what can you do . . . ?

This will seem much less unfortunate than sipping something on your own and, in an unforgiving world, what can be wrong with reassuring falsehoods?

But try not to give the impression that you're actually waiting for someone. They will—naturally, because you *aren't* waiting for them—be unable to arrive and this may seem sad to your observers.

Another option, then.

153

d)   Should you have such a thing about you, there's always your phone to bring relief. It can provide the necessary chore of weeding out your messages, or just reviewing them, reflecting on the fact that several people, people who know you, have formerly made efforts to get in touch— some of them wholly unsolicited. Thinking this, projecting this satisfaction, can be warming and easily done. Or you can text a random friend to say you're bored—you need not mention being solitary—and then you can smile quietly, as if you are in love, as if you have just done something new about your love. This will be additionally warming and will make you appear more attractive. Not that you aren't attractive and may not genuinely be in love and entirely appreciated: it's simply that your love is not here and not now. So you need a touch of proof, witnesses, reassurance. A gently enhanced presentation will mean you seem accurately yourself.

Although there is always the danger that, if your love is an absence or else a repeated mistake, the darkness of this may creep in and cloud you. Or it may happen that nobody calls you or texts you back. Not that you needn't still pretend they have.
Being publicly ignored is, once again, sad.
And miming that you have a small phone palmed in your hand when actually you don't, going through the motions—that would be even sadder. Don't do that.

h) Make little notes on scraps of paper— frowning, serious lips—as if an especially vital point has sprung to mind and must be recorded.

154

Or make the effort to carry a laptop and use it—behave as if you're doing business, an unassuming figure at the heart of invisible empires, or someone who's working on sonnets, a biography of Houdini, a *roman-à-clef* with more keys than a piano and no locks.

Which would be very, very, very sad.
So perhaps not writing.
Reading then: that's involving, that's company.

i) Study the menu, or flyers, advertisements, scan through orphaned newspapers and wonder who's held them before—let this consume your time with a merry glow.

And bringing your own paperwork need not appear defeatist: you can peruse your chosen material as if it is challenging, abstruse, work-related, essential to a course of study—or else something you can demonstrate, with plentiful nods and grins, as exceptional, a book that everyone sensible should be reading. It would be good if any covers or bindings involved could be stylish.

l) Play yourself preoccupying music—pipe it in gently through whichever headphones you prefer. Make it clear that you are enjoying yourself, that you inwardly thrum.

Don't simply stare into space as you might quite reasonably do while listening to something not unpleasant—this will make you look mentally stunted. But don't enjoy yourself too vehemently, either—not if you're over twenty-five. Avoid anything

155

beyond mild finger-drumming and possibly foot-tapping. Mouthing lyrics, graphic physical commitments, the playing of imagined instruments—these are all to be eschewed.

Don't begin to fret in case your isolation indicates that parts of your life have gone wrong or astray.

That would be intolerably sad.

m) So you should turn the ugly pressure of being observed into observation—watch the other customers and staff and stand aloof from your species.

This will allow you to see that—let's say—couple G are in the first six months of a warm, but rather juvenile pairing—that couple E have not had sex, but are going to soon, although she is less interested than he is—that child N is a sociopath and his mother O isn't helping. She is swayed by his blue, blue eyes and his fair, fair hair and he's already using his beauty thuggishly, enjoys worship, believes every other woman he meets should offer it and that he should be perpetually able to do what he'd like.

But conversely, a not dissimilar child shouldn't be neglected. No one, for instance, should hold back her motherlove from a clever blond boy, or never fully meet her son's extraordinary eyes full of sea and want. This would harm him. It might drive a probably unpeculiar soul to fold himself away and make a package, a distasteful secret, of whoever he turns out to be. A good mother would study statistics and then avoid likely causes of injury and death: traffic accidents, choking, drowning, poisons, electrocution, falls. She would be aware. And she would be kind—she would love and be amazed by him and kind; she wouldn't want him growing to believe he's been defective from the start. She wouldn't want to make him alternately abject and untrusting in affection, both angered and paralysed by inrushes of hope—in short, ruined for any other woman he might care about.

Although none of this should matter to you. It's as irrelevant as the man A who might sit there, reading a book in the coffee shop. He might be both unashamed and undemonstrative about it, just reading—could always carry a book or a paper for dining out, could usually expect to eat and drink alone, stay neither happy nor unhappy, but wholly suspended in a resignation he isn't stupid or numb enough to call content. And possibly he used to be loved and a sliver of him still expects it, is alert, betraying him to every disappointment. Touch him with sufficient gentleness and he might kindle, smile.

And that would be very intolerably sad and sad and sad.

And none of your business. You have no connection to any of the café-dwellers you'll ever watch. Because you don't watch friends. At least, you shouldn't.

But anonymous lives, their being close, can sometimes seem a kind of safety, a comfort. If you let your mind out to touch the idea of someone and hold that—who they might be—they can soothe you. They're people you can decipher, who can warm you, but you'll never have to meet.

This does no one any harm. It's not intrusive.

Strangely, if you recall when you've been most lonely, you won't think of being alone, of guessing at unknown occupations, interiors. You'll remember

157

having made an effort, perhaps being well-dressed and yet entirely certain this does nothing but highlight your obvious lacks—and there will have been crowds and laughter not your own and the shock of your friends' and of your love's inaccessibility. Those who should have been closest have stepped away.

y) Consider your love, focus, perhaps briefly close your eyes and entertain its full effect, let it come awake, flare in you like music, so it touches your sides and tickles, turns and strains against you, like the finest music—no electronic assistance necessary—like the songs that change your heart, that walk you through public places as if you're dancing, that make you feel like dancing, as if you're running out beneath close thunder and letting it lift your hair and make you dance.

But not if your love is gone, or spoiled: you couldn't bear it near your thinking then. Don't try.
Because you can't.
Shouldn't.
Can't.
Shouldn't.
Can't.
A little bit of crucifixion in each palm.
Find yourself rubbing the skin.

Elizabeth hopes to get though her afternoon by watching a film, sampling the vessel's lively schedule of current hits.

Don't think of a man A and give him a name, a line to his back and knowledgeable hands. Or if you must, then imagine that he's cultivated solitude because of his own guilt, has made sad habits by choice, prefers them, and is in no way your responsibility.

You ought to leave him to himself.

Too many things have been his choice and have been wrong, untouchable.

It's been two days.

No Arthur.

She let him go and he has gone.

Which has left her—predictably, pathetically, as if she were seventeen, and helpless and knew no better—has left her with chafing evenings, hours that gnaw, with walking and waiting in public places and drinking too much coffee, because there is no more harm caffeine can do her: she doesn't relax, she can't get sleepy, she has moved beyond espressos and their minor damages, but might as well add them to the general, miserable, bad inward thrumming. She likes their taste. She wants to have something she likes, for it to be there and simple.

Two days—not a sign of him.

***Two* days—Smile at me.**

Two.

Man.

Is he trying to tell me something, or not saying anything at all?

Was this the end of it?

Derek is with her. 'It's like a fucking prison.'

'It's like the opposite of a prison.'

'Why are you drinking so much coffee?' Derek smells of their cabin, of stale sheets and boring skin. 'Coffee always makes you weird.' Derek beside her in the cinema.

Beth, it's true, is nursing a cardboard cup of coffee. 'I've never not drunk coffee.' She has it mainly because its warmth calms her hands, because walking with a cup has always made her feel at ease—as if she were at home in a street, or an office building, or a multi-purpose auditorium plunging forwards and forwards with a ship. 'I've never not drunk coffee. Are you saying I've never not been weird?'

'Yes.' He would have started laughing by now if he was well, if they weren't trapped, if she was better at being a nurse, or being a girlfriend. Or both.

I nurse my coffee, but not my boyfriend. What does that say about me?

What does that say about him?

Beth wanted to be here, where the air is thinned with theatrical height and inoffensive and the weather is far away and does not whip, or punch, or moan and this is a dark place where nothing half-recognised will catch her eye and then hurt her.

Derek starts again, 'No, I don't think you're weird. I think . . .' And he sounds uncantankerous and small, as if he is trying to begin a sentence that is about how his plans have foundered and that all is not well with the week and perhaps them, perhaps there is something wrong with what they are.

We don't want to deal with that, though—not with so many days still to cross. Jesus . . . Especially if it's true.

She ought to rub his shoulder, his knee, be consoling, but she's tired of not being happy with

160

him and guilty if she leaves him and is without. She is also sick of weaving him along to his sun lounger—it is now effectively his and he gets ratty if anyone else is in residence. She would like to ditch fretting beside him in the Winter Garden with the blankets, the mugs of hot water, the mayhem through the glass.

'The film will distract you—it's a boyfilm with stuff blowing up.'

'Don't fucking patronise me.' Derek is clamped in his seat, virtually phobic about motion, tensed in the face of everything he can't avoid. 'This is the bow—we're in the bow—the bow goes up and down the most—we need to be in the middle.'

And, indeed, the lighting bars hung ready for the shows (all dancing displays currently cancelled, due to bad weather, the performers being unable to leap or frolic safely on an uneven surface) and their state-of-the-art lights are creaking, swinging, while the screen sways gently in the manner of a sail on a soft day.

'If you focus on the picture, it won't move.' And she does say this patronisingly, perhaps even intends to.

I know he's ill, I know he hasn't eaten properly in a while—and I will get him to the doctor tomorrow—he can have the injection, they've said that might work—but sod this. I am not responsible for his condition.

He should complain to the captain.

Several passengers already have, made requests to the skipper suggesting he ought to do something about the waves, take steps, get them not to bang against the hull . . .

Francis would be happy to know that his joke came true—any word can work a spell.

161

Or no word—doesn't matter who you are, the weather can still fuck you. The wealthy, though—they want what they want and they have to have their say—their word.

Or else they're simply optimistic.

Maybe they just have a sunnier outlook than normal when it comes to the human condition. Maybe the wealthy just believe we can change, or survive anything.

'Fuck off.' Derek's voice flat and nasal.

Survive anyfuckingthing.

It doesn't kill you to assume that.

Just sometimes other people.

'Fuck off.'

Maybe there's something about me that seems to be leaving, left, and maybe he wants to change and deal with that—decide in advance that he hates me, then he won't mind when we're over.

That's what I'd do.

That's what I am doing.

Beth has decided to hate elsewhere: a man who sits in cafés with the one book he always carries, reads and reads it like a meditation, a repeated song—stylish cover.

A book from me.

I used to give him presents.

And he gave them to me.

Now we give each other discontent.

Could be worse. The proper subject for consideration would be what he gives to other people—Arthur—the man A, full of keys to private locks.

In he comes with gifts you shouldn't want.

162

There's a wife at home amongst the furniture and ornaments and all the beautiful litter of a shared life and she keeps on asking for her husband, even though she's completely aware that he is dead. And it is nothing but human to breathe and feel inside a skin that knew him and to grieve—to think with a mind that heard him and to grieve—to still carry the needs that meant she would, over and over, touch him before she could even intend it, her love faster and deeper than her will, and to grieve. And it is normal, reasonable, for her to reach out and seize absurdities once he is gone.

It is, after all, absurd that she continues and he does not.

It is much less absurd to demand he come back: to be, in that way, optimistic.

To be absurd and optimistic is not the same as being stupid.

The wife, the widow—she isn't stupid.

She is hurt.

And she is—though it seems rude to mention—a millionairess. Properties, stocks, shares, she is both cash- and asset-rich, has several millions. Lucky her.

And if there was once a probably unpeculiar soul, a boy who folded himself away and made a package, a distasteful secret, of himself—who grew in a box of his own making—then he might later have become an adult specialist in hurt. And he also might be a connoisseur, a collector, of the wounded and prosperous, might gain an interest in their fortunes. Lucky them.

Or him.

There might, of course, be innumerable times when he doesn't even mention charges as he carries out his work. He might simply make it excellent, effective and an act of love and cherish the days when his spine feels upright, evolved, and he is clean and takes pride in the services he embodies: his restoration of lives through—admittedly—grotesque and intrusive lies, but if the lies are beneficial where's the fault?

In other contexts, though, there is this compromising truth: that he has to earn a living, pay his bills. Which gives rise to the question: why not pick out a few, a ludicrously wealthy few, and have them pay for all the useful happiness of others?

And there are many reasons why not—good, sane reasons—but they may be less convincing than the discomforts inherent in poverty and powerlessness: he wouldn't wish those on anybody—including himself.

So, having made his dark decisions, his compromises, he can choose his marks.

And, for them, he becomes a smiling and attentive parasite.

He would rather not.

But he does have to.

And maybe he goes to the wife, the widow—who is called Peri Arpagian and who misses her husband, who was called Mels Arpagian. And maybe the man fixes her inside the sort of assistance that will never set her free. And maybe she knows no better and is glad and grateful to him while he manipulates and deceives her and rations the warmth of his attentions to keep her weak, because maybe he needs her to be addicted—to him—and so he makes sure to arrange it.

And this means that in many other ways he'll be tender; he'll fly to New York—where Peri lives and he mainly does not—at her request. He will get on a plane, although he loathes them—although his too many air crash seances have left him soaked with pitiful, lengthy deaths, falling and lonely screaming amongst strangers, the tumble of belongings in vicious air. There are rooms and rooms inside him filled with the abandoned living, the guilty living who still remember sick confusions of flight numbers and the way they begged reality to offer survivable options: that their loves had altered flights, that plans had changed. They prayed for the salvation in mistakes—*she might not have boarded, he did mention he might stay an extra night*. Nevertheless, the man climbs aboard to be with Peri in hours, almost whenever she says he's needed. Almost. And there are Sundays when he'll go with her to garden parties, evenings when he'll agree to dine with her at the Metropolitan Opera Club, when he'll walk her on his arm into her parterre box and then sit through the onstage posturing and repetitions: the big women shouting, the men with unruly arms, the unlikely conjugations of their fat romances.

Although he dislikes opera heartily, he never suggests that she shouldn't endow it with vertiginous sums. There is plenty of Peri to go around.

He has glanced towards the Director of Major Gifts at this or that black tie occasion and known they were both thinking—*There is plenty of Peri to go around.*

And Peri has the man's numbers and, quite often, he can talk her through an empty night and into the grey hours of morning if she wants it. His silences and absences are very rare—the minimum necessary to spike her need—because he mainly aims to please.

Then again, it's not hard to please the addicted:

165

only starve them a very, very little and then feed them their substance of choice. *Let them score and they'll adore.* And if *he* is the substance, then what could be more beautiful than the way he'll descend through the cloud cover, place his seat in the upright position, secure his tray table, grind through the landing, the trudge to Immigration—*here for pleasure, visiting a friend—yes, I do visit her a lot—nothing romantic, no, she's old enough to be my mother—no, I'm not into that*—claim his bags and then look for his name on a sign in smeary block capitals—*A. LOCKWOOD*—a nod to the limo driver holding it, and the slide out of Newark, relax and roll straight for her building, walk in and chat politely with the doorman—who is called Richard and who likes A. Lockwood, thinks of him as a friend, and invites him to head on up. And then he'll ride the elevator—art deco, all original—while it rises fifteen floors and then opens, always slightly disconcertingly, right into Peri's home, which is an apartment in Beekman Place: French antiques, bay windows, East River views and a balcony furnished with manicured shrubs.

He visits with Mrs Arpagian regularly, has cultivated her devotion, her craving, over a period of years. He has sought out her wounds and then closed himself inside them like a bullet fragment left there to corrode. And he takes care—professional and conscientious—to note her furniture and ornaments and all the beautiful litter of her previously shared life and he continues to learn from them. He is in the habit of asking to use her bathroom and then trotting about through her flat: gliding into bedrooms, armoires, closets, medicine cabinets. He has gradually fumbled and investigated every tender place within

166

her privacy. He has made it his business—because it is his business—to gather information.

Not that she doesn't flat-out tell him virtually everything he could require without his asking. Not exactly a challenge, Peri Arpagian.

Treated me like a sickly nephew from the outset, like a lost son: patted and doted and, in her way, spoiled. Gave me a scarf—not a Patek Philippe, or a Gauguin study, or an Alfa Romeo, not any of the marvels that she could afford—just a scarf and some cake. Personal gifts—no desire to impress, or dominate.

You know that you've got them, the rich, when they give you presents anybody could, when they try to be ordinary for you.

*First time I went over, it was snowing unstoppably and the weight of Manhattan halted under it, but I'd said I would be there, so I was. I walked—for an hour—round and round, up Sixth Avenue and along, down First and along, that hideous sting every time I turned into the breeze—a punishment for what I have to do, a little fee—**I couldn't see a cab anywhere and I've never got the hang of the subway**—the subway doesn't run near there: no one who matters would want it, so it doesn't approach—**I'm so sorry, I think I'm late, am I very late?**—arrived damp, dishevelled, perished—the cruel air off the river had murdered my ears—Richard looked askance. If it hadn't been for the tailoring—has an eye for a suit, our Richard, quite the dandy on his days off—if I hadn't pointed up the British accent, then he wouldn't have let me in—expected or not.*

But arriving in genteel need, I knew she'd love that, want to fuss: summon Imée to dry out my shoes and socks, make arrangements for slippers. A man in your house in slippers—you'll keep him for longer than you

167

ought. You'll talk to him. You'll give him stories that he really shouldn't have.

I stayed the night—spot of dinner, nothing fancy, meat, veg, figs with cheese, more conversation—confide in her and she will be confiding—and then we watched a Rock Hudson movie: likes her Home Entertainments does Peri, has the Recreation Room with the walnut, out-of-tune piano and the fancy sound system with walnut speakers and the fancier projector and the specially painted wall to enhance the image and the floor-shaking speakers you know she'd enjoy even if they weren't upstairs in a two-storey, soundproofed apartment—cranks them up for Saturday mornings with Dizzy Gillespie, Benny Goodman, Artie Shaw: shivering the windows, swinging the walls back a little, waking the floor almost to dancing, almost to that— like a type of fury, her need for noise, huge music, her hunger to be touched by it. She wouldn't care if she damaged eardrums throughout the block, left her neighbours sleepless, cracked their walls.

Not that she does, but that's her choice—her behaviour is always her choice. Millionaires don't like restrictions: laws—even natural laws—are so rare an intrusion, they'll always seem clumsy, blasphemous.

After the film I'm kitted out in a dressing gown and pyjamas—not her husband's, they're from the days when she had guests, when they had guests—and then a quiet goodnight and off to sleep in Egyptian cotton. I kissed her cheek before we parted—made the gesture crisp and English, gallant, non-threatening. She smelled of imported honeysuckle soap.

No work until the following afternoon and only a brief session then—asking her to lead me to an object— clasp my fingers round her wrist so they can listen— thinness of ageing skin: shy, fuzzy, indecisive and then

168

*this hardmetal, proudmetal, fierce intention, it lashes in. I'm walking with her, quartering the room, and she can't help but lead me, shout with her bones that we have to head for the little table and her husband's wristwatch. We almost stumble when we reach it, overly anxious to arrive, and there's a triumph in her, a glee, when I lift it up—**oh, yes, he was asking you to think of this**—and then letting it speak to me—**something that touched him every day: he knows my business better than me, he's very strong in this, strong man**—remains of Ralph Lauren cologne in the leather—she still keeps the last bottle, evaporating, fading: probably inhales a little when she can bear to, can stand the pain. No son to inherit the watch. No child to inherit anything. But now she has me and I can tell her about Mels, be somebody else who remembers him, who knows him.*

It felt as if we'd just been introduced.

But Peri was mine from the start, from the shoes.

That's all it took.

Sweet Peri—bending while her servant watched her, undoing my laces, removing each snow-ruined shoe, inviting me all the way in.

She was nothing but ready.

And necessary—a valued contributor to my own little Welfare State of the Beyond—from each, according to their capacity: to each, according to their pain.

But it's still like stealing, like watching a neighbour's windows while I wank, like slipping my fingers inside an old lady and working her until she pays, until she wants and pays me every time.

She sent me home with coffee cake and the scarf.

Coffee cake wrapped by the silent and observant Imee who disapproves of me, but who makes up a package which is both waterproof and lovely—sets it in a blue paper bag with blue cord handles, from a stationer's uptown. Peri's household economises and helps to save the planet by reusing bags, which is cute—relatively cute. And then Peri brings the scarf— new, Italian cashmere—a little treat once meant for Mels Arpagian, although I don't say so yet—but I appreciate it, offer effusive thanks and then throw in a moment when it seems to strike me, have significance, and I let my eyes well, but control it. I intend her to notice, but also be controlled, so she can navigate our goodbye without breaking fully up against the thought of Mels—the man she lived with for forty-three years and who was named after Marx, Engels, Lenin and Stalin as a joke. Mels, who happily fed America its own uranium. (And who also mined copper and silver and gold—mainly those—and had some other interests; he did diversify . . .) Mels who defended the price of his shares, who wouldn't pay to seal abandoned workings, who contaminated water, who poisoned Navajo miners—and their families—who had a sunnier outlook than normal when it came to the human condition, believed we could change or survive anyfuckingthing—a true optimist who burrowed far and wide underneath Utah. Mels who enjoyed a joke.

Good sense of humour—clearly, in various ways, a nice man—started up from cabbage soup and chilblains, too many brothers and sisters, the unwanted offspring of unwanted immigrants—and he didn't completely erase what that was like. He could be charitable. His family had been touched by the Armenian genocide— could tell you stories that made you weep, him too. He was not socially inactive, was benevolent to people often—as long as they weren't sick or destitute because of something he had done.

I might have been his friend.

If it weren't for the poisoning issue and the breathtaking

170

greed.

Breathtaking. Like lung cancer—which is what killed him. Mels with the same illness as his miners and downwinders—unfuckingsurvivable—the adults and children who kept on breathing and eating and playing near the gaping tunnels, the abandoned tailing heaps. It's good to share, see the results—reminds us that we're all in the same species. His disease metastasised so quickly that he was finished in months, despite exemplary treatment.

Peri laying the cloth, soft around my neck—around delicate and important lymph glands, an unscathed throat—knotting it in front and then tucking it inside my coat.

Like my mum.

Not like my mum—like a mother.

And she gets my finest, close to my finest work: accurate details, conversations, songs, jokes—old Mels and his wisecracks—his pranks—his ironic phobia of smoking: immaculate material, irrevocably convincing. It is a dirty thing I do to her, but that doesn't mean I can slack—it provides me with more motivation to excel. And she'd have been dead long ago without me. Her health has improved since we started, her posture, her skin—she's back at the fund-raising dinners, the charity silent auctions—she likes off-Broadway, looking at edgy art: having safe adventures—Martin the smartly gay PA in a good suit at her elbow, the chauffeur parked close by and waiting. She no longer repeats herself, or forgets things, because she hasn't forgotten Mels, has neither lost him nor what she offered him, was for him, in herself. He's back and so is she.

Sophie Myers passed on my name to her. I do mostly rely on recommendations, on women who've had me who talk to women who might need me, pass me on

171

like an infection.

Always the women.

Sophie vouched for me. Sophie Myers, widow of Christopher Myers III—the much-lamented Kit—who heartily enjoyed his yachting and weekend jaunts to Venice and raping a range of wetlands and African countries.

Made him regret it after death. Sophie's big with AIDS orphans and conservation as a result—pays for drugs and schools, well-building, micro-loans for mums, mosquito prevention. And then there are the film crews she supports who document dolphin kills and shark-finning. She dabbles in seabird-rinsing whenever there's an oil spill. She gives generously to pelicans and gannets.

As generously as she gives to me.

But she'll never be quite as generous as Peri.

Because Peri gets scared. Her mother married up the second time around—Big Bad Step-daddy Warbucks— and, by all accounts, enjoyed it—her spirit drops in, from time to time and I have her say so—but Peri's never had faith that her own situation is secure. Enough capital to pamper villages, indulge a dozen lifetimes, but she lies awake anticipating threats.

And I help with that.

Because I am a bad man.

If I believed in hell, I'd be sure this would send me to it: frightening Peri then selling her protection.

Ask any one of the bastards who do this because they're sadists, psychos, inadequate, insignificant, blood-drinkers—who love it because headfucks get them horny and power makes them come—ask any of the usual practitioners and if they're honest—which they never will be—they'll tell you the serious money, the best way to earn, is with fear. Give people a heaven

172

with bells on: further education, enlightenment, everyone cool they've ever wanted to hang out with: and, yes, they'll pay for that. Return their dead, let them hear, speak, touch, kiss, let them reconsummate— dig in and make your prostitution limitless—and they'll pay for that, too. But give them the truth of a world that doesn't know them and won't care, enumerate their frailties, nudge them—gently, slightly—towards the sewer which is human nature, and of which you are a prime and predatory example, and have them peer in—then they'll beg you to defend them and believe every unseen monster you create. And they will pay you everything you ask.

And they will thank you.

'But we were informed that it had been a bear . . . Mr Williams, he called and told us a bear did it . . .'

The man knows about Peri's cabin in Montana— Mels heading there with her to act like a hunter; plus, youthful lopes across the country as a couple on matching caramel-coloured quarter horses— idyllic. They found the insects trying, though, the isolation—the place was more a topic for conversation than somewhere to stay. But its memory is laden with thoughts of health, incautious love-making on blankets by the lake, bug bites, roughing it with a deep freeze and a helicopter kept on call for them in Missoula.

The cabin means trust and relaxation, skinjoys and sunlight, log fires, lunging evenings, a past that was smooth and fit.

Inevitable, then, that the man attacks her there.

The way that a bastard would—a sadist, psycho, inadequate, insignificant, a blood-drinker.

Peri neat in the hard chair beside the man's—his knee could be touching hers but it's not—it

173

won't—and the drawing room is cool and cream and linens and silks and possibly not the perfect background for his skin—it makes the man slightly invisible, puts too heavy an emphasis on his suit—but she feels relaxed here, prefers it for sittings.

Not that she's relaxed at the moment. 'Wasn't it a bear?'

'I'm not seeing a bear. I see someone breaking in, breaking the door and—it's very pretty inside—or it *was* . . . you chose the things yourself—I like the colours, lots of reds—and you enjoyed the fireplace . . .' Because he needs a lock on her thinking, a blush, the flicker of screwing by firelight—that way he can pull her further in, fracture the mood, introduce damage, get her hands rubbing each other.

That's right.

She doesn't have to tell him anything—her worried hands are more than enough.

'But it ended up such a mess—a waste—all your pretty things—he left it—they left it a mess—two men, they hiked in.'

'Goodness.' He knows Peri's imagining how hardy and fit two such hikers would be—and surely armed against cougars and, of course, bears—how dreadful if she and Mels had been there—two men armed against people. 'Two? There were two men?'

'They broke up the rooms afterwards . . .'

'Afterwards . . . ?'

So much more penetrating, if she drops into a sentence he leaves unfinished—suffers its possibilities before he pretends to rescue her. 'They used knives to make it look like bear's claws.' Blades lacerating delicate air, personal belongings—he doesn't have to say it, she tells herself.

While he spins off into random thinking he

shouldn't permit.

That's a dessert, though, isn't it? A bear claw. It's a cake, or something . . . Jesus, the mind does wander . . . because it is unhappy and wants to run . . . but it can't so fuck off with that.

The man's face grim as he disciplines himself, becomes purposeful, intent—which makes her flinch, but he drives in anyway, ungentle. 'But that was afterwards . . . They spoiled your things afterwards— once they had what they'd come for.'

Which is frightening, but not as bad as, 'Once they had what they'd been sent for.'

Better.

Or worse.

Depends if you have a conscience and if you can still hear it.

But I never listen to mine, so fuck off with that.

'Somebody sent them?' Peri, like many of her kind, assumes that envy and conspiracy surround her. This flames through her like phosphorus.

So he ignores her, digresses. 'Frank. I think one of them was called Frank.'

Can't get it wrong when he doesn't exist and therefore cannot contradict me.

'Yes, he was definitely Frank. No name for the other one. They spoiled your flatware . . .'

Peri cares about crockery, having side plates and fish knives and spoons for honey and all the special tools for shellfish—doesn't feel born to it, so everything matters.

Flatware, which is plates and dishes—which are flat—but also cutlery, which isn't . . . you can suffer over here, for lack of vocabulary . . . Or double your chances of being right.

'They spoiled your flatware, but they also took

175

things—some clothes.'

'Oh, no, Arthur.' *She can call me Arthur, but I can't call her Peri—she's always Mrs Arpagian, as if I'm a servant. When I'm the master.* 'Do you think so, Arthur, I don't think so.' She's not really contradicting, more highlighting that he's infallible and she knows his news is still unfurling and will be bad when it's completely visible, surrounding her and cinching in. She starts patting Arthur's forearm with her hand. 'There was hardly anything left there—a few shirts, boots . . . Mels had a work jacket, I think . . .'

Outfitted to suit the territory.

As am I.

Made Richard especially happy this morning—twin vents, hand-felled lavender lining, flower loop, ticket pocket, functioning cuff slit, the usual: my work jacket.

'Small, personal objects will have gone missing and older clothing . . .'

Her voice quick and thinned with anxiety: 'But not worth anything. Why would they take things that are worthless . . . ?' Although she's already convinced this was not a normal theft, is something that obeys the rules of worlds only the man can navigate.

'Clothing that's been with you and carries your shape—surfaces that have absorbed a little something of your personality . . .'

*I'm not saying **aura**. I never have and I never will. I will not talk bollocks. I won't. I don't have to. This is bad efuckingnough without that.*

*And I'm not saying **essence**. I'm not saying **emanation**. Won't have them in my fucking mouth.*

Peri's mouth a whisper open, her horror silent, palpably chill.

Slender lady, born in the thirties, has a fragility and openness that makes Arthur want to hug her,

176

see her laugh, bring her roses, listen to jazz with her until they both get sleepy, sit on the side of her bed and kiss her forehead like a proper son.

But instead I do this—I hound her.

'If such things are passed into unsympathetic hands—envious hands, jealous, malicious—then a skilled reader can find your weaknesses, can work against you with contagious magic.' Arthur pauses until she looks at him—gaze flickering between his eyes and lips—trying to decide which she should hide from most. And then he delivers the three small, fatal words—'I am sorry.' As if she's beyond all saving, including his.

I'm not sorry. I am a bastard. I am a cunt.

And then he waits.

One thousand and cunt, two thousand and cunt, three thousand and cunt . . .

While she cries in a small way—neat little girl in a big house crying—and she glances across at him as if she is being foolish and would like to be much more brave and

Four thousand and cunt, five thousand and cunt . . .

He can't relent.

Six thousand and cunt . . .

Liberty print handkerchief tucked in her sleeve, then dabbing, keeping good order, being presentable because he's watching and—there it is—the moment when this horror flows down and in and meets its more established brother—the loss of Mels.

Seven thousand and I'm not that much of a cunt.

Finding her wrist and kissing her knuckles, the salt, he strokes her arm, and takes both hands at this point, holds firm around them and—hush, hush—the comfort of this provoking a further collapse but he'll squire her through it and could weep himself, could and does—it's the direction to take—and only very slowly, only after minutes, does he say anything else.

'All right? Peri?'

'Oh . . . I . . .'

And she can't tell him that she was recalling the funeral and wishing she'd known him back then— seeing how dapper he'd be in mourning, her tall protector, dipping to take care—she can't be particularly informative, but he nods and, 'I know. I know. And the thing I know most? Is that I will fix this and it will be fine. You will be defended and any ill-effects will be quite overthrown. That little cold that turned to flu—I'll bet you it wasn't a thing to do with you—you see your doctor every week, you're fit and healthy and—'

'Now, Arthur . . .' She gives him a smile that he feels in the pit of his stomach, like someone dropping cold coins there. 'I'm not young.'

'Well, *I'm* not young, Mrs Arpagian. We are neither of us young, but neither of us ought to catch a cold that turns into flu.' She pretendfrowns to say that Arthur hasn't fooled her and he pretendfrowns to show he has been caught in this the very least of his lies, which is hardly a lie at all—she is fit and healthy, she could last for years. He could have more than a decade of income left. 'Someone out there is practising against you and I will prevent them and overcome and we will triumph. They may have used foot track magic at the cabin and I've heard more and more lately of the *Pulsa D'Nora* . . .'

A gift, the Pulsa D'Nora—*some nonsense with tongues of fire that can pray you to death. One recitation and that's that—every opponent just vapours*

178

and ash—as if there'd be anyone left if it was true. As if I wouldn't use the hotel shaving mirror and cast it on my fucking self.

'The *Pulsa D'Nora*?'

Some Kabbala freak has already mentioned it to her, so he slides his grip and squeezes her arms and grins as if she is making him courageous and he explains, 'It's words, a thing built up from words— but every word has an antidote—and every word is letters and each letter has a value and a value is a number and I'm very good with numbers, always have been.' And he sits up straight, releases her, acts the manly man: competent, commanding. 'So then. There are ingredients to gather—some of them rather rare—although I have many—and ceremonies that I will perform. One has to wait for the old moon, one more for the new.'

Have to get a planet in there somewhere. And girls do like the moon.

'For the rest, it will take me a week to fast and watch—I must sit with a rabbi and a priest and another . . .'

Can't be too specific, makes things humdrum.

'And then for three days I will confuse and then destroy their intentions, I will cleanse your street, home, interests, your health, your peace of mind, your present and all visible avenues of your future.'

Although further paths will be revealed and need attention, further challenges will arise, which I will conjure, address and defeat—not complicated, defeating my own fictions. A form of therapy, you might say. I make the dreams and Peri swallows them—each of my ladies does—and Mr Walcott, my solitary gentleman—they eat my dreams: my endlessly vanquished and resurrected, my ingenious dreams.

179

'And then we'll have our ritual here—for us—and I'll position protection at thresholds—'

Which Imee will remove. Loves to dust and polish, remove feathers, powders, lines of silk. Naughty girl.

Not that she shouldn't—they serve no purpose.

'Windows and doors, the balcony rails and so forth. You'll be cosy.'

'Do you need the money now?'

'I don't need the money now. I don't need the money now at all. I don't want to talk about the money.'

And that's true.

'When this is dealt with and you're happy—extremely happy—and well—and sleeping well . . .'

I have to suggest that she isn't, so that she won't. That's also fucking true.

'Then I'll write it all down in an invoice and you can pay me.'

Oh, and that's as fucking true as I can get.

Or just about.

But I didn't invent it. I am nowhere near the worst.

It's just the Dream Game—strong as a dark spell could be, if dark spells existed. The Dream Game created Mels Arpagian's fortune—uranium for the cold war, the rare and precious substance to rout the phantom hosts of enemies, the overestimated peril, the reasons for spending money on ideas of death, on murder. In other times and other contexts, it has other flavours—it's still the same game. Build a stone step into your chimney, it'll make the witches rest outside and leave your house alone: no witches, then the step must be working, must be needed—it can't be that there aren't any witches, that you don't need the step. **Buy this juice or your kids will be blighted—use this cream or your skin will be haunted—give up this right**

180

or your country will founder—bail out this company, bail out this bank, or you'll live in a wasteland—change your life according to this plan or you'll never be happy, you'll never have sex, never properly fuck, never please or even tolerate your cock or cunt again.

It's all shit magic, nothing more.

Our current crop of Dream Games want sacrifice and pain and heroes and terrors to burn the world and the energy of righteous torments implacably exacted, and sufficient funds to stoke our problems, not remove them—to keep the craving and the sense of arcane threats, of powers facing powers and miraculous escapes. They want hate. They work for money and hate.

It disgusts me.

As much as I disgust me.

Perhaps more.

At least I work for money and love.

And my dead are already dead and I didn't make them and I wish for no more, have enough, and all of us walking and turning and dancing to our graves in any case, no need to rush. We'll get there.

I won't work for hate.

But still . . .

He is no longer anyone close to what he'd like and occasionally he can picture this restaurant—Italian place—and he wasn't there alone, was with a woman, a cause for love, uncalculated faith. Long time ago. And the waiter—perhaps for comedy effect—had idiosyncratic English and said, with an air of concern, 'If you is me,' and went on to advise on the choices of wines—which were limited. And A. Lockwood looked at the woman's face—the pair of them amused but not quite laughing, enjoying that edge—and he tasted in his mouth—sweet,

181

sweet, sweet—*If you is me*—and the phrase seemed significant and not a mistake. It seemed that the woman could be him and that he could be her, that they were interchangeably themselves and this was glorious.

If you is me.

Then all is well and I will manage very nicely.

I will not, in the spring that follows this autumn, lie on a hotel bed still wearing my stage clothes, tainted with sweat, my evening done with—leukaemia kid, feisty grandma, car crash kid, feisty grandad, boring aunt, eccentric grandma, unresolved mother brought to her full stop, tears for two inadequate dads, thanks to the husband who cleaned up his father-in-law, dressed him and dealt with him decently in his last days. Decency should be rewarded.

And so good that such a thing is so common, is such an easy guess.

So good that we are so connected, human beings, all of a piece.

So I ought not to end up lying cold on a hotel bed.

I shouldn't be alone.

I shouldn't be without her.

That ought not to happen.

Except it will.

No words to stop it.

And I'll lie on the bed and be alone and be alive, but not exactly.

And I'll be aware that I have set myself down precisely as I was before I left to give the punters what they'd want. I will be troubled by the circularity of this. I will check my watch and it will be approaching midnight and no one I can call and no one who will call me and I will start writing—words that are letters that have values that are numbers, that will be no use to me.

But I'll write to her anyway—an angry, inadequate, pleading thing—and I will wish for magic, that she will touch where I touch the paper, I will tell her my wish, my little wish that I know will fail and not bring an answer.

And after I have written and felt sick, I will seal up my failure in a hotel envelope and I'll need to be inside with it and sent to meet her—to let her lift me, hold me—but instead I will tear up my effort, throw it away. Might as well speak to the dead.

Might as well be truthful and say I'm the dead speaking—writing.

I can say anything—she won't hear.

Then I will stare at the mirror and what it shows of a sepiaed spilling light and wallpaper that's turned alien, that seems older than it should. I will think I could be peering back into the 1950s—no, the 1940s, somewhere nicotine-stained and harsh and accustomed to loss. It's not that I'm delusional, I am simply struck by how appropriate the feel of the forties could be—that they will assist me in the work—and I have to work, have only the work and will be the work and will love the work and the work will not leave me or find me inadequate, insignificant. I will be busy with drinking my own blood and I will have nothing because nothing lasts and I will last—I will be busy to death—I will be busy with death—I will be busy.

And tonight I will shave—no more beard, or moustache—short back and sides in the morning from somewhere traditional and cheap and begin improvising clothes that will fix me in a sympathetic decade—a time before I met her, before I was born, a time for the dead.

I will be him: the man who could stand at the mirror, step into it and disappear.

Elizabeth Caroline Barber is thinking—*this is my birthday and so I should have what I like, that should be what happens, not this, which is what my dad likes, which is what my dad **always** likes—and my mum lets him always get away with it: they are not grown up.*

Elizabeth is ten which is double figures, which means she *is* grown up. Having double figures makes you grown up and only great efforts and acts of will can overturn your natural state into something that's messy and less.

Both her parents—but especially her dad—make constant efforts and acts of will.

Today, in all this unrequested crowd—her dad's too many guests—her dad is the one with the shiniest, curliest hair—black, black, black—and the long arms—also darkfurry and curly—and the mildly hitched up shoulders, as if he was hung on a peg by the back of his jacket and left to hang for a long while and has never quite got used to being freed—as if he expects it to happen again.

Her dad is the man in a black suit.

One of the men in a black suit.

The living room is currently stifled with black-suited men: they grin and lean and bump against each other, they wave and gesture, scratch their ears, pat their pockets, cough, they are all over the furniture like a murmuring infestation. Amongst them are rainbow-coloured shirts, or wild ties, big cufflinks, startling waistcoats, garish and elongated shoes—*like every time they step, they're squeezing out something ahead of them from their feet, can't help*

184

it, here it comes—like they're walking on big shouts, embarrassing wails, or on being stupid—yes, like they're walking two planks made of being stupid, stepping out along stupid and it's holding them up—and they have striped socks, or checked socks, or idiot socks, or no socks, or too-short trousers, or turned-up trousers, or on-purposely odd-shaped trousers and their handkerchiefs are mad with colours, luminous, and their hats, should they possess hats, have been borrowed from cartoon characters, or old films.

In short, if someone now takes a photograph—and her father may at any moment, he loves snapshots—then Elizabeth will look as if she's caught inside a tasteless funeral, a bizarre wake: perhaps one to commemorate a clown. It will seem to have been a quite happy occasion—as if the deceased was not well loved. She will, in fact, appear to have been the only person there who was upset.

Because it's her birthday.

But not her birthday—that's been stolen, as usual.

But here Beth is, dressed for celebration in her neat red tartan dress with the scratchy white lace at the front and wearing her new TickytickyTimex watch and standing on a small wooden box which is painted blue and with silver stars, and she is surrounded by her father's friends and not one of her own—she could have invited a few, but she didn't want to—and her hands are by her sides and she isn't to close her eyes and isn't to stare, she is simply to look about in the way anybody might at the men who loll and gesture with studied carelessness, who occasionally giggle, or sip drinks while they sing—as raggedly as ever—'For She's a Jolly Good Fellow,' over and over and over.

Beth is not a *Fellow*—a fellow is a man.

185

Beth is not *jolly good*—jolly good people do what their parents want—and she is only halfway to that. She is standing on the box, but she isn't really *joining in and enjoying yourself*—she isn't properly smiling and whenever her eyes meet her father's she can see that he wants her, needs her, to be happy and that she is spoiling his treat. This makes her sad, which he notices and so he gets sadder.

Her dad—Mr Barber—Michael Barber—*everybody calls me Cloudy, Cloudy Barber, that'll do fine*—has arranged the same treat for her every year she can remember, which is seven years. What he did when she was very small, she has no idea, but he has certainly given her this for at least seven birthdays—this silliness for her with the blacksuitmen.

Since 11.26 this morning when Elizabeth grew up, passed ten, she needn't want this any more, but still she gets it—here it all is: for her, to her, *at her*. They are singing and grinning *at her*, aiming themselves too much in one direction—which is her direction—and, while they do, they pass her money. She does not understand precisely how this passing is achieved, but knows that the coins and even folded notes—the warm postal orders—do not arrive by magic. The blacksuitmen are, like her father, magicians—*professional* magicians—but they don't have the kind of magic she reads about, the sort which is to do with wizards and talking animals and wonders. Her presents appear by the kind of magic which is her father's job and which is for children—strangers' children and their birthday parties, or sometimes grown-ups who are having weddings—it's a magic which makes him tired and sometimes annoyed when she interrupts him practising things that are secrets. Her father's magic is unmagical.

Although once, really once, it did amaze her—did terrify. She was sitting in the bath and little—five, or six—and she could hear her father's walking up to the door and then his shout, 'And now—let there be *no light at all*!' After which there was a brief, dense pause and then the sound of him clapping—a sound like her nice, warm, aftershavey dad clapping his hands—and after that it was, indeed, absolutely and violently dark.

And she had seen that the bathroom door was shut, she had closed it herself when she came inside and pulled the bolt across—she likes her privacy, Beth, and to never have draughts, and has drawn the bolt across for as long as she's known how to manage it without letting her fingers get nipped—and she plans, when she is older, to own many locked and bolted doors with secrets packed behind them: she will think up secrets. But this was not her secret, this was the door safe shut and her father not touching it, not opening it, and the light switch being in here with her—on her side of the door—but the light still going out—magic—the darkness coming—magic—the room dropping into magic—and it was winter, an evening in November and deep night outside and she was alone in her bath of suddenly thickened water, the threat of it against her—magic.

And she had seen it: the real magic, like in books. She had seen, honestly seen, her father's hand reaching in right through the door—like a horrible grey dream thing—this pale and unnatural hand pressed through the wood of the door and reaching the light switch and—*click*—off it went.

Except there was no *click*, just the pause and then her dad's hands together—normal, normal, normal hands to hold and know and mend things—her dad's palms together and safe outside the bathroom—*clap*—and then her voice being very loud and screaming and echoes and splashes and this choke of wet lostness reaching into her and through her.

And then the light came back.

Good.

No signs of how.

Just a different magic—the kind to restore things, save them when they're lost.

Good.

And the door was still bolted and there was still no noise except her own, only then her dad's voice was there also, sounding worried and gentle beyond the bathroom and she couldn't hear his exact words, because of the din of herself, how it bounced against the tiles, and her mum audible next, joining her father with footfalls and then shouting, not letting him get away with anything, not this time.

Their fight coaxed Beth into quietness—a dreadful, large silence—before both of them called and promised and argued and reassured her up out of the bath and past the haunted light switch and close to the door frame. They spoke to her until she could believe that she was brave and pull back the bolt—her fingers shivering and the metal pinching her for spite: when one thing goes wrong, then all things go wrong—and she opened the door for them and they fell in at her and half tumbled and half lifted her into this thump of a hug.

Shaking and dripping with magic—this marvellous, terrible thing.

Her dad rushed a towel around her—always quick as snap when her mother is unhappy with him and means it, always cowed and puzzled and, somewhere, faintly pleased.

Beth was put into fresh pyjamas—something healing about fresh pyjamas, not that she was wounded, not exactly. And she was given hot chocolate and then brushed her teeth with her mum in the bathroom in case it was scary to be there and then she went to bed—her bedroom door open and not with a bolt even attached and no secrets inside it except that she sometimes listened to the old wireless under her covers, went to sleep with the mewling and whispers of static between stations, trying to make a new language out of them—and this wasn't a secret: everyone knew.

She sat up in bed feeling not frightened—more happy, racing, sleepless. She had survived and now she wanted to survive again, be proved impregnable. Beyond her in the corridor she could hear her father saying, 'I thought she'd like it . . .'

Beth did like it. Afterwards, she loved it. She wanted more.

'Idiot.' Her mother's voice angry and slightly amused, which was confusing, but also familiar and to do with who her parents were.

Because of her parents, Beth will never quite understand arguments—the first she saw being so pleasant, a form of flirting: raised voices and helpless glances, touches at arms and shoulders, lips trying not to part, to give themselves away. Her mother and father offered each other rows as a concentrated kind of affection. Their silences were the bad thing—the infrequent, but very bad thing. When they made each other sad, there were no words.

'I thought . . .' Her father shuffling his feet in the corridor, wriggling—she could tell—with small pleasures, as well as concern, 'Well, she might have

189

'. . . I thought.'

'You *didn't* think. Because you're an idiot.' Her mother pauses. 'Go in and make it all right . . .' This is a voice which Beth knows she is meant to hear and believe. 'You're the magician—you can make it all right.' And then softer, but not so soft as to disappear, 'Or you'll be dealing with it when she wakes up full of nightmares for a month.'

'It'll not be a month.'

'How do you know? Anyway—you'll be the one who copes, because I'll be asleep. You're the one who gets the lie-ins in the morning, the bloody night owl . . .'

'Because of my not-proper-job . . .'

'Because of your not-proper-job. Slacker.' Her voice with a grin underneath it.

'Always wanted to be a kept man.' His, too.

'Don't know if I *will* keep you. Might throw you back . . .' And a noise which was the noise of them kissing—her mum and dad kissing—which they did a lot, more than other mums and dads. It was moderately shaming. 'What on earth did you expect, Mike?'

'That it would be . . .'

And Beth will never know if he was going to say *fun* or *beautiful* or *horrifying* because he doesn't finish the sentence, only makes another kissnoise and walks into her room straight afterwards and sits on the edge of her bed—give, give, give in the mattress— the feel she will always love, of somebody's weight on her bed, such a kind and simple thing—and he tells her, 'I'm so sorry, wee button. Really.' And he holds her hand, eyes focused on the floor. He does mainly look away, her dad—unless it's for something important. He's paying attention, maybe too much attention, so that he can't always look, except in darts and flinches. 'Really. Your mum's going to kill me later.' And then he swallows loudly and stares as if he has made another bad mistake, while also smiling. 'A bit—she'll kill me a bit. She won't really kill me dead. She is cross, though. With me. Not you.' And he peers at her. 'You all right, Beth?'

'Uh-huh.' She likes him being sorry and so is stern.

'Sure, love?'

'Uh-huh.'

And his face, by this time, is pained, fretting, and so she relents, squeezes his fingers, hugs his arm.

'Oh, good. Glad you're OK.' Relief lets him gaze away again and explain, 'I didn't mean to scare you. Not that much. Not much at all.' And there's this purr in under his voice, this bedtime story purr, that makes an ease, a peace, around them. 'And the light will serve you now, I've told it and I've sprinkled it with magic powder and –' he opens his fingers and wriggles them so that sparkles of white and green and blue fall to the coverlet and shine—'you get some too. And it's *all right*.' Beth knows the magic powder is out of a jar: she has gone with him to the special shop that sells it. The powder doesn't do anything, is just pretty. It's his voice that lets her rest. 'I didn't mean you to get a big scare.' She expects the music of him will be for ever, permanent in her life—a sound to stroke in her spine, to be home, to be there, reliable. 'Not a big bad one. Sorry.' It will be wrong beyond all understanding if this isn't true.

When Beth is an adult full of PIN numbers and passwords and information and memories and preferences and doubts, then she won't often consider how frightened she was in the bathroom, or how she saw what wasn't there to explain her terror. She conjured a ghost: her father's hand, but not her father's: the way he would be if he were different, wrongly different, reaching in from somewhere else. And she won't especially remember hoping for other shocks, further plummets into strangeness which never came—or being kissed by her father *night-night*—doesn't sound the way it does when he kisses her mother—and rolling over while his weight on the side of the mattress stayed, guarded, kept the blankets tight.

It will be years before one day she thinks, out of nowhere: *Of course: the fuse box was in the cupboard beside the bathroom. He just took out the fuse. Nothing to it. I bet he had it planned for ages, waiting until I'd be old enough so I'd be impressed, or pleased, or something—not freak out. And I disappointed. I made it a much better, much worse trick. I made it the start of an appetite.*

Standing on a silly box—standing just over the edge of ten years—she knows nothing about her adult self: the strains and lines and likings of who she will be are settling quietly like sediment where she can't see—later there will be fractures, extraordinary heats and metamorphoses, but she currently takes no interest, can predict none of them. She is simply miserable and glad that her friends aren't here. She has never let them watch the blacksuitmen and their work which moves in the room like a series of bubbles, warmths that ripple towards her and fluster. If she were to be honest about them, she would say the men irritate her because what they do is close to being still pleasant, almost appropriate, it could drag her back to being a baby, just a girl. Once she is older, she will be able to break it down into a series of benevolent deceptions: loading, ditching, passing, palming, misdirecting—an odd display of love. At present, it does seem enticing, appealing, that somehow—from hand to hand and man to man—intentions are approaching her in ways that aren't explained, but it mainly makes her feel excluded and not clever enough.

She will eventually become familiar with this sensation. When she is a jolly good and studious teenager, school dances will nag at her. Discos will be worrying—and the headmistress will insist on calling them *discotheques*, which will make them seem French and complicated and shady—and going out to clubs will be worse. Kisses—harmless old kisses—will suddenly be redescribed, for no clear reason, as *French,* and will change, become complicated and shady. Beth will find that ugly boys, boys she doesn't like—and there are very few boys she *does* like, she already has quite particular tastes—any boys at all can still light her, trouble her with what they start in rushed and brave and slapdash kisses, in how they speak to her body, wake places she won't let them see, in how they work transformations, imitation magics, have blunt but effective hands. Boys will startle her too much at first, or make her frighten herself with herself—she'll gain a reputation for inviting and then bolting, running away.

And the men in black suits help begin it: her confusion, resentment, fugitive nature. They stare at her while she stands out on her box and whoever is closest pulls gifts from her hair, or slips them—soft as whispers, as kisses, as lips—into her dress's pockets, or tucks money into the air close round her

193

father so that he can retrieve and then present it to her.

They are doing their best.

But they're interfering, too, they are making her a spectacle and she wishes they would not.

She really does like her privacy, Beth.

No, she *loves* her privacy.

She wants bolts.

She wants boxes that open and swallow everything, hide it, close, lock, and then seem innocent and portable as ever. She wants to be safe in the blue box with the silver stars, which will be prettier than her to stare at and peaceful.

And she believes it will be good if she can box her joys, control them—no more of her birthday money exciting her more than snow, or wishes, or the seaside, or fruit growing on trees—just growing, straight out of trees, or even little bushes—and more than ice cream with bits in, or big dogs—no more of these things being able to make her laugh, whoop, run to burn off the so much wonder of reality, the pleasures she expects, the escalation of delights.

In a while, her mum will come through with a cake—it will be big and have Orinoco Womble on it in colours of icing and *Happy Birthday*—and there will be more singing and her dad will fetch his camera—which is called a Polaroid Square Shooter—from the table by the door and he will take her picture and everyone will look at it while it develops—because in 1976 self-developing photographs are exciting. They will watch her conjured out of nowhere and she won't even be involved.

Beth will keep the picture with a number of others in a box under her bed—under her succession of beds. Eventually, when she looks at it she will see

194

a blaze of cake, gone faces, a record of dead faces—
her mother slightly blurry, but smiling in a mauve
paisley patterned dress, skin warm with the candles'
shining—her father not there, already not there, but
only because he is holding the camera, tilting the
image slightly to the left and down, which was a
habit, is characteristic, makes her feel his fingers,
still holding on to the edges of everything. And she
will see an inrush of silences and a small girl who
was petulant, frowning: who was wrong—joys
controlled aren't joys at all, that's why they are so
terrible.

'Cloudberries.'
'I'm sorry, what did you say?' Beth is sitting and
frowning up at a tall, nervy man in a pebble-dashed
jacket and bad shoes. He is standing beside her and
is someone she has never seen before.

It's 1989 and not Beth's birthday; close, but this
is just a party—one of her own making and in her
own flat. At least, it's in the flat she shares with two
other students, both of whom are slightly dull. She
picked them for their dullness—uninvolving Sarah
and boring Elaine. She wants to get her PhD—which
would please her dad: she doesn't have to please
her dad, but she would like to—and Sarah and
Elaine will not be a distraction. She has shared
accommodation before and been through the shouty
boyfriends and strange compulsions and sad
compulsions and haphazard mental collapses of too
many strangers and acquaintances and very-much-
former-friends to expose herself again. She is tired

of being a student: of bar jobs and waitress jobs and telesales jobs and learning the words and numbers of what seems a pointless game. It doesn't feel as she'd hoped: like owning secrets, like enlightenment. And she's older: this sad case the campus can't shake, because where else would she go? At least she'll have peace with Elaine and Sarah—if both of them exploded, burst into flames, they still would be proudly unable to draw a crowd.

'I said *cloudberries*.'

Beth is tucked at the top of the stairs, just inside the dim quiet of the landing—no lights on up here, guests being encouraged to stay below, keep tidy and not creep off for sly shags in or on other people's beds. The man must have crossed the landing behind her soundlessly and is, in a minor way, an intruder. The idea of this is disturbing. She doesn't know where he's come from and had assumed she was alone—meaning that, for a while, she has been defenceless.

He drops to sit beside her, knees high to his chin. 'Like when you were a kid, isn't it?' And he is, all at once, companionable, easy. 'Up late and peeking at your parents' noise.'

But he is not her companion and shouldn't be easy so Beth tells him, 'You can't peek at noise. You can't see it at all. In fact.' She feels he may be uninvited—he certainly isn't Sarah's or Elaine's style—long blond hair and a fussily shaped beard, a sense of intelligence about him.

Which he's probably faking.

He looks like General Custer—so he can't be that bright.

He looks like a fake.

He doesn't look like a part of her future—a long,

fluttering tear in years and years and years. She has no prediction in her pocket which reads *On the 4th day of the 3rd month in 1989 Elizabeth Caroline Barber will meet Arthur Peter Lockwood and they will be bad for each other, ever after.*

She doesn't even fancy him—not especially.

He sits as close as he can do without touching and there is something hot and interfering about the empty space he leaves against her. He is hard not to notice.

She doesn't fancy him—she *notices* him.

'I'm sorry?' Beth wondering why people say this precisely when they want the other person to be sorry and when they are themselves not sorry at all.

He repeats, 'Cloudberries.' And peers down through the banisters as if he has never watched flirting and drinking and smoking—the slightly pompous passing of spliffs, poor dancing to Sarah's disastrous music, relationships thriving, changing, being knocked out of shape. It seems these things are lovely to him, almost hypnotic. Then he peers at her, his face mainly in shadow but clearly enjoying its own curiosity. 'Cloud. Berries. You wanted to know.'

'Oh.' And she wishes that she was more sober, could deal with him effectively and get away. 'Yes.' He gives the impression of being safe, if eccentric, but it strikes her that no one should actually be able to seem *that* safe, *that* quickly—it's not normal. 'I see.' But meanwhile he is right: *Cloudberries* is the answer she was after. Downstairs in the living room Beth had been passionately describing—she can't think why—her long-ago Orinoco Womble birthday cake. This had led her to realise—with four or five glasses taken of Elaine's disturbingly bluish-green and very sweet punch—that she couldn't remember what Wombles used to eat. And Beth had been a big Womble fan—read all of the books and had an Uncle Bulgaria doll and everything. At that point in the evening her knowledge of the usual Womble diet became important, even vital—she had been loudly distressed on the subject, only slightly joking when she tried to explain that who she was, who she *really was*, might be wholly bound up with being certain she could feed, should she ever have to, all of the fictional animals who had softened and blessed her youth.

But by now the information was less precious, almost irrelevant. 'Yeah . . . Wombles ate cloudberries.'

She hadn't been aware of the man when she was talking about cake, hadn't seen him, which indicates that he is good at sneaking, listening, that he makes it a habit. It may suggest—although she doesn't think of this—that her need, her dismay, were why he listened, what brought him, what gave him a chance to catch her mind slightly opened—like slipping his finger inside a book, keeping his place.

'Hi. I'm Arthur.'

Arthur the spy.

But you can't have a spy called Arthur, that wouldn't suit—like Hilda, or Bert, or Mavis—none of them names for a spy.

'Call me Art.' This said with the air of someone trying to set his first nickname, make it a good one.

Don't want to call you anything, thanks.

'Well, Art . . .' And Beth gathers her forces to leave. As she does so, he places his palm firmly, briefly, over the back of her left hand and smiles before letting her go, turning his head back towards the banisters and his study of her other guests.

She doesn't really want to go downstairs, sink into the muggy crush and fumble. Something horrible and Eurovision is playing when she would like the Kinks or Cream, or any other at least plausible musicians from a period when it was cool and influential and dignified to be a student. She was a toddler in the 1960s but she'd swear she still knew they were springing up nicely, being magnificent, and understood that her own generation would be dogged by mutual disappointments. She can remember, is keen to claim, her early-onset nostalgia: small, earnest five-year-old Beth in a range of handmade cardigans telling people, 'When I was four . . .'

Plasticine and blunt-nosed scissors and a gold star every day for being middle-aged . . .

Beth doesn't examine the back of her hand for maybe half an hour, doesn't notice *BETH* written there in purplish letters between the knuckles and the wrist—not until an engineering student pal of Sarah's points it out. 'Worried you'll forget your name, are you? Is that it? Worried you'll wake up in the park? Yeah? Is that it? I woke up in the park last summer . . .' He sniggers and spills some snakebite down the front of his rugby shirt.

Beth misses any further exciting details of the park incident, because she is working her way round to face the landing.

It must have been him—call me Art—just what I need, more bloody nonsense—amateur magic.

Art remains compressed in a bony crouch at the head of the stairs. She waits for him to raise his head.

They're always the same, the ones who like to play: once their trick's been started they have to see its end.

But he doesn't move, gives every appearance of being densely, absently relaxed.

So he makes her climb to him, seek him out.

'You transferred the pigment when you touched me.' Beth sits beside him and when their legs brush, he retreats just enough to avoid the contact, compacts himself further. 'Overheard my name?'

He lets her take his hands and lift them, see that he's now wearing gloves.

'What the fuck?'

Art keeps placid, quiet: tugs off his right glove, shows her his palm, the purple mirror-writing, her name in smeary block capitals. He clears his throat and says carefully, 'Isaiah 49: 15–16 . . . "Yet will I not forget thee. Behold, I have graven thee on the palms of my hands . . ."'

'Does that work with anyone?'

'Sometimes.'

'Seriously?'

'I don't know—you're the first time I've tried it.' And then he mumbles, struggles his glove back on. "Thy walls are continually before me."'

'What?'

'That bit doesn't help at all . . . the walls . . . and I think it sounds too religious.'

'Quoting the Bible? Yes, that might sound religious.'

'*Too* religious?' He's smiling, his mouth seeming soft and bewildered by itself, by what it might start saying. It's hard to tell if this is more of his act—being disarming.

'Maybe.'

And he leans for a moment against her, shoulder to shoulder, gentle and then away.

'Do you want me to ask you about the gloves?'

'No.' The smile again, aimed at his knees. 'No,

200

you'd better not.'

'Then I will. Why are you wearing gloves?'

And he takes this small, inward sip of air—fish out of water—fish liking a risk—and begins, 'Because I wear gloves almost all the time. I sleep in them.'

'Almost all the time . . .'

'Yes. I just said that.'

'In the shower? In the bath?'

'You're being silly.'

'Oh, of course—'

'I wear rubber gloves for that.'

'Oh, even more of course.'

He leans against her for another breath, face deadpan, voice earnest. 'It helps me feel. I sleep fully dressed and in the gloves, I keep covered and then when . . . It makes me feel better.'

'I should go.'

'If I take off my gloves and hold your shoulders . . .' His voice changed, revealed, somehow *at work*. 'Then you'll tell me your favourite person here—or which is your bedroom—or what you think is your household's ugliest ornament—that one isn't fair: it's the big glass seahorse sculpture thing in the living room which belongs to the blonde girl who likes it, but you want to break it: tonight you're going to break it and blame a guest—you ought to blame me—or you could tell me which is your bedroom, could lead me to it.'

'You've already said that.'

Tiny voice now, factual. 'It was an example.' And he takes off both his gloves—dark, thin leather, lined and creased and folded with use, like the skin of other hands—and he puts them in his pocket and he sets his fingers on her shoulders. And he eases the words in again, is himself—what she already,

201

mildly, thought of as his genuine self. 'You simply think and let your shoulders tell me. Think what you want me to know . . . Yes, I'm an arse and quite sad and quite sleazy, but not that . . . Thank you. Think that your name is Beth. Thank you. Think that you're not called Sarah, because then you would sniffle and mouth breathe in a deeply irritating way—bad sinuses . . . and why are you with them, both of them? They don't suit—you must want them not to suit . . . but that doesn't matter—why not think of your favourite person here, of the one who interests you the most—thank you—let yourself tell me that—thank you—let me know that. Your favourite person. Thank you, Beth. Thank you very much.'

Thanking her and thanking her—as if she is slipping money inside his clothes.

She feels that he may be smiling—that she can feel him smiling in his touch and in the pressure of his side, the rise of his breathing against her back—and then he lifts the contact, removes it.

They sit for a while in silence with the party beneath them.

Art withdraws, replaces his gloves, winds his arms round his knees.

And Beth hears herself say, 'That's a lot of effort.'

'Which you'll remember.'

'Really.'

'Oh yes—you'll always remember how we met—it'll make a nice story for the kids, the kid, the puppy, the cat . . .'

'Then again, maybe it wasn't *enough* effort.' Beth deciding to worry now that he has her address—is currently *at* her address—that he may be more peculiar than he looks. It would be hard for him to be more peculiar than he looks.

But he keeps on hugging himself, staring at people who are not her, troubling Beth only with little sentences, murmured in. 'Probably. I don't know. I'm guessing. I saw you tonight and guessed . . .' He rubs his chin against his forearms and she hears the rasp of his ridiculous beard. 'I am of the opinion that you should have efforts. I can't guarantee their results.'

Two or three hours later—afterwards she won't recall how long she waited—she will go downstairs through the party wreckage and half-dark and knock the big glass seahorse sculpture thing off the mantelpiece, smashing it irreparably. No one will hear her do it and she will blame Arthur for the loss.

'How are you this morning? Good morning?' Mila is the stewardess for Beth and Derek's cabin. Mila is weatherproof and cheery, her conversations melodiously penetrating. 'Your husband? Three days ill, four nights ill, that's no good. He is a little better?' Mila's interest in her charges is both heartfelt and exhausting.

Beth no longer tries to explain that Derek is not her husband, that he did, until quite recently, want to *become* her husband, but this is almost undoubtedly no longer the case, that he is currently barricaded somewhere surly and disappointed inside his head. Their room feels like his skull, somehow, like being locked in an uneasy skull, wearing itself smooth from the inside out—rabbity and stale. 'No. He isn't better. Not really.'

He isn't the better man—only looks like him. Bloody depressing to think of how often I've gone for the tall and the blond and then been sorry, spent all manner of awkward coffees, dinners, clammy nights, with the sense that I've misplaced something, that I'd glance away, turn back and see what I want.

Who I want.

And is that because of Arthur, or is that because of me: am I someone inclined towards wanting things like Arthur? Men like Arthur. Is he a genetic weakness, like diabetes? Or does some part of me harbour Nazi cravings for blue eyes and blond hair? And something broken.

Does he mean I'm a racist?

He does mean I can't think of him for long without distracting—he's too much, otherwise.

It's not that I wouldn't love to concentrate—Jesus, please—to be clear and single-minded, but not about him, it can't be about him—because then it turns out that I'm not a bigot, I'm alone. And I don't crave a type.

It's just that I know how to learn things and I learned a man, but I can't have him, because in person he's a toxin. I keep him in my skin and I don't forget, but I can't be with him. Even when we're together, we're not real: I'm not me, he isn't him.

And this is my finest time—what he doesn't get. Back when I had the skin, the bloom, the sort of ease, I wasn't ready: it's now we should be together, when I think I might have found the start of what we need to do, how we could be.

*It's different with men and women, I realise—I did read the manuals: **Female 45–55, Male 50s Professional, Immigrant Female 30s**: I memorised the classifications,* *the life paths, studied what to tell enquirers.*

Gentlemen peak early and ladies are late.

But that's a very incomplete story.

Gentlemen peak early, but then they can find out who they are, how to apply themselves.

Ladies peak early and then can keep peaking. This can be a conflagration or a tragedy, a wound.

When I came in my twenties it seemed significant: today I could bang my elbow and find myself more deeply moved. I have capacities I barely understand.

And sometimes we almost really touch, but never quite.

We get theatrical instead. We waste ourselves. We don't hold each other and catch light. We never rest, enjoy the peace of ourselves. We are never properly naked. We do not ever truly fucking meet.

I miss him. And he misses me.

We are stupid enough to wreck ourselves at heart.

From which I should digress.

And there are very many varieties of digression.

In word, in thought, in deed.

My digressions involving the wrongly fair-haired and imperfectly tall—the spidery, washed-out imitation Arthurs and my being unable to like them. Clambering into stupid situations in case they might be feasible— trying to be under someone and to touch them but not that much—proving I'm alive and capable without Arthur and being with whoever else, but not that much. They don't quite exist—are just someone who isn't Arthur.

Like Derek.

Don't know what was I thinking. Then again, that's what I aim for—to not know what I'm thinking.

And so it's closing the eyes and lying—in every fucking sense lying—and holding whoever's shoulder as loosely as I can—imagining there's a lace doily, or a napkin laid between us, something insulating and polite—and closing my eyes and needing to feel the better man, but he isn't there because I settled for safer and stupider and less. Again.

It passes the time.

Christ.

Beth puts the Do Not Disturb sign on the door, because Derek has promised that if Mila comes into their cabin again while he's trying to sleep he will *glass her in the face*. He's in no condition to harm anyone and isn't a violent person, but he may make a scene, insist on indulging in complaints.

Mila leans on her trolley—her *luxury Porsche trolley*—which rattles with each surge and is laden with nice clean facecloths that no one will get and pillow mints that no one will eat and shampoo that no one will have the strength to use. 'He needs dry food. Like toast. Like biscuits—the way you have biscuits in the lifeboats. When we have lifeboat drill there is biscuits in the boat and water only and they say someone will give you two pills when you come in—I don't get sick, but I would get two pills, because in those little boats you will be sick and then everyone else will see you be sick and will be also sick—more than thirty people in a little boat, being sick, that would be such a terrible thing.' Mila is, no doubt, audible to Derek, and Beth is not remotely attempting to move her away along the corridor. 'I can fetch dry biscuits and give them to him, but not now—if the DND sign is on the door then we cannot knock even, we can do nothing.'

'I think nothing is what to do.'

'You are sure?'

'This evening, we can give him water and dry

206

biscuits. He's had the injection and I think he's sleeping.'

He isn't sleeping—he's flat on his back and venomous and staring, he's turning himself into something I can't love, can't like.

I used to be able to like him. Liking is OK.

Settling for less. Settling for decent and reliable and normal.

Which is less.

'We drill all the time, have exercise for when the ship sinks.' Mila says this happily, confidently, and it is plain that she would be equally sanguine in a lifeboat—her liner going down by the stern, its harpist perhaps still playing on the ever-more-slanting deck, and Mila quite content, asking after everybody's health, handing out biscuits and perhaps one or two of those mints. 'Look at this today, this morning—the whole way is DND and DND and DND . . . I will have to make report, say why I don't go in and clean . . .'

It's true: the passageway is thick with plaintive Do Not Disturb signs that swing from the handle of each door and indicate distress within. Elizabeth walks past them along the press and give of carpet, the perspective dipping, twisting ahead. She moves through the section that rattles like walnuts in a tin, the section that whines like a metal-on-metal puppy, the section that constantly bathes in a mild howling, and then she ascends, staggers round and round the stairwells. She wants to be outside: not on the circumnavigating deck, still haunted by a few mad walkers, brisk and smug in their waterproofs, clocking up miles—not where Arthur leaned at the stern, where the stain of him leaning will be by the handrail, a salt and judgemental shape—she's heading higher, high as she can, up until she runs out of ship.

Fucking Arthur—who is more, rather than less—too much and indecent and unreliable and abnormal and I didn't love him at the start. He did that to me—I think—he made it happen—I think—or I did—or we both did. We saw something in each other, something bad, and then chased it and it didn't run away.

*Lying—again in every sense—by myself in bed after the party—after that first night. And I'd broken that sodding glass abomination and I wanted to anyway, but I know that I did it so I could tell him later—which will have to mean seeing him again. I already want to see him again, but I don't fancy him—it's definitely **noticing**, not fancying.*

Only I want to be near him again and that leaning against each other thing was nice and hand-in-hand was nice and maybe this makes me nice—my sudden fondness for small and friendly gestures.

I could be nice about him.

It's not as if I really want a wank.

A wank would be rude. And the fact that it's rude and to do with him is not in any way another layer of attraction.

Dear God, the utter rubbish you tell yourself.

When really you just want a wank.

When your mind's already out and predicting, sketching how he'll be, playing the cheap psychic, the way we do with everyone we love—building how they are when they're without us, how they'll be when they come back.

Habit of a lifetime.

And he made it worse.

Arthur there at arbitrary parties, at some and not others—nobody seemed to invite him, but he'd get in all the same—and seeming to know which pubs I went to and being about the place, then elsewhere, more tangible when disappeared.

Be available, then not: make your appearances random, a long tease—it never fails.

He would have realised that, but I never did feel he was playing me. He felt reassuring, let both of us be unwary in this gently hungry place. It was almost like friendship, as comfortable as that.

While—absolutely and of course, this would have to be the case—I'm studying MAD—Mutually Assured Destruction.

You couldn't make it up.

That was the subject for my thesis—great conversation-stopper, not bad at emptying rooms: simply tell them you're learning how to get a population of sane and ordinary people to be happy with MAD and convinced they could survive any conflagration—convinced they'd want to survive—how to make them optimistic enough to believe we can change, or survive anything.

Survive anyfuckingthing. Protect and Survive: take your doors off their frames and hide in underneath them, shove your head in a brown paper bag—as if you're a pound of apples. I spent months with all of those lies: the Public Information films, the plans that were no kind of plan. The bad spells, shoddy enchantments.

And then I'd come home and maybe Arthur would be there, or I'd go out and maybe Arthur would be there—and maybe he happened to be in my living room while a bunch of us watched the Berlin wall come down and were happy for other people and for a good change, an achieved change—and this was history and when I remembered it, I was going to remember him also—it'll make a nice story for the kids, the kid, the puppy, the cat: that while we weren't *exactly dating, the world turned wakeful, tender, changed its dreams.*

*We kept ourselves unerotic for so long—which is almost more erotic than anything else—and maybe that's what he intended for those nights when I'd go to my bed alone, the nights after we'd chatted, leaned a bit—maybe he knew the condition that I would be in and was lying in his own bed and hypothesising, breaking a sweat. I was certainly thinking about him and I was a grown-up and at liberty and it's not unusual or peculiar to touch yourself on somebody's behalf— you know them a bit, but not like that, but not exactly **not** like that—actually, you know them just enough to make this awkward and yet lovely—if you imagine them being aware of what you're going to do—may do—could do—will do—why fool yourself: the pausing is preamble to a definite end—it's what you will do— you're going to fancy yourself enough as their replacement to make yourself come—but you feel naked, shamed, extraordinary, if you think of them knowing, of informing them: **yesterday, I wished my hands into your hands and improvised from there—** then it's almost too uncomfortable to continue.*

Almost.

But when we were together we digressed, we made distractions. He took an interest in my work: found me descriptions of mass shelters, their lists of provisions, amounts of fuel stored for running generators, the rules for admission and denial—survival not always the kinder option—some things intended to be unfuckingsurvivable—your wife dead outside, your kids dead outside—kid, puppy, cat—your life dead outside. No doors on the toilets in case you hid in them and tried to top yourself.

We listened to Patrick Allen being the last voice we'd

ever hear: all his announcements—sensible and inevitable wartime advice with this stink of a hell underneath it. That shouldn't be sexy. But it was.

Me full of mass casualties and damage and him full of I had no idea what—man in gloves, magic man, quiet man, man who works in a florist's sometimes, who can build things for you: cabinets, bookshelves, makes little boxes with sliding panels, private places—handy—secret—whose aim seems to be elsewhere and as yet unrevealed.

He didn't tell me what he really did for months. Took off his gloves and held my face and told me, kissed. And why not try it together—give the wounded their dead together—Mutually Assured Eternity—bombproofed.

And it made sense. It did. It seemed a beauty.

Although I was not exactly at my most coherent: lack of sleep—presence of love.

And next I'm stealing my dad's secrets, palming them, adapting, learning my new lessons on most nights—clean nights.

Leastways, they stayed clean until I was alone. Then less so.

But I could have just had sex with him—it's not as if we couldn't have started if I'd asked. I believe that's the case. But I waited. I didn't try for months. No obstacles then, and nothing wrong with me, not especially—I was only angry, justifiably, furious about things that were appalling. I cared about him, but also about strangers. I wanted to help. I was getting my education so I could help.

And I knew—start love with Arthur and it wouldn't be controlled. I'd get lost in it. We both would.

Ecstasy.

Nobody actually wants that.

So we restricted ourselves to lessons and structure and practice—hands with hands and hands in hands and thinking leaned in against thinking.

And we had the code—the simple one—our first code.

1—Please listen
2—Man
3—Loss
4—Child

Easy.

When she reaches it, the door to the upper air feels locked, there is such a weight of gale against it. Beth has to lean in, shoulder the glossy wood, manage a final shove when the pressure eases and lets her barrel into a merciless space. For a moment she can't see, can't breathe, is simply held—the shock of weather, its beautiful offence prevents thought—and then this joy comes, this immense, horrific pleasure in every gust that comes at her like a big dog, that flattens her clothes to her body in a knock, that maddens her hair, that can hammock around her in any direction, every direction, and push her, draw her, stumble her where it likes and the sky is above her and swooping to each horizon, a howl of blue: a tall, fierce ache of blue and its clouds in lines, in streamers, banners, dazzles, flares—it is all alive and makes her laugh.

Better.

Best.

In the end, you seek them out—your ecstasies. The ones that you can bear.

The deck dry underfoot and light, shining as if it's been bleached by sheer speed and the shuttering sun.

She stands and rests against it all, turns her neck

to let it be touched, closes her eyes.

5—Help
6—Betrayal
7—Love
8—Accident

The useful words, they had to be numbered to let us work them as we'd wish. Five steps, eight breaths, six seconds of silence after Art steepled his fingers together—we had endless variations. A word could repeat and repeat and repeat and give you loss underneath its own meaning, a stranger's little gift. Whatever we said, thought, did, the numbers ran through it, illuminated, were additionally generous, complicated.

In the end, I'd wonder how people spoke without them. As if we were normal and everyone else was too small. And both of us in the same beat, in this invisible motion. Can't think of the hours that we spent in his bed-sit counting—silent and marking the time until we were always synchronous.

As if we had one pulse.

But anyone can do it, if they want to be peculiar enough.

9—Pain
10—Now
11—Fear
12—Work
13—Sex

And on and on and on and you don't get **Woman** *until* **20,** *up with the reassurances and compliments—* **Brave, Artistic, Honest, Forgiven**—*the treats.*

We did give them treats.

We.

Us.

*We were the people who understood: **1** is **Please***

213

listen—and later we made it **Look At Me**—but also it was **the first thing to think of** which is **death** and **a passage of time**—in **time** we all do get our **death** and then **time passes** beyond others' **deaths**—and fuck me, the pair of us started to operate like this, we had to, hopping about from thought to thought for the punters, from word to work to number to symbol to—**time** is a **watch**—you may be getting the code for **watch**, so you'll imagine it in your hand, coddle it in the mind's fingers—or else announce its status as a messenger to your audience, if required—or picture it pointing to particular numbers, if you'd like: it can mean you'll remember them, group them together, a set of coded details you fit to an enquirer, something to keep you steady through a long sitting, or in case the punter ever comes back—for another sitting, that is: you don't expect to hear from beyond their graves—or else you can allow it to be just a **watch**, the enquirer's own **watch**—so many people have a **watch**—even if they use the clock on their mobile phone, that's like a **watch**—you can tell them about their **watch**—or their phone—or their kitchen clock—or how their years are passing—or their loved one's, lost one's **watch**—as you talk to them, you can feed them anything, change, qualify, redefine—and **watch** is also **Now, can you** . . . slip in 'Now, can you . . .'—Arthur can tease any sentence apart and make it fit—and he'll mean a **watch**—and **1** is the symbol of **a man standing in a doorway** and, 'I'm seeing **a man standing in a doorway. Does that mean anything, can you think?**'—an eloquent image to start, adaptable, the punters will interpret it to please them—and my whole head packed with this, streaming with, 'A dream of rising upwards and a door number which is important and has a 2 in it and a death, a passing that took place on or near to a special

214

occasion, that happened close to something like a birthday or an anniversary . . .' Frowning into the middle distance—the place where observers assume all this shit is stored.

And on

And on

And on

It doesn't go away—my head's still caked inside with the arithmetic of lying.

The deck isn't empty, not completely. There's a woman in a flying raincoat standing behind the funnel, a couple attempting to walk. Everyone, Beth included, is grinning.

Weather junkies. We love it, want the shake, the being so kindly defeated by what could kill us—it doesn't know us, doesn't notice, but it feels like playing, like something big taking an interest in us, paying attention—as if we could influence nature by catching its eye. It makes us comfortably tiny and hugely important, both at once—like being kids again.

We're up here, leaning against nothing we can see and willing it into more than physics: inventing a story—a scene where we rough and tumble with an attentive and jovial reality. We're people, and people do that: we live in stories.

I have the story of my family, my mum, my dad, my health, my shameful and redeeming and unforgivable acts—the story of who I am and wanted to be and could be and never will and never tried and failed to be.

I have the story of my good, clean, honourable country where I live—not perfect, but what's perfect?— not perfect, but not the purgatory in newspaper horror stories—not perfect, but not the shallow paradise in television wealthporn stories—not perfect, but not the

215

comforting, smothering, jealous and noble stories of the fucked-up past—not perfect, but not the threatening, beautiful, beckoning, stupid, pain- and death-free stories of the fucked-up future that anyone will tell you if they want you to do something for them: to buy, to vote, to die, to kill, to believe, to torment beyond believing—not perfect at all.

*I have the story of my present: the **here** and the **is**: me on a patch of somewhere arbitrary and the hugeness of each unprotected moment under its racing sky. A beautiful and terrifying story.*

All fucking stories: what makes us nice, what makes us talk, what lets us recognise ourselves, touch others, be touched ourselves, trust loves—the fucking stories.

And they're what works the magic: the hard-core, bone-deep, fingers in your pages and wearing your skin and fucking you magic—that magic. Inside and out.

What he gave me—the power to be in other people's stories.

Something I took to as hard as he did.

He didn't make me, lead me astray. I adored it as much as he did and as much as him.

And the raw air screams, sings, cries, rocks her in place, keeps her looking at the furrowing ocean, the ways it breaks and mends and breaks and mends itself. Stare long enough, you see things: heads, rocks, wreckage, darknesses, fins.

*First time out and doing a platform gig I wasn't scared. It was a way to be us—I could be him and he could be me—and, just before we started, Art turned as he stood up from the table and he faced me—back to the audience and shielding me, and he let us look, have that serious look—**here we are and working, nobody like us when we're working, when we're hot as fuck**—and he almost smiles, parts and might begin to* *lick his lips, but doesn't quite because this is about different satisfactions.*

Christ, he was really something.

And so was I.

This woman—Sally—looked bored, chilly, a bad choice, but still I'd picked her and that seemed not incorrect, not entirely unwise, and I'm throwing her names and getting no hits and the minutes are winding by and the room apparently sagging and my voice getting quiet, dry and smaller and I'm vamping with stuff about her being off-colour and maybe not taking care—hardly a wild leap to say so: she was puffy, self-punishingly fat, cheap haircut, unloved skin— engagement ring, wedding ring, probably early forties but seemed older—and she's giving me no signs, has been taught by domestic circumstance, by close experience, that you shouldn't give signs—I want to tell her 'Your husband is a bastard. He is almost undoubtedly a bastard and everyone dead and here with me would like to say so' but other than that— which is impractical—I'm close to having nothing left, to giving up.

Inexperience.

Arthur behind me, but I know, I am aware, that he's unconcerned, so I lean in harder, insist—she can't have come here for no reason.

Which is when she gets angry—wonderfully, silently furious—she's close to shouting that she thinks I'm crap—I can see it—and it's because she's scared— these frightened eyes—so fucking scared. No one who isn't terrified needs anything like as much bitterness, as much rage, as that.

She's hiding inside it.

I pace—and I know that Arthur's sitting with his arms crossed—softly, gently—both hands visible, the

217

fingers, but I can't break contact with Sally and really check—I think he's showing three fingers and four—that's his opinion and I agree—didn't tell me beforehand, so it may be a guess or a detail he forgot—except that he never forgets—three and four and that's Sally, her story—she lost a child.

I'm sure because of one glance—one tic of the head down and to the side and when she faces me again, raises her eyes, she's younger—for a flinch of time she's younger and just at the start of that fresh tenderness, mother tenderness, and already it is purposeless—stolen away—the woman that she had intended to be is disappearing.

A day when the world jumps up and tears out everything, but lets you live, makes you live, leaves you here to stay without the everything you needed.

They didn't take care in those days, the hospitals—not much better now—so you edge what you describe into some sense of difficulty about seeing, you say that she was in hospital and wanted to see someone.

And then you watch her break, a whole woman harrowed down to sobs. They didn't let her see the baby—and no grave—speed and corridors and numbness and never knowing—fuckers—she never knew—fuckers—she never knew her child, or started or finished or had any help—they abandoned her to this.

'Little clothes, talking to your mum about pink or blue . . .' Pink gets a hit, a sign of laceration, her shoulders tense—so a girl then, a dead girl. 'Your girl knows you had a name for her and she hears you say her name.' It's a risk, but the mouth is such a soft place, so used to speaking that it's an easy bet: if I set her thinking, then I'll set her speaking in herself—and she does, she starts to say it in herself—she permits

218

it—the unnameable name. 'Pa- pa . . .' I decipher her lips—doesn't have to be precise. 'I'm getting . . . It starts with a P.' And the mother speaking it out loud then, like a love, a pride, 'Pam.' She can't manage any more, has to grip the hand of someone to her right—she doesn't know them, just holds on for fear of falling, being drawn into the place that's always there and always hunting for anything good, that takes it away.

I risk the possibility of mentioning a graveyard—she went without her husband, of course, because he's a bastard, as previously established—she's somehow in a graveyard—she didn't quite mean it but there she is—not at her daughter's grave, she has no idea where her daughter is buried—may simply have been dumped in a communal pit, but that's what we'll never mention, I'll only imply that Sally's looked and couldn't find— and in the graveyard she's at one of its edges, an untidy place where they've grouped the untimely dead—a line of memorials, fading toys and playroom colours, cheap and obvious and sentimental and clawing you down by the legs, by the hollow in you where she grew, until you're in the turf and sinking and gone to that place— she's felt it, has often thought of the permanent numbness, the blank she doesn't want to think is all there'll be when she runs out over the edge of her life—she has wanted to leave and go to her nearly kid—she has wanted to leave and be nothing.

And when she swallows I do too and I am in her, I am her.

I am out of myself and in the miracle.

And if she believes that her child still sees her— knows, accepts, forgives and loves and loves and loves—then she'll be altered.

Better.

219

Maybe.

The deck here is painted ready for sunshine and games, shuffleboard, quoits.

But that isn't why I did it.

I did it because it was wonderful. I enjoyed it.

Cupboards rattle against securing ropes, filled up with summer chairs, cushions, toys to keep little ones occupied when they're not in the paddling pool.

Love to paddle, kids.

Love all sorts of things—love their mothers—and they are loved.

She tries to focus on the sky, the way the clouds seem so languid, while everything here screams.

It was a thing we were good at—that I was good at—not as good as he turned out to be, but nevertheless we were something. And we felt like nothing ever has or will.

She angles her face to the cold sun.

Arthur and me, we could get tight up inside somebody's story—we could make them invite us in.

I'd start with a name, any name—doesn't matter—certain ones imply ages, nationalities, religions, others are more neutral—play it safe, or take a risk, I could pick—the enquirers are the ones who do the work. If the name gets a hit from the hall, if people claim it, then I keep with it, move on with it—switch in through descriptions—one detail, two, three—until I've knocked down all the possibles amongst my audience to a handful of enquirers, a couple—my woman, my man, all mine—I narrow and narrow what I give them until only their love fits. They think that I've found them, become more and more precise, when all that I've done is allow them to identify themselves.

And Christ, they do want to identify themselves.

The process is sly and irresistible and cheap and it

will always impress, because enquirers have no understanding of probability: they don't know how very likely it is that somebody else in a relatively modest gathering will share your birth sign, or will believe in birth signs, or won't like opera, or will have a scar on their right knee, a bad back—get enough people together and someone is bound to qualify for any competent opening description—and then they'll get to be the heroine, the hero of a story, not just an also-ran. And they want as much for their departed— who maybe had a chest condition, bad legs—or someone they knew had bad legs—or forget it and slide on, keep talking—they had blond hair, wanted blond hair, had a friend with blond hair, had hair—they worked indoors, in an office, in a serious office, like a legal office, they were important, good at their job, they made a difference, didn't go on about it, not really, they worked there many years, had a send-off to mark their retirement and a gift, at a bit of a loose end after that, although still with interests, sometimes they'd say that they couldn't imagine how they'd found time to have a job.

The more is known, the more it's possible to guess, the more it's possible to know, because close in the places where we think we'll be unique, we are anything but—we have first jobs we got through a bit of a fluke, an element of luck, and something happened when we were children that was nearly fatal, that gave us a scare—gave other people, the ones who cared for us, a scare—involving water—and when we are with our loves, we can be clumsy and worried and happy and scared and sometimes racy—we can surprise ourselves— and we can get so happy and so complicated and also simplified in our pleasures that we sometimes wonder how the fuck we could ever be this lucky and we also

221

don't know why the fuck we have ever been this hurt, this marked, this damaged, so that anyone who knew about it would wonder how we move, how we can stand—only nobody does entirely know, they would have to be psychic to know, they would have to be in possession of strange gifts and able to see us in our deep, sweet, bleeding places—to go further than love.

Except no gifts are necessary: in the deep and sweet and bleeding, that's where we are the same. In the heart of us, we are together—joy, hurt, fear—if we paid attention, just held on, we would feel it beat.

Beth stays on deck until her head aches, her cheeks, until she is mortified, shivering helplessly.

And when the gig was done, I'd go back home and be without him, but next to the Arthur I'd built from his absence, I'd lie beneath the weight of that. I made him irremovable with too much thinking—didn't mean to—I was just scared—and rehearsing—and scared— and I thought the story of him would be more controllable than his skin, his mouth, his fingers—I didn't want to spoil what we seemed to be.

Thinking their name when you come—you shouldn't. You'll always want to make it true, summon your love so they can hear it—your spell.

Working towards the nearest doorway seems an absurdly elongated process and very distant. She observes herself fighting her way back inside, yanking, jolting the door until she is finally accepted, lost in a deafened, broiling stillness.

Francis sees her in the café before she can avoid him, before her hands are ready to gather a bland warm drink from the many bland-warm-drink-dispensing machines.

'Now.' He rises and marches at her briskly, Bunny waving, staying where she is. 'For goodness' sake— you haven't been outside?'

'Yes.' Beth's mouth almost incapable with cold.

'Mad woman.' But he grins. 'Was it very exciting?'

She nods, because he wants her to nod and because it is true.

He takes her arm and wheels her round, 'You will sit with Bunny and tell her all about it—exaggerate as much as you like—and I will get you a hot chocolate, because that is the only thing that will do. It will be extremely sweet already, but would you like more sugar in it?'

She shakes her head and lets him father her, mother her—there's no harm in it, the ways we can adopt each other and this time he won't make her cry, she is too cold to cry and too suddenly settled in her mind.

'Bunny, here's Beth again—obviously. You'd have to have had a funny turn not to remember.'

Bunny, tired perhaps, but shaking her head in a manner which is pointedly contented, 'Just ignore him. I always do.'

'I'm going to get her hot chocolate and also cake. She isn't eating enough. Look at her.' And he hands Beth into her seat, is briefly and tenderly grave when he looks at her. 'Is there any type of cake that you don't like?'

'Um . . . No. I . . .'

'I think she has hypothermia, should we tell someone?' Stroking his fingers against his wife's neck, intent on her, hungrytender.

Bunny inclining to the touch, 'Go away.'

Which Francis does with a kind of bow.

'He's an idiot.' As Bunny examines her husband's back, its retreating, mildly self-conscious line, its resilience. 'Now tell me about the waves and tempests—I can't get out in them myself, he won't let me. And we'll have a nice afternoon tea together, if you'd like—it is the afternoon, isn't it? Every day I change my alarm clock and my watch—except for today when I shouldn't have . . . I think. The ship's magazine said I should, but it was mistaken, apparently. Or else I am. And we do nothing but eat and sit and wander about and eat and then dress up and eat . . . most disorientating. I have a suspicion it may be Wednesday, is that right?'

'Yes. It's Wednesday.'

'Well, that is a relief.' Bunny pauses, checks on the patisserie area and then on Beth. 'I was in a slough of despond because I missed the Napkin Folding Tutorial this morning—honestly, does anyone attend half the things they suggest we might like?' She pauses again. 'Sloughs of despond are unpleasant, but we overcome them, don't we?'

'Yes, we do.'

'Strange situation—the ship, the crowds, the bobbing about, the dreadful couple from Windsor with whom we've been forced to eat dinner every night—they've only been married for fifteen years and clearly want to kill each other—amateurs . . .'

'You don't want to kill Francis.'

'Not often. Not lately. We've had our times.' Patting Beth's arm for a second as she raises her hand to beckon him in.

'Stop flapping at me, woman.' Francis, arriving perilously with a laden tray—three mugs of chocolate and a variety of cakes, tiny cake forks, plates, napkins, the whole weight and balance of it slithering and clinking until it's set down at rest—or as much at rest as anything aboard seems likely to get. 'I can see you perfectly well.'

'No you can't, I've got your glasses in my bag.'

'I can see you perfectly well enough.' Smiling at Beth so she's in on the joke. 'I'd know you anywhere.'

And they sit and they have what Francis declares *an illegally early tea* and they talk about the storms— the good and bad weathers they have seen. They spend an intentionally pointless hour.

And Francis and Bunny tell Beth a story, give her an image of Bunny running in a downpour, chasing across a field and Francis there and also running, holding a newspaper over Bunny's head until it's no longer a protection, only this heavy, tearing thing, and so he throws it away and they stop hurrying, are dignified and—by the time they reach a little village—they are stately and do not mind that people laugh at them, because the rain is warm rain and they are together. Together and soaked.

And it is difficult to leave them.

Once she has, Beth doesn't return to her cabin, doesn't discover if Derek feels better, or worse, or the same. She goes to the Purser's Office and makes an enquiry—slightly bored manner, no commitment, even faint irritation—delivers it well: 'Excuse me. Mr Arthur Lockwood . . . He's in one of the Grand Suites . . . I think that's what you call them. Could you help me with that?'

She no longer knows what else to do.

'I am expected.'

And this is when your book can tell you about the man and about the woman and how they're both young and in a cold town, rainy, scent of dead industry thick in the breeze as they walked from the railway station this afternoon.

It's dark now and they're tired because all evening they've been concentrating and remembering and talking to strangers about other strangers and watching them cry. It is beautiful, but also tiring to watch strangers cry.

They lean in to each other while the rain flusters and link arms, working their way back to the hotel— station hotel, Victorian monster of a thing: big rooms and draughty and patches on the curtains that the sun has faded, patches where rain has caught the cloth and stained it, weary carpets, chipped tiles and thin towels in the bathroom, potentially fatal electric fires. The man and the woman don't mind the mixture of grandeur and shabbiness, it amuses them, is part of a world filled with pretending.

Although they don't have an umbrella, they almost amble, not speaking, past the ugly town hall and the emptied municipal flower beds, the brightness of shops. It takes them a long time to make a little journey and they even pause before they mount the hotel steps, as if they might wander further on.

But they do come inside, grin at each other as they stroll across the foyer, their clothes clinging. The man's thumb leaves a damp mark when he

226

presses the button to call down the lift and when it arrives and the doors open, they already know that his room is on the third floor and hers is on the sixth, because they are good at keeping hold of numbers. And a stranger who's wearing a grey mackintosh trots up—he has this jerky, trotting step they will both recall very clearly—gets in with them, smells of cigarettes and Brut and some kind of dark stout. They grin at him, too. They love that the stranger is here and let him stand between them, flurry and heat the absolute truth between them which is that they will both go to the woman's room and they will undress in the quiet and chilly dark and then they will climb into her bed and find themselves there and waiting with the story of who they are and want to be and could be and never will and have to try.

There are so many things you ought to know—for your safety, for your happiness—and your book would like to tell them all to you. It sees that you do love your friends, but you don't trust too easily, your intimacy needs to be won and sometimes you can seem inaccessible and this is unsurprising because you've trusted and been hurt before. Although keeping yourself too solitary can become abrasive, there have also been individuals, personalities that you've sidestepped and you had every right to, because they meant you harm. Others have simply been easy to forget. It's slightly embarrassing to acknowledge that there are people you went to school with, worked beside every day, and now you don't have their numbers or a current address. And there have been occasions when you've told your problems, even the large secrets of your self to total strangers—you've let them look clear into you, and this has been surprising, but also liberating. And after they'd heard all you could say they were nothing but compassionate, affectionate, humane. They owed you no courtesy, yet you inspired it. This is because you have a good heart, a quite excellent heart. And you're interesting; sometimes you doubt it, but you are. You know how to tell a story and when you do people listen. You can make them laugh, which is relaxing and a tonic—they appreciate it.

And you're beautiful.

Again you're by no means sure of this, but you do possess beauty and it can be something you ought to protect, if not celebrate. When you were younger you occasionally felt slightly muffled, you looked for ways to be expressed and—although you might not say this yourself—you wanted to let your beauty be expressed. You've allowed some of your plans for this to slip, though. They were over-optimistic. To be truthful, the creative side of your life has worked out unexpectedly—is still working out. You are not a disappointment to yourself, but equally you aren't quite who you intended you'd be.

And your excellent heart has been broken and since then you haven't been the same. You came back from your troubles in some ways stronger and you don't go on about it—you've had courage that no one can fully appreciate—but you were injured deeply. You can't say you weren't. You hope this has made you more patient, generous, but you're aware that you can also be bitter and

228

self-punishing.

And these days you don't walk into situations with your eyes shut, not if you can help it—you like to be forewarned and forearmed. It can amuse you to be cynical, before you catch yourself sounding ugly or someone corrects you, or questions what you've said. Then you can stop, take stock of what you do have, what is here for you. You undoubtedly have reasons to be grateful and when you are, you feel more comfortable—not in a pious way, you'd hope—only with this slight peacefulness about you, a content.

There was a period when you might have attributed the good things in your life to higher powers: luck, God, willpower, effort, the stars, fate, the benefits of this or that philosophy, or system, your mental fibre or moral discipline. Now these kinds of simple assumptions seem rather naïve and you are less sure of your place in the fabric of reality—or if reality has a fabric, a pattern.

When you were a child you found it easy to believe—were apparently primed to have faith in almost anything and anyone. This has changed, partly because by now you've been fooled too often, scammed and disappointed. You also believe less firmly because you keep learning: you're open to new information and this can adjust your points of view. Your opinions aren't set in stone. Nor are you changeable for the sake of it, or shallow—although everyone can enjoy being shallow now and then and it need do no harm. You are perhaps more flexible and, indeed, thoughtful than average.

There have been television programmes and movies that you've watched ironically, or not at all, but you're aware that others took them at face value and accepted what you couldn't. You often read the papers and then hear their headlines repeated later, undiluted by an intervening thought, stale ideas in strangers' mouths, and this can disturb you. You worry true believers are out there, like fierce toddlers needing to have their own way, hoping to turn their whole species their own way: to unleash the unbridled market, unbridled government, unbridled precepts from unforgiving gods. You suspect they want to mark you with mythical whips, prepare you in their stories, dreams, laws, so that you will bleed in this world and the next. Their posturing can seem ridiculous, but also a genuine risk.

What you might call your current beliefs are complex, mature. God and death are changeable ideas for you: threatening, mysterious, blank, laughable, beyond reach: both of them can be odd comforts and bad jokes. You would like to inhabit a universe that's intelligent and loving, but it has shown itself unwilling to be either. Still, you have consolations: animals, landscapes, natural phenomena, the song of birds, the continuity of genes and minerals—blue eyes begetting blue eyes, carbon in stars and bones—and so much, so much, so much music. These can be joys, whereas many of the rituals from your childhood no longer impress and there are days when you may feel disturbed if you consider them in any depth.

And you aren't superstitious.

Habits and talismans of this or that kind can aid your confidence, that's accepted, but you wouldn't want to rely on them instead of proper preparation, instead of relying on your personal qualities. You'll admit they can give you a boost during tense situations. You may read your horoscope in the papers, but that's only a bit of fun—journalists make them up, they're patently generic guesses, veiled compliments and less-veiled threats. Surely, if astrologers were genuinely insightful, they could have told everybody about those extra planets out there, circling the sun: Sedna, Eris, Vesta and the rest—surely they'd have mapped them long ago. Whole planets—they're not like your spare keys, or your glasses—you can't just mislay them. You don't think that's an unfair point to make.

Under pressure, you may be a touch irrational and this can mean co-workers or family members may appear to be obstructive, or else your surroundings may seem malign for a while: the streets and traffic clotting, geography squirming away from available maps. Some days apparently have a grain and you can feel yourself going against it, but your anxieties do pass and they're rarely so great that you can't control them. Perhaps you do knock on wood, throw salt over your shoulder when you spill it—that's more about keeping a culture in place, about practising something your grandparents or parents might have done. None of this means you'd be taken in by any kind of mumbo-jumbo.

Although not everything has a rational explanation—you know that. You've talked about this over the years and found most people have one story, one place in their lives where the ground gave way and let them fall to somewhere else. They have been amazed. And the stories they've told you weren't the usual, fragile rubbish: that someone came to mind and then that very person called them. (No one remembers the endless thoughts that are followed by no call.) Or else some scenario, object, animal, human being was very clear to them while

231

asleep and was then reproduced, or near enough, when they awoke. (No one remarks on the visions, intuitions, portents that don't come to anything.)

That kind of nonsense is easily explained. What shakes a human being is strong magic, the apparently real thing: someone is stopped by a flower seller in a foreign street, or an old man in a bar, an old woman, an uncanny child—whoever and wherever they happen to be, they make some announcement, statement, which proves miraculously accurate or useful at a later date. Or objects, circumstances, actions collide with an insistent significance which turns out to be of material assistance in vital decisions, or trying times. Or someone goes to see a card-reader, palm-reader, aura reader, colour reader, I Ching reader, psychic, obeah man, medium, santeria wise woman, healer, crystal gazer, cyber-witch, someone who claims to be a gipsy on a seaside pier—however it happens, an enquirer *is told something important*.

A magnificent force has touched them, sought them out, and a deep and golden fact is shown to them and it could never have been known in any ordinary way and it comes true—it is true, could never be anything but true—and it proves the pattern in reality, it unveils the threads and shows how they shine.

For anyone this would be special and would make them special and you realise they wouldn't like you to take it away.

Because it's happened to you, too—you've had your turn at being special. And you believed in it. It was made to be believed.

A man standing in a doorway.

It might have been something like that—an almost

infinitely adjustable and eloquent bundle of words. It might have been something you'd heard before, or words not even meant for you, but still they hooked in and stayed with your thinking and spoke to you until you sought them out, began to search for their vindication.

And when you look, you find.

* * *

Beth looked.

A man standing in a doorway.

She's good at looking, is doing it now, walking her way towards whatever a *Grand Suite* will turn out to be, to whatever the rest of her trip will turn out to be, to however, for fucksake, she may spend the rest of her life.

No pressure.

Only walking to Arthur's suite. I have walked before and have walked to hotel rooms and suites before and he has been inside them before. This doesn't have to be a challenge if I think of it like that—bite it into little pieces and then I can swallow it.

And focus on the irrelevant and harmless—everything he's not.

So.

It has its own name, like a pet: the Astoria Suite. Art's staying in rooms with a name. Because things for important people can't have numbers, they need to be personalised—the rest of us get the numbers.

She winds herself up the stairs.

'Ask, and it shall be given you; seek, and ye shall find; knock, and it shall be opened unto you.' When he still did the platform work, he'd chuck in bits of Bible—enough to add ballast, but not provoke.

233

Eventually, I learned them, too. I can quote fucking scripture like a fucking nun if I fucking have to.

For a while it had been his favourite—**seek and ye shall find**—he'd used it too much, in fact, almost as much as **a man standing in a doorway**—and when she left him, the image of that left with her, lodged and watched until September 1999—when she'd passed almost five years without him—and then it lit her, made her see.

She had taken her mother for a break—Bank Holiday weekend.

Can't resist a Bank Holiday weekend.

They'd got rooms in a spa hotel with nice toiletries and complimentary bathrobes and a selection of treatments and procedures guaranteed to be cleansing, or detoxifying, or relaxing, or just nice and hot tubs and a fucking swimming pool—as if this would be a sensible idea and as if they ought to be alone somewhere like that with too much time to think—alone because her father wasn't with them.

It was in Beverley—no reason to pick Beverley, but I did.

Beth's mother had walked the grounds when it wasn't raining and read when it was and, although the rest of the spa's suggestions didn't suit, she got a haircut and a new perm and had her nails done—nothing garish, just a nice manicure and a little bit of shine. She'd explained to Beth how the ladies who did it all—who encouraged her into it—had been very outgoing and pleasant, they had made her laugh and first called her Mrs Barber, but then later they called her Cath, because she asked them to, because Cath is unchangeably her name and isn't reliant on anyone else.

Cath had come down to dinner looking pretty for

nobody, hands holding each other, unwillingly self-contained. She wore her first new dress since her husband's funeral as if it were a sin.

Beth had paid what she couldn't afford to for massages—face down and tensing more when they touched her, when they tried to let out what her muscles were barricading in: the thoughts and thoughts and thoughts. She'd guessed this would happen and wasn't alarmed—she was only embarrassed when she got her money back for one session because she had started sobbing—full, jerky sobs—and that meant the masseur had noticed and stopped.

It wasn't unreasonable—guy by himself with an upset naked woman under a sheet—could be awkward.

Everything stops for tears.

As a general principle that would never work. Put the whole bloody world into gridlock, that would. It would send everyone chasing round boats to no purpose, set them adrift.

No. I do have a purpose. It is a bad purpose, I think. I'm not sure. It may be the wrong way to do right.

Beth has reached Arthur's deck, which is Deck Seven—of course, it would be seven—and the light fitments are more aspirational here than elsewhere and the air tastes cleaner, subtly conditioned to please those who've paid for it.

The scent of people faking it—Kings of Glasgow with looted pensions, Duchesses from Solihull who are blowing their redundancy money, couples who want to be twenty years ago and newly-weds—and they want to have white glove service and little sandwiches cut into shapes and their picture taken with the captain and dancing the night away and pretending that being British should mean you are running a loving empire,

235

keeping the less-blessed and foreign in line and teaching them how to boil vegetables into submission and forget themselves and salute the Butcher's Apron when it creeps up the bloody flagpole every morning.

They don't want to be ashamed.

Or they just want to fake being film stars.

And the Germans fake being Brits and the Americans fake being Brits and the Brits fake being Brits—fake it harder than anyone else so they can be imperturbable ladies and firm but fair gentlemen.

The French stay French. They have their own problems. They have their own flag.

Everyone has their own flag. How would you know what's yours if you can't stick a flag in it?

Me, I'm flying a white one. For surrender and undecided—blank sheet.

It takes her an effort to move along the passageway— going against its grain.

Did he want us to be here because we're both fakers? Did he think I would be at home in this many lies?

And she'd knock on wood if there was any—*Does veneer count?*—she'd throw salt back over her shoulder in a trail if she thought it would help.

It has the scent of a good hotel, that's all—no need for me to get hysterical.

Arthur is a collector of good hotels.

It wasn't unlikely I'd meet him in one. In, for example, sodding Beverley.

In sodding Beverley, Beth had stalled outside her mother's room, had missed the moment when they ought to kiss goodnight, or hug, should do something compassionate. Eventually Cath had thanked her again for the lovely time she clearly wasn't having and had given a small, stiff nod.

'You don't need to thank me. I wanted to . . . It's

236

good if we . . . And the office has been busy and . . .'

'You can't work all the time.' This only a quiet statement, not accusing—which naturally made it accuse Beth more and then widen to suggest a background of daughterly neglect, the waste of a university education in mindlessly administrative jobs, a consuming lack of positive direction that was clear to anyone—the usual themes.

Beth was unable to explain that she wanted to be busy, not fulfilled: that chasing fulfilment would be dangerous, would wake her. 'No, I think I *can* work all the time, actually. I think . . . Sorry.' Beth watched her mother's lips, the sadness briefly plain in them and then the irritation. When she spoke again Beth sounded childish, whining, 'It's what I do, Mum . . . Coping . . . Sorry . . .' She had no strength to be kind and do better. 'Sorry. I shouldn't . . . We should have breakfast late tomorrow—last day. Or in bed— you could do that.'

'I'd rather have breakfast with you.'

The need to have Beth around had never been there before; at least, not in this ravenous, sad form. It made Beth want to leave.

So she did. 'We'll do that, then. And I'll get off to bed. Tired. Sorry.' No sitting up in her mother's room and ignoring bad telly again, both reading to avoid being companions, or having a conversation. 'See you in the morning. Sleep well.' But they would have been together, nonetheless, which might have been bearable for Cath but Elizabeth couldn't deal with it, not yet. She only ever saw her mother with her father. Now she can't sit next to one and not expect the other, assume he'll fluster in with apologies about a gig that ran much longer than

237

expected, an awkward audience, a birthday girl who cried.

I should be more help to her. But I won't. As ever, not a jolly good fellow. But I can only stand what I can stand.

And she'd headed upstairs to her own room, padded along the carpet between perspectives of calming, Zen-flavoured pictures, door frames, doors.

Heard the noise of an opening door and I looked round. No reason to do so—I wasn't expecting anyone.

A man standing in a doorway.

And I can't recall being surprised to see him. I don't think I felt anything—no dip in the stomach, no swing—it was only like being suddenly in a wide, high empty space and having no breath.

Arthur was standing in his doorway, barefoot in an upmarket suit—thinner than she'd remembered, paler, wearier, clean-shaven and with a poorhouse short back and sides. He was holding a Do Not Disturb sign, about to close up for the night.

He looked at her.

I don't think he was feeling much, either. Although the sign shook in his hand. I noticed that: a jolt and then he made himself steady.

And there had been something naked in his eyes, caught in the open for an instant and then gone.

And I could have decided to think—'What are the chances of both of us staying at that hotel and at that time and of my passing precisely when he would be standing there and I could see him?' I could have imagined our meeting was so unlikely it must be a sign of some larger intention at work—our destiny.

But there are so many corridors inside so many hotels and so many people who have met—at other times and in other places—so many other people and there

238

are so many nights when so many sleepers might wish not to be disturbed that the chances of somebody somewhere encountering somebody else—even somebody they have kissed in the past—those chances are quite high. Even though the greater the number of variables, the less likely the event, it's still not that miraculous for someone, somewhere to see someone stand in a doorway—someone whose palms they have kissed, whose stomach they have kissed—someone they have kissed right to the root where he's hard and sweet and clever and where he wants.

She stops in the rising and recoiling passageway and can no longer think of going forward.

And he kissed me. We might have been kind and done better, but we didn't even speak that much—just acted as if we were following a plan and had decided to give each other what would keep us from having to think.

Of course.

But there wasn't a plan, not anywhere. Our meeting was a coincidence, not a hint, not a gift, not anything that means we have been sentenced to a life spent faking—play-acting that we're a pair of horny strangers, chasing the cum.

Deck Seven waits—all swaying perspectives and a reddish carpet for the movie star touch.

I can't recollect if I told him my father was dead.

I'd have told a real stranger—it would have been the first thing I'd have said.

And Beth waits, too. She can't go back, but she also can't move any nearer to the curve that will lead round the line of the stern. Turn the corner and she'll find Arthur's suite and he'll be expecting her, because the Purser's Office told him she was on her way, because wealthy people should not be

239

subjected to surprises. Beth can imagine she feels his concentration drilling and humming against the walls.

But he could have gone out—avoided the issue, done what I might do.

I am out and avoiding, in fact.

She decides she should stand and worry that she isn't properly dressed. This will pass the time.

And what exactly would the dress code be for this? What's the proper costume for not quite adultery, or for various grades of betrayal, or for the new start of something old? I couldn't face that. The new start of something new, then. Which I can't face either.

Should I be naked, get it over with, cut straight to the way we end up?

Or fancy underwear? We tried that. I tried that. The guy never has to, it would seem. He just brings fancy sheets.

More things to not face.

Nondescript appearance, that's what I'm aiming for, noncommittal, non-combatant—an ensemble that might suggest I'm not making assumptions.

I should have tied my hair back, sprayed it down, worn a bloody balaclava—it has a mind of its own. One of us ought to.

I'm not going to be as I should and he's going to see it. And I'm ugly enough where it doesn't show, so I would rather be presentable on the surface.

She closes her eyes and begins to step forward—being blinded helps.

The jeans because they fit, they're comfortable, a comfort, the sweater because it's cashmere and it might not look terrific—green, it's draining and it's clashing with the carpet—but it's soft and I need soft.

Low shoes because I would rather not fall.

240

Already a fallen woman.

While she progresses, the ship's life works on her, its motion making her heavier and then lighter in a long, slow rhythm, as if something is hunting along her bones, squeezing out the thoughts she doesn't want.

Derek might be awake, he might be rallying.

I'm not even sure what time it is.

It's ridiculous that she may be found like this by a steward and asked to explain herself, which would be shaming.

I don't want to be ashamed.

So I shouldn't be heading back to Arthur.

People who don't want to be ashamed should avoid performing shameful acts.

And the floor, walls, ceiling keep on shifting and her mind also shifting, running, shuddering, until suddenly it locks, is still—perhaps exhausted—and she thinks this is what it's like to be him, Arthur—a man so filled with everything that he twitches and flails on dry land, unfitted for anywhere stable, but shake him out into chaos and then he's a piece of peace.

If I knew how to be him well enough, I could maybe get by without him. I could fake that and be safe.

Bollocks.

I want to kiss him.

It isn't complicated.

I want that.

A man standing in a doorway.

The man ought to be Arthur, but Arthur has arranged other arrangements.

Loves his arrangements—surprises for everyone but Art.

When she rings the bell, Art's suitably impressive door is opened to her by a man in a dinner suit who wears white gloves and a shipping line name tag—*Narciso*. 'Good evening, Miss.'

Arthur is the one in the living room, sitting on a sofa with not enough space for his length of bone. He is concentrating on his bookshelves—this level of accommodation provides both bookshelves and books—and now he tells a random selection of tour guides and holiday mysteries, 'This is Narciso—my complimentary butler. And he is. Very.' Arthur winding his arm round under his knee, frowning. 'I think he'll be staying. He can serve us things. Snacks. Champagne.' Art is in jeans and a very fresh shirt the colour of his eyes and this is a plausible choice: not unattractive and it doesn't emphasise his skin—the pale shock of his skin; better to highlight the blue where he looks, the dodge and sudden focus of that. This isn't a working outfit—the idea would be that he's trying not to try—but it's formal enough to let him be relaxed. The shirt will have been made for him by somewhere double-barrelled—Payne & Hackett, Needham & Markham, Markham & Dunne—a place with bloody names.

'They've been trying to give me champagne since I boarded, but I don't like it because it's for celebrations and I don't celebrate.' While Arthur speaks, Narciso smiles like a man who is only half

242

listening and used to eccentricities. He ushers Beth into a seat and stands behind her shoulder.

'We're close. Aren't we close, Narciso? We're as close as a temporary, rented butler and his not-really-employer could possibly be and we have no secrets. So he can stay. I think he should stay. What do you think?' He turns and blinks at her and is slightly out of breath. 'We could watch telly.'

And Beth feels as she is intended to: insulted and a little sick and she snaps back, 'Or you and Narciso could watch telly and I could leave you to it.'

Arthur calculates his way through shrugging, sniffing, demonstrations of unconcern. 'We could do that, we could . . .'

And the ocean is dark and torn through the windows and the weather lunges round the balcony which would be perfect for summer entertaining, but is useless to them currently. Beth watches the rain streak and shiver on the glass while the silence thickens and what else did she expect—that he would be straightforwardly pleased to see her and this would be easy and not very possibly the last of their last chances?

Narciso paces neatly away to the tiny kitchen, returns with a tinier dish of rice crackers—which are tinier still—and sets them down, stands at ease.

'Thank you.' Arthur letting this be a murmur and deciding to claw both hands through his hair. 'And I think that even though we are not in any way celebrating, you could bring us the champagne and then, as it turns out, we won't be needing you this evening and you can put out the sign on the door to that effect, because being disturbed is not a good thing and I have had enough of it and from here on in I will avoid it at all costs.'

Narciso tranquil, 'Yes, sir. Of course, sir.' And bringing the champagne, tucked into its ice and, 'Good afternoon,' then vanishing away.

It's almost intolerable when he goes.

Ought to wave the flag—run it up and wave it and admit defeat. But he'd never trust that and nor would I.

Arthur faces her, quiet, clear. 'Ahm, look. I don't know. Nothing of this is . . . and I don't know what would . . . for the best . . . I, I do want the best. For you. But also for me.' And he swallows. 'I'm very tired. Can I start with that? Should I start with that? I go every day to the spa place here and they try and put me right, relax me and I lie in the pool— sorry—I . . . mainly the hot tub and then I'm here and they bring me the fish with the seasonal vegetables and the fruit which is good for me because that's what I ask for and it's OK, it's a reliable meal and I can eat it every day if I have to—I need things to be reliable . . . And I am . . . That is, I don't sleep.' He is wound into himself, elbows and knees folded tight, long feet tucked away from her and there is something distantly horrified in his expression and she doesn't want this to be her fault—she doesn't want him horrified at all—and he keeps on. 'You know how I don't sleep. Nothing to do with conscience, just physiology—I actually sleep more when I'm working—sorry—but it's starting to matter, the insomnia—because eventually I need to sleep and I still don't, not exactly, and the problem is— apart from anything else—that I sometimes dream and you're there—and so I am avoiding sleeping, because I am avoiding dreaming—sorry, but I am— but you are there when I do get to sleep and I do want that. I think. Waking up is bad, because that

244

means you go, but I do think I want that—to dream. So I'm not sure why I'm trying to keep it away . . . I was kissing your neck the last time, that's all I remember . . . I can't . . . ah . . . I can't do what we've been doing. I can't. The visits every now and then.'

'I know.'

'It's not . . . I can't do it.'

'I know.'

'Well, then fucking help!' The start of this shouting, but then it snaps down low again. 'Stop fucking me about.' He rubs his knees, rocking slightly against the will of the ship. 'Just . . . I fuck you about too and I don't intend it . . . and . . . but I do.' He subsides, bends forward to study his hands before he lifts them to rub at his eyes and then cover his face. He keeps them in place to hide him. His back rises and falls unevenly.

'Arthur.' Beth's voice strange in her throat and she's wishing for codes to solve this, give him meanings. 'I . . .'

I can go and sit beside him and get him to believe in me, that's more effective than talk. I know how to feel trustworthy—just imagine that I love him and I wish him well and the rest will take care of itself, automatic. He'll understand.

A drumming scours through the ship and almost makes her stumble, but she does go to him and doesn't touch, does not disturb, only concentrates and then begins with, 'There was that place where we stayed—Fife, wasn't it? The baby castle with a sort of tower and it was genuinely old, but peculiar, weird furniture and made-up coats of arms on papier mâché shields.' And this is chatting, which won't be frightening.

Chat and the world chats with you, strive to address your issues and you'll be doing it alone.

I wouldn't even be doing it with me.

But Beth would prefer to be here and herself and not alone and not frightened, 'There was no staff— just that guy who owned it and pretended there were staff, but then when he's serving breakfast and he's clearly also cooked it and there are no other guests, he admits that he's all by himself, but not to worry because he hires the place out for weddings and that goes quite well—wedding in a castle.'

Arthur is still leaned over, but his hands have eased down and he's beginning to relax. He's letting her in.

But I mustn't notice, I'm just telling a story and he can listen and we'll be like friends, old friends, and I do love him and I do wish him well, so there's nothing here that could disturb him.

She isn't performing a shameful act, 'Our room was the library—great big purple room with a four-poster bed and these abandoned hardbacks, nothing newer than the 1950s, and . . . it was . . . that seemed . . . there was the lake at the back and tall, tall foxgloves—so many colours and as high as you.'

His spine straightens a fraction at this and shows how she is working in him and she keeps her rhythm, her pace, the engaging details, 'And tiny frogs, when we walked there were these tiny frogs—perfect little babies scampering away to be out of danger only we weren't going to hurt them and we . . . it all smelled of cut pine wood and I wished it was cold so we could have a fire and sit by it and instead we sat on the patio by ourselves and there was confetti left in the gravel—silver metal confetti cut out in the shape of a couple dancing, which was very tacky, but I kept a piece. I've still got it. I found it with you and it made me remember dancing with you. I keep it because it makes me remember remembering.' So that he knows she wasn't blankly absent, was imagining her ways back to him all the while, all the months, was puzzling out towards him.

And he joins her, joins in, gives in. 'The confetti people, they had rather distanced upper bodies and high arms. That's what I remember. It didn't look like dancing. It looked like two people throttling each other. You could take your pick. Both intimate in their ways.' Which is him testing her, not making himself easy, but still willing.

He pauses and she lets him and likes that she heard a smile under what he said, but doesn't check him. It's too soon to check. He mustn't feel examined. The next thing he'd feel after that would be that she's playing him.

When playing him would be a shameful act.

Beth starts in with a gently different direction, something warmer. 'I didn't dance with you that time.'

'No.'

'That was . . .'

'Galway.'

He doesn't move. 'Galway.' But the purr is beginning in his throat, the low and comfortable sound.

Two men who had that—two men with that exact sound. And Arthur's the only one left.

'We were in Galway.' And he shifts and turns further from her, but leans until his back is tight to her side and rests with a small flicker of something like regret, misgiving, and then a fuller pressure. 'And it was another bloody wedding . . . Big

247

hotels—you'll get weddings—weddings, or honeymoons and all the fucking—and I mean that literally—all the *fucking equipment*: remote control ignition real-flame fires for romantic atmosphere, scented candles for overpowering atmosphere, built-for-two tubs with bubbles and funny lighting . . . *Christ.'* His ribs move when he jerks out a small, fast breath and she knows this is like a laugh—the way a sad man laughs.

But she can't have him sad—'We like them, though. The big hotels. The facilities . . .'

Arthur's body tenses slightly and no training or insight is required to help her read that he doesn't entirely want to start recalling the glide of soaped skin in hi-tech showers, the coddle of warm water and the tease of cold and the splaying and crouching and mouthing and the ludicrous, never-ending cleanliness of staying dirty—Friday night to Monday morning checkout of straining to keep themselves spiked, taut, stiffened, adequately bewildered to hide from who they are and to be fucks. Three nights of being a ride, faking that you're a stranger's little gift.

And this will hurt him, so he shouldn't think it and it's OK to change his thinking if it saves him from a hurt.

'Galway—it was nice.' But he's closing down into himself.

Catch him then, steer him.

'Yes. We liked Galway—and downstairs in the function suite there was a band and it didn't seem likely it could be that bad . . . and loud.' She sounds as casual as she can while the floor writhes under their feet.

He edges out to meet her again. 'Probably everyone

248

else in the place was down in the function suite, banqueting hall, whatever—there with the wedding. Us the odd ones out.'

'Like always.' And she tries to make this sound like a good thing.

'Like always.' And he makes this sound as if it's not.

'We're more the honeymoon.'

Which is the wrong, wrong, wrong thing to say.

Amateur.

'We're not any kind of honeymoon.' And he sits away from her, coughs. 'Sorry, I don't want to lose my temper and I don't want to be talking about this. I can't. But people on honeymoon are together and that isn't what we do and please don't insult me with that kind of . . . I realise you like to hurt me and you have your reasons and I have my own reasons to hurt me and they're better than yours—I know me better—but please don't.'

Twitch in his shoulders, as if I've hit him which I'd never do—only ever did that once which I regret—and arguing fatal now—we can't—I can't—but chatting—run back to the comfortable and easy chatting—he needs to be comfortable and easy—then we can do what we need to.

'They played covers from *The Blues Brothers* and *The Commitments* . . . I think they played "Mustang Sally" three times, four times—a lot.'

'Just a lot, Beth. Let's do without the fucking numbers, they give me a headache.'

Concentrate and concentrate and give him what's right.

And love and love and love and soft and smile.

And, 'No numbers, then. I'm sorry. We got out of bed and we had a dance. All those layers of

249

floorboards and the carpet, so we were having the music filtered—still not great—but OK at a distance and . . . it was like when you'd only just stopped that wearing the gloves thing and all the rest, being wrapped up all the time—way back then . . . You were so . . . As if you weren't used to it—the touching . . . and your skin was . . . It felt . . .'

I've got this whole speech ready—about how there's this other man he keeps inside and he's always dancing and he shows, not all at once, but he's there: in the shoulders, or the snap to an arm or a spring in the walk, the melody in under Arthur's walk, and he's there, he's properly there, this happy man, the truly happy man and I love him and I danced with him in Galway—with almost all of him.

Too long.

Just hold his hand and give him the summarised version.

'You were blinding. Sort of blinding.'

'That doesn't seem likely.' But he lets her close the distance again, ghost a contact, an invitation, hip against hip and when she smoothes her hand across his back Arthur's spine is audible through his shirt and the bite of it, its kind of exposure, catches her—he is habitually lean, but now he's thin, harrowed—and this is in some way utterly appalling. Too much of his structure is showing through.

And there's his heat, his intention beneath her fingers—muscle, ribs, thought—it's labouring, slowing, adjusting, before, 'Sorry, Beth. Sorry . . . I . . . I like your stomach against my stomach. When we danced . . . That's a clumsy way to say it, but . . . In my stomach is where I get scared and when you . . .' But he changes his direction, retreats, 'We're all done by kindness—it's never ineffective . . .'

250

'Come to bed.'

'I don't want to come to bed, I don't want to be near a bed, I don't want—' And he hugs himself around his shoulders and drops his head on to his arms.

She does not kiss the back of his neck where it is pale and soft and burning, because this would be impractical. She leaves him be and says, 'I know. And I don't want. Not that.'

'I was going to take ice cubes from round the champagne and make your nipples hard with them— numb you up then suck you—some kind of crap like that—the usual . . . We make plans, you see—people make plans and they are the wrong plans, so they are laughable—but you shouldn't laugh because they can't . . . can't help it and they hurt. They hurt everyone.' Mumbling into his Jermyn Street shirt and then failing, stopped.

The horizon soars and shakes and Beth waits.

Takes as long as it takes—five minutes, ten minutes— until he's calmer. But he's mine now—all opened, all ready. And listen to his breath—smoother and smoother—he'll be able to hear and we'll begin.

'I worked out why you take the ships, Arthur. I understand. On the first night, I realised and it made me . . . When you lie down in your bed and the boat moves—the tiny rock—the tiny flicker in the mattress, the give—it's like when you were a kid and somebody came in and sat on the side of your bed—it's that kindness again—it's the best—it's . . . nobody's ever going to do that who doesn't . . . It would be someone at least looking after you . . .'

'Has he touched you today? Derek. Did he touch you?'

'Sssssshhh.'

251

'Has he touched you?'

'No.'

'Why the fuck not?'

'Christ, do you really . . . ? Because he doesn't want to, because I am being a bitch and inexcusably cruel to him, because he is ill, because I wouldn't be able to let him. He hasn't really touched me since dry land. The first night on board we were just very sleepy and ever since . . . Arthur, the pills I've been giving him aren't for seasickness. I break those out of the pack and palm them and take them myself—he's been eating . . . it's a homeopathic remedy for sinus infections. Does sod all. Won't harm him. But it also won't stop him being iller than anyone should have to be.'

And no one but Arthur would find that romantic—but he will—he does—there he is, my boy—looking at me like he's waking up.

But she takes care not to smile. 'You didn't make me do that—I did that, it was my choice.' This is a confession and therefore serious. 'It is not to do with you, but I might not have done it if you hadn't been here.'

'No. You would have got engaged.'

Which is the last little fence that he'll throw at her and so she ignores it, 'He might have asked me to—I couldn't have. With or without you, I wouldn't have done that . . .' The ship swooping and reeling with her when she realises she's supplied herself with the perfect cue—an accident, so it should sound genuine. 'With or without you—Arthur . . .'

If you're being honest it's all right to sound flat, jangled, amateur. So aim for that.

'Arthur, can I be with you? Please.'

'He kissed you. I saw him.' This isn't an objection,

252

it's an invitation.

And my boy gets to be my boy, my own boy.

'And so will you.' And she gets up, slides her hands under his ears and holds him.

When they walk to his bedroom they are exactly as unsteady as they should be.

My boy.

And Arthur climbs on to the goldenish coverlet like a very orderly boy, simply lies down across it, curls away on his side, faces out to the balcony and his dangerous view.

Beth sits on the side of the mattress, lets it give, give, give, then swings, moves, rests herself up against the headboard, the pillows. She slips her hand in under his skull, his cheek. She is glad of his weight.

'I go on marches, Beth.'

He'll talk now and I'll let him.

And she's glad of the shape of his voice against her fingers.

'You'd be proud of me. Maybe.'

She doesn't imagine the craft lying thick in his mind, the darknesses and strategies and lies. They have a weight and a shape and are beating in him, too.

And I have my own and today I don't save him from myself.

He rocks his head back and forth, warm and away and then warm and then away and, 'I think you would be proud. Not because of . . . I mean . . . I met these soldiers' mothers—in the way that I would meet the mothers of dead sons—I'm sorry, I know you hate it, but I have to say and . . . but I . . . What do they have apart from me? Their boys, they were teenagers and they wanted free driving lessons and

253

a fucking job and they looked smart with the haircut and the new dress uniform and people talked to them about loyalty and self-respect and discipline and they got very good at pressing in regulation creases and bulling their boots—I do know a bit about it—the research—some of it I read about and the people, relatives, other fucked-up soldiers with other dead—with dead friends—they told me some of it and it doesn't, in this context, I believe, matter what I was doing—or what the reality of that was—I still have the right to be fucking outraged, fucking beyond it, that they went off with minimal training to a country where they never should have been and were killed for predictable and fucked-up reasons, because that's what happens, always, when people pay no fucking attention to each other. Always. All neat and kissing you goodbye and photos in the post and emails and, after that, home in a box—how do you make sense of that without me—you aren't going to get apologies, or justice, or an undertaking that the recruiters won't hang round your shopping centre, your scheme, your school, and pick up more boys and use them to make more dead and . . . You know what they used to say?—in the First World War?—in that one? Believe me, I know my wars— half of my job has been learning fucking wars—they used to say there was one time when a king would have to salute a private soldier and the soldier could ignore him—which is when the private soldier is dead. I get tired of all the respect being given to the dead. I respect the living. The *living*—the ones who have to live, keep doing that—they're the ones I work for. And I march with them.' He pauses for a breath, presses his face against her hand. She holds where he's frowning. 'These women, they're different now: they're not just bereaved, they're activists—they're not the way women in housing schemes are meant to be—they don't just shut up and take it. And I'm there with them sometimes—no particular use in that context, but I'm there, I want to be there—when I can be, where I can be—and people come round on the demos and give you signs, placards—usually the faces of hurt kids, dead kids, and you carry these dead kids with you and I walk behind the mothers and they wear T-shirts, they wear these T-shirts with numbers on them, their sons' serial numbers—because their sons were numbers, are numbers—everything they did and cared about and trusted and all that's left is these T-shirts and a number each—women wearing their sons. And I march and I give them money because my job makes me money and I *try to fucking help*. I try.'

He stops to let her contradict him, rolls on to his back and gives her his hand, makes the grip tight. 'On the last march—because I do as many as I can, because you get to know the . . . it's not just research—the organisations, they tell you about more and more and more of this shit—this death shit—and the last march I was on was for refugees, asylum seekers. Three of them had killed themselves—my government, your government dumped them in a block of flats where no one could live—no one—no one *un*traumatised, no one *without* ghosts—the flats, they're just an invitation to top yourself—if you looked up: lousy balconies, rotten wood, shit paintwork and the whole place is just telling you, *Why don't you piss off and die?* There's this guy there and he's just a punter, he's local, has all these relatives—cousins, pals—and they've jumped—they weren't refugees, they just lived

255

there—which is being another kind of refugee, isn't it . . . and the guy, he's telling me this stuff and he's not playing me, he doesn't need me—I'm just listening—and it's clear, more than clear, that anybody sane would jump. They would jump to not have to be in the normal blocks of those flats—and inside the block for the refugees . . . they're not allowed washing machines in their flats—there are four fucking washing machines in this one little utility room—that's all there is among Christ knows how many in the whole block and half the time the machines don't even work—and no door locks that the concierge can't open—and checking you out and checking you in—that's not a concierge, that's a jailer—Christ, we've got prisons with children in— refugee prisons—and what have they done? They've been the weakest of the weak, so we put them in prison—it's all . . . it's because we don't see each other, we don't even try . . . So there's this family in the high flats, they kill themselves—patch of the grass with some flowers on where they landed— covers up any indentations, I'd suppose—cheap flowers—and these people, concerned individuals, they turn up—call goes out and they're there—and me—and we march—with some of the guys, the asylum seekers from the flats, and eventually, you know, there's a quite a lot of us under way, we're off and we're filling the street and we're coming into town, from where the thrown-away people are to where the proper shops are and the good buildings that aren't trying to kill you—where the respect is—and these refugees, these human beings from nowhere, from hell, from nothing they can stand to remember, they're walking down the middle of the road and holding up traffic and being *guarded* by

256

police—escorted and looked after *by the police*—who are behaving themselves—and the refugees, they're not allowed to earn, they can't vote, the Border Authority can do what they like with them at any time and no one seems to care, but today they have policemen helping them to be a parade—and there are total strangers there to prove that someone gives a shit—not just politicals: couples and kids and students and whoever—and it's not practical, not really, it's just giving up a bit of a Saturday morning to prove a point and not achieve, you might say, anything much—but the asylum seekers they're so bloody happy about what's going on—the almost-nothing that's going on—that some of them are *dancing,* they're *singing*—'cause it seems like they might exist, they might be real again and in the world, might be able to have a bit of it, and I am *absolutely certain* I could help them, what I do could help them and it would cost them nothing and I could have helped that family, they needn't have tied themselves together and walked off the edge of their lives. They had nothing, Beth, and nothing is the code for nothing—for fuck all—and no one should be left with that.'

And the sound of this seems to frighten him and make him want to pretend he wasn't suddenly thinking of himself and of small problems—she can see him blush, consider the largest options he can muster. 'I just . . . I'm not the worst specialist in death—I do not personally, directly *make* anyone dead, I do not earn my money by killing, or by allowing other people to die, I also do not go through my life under the impression that my everyday decisions *aren't* murdering people I'll never meet and I make an effort to be responsible in my

behaviour and I do expect—I insist on expecting—
that other human beings might try that, too. Thirty
years ago—I can't get this out of my head—thirty
years ago—what's 30 again? **30** was sport, wasn't it?
Something sport related . . . inappropriate . . . Thirty
years ago, the UN promised that every member
country would give 0.7 per cent—which is the
mathematical way of saying fuck all—of their Gross
National Income to stop the poor dying, so that
mothers and kids and other ordinary normal members
of our species wouldn't just cease to exist for no
good reason—wouldn't be executed by the nature
of their lives . . . in 2009—this is research I do for
me, it's for nobody but me—it's not practical, it's
because I like people and I don't want them to need
me and it's only when your dead have gone the
wrong way that you need me—and because I do the
research I know that in 2009 *five* countries were
actually giving 0.7 per cent. *Five*—out of all the UN
countries—five out of 102. Sweden, Denmark . . .
none of them amazingly big countries with huge
resources, just merciful and civilised.

'Five from 192—that's code for almost everyone
being a cunt. Or for the people who represent almost
everyone being cunts.'

'Sorry for the word—as a thing and a place, it's
. . .' He lets his breath struggle in his chest for a
moment. 'You know what I mean. We are not well
served by the allegedly great and the allegedly good
and the powerful.

'But I can say, Beth, I can tell them. Because of
my job, I can tell the people—some of the people—
who would otherwise spend their surpluses on
medieval tapestries, or jade, or German armour—
who would otherwise gather over-priced shit with

258

dodgy provenance, or no provenance, or fakes—the people who want their names chiselled into everything with gold inlay because it's classy—I can say to them, "Collect lives. Why not?"—I would say *save* lives—but *collecting*, that's easier for them to understand. They can keep a running total on a collection. They can turn up in tropical gear, fresh off the Lear jet and meet kids who'll remember their names for ever, no gold inlay necessary. The kids will be able to remember and have lives, because the people with more money than sense—me included, that would include me—did something to help—did more than they thought they could to help—or just stopped doing things that harmed. I can get people to collect other people being happy because apparently their dead will come back and suggest it, demand it, because the afterlife can be merciful and civilised if we would like. It can be what this life is not. And quite possibly never will be. The dead—the ones I bring back—the ones that I say I bring back—I can get them to tell anybody you'd like the truth: that there is inexhaustibly more and more damage to undo, more pain, and I'm tired and I'm tired and I'm tired, but I'm . . . I try to do things, I . . .'

And Arthur turns to find her and she lets him cling as if they are falling, as if he is falling, as if he is angry and afraid and the bed gives and gives and gives and he is her boy, her soft, sore boy being taken into silence.

Here now.

Here now and you can sleep and everything you've said can be true and everything you've done can be acceptable, forgivable, normal and we can be together.

I can believe that.

If I believe it, then it isn't fake.

259

Your book doesn't understand belief, it can only tell you what it sees: a hotel lounge with a duck egg and caramel carpet, fat chairs and the quiet of hospital waiting rooms. Beth is sitting in an armchair opposite her mother and staring at a magazine filled with snapshots of people she doesn't know having parties, and true accounts of horrible diseases and assaults and accidents—also with snapshots. Everyone pictured appears to be having enormous fun, regardless of whether they're toasting an over-dressed table or undergoing skin grafts.

Sodding Beverley, the morning after.

There is a grandfather clock in the hallway knocking out the time and further away, in the dining room, breakfast crockery is being cleared and places are being set up ready for lunch. The meals here are both unremitting and niggardly—neither woman is sure how to wear away the hours that are left between them. Beth can't have another massage. Cath can't have her hair cut again.

Up in the rooms there is cable television, there are pay-per-view movies, but Cath would think watching a film would be wasting the day. And probably it wouldn't occupy her mind enough. Particularly not today.

Today is her wedding anniversary, but she can't be married any more.

That's why they're here. This is the first time Cath would have spent the day alone—first in more than forty years.

Beth would be relieved to go upstairs and lie down,

but that would involve abandoning her mother and she's been doing that too much.

Beth is stupid with exhaustion and vaguely tearful. For little minutes she drifts into numbness and then she snaps alert, glances at her mother and, once again, wants to cry but doesn't. And Beth's clothes don't seem quite able to drown out the memory of Arthur and finding him. The rediscovery.

Sodding Beverley, the morning after.

Outside there is drizzle, so it would be unpleasant to stroll. There are tall Victorian trees in the grey distance across a lawn, planted to climb artistically up a hillside and Beth studies them, heartily admires them to prevent herself from feeling where she has been bitten and where she was most touched and how unwise it would have been to sleep with Arthur, to give him that trust, and how terrible it is that she didn't.

They parted in the small hours: phone numbers, brisk kisses, a slightly embarrassed rush.

Arthur was leaving early.

So he'll be gone now—would have headed off before she came down.

He would have walked across the entrance to the dining room, past the clock and out to his car and neatly away from any chance of her mother seeing him, recognising him, making half-right and half-wrong assumptions, shouting.

And he's neatly away from me, too.

A rising breeze makes the big windows rattle.

But there's another sound inside that.

There's a tapping—perhaps from twigs dropping, or debris, Beth can't be bothered deciding which, but her mother is standing. That's what makes Beth look up: the sudden movement, the lurch of odd

261

hope. Her mother is standing and walking, easing, slowly, slowly towards the window and gazing straight ahead and there it is.

Tapping.

There's a magpie—large and handsome bird, dapper black and white and that special sheen along the feathers—the dash of glamour that you always get with jays. And he's tilting his head and thoughtful and considering and tilting again and he peers in and then taps. He steps, deliberate, taps once more.

And Beth is also standing, didn't quite notice how, and her mother is inching closer to the window and the magpie nods and eyes her, steps, taps. He has a circus air: costumed and tricky and unnatural—clever bird—pickpocket bird—magician bird.

The magpie is unfearful. He taps with his beak and then rests—as if he's awaiting some response.

'He wants to come in.' Her mother's voice careful and joyful, delighted. 'He wants to come in.' Cath brings herself all the way close to the glass and touches it with her hand, her palm pressed flat where it should surely disturb their visitor; but he remains tranquilly determined, ponders it and then taps again not far from her thumb. 'Oh, Beth.' A girl's voice. Young and happy.

And if her father was going to visit them as a bird, come back and please his wife, give love to his wife, then a magpie would have been his choice and here is the magpie, their magpie, in a nice black suit with pantomime touches and jocular and peeking at them, familiar as family.

But it isn't him. It's a bird. It's a story her mother will tell and that will help her and will be special and will never be taken away.

'Oh, Beth.' And the broad flare of wings when it

leaps, finally takes flight, renews the loss and her mother's weeping. Tomorrow she'll say that she slept well and dreamed of her husband and the way he smiled, and of flying.

But the bird wasn't him. Beth can't believe it. The bird was just a bird.

With Arthur, she's the only one who doesn't get her consolation.

'Arthur.'

Beth wakes in the suite before him.

'Art.'

Panicking in case she has slept too long, because she has slept at all—the windows showing spills of shiplight on the dim balcony, rainwater glimmers across tables and chairs provided for fair-weather entertaining, elegant guests. Beyond that is a vertigo of black—it's full night.

'Fuck.' She's been lying awkwardly, they both have.

Clothes will look as if I've gone to bed in them—because I have.

'Fuck.'

'Hm?' Arthur stirring, taking little sips of air and he shifts. 'You . . .'

It's painful when she tries to move. 'I'm here.' She must have fallen asleep and never shifted. One of his buttons has been pressing near her eye and it hurts when she lifts her head.

He swallows, 'You're?' Voice in his chest and moving like a deep and red and dreaming thing. 'You're . . .'

Arthur's hand briefly, muzzily patting her hair as

263

he twists his shoulders and hips and retreats until she is lying without him, unembraced. He turns on the lamp—the small glare stings her—and checks his watch. 'It's past seven.' Rubs his face, 'By which I mean, it's past seven o'clock. Not any other meaning. I don't mean anything else . . . I'm sorry, it's probably late for where you want to be . . . and I'm sorry . . .' He sits up and closes his eyes. 'I'm sorry, this is the last thing, the worst . . . this is the worst thing I could have . . .' Rubbing the back of his neck to be a comfort while he upsets himself. 'Waking up with you . . . I think when you go, that you shouldn't come back. I think that we would just . . .' His good shirt creased. 'I can't.'

'It's all right.'

It isn't all right—it's us on a ludicrous boat in a blind ocean and everywhere else, they're dying— willingly, unwillingly, violently, unnecessarily, badly, well, at the limit of their natural term or long before— the world is spinning with it, ruined, and I am guilty and we are guilty and everyone still living has to be guilty because of it, but I'm not having that tonight— not tonight—and I'm not having you try to end this now because you've panicked that it's going to end later when you're in too far.

Arthur is sitting with his fists braced against the bed, thumbs rubbing his knuckles. He keeps his eyes shut.

You're in too far already.

I know it, because you're next to me.

Beth kneels on the bed and it gives, gives, gives.

But I'm not going to argue—I'll speak to your skin.

'Arthur, I'm going to take off your shoes.' He doesn't answer and so she undoes his laces, pulls at the weight of stiff leather until it gives, gives, gives, until he lets her steal his shoe.

And again.

Gentle and warm feet and red socks, his not-at-work socks—' And I'm taking off your socks.' He makes a little noise when she does this, a younganimal noise. 'I'm putting them over here, out of our way but this is me back here and I'm going to stay back.'

She stands next to the bed.

Bare feet, long toes—and he won't prevent me, but he won't assist, but he won't prevent. So we're all right and I can be doing this and reading him because it's needed, not an intrusion, not a theft.

She has the impression he is thinking of being heavy, of being sunk into the mattress, of being a man who cannot give himself to this.

But we both know he will.

And she bends to him. 'And this is me kissing your feet, this is the feel of me kissing your feet.'

The Magdalene thing—it'll work. He's not a Catholic, but he had a funny mother, that's like being a Catholic. Mary Magdalene will reach him.

Lips on his instep, more respectful than erotic, 'I know you'd kiss my feet, but I'm doing it for you. I have decided to.'

The complicated bones, the smooth skin.

This isn't a violation.

'And this is my hand on your stomach where you get scared.' And slipping her fingers inside his shirt, between the buttons and there he is, alight.

Arthur sways his head to the left, as if he's trying to think something through, angling his thoughts. Obviously doesn't intend to open his eyes. He arches up in a small way to answer her, but then lowers himself again, withdraws.

Which means he'd still like his privacy, maybe his

265

dignity, and so she removes the touch. 'Arthur, it's where I'm scared as well. And this isn't going to be what we do—the way we've been. This is about . . .'

I think he'd be more convinced if I can't help faltering and anyway it's too late if it would have been stronger of me to roll on and make the statement, be matter-of-fact.

'Arthur, I love you. I want you to believe that.'

And who says they love anybody without wanting to get the love back—it isn't a generous emotion.

'And this is me unbuttoning your cuffs and this is my mouth. On the inside of your wrist, which I also love.'

Starting an inventory because that will give them a structure and a pace, 'And the other one. Can't have favourites.' Which should make him smile, but he doesn't—he's listening too much.

He's reading me—I can feel it, taste. I can read it.

So I'd better get this right.

'And you know I have to do this.' Kissing his palm, his too hot and too clever palm. 'And I need to take off your shirt.' And fast with the buttons, smooth with the buttons—determined enough to make it seem inevitable and right.

And here he is—Arthur—all blue-white and tender breath—like he's hurt already.

'We have to.'

Now, slowly, slowly—kiss his throat—him swallowing beneath you—kiss the notch in his collar bone—nipples—kissing the hair—his ribs—poor ribs—poor boy ribs.

Shadows and hollows and silk, 'And I love this.' And Arthur the man and Arthur the boy again, too. 'I love all of this.'

Needs someone to get him through it.

266

Flail of his arms as she struggles him out of the cloth, tugs it away.

Kiss where he's scared. Me, too.

'I want to see you, Arthur, and I want you to feel me looking.'

Kiss over his heart and feel it startle.

'I love you.'

Not a lie.

Kiss his mouth so he can't say it back—so he can't fail to say it back. Either way, it would be our problem—and a joy and a beauty and a trap.

Kiss his mouth.

And I don't want to think, not any more.

Belt buckle—tricky and sleek and tricky.

Jeans.

Clumsy.

Unfasten.

Unfasten.

Unfasten.

Unfasten.

Break him, peel him free.

'I do love you.'

Silkhotsilk.

Crest of the hip—hummingbird tremor in the thigh— inside—under—kiss the fur—shift of the skin— shiftingundertheskin kissed balls—fleece and lovely—where he wants—round and blind and speaking and head and rim and head and shaft and this is everything and sorry and angry and sorry and perfect and tongue and mouth and needs and take him in and keep and lose and keep and play and the first taste of almost and almost and the softesthardestlostestnakedest thing in the world and he's dancing and taste the dancing and running against the tongue and taking him in and lips and taking him

267

*in and hands and taking him in and never leave him
be and take him in.*

Say nothing.

The idea of calling him darling.

Say nothing is best.

Arthur opens his eyes. The blue of them is terrified.
And she doesn't know what this could mean.

*Please not that I've hurt him. Please not that he
doesn't believe me. Please not that he didn't trust me,
but let me in any case.*

Please is it love?

She wants to tell him that she's sorry, but is a
coward and worried that he might ask her what she's
sorry for and so she lies beside him, edges her head
on to his chest. 'Can we stay like this? For a bit.'
Like this, he can't look at her.

'Of course.' Unforthcoming voice, small and
private.

And she thinks about Beverley and the night when
they started again and how in the grey, in the
pre-dawn, he'd got out of bed and gone off to the
bathroom and she'd dozed and then something had
fully woken her—the electric sense of somebody's
attention—and she'd sat up and found him there
watching her, standing in the doorway with the light
at his back, being this curious shadow—and he'd
said, 'You feel different.'

'I am different.'

Arthur waiting, his head seeming to shift and focus
on something beyond her.

Always does that—indirect.

He does see, though.

*The distracted man who's looking somewhere else—
that's who'll catch the trick. The ones who stare and
are intent, they're not a problem—any magician will*

take their careful observation and lie to it, because it
is solid and therefore can be moved, aroused, betrayed.

Arthur looks away to catch the truth.

'You *are* different?'

'Yes.'

She seemed to feel him testing her silence, pressing against it, but then he nodded, walked to join her, his body cooled. 'I'm going to sleep now. If you don't mind.'

'No. I don't mind.'

'I have to leave early in the morning.'

'Well, I'll . . . once you're asleep I'll get out of your way . . .'

And he rolled on to his side, stilled his breath, but he didn't sleep—she knew he was listening when she left.

It is perhaps foolish, but happiness can scare you. The big kind, the real kind—it can be too much like a new country opening round you, strange and wide. You do love it, naturally—you'd be insane not to— you dance in it and it's the best music you've ever felt—but you can still wonder how you've come to be so lucky.

And beauty, you can't be near it without changing and what if you change to suit it and then it goes— then you won't be the right fit for anything else. Or it can be as if saying a lover's name will make them disappear—abracadabra—or as if they might say yours and you don't know what would happen if they did.

It can take a while for you to adjust.

269

But you can.

You could.

You should.

And your book would love to see you happy—the big kind, the real kind.

So your book wants to play with you.

Just a game.

For company.

For you and your book to be together in a little game.

In this game, you could—if you wanted, you don't have to—you could pick a number between one and nine.

You would usually be asked for a selection between one and ten—that's the standard for many illusions that might trick you. Statistically, you'd be most likely to choose seven in that case. Most people prefer seven—it has a nice corner, was easy to draw when you learned it and hasn't too greedy a value, but isn't too low—it's a number of moderate, comfortable self-esteem.

A magician, a trickster, would tend to pick a three. They favour threes. They favour three of clubs—almost worthless, a dark and peculiar card, shows a symbol like a paw print, the sign of an odd beast. This sets them apart from those they deceive.

But you can have any number, any at all between one and nine.

You'll probably avoid seven now.

You don't have to, but you can.

You probably will.

Or not.

What matters is that you know you do have a free choice.

So pick one number.

If you'd like.

Your book can wait.

It would be happy if you'd pick.

And once you have picked—if you have picked—it would like you to multiply your number by three.

And note the answer.

And then add three.

And note the answer.

And—why not?—you can multiply that answer by three once again—by the magician's number—that way you have three threes.

For luck.

There's no such thing, but if it could, your book would promise you good fortune—books have made similar promises before. Your book might have said you could be defended from every harm and that nothing will ever reach you but tenderness.

That ought to be possible and in a book anything at all is possible: once you're tucked up neat inside a story, you can find all kinds of things convincing.

But your book will only give you something honest—the magician's number. The number which can be *Touch me* or *Loss*. 3.

The magician's number changed your first thought to something else and then again and then again.

It altered your thinking and something which alters your thinking can alter you, alter your world.

If you choose to play.

Just a game.

Where you multiply your number by three, add three, then multiply by three and note your final result.

That's all.

Your book—because it never wants to lie to you—will tell you this.

Or you could pick one of its meanings in the codes, whichever spoke to you the most.

Or you could pick both and the good luck, too. Why not—you deserve it.

Or our game might have been a type of manipulation when manipulation is usually wrong, although not always—not when it might make you happy, or satisfied, or keep you from being alone.

It's sometimes hard to say what's right, what's wrong.

But because your book doesn't want to trick you, it won't tell you that it knows you, can slip into how you think, has sat quiet in your life and watched you, been with you, has spent this many pages with its voice curled in your head, with its weight against your fingers and working at you. It won't say it predicted your choice long before you first met.

It won't deceive you.

Derek is sitting on the bed in his bathrobe when Beth slips into the cabin. He's entirely awake and alert.

Shit. Say something.

'Hello.'

More than that.

'You look better.'

'I know.' Derek nods as if he's handing over a school report, or some kind of challenging but completed project: here's his health, present and virtually correct, all neatly boxed and polished.

If I don't tell him now, I'm not sure when I will.

On shore.

But the shore's too far away.

'Really healthy, Derek . . . Well done.'

Well done?

Well done and by the way I have been with—sounds biblical—another man—Christ, this is giving me a headache—another man—made love with—trying to make love with—another man—I think I'm ill—not pleasantly ironic if on a boat full of geriatrics I'm the one who ends up having a stroke—no pun intended.

I have no idea what I'm supposed to say—how to explain that Derek is no longer my concern, not at all, that I look at him and get vertigo because he is so far away.

I could ask for it to be included in the ship's daily newsletter—GRAND SUITE USED FOR MAKING LOVE WRONGLY, WOMAN TRAVELLING IN CHEAPER STATEROOM EXPRESSES REGRET, BUT RETICENT ABOUT HER REASONS FOR DISCOMFORT.

Beth concentrates on the TV which is currently showing a map of the ship's progress, accompanied by the kind of charmless music she associates with crematoria.

I think I will hurt him and I think that is hurting me.

WOMAN UNWILLING TO SAY WHO SHE MEANS BY 'HE' FOR FEAR OF SCREAMING AND THEN BEING UNABLE TO STOP.

A jaunty orange dot in the Atlantic shows their position and it's not a wild guess to imagine that Derek is willing them fast into port.

WOMAN FOUND REPEATING INTERNALLY 'I CAN'T TELL HIM'. UNABLE TO SAY WHO SHE MEANS BY 'HIM' FOR FEAR OF FINDING OUT.

273

I am not a jolly good fellow.

Derek wants to be back with normality.

And I think I will hurt him again.

Derek hopes to be the way they were, because he misunderstands what that was. If he knew more, he would want her much less.

I no longer know what I am: but if I owned something this broken, I'd throw it away.

I should be thrown away.

Derek is no longer seasick, just homesick, but he also seems contented. 'I do feel a bit . . . you know—good. I slept for a long time.'

And how almost beautiful it is to be this scared—cold, sick, as if something is dying. I haven't felt this much in years.

Like ecstasy.

'Well if you slept you must have needed it'—*rules of civilised conduct*—and she kisses his cheek and not his mouth—*never kiss a man*—'Glad you're getting better'—*with another man's spunk*—'Very glad, love'—*still in your mouth*—'Very glad to hear it.'

She eases round the cabin to avoid both him and the bed, tries lurking on the sofa.

Not still in my mouth, that's an exaggeration. But it makes itself felt, nonetheless.

Derek's concentration follows her like a clumsy fumble, he irritates, but she doesn't respond.

Another man's semen, seminal fluid, cum, spunk. Which is the simplest part of this.

Beth arranges—*pressure flutters*—her limbs as if she—*in his balls*—as if she has never—*get him to where he can't help it*—as if she has never had limbs—*which isn't fair*—to arrange before—*tastes of home*—they are all shining and distracting. *He tastes of home.*

274

Not an unreasonable rule, the No Spunk Rule.

He tastes of home, he tastes of where I could live and I stole him away from himself and he knew it.

Not an unreasonable rule.

And Derek has to ask, 'Where were you?' because this is not unreasonable, either.

And it's not as if—'Massage'—*I hadn't prepared an answer—*'I went and got one'—*good answer, allows me to seem rearranged for an innocent reason—* 'Bloody expensive, but you know . . .' *And I do smell different, but not of cologne, no aftershave—no scent but Arthur's skin—*'I was tense'—*Close skin on me, hard to catch—*'Still am, really. Funny' *as if he'd designed himself to be undetectable, to make this easy for me.*

'Well, that's nice, then, Beth.'

Nice. Yes—that is precisely the word I was searching for—this whole week has been, beyond question, as nice as nice can be.

'Yes. *Nice.* Did me good.'

I could have said I'd been decorating hats, there was a hat decorating class: started more or less exactly when I pulled down Arthur's jeans.

The class not involving cock-licking, just hats. At least that's what I would imagine.

Fuck.

He didn't stop me.

I knew he wouldn't.

And I know I can't be me and I can't be here and I can't have—I can't have.

She turns to Derek without meaning to and he grins. 'I'm only just awake.' He's glad of her.

'Yeah, love—you look a bit . . .'—*may I suggest*—'Drowsy.'

'They've given me a scopolamine patch. See?' And

275

he shows her the little sticking plaster thing behind his ear. 'It'll last three days.' He is as bashfully pleased as he might be if he'd grown it.

'Three days. Wow. Strong stuff then, Derek.'

So he'll be in the way for the duration—transdermally delivered interference. Which means I have to tell him.

I've already said that.

I do have to.

He blinks docilely. 'And we've only got another two nights on board . . .' and brings back a gentle and genuine smile that she hasn't seen all week. 'Have you been very bored? On board.'

'No.' And if she wanted to, she could like the deception. 'Not bored.'

'I am sorry, though.' Derek manoeuvres himself across the bed, gently preoccupied because he is testing his reactions and finding them healthy and promising. His robe falls open unalluringly. He gets himself within arm's reach.

And I wish that arms wouldn't.

But he keeps himself delicate, only takes her ear between his forefinger and thumb, strokes her cheek and she has to let him, because not doing so would be unusual, and here he is, undeniably Derek—looking and acting exactly as he has at other times when he has been endearing and lovable. But today he isn't.

That's all gone.

She is embarrassed for him.

But I also want to laugh—like giggling at our funeral. What am I that I'd feel this way?

He is trying to make good. 'I'm very sorry, Beth. I've been . . . I wasn't the best company and I didn't mean it, but . . . I've never felt that lousy . . .' Which is what people do when it's too late.

'It's OK.' *He needs a shower. Mouthwash. To get away from me.* 'I understand.' *And I'm sorry as well, but saying so would be misleading.* 'You must be hungry. We'll go out and have something to eat.'

'Do we really have to leave the cabin . . .' and he gives her the foreplay smile, which isn't any more and never will be.

'Yes, I think we should.' Standing up and away from his hands—*no finesse: I used to think that was honest and maybe it is, but I still don't like it: he has bad hands*—a slight brush of his forearm as she goes, to prevent offence. 'Fresh air . . .' She holds her back to him, reconsiders the television, apparently fascinated by the details of wind direction, sea temperature, heading. 'Then Mila can get in and have a good clean while we're away—she's been waiting to for ages—born to clean, that woman—a natural taker of cares.'

'Bugger Mila.' And maybe this is who he really is: a mean-spirited man with a sour tone, the one she would end up dreading once they'd married and he'd stopped putting up a front.

Which is a comforting thought—that he was betraying me, pretending, and would have turned out to be somebody else.

He needn't have bothered. Somebody else was already there.

'Mila was very worried about you and is a nice woman.' Staying bright and firm. 'Get a shower and then we'll have a stroll, a bit of food. There's this lovely couple we can maybe hook up with—they've been keeping me company.'

I think I'm shaking.

But Derek slumps back into his mounded pillows, squinting up at her and failing to be charming. 'You

277

really want to go out?'

'I do want that, yes—that is exactly what I want.'
No it's not.
Derek sighs, stalks to the bathroom.

*   *   *

The buffet isn't crowded: the dinner rush has passed. Couples are lodged in angles, enjoying shadows—or some passengers are merrily in fours, teams by now, settled into patterns of which they feel protective on this their second-last night. They are delicate with nicknames and jokes, references to shared events and enjoyable complaints, their tiny history together. They are planning they honestly will keep in contact and meet again, go ashore with this extra comfort: *it's always wonderful on cruises who you'll end up talking to.*

An American woman in a tentative sweater sits down at a Geordie man's table. He is unpromising.

'It's always wonderful who you'll end up talking to.' She can say this because she recognises the Geordie from yesterday's lecture—which was about sand—and her announcement of their provenance is desperately confident, unarguable, and so he lets her join him and they shake hands and this will not be the beginning of a romance, or even an acquaintance, but they won't eat alone. They'll demonstrate they can be interesting and entertaining if they wish. They can be at least as wonderful as sand.

Beth scans the tables—recognises the so many faces who have seen her rushing, or weepy, or miserable with a coffee, or outside in the blustery light and staring—seeing the hinge where the world

278

swings—air into water, water into air.

Big-earring couple, still pursuing their week-long pirate theme—surprisingly tattooed Floridian woman who misses her kids—dim, military husband and silently damaged wife—gay guys from the West Country: only one of them joking when he eyes up the Filipino waiters—and Bunny.

'We should head over there . . .' Beth so relieved when she sees Bunny that she fears she may just have surrendered to hopeful delusion.

Derek is trying to slow and incline towards a series of seating options which would mean he has her to himself, but she pretends she doesn't notice and drives on. This makes him less subtle. 'Do we need to be with strangers?'

'They're not strangers. They're . . . ah.' Beth waves.

Because Bunny loves waving and ought to have people that she can wave back to every day—Francis and friends and visitors every single day.

Bunny waves back.

'This is Bunny.' Beth almost trots Derek along to present him. 'This is my . . . this is Derek.'

'Oh, you poor dear.'

Bunny taking Derek's arm and settling him beside her while she gives Beth her instructions. 'I am going to see how your friend's recovery is progressing and I'll tell him all the best ship's gossip that he's missed.' She deadpans at Derek and then chuckles, 'Don't worry, I'll make it racy. And Beth will go and fetch you appetising morsels. But you'll have to pace yourself, you know.' An ill person being businesslike about recoveries and weaknesses. 'Beth will also be very kind and locate my missing husband and then he can help her to carry things back.'

Bunny's in a trouser suit—purple, mandarin collar,

a tidy and sensual fit which Francis will like and her favourite jewellery again. 'I haven't a clue where he is—habitual with him, the wandering off. Watermelon. He's been on a mission for watermelon all day. I should never have mentioned it. By now he's probably insisting they lower a boat to fetch some.' Derek isn't responding to her, so she changes her focus to Beth. 'What will we do when this is all over?' The sense of a weight returning when she says this, so she adjusts, 'When we don't have servants . . . poor us.'

Beth kisses her—*with a dirty mouth*—gives her a peck on the ear—*with a lover's mouth and Bunny understands about love*—and reassures because this is expected and can be playful, 'You'll have Francis at your beck and call. I've never seen anyone more anxious to be becked and called, in fact.'

Bunny agrees to be distracted by the thought.

All of us masters of distraction.

Mistresses.

Sounding louche is the least of my troubles.

Then Bunny moves on to being coy, enjoys it: 'I don't believe we can describe him as staff, though. There are certain things one doesn't do in front of servants.' Her smile is coloured with Francis and how he would smile if he could hear her. 'Or with them, for that matter.'

Derek is, meanwhile, sullen and clearly doesn't want to consider geriatric sex or listen to Bunny, but Beth pats his shoulder and goes in search of Francis—*because I would like to eat my dinner with a gentleman.*

'Oh, I'm not, you know.' Francis quietly tired when she finds him, his tray laden with fruit—especially watermelon—and cheese, his pockets full of crackers as usual. 'No, I'm just me. And she puts up with the me-ness of me. And that's all right. That's very fine. No one else would.' A fingertip smudge of blue beneath each eye.

He's spent the week breaking his heart to be cheery, a jolly good fellow.

'No, you'll always be a gentleman, Francis. It's how you're built.'

I don't give compliments. It's not a compliment, though, is it? He's a gent.

'You're very kind. Thank you. Should we meet on any future occasions—not at sea, I don't just mean tomorrow—it would be my pleasure to try and not be disappointing.' He peers at the plates of watermelon—neat chap in a blazer and slacks, doing well for his age, only really needs glasses for reading—*but it's not his health that scares him*—a tray full of gifts for Bunny, treats, expressions of affection.

What will he do when they're pointless?

Some people have problems they did not make.

'You're very good with each other.'

'What?' Francis close to alarmed for an instant— he doesn't want a eulogy yet and she should have known better than to start one—but then he simply rolls his eyes. 'We've had our moments. In both directions.' Then he stops, doesn't want to hear himself almost speaking his marriage away, out of existence. 'And I'm sure we will again . . . Christ, it can make you bloody miserable.' He pauses again, picks an unthreatening meaning. 'This *end of the voyage* bit, it's glum. Even though it's not as if you'll actually miss almost anyone you've met and you're going straight back home with whoever you came with—I mean, it's not an emotional time, or anything.

281

It shouldn't be.' He rests his hand on her shoulder. 'You, though—you have to come and see us. And I would recommend you do that almost as soon as we land. Unless you're busy, might be . . .' He stumbles when what he meant to be enthusiasm sounds as if matters are urgent and Beth ought to rush.

'I will come and see you. Both of you.'

Because any word can work a spell and then Bunny will have to be there, still all right.

Francis gathering his poise again, summoning up mock-serious nodding. 'Excellent. And that's contractually binding, you know—a promise made at sea, I'm sure that's something legal. Not the standard holiday fib. Let me give you our address.' And he moves deftly through his procedure for finding his card and presenting it. Beth suspects there was a time when having a business card was a big deal—it still pleases him. 'Here. Don't lose it. And then you can come and stay—we're deep in the country now and it's too far to travel and not stay—and if you stay for a night, then you might as well make it longer . . . See?' He winks at her. 'You were warned you'd be kidnapped . . .'

After this, both of them are aware they will need to joke and talk nonsense and not act as if anyone is dying or ever could: they will behave like human beings and make the very best of ignoring the long term.

Which could make me proud of us. I'm definitely proud of Francis.

So they improvise and she *forages*, as Francis puts it, with him in attendance, encouraging and advising and flirting in a way which implies mutual respect.

'This is very wonderful, Beth. Your being here.

And you've made the sun come out.' He steers her round to a window and proves his point. 'More wonderful. Gorgeous.'

Out on the deck a jogger in a knitted hat fights his way past the glass and they watch him and then survey the restaurant and its quietly pornographic butter sculptures and carved fruits and busied heat lamps. The room seems to halt before it drops with another wave, rolls and sighs, and while it does Beth looks at Francis and tells him, 'I'm not going to say goodbye. I would if I was going to, because it seems like the right time, but I'm not.' And she kisses his ear and he grins.

Then he kisses Beth's hand and when he raises his head again, the grin isn't hers any longer—it's for Bunny. 'Very wonderful. Now, we're late and there will be rumours and alarms. And I have already been severely scolded for eyeing up the butter maidens. Dairy produce—it makes the sculptor overly focused on milk and its associated physical attributes. Come on.'

'I can't think what you mean, Francis.'

'And Bunny says neither can I.' Still grinning as they progress round to the table.

When he arrives, Francis kisses his wife and she frowns at him until he pantomimes being sly and then they both giggle and she kisses him back. 'Did he give you any bother, Beth?'

'No more than usual.' Beth sets down her offerings alongside Francis's careful array. Her efforts appear random: cold chicken, grated carrots, dumpling soup, a slice of pizza, watermelon, something with fish in a pink sauce—the kind of things she'd bring a stranger, trying to guess what he'd like.

When I no longer care about what Derek likes.

And what would be a suitable meal to share with a soon-to-be-ex-almost-future-husband?   Sexual Etiquette For All Occasions—I think that's a lecture I missed.

Derek has decided to be baleful. 'And what's the usual?' But then he seems unable to think of anything more to say, so he prods at his chicken suspiciously. He may have thought it might be impressive to refuse nourishment, but then Beth watches as four days of fasting kick in and he proceeds to eat everything she's brought him and then to insist on more. Otherwise he is mostly silent. Bunny, who has clearly been steadfast in trying to draw him out, makes a further attempt. 'We live in Dorset.' Although she's beginning to tire.

'Really.' Derek stokes in a forkful of risotto with a studied lack of grace. 'We don't.'

Absolutely inexcusable.

Bunny was enjoying a little slice of cake, something pistachio and ornate, but now she doesn't touch it and only studies her hands and is too quickly too frail and Francis is on his feet and patently disgusted, breathless with it, incredulous.

Taking his hand, Beth stands with him. 'I need some dessert. Francis, we'll search for dessert.' She leans into his shoulder. 'Could we. Please.'

Francis unwilling to move, his hands getting angry and considering bad things—Beth can feel when his forearms twitch.

Bunny takes a breath, steadies and then tilts her face up to her husband's. 'And a cup of tea, darling. I'm dry. If you wouldn't mind.' She gives him a tiny shake of her head, 'Go on.' Which allows him to exhale and hook his arm in Beth's.

As they step away Beth hears Derek add, too loud,

'And a cup for me.' And she has to work hard to keep Francis with her. He is trembling.

They make it as far as the tea urns before he dodges to stand in front of her, holds her quickly by both shoulders and then releases her, abashed. 'Look, I know he's your—'

'He's not.'

'He's . . . ?'

'Derek—he's not my anything. He was but he isn't and I haven't been able to tell him and I thought he would do, be all right . . . I thought he would be a safer, a saner . . . There's another . . . There is a man and Derek isn't him.'

'Well, thank fuck for that, love—because he's a *tosser*. Sorry, but really—what a *fucking* arse.' Francis blinking and checking her, wary. He winces out a minute smile when she doesn't seem upset. 'But . . . you know that.' Shakes his head, smiling more, glancing back at Bunny, watchful. 'Sorry. Of course you do. You're, from what I know, extremely bright and attractive and . . . I'm sorry, it's none of my business, but I do get tired of seeing fantastic women with appalling men. It's like some form of blood sacrifice, self-harm. I can't be doing with it. Not that I'm any great catch or one to talk, but . . .' And his fingers remember their previous intentions, tighten momentarily.

'I wish it was your business, Francis—you'd have made it all . . . neater, or . . . And I'm so sorry he hurt Bunny's feelings. I should never have brought him anywhere near her—or you—I was guessing I could manage him if you were around—and I am, I'm really sorry. And you can punch him if you want.'

Francis factual, 'I do want.' And keen.

'I know you want.'

'I wasn't always a gentleman—it has grown on me over time, like moss. He is, in point of fact, lucky I do not *punch 'is fuckin' 'ead in*. As it were. Ask Bunny.' Enjoying his accent, a gleam of who he could still be.

Can imagine him—sharp and handy and Bunny fancying this dangerous young man. Not too scary, just right.

'I will ask her. When we're alone. And I—'

He grips her shoulders again, this time slightly fierce. 'Look, this isn't the time and I truly do not normally take advantage of being incredibly ancient to give advice. Nobody ever wants it, for a start—of course they don't: *it's advice*. But I have kids your age . . . No, I don't . . .' He's rueful for a beat. 'I was waiting for you to contradict me there. My sons are in their twenties. Nice boys. And I wouldn't let them anywhere near you, you'd break them in half.' Another beat so that he can smile if Beth does, which she does. 'No offence—in fact, I mean it as a compliment. But—back to the previous topic—if I'd had a daughter . . . you can say this kind of thing when you're 180 . . .' But he can't phrase this kind of thing in a way that suits him. 'Oh, sod it. You and *that* doesn't work.' He cocks his head towards Derek, as if he wants him taken away. 'You and whoever else seems to be excruciating, but at least you care . . . Obviously care . . . So maybe that would work. If he's whoever made you look the way you look today.'

'What do you mean?'

'This evening something is not the way it was with you—and it's the sort of difference that's . . . This is a being 180 thing again—seen it all . . . Almost all . . . Some of it . . . That is . . . In the words of the immortal Jimi—*Have you ever been experienced? Well, I have.*'

'He likes Jimi. The other—'

'The other chap. I know. It wouldn't be *Derek*. And the liking of Mr Hendrix is in the other chap's favour, of course . . . Not that we're necessarily discussing quite the same experience as Jimi's . . . Then again, it's all intoxication isn't it? Eventually . . .' But he'd prefer to be with Bunny—she's upset and he has been brave for her and will again—will have to be much braver—and he would like to be more helpful for Beth, but Bunny is Bunny and is everything. So he's brief: 'Give it a go.' And then regrets it slightly. 'See if you're kind to each other. Try it. Maybe. It won't kill you.' And he shows her his face, his unarmed, unprepared face—'Lots of other things will. For sure.' He gives her that, then fusses at his collar, brushes his shoulders free of invisible lint, retires into being jovial for her—and then stern. 'Right . . .' The voice of a father with sons. 'The tosser. I need a word with him.'

'No, but—'

He won't actually punch him, though, will he?

Francis marching, bearing down and—despite a manifestly absorbing attack on a bowl of Thai green curry—Derek glances, falters, is dismayed and Francis tells him—carefully—'You are not going to eat any more. You are going to escort Elizabeth to the theatre. Don't act as if you've never heard of it. You're going to escort her courteously to the theatre and not take out how thoroughly disappointed you will soon feel with yourself on her or anyone else—you will not bother any of the staff.' Derek's head low and Francis maintaining his tone while his eyes look wicked and happy at Bunny and at Beth and he lies, 'I've been in the service, I've seen your type.' For a breath, he is joyful with how unlikely this is and then pointed, sober. 'You will watch the show. That's what a gentleman does with a lady. *You escort her.*'

Derek flounders his gaze up. He can't work Francis out, doesn't know who would actually win in a proper fight, because Francis is beginning to look quite useful and threatening and it would be just all upside-down to be beaten by an old man. Mainly Derek's face is turning scared, but he's also trying to present himself as polite, unwilling to contradict a senior citizen, 'I don't, I—'

That was a bleat—definitely an unmanly sound.

I shouldn't be enjoying this.

I am, though.

Derek blinks. He is being humiliated.

But he hasn't a clue how much, how deeply and that's the part I'm not enjoying.

And Francis is right: the only place tenable for us will be the theatre. Where Derek can be diluted, where our position can be diluted, by an audience.

Francis is insistent—like an elegant cosh. 'You don't what? You don't know what the show is? I don't care if you don't know what the show is. Whatever it is, it will be a delight. And, on your way, you can reflect repeatedly on your good fortune and continuing health.'

Derek puzzles at the silence.

Then, 'Off you go.' And for a moment Francis puts his arm around Beth's waist—warm, light— kisses the top of her head. 'Starts at 8.30. Don't want to be late—it'll help you both to get a good night's sleep.'

And for saying this Beth could kiss him—so she

288

does and this time she can't avoid it feeling like goodbye.

Kiss him with a lover's mouth. Francis also understands about love.

And then she kisses Bunny, 'You have a top-quality husband there.'

Bunny who smells of Chanel and powder and constant moderate pain: 'He's not bad. But I can't tell him that—he's unbearable as it is and in a funny mood at present.'

They conduct their conversation as if Derek has already gone and he soon does bump away from the table, heads out, fast and ungainly, between the other diners and then loiters at the far door.

'I am not in a funny mood.'

'He always says that when he's in a funny mood.'

'And you always say that.' Francis sitting down beside his wife, attentively snug beside her and slightly pleased with his recent performance, excited, and Beth leaves them being themselves only mildly louder for her benefit and thinks that when she's gone they'll drink their tea and maybe have an early night and continue from there.

Derek escorts her so effectively to the theatre that they arrive fifteen minutes early.

Actually, he didn't escort me—pacing a foot ahead of me in a morbid sulk isn't escorting.

I should tell him—then he could go, or I could go. Put us both out of my misery. Let us get away, each to our own.

But I'm a coward.

After the show. I'll do it then.

After the wait for the show and then the show.

I promise.

We can manage the wait—quiet wait. Quiet as staring

289

numbly in a resentment-filled lift while Gordon from Nuneaton (with wife) and Ted from the Channel Islands—he doesn't say which island, or maybe he lives on several—I know a man who lives on a single specific Channel Island, who talks about it—so this Gordon (with wife) and Ted (without wife)—Ted's wife having an early night: he says it gives his ears a rest and we all smile at this, complicit in its minor hatefulness—all of us smile, that is, except Derek, who has troubles of his own, which I will add to and that's why I despise them and myself.

Despising is as good as anything, though—it's an adequate diversion.

So Gordon and Ted discuss their knee operations— and then, the lift finally letting us go, precede us into the auditorium while I ponder—as they have at great length—the benefits and drawbacks of keyhole, as opposed to open-cast, orthopaedic surgery and yet find myself truly more interested in whether Gordon's silent but deep-eyed wife will one day strangle him with a pair of pastel golfing slacks—he needed the plastic knee to continue his golf—or whether perhaps she'll swap murders with Mrs Ted, disguise herself as a hooker who looks like his mum—his preferences would undoubtedly lie that way—and then bugger him to death with some large unbuttered vegetable while he's strapped to his own kitchen table.

I don't mean that.

They were all right.

Probably.

Even Ted—sexually frightened and too old for his current persona, Ted. He thinks his world isn't working because fox-hunting scenes have been banned from Christmas cards by socialists and Muslims and the UN. This, when the Prince of Peace's tender birth, his

290

virgin mother's baptismal kiss, the harmoniously
crowded manger, should obviously always be
commemorated by drawings of borderline Nazis and
admirers of Pinochet galloping out across farmland
they no longer own to prove a point before watching
dogs rip an almost-dog to pieces—or a cat, or some
other equally tasty domestic pet.

Christ, I don't want to be like this.

Or here—waiting for a magician.

Naturally.

Beth is almost relieved she has ended up having
to watch 'Not to be missed, the personality and
magic of Matt Mitchell'.

And I have to be grateful for him because he'll keep
Derek out of the cabin and awake—until the heavy
meal and the scopolamine kick in.

I hope.

Francis hoped.

When Francis ought to be saving his optimism for
better things.

The house lights dim and then go out, but mean
nothing melancholy by it.

If Derek's sleepy, docile, then we can be civilised.

Or, putting it more frankly, I would like him to be
temporarily disabled, because this will work to my
advantage when I admit what I have to and should
have long ago and everything becomes my fault.

A swirl of portentous music clambers up to the
balconies and then washes back.

And here's the lovely Matt.

Matt is vaguely tubby, something failed in the line
of his shoulders.

It seems he hasn't brought his personality with him
tonight. I wonder if he's got his magic . . .

Arthur said I was merciless.

291

Matt begins his routine, manipulates his velvet-draped props and scuffles limply round his strangely proportioned tables, as the stage creaks and heaves.

Black suit, orange waistcoat—I'll bet he's wearing, yeah, the orange socks to match . . . and the ladies and gentlemen adore him—and they adore his newspaper which he will now tear up and restore and then, I suspect, form into a tube and fill miraculously with milk.

This truly is the 1970s—'74, or '76.

And we're all at a sodding birthday party.

Dad, he'd have rocked the place. He had proper patter and style and he could do it—genuinely prestidigitate—I thought that word was so magnificent—he'd throw in an extra pickpocketing, or a levitation, or move that card to where it couldn't be, because you were sure it couldn't be, because you'd looked, you'd concentrated, you'd expected to be fooled and you'd been careful, but there it is: inside the card box you'd covered with your hand for all that time, for surely every minute—you wouldn't be confused about such a simple thing, or about when a trick is started and when it stops.

He would make you amazed.

Yes, he did the kids' stuff mostly, but when he performed for adults—only once in any evening—he'd shake them. He'd move their thinking; not far, but he'd move it. I saw.

And the milk is poured into the newspaper and—goodness—now it's gone.

How absolutely fucking amazing.

If I could make anything I wanted to appear, if I could take the broken and the ripped to pieces and make them whole and show the multitudes that here is a genuine, absolute miracle — would I waste my

292

gifts on newspaper and milk?

And here come the scissors and the bit of dodgy rope.

This is purgatory and I deserve it.

He didn't like Arthur, my dad—and I wanted him to: two men with beautiful voices, strange interests, they should have negotiated an understanding.

Very clear that they wouldn't—how could a dog like an almost-dog? And both of them thinking the other is only the almost-dog.

But I was being optimistic and introduced them.

*Mum was making an effort: first meeting and I've said Arthur's important and I've never brought a bloke here before and me and him, we're braced for dinner—the **finally we have to do this and just bite the bullet, catch it in our teeth, which is a dangerous trick and can kill you** dinner—and she'd got the house pristine and there were fresh flowers and candles and she was treating Arthur like a blacksuitman, a member of the tribe, one that she'd accidentally missed and should know better and that's as friendly as it gets. She made him eat too much dip—he hates dip, but he was also beyond his own skin with the effort of being the gentleman they'd favour: swallowing down this pinky goo and wearing a tie and a suit—blue suit—and taking her hand and kissing it. Dad leaning beside me but not speaking, a palpable shiver in the air around him indicating his need to be sitting in a Mississippi rocking chair, set out on a broiling porch with a shotgun on his knees and ready loaded.*

Which was only the usual fatherly feelings and I think we were aware of that and managing. Dad cared. He was supposed to. He was expecting—just quietly, not getting ridiculously demanding—a presentable wedding with tail coats and hats and photos and his

293

wife in enjoyable tears and then kids and more photos.

Only none of us could make a magic to manage that.

We were sitting down to eat—Mum and Dad and me and Arthur—a cheery four. She'd laid out the posh Christmas place settings, only minus the berries and tinsel and we were not without tension, but working on it. Arthur and I were working, concentrating out into the room harder than we'd thought we could— trying to harmonise with Mum and Dad and each other and to calm things, trying to help. And, on the other hand, it did not help that Arthur was teetotal. He had decided he needed an ultra-clear head always, so no additives or fixes. The teetotal phase came after the gloves. Dad viewed teetotal as peculiar. Christ knows what he'd have said about the gloves.

And early on, the evening still stiff and early on, before we were done with the home-made beef broth, Dad asking him, 'And what do you do, Arthur?'

And Arthur told him the truth.

When he could have said anything and been believed.

Matt shows his audience rope in pieces, rope complete, rope knotted, rope pulled through the neck of a small and unharmed boy.

Tricks for a grandson—Dad was born for that.

The current magician laughing with his audience— an inward, piggy snort of laughter. He's filling his hands with sponge balls—dear God, sponge balls, not even billiard balls—a wilderness of sponge balls and he's snorting and shuffling his feet.

He is terrible.

Which is why they love him, why they will clap when he pushes that long needle through that big balloon— which, to be fair, is moderately tricky when the ship's moving this much.

294

So tricky that he bursts the balloon.

Well, that's fine, though—try again. The audience can wait.

And again.

There are two reasons for watching performances of any kind. They are both human and understandable reasons.

We can come out and see people, members of our own species, excel themselves, transcend expectations, burn in their work. And clearly these performers are bigger and finer and more amazing than we can be, but this is a good thing, this is wonderful, a gift—and maybe they have reached a place where we can go, are the truth of ourselves revealed. Maybe we have in us an equivalent light. They are people and we are people and when we stand up and applaud them, discover that we are standing, have been drawn up by this wonder they've provided, then we are applauding something of which we're a part—we have humility and pride both avid in us and are delighted. We let them heat us into being slightly someone else.

Or we can come out to see people, members of our own species, fail and be uncomfortable, unhappy, deluded, ridiculous, cheap. And perhaps we have been all these things, have felt ourselves be all these things, but tonight the performers suffer and we are safe and more competent and poised than we believe they could be. They are people and we are people and we abandon them. We aren't overwhelmed, uncovered, we get to stay the same and be quite sure we're adequate.

Tonight I am sitting in the second kind of audience. They are why I no longer have a television: too much of the second, not enough of the first. Important not to hate them for being as they are—because they are as merciless as I am and the truth is that they can transcend themselves and blaze, astonish, be amazed—probably have and could still—and, as repeatedly established, their hearts will be broken, perhaps more than once, and at some inevitable point they will cease to exist—they will be a tragedy—these things are certain for them. So they can deserve only tenderness.

But these are the people—and I'm not unlike these people—that I would want Arthur to headfuck—to take advantage of their rigidity and their hatreds and their fears.

And really that's almost saying they're the ones who deserve the best magic: not pulls and cards and linking rings and disappearing women, but eternity and love for ever, loves restored.

I think maybe Arthur imagined my dad would be able to see him that way. As a magician—as someone who offers wonders.

But when Arthur was working he said that his wonders were real—they couldn't be wonders unless he could say they were genuine—and there's only one rule in magic: you can't claim that it really is magic. That's the lie you can never tell.

'Don't bring him back here.' Dad gone from the table and Mum in amongst her best napkins, her nice things, and stricken, but I had to chase my father, find my dad.

He looked the way Francis did about Derek, 'I can't, I can't stop you . . .' the same fury and he's embarrassed for me as well and protective. And he wants to start a fight. 'Can't have him in the house.' But he has no one that he can bear to fight with.

*Don't remember what else he said, but **can't have him in the house**.*

Mum had made the special fish pie with extra veg,

296

and a cherry flan and optional cream and nobody ate it.

She was crying, but I was busy and Arthur was sitting in his car, not gone, but not in the house.

Can't have him in the house.

Dad holding on to my arm and we can't believe ourselves—we've been changed didn't mean to and I have to go and be with Arthur.

Can't have him in the house.

If they could have liked each other, borne each other.

The audience are clapping again. Derek huffs and shifts his legs. Matt Mitchell and his personality have skewered the balloon and yet it remains healthy.

Not even a drop of blood.

Perhaps maddened by his impossible success, Mitchell walks down amongst his spectators, pressing out minor waves of unease—they would prefer him to be neatly far away. He reaches out unsuavely and plucks a young lady out of her seat. She is manifestly fitter and thirty years younger than almost anyone in the house and walks like the kind of dancer who might take part, for example, in a New York Arrival Cavalcade of scenes from popular musicals in just such a venue as this, perhaps tomorrow night.

Matt leads his in-no-way-suspicious companion up on to the unruly stage, mugging and flapping mock applause until he is rewarded with a burst of relieved appreciation: he is back where he should be and the show is no longer a threat. A stagehand trundles out an improbable trunk that's draped with a yellow cloth.

Metamorphosis—that's going to be his finale: an effect which was already boring when his grandfather walked out of the music hall showing it because it was FUCKING BORING.

That's if his grandad took an interest in magic—someone in his family should have . . .

Or not—it doesn't exactly seem to foster functional relationships.

Matt whisks the cloth lumpily away—it is stiffened by a rod that runs along one of its shorter sides—and shows the trunk to his assistant who is amazed by it in the way that women in bad porn movies are amazed by their own and others' nudity: on a kind of big-eyed time delay. He then takes a velvet sack out of the trunk and waves it at her. He tells her loudly and clearly—the way he might speak to a senile relative or a puppy—that she must hold this sack open while he steps inside it and then fasten it round his neck before she shuts the trunk's lid over him and fastens that *very securely.*

Arthur gave me a vibrator once that was sold with a black velvet pouch to keep it in—just like Matt's sack—excuse the doubled meaning—drawstrings you could tie. It was smaller—but still a container for a dick—a fake dick.

That was in one of the London hotels—on the Strand. Our room had a window that looked on to white—a type of light well tiled in white—and he'd been to a sex shop before he arrived, bought stupid things, was in a funny mood: 'You could take this with you and think of me. I know that you won't take me.'

He's never fair.

And nor am I.

The assistant, as instructed, stands on the locked trunk. She holds the yellow cloth in front of her as if the audience have interrupted her while bathing. She attempts to look confused, nervous and sexy—each of these emotions proving too stern a test for her acting abilities. She raises the cloth. The rod

298

inside its top edge allows it to serve as a curtain that hangs sufficiently wide to obscure the trunk, her legs, body, head. Her arms are lifting high and she's swaying on tiptoe along with the general swagger of the ship, of everything. For a moment only the cloth is visible.

A synthetic melody is playing. It grows louder and therefore more sickening.

And everyone wants to see behind the cloth. We can't help it—we're all sure, will always be sure, that what's behind it will be wonderful. It's never quite as good when it's revealed, but next time—then it'll be amazing. Next time the secret will be beautiful.

Bodies under sheets—is that why we do it, put our dead under cover? So then maybe magic will happen and we'll pull back the cloth and look at them and they'll be looking back—restored.

The curtain is let fall and—alacazam—Matt is standing thrillingly on the trunk. More exciting still, when he unlocks that very trunk, his assistant is inside and tied up in the sack. There are whistles and cheers mingled in the applause which Matt dips forward into, bowing open-mouthed, the way that he might dunk for apples. His assistant bows, too—professional about it, forgetting who she's meant to be.

*It's the speed that impresses—how quickly they change places and the man can become the woman and the woman becomes the man—Houdini performed it with his sweetheart—**if you was me**.*

Funny couple, the Houdinis—the Weisses, to be more accurate. No kids, so they just invented one, made him a story between them.

The house lights nag in and obediently the rows of seats begin to empty.

Beth nudges Derek, who has been dozing, when she'd rather he saved unconsciousness for later.

But I don't think he will sleep later.

And I won't be there to know.

Because it stops now.

We stop.

He sniffs, wriggles his shoulders and seems as tender and clean as anyone just woken.

I think what he liked was how unavailable I am. He read it as a complex interior passion, something to be cunningly unveiled.

But pull back the cloth and he'd see—I'm all in pieces, no use.

'Let's get out of here.' He does sound a touch groggy.

And he's the real audience volunteer—a genuine innocent—so no matter what he does, the trick's against him.

They slip themselves in with the last of the crowd, the murmurs and perfumes.

In most paintings of the crucifixion they get it wrong—they show the nails fixed through his palms, when that would never work: you had to be pinned through your wrists or you wouldn't be adequately supported. But the artists understood: blood and metal at the sweet spot, that's what to show—everyone's had a taste of that.

Which isn't going to make what I do to him all right. I am aware of that.

Beth lets them be drifted and bumped towards an exit.

Francis and Bunny will be in their cabin, each one of them with their love, in their love.

'Derek?'

'Yeah.' Short, flat syllable.

300

'Do you like Jimi Hendrix?'

'What?'

'It's OK. Forget it.'

They are outside the theatre by this time, paused on the insistently high-quality carpet and Beth is simultaneously tired, tired, tired and beyond herself, starting to live in another place, somewhere thoughtless and taut, and this makes her unwary.

'You fucking cunt.'

She doesn't expect that Derek will grab her elbow and, loud in her face—not fully shouting, but drawing in wider attention—he will announce, 'You fucking, *fucking* cunt.'

'What?'

'I was *ill*!'

'You were . . . Of course you were ill, I was . . . I was feeding you pills for days.'

The badness of saying this thrumming in her fingers.

'Cunt.'

The foyer unhappy. A boxy-headed man in a dinner jacket jerking his head as if he's been slapped by the first use of *cunt* and—after the second and third—clearly torn between physical intervention and removing his wife from further exposure.

Further exposure to words for a place that she has and an activity to which it has quite possibly been subjected.

'Derek, what are you . . . ?' *But Mr Box would not have called it fucking. He peaked early and now he's lost.* 'There's . . . why are you doing this now?' *He'd never have said cunt.*

Lovely, round, firm name for it—cunt.

Mrs Box might have said it—she has hidden depths— hidden from him—bet she dances alone at parties and

301

scares the shit out of him when he sees her, bet she flirts with waiters.

And why am I reading them when I ought to be reading Derek?

Derek whose colour has risen and thickened, who has lost his dignity, thrown it away—upset much more than angry, eyes wet and large and steady on her, as if he can force her to reveal some strange capacity to strike him, or be poisonous, or a physical abnormality which will prove her wickedness. 'I was ill and you were . . . All today. *All* today. And where have you been all this week?' He wants to point at her and shriek.

He basically is pointing and shrieking. And all the discontented couples loitering to stare because we're obviously much more discontented than any of them.

'I'd wake and you wouldn't be there and you wouldn't be there and I wouldn't know why and then you'd come back and be . . . today, you were—'

'Derek, like you say'—*I am a coward, Jesus I'm a coward*—'You haven't been well. I've been around.'

'A-round?'

We're an extra show for everyone. 'I've been . . . you slept a lot. You don't know—' *They should thank us. We're pretty much as mediocre and predictable a gig as they would like.*

'I *know*!' This a full yell and the crowd fluttering back in case things get genuinely untidy. 'Were you with him?'

They'll send a steward, security—we're letting the side down, being inelegant and not dashingly dressed.

Soft sweater.

'Him? Derek, what does that mean—*him*?'

Soft sweater.

'That old bastard—he was all over you. Is it him?

302

Were you with him?'

'With *Francis*?'

'I don't give a fuck what he's called—is it him? He has a wife. You're screwing a pensioner with a wife.'

I need to be quiet and elsewhere. I need to walk away and leave him and he is giving me every reason to. 'You were rude to his wife.'

'And you're *screwing him*!'

It's not you, it's me. *Does anyone actually say that? Goodbye, it's not you. When of course it is you; if I'm leaving it would obviously be you.*

And me.

Why don't I feel anything?

'Francis has been very kind to me—'

'Yeah, I bet he has.'

This shouldn't be fun—to pace him, and pace him and here's his shoulders in the angle of mine and our feet—not agreeing—but now they do—and feeding him calmness and see if I win. Make him a game and he can't scare me, although he doesn't scare me—I'm not scared, shamed, not anything.

I'm not anything.

'Derek, this is absurd.'

Derek glares at her, but he would rather be pacified and convinced.

'You're being absurd. Francis is married, he loves his wife, he's . . . a nice guy. I don't know what you're talking about.'

And she leads and he follows and slowly, clumsily, they straggle into a lobby, past a winking clutch of lifts. She is taking him away from the scene of his crime and nearer to the scene of hers, while both of them are more or less forcefully ignored—some observers missed out on the previous scene and

303

others are of the opinion it shouldn't have happened and therefore did not.

Can feel a tickle and giggle in some of the bystanders, though. The woman in the tan trouser suit especially— she's hot and wet with speculation and she'll talk. They'll all talk. By tomorrow morning this will be exciting the whole ship: perfectly sordid gossip.

Derek is also aware of the hungry and disapproving pressure set against what he would like to do—he wants the full-tilt drama and then probably a reconciliation. 'You cunt.'

I don't want Francis to know, though—not Bunny and not Francis.

'Derek, do you know what I did today? While you were asleep? Asleep again'—*always classy: blaming the victim*—'I went to the duty free perfume sale on Deck Three—a thrilling experience: village tombola meets *The Poseidon Adventure*'—*lying this much, it gets you light-headed*—'And I had lunch and I read the ship's newspaper for the day and tried learning how to recognise ship's officers according to their epaulettes'—*the story to replace reality, that I will believe so that it will be believable*—'And I had a massage and that meant I could use the pool and the sauna and sit in peace and read a magazine and—yes—they only had magazines for the elderly, talking about how sixty is the new forty and eighty is the new seventeen'—*and he is wishing every word into truth*—'And how to deal tactfully with double incontinence and how to bring cleaning materials with you when you go into hospital so the general lack of hygiene won't kill you'—*I'm being kind, something close to kind*—'This did not make me want to screw a pensioner. And I care about Bunny and I care about Francis.'

304

'Why don't you care about me?' Clean, small words. 'Beth?'

'Wh—?'

And she didn't expect this and hasn't stopped herself from facing him, studying, so that now his pain jumps up at her and sinks clear in.

'Why don't you care about me.' Soft—as if he is tired, tired, tired and would just like to know.

'I . . . Derek . . . I don't want to hurt you . . .'

Which is not a lie.

'Oh, Christ.' And he buckles and she puts her arm around him, as if he is once more sick and she walks him to some chairs by a little window full of nowhere, 'Oh, Christ. I . . .' The wave tops are closer to this deck, the blurs of disturbance flickering and plunging.

'I'm sorry.' *And I am.* 'I'm so sorry.' *Please be angry, instead of like this.* 'I didn't mean . . .'

Derek is sitting with his hands slumped in his lap and he starts weeping, 'Christ.' Making no effort to hide himself, nose wet, tears dripping off his chin.

As if he's five and needs his mum to get him through it.

Christ.

Little knocks of breath shaking him and then a halt and then another wave of losses tearing in him and she can't touch him any more, because that would be unfair.

When every part of this is unfair.

'Derek, you're a good person.'

Beth watching the cliché hit him, set him further adrift in this new place which is unbearable, but where he's still managing to plan and hope that if he breaks, genuinely breaks, shows it, he will be rescued and by her. And she can't let him think this. 'You are, though . . . good. And I'm not. I'm a bad person and a bad person found me and you need a good person and a good person will find you . . . and this is shit . . . this is such shit. I'm ruining you . . .' And he holds her hand—wet fingers, hot fingers, chaos all over them—and he clings while she tells him, 'The last thing you need is me.'

Derek surfacing, gulping, 'But . . . I do . . . But . . . Is there someone? Is there someone? Is it him?'

Impossible to guess if saying she's leaving him for another man will be worse than saying she's going to be with no one. *All done by kindness*—'A long time ago . . .'—*Once upon a time.*—'Me and this guy, we were the same . . . I'm not explaining this well. But don't blame . . . It's not Francis. Please don't speak to him. Or talk to Bunny. Neither of them ought to be upset.'

WOMAN IN FRACAS FINDS HERSELF PATHETIC AND DISTURBING.

'I know if you were yourself, you wouldn't want to upset them.' There's an acid curl of a smile from him—disgust—and he abandons her hand and she lets him start to be alone. 'I know, I know, who on earth ought to be upset, or would want to be upset . . . I am sorry'—*And tell the good lie, at least do that*—'I wish it could have worked.'

'I was going to . . . I was going to . . .' A sort of horror in him and he can't bargain himself free of it, but even so—'I bought a ring . . .' It should be an influential confession.

'Derek, this is terrible, but—as well—you're really tired and run-down and . . . it'll seem worse . . . not that it's . . . Derek, nobody's died.'

And his focus snaps in, boils, 'I wish you fucking had.'

Which is fine. It's good to hear.

306

'Yes. And you're right to and . . . I'll leave you alone. I'll leave . . .' *He has my luggage and I can't go back.* 'I'll be out of your way.' *I'm worrying about my fucking luggage—I am a cunt.*

'Fuck you, Beth. *Fuck* you.'

Stand up and walk. He won't harm himself and he'll recover. Without me, he can be happy. Without me, I could be happy.

But he takes her wrist, pulls, harsh grip, kisses her knuckles—*every time, like punching him slowly in the mouth*—while her fists curl to keep their privacy and he scrabbles, clutches, and she has to tug loose and this is unwieldy and will make him hate himself as much as her.

But later he'll only hate me.

I hope. In the end he should do that and then he should forget, but not forgive because I'm unforgivable.

WOMAN FINDS HERSELF A COWARD, KNOWS SHE WILL BE AGAIN.

There's a man in a doorway. He is leaning at the brink of a bedroom in an unfamiliar flat and it's dark but he hasn't turned the lights on. He has a name, but he doesn't like it, so he's leaving it be.

Outside is Pimlico and it's a Friday evening but quiet because the rain is hammering, punishing down, keeping the weak and the prudent indoors. The man is staring at the pelted window and the mix of lights worming and shattering on it, caught in the loose water: the colours of the shop signs across the street: 24-hour mini-market, Fish and Chick Inn, newsagent, off-licence: open late.

The man is thirsty and cold, maybe hungry, but not taking an interest. What condition his condition is in does not concern him. He may have been leaning for a while, perhaps since this afternoon.

It gets dark quickly—November—uncivilised month.

A siren peaks and slews somewhere to his right—injury, emergency, crime—and then diminishes, disappears while a woman's voice yells. The same voice has been yelling, on and off, for a number of hours. The man has assumed that she is mentally unable not to yell.

Funny area, Pimlico—seems like it's on the way up: calm and cream-coloured Regency perspectives and high-design shops and Dolphin Square—naturally Dolphin Square, the nest of scrimping aristos, MPs and spies and shaggers, singles and nutters and incognitos—could almost be Chelsea, those bits—and then there's the iffy hotels and launderettes—did you ever see a cheery launderette—and sections of street like this one, it's got a grudge this one, off-kilter, an atmosphere of brokenness and bad stuff being done.

Not where you'd pick for your mum to live.

Not that his mother is living any more—she died last Wednesday and is gone now, passed on, called up yonder and out of the way.

She dwells forever in the Happy Summerland.

The man had not seen his mother since—he isn't absolutely certain—but probably 1984. Still, he is her only son—her only child—and so, naturally, he was located and called to identify her body. He wishes she'd had someone else to do it—not to save him the trouble, but to let him feel her life was populated, contained an affection she understood

308

and could accept. But this was what she'd ended up with: his absence and then too late arrival to view a small body, grey body, lesions on the skin. And her poor hair—it had been pretty when he first knew her, she was proud of it—crowning glory, brushed it each night—the tamp of the brush and the dry, long sound of each stroke, he recalls that clearly—her poor hair had thinned and coarsened and become sad.

Terrible to know her at once when she ought to have been unrecognisable. That would have broken her heart.

You're not seeing me at my best.

Medication.

Mental health issues.

And difficulties.

Her flat has the sweet, heavy stink of anxious drinking and is brown, everywhere brown, and there are cigarette leavings, saved newspapers with the crosswords completed neatly and less neatly and very wrongly and tinned salmon in the kitchen cupboards and microwave popcorn—that would have been festive—no guests, no sign of guests—but popcorn, nevertheless, and in the little freezer compartment hunched at the top of the fridge there are ready meals for two. So manifestations of hope. Or hunger.

Still a double bed.

He can't touch it.

Earlier, he packed up her clothes—no resonance in them, nothing to connect with except the sense of colour, a remnant of her style in certain items. It all went to a charity shop where there was conversation—you do have to explain when you bring in so much—about the sad demise.

He found that he couldn't say *mother*—couldn't use the term in public—was convinced it would be thought unseemly that he was so unsuitably far away from her—that her clothes smelled unpalatable—that she wouldn't like it known. So he told the assistants his aunt had died and here was everything.

Held in two bin bags and a cheap suitcase.

Everything.

Once he'd folded and packed her things ready—her effects—he'd made a sandwich. Had to clean the kitchen worktop before he started and then used the hard bread that she'd left, that she'd opened with the same knife he was holding and then left.

You get a proper loaf and you cut it with a bread knife—she never liked the ready-sliced, said it tasted clammy.

Stale bread and home-made jam with a scrawly label that read *blackberry and apple* and a sticker marked 50p.

Christ knows where she got it.

And it doesn't taste like anything except of purple-red and sweetness.

Mildly spoiled butter—it was out on the counter in a dish, had been for days. Cold in the kitchen, though—so it wasn't as ruined as he'd thought.

Small mercies.

And he ate the jam sandwich standing up, making crumbs.

Almost inedible.

Then washed his hands.

Came and leaned in the doorway.

On the 12th of November 1997, my mother died.

Birthday on the 9th of June.

Never knew where to send a card.

And she might not have liked it.

Medication.
Mental health issues.
And difficulties.
*When somebody dies, you're not always sorry, you
don't always want to talk.*

His voice seems scoured, cleaned back to the bones
where it's only pedantic and wary, where it's made
of darts and shadows. 'My turn, is it?' Arthur stands
in his suite's living room watching his windows and
their sparks and flickers of uneasy rain. He's arranged
that one lamp is shining, angled down, which means
the furnishings and special touches guaranteed to
make his suite a home away from home are dimmed
to irrelevance. 'Is it? Me now? Me again? *Lucky me
. . . ?'*

Beth called him from the Purser's desk, but that
was a while ago—she's been walking, the mind of
the ship turning beneath her, and she has kept as
empty-headed as she can, getting ready for this.

Ssssshhh.

To please him. Mainly to please him.

To let him be pleased.

Keeping herself a secret from herself so that she
can manage, be as she must.

*Nothing in me for him to read but what he wants
to find.*

Once she's arrived, it's clear he's been getting
ready, too. He's made sure that she's the one held
in a doorway this time, framed and feeling herself
ugly while the nicely detailed woodwork of the door
nudges her arm and then retreats.

311

He is difficult to see, slightly hunched, head tucked and he keeps beyond the lamplight even when he turns—in a dullish shirt and probably jeans, and barefoot: pale shapes, ill-defined as his moving hands, his face. 'I thought I'd leave it open for you, so you could *just walk in* . . . You needn't shut it— not if you can't be bothered. I have to assume that you'll *just walk out* at some point. It'll be convenient for you if it stays like that.'

'Arthur—'

'I know you always enjoy your symbols—so what does it mean? *Woman in a doorway*. What do you mean?'

Beth stays outside in the passage, the dark space beyond the lintel is tensed against her, thick with him, and it seems that stepping forward would be like walking into water.

'Are you going to come in? Which is to say, what do you want?'

'I . . .'

Sssssshhh.

'Please make up your mind about something, Beth.'

So she breaks the surface and then shuts it round them with a dull snap of the lock. 'I left him.' Three little noises, meanings, they blur and drop in the blinded space while her eyes adjust.

She can hear him rubbing at his hair.

'No. You went to him. I'm the one you left. As usual.'

And she can pick out that he's looking towards her and so she tells him the first truth, 'I said I'd be back.' He should have all of her truths; it will be difficult, but he should. 'I said.' Tell them properly and they won't hurt him, won't want to hurt him,

312

will not be intended to injure anyone.

'You've been hours. It's past midnight.'

'I didn't know that . . . I didn't know.'

'You called me at *ten*.' Little threads of panic in this, which is going to mean that both of them are frightened and their fear will be dangerous—her fear more than his.

Ssssshhh.

So it isn't manipulative or deceptive if she stands and doesn't snap at him and pretends that she's not frightened, is no more than bemused. And inside she plays the trick on herself which means she imagines her pulse as languid, as a tranquil circulation of content and this will fool her and spread to him, because comfort is just as contagious as despair. He would rather be comfortable, comforted—anyone would—so she will be first. There's nothing wrong about this. It isn't the same as with Derek. It matters.

He sits, seems to press in on himself and his shape darkens. 'Are you going to say what you were doing? Or am I not worth keeping up to date—no bulletins on your movements? Or is this another punishment?' He sounds brittle and as if she should touch him, but she can't—not yet—he wouldn't like it. 'Because, I . . . maybe, maybe that would be—if that's what you want. If punishment is what you want . . . We could . . . You and I, we . . . if we're together and this is what you want to do to me, maybe . . . Maybe if I'm allowed to know what's coming then I can agree to it and you can punish me and I deserve it, so that's what we'll do. Is that what you want? If you want to punish me, then you have to be around to do that and I would be sure you were going to be around. That would be a *fact* . . .'

'Arthur—' Easing forward to him in the way she

313

might towards an animal, a fugitive thing. 'We . . . what are you . . . I couldn't do that, you couldn't—'

'Then tell me what I *can* do!' His voice with a tear in it, a boy's voice, something too lost to be borne. 'What can we do?'

As she reaches him there's a confusion, her being clumsy, catching his shoulder, his chair in the way, their arms colliding as he twists to avoid her. 'Don't start that again. Please.' But—accurate, quick—he reaches and traps both her hands in his and turns them sweet side up, kisses each at its heart with a wary mouth, an intelligent mouth, an asking mouth. He gives her the small, sharp presses of his breathing and the sense that he is thinking, puzzling through until he can risk, 'So you saw him and he made some kind of fuss and then you left him. Or you saw him and then you left him and he made some kind of fuss. I would prefer the second . . . And you're happy if I do this . . .' She stands and waits in front of him, her hands lighting, and he restates for clarity, 'My doing this is permissible and not unpleasant for you.'

The sound of touched skin. Lips. Tiny noises. Beautiful. No more to consider than this.

Ssssshhh.

All done by kindness.

Undone by kindness.

'It's not unpleasant for me, no. It's . . . very pleasant. And I'm happy, Arthur. Yes.'

Almost true. Soon could be true.

He keeps on, 'And you're happy if this feels like love? Which is important. Because it is.' Syllables tiptoeing out between the dab and cling of his mouth near her thumb, her wrist, where her fingers part. 'And you made what you did—what we did—the last time you were here, you were making that feel like

314

love to me. And it made me happy when you did that.' He tenses at each point of contact and the small shocks of this travel in her arms. 'When you were here, Beth. When you were here today. With me. Yesterday, now, I suppose . . . When you were with me. I did believe it.' He lifts his head. 'Was I right to believe it? I am right to believe you.'

And the next truth, 'Yes.' Chill on her skin.

A twitch in his grip, 'You're sure?'

'Yes.'

Ssssshhh.

And the breath leaves him, rushes him empty, and Arthur raises her palms to his face and then lets her go, lets her smooth his hair back from his forehead, from his temples, stroke over the crown of his head, while he weathers something that jolts his spine, some internal decision, and drinks in what she knows will seem new and clean air for him, the scent of possible optimism.

He angles and turns his head and she holds it as he does—cradles the weight of what he's had to teach himself and who he's learned to be and where he lives and he leans to press his forehead against her stomach, to rest. She kneads the back of his neck, the tight wire in it, the signs of the fight to keep him steady and operational. And when he breaks off and sits forward she touches his smile, his proper smile.

'Beth? Do you want a seat?'

'No.'

'Do you want to lie down?' All the words shiny with smiling.

'Yes. Yes, I do.'

'Do you want to lie down in my bed?' And the shine thins to a mutter, creeping out, almost beside itself with want—and then the closing rush, 'And you can be naked now and I'll be naked too and we can feel like love, we can do that.'

The ridiculous, naked, ridiculous things we say. Because we feel like love. Which is a terrible word and a terrible thing.

Ssssshhh.

'Yes. We should do that. Let's lie down.'

*   *   *

And they keep his bedroom blank: no lights—edges and furniture offering mild assaults and the darkness tilting and counter-tilting and they are unbuttoning, unfastening—they are apart and then together—her stomach meeting the warmth of his: warm and not afraid, but nervous—as if they are younger, as if they have never—and they fix in a simple hug so they'll know they're both there and both safe before they start again—fingers unbiddable—too numb, too electric—and stumbling out of jeans and then clear of everything.

Everything.

'Come here.' What you always end up saying before you know you have. 'Come here.'

And opening the bed for each other, peeling it back and clambering, kneeling, lying on how smooth it is, letting it sleek them together and into a slow embrace, an exploring embrace—live skins and astonishments and edges—both of them middle-aged, halfway, more than that, the downward slope and not what they were, but more than they were and they taste of each other and of amazement.

And he's holding her breasts, supporting her breasts, as he licks and mouths, tests them with his

316

teeth.

Takes care.

And he suckles until the ache of it draws in her spine, until it's yelling.

Sssssshhh.

Have to take care. Always. Of every mortal thing.

Everything.

She uses fingertips, only fingertips, to chart his back: shoulder blades and the insistent frame, the bone, the sweet purpose in his fabric, moving, and she has met this before, these pieces of Arthur's information, but not known them. They simply became familiar—they weren't known.

The room filling with who they might turn out to be if they'll risk so much newness, nearness, faith, and what they need, might find and the movement of sheets and half-words and mumbles and strengthening breaths and how they shift and roll, lie face to face and halt on their brink, get stung by their forward momentum as it rolls back through them, complains while it eases and slows, but they don't indulge it—little rubs and reminders, but no more, not yet.

Arthur swallows, worries his cheek on the pillow, settles. 'Why wasn't it like this? Before. It was . . . even at the beginning when . . . When we were together, I thought we were so together—I wouldn't have said that anyone could have been more . . . It wasn't like this, though. And, I mean, thank you, but . . . When did you start hating what I did? Was that it ? When did you start hating me? It must have been the whole time, almost the whole time . . .'

'I didn't hate you.' *True. But not enough true. He ought to have all of the true.* 'Eventually I did. But

317

not really . . . And I didn't hate what you did. I was doing it, too . . . I loved it—the first year, maybe longer—it was . . . there was that one part of it that was always so . . . being *in* other people, *being* other people, feeling into who they are and how they are—and being with you and that close to you and . . . but . . . No, I couldn't stand what it meant—if I thought about it—I couldn't stand what it was. So I didn't think about it. I would tell myself *Ssssshhh* and I would concentrate on what I expected would happen which was that I genuinely thought eventually someone would stand up at some evening, some service, some gig, and say—"This is ludicrous, this is obviously, obviously fake, nobody sane could take this seriously or trust it, and you are a fraud—you are both frauds and you can go away now and stop."'

Beth brushes his shoulder, his arm, because he is too still, as if he is going away in himself. She needs his company or she can't continue. 'I assumed it would be stopped. From the outside. Kind of. I avoided doing anything about it myself by hoping we'd be prevented. But no one said a word. Nobody didn't believe. So many people, so hurt—they're not sane, not in the places we get into—they're not going to unmask us, kick away their sole support—that would be making them eat what's left of themselves alive. And we weren't big enough to get the sceptics turning up and throwing their weight around—they couldn't be bothered: not enough profile in it for them. No one was going to intervene and you were . . . committed. The enquirers, they had nothing else, nothing but us and we were less than nothing, we were giving them less than nothing. And then the money was getting serious. We were earning a living out of it, turning big. I couldn't deal with that.'

True.

She eases her knee a touch between his, because this should remind him he's beautiful—it's not to keep him from paying attention, not to obscure what she means, 'I didn't hate you, but when we were together and like this, you felt as if you were working and I was work—like when you'd take off those fucking gloves and then you'd undress . . . like you were going swimming or something—just *fast*—just business—not that you weren't excited, but . . . not about me. Even after you'd finished with wearing the gloves. It didn't seem to be about me. Not that you'd have to be about me, but . . . And not that I didn't still . . . We'd start and the whole of you would be listening, but not like this—it would be like a gig. You were—I'm not saying this is true—but I thought you were turned on by practising—by reading in so close—and I was another gig. Like I was a rehearsal.' Her arm tight over his waist and paying attention. 'I'm sorry.'

'No.' His voice fragile again, young. 'I'm sorry.'

'I'm not a good person. I didn't give it up and leave because I was trying to be a good person . . . I was lonely, Art. That's what it was.' And she pulls her arm in tighter, so she won't lose him. 'But I could have done . . . something. I wasn't sure. We got so fucked-up . . .'

'I made you lonely.'

'You didn't mean to.'

'I made you lonely.' He kisses her forehead, eyes. 'But you're not lonely at the moment?'

'No.'

'Tell me if you are. Because . . . I can't get it wrong again and you have to *tell me* if I'm heading that way and . . . I can . . . improve. If I know—can

319

attempt to, possibly not, but I'd have the chance . . . I mean what is the point of us both over-thinking if we can't get any use out of it.' And he kisses her again. 'I'm sorry. I'm very sorry.' With a kind of furious searching: face, neck, collar bone, breasts.

Beth has no answer for him until he slows and she can meet his mouth with her own and—*true*—'I'm not lonely. And I don't think I will be. I think it's all right.'

And something scrambles in her chest to be nearer than she is to him, to be fastened—arms straining with being so very hard fastened—and round his breathing.

He tells her, 'Yes. Hello. Yes. It's fine. Yes. It's fine.' Until she can be more sane, less almostpainful and Arthur clears his throat and quietly offers, 'But the work—my work—that is a problem. Currently. And permanently. We know that. I know that . . .' He draws one finger down—slow, slow, slow—finds her nipple, begins to wake it. 'I know that . . .' It's easily woken, grows fretful for him, but then he relents. 'Sorry. Mustn't distract—we have to concentrate . . . No hiding. Not the way we do. Because at the moment we should . . .' He leans the next sentences in, careful. 'It has to be only the scary type of thinking—one thing at a time and *about what we need it to be about, not running off*. Because I do that and you do that, too and . . . we won't. No distractions. Not at the moment. So I won't lie here and feel this and just . . .' He brushes the crown of her nipple. 'Except for feeling it then. Checking it's OK . . . You distract me. A lot. But this of you mustn't distract me from the rest of you . . .' A grin in this, an ease.

'Or vice versa.' Because she agrees and because

320

it's true.

So no more thoughts than necessary. Which is good.

One thing at a time and about what we need it to be about.

Not everything.

Everything would be too much.

Which suggests to her that she's being distracted by how she shouldn't be distracted, 'I mean, I want to talk.' But there are worse things.

Ssssshhh.

'And I want to talk, Beth. I do. And I have to behave. Not get disgraceful . . . I do love you being here, though—if I haven't said. I do.' Then she can feel him focus, still himself. 'I didn't know the work was between us when we were like this—or not like this, not as together as I imagined—but in this position and I am sorry. I've said I'm sorry . . . but I am additionally sorry for that. At least it shows I wasn't reading you. It shows I was paying no bloody attention at all. So sorry.'

'Or else I was too good at hiding.'

Ssssshhh.

'Well, we both aren't going to hide any more. And so . . . I want to ask you, if you don't mind, I do want to ask you . . . please don't—if I can ask—two things—please don't ever be—if I can use the word—*polite* that way again. Do tell me when I've screwed up. I'm repeating myself, but do tell me . . .' And a sense that he is calculating a drop now, judging if he will be harmed when he jumps and, 'Second thing—if this isn't what you want any more—if I'm no longer required—and you have to go, please say so and then go. Don't, please, do the slipping away thing and seeing whoever is next and pretending you're still with me. I'm not saying that

321

you would, but you might want to be kind—you are kind—but please don't let me think you're with me and we're together when we're not and you're also with somebody else. You've been slipping away to me all these years and it's the last thing I can comment on, or complain about . . . it kept me going . . . But if you do that to me, then . . . Sorry, no ultimatums—no ultimata, whatever the word is. Just, please, just, don't hide it when you're going—*if*—if you're going. I'm not criticising, I'm not . . . it's a skill, that kind of hiding, not a moral failing, and I'm not saying it's a failing of yours, or that it's habitual—it's my fault, in fact, if anybody's, in a way . . . it was circumstances . . . But please just don't, though . . .'

'I won't.' *True.* 'I promise.' *True.*

'You don't have to promise.'

'But I am. And I think I do have to.' And she feels in him how his body is restless with driving to be precise and to keep his emotions tidied away from hers and leave her free, unpressed. The gentleness in this bright against her. 'Arthur—' And if he can be precise, brave, and they are alike and with each other and together and they have love and are in love, are inside love, then it ought to be possible for her to tell him everything. Her everything.

Ssssshhh.

But he prevents her confession with his own and she lets him.

Because I am a coward.

True.

'You should know, Beth—what I do . . . It's insufficient, it's only a gesture, but something with me has become habitual . . . It developed. That is, I'm more insane than you might suppose . . . I

322

presume you do suppose that . . . You should. And I live incredibly well, unnecessarily well, and I'm used to it and I wouldn't want to lose that. I give some of the money away—of course I do—but I don't give it all away—easy to forget that you didn't have money, very hard not to remember that you did . . . I've seen that. The refugees, some of them . . . losing your money, it isn't like losing a relative, a love: but it's being less, having worse health, bad food, fewer freedoms—it is losing a part of yourself. A partial death. For them it's . . . it can eventually kill them . . . Me—fuck . . . I'd miss the boats, the tailors, the pretty hotels . . . that type of selfishness . . .' And he strokes his knuckles absently across her stomach, there's no intention in the touch. 'And . . . I'm not trying to make a point with this, but if I kept on with the work—and I did keep on with the work because it made me money and it makes me money and because I believe in it, some of it, some elements I can render acceptable to myself—if I kept on with it, then I understood that I couldn't have you—I would only get whatever you decided you could bear, the number of days you could cope with, or that you sneaked away from whoever was saving you from me . . . um, an occasional . . . well, I'd get an occasional fuck. Sorry, but that. I'd be an occasional fuck. And I believed, as I've said, in the work, but I also believed that the work is a terrible thing, so I decided I should pay for it and there's this . . . there's a plant called Jack in the Pulpit—I even enjoyed the name . . . This plant, it grows big, dark, glossy, tropical-looking leaves and in the autumn there are clumps of berries—orangey-red packs of berries at the end of a single stem. I see them growing when I'm upstate in New York and

323

brain-fucking people who are pleasant and very grateful to me while I'm earning my comforts and my stock tips and my little gifts—there are the Jacks in their pulpits: watching, growing, building up to the autumn. I always make a trip over then and I don't see anyone. I don't consult. I go and I'll pick the berries and I take them back to my hotel—to the Carlyle—where they look after me and are used to me and what I like and the guys on the door and in the lifts, they shake my hand and call me Mister Arthur, because that's friendly and respectful at the same time—first name, but I'm also a Mister—and I go to my suite, which has very pleasant views down on to Madison and 76th and I wash the berries, because they've been outside and you can't be too careful and then I sit on the sofa and I take one and I chew it. And it hurts me. If you chew the berries, they hurt. If you touch them, they sting your fingers. They contain oxalic acid and in your mouth they burn like fuck.'

'Art.' A bleak turn in her stomach and then angry with him, outraged. 'Arthur—'

'Ssssshhh.'

'Arthur.'

But, 'Ssssshhh.' And he shakes his head and is placid, factual. 'They burn. Certain indigenous nations would use them to poison their enemies: give them spiked meat, because it does act as a poison. Or peoples used it as a trial, an ordeal. I was told that . . . I'll chew a berry but I don't eat— you mustn't: the acid causes inflammation and the swelling in my throat could choke me, so I avoid it, because I don't want to die. I want to be in pain. That is, I don't want it, but I should have it. I punish my mouth. I say bad things, so I punish my mouth.'

324

Beth sets two fingers on his lips and cannot imagine, does not want to imagine how he has been living, how he has governed and ruined his days. 'Don't do that again.' His soft mouth, the soft of his mouth.

'It helps.' Words on her fingers, between her fingers. 'Then I wash my mouth with milk.'

'Don't do it again. Arthur? I want you to promise me that you won't do it again.'

He turns and frees himself to speak, 'That's . . . Yes . . . I can't. I can't do it again. If you don't want me to, I can't, Beth. If you don't want me to I can't do any of it again. I can't have anything in the way any more—there has to be you and . . . I'm giving it up, Beth. I'm retiring. Early retirement.'

'You wouldn't be happy. You'd miss it. If you still worked . . . I could deal with it. I could . . .' A misuse of her mouth.

'You wouldn't deal with it—you might tolerate it, but then eventually the tolerating would wear you out and you would leave me and I can't . . . I couldn't . . .'

His knuckles drift lower and she wishes them lower still, because otherwise this is hearing him tear down his life for her, hearing him offer everything, and how can she reciprocate and this morning is a beauty for them and it should be that they can have the beauty and Arthur can be here and happy and allowed it and she can be here and happy and allowed it with him and they can be uncomplicated.

Surely that isn't a criminal possibility.

Beth shifts her hips a fraction and he responds. *Beautiful.*

Beth feels his thinking glide until his thumb is tracing back and forth to the root of her thigh while

325

his fingers reach into the hair and tease, press—once, twice. But then he simply moves to hold her waist, snugs words beside her ear—there's a heat in them, but his need to explain is hotter. 'This lady called Peri—a few others like her, but especially I have Peri and I can't just cut her off and I can't tell her what I am, that I've lied for all these years. It would kill her. I'm not being dramatic, I'm almost certain that's what it would do and I can't risk it. I like her the best and I do the worst things to her and I have made her need them . . .' His thumb makes tiny arcs at the small of Beth's back, requesting, irreversibly interested. 'But I can, I can . . . I won't frighten her any more. I'll tell her that everything's fine and that she's protected permanently. But that will involve an amount of convincing. And she'll miss her husband, I would have to . . . I'll have to keep seeing her. She wouldn't understand if I just went away. It would take a while to finish, if you'd allow that.' And then his hand gives in, returns to her thigh and then runs and seeks and slips, it grazes the furrow that will mean there is no more thinking, only opened distraction, only themselves. His fingers prove her wet, let her be wet, make her wet and prove her wet and round and round. 'That's . . . that's for in a minute, though.' Before they calm, brush so faintly they are almost absent, so faintly that her mind aches and yelps with trying to feel them, have them more. Which he understands, 'Beautiful. For in a minute.' And chooses to ignore.

Beth needs to see his face, but they aren't going to turn on the light.

Ssssshhh.

So she tastes his mouth again—tender place, clever

place, hurt place—and he continues, 'Some of them—the ones I've used for money—they'll still want to talk to me and I can not take their money— make them think it's to do with purity, or something . . . that it's no longer pure if I do it for cash. I've . . . But I would have to keep . . . There would be maintenance—especially for Peri. Closing it down would take so long . . . Christ, Beth. I don't want to harm them.'

And she's moving for him, lifting as he plays in the groove of her, flickers a spark and then down, precise, and pushes in, clean in and, 'How many fingers am I holding up?' She can hear his purr—and his smile—Arthur happy because of her.

Like him happy.

Love him happy.

Feel in him the way he's dancing, close to the surface, the boy who's dancing, the man who's dancing—full of happy.

'How many fingers?'

'One.'

'And now.'

'Two.'

'And we won't do three because three is a crowd and two is absolutely perfect. Two is just exactly right. And I'm sorry, I can't talk any more except about you and this and that it's perfect. Can't tell you anything else about anything else. Can't. Should, but I can't. Hiding.'

'We can hide.'

True.

'Sorry, Beth.'

'I'm not sorry.'

True.

'Hiding my fingers first . . . I like it when you hide

me. Good place to hide. Best place to hide . . . But if you won't hold still, you'll end up coming. You know that. You do know that. And if I keep doing this. Then you'll come. Would you like that? Would you like to come round my fingers? I take off my shirts with those fingers, stir my tea, they get all about the place. And. Right. Up. You. That's their favourite. They love that.' Good hands, always good hands, speaking and dirty hands, fucking dirty and fucking extraordinary and in tight with the strength of his voice. 'And I'll love looking at them and thinking: Beth came round those fingers—we started all over again and we started with her coming and that's a good thing—she had a nice come, she had a lovely little come round those fingers—want you to come round my fingers, Beth—so it gets in my bones—and you've been wanting it for ages—and all today—it was such a bad day, love—not bad now, though—and you should have a come and I've been wanting it . . . I have . . . I have . . . Or maybe . . . If I take these away and just . . .' And the beautiful leaving, the withdrawal, almost enough, but not, 'Oh, I'm sorry darling, were you nearly there and I stopped . . . That's such a shame, Beth, when you were very close. You were. You were really very close to such a nice come.' While he folds and rolls with her, holds, sways, the small warm tic of amusement where he's neat against her. 'And then I don't let you . . . that's really very inconsiderate of me.' Almost unbearable against her. 'But there's always the possibility that we could do this instead.' And the rock of the bed and the rock of the room and his weight on her and he's feeling out and finding out his way, looking and shifting and the blunt nudge and here's itself and searching and playing and the in and in and in, and the rock of him, 'And that's because I love you and that's because I love you and that.'

Flare in the skin where it works and knows and learns and wants and parts and she bites, doesn't know where she bites him and he shudders while she does and then speeds, is driving, arches his neck before he catches himself, soothes back, is sly at her cheek while he feeds her his fingers, lets her taste herself, 'Which is gorgeous—the way you taste.' He draws in a breath between his teeth, 'Oh, makes me want to fuck you. Makes me want to screw you so much. Makes me want this. Making love. Makes me want making love.' His pace lifting for a thought before, 'You're quiet, though, Beth. Why quiet? Leave my fingers.'

Which keep the mouth from speaking, from going wrong, from everything.

'Leave them, Beth—'cause it's turning me on too much . . . And I need to think. I think I need to think.'

*Almost unsurvivably arousing, the tiny idea of calling him **darling**.*

'Speak to me, Beth.'

If my absence would please you, I'd disappear.

I'd have to go.

But I can't go.

So she says to him, 'Darling.'

He flinches. Happy flinch. 'Good word. Like that word. Can I kiss you?'

''Course.'

And he does, licks the taste of sex under her tongue. 'You happy?'

'Yes.' Blurring into him, flexing to meet the clean length of his body, how he is opened and home, and she fits her legs close round his waist, catches him and the way he's himself, is the whole of Arthur and delivered and here. And she whispers—simpler to say when it's smaller, 'You make me happy.' She whispers so they can dream each other and not be disturbed, 'And you're my darling.' They could walk off the boat in New York as a couple: true and changed and joined. They should be able to do that. 'I dream you. I dream this, I dream all kinds of . . . I dream you. I learned you, Art. I learned you and I dreamed you and when I'm away—when I was away—I kept you. I could feel you.'

And here's the leap in his spine, this delight in him—milksweet thing—that's fast and faster and deep in his lungs and the hook and the kick and the cleverness of his hips, and when he whispers, 'D'you want to come, Beth? D'you want to come with me in you, because this is me in you, this is me right in you, this is my cock and it's in you and I love you and come with me. I do love you.'

And you know his sweat, new sweat, and he knows you, he allover knows you, knows you wet and you know him dancing, know him inside naked and here and here and here and here and here and he's here and you're here and here and here and here, you're fucking here, you're fucking here, all here.

They shiver after.

Slowly the ship's din coming back and the swing of the bed and who they are and not being each other, only themselves, but also each other, this excellent bewilderment.

He curls in behind her and is dapper, nuzzled. He allows himself a sigh, reaches and winds his arm around her and under her breasts. 'I love you, Beth.'

The ridiculous, naked, ridiculous things we say.

'And I love you.'

And Beth is certain that he should have and see and know everything—all that's left. The whole story.

Everything.

True.

True.

True.

Put it in his wonderful head—give him what's ugly, what's me, like hitting him, like making him bleed.

Sssshhh.

My darling.

I can't.

I can't do that.

So I shouldn't take his hand and shouldn't kiss him. I can't have what I don't earn.

'I love you. I love you, darling. I love you, Art. I love you, Arthur Lockwood. I love you.'

Burns in the mouth, burns like fuck. Never said it so much and it burns me.

But I do take his hand and I do kiss him.

Sssshhh.

There's a boy sitting outside his bedroom, leaning against the wall, one knee bent high and his other leg extended across to the opposite side of the passageway. He is staring at his shoes which are off-white Converse All Star Hi-tops. He bought the trainers for himself and enjoys them—the way they seem cool and also seedy and also laughable: when he wears them he gets close to being all those things on purpose and can own himself. Before, when he was really a child, people would peer down at his feet—his long, long feet—and say, 'You'll grow into them, then.' And he got tired of it. This is better— being his own joke—tall and getting taller, bigger, like a threat.

The boy is quiet, perhaps listening, hands loose on the carpet to either side of his hips as if he is consciously controlling them, not making fists. Inside his room there are the sounds of his mother breaking things.

This happens.

It is not his fault.

It is not her fault.

Every six or seven months it is now simply necessary. She has to destroy as much of what he has as she can find.

So he tries not to acquire belongings, or else makes them disappear, slides them under floorboards, buries them in taped-up boxes—but the best is not to bother with them in the first place. For some reason, she doesn't damage what he wears and carries with him. And the stones he has kept from the island she only throws about and hasn't broken, although his favourite is always in his pocket, just to be sure—the one with the brown and mauve and sepia wood grain, the beach agate. For luck.

He is waiting for her to be finished. Then she'll go and cry in the kitchen and he'll tidy up.

He takes the pebble and holds it like a wish. He lends it his heat.

He doesn't know that in thirty years' time he will be in Pimlico and it will be raining—will have poured all night—and these days he will be mainly Mr Lockwood, not so much Arthur and almost never Art—only one person will call him Art and she will not be with him.

And he will be standing in a sodden jacket at the pavement's edge, his feet in amongst all the wandered colours of the shop signs, the confusions of light, and he will be holding a jar, lending it his heat—dark blue enamel bands laid around turned brass that shines vaguely as it tilts in his hands—it looks like a prop, a suspicious container for onstage skulduggery. But Mr Lockwood will have no audience, no one to see when he unscrews the lid and empties the jar into the gutter and the fast, thick flow of water and of darkness.

It won't make Mr Lockwood happy to tip her away and then set down the urn, wait until the rain has washed his hands a little and then walk, leave her. He may have the sense there is something troublesome he needn't carry any more—but it might only be that he's rid of the urn: heavy thing and awkward, solid metal, respectful option, quite expensive.

Coddling the stone warm in the heart of his palm, the boy shouldn't know this—it would scare him. It's nothing he ought to be able to predict.

If this book had been with him, could be with him—company for him and the blue of it resting faithful against his skin—then he couldn't be allowed

333

to read it, not yet.

So naturally he would want to read it, because forbidden things are always best. Looking under the cloth, the sheet, behind the curtain, to see and find the tricks of things—he can't resist that. Human beings love to look and he is a human being.

Last time his dad came back they'd make trips to a wax museum—not a good one—a dusty, small place—the clothes on the models didn't fit, and everywhere had this sour, strange smell that almost suggested the use of remains: true body parts, hidden beneath the wigs and unconvincing surfaces.

The room for horrors was most popular, the fullest on Saturday mornings: it had a guillotine equipped with victim and operator and an Inquisitionist and there was Jack the Ripper, Sweeney Todd—all these glint-eyed figures who worked with death, could treat it with familiarity, let it in. And beyond them was a curtained doorway—greasy red velvet and a sign that said no one should pass through it unless they were over eighteen.

The boy is not over eighteen.

So his dad wouldn't let him go in—avoided that corner on each visit. But then the old man fucked off again, his goodbye very final, desperate, and accompanied by sad offers of money and advice and Arthur not happy about this—except that he spent a bit of the cash on his shoes and afterwards he went to the museum by himself and slipped in behind the velvet and was where he should not be and got educated.

He'd guessed it would be about shagging, whatever was being kept from him, and he wasn't quite mistaken. He stepped inside to face rows of bleached-out medical models: elucidations of sexual diseases, the pitfalls of pleasure: blisters, rashes, pockmarks. It was disappointing and repulsive—the worst of what human beings could be, their destroying. The worst he knew then.

'I went back, though.' Arthur Lockwood with Beth and telling her the waxworks story and there's full, grey day at the suite's windows and outside in the corridor the speakers are carrying their captain's last announcement—Manhattan tomorrow and it's been such a pleasure having them aboard.

Beth and Arthur have turned on the lights so they can see: blushed skin and busied and pulled and stroked hair—resting now—and lovers' faces—still almost the faces they had in dreaming—and plain white sheets, surrendered sheets—and Beth beside the man who is not being Mr and not being Arthur—who is being Art for her and here and over eighteen and stretched across his bed, in his bedroom, in his suite—which she supposes has become their bed and bedroom and suite and which is balanced on the ocean's skin, swaying on almost three miles of water that's relentlessly beneath them while she looks at him.

We love to look.

'I went back.'

'I know. You would.' And Beth not long awake and Art having laid himself flat, setting the back of his head just below the finish of her ribs. His weight and his thinking press at her breath.

'Of course you'd go back, Art. Can't leave well enough alone, you . . .'

'You weren't saying that earlier.' He glances along at her. 'You weren't saying anything of the kind earlier.' And he reaches his hand out to be held.

And she holds it. 'Earlier is why this bit gets to be

romantic. I think. Maybe. All new to me.'

'Not really my area, either.' He repositions his shoulders slightly. 'This *is* romantic. I would say. Because I would also say—am saying—that having to look is almost always like that—at least disappointing: you go past the curtain, or you lift off the cloth and there aren't any wonders—the secret's no use, or it doesn't exist, or it's terrible and you shouldn't have to see.'

'I know.'

'I know you do . . . But *your* secret—under *that* sheet—not that you currently are under that sheet, but there were rare occasions when you have not been completely naked or covered in me . . .' And he shifts his head so that his cheek is by her hip, blows softly, lends her his heat. 'What was I . . . ? I got distracted again.'

Although she has her own heat: 'No mental discipline, Art—that's your problem.'

'Yeah . . .' He pushes out a dry breath, his almost-laugh. 'That's my problem . . .' Then he turns back from her. 'My point was . . . there are occasions when you are very covered in very many ways . . . But I have worked out your secret . . .'

Ssssshhh.

In his lazy voice, early morning voice, unprotected voice, 'Which is that you're more beautiful than you'll let anybody know.' He squeezes his hand round her fingers, 'But I found you out.' Meeting her eyes directly, plainly.

Sssssshhh.

And she's the one who sits up to stare across at nowhere, a numb wall. 'No.' While she thinks that she wants to save this afternoon, loop it and stay in it and never move on to what comes next. 'The secret

336

is that you have no idea what I'm like for the rest of the time. You only ever see me when I'm with you.'

'No—'

'Yes. And often I have not been . . . but I've been all I could . . . I mean, I've been uglier elsewhere.'

'And elsewhere, ugly is all I can be.' He sits up in the nice wreck of their bed. 'Sorry. That's . . . That really isn't romantic . . . It's just that—in Pimlico I didn't *feel* anything. I feel with you. I always feel with you . . . it hasn't always been . . .' He goes for the diplomatic choice, polite as a stranger. 'There has always been feeling available even if it hasn't been positive. But there was nothing then. For my *mother*.' He says the word as if it comes from another language: a strange, demanding country. 'Nothing at all until I was—sorry to . . . but I'd gone to London for work . . .'

'You don't have to keep apologising.'

He twitches his head, but doesn't contradict. 'Anyway. This guy had got hold of my number—I'm still not sure how—and he kind of didn't want me and he also kind of did.' Art taking her hand again, keeping it. 'His name was supposed to be Drazan . . . I have no idea if that was true—didn't seem it—and he kept telling me that he had a ghost. And what exactly I'm supposed to do about a ghost, I can't imagine . . . wave a bible at it . . . This is not stuff that I do. And his ghost lived in his flat in Talbot Road—it didn't break things, it didn't move things, it didn't appear—he just knew it was there— and his girlfriend had left him because of it . . . Naturally . . . I nearly couldn't be bothered, but I was in town anyway, so . . . We meet in a pub opposite his building and he's fucking me about immediately.

It's a quiet and early pub—all bleach and last night's piss—and he's fucking me about in it, nearly giggling and talking shit, very nervy and clearly a wanker . . . but I also know . . . I *know* . . . he *does* have a ghost. He's telling me, but *not* telling me and he doesn't *need* to tell me, because of his face—what it's saying—because I have the same face—his ghost isn't a child, or a man, or his sister, or a lover, or a friend—it's his mother. His mum. I know what a bad son looks like.' Art's thumb fussing, thrumming over her knuckles, back and forth. 'He didn't like her and then something happened and he's not sorry, except he is—because he knows what happened, what killed her—doesn't need me to tell him, doesn't want me to tell him, because it was shameful—it was so bad that he thinks it shames him. He was a narcissistic bastard. Like me . . . He kept me there until lunchtime, till the place was full of punters—not our kind of punters, just . . . punters. Eventually I just said, "It's your mother. They shouldn't have done that to her. It was wrong, it was absolutely wrong." That's all I said.' The colour of his professional tone there, authoritative and gentle—the most effective blend—a flicker of who he can make himself be—and then it's gone and he's only Art, sheets gathered at his waist, thin shoulders, the long arms and their sensitivities, their tensions.

If you weren't sensible, didn't study him enough, then he would probably seem weak. But he never is. Things hurt him because he allows them to, because he wants that.

Doesn't mean I should help them to hurt.

Sssssshhh.

He waits, heaves in a long breath, then. 'I've had other Bosnians, Croatians, some Serbs . . . of course—anywhere like that and eventually, I get them, get the grief—but I wasn't up to speed—mainly because I didn't want the job and I didn't trust him and I didn't like him, so I hadn't prepared. I intended to be unimpressive, but then he's . . . it's like this . . . this rancid taste that's . . . it's permanently there—it stains what he eats—I can see it on him—and he's so angry and so scared and so disgusted with himself and it can't be touched, or cured and . . . and it's not unfamiliar.' He closes his eyes, then gives her their blue when he opens them again. 'And I bounced him those three sentences—banal sentences—and he let go—spilled the lot. I was there until bloody dinner time. This woman he hated and hadn't seen in years, but he's found out they took her away from her house in Donji Grad—I remember, you know I remember, I have a mind that keeps the details—and she was held in the rape camp at Doboj, in the Bosanka factory. And the rest is self-explanatory. And it also lives in his flat . . . She was called Merima . . .' Art frowns at the air ahead of him, seems absent, or forsaken.

So she pulls him in and down with her until they are lying again, but he turns on to his back and faces the ceiling and, 'I was home and clear of him, clear of it by the end of the week—on the island. On the first day back I headed over La Coupee, kept on and then into the Pot—it's this tiny, closed-up bay and it's my place—it's mine. And all the way there along the cliffs the sea was unnatural—was beyond stillness, so flat you could see the grain of the water, its true nature—like an agate, all these blues, and every boat that crossed would leave this trail, this mark like a finger writing on glass. You could see all of where they'd been—they wrote it out for you to read.

'But you weren't there, Beth. And I dropped into the bay—it has these big walls—and then went out through the new gate—I call it the new gate. There used to be a single tunnel that let you leave, but a fresh one's opened since I was boy. There's been an additional collapse. It was a low, low spring tide and I ended up standing on the shore where there should have been feet of water, was way out amongst things I never should touch. I ought not to be able . . .'

There's no particular change in how he's resting, how he speaks, only this knowledge that he is, somewhere, fracturing and no longer minds. He will be undone with her and expects her to be kind.

'And the ravens are complaining at me—there's a pair that nest round there and they're up and shouting, grumbling—and the sun silvering their backs and I don't want them worried, because they're my favourite—not 'cause they're underworld birds, the Other Dimensions thing—because they're clever and like small, flying people—and they worry the way that people do and so I sit—and when they settle down and stop talking—they do almost talk—I can hear them flying. It's so quiet that I can hear the air pulling through those fingers at the tips of their wings. I'm up on my best rock and sitting and then they've settled too—they've landed and mewed a bit longer to each other, but now they're satisfied and the only noise that's left is in my head. It's this impossibly wonderful morning. And you're not there. You're not beside me and not saying how hot the stones are, or looking at the glitter in the quartz, or . . . and why should you be . . . There was no reason for you to be there.'

And she has never seen him cry, not in more than

340

twenty years—all the times stolen out of more than twenty years.

But today he does. 'And it's about you, but then it's her and . . . she was so sad . . . My mum, she was sad the whole time. And . . .'

And she kisses this other salt of him and, 'Ssssshhh.' And this makes him worse and his hands are wrong, lost, needy and he's labouring and broken back to the noises of a boy, back to the heart, and they hold each other and she can read, can feel the cold and deep and wrong shifting in his chest. It stings her where she touches him.

'I'm sorry, Art. I'm sorry.' And he shouldn't have to be this way, not for anything, should always be defended against it. 'I'm sorry.' Anyone who loves him would take care of that.

*   *   *

He's better once they've slept again and gathered themselves. And it seems to Beth that he's made a decision, some large undertaking around which he is building, a man at work.

Arthur leans just inside the bathroom. 'You don't mind, do you—if we don't do the two-in-a-bath thing . . . ? It's quite a small bath.'

'And it would be too much like how we were.' Beth not wearing Arthur's shirt for the same reasons— nakedness seeming more straightforward.

'There's that—yeah . . . There's that.' Arthur wearing the not-that-luxury robe provided with the toiletries and towels. Its sleeves are short enough on him to be comical, which he notices her noticing. 'It's one size fits all and the one size is not my size. They don't make allowance for the more elongated

341

gentleman.' And because this could be rude he is smiling, but only a little, because they can also ignore the doubled meaning and because he is comfortable with himself.

Eventually, they dress—Beth in yesterday's clothes, which remind her of yesterday and complications— and then they eat an extensive breakfast, served by Narciso with an exemplary lack of surprise. He is purely benevolent, attentive. The suggestion that he should call at another cabin, perhaps with a steward or two to help him, and repossess the lady's belongings, rescue her baggage and bring it back is something he treats as if it were commonplace.

Beth's stomach doesn't like the idea. 'We shouldn't really ask him to do that and Derek could be . . .'

'Derek won't be anything if they go in mob-handed. It'll give him something else to resent, which will help him.' His mouth dainty round this unpleasantness. 'I'm not absolutely callous to say so. I'm being practical. It won't be fun for Narciso and I'm sorry for that.' Arthur considers some porridge and a fruit plate with brutally ornate garnish. 'You do need your things. You need clothes. Unfortunately. And if we buy a new wardrobe onboard you'll disembark looking like a colour blind dowager or a ladyboy with troubled self-esteem—those are the only options they provide. It goes without saying— although I am saying it—that I would still love you whatever you were wearing, but I feel both those options would be undignified.' He perches a celery baton behind his ear like a pencil, perhaps to make up for having little appetite.

'You're cheery.'

''Course I'm cheery. Entirely.' He grins at the fruit. 'I've got what I want.' And he closes his eyes, the

342

grin becoming private—as if Beth is his secret, as if he keeps her even from herself.

They pour each other coffee, exchange dishes, Art picking at bread, but clearly enjoying their domesticity. 'You'd think we'd been doing this for years.'

'We sort of have.'

'No we haven't.'

'No. We haven't.'

'It agrees with us, though. Pass the milk, could you?' He's playing—maybe the doting husband on holiday, the familiar man, the permanent fixture. And it does agree with him: deft with his cutlery, sitting up straight in a fresh fawn shirt, immaculate brown suit—enjoying a little formality—bare feet to say he's at the seaside.

Beth reads him the ship's newsletter for their day— the last before New York—and they agree to be unconcerned that they have not attended the Detox and Weight Loss Seminar, or the Improvers' Bridge Class, or the Singles Coffee Morning.

'Won't be needing that.' A tiny sharpness when he says it.

'We could go and be smug.'

'It's a while since I was smug . . .' Arthur pours himself more tea—they have a choice of three beverages—and looks up when he's done and is shy for her. 'I think I might like it for a bit.'

And he should stay like this: contented and happily sleepy, sleepily happy—all won, all well. Beth watches him, can't stop watching him, until he asks her, 'What?'

She dodges on, 'We're exactly too late for the Afternoon Champagne Art Auction.'

'Have you seen the art?' This because he wants to make her laugh. 'I'd rather be keelhauled . . .

343

Which they can do—it is a ship and they have a keel and everything.' Waiting for her to react and then dipping up from his seat, leaning to kiss her cheek. 'Not all the generic champagne in the world could make me gaze on it again. A stoned monkey with a brush up its arse could do better.' He winces minutely because this isn't quite as stylish as he'd like.

So she teases him very slightly because he will like that, 'A stoned monkey . . .'

'I'm tired . . . I'll do better next time . . . Need practice . . .' He does like it, is helplessly comfortable as he points out, 'And we'll need to get back into bed—as soon as your clothes have arrived. Can't come to the door in our dressing gowns—Narciso will think badly of us.'

'We've only just got dressed . . .'

Quietly: 'Love you dressed. Love you undressed.' And he divests himself of the celery and becomes serious. 'Plenty of time for both . . .' Predicting their future—gentle and authoritative. 'And we need a lot of sleep because . . . of the not sleeping. And tomorrow we'll be up on deck for . . . oh . . . Narciso suggests around 4.30 in the morning, maybe five. With which I concur.'

'What the hell for?'

'To see the sunrise.' He ghosts a smile, but almost hides that he is contented, because he is being pushed, teased, having to explain himself—because of these different touches of being with somebody else, nicely interfered with. 'It's an occasion, a tradition. End of the voyage . . . Stuff to look at. That big woman on the island with her arm in the air—she's good value. She's all lit up at night . . . Like you . . .' Almost swallowing this last. 'That is romantic, though isn't it? That is quite romantic. It will be. I promise. I'll be putting the effort in.'

'Art . . .' *Sssssshhh.* 'Art, I read this story.' *Sssssshhh.* 'There was this woman, young woman—youngish— and respectable, but she started to be a medium.'

'Do we have to talk about this?' Too hard a touch, he doesn't want it.

'It was—I can't remember—the 1890s or so, round about then, and she was a medium for her lover, this man who'd been . . . and she would talk in his voice and write things and . . . he would inhabit her.'

'Yes, I read about it.' He's only being brisk, not harmed, wants a return to the good of their day.

'And it was all sort of the usual—except that he wasn't dead. He just wasn't with her. He'd left. And . . . she still needed him. So she made him up.'

'It's a sad story, Beth.'

'It's romantic.'

'It's about someone going mad.'

'There were . . . There have been times . . . It's not that I didn't miss you.'

'Sssssshhh. Too sad, Beth.' But he isn't sad, he's relieved, he's complimented. 'And I can't do sad today.'

He'd thought he might not like what I would tell him.

He looks at the tablecloth, coddles his joy for a moment, keeps it inward. 'Not when we're saying goodbye to the ship and the suite and the bed. Nothing bad has happened here . . . I'm very fond of them suddenly. I'm very fond of everything . . .'

'I know.'

'I know. I know you do.'

Your book is an honest thing. It wants to be true for you, always has, and it can't hide that it's almost finished now, it wouldn't want to if it could.

Everything stops.

You've realised this.

You can remember the taste of Sunday evenings as they dwindled down to sleep and then school in the morning: that change. Or a favourite teacher left and was replaced by someone dull, or frightening. You've stumbled through the vague melancholy of childhood holidays in their last hours and the usual forked desires: wanting to eat up those places you've found and learned and cared about, those new kinds of fun, hoping to roll in them, hold them so hard they'll be for ever, incorporated, will speak in you beyond their limitations—either that or you'll sulk and wait with not enough time left to be as you were and more than enough to feel injured and robbed. You've adopted both positions, sometimes simultaneously.

Over time you slightly, slightly, slightly began to resent those glimmers, shivers, little tunnels into your affection, reaching out from temporary joys: other people's pets, toys, gardens, loaned clothes, loaned rooms and houses, the passing friends of friends, the other people's parents, the here and then gone—you were fond of them, but also blamed them for being transient and therefore hurtful.

And you dislike the knowledge that, once you have stepped away, events will heal behind you and continue. Your presence is never entirely indispensable.

Since you've got older, have been independently

346

in motion, there have been landscapes that were generous and striking, special hobbies, kind hotels, gala occasions, different pets, toys, gardens, clothes, rooms, houses and you have, as usual, agreed to be fond of them—but the more you love them, the more you cannot keep.

You're aware of this, too.

So you let go—which is healthy and adult—and occasionally wonderful. You have sometimes adored those fast days and small plunges into moments you wholly inhabit, because they are all that they ever will be and so there's no sense in having to ration your commitment. You can be breakneck, full tilt. You've tried pastimes and excitements, dangers, precisely because you were certain they wouldn't last—as if you were testing alternative versions of yourself.

And short-term exposure to people, that can be a remarkable mercy: having no cause to consider others' failings and no reasons to make you exercise your own—appearing just as you'd wish, taking part just as you'd wish and then being done, performance over. No loose ends, just experience, pure existence—this can have its place.

There have been days when you'd like to explain how perfectly fine it is to close a door and be outside it, to head off alone and have peace. Peace for a while, space and liberty to come back in refreshed.

The hardest of your losses at least always give you this consolation—a too-large freedom. That big, deep, unworkable love: that absence that still punishes, catches you in anniversaries, old photographs, silly stories; those chances you can't have—they throw you into open air. And perhaps you fly. You can be who you want now, maybe—but

347

with nobody there to see you try.

Everything starts.

You know this.

Beth and Arthur—Arthur and Beth.

I'm not sure of our billing, or how strangers might refer to us if we were presented as a pair, the names and terms we would suggest.

Not sure.

They are together, certainly that, arm-in-arm and up on the ship's highest deck with the early crowds, the handrail-leaners, camera-carriers, the knots and straggles of murmuring shapes. Everyone seems a little stunned and delicate with lack of sleep and the large cold around them which is relatively still, but has a suggestion of merciless places in it nonetheless: Hudson Bay and the farther north, the solemnity of fatal wastes. The dark, though, is familiar against the ship, close to affectionate as they begin to abandon it: a clouded starless sky overhead, but the curiously intrusive signs of life beyond themselves now peering through to either side: low strings of shore lights and the shadows of Staten Island to port, Brooklyn to starboard.

'We're in the Narrows.' Arthur being manly for her and giving unsolicited information of a technical nature. Right across the deck, husbands and lovers and partners are doing the same: instructing. And wives and lovers and partners are consenting to be instructed, enjoying the game of it.

We should have our picture taken—it'll last.

Beth is deep in the pullover and waterproof she'd

348

packed for just such an occasion. She has most of her things, more than she'd expected, courtesy of Narciso and a pair of largish stewards. She didn't ask them how Derek was or what he said and they didn't mention. Arthur kissed her once the bags had been set down and the men had gone, as if some momentous barrier had been crossed.

Art is in his long overcoat. When she remembers him, she will only have to picture him in this and so the image will stay precise. Which is a good thing and mentally economical.

It's not a very substantial coat, though, and she doesn't want him catching cold, or being uncomfortable.

Enough to make you weep.

She squeezes his arm.

'What?'

She asks him the second thing that comes to mind, 'Are you warm enough?'

'Yeah. In parts. We might have to stroll shortly or I'll seize up. Why? Or—if it isn't annoying—might I suggest that you have decided to be responsible for my temperature and well-being . . . I am, of course, happy that you should.'

She doesn't answer but hugs him while the tamed breeze ruffles them, smells of land and later today and another country.

He kisses her neck, 'Hello, Beth,' and reminds her of bed, of earlier, of yesterday and lets her feel where he hasn't shaved. 'Who's here with me.' It isn't like him not to shave, not to be polished. 'And mine.'

He subsides and they begin to move forward on boards which are hardly in motion, have faded.

I think he would like it if we took a picture. But we

349

don't have a camera.

If we see Francis, I'll ask him and he'll help.

I'd like to see Francis. He would make me believe that I know what to do.

And she slips her hand to the small of Arthur's back, steals the fall of the cloth, how it will still fall if she's not with him and the long beat of his walk and the way he is liking the touch of her, the attention.

Monologues about tonnages and draughts continue around them and Arthur halts, turns gently, rests his chin on the top of her head and sways with her, although the boat is still.

She will be able to recall this exactly, perhaps for ever. She would prefer it to be for ever.

'What's wrong, Beth?' But he doesn't sound concerned; it is only that he has the right to take an interest.

'I'd like to play a game.'

WOMAN WHO FINDS HERSELF A COWARD COMMITS HER CRIME THE ONLY WAY SHE CAN.

Absolutely inexcusable.

'I don't really want to play anything, though, Beth. I thought we'd just . . . see sights. Wouldn't that be OK?' He strokes at her shoulders, enquiring. 'If that would be all right . . .'

Her mouth unwilling, full of the cold, 'One game. Please.' A merciless place.

'Well, if you're saying please . . .' And he is almost beginning to be cautious. 'What's the game?'

'There's a list.'

Art stands apart from her. 'I don't like lists.' His feet braced on the wood. 'Not any more.' He folds his arms, but waits, angles his head to hear her properly. 'And if there's a list, then it isn't a game—it's a trick.'

'There's a list.'

And this makes him step to the side and then close again and then away—the anxious walk of a man back on ice—one shoe splaying out. His shoulders are rising, tensing, penning him in, so that he can be the hurt man she doesn't ever want him to be.

Which means she should shut the fuck up so they can be themselves again, come home to be as they were.

Except we would be broken and pretending and a lie and I can't give him another lie—not my love.

He clears his throat and then sounds like a stranger she might meet in a hotel. 'Is this something you prepared earlier—your list?' Each word harder than the last. 'Is this something you have memorised?' The sentence nailing in.

'Because we used to.' Her hands are stinging. 'It's a list of eleven words.'

He walks to the rail—the faltered, breaking walk—and leans, looking out to where there is a tiny, greenish blur that will soon be larger and the Statue of Liberty and that will make people excited and possibly inspired. He doesn't speak.

And this is the back of his hair, the line of him, how his weight rests to the left, the dare in his hips, the thoughtful, hurtful, lonely whole of him. He is the sweetest place.

And she has to explain, be very clear—without clear instructions nobody can be with you inside your trick. 'So, there's the list.' Very small words to bring on the end of them, what they are and what they could be, 'And the list—it's what I'll give you now.'

'Can I assume I should number the words from one to eleven?'

She thinks that she would be afraid to see his face and that she also misses him. 'Please if you could. I'm sorry.'

'Don't be. Please.'

It is impossible to take his hand, because it's too late.

'The words that I have for you are

'PALM

'BOY

'BLUE

'SWEET

'BOOK

'DROP

'BURN

'FIND

'SPEAK

'RIGHT

'BLOOD.'

So no one is touching him or looking after him and he is by himself when he says, 'I don't understand your list.'

'Please, Arthur . . . just . . .'

'I will.' He doesn't shout, but is near to it.

'Pick a number between one and ten.'

Winding quickly, quickly round from the rail and his hands high and, 'Christ, Beth . . . just . . . what do you want to . . . you can tell me . . . *Christ*. You let me . . . *Beth, you let me.*' Before he shakes his head and is soft, 'I'd pick seven. I would always pick seven. Seven.'

'So I count from BLOOD, RIGHT, SPEAK, FIND, BURN, DROP and BOOK is the seventh word and that means I give you BOOK.'

He addresses the bulkhead behind her, 'But seven wouldn't be right, not for today. I ought to pick six.' Testing the trick, extending it, because he knows that when it's over something bad will have followed it in and because this will make it tell him more and he's always the man who wants to know.

'Then I count off BLOOD, RIGHT, SPEAK, FIND, BURN, DROP and that makes six and you are left with BOOK.'

She watches anxieties hit him in flickers: skull, muscle, breath.

'Or three's the magician's number. I could take that.'

'And then I'd count PALM, BOY, BLUE.' She sounds angry, she shouldn't be angry, isn't angry. 'And the third word is BLUE. I give you BLUE.' He's the one who should be angry—she wishes he'd be furious.

'Two was for me, was for man. What I used to be.' Flat statement.

'Please, Arthur . . .'

'Two.'

'Then.' She's shaking—her hands, throat, breathing. 'Then I take away PALM and BOY and I give you BLUE.' All untrustworthy now.

He cradles his forehead with one hand, rubs his hair with the other. 'But in the beginning, I didn't lie.' And then he looks at her and seems tired, tired, tired. 'I'll always pick seven. I have no choice. Seven.'

Arthur smiles the way a human being does when they understand tricks—*there never really is a choice.*

'I know.' And Beth looks at him and keeps looking because this is a kind of holding and because she understands tricks, too and because she wants more than tricks this morning. Just this morning, just once, she wants the miracle and she has asked before and didn't get one, so she's owed.

There ought to be magic, just this once.

And in her pocket there's the prop.

There has to be a prop. Self-working.

And she reaches to find it, fingers blind with the cold. 'I have something for you. I made it.'

'Beth, please—'

And he stops when she brings out the book—it's in her hand, a kind weight in her hand, less than a pigeon, or a plimsoll, or a wholemeal loaf. 'It's yours, Art. I made it for you.'

And, 'I can't.'

Because it might hurt him like fuck.

'Beth.' But he takes it from her anyway and both of them are unsteady and the camera flashes keep firing, saving the moments as they die, and the shining statue is overblown on its island and falling behind and Beth only has one instruction still to give.

Too fast. The end always catches you too fast.

Then she has to leave him.

But I'll go where he can find me, where it would be possible to find me, where it would be possible.

And Beth tells him, 'Read the end first. Please.' Wishing the night would press the words back and into the quiet of her mouth. 'You always read the ends first.' Wishing.

'If you want me to read it then, please, I do have to know what it is, Beth. Please. Because I can't . . .'

Every moment racing down and disappearing.

'It's your book, Art. That's what it is—it's your book. Because I know you and I learned you and it's your story. It's the story that I wrote for you and it's your story and all the parts of it that matter, they're all true.'

Read the end first.

And I promise, everything that matters here is true.

This is for you.

This is for you, your blue book.

And it's here in your hands and it wants to feel like touching and like trust and it wants to tell you everything, but it's scared and in your hands and incomplete unless you're with it and can see. It wants to be able to live and see you back.

And it wants to start gently, evade just a little and remind you about blue books—that they are secrets.

Blue books keep the privacies of trades and crafts and carry years of practices made perfect and they are cheats and tricks and shameful and denied.

And no medium will ever say they have one. No medium will ever say they've stolen what they need of you and noted it, kept a record to help them lie at you.

But this blue book is true.

Built of one life.

This is your book. This is your blue book.

And your book has to tell you about a boy—that he was funny and clever and when he was born his hair was honey-coloured and warm and would have made you want to touch it and his eyes were the blue of love, blue enough to shock. And, as he grew, his hair would change, become more coppery and complicated, but his eyes were perpetually a startle, like a light caught in glass.

During his earliest hours the boy beguiled his nurses. Then he moved on to charm elsewhere, although he was an unflamboyant baby, generally ruminative, like an old man returned to little bones, starting again and lolling and lying in state—that, or else he would panic with all of himself, be expressed to the soles of his feet in his distress.

His mother learned what would rescue him: sometimes motion, sometimes holding, sometimes music and sometimes his own exhaustion would defeat him—and in this she knew that he was like his father.

His father who wasn't there—the boy coming home from the hospital to his granny and grandpa's house. His accommodation had been problematic to arrange, had involved shouting and types of breakages and disbelief. But then the boy turned up one afternoon, as fresh as milk and in his mother's arms—new to her arms—a wonder shifting in her arms—and finger-gripping and nodding and looking and looking and looking more than any human person ever had—eating each of them whole: grandmother, grandfather, mother—and almost immediately the household fell into kinds of peace and comfort and the enjoyment of strange hours and occupations. He made everything different.

And he became their fascination and they brought him their best. His gran fed him puréed versions of whatever the household was eating and sang to him and attempted knitting, became as compulsive a photographer as her husband had once been. The boy's grandfather resurrected old illusions to offer him—could hardly be kept from producing silks and sparkles unless the child was sleeping—and even then there were moves to practise for him, there were novelties to invent.

The boy took disappearances, substitutions and transformations quite for granted, but was amazed by his grandad's eyebrows and by faces in general, and by a toy purple dog made of corduroy who had embroidered features, because buttons or anything like them might be dangerous, might work loose. The boy adored his dog. Later he was going to have a pup he would grow tall and run about with. By the time he was almost two, he'd expressed this opinion. He had many often vigorous opinions.

His mother seemed best at worrying: the boy fed nicely, but he was long-boned, basically skinny from the outset, so he didn't look like the other babies being checked at the surgery, or the ones trundled up and down in shops. He also wasn't turnip-headed and sluggish or ugly the way they were. He was extraordinary. And extraordinary isn't always good. It is outspoken and unusual, which may come to be a problem later on. And he was quick—maybe walking too soon and damaging his legs—but no way to stop him walking, pottering, tumbling— another worry—although he was usually unconcerned by falls unless he caught sight of her fretting—then he would yowl. And his mother wasn't sure if a grandfather and no father would be enough.

She wanted her boy to have enough. At least enough. If not everything.

But she wasn't with his father any more and it had been too difficult, so difficult, to leave and she couldn't go back. She couldn't. It would have hurt everyone.

His father having been who she'd lived with and worked with and thought with for months, years— not very long, not all that long, but years, five years—and his father was extraordinary and his being extraordinary wasn't always good. His heart was clean and hot and right, but other things weren't good.

And, almost as soon as she'd left the extraordinary man, the first signs of their boy were irrefutable and more arriving, along with this sense of the child puzzling, assembling himself, coming clearer and clearer.

But it had seemed there was no fair, or kind, or always good way for the mother to say what she ought.

You have a son. We made a son together. We have excelled ourselves.

But don't see him. Don't see us. Don't hurt yourself that way.

Don't hurt us.

Don't hurt me.

Don't hurt him.

Except when she first met the boy and took him up, all alive and thinking and who he was going to be there and sharp in him already—and his father in him, too, clean and hot and right—she could have made the phone call then.

She would have.

But she was busy.

The boy made her very busy. It doesn't bear thinking about.

And he was a summer child, born on the 14th of June—14th of June 1995—and his grandpa full of plans for birthdays, although his mother did try to restrain them.

When the boy turns one, there is cake and there are balloons which he receives graciously, as his due, along with the way his granny and grandpa's hands

358

throw shadows up on a white wall—small magics, making animals and adventures—these he studies in deep silence and then screams about when they go. And his grandpa works through an elegant effect involving a butterfly which bores the child until he can hold the butterfly and suck it. He does not have his little friends round—they aren't real friends yet, they're simply random people of his age who are stupid and unattractive and who waste everybody's time. His mother feels their first year is something to celebrate with his own people and in his own home.

He does keep often with his own people and talks to them and asks them for only red jam and how to say hospital and what dark is for and he kisses them goodnight and goodbye, but not hello. And he totters and jumps about naked in front of them between bath time and pyjamas, because there are few things finer than being naked when nobody else is allowed it, because of being old. And these are the people who love him, the people who go to sleep thinking of what he'll do next and of how he'll be slightly more of himself in the morning, more every day.

His second birthday is different: there are plans, outsiders will be coming—not magicians—other children and their parents. And it's hot, fully hot already, so there will be maybe a kind of picnic—which can happen indoors when it, naturally, rains—and there can be games and naps and, yes, some tricks, a small amount of tricks from Grandpa.

Because the boy is fond of splashing and having his skin in the air—with the jaunty hat and the sunblock: he's ambivalent about the application of sunblock, but he gets it anyway, is protected anyway—because he wants water, there will be the paddling pool—a small thing, inflatable thing. He's tried it before and been demented with how remarkable it is. It renders him speechless—and then compelled to sing.

'Addle Pool.' He demands this more often than he gets it.

'Addle Pool.' He can say *paddling pool* perfectly—his speech is well advanced and modulated and a gift. He just doesn't want to say *paddling pool*—the Addle Pool is so magnificent it should have its own name. His purple dog is Uff and then there is Addle Pool—two glorious things.

The weekend before his party is sunny. Saturday afternoon is spent in the park with his family and judder- running after pigeons and dropping ice cream and the boy has a balloon—he does appreciate balloons—and this is a posh one with silver sides that bobs beyond his head as he walks with it. He will let no one else have it—until its string escapes him and it flies, soars.

The four of them are hypnotised by its ascent and the boy not unhappy—it climbs so marvellously, he is proud of it. But all the way back in the car he asks if his balloon will be waiting for him when they get home and where has it gone and what is it doing and when will it be home and it ought to come home. The balloon is his first trouble. It is the beginning of his being sad.

On Sunday, his mum and grandpa set up the Addle Pool and fill it, because—apart from being delightful—it may compensate for the lamented balloon and prove a distraction.

The boy does, indeed, splash and run and slide in the pool until he's rendered fuzzy-headed by his undiluted pleasure and agrees—eventually—to be dressed and re-sunblocked and to lollop on his blanket with his cloth books and Uff.

And his grandmother's in the kitchen and making a roast chicken dinner which she won't again.

And his mother is in the garden and talking to his grandpa and also shouting towards the kitchen but not hearing any answer and—this will only take a moment—she trots to the kitchen door and peeks in and she is distracted, she gets distracted and she's backing out to the garden again, because she's asked what she wanted to about the dinner—when it will be ready—and this doesn't matter, could never really matter, cannot be important—but then she's thinking of what might come after, of how their evening could turn out to be. So she decides she'll make arrangements for later and drifts in from the sun again, re-enters the kitchen and chats.

And it's hard to tell if even a minute passes.

And then the child's grandfather is standing in the doorway.

He is standing in the doorway and his arms are wet and the boy too—the clothes the boy has barely worn are soaking wet.

There is a confusion.

There has been a confusion.

The mother was distracted in the kitchen. The mother had said she would be a moment, would glance in and then be back, hardly gone.

The grandfather was misled. He thought he saw his daughter emerging—heading for the lawn—doing what she ought to and walking towards her son, seeing her son, calling him into the rest of the day, into the rest of their time, his time.

The grandfather had turned for the shed and left, as far as he believed, his daughter and grandson safely together. The grandfather kept his secrets in the shed and had intended to nip in and fetch some magic powder, bring a pinch of it back to the boy because it would look very fine for him in the sun.

And the boy had been on his stomach on the blanket, summer blanket, soft blanket and with his toys.

But he's quick.

And maybe, maybe, maybe the boy had believed that Uff—who is very like him—would enjoy a swim and so he took Uff to the water and dropped him in, saw him changing, sinking.

There is no way to know if this is how it happened.

It is impossible to ask the boy how everything was lost.

It will always be impossible to ask him.

The boy is called Peter.

The boy is called Peter Arthur Barber.

The boy is still warm.

The extraordinary boy.

Still warm.

They try everything.

It is unforgivable.

Peter Arthur Barber.

He shouldn't have been alone.

It will always be impossible.

And you know this.
346
346
346
losschildbetrayal
losschildbetrayal
losschildbetrayal
18
18
18
Pleaselistenaccident
Pleaselistenaccident
Pleaselistenaccident
345
345
345
losschildhelp
losschildhelp
losschildhelp
3
Touch me
3
Loss
3 times 3 is 9
9
Pain
9
Meet me
You learned this.
You taught me this.
Where we could meet.
How we could meet.

And, Arthur, this isn't a book. This is me and this is you and you were meant to see him. Once things were settled and he was confident in himself, then you would have been with him and known him.

I promise.

I thought there'd be time. There wasn't any reason to think that there wouldn't be time, but I stole him from you, because I was stupid. I stole every part of him from you and I lost him because I was stupid and now I'll lose you.

And I'm a coward, so I didn't tell you.

I didn't want to lose you.

When you said I felt different, and I said I was, that was the closest I got to saying. But we were happy then and you were beautiful—we were beautiful—seemed it—and there hadn't been anything beautiful for so long.

And I understood eighteen when you said it to me in the queue. You know I did.

And you understand me.

And this whole thing, it killed my father, left my mother without both of them and how would I tell you this and not hurt you, too.

And you were smiling today and you have his smile.

And I never didn't love you, but I avoided it, I kept distracted, because that's what I do, because I am a non-working human being.

And before this I always have kept distracted.

But I remembered you. I always remember you.

And this morning I saw you, with nothing in the way. I saw who you are and you saw me.

And now you know the rest of it.

And that I made you a book.

Because you can have this and hold it and you can look at it and see it looking back and where your hands are mine have been.

And I do love you.

And if you don't want that, I understand.

But I do love you.

And there is nothing I can help or solve and I am wrong, a wrong person, but if it would please you I can give you this which is my voice to be with you, my mouth with your mouth and soft.

And you should have the story of a man who stands very still on a ship's deck—broad wood under his feet: tiny shifts in it, gentle—and he watches an island city as it grows to meet him, bluepink in the first hour of the day. He is facing east and the new sun boils at the foot of every cross-street as he passes along the shore—it climbs the sky and is a fury of colours, a hunger, a beautiful rage between buildings that seem cleaner and better than they should be, perfect and eternal as dreams.

And this is beautiful and dreadful and the man is used to beautiful and dreadful things.

And windows gild and flare and are extinguished and the water burns, silvers, splits and then heals behind him, while quiet gulls kite above. There are no sounds except the calm of the slowing engines and the man's thinking, the words in his head.

And when the man comes to land, walks on solid ground, the ocean will stay with him, will rock with him, and when he stands the world will roll, will dance, be an amazement. And this will make him feel that it isn't impossible, that it isn't completely impossible that he could be happy, that he could come home and live.

He could be happy. He could be loved.

He is loved.

You are loved.

If this is a spell and there is magic and everything that matters can be true, then you can be happy and be loved.

And if I was on solid ground and with you I would give you my hand if you wanted.

I would touch you.

I would touch you.

I would touch you.

I would touch you.

I would touch you.

I would touch you.

I would touch you.

This is the best of me.

But I'd give you my hand if you wanted.

I'd give you everything.

ACKNOWLEDGEMENTS

With many thanks to Derren Brown, Julia Cloughley-Sneddon, Coops, Peter Lamont, Ian Rowland, Ros Steen and Shelby White. Thanks also to the island and people of Sark.